933

D1032093

A History of the British Economy
1086–1970

A History of
the British Economy
1086–1970

Brian Murphy

LONGMAN

LONGMAN GROUP LIMITED
London

*Associated companies, branches and representatives
throughout the world*

First published 1973
ISBN 0 582 35036 0

*Printed in Great Britain by
Western Printing Services Ltd, Bristol*

Also available

A History of the British Economy 1086–1740
paper (part I)

A History of the British Economy 1740–1970
paper (part II)

Contents

CONTENTS

PART II

Graphs and tables

Chapter Three

Chapter Four

Chapter Five

Chapter Six

Preface

Apart from the physical sciences, few academic disciplines have been the subject of as thoroughgoing a revision in recent years as has economic history. It has been revision on two levels: on the purely factual, where greatly intensified research activity has both deepened and amended the received version at a variety of points; and, perhaps more tellingly, on the interpretative level, where the revision has been characterised by an endeavour to apply the lessons, or, at least, the inspiration, of post-Keynesian economics to the facts of history, and to supply a picture of a dynamically articulated economy in place of the essentially static representation of economic institutions and events which an older historiography had proffered.

This book represents an attempt to gather together the fruits of this revisionary work in such a manner as to provide the 'A' level student with a comprehensive textbook, and higher level students with a basic work of reference. As to the efficacy with which this aim has been realised, the reader will judge for himself. But if there is any one central test of the worth of a general economic history, my own conviction is that it must be the requirement that such a work should be both *economic* and *historical*. If the fault of the older economic history was that it was insufficiently economic, the danger of the new, perhaps, is of being insufficiently historical. An approach which does not seek to push beyond the quantifiable and which looks to the past only for testbeds for econometric models may be a useful branch of economics but it is not history – which before it is anything else is an acknowledgement of the past in its own right. Nor, by the same token, is it history's essential business to indicate how things came to their present pass. In this book the division into periods has, among other aims, that of containing the past in historical time, where it belongs, and preventing its being swallowed up by the present, or by some particular historical phase to which, for one reason or another, a special importance is ascribed.

As to the requirement to be economic: a book of this kind labours under the difficulty of not knowing what degree of economic literacy may be assumed on the part of its readers. The safest thing seems to be to assume none; and to supply as much economic theory – and no more – as is needful in any particular context. To the initiated economists, who may find some of it rather *simpliste*, my unblushing apologies. To the non-economists, whose apprehensions may be aroused, my assurances that, for the purposes of a general work such as this, it involves nothing more than the application of a modicum of native horse-sense – and the reflection that if they find themselves picking up a little elementary macro-economics as they go along, they will hardly be any the worse for it.

A final word on geographical coverage. 'Britain', throughout, is the area covered by the designation at any one time, including Scotland after the Union (here in practice, after 1740) and Ireland never. However, this general principle has not been clung to with a scrupulous pedantry. Moreover, the book does not aim at a comprehensive regional coverage, and, in general, has little or nothing to say of particular localities which at any time stood aside from the main stream of British economic history.

My thanks are due to the army of scholars, most of them unidentified in the text, on whose work the book is founded – with the hope that those of them who may read it and recognise themselves will not feel that they have been dishonoured; to the authorities of Norwood Technical College whose cooperation has facilitated the undertaking; and, very specially, to Mrs Audrey Munro, without whose talent a fearful mess of a manuscript could never have been translated into print.

Maidenhead, February 1971   BRIAN MURPHY

PART I

1086-1740

One

England in 1086

The sources

History begins when records begin. Man is perhaps a million years old but his history for all but a small fraction of that span is nothing more than what is revealed by a few skeletons and some roughly fashioned stones. The history of the economic activity of men who lived in England covers only a microscopic section of the span and only over a further fraction of that microscopic section can we answer most of the questions which we would like to pose. The tools and instruments which survive enable us to tell with some accuracy when stone was replaced by bronze and bronze by iron; when crops were first planted; when woven fabrics were substituted for skins and furs. Other archaeological remains, such as pottery, coins and the traces of buildings, add a few further details, and as we move into the Christian era and the coming of the Romans to Britain some written evidence supplements the scanty picture. With the departure of the Romans the view clouds over again. From the seventh century onwards a few precious facts of economic import can be squeezed out of the charters recording grants of land, the legal codes, the histories of Bede and later chroniclers, and religious and secular literature. But the authors of these documents were not writing with a modern economic historian in mind and such information as he can find in them more often sharpens than satisfies his curiosity. Patient and imaginative scholars have performed prodigies of reconstruction out of these meagre materials. But even in skilled hands the records rarely yield adequately detailed answers to the questions: what was produced; by whom; organised in what manner; using what techniques; distributed to whom and by what means; how was wealth divided; what were the economic relations between England and the rest of Europe; what changes occurred in these respects over the years and why; and above all, in any connection, the question to which economic history must have some sort of an answer; how much?

It could be said that a truly *economic* history can only begin where contemporaries start to ask these questions about their own times and leave us the results of their inquiries; and in England this, generally speaking, did not happen until the seventeenth century, while we have to wait until the nineteenth before such inquiries cover the greater part of the field of economic facts. This development, when it comes, is the product of two new mental attitudes: the spirit of academic curiosity and belief in economic planning. Before these attitudes become effective, our only abundant sources of information are the records kept by individuals and institutions for their own financial purposes. Of these, two principal classes stand out: the estate records of landowners and the tax records of organs of government. Economic history can make a useful start at that period in time from which these survive in significant quantities. For England, uniquely, there exists an exact date which marks the beginning of such a period: 1086 – the year of the compilation of Domesday Book.

Domesday Book

In the strict sense Domesday Book is probably not a tax book. Modern opinion is that it was in effect, although not in form, a census of 'knights fees'. That is to say that William I, twenty years after the Battle of Hastings had secured for him the throne and for his Norman fighting men the possession of most of the land of England, sought to determine how many of the armoured and mounted soldiers who made up the hard core of his military force could be supported from this land. If it is not a tax book then it is something very close to it. The knights in a Norman army were not paid. Instead they received grants of land (fees) the revenues and produce of which enabled them to equip themselves when needed for war and to maintain themselves in some modest dignity in time of peace. A calculation of economic resources would indicate the potential size of the military resources available to the crown. The more precise the calculation the more precise the indication, and the more valuable to a later inquirer interested in the economic resources themselves.

The inquiry was meticulous. Excepting the counties of the far north

(Cumberland, Durham, Westmorland, Northumberland) every rural community in the country reported on the amount of arable land, the number of householders, and the number of ploughs within its bounds, and in so doing distinguished, with various degrees of fineness, between different classes of inhabitants and the amount of land held by them; and further provided some information about pasture land, woods and other productive resources. The returns from the towns are usually less informative, but they do report the number of houses and their rental value. All this information was then collected and within each county listed under the names of those to whom the property had been granted by the king, and by them in turn granted to knights whose service was ultimately owed to the Crown. This was the form in which the information would best suit the king's purpose of determining to whom he was to look for knight service and in what amounts.

Domesday falls well short of being a comprehensive economic survey. It speaks of the amount of arable land but not of the crops sown nor of the output achieved. Only in some cases does it enumerate livestock. It gives no indication of the amount of produce sold. It says little of the occupations of townsfolk. And so on through a variety of omissions. But on some points it provides information which would otherwise be totally lacking, and to others it brings a precision where otherwise there could only be vague generalities. All in all it means that more is known of the late eleventh-century English economy than that of any other comparable part of contemporary Europe, and in some important respects, than that of England itself in later centuries.

The population and the land

The picture which Domesday, in conjunction with other sources, presents is of an England whose population was probably around one and a half million of whom some nine-tenths lived in purely rural communities. About a twenty-fifth lived in the towns, about ten in number, with a population of over 2,000, nearly a half of these in London; the remaining twentieth or so resided in what were essentially outsize villages, or centres where the presence of a bishop, a sheriff, a military garrison or a junction of travellers' routes had caused a knot of non-agricultural population to form, but where many of the populace were still engaged in agricultural work. Altogether close on ninety-five per cent of the population lived directly off the land, or in immediate dependence on those who did, the bulk of them clustered

3

in villages of from fifty to two hundred persons, although the in-habitants of the mountainous northern regions, the hill country and moorlands of the west and some forest areas, were scattered in isolated homesteads.

There was little trade or manufacture and of what there was our knowledge is small. But we are dealing almost entirely with communi-ties the range of whose material wants and expectations was very limited: food, drink, shelter, warmth, clothing and the tools necessary for the provision of these things. The first four could normally be supplied entirely from local resources, by individuals for themselves. The extent to which clothmaking was a distinct function is not clear – specialist weavers certainly existed but how far this division of labour had proceeded is uncertain. Iron used for tools had usually to be obtained from outside the community and would be fashioned by a local smith, but iron was used only for working edges, the rest of a tool being made of local wood. Salt too would have to come from outside, sometimes from abroad. Here the effective wants of most of the population stopped. The five per cent or so who lived by manu-facturing and trading catered largely for the extra wants of the minority with means surplus to subsistence requirements and were heavily con-centrated in the regional centres: London, Winchester, Norwich, York, Lincoln and Bristol.

The location of these six towns affords an indication of the general distribution of population: heavily biased to the east and congregating particularly in the middle section of the eastern half. The Domesday returns show that the population was heavily concentrated on the flat lands between the Humber and the Thames, and especially in the counties of Suffolk, Norfolk and Essex, whose light soil could be ploughed the most readily. Here the work of two millennia in pushing back the wilderness – forest, scrub and waste – had gone furthest. But almost everywhere in England the achievement of a hundred genera-tions of predecessors was evident. The great weald stretching across Sussex and Kent still formed nearly fifteen hundred square miles of forest and there were lesser forests elsewhere, but over most of England it was isolated, though abundant, woods or belts of treeland which in fragmented and attenuated form continued to give testimony of the prehistoric forest.

It was the plough that had thrust aside the trees. Eleventh-century England lived off arable land and the low yield obtained per acre meant that an extensive area was needed. Pastureland was merely land that was unsuitable for cultivation. Every acre that could bear wheat, barley, oats or rye was pressed into service; for simple sustenance had to be the overriding aim of a society whose productive techniques were such that one family's labour yielded little more than one family's basic needs; and an acre of land under cereal crops yields significantly more nutrition than the same acre grazed by livestock. The concentration on arable farming had a triple effect on the number of animals kept. It obviously limited the amount of land, especially good land, available for pasture. It further limited, on such pasture as there was, the grazing for animals other than the oxen needed to draw the ploughs. It also limited the amount of meadowland for winter fodder – this especially severely as, while rough summer grazing could be had on waste land and better grazing on the arable between harvest and seed-time without cutting across the primacy accorded to cereal crops, meadow could only be had at the expense of grain and was only very grudgingly conceded. As a consequence animals were often slaughtered in late autumn, the hides and wool converted into leather and cloth and the meat salted. (It was commonly putrid by spring as salt supplies in many places were inadequate.) Of the meat-yielding animals cows were the most restricted in numbers by this near-obsession with arable. Pigs, which could feed off mast and acorns in the woods, were fairly plentiful, and sheep, which would crop on nearly anything, were kept in large numbers for the sake of their manure. But denied good grazing and totally without additional feeding all these were lean, scrawny animals providing nothing more than a marginal variation to the bread diet which was the staple of most people.

There was one seeming extravagance Domesday men allowed themselves – ale. As much as a third of the arable may have been planted with barley. Doubtless a good deal was used as bread-grain and in times of need the whole crop could be thus employed but the true destination of much of it was the ale vat. We may think it remarkable that a large proportion of such scanty resources was dedicated to inebriation but the bare, monotonous, shortage-threatened life of medieval England would have been intolerable without it. It belonged with bread among the necessities of life.

Sheep-dung was invaluable in supplementing the soil's natural fertility but its use could not permit of the uninterrupted cultivation of the land. Earth must be refertilised periodically. In Domesday England, as everywhere, this was done by allowing the land to revert to grass – fallowing. In general, land was rested in this way every other year so that at any one time only one half of the arable was actually in use, perhaps sown and harvested at the same time, more probably divided between crops reaped in late spring (barley, oats, peas) and crops reaped in late summer (wheat, rye). This is what later generations have called 'the two-field system', and in so doing have perhaps given an impression of a stricter uniformity than may have prevailed.

The semicommunal nature of farming must certainly have given a considerable rigidity to whatever was the normal practice in any one village but account may have been taken of variations in the quality of different pieces of land and the worse fallowed more frequently and the better less frequently. The practice found in the north-west and south-west of farming a heavily manured central core fairly intensively and from time to time taking in portions of an outer area which would be worked for a while before being allowed to revert again to grass for some years may not represent a Celtic system of agriculture as distinct from an Anglo-Saxon one (as has been suggested) but merely a distinctive variant of the one system necessitated by the nature of the land. In this case one would expect less marked variations all over the country. However something approximating to a textbook two-field system was widely prevalent and the fact that not much more than half the available land was concurrently used is crucial in any appreciation of the productivity of eleventh-century agriculture. It was in fact very low by modern standards. But any invidious detailed comparison between it and twentieth-century agriculture would be grotesquely unhistorical. The useful question is: how capable was it of meeting the contemporary demands made on it? The rough answer is: just barely capable. It was asked to do little more than provide those who worked the land with enough to eat. In good years it probably served well enough. In bad years men went hungry, though few would seem to have died of outright starvation.

Village and manor

One important set of questions remains unanswered. What were these village communities which we have discerned as the characteristic social and economic units of Domesday England? Who composed them? What were the relations of the inhabitants to the land, with each other and with those Norman lords to whom William had granted the land? The only simple answer is that there are no simple answers. The difficulty is not only one that we experience looking back, but one which the compilers of Domesday themselves must have felt acutely too. They brought with them from France their own notions of the relationships between men and men and between men and property. But it was William's policy to preserve English customs as he found them – otherwise his claim that he came not as a conqueror but as one entering into his rightful inheritance would have been an empty sham. Thus the Domesday commissioners had to fit their own words and concepts to social and economic facts for which they were not designed. The Englishmen to whom they addressed their inquiries employed a variety of terms to designate men of certain social standing, or possessed of certain legal rights and obligations, or vested with a certain amount of property with, perhaps, attendant duties, or of some combination of these elements. The distinctions may not have always been clear to the Englishmen. They were quite mysterious to the Normans.

Amid this confusion of two languages certain facts can be made plain if not simple. English society was more variegated than Norman. In particular Norman society conceived solely of a relationship between superior and inferior, in which land was the bond: the inferior held land 'of' the superior and owed him certain services in return. English society conceived of such a relationship into which land did not necessarily enter: in return for the protection of a man of weight a less powerful man might submit himself to certain obligations, but these admitted the superior to no necessary rights in his land and he might well enjoy this kind of relationship with more than one superior; in addition, he might rent his land from someone who might be his superior but who might equally well not be. Thus, while the Normans thought of one lord, one piece of land, one man, as a logical progression, the English thought of anything from no 'lord' to several 'lords' as one thing, and of a man and his land as another thing. Further, the Normans conceived of all land as fitting into their simple scheme of things so that for every piece of land there was a lord who had both rights in the land and power over those who occupied it. Since the English had no simple scheme they lacked the notion of *Nulle terre sans seigneur* (No land without a lord).

Neither society, it should be noted, had as yet a simple notion of landownership. Men had rights in land and usually more men than one had different rights in the same piece of land. We must be wary of defining a situation where one man receives a certain payment in respect of a piece of land and another man occupies it as a modern landlord–tenant relationship; the 'tenant' may well in practice possess what we would consider to be the distinctive rights of 'ownership'. More particularly we must not think of lordship as synonymous with ownership and must realise that what William granted to his followers was the *lordship* of land.

The next plain fact that emerges from Domesday is that while, even in the twenty years since the Conquest, 'Normanisation' has made notable headway in fact and practice, the commissioners' use of French terms does not indicate a determination on their part to impose French ways – they are attempting to fit the words to the facts, not the facts to the words. Finally, while it is proper to stress the clash between these two societies, there are considerable areas of overlap. Both are products of the same general culture. There is evidence that English society had been moving of its own accord in the French direction. Furthermore the two societies shared a largely common economic background. In particular land and labour were, in a starkly direct fashion, the principal sources and forms of wealth. If one man conferred the use of his land on another the likelihood was that the only valuable consideration which he could receive in return was labour. Once either society had come to the point where some men had more land than they needed and some had less, labour services were bound to emerge. The Normans might tend to look on this as a distinctive mark of bondage on the part of the labourer, while to the English it could be fully consonant with personal freedom. But the outward identity of the two approaches made it inevitable that one would be largely assimilated to the other once they were brought into close contact.

The Domesday villagers of England, then, were men who ranged over a wide variety of ranks from completely independent owners of their own land to those who were the mere servants of a lord, allowed the use of a small plot in return for their labour. Behind them all, there lurked a Norman lord who was in course of making effective over them the power which his language induced him to believe his grant of land had bestowed on him. So far, perhaps, in deference to the royal wishes, he had left them very much to their own strange ways, but he could not help but think of them as belonging to the only two classes he understood: freemen and villeins – those who owed him only certain stipulated payments or services, if anything, and those who owed him whatever he required of them and were permanently bound to his service. (No implication that serfdom was more widespread in Normandy than in England is intended here. In fact it was much less common, but where it existed it was of a more unambiguous nature

8

than in England.) This is without speaking of slaves whom Normans and English alike had always possessed. Landless, propertyless and completely their lords' to command, they constituted about a tenth of Domesday population.

The land occupied by those who owed duties to a lord along with the land exploited directly by him (the demesne) composed that lord's manor. Such a manor may have covered the whole of a village or may, on the other hand, have been made up of land scattered through several villages and even have included some town houses. In such a case of dispersed property the only unity that the manor possessed was that it was administered from one centre; if the property was very extensive there would be several such centres and the lord would be owner of several manors. Much of the land of England fell under the great lay and ecclesiastical lords of twenty, forty or more manors. On the other hand, Domesday ascribes manors to owners of a few acres whose only distinction was that they acknowledged no lord and belonged clearly to no community. A Domesday manor is just an autonomous property unit. Conversely, the whole of a village may have been included in one manor or may have been divided among several manors of several lords; where the idea of one man, one lord, or of lordship at all, had not yet rooted itself it might be impossible for a Norman to determine in whose manor, if anybody's, a particular piece of land lay or to which lord, if any, a particular man was attached. In general, at the time of Domesday the identity of village with manor and the classification of the villagers in accordance with Norman ideas were clearest in the thick belt of territory running north from Hampshire to Nottinghamshire, and were least evident in the densely populated counties of the east. To some extent this seems to reflect pre-Norman differences between the two areas.

Even in places where lordship was strongest the village economy might be largely unaffected by it. Services owed to a lord, whether in money, in labour or in kind, were clearly a drain to some degree, perhaps a severe one, on individual resources, but the manner in which a livelihood was secured was the same whether there was a lord to be reckoned with or not. A breakdown of the villagers in terms of the amount of land held by each would often reveal a simpler state of affairs than even a Norman one in terms of status and obligations. Two classes emerge: those who hold enough land for subsistence and those who do not, and within each class there may well be a very high degree of uniformity in size of landholding; the first group hold a standard unit

9

(known variously as a virgate or a yardland or, of half-size, an oxgang or a bovate). The unit would, from area to area, vary in size from 15 to 80 acres but it clearly represents the amount judged necessary for one household's subsistence and usually approximates to 30 acres. Those comprising the second – and rather smaller – group hold some 5 acres or less and are largely dependent on employment by others for their livelihood. They are usually described in Domesday as cottars or bordars. Thus we have a community composed of peasant farmers and agricultural labourers. If we look at the land itself we must, in all probability, add a third element: the demesne lands of a lord or lords who may or may not be resident.

Few villages would correspond perfectly to this picture. There will be some variations in size of holding but rarely such as to blur completely the distinction between labourers and farmers or to conceal the essentially subsistence nature of the holdings; where larger or smaller holdings exist they will often be seen to consist of multiples or fractions of a virgate (e.g. 45 acres [$1\frac{1}{2}$v] or 20 acres [$\frac{2}{3}$v]) testifying to recent additions or subdivisions. If we could actually physically view the fields, little of this would be evident. In rough country, irregularly scattered patches of cultivated land would afford little indication of the pattern of land ownership. In gentler country, some 500 to 2,000 acres of arable land would stretch unbroken by any fence, hedge or ditch distinguishing one man's land from another's. Here the only continuous marks would be those of the plough, in blocks of gently curving parallels; and at intervals amongst the parallels some kind of boundary sign dividing the land into conventionally quarter-acre strips, roughly forty times as long as broad. Each man's land consisted of a collection of these strips – not of adjoining strips but of single strips scattered over the whole arable area and apportioned within the area so that whatever fallowing practice was followed he would have the same number of strips under cultivation each year.[1] These were the 'open fields' whose beginnings and original motivation are lost in unrecorded history. They were ploughed in common. It would have been a gross waste of time for each individual to move a plough and team the hundred yards or so between his strips after each had been ploughed. More significantly, few had a plough and team of their own. Eight oxen made up a stan-

[1] In Kent holdings were originally in the form of single rectangular blocks although 'gavelkind' (equal inheritance by all heirs) which prevailed there had often broken these up into small irregular lots, and with multiple inheritances or acquisitions of extra land a man's holding might consist of several such lots. This Kentish peculiarity is probably racial in origin, the area having been settled by the Jutes at the time of the Anglo-Saxon invasion.

dard plough team on the heaviest soil, although six, four or even two oxen teams were used on lighter soils. The typical virgater owned only two oxen and thus usually had to join with others to provide a full team. The ownership of the plough itself in such a group is a point of uncertainty. It may have been jointly owned but more probably it was in individual ownership and exempted the owner from providing oxen or qualified him for a portion of land or a share of the produce. This composite plough and team did not, of course, confine itself to the land of its co-owners but worked a whole section of the arable while other ploughs did likewise.

How far communalism was practised in other farming operations, harvesting, sowing, etc., is not clear. It certainly prevailed on the arable between harvest and seed-time, when everybody's animals grazed on everybody's land, and perpetually on the ordinary pasture where there was no question of individual ownership of land, though if there was too much pressure on it, the number of animals each person could keep there might be regulated according to the amount of arable he held. 'Commons' was in fact the universal designation for this waste that served as pasture. In an extended sense the word also covered woodlands in which again there was normally no individual ownership, but unless it was very abundant the right to wood was fairly closely controlled and incoming Norman lords often conceived of themselves as having unambiguous rights of ownership. (The forest proper, with its hunting, was jealously guarded royal demesne.)

Looking at these provisions as a whole it can truthfully be said that the typical English farmer was the subject of a communal discipline.[1] The system would have been unworkable without a certain degree of cooperation and theoretically an individual farmer could not always do exactly as he wished. Amongst an earlier generation of historians some, conceiving economic history as essentially an object lesson in the virtues of untrammelled individual enterprise, entertained images of vigorously minded, profit-conscious villagers, frustrated by the inertia of their neighbours. The time would come when some men would seek to trangress the bounds of custom. There is little reason to suppose

---

[1] The view that the agrarian arrangements described in these paragraphs were of ancient origin and well established by the time of the Norman Conquest is conventional orthodoxy. It should be said, however, that documentation on the matter is very sparse and the received view depends much on reading back into the eleventh century what is known in detail from later centuries. In two articles in *Past and Present* (nos. 29 and 33) Dr Joan Thirsk has suggested that these arrangements may have been much slower in developing and may not have attained finality until the fifteenth or sixteenth centuries.

that it had arrived in the eleventh century. It is true that if the village was planting oats then everybody had to plant oats (or at least some crop with the same germination period so that all strips were clear at the same time to allow the animals in), but since everybody had the same simple object of sustenance to wish to do otherwise could only have been mere caprice. And to speak of a more discriminating awareness of the alternative uses of land, pasture as against arable, would be to ignore even more fatuously the beginning and end of the whole activity: subsistence.

Over a considerable part of the country the nature of the terrain rendered this village-centred open field farming impractical. Throughout the Highland Zone (roughly the area west of the line Berwick-on-Tweed to Dorchester in Dorset) it was only in occasional stretches of fairly level country that it would be found. The scraps of cultivable land to be had from hillsides, mountain slopes and moor could never have lent themselves to strip division. But such regions were only very thinly settled, if at all. Even within the Lowland Zone there were farms standing outside a village community, individually owned and individually worked. Sometimes they were quite large, maybe 200 acres, and required a hired labour force; sometimes they were merely subsistence size – these latter were especially common on the easily worked soils of East Anglia where a light and simple two-oxen plough sufficed for cultivation. But, overall, the acreage of such individual farm units was only a fraction of that of village land.

The village with its semi-communalism, its traditional farming practices, its near isolation from the world outside and its intense preoccupation with raising enough grain to feed itself, was not merely the fundamental but the only important economic institution in Domesday England. We could wipe off the board towns and townsmen, manors and lords great and small and, from an economic point of view, we would scarcely alter things at all.

Two

1086-1348

The nature of economic change

Change is not something that an economy necessarily undergoes. At least it is not if we mean by change the coming into existence of new forms of economic organisation or new techniques. Differences, of course, there will always be, but there have been economies which have gone on for centuries without experiencing any noteworthy organisational or technical advance or regression (the Bedouin of the Arabian desert, the inhabitants of the interior of New Guinea, the Indians in the remoter regions of the Amazon jungle are still extant or very recent instances). In the very long run it is probably true that societies must change their methods of supplying their needs or die, for nature changes over the millennia: the sea encroaches or recedes, the weather becomes colder or hotter, wetter or drier; rivers change their courses, dry up, or emerge in new places; forests spread or wither; the soil gives way to sand or sand to soil; animals and fish change their habitat; mineral deposits become exhausted. Societies which do not adjust accordingly must vanish. In any shorter run there is no law of nature or history which dictates economic change. Or if there is such a law, it is, in essence, the Malthusian law: population tends to increase in geometric proportion, the resources available to support it only in arithmetic proportion. But allowing that the law does express an important truth, it could operate for a long time without evident consequences if the potential increments to resources were large in comparison with the ratio of population increase (i.e. if resources ran in the manner: 1, 51, 101, 151, 201, etc. and population: 1, 2, 4, 8, 16, etc.). Put more plainly, if there were plenty of land which could readily be brought into agricultural use a population could go on increasing in numbers for a long time without experiencing any great difficulty in feeding itself. However the 'long time' here is shorter than the 'very long run' of changes in the physical environment and we can perhaps discern demographically engendered 'crises of subsistence' within historic times. (The Roman Empire may have experienced one and possibly collapsed because of it.) Perhaps then there is a law of economic change which states that societies eventually come to a point where they must either effect a major economic advance or submit to a profound regression. But we would have to be very careful in applying such a law, and the mere coincidence of economic change and rising population is unlikely to be an instance of the law in operation. Men respond to stimuli other than those of their stomachs.

There is, of course, a simpler way in which population has a bearing on economic activity. As population rises (or falls) more (or less) goods are required and (assuming that the factors of production other than labour adjust in the same proportion) more (or less) are produced. Thus total output rises and falls in relation to population. But if the variation is a flat quantitative one (i.e. simply more or less of whatever was produced before, in strict proportion to population change and without any alteration in methods) it is not particularly noteworthy. However, the assumption made above that other factors of production adjust readily to a change in population is questionable. Consider the simple case of a medieval agricultural community. Land may exist which can be brought under cultivation, but first it must be cleared of trees, scrub, gorse, heather, stones, etc. and be broken up by repeated heavy ploughing. All this involves a diversion of resources of labour and equipment from their usual task of meeting consumption needs. Doubtless as much of it as possible will be undertaken at normally slack times, such as the winter months, but it may for a short period necessitate some sacrifice of normal output for consumption. Further, there will be a timelag between the need for extra food making itself felt and the coming into production of the new land, during which interval a relative shortage will have prevailed. Thus the relative difficulty of bringing into effective use an additional amount of some factor of production will at least temporarily upset the economic equilibrium. The new land once in use, balance will be restored and things may then go on just as before. But in the interim a process of change may have been initiated. Conceivably, individuals will have been prompted to seek out new activities or new sources of supply. But unless the problems of extending the cultivated area are grave and persistent such internal shifting is unlikely to engender any significant change in the character of the economy. Economic change in fairly primitive societies cannot be interpreted by some general law defining the dynamic of a closed system in purely economic terms. In most, if not all, cases we must look for some external agency or for some impulse which is not specifically determined by material environment.

Demographic developments

Domesday Book is a unique document. After William no other English king ever attempted anything of a similar kind. For population purposes we have to wait until 1377 before the poll tax lists provide a further direct indication of the number of people in England. However, from the thirteenth century onwards sufficient stray data of various kinds exists to permit of estimates for earlier dates. These would suggest that on the eve of the Black Death (1348) the population of England may have been some $4\frac{3}{4}$ million, by comparison with the $1\frac{1}{2}$ million or so of Domesday.[1]

This change in population did not occur at the same rate over the whole country. It was at its least in the already crowded counties of East Anglia, a little above the national average in the territory immediately to the west of these and at its greatest in the north and west. These geographical variations are hardly due to differences in the natural rate of increase. They must represent migration and the clear tendency is from east to west, leaving aside the special case of the move into Yorkshire and adjacent areas for which there is the particular explanation of their unnaturally low population at the time of Domesday as a result of their devastation by William after the revolt there in 1069. The mechanism of this migration is unknown to us, but we can be fairly confident that it did not consist principally in transplantations

[1] The inevitable unreliability of any estimate of medieval, or even later, population should be stressed. In this book all demographic detail for the centuries up to the middle of the sixteenth is drawn from J. C. Russell, *British Medieval Population* (University of North Mexico Press, 1948), adjusted in the light of later criticism by J. Krause, 'The medieval household: large or small?', *Economic History Review*, vol. 9 (1956), T. H. Hollingsworth, *Historical Demography* (Hodder & Stoughton, 1969), pp. 375–88, and that contained in J. Z. Titow, *English Rural Society 1200–1350* (Allen & Unwin, 1969). However these various criticisms are not always fully, or at least readily, compatible with one another. An adequate discussion of the matter would be beyond both the scope of this book and the competence of its author. The figures quoted in the text represent an attempted blending of compromise and credibility.

of men over distances. Occasionally a lord of many manors may have moved men in a body from densely populated property to under-developed territory in the west or in Yorkshire. Along the Welsh border, the Crown or the marcher lords promoted settlement to block the paths of Welsh invaders. But it is in the cumulative effect of moves of five, ten, twenty miles by individuals seeking land or employment that we must probably see the formation of this westward ripple. And to imagine this we must modify a little the traditional view of the medieval villager being born, living and dying in the one parish. For most, and virtually all of those with land, this was doubtless true, but many of the landless must have got at least as far as the next parish.

There is no need to associate this social mobility with a widening of mental horizons or with an intensification of economic links with the outside world. It does not require much imagination to travel a few miles in search of a livelihood, nor does it require the traffic of goods to make one aware that there is another parish a few fields away. Nor is there any essential economic difference between an individual making a move from one community of arable farmers to another and in his being accommodated at home when more land is taken out of the waste. The shift in population was pronounced, but it was neither the consequence nor the cause of significant economic change. Nor did it radically alter the balance of population distribution. Of the fifteen most densely populated counties in 1348 Oxfordshire was the most westerly and Norfolk headed the list. The tendency to edge westwards was probably older than Domesday and must be largely considered as the result of those interim difficulties attendant on bringing new land under cultivation.

Urbanisation

There was, however, one form of migration which had a more signi-ficant character: that from country to town. In 1086 some four per cent of the population lived in communities of more than two thousand people; by 1348 this figure had risen to about seven per cent and the number of such communities from about ten to perhaps twenty-five, among which London, with probably something between fifty and sixty thousand inhabitants, was as always the giant. These were economic units with a distinct identity, consisting essentially in the fact that within each the populace lived largely off one another; they made goods for one another, they sold goods to one another, they provided

16

services for one another.[1] Of course they undertook these functions for outsiders as well. Indeed the very existence of the community as an entity depended on this, for one thing it could not do was feed itself. It had to earn its bread by 'exporting' a surplus of what it did provide. In a society where agricultural produce (including wool, hides and wood) still accounted for the bulk of most people's needs, this exportable surplus had to be large, but in these twenty-five or so communities of 1348 few individuals secured such commodities directly by selling their own wares to those who supplied them. The pattern of economic relationships was more complex.

Of course the dividing line of two thousand is arbitrary. But whether we draw it at a higher or a lower level, or decline to draw it at any particular level, we must distinguish between communities with this kind of economic identity and those which, while non-agricultural, lived more directly off the surrounding countryside. The latter were just an element in a rural economy. The former constituted a distinctive urban economy. During this period, as had been seen, they grew rather more rapidly than population as a whole but nobody can represent an increase of four to seven per cent as an economic revolution. Small as it is, however, this disproportionate growth does demand an explanation. It represented in a clearer manner than any other change a tendency towards a higher degree of specialisation of economic activities than had prevailed at the time of Domesday. It meant that some material needs formerly met by individuals for themselves were now being met by workers devoting themselves exclusively to that activity – or, at least, that isolated village craftsmen had become town craftsmen in company with others, with consequent improvements in skill and technique. It was in the manufacture of woollen cloth that this development was most prominent but in various degrees it occurred in many other crafts: the making of leather, metal and wooden goods with the numerous subdivisions to which these are susceptible. Moreover, middlemen of various kinds were buying and reselling goods which formerly were either not produced at all or were consumed by the producer himself or disposed of directly to a final buyer in the immediate vicinity. Again it was in cloth and in the raw material, wool, that trade developed most conspicuously.

The causes of these developments do not lie within the narrow

[1] This is essentially a mathematical phenomenon, capable of being represented by a finite series. Each extra person creates a fractional demand for goods and services. The larger a town grows the wider the range of demands which it is itself capable of meeting.

bounds of positive knowledge but outside in the wider regions of speculation. That there are distinct advantages in specialisation, whether of individuals or of regions, is evident. That these advantages will be perceived by a particular society at a particular time does not necessarily follow. Why one time rather than another? And if they are perceived why are they not carried further? A notion of economic history as the record of a beneficent evolutionary law destined to culminate in the optimum employment of resources is an attractive one. There is even some kind of plausibility about it. Once having hit upon a better way of doing things, men are unlikely to revert to the worse way, and just as a monkey chained perpetually to a typewriter will eventually produce the complete works of Shakespeare, so men will, in the course of time, hit upon such a better way. Yet we would be reluctant to believe that it is all quite as haphazard as that. Men do not just hit on something. There is always an element of purposefulness about human activity. But the historical sequence of purposes and triggering circumstances which resulted in the closely associated phenomena of urbanisation and specialisation cannot be identified with any confidence. As a problem in English history the question can fairly be begged by ascribing the development to influences from the continent, trickling into England from perhaps the early eleventh century. And considered as a general European phenomenon it may suffice here to refer to the persuasive, though disputed, thesis that towns are essentially the outcome of the expansion of trade on land and sea as the barbarian bands, Viking, Magyars, Saracens were repelled or settled down to more peaceable ways. Points convenient for the interchange of produce peculiar to certain regions attracted a small permanent population to cater for the personal and commercial wants of merchants resorting to them, thus initiating a cumulative growth process.

So far as English towns are concerned we lack the data for useful case histories. Such information as we have relates almost entirely to their politico-legal history. And although this is of some real economic import it must be borne in mind that what follows here on towns and townsmen is governed less by what an economic historian would wish to say of them than by what the available sources permit him to say.

The sources speak above all of the distinctive constitutional character of towns, a character which conferred distinct economic advantages. A town with a fully developed constitution acknowledged no lord or superior official other than the king himself. It managed its own affairs, had its own courts and collected its own taxes, apportioning them amongst the townsmen in its own way. This is not to say that we are confronted with an urban democracy on the ancient Greek model. These functions were not undertaken by the citizenry assembled together but by a mayor and a body of aldermen drawn from the townsfolk, whose mode of appointment varied but was not in any event by way of universal suffrage. However, within this period they represented the townsmen and their sentiments fairly enough in the huge majority of cases. They provided a form of administration, a code of justice and a tax system adapted to the needs of a community of craftsmen and dealers. Equally important was the fact that not merely was the town as a whole free of lordship but so was each individual townsman. No lord had any claim on his person, his property or his labour; no outsider could interfere with the pursuit of his trade or his enjoyment of the gains from it – a security which the lord-ridden countryside of contemporary England could not offer with the same certainty.

Not all towns had this full range of privileges but by the end of the period the great majority of communities of, say, more than a thousand persons and some smaller ones had. Towns of ancient standing had always possessed a fairly distinct autonomy from whatever type of government prevailed in the surrounding countryside although many would, at this time, receive some formal recognition of their status. Towns which only fully emerged as such out of a rural manor had to sever themselves, often very gradually, from the control of lord or sheriff. The instrument of severance was the charter, granted by lord or king, setting out the liberties and rights bestowed on the town. A charter might create a fully autonomous community at one stroke or, as was more commonly the case, a piecemeal granting of concessions by successive charters might be involved. A charter was rarely a free gift on the part of the donor. It was something of value, and value in money was usually given for it. Apart from the initial purchase price the terms of the charter generally included the *firma burgi*. These were an assessed equivalent of the value of the financial privileges of lordship – market tolls, court fines and fees, and the right to other payments from the townsfolk – to be paid annually, or at some regular interval, to the lord. They might be quite onerous but once fixed by charter they were thereafter invariable.

The most prolific granter of charters was the king, in respect of towns standing on his own personal property. There were perhaps three reasons for this. The king, despite his very extensive property, had the most acute need of money, and sale of charters was a valuable source of revenue. The king, already possessed of sovereignty over the whole country, was less jealous of the power which he possessed in his capacity as landowner or manorial lord than an ordinary lord might be. Finally, the king might see in prosperous and strong autonomous communities a counterweight to the power of the territorial aristocracy which was a standing menace to his own security. Other secular lords followed the royal example on their own manors[1] but the great ecclesiastical lords, bishops, abbots, cathedral chapters and collegiate churches, rarely granted complete autonomy to towns, or potential towns, on their lands. Churchmen with their keen sense of being mere trustees for an institution destined to endure until the Last Judgment and consequent reluctance to cede property or power well earned the legal epithet, *mortmain* (literally, dead hand).

These charters have a special value for the historian. They mark in a rough fashion the emergence of concentrated communities containing a large enough element of non-agricultural population to feel the need of and justify a special form of organisation. Within this period there are 113 such charters known. The huge majority of the towns thus legally created were far from forming what we have already defined as distinctive urban economies. They were what might most handily be called country towns. They were part and parcel of the immediately adjoining countryside. Many of their inhabitants earned their living on the land; many more engaged in agricultural work at special times such as harvest. The fields touched their doorsteps. The economy of the non-agricultural element depended heavily on the sale of its wares to the surrounding country-dwellers and, with almost frightening precariousness, on being provisioned from such surplus as its rural neighbours could raise. The weavers, tailors, hatters, shoemakers, smiths, millwrights, wainwrights, wheelwrights, coopers, carpenters, ale-house keepers etc., who in twos and threes made up this non-agricultural element, were little different from the single ones to be found in many villages. These country towns, by significant contrast with the genuinely urban communities, grew only in proportion to total population. This is to say that, on balance, there was no movement from the land to such communities or, alternatively put, that their growth does not represent any really new economic departure. How-

---

[1] In some instances lords took the initiative themselves, seeking to create planned towns on new sites by offering inducements to craftsmen and dealers to settle on the site in the expectation of adding tolls etc. to their domanial revenues. A handful of these were founded in real commercial prospects. More, probably, rested only on wishful thinking and came to nothing.

ever, it should be allowed that the larger a community the more scope there is for economic specialisation; it is therefore probable that by 1348 a slightly higher proportion of the rural populace was devoting itself to non-agricultural work than had been the case in 1086 – a development which would be as evident in the village as in the town.

The guilds

The increase in the size of non-agricultural elements brings in its train that institution characteristic of the medieval world: the guild. One can almost say that anywhere in medieval Europe where six or seven of a like kind are gathered together they will form a society. We are here concerned only with such societies as have an economic character, but we would seriously misunderstand these if we did not recognise that they are just one form of a much more general institution and that while these may occupy themselves principally with economic matters their origins are not to be sought in economic motives, nor are they subsequently sustained by economic impulses alone. They really belong to religious or cultural history, even though it has been from the economic historian that they have received most attention. The cultural roots cannot be probed here. We can only say that a medieval townsman seems to have felt himself incomplete except as a member of some society whose founding principle was common devotion to a particular saint or attachment to a particular form of piety. In England the first such societies whose membership consisted of those following the one craft appear to have been guilds of weavers which already existed in some places around the time of Domesday. But for the moment we will pass over those to the guild which we find almost everywhere when a town comes into formal existence through a charter. This is the guild merchant. Quite commonly it too received a charter but it is improbable that the charter created the guild. Rather the charter conferred on a pre-existing organisation a special kind of authority within the town. It is far from clear how this authority was distinguished from that of the mayor and aldermen or if indeed, in some cases, there was any distinction at all and if the two bodies were not the same thing. Certainly the senior membership of the two was often identical and even if a formal distinction was maintained between them, in practice they functioned as a single authority.

Theoretically the authority of the mayor and aldermen extended over all those living within the town, while that of the guild merchant extended over only its own members. These members must have consisted of all those engaged in manufacture and trade. We have no certain knowledge about this but it seems incredible that 'guild merchant' really meant what it would mean to a modern ear: a guild of merchants. Some of the larger towns may have contained enough merchants to warrant their forming a special body, but there must have been smaller towns which did not contain a single merchant (in the sense of one who buys and sells the produce of others) but yet had a guild merchant. This is only explicable on the assumption that merchant here signifies anyone who depended on the sale of what he produced or handled to secure his material needs by contrast with the more familiar kind of individual in the countryside who consumed what he produced and produced what he consumed. Once the numbers of such 'merchants' reached any size they formed a guild. And at the same time they posed an ethical problem. In the case of someone practising a subsistence economy his return was directly and necessarily proportionate to his labour: the more seed he sowed, the more land he ploughed and the more diligently he tended his crop, the more he had for his own needs. Here there was no problem of value in exchange to be settled. Quite otherwise with the man who depended on the sale of his produce. What was he entitled to in return for his labour? The modern answer is: whatever he can get for it. If he is greedy and asks too much he will be unable to find a buyer. The rule of the market determines, in an equitable manner, his return. But the medieval mind lacked the law of supply and demand. Justice required that, like the subsistence farmer, the seller receive a return proportionate to his labour. And justice it was then that determined, or was supposed to determine, the price of his produce.

One of the primary functions of a medieval town authority was the control of the market to ensure that the 'just price' prevailed. The problem was complicated by the fact that nobody ever succeeded in evolving a practicable way of calculating the 'just price' of particular articles. Ultimately the matter was one for the Church – indeed without Christianity men might have been well content in practice with the law of supply and demand even if they never recognised it as such. The Church, God's own instrument in the world, was the arbiter of justice, for justice was the way in which God, from time eternal, had determined in his perfection, that men should conduct their affairs with one another. Theologians devoted endless thought to teasing out the idea of the 'just price' and some even came close to a modern theory of supply and demand in so doing. But few medieval townsmen read their scholarly treatises and in the market place a rough rule of thumb fixed a price that ensured the seller enough for modest comfort – in effect a 'cost plus' principle which, doubtless, in ordinary circumstances, led to much the same price as would have prevailed in the absence of control. The same sense of justice compelled a similar supervision of quality. Goods offered for sale had to measure up to the standards of competent, careful, and honest workmanship.

These then were the special functions of a guild merchant: to ensure that justice prevailed in respect of the economic activities of its members. (In the case of two commodities of supreme and pervasive importance, bread and ale, the special device of regular courts – 'assizes' – to regulate their price and quality was employed. The assizes of bread and ale were conducted by the corporation and were vested with punitive powers which the guild merchant seems to have lacked in the disciplining of its members.) Justice cut both ways. Both buyer and seller had to receive value. Further, the seller was entitled to protection not only against a buyer but also against other sellers. He had a place in society; he was part of the social order, an order conceived of not as man's doing but God's. Anything that threatened his livelihood was an offence against justice, and for a guild member to seek to expand his own business at the expense of a brother member was an obnoxious offence. Price and quality control then served also to ensure equality amongst guild members by preventing competition amongst them. Against competition from outside the guild member was protected by the simple exclusion of outside merchants except when they brought raw materials which were not available locally or goods which were not produced in the town, or came to buy, in which circumstances they were admitted on payment of a toll and subjected to a close watch on their activities; if the town had merchants of its own the stranger might be forbidden to buy particular commodities which provided them with a profitable part of their business, and he might be forbidden to buy raw materials needed by the guildsmen themselves. If he brought in a consignment of goods all guild members interested in buying them had to have an equal opportunity of doing so.

Clearly all these forms of control, placed here in the context of an idea of social justice and a spirit of confraternity, were capable of abuse and were theoretically a check on individual enterprise. But even if one were crassly to ignore the matrix of ethical and customary attitudes in which guild control was embedded there would still remain the truism that as consumers themselves craftsmen had a direct interest in preventing such control being used as an instrument of consumer oppression; while to dwell on the possible inhibitory consequences of control would be to ignore even more foolishly the economic environment. The state of affairs would have been little different had the controls been completely absent. We are dealing with small-scale producers, using simple techniques, catering for limited local markets and differing little from one another in point of efficiency; and this situation was the product of the economic and technological circumstances of the times which provided neither the scope nor the incentive for anything very different. When, later, opportunities did arise for the talents of the adventurous, vigorous, risk-bearing captain of industry – the heroic figure beloved of Victorian historians – the system of controls was brushed aside. They lasted only as long as they served economic needs. They are the creation, not the creator, of the conditions of the day.

By the late twelfth century in some towns and in nearly all the larger ones by the middle of the fourteenth, the guild merchant had started to disappear; on the one hand merging into the corporation, on the other giving way to the newer craft guilds. The extent to which these had emerged and were playing a significant economic role at any particular time throughout the period dealt with in this chapter would seem to be fairly strictly a function of population. In characteristic fashion men engaged in the same craft formed themselves into guilds whenever there were enough of them to warrant it. As the numbers of craftsmen of all kinds increased the guild merchant must have found it increasingly difficult to exercise efficient control over their activities and had to delegate this duty. The craft guilds lay ready to hand to assume the responsibility, answerable always to the senior organisation. As the guild merchant shed these particular functions and confined itself to general supervision and concerns common to all, the already shadowy line of distinction between it and the corporation vanished entirely, and the one became lost in the other – except in some cases where it survived as a guild of merchants. In point of economic function then the craft guilds represented no important new development. They were unambiguously subordinate to a higher and older authority. (There were some exceptions to this in craft guilds of long standing, mostly those of weavers, some with charters of their own, who considered themselves to be autonomous; their claims were eventually overborne everywhere by the corporation.)

We do, however, find the craft guilds regulating two matters with which there is no evidence that the guild merchant had concerned itself, presumably because these matters had not reached a point where regulation was necessary. The one is apprenticeship. Nearly all craft guilds had quite elaborate apprenticeship regulations laying down the financial terms under which a youth was to be admitted to an apprenticeship in that craft, the manner in which his master (in whose house he lodged) was to care for him, the age at which he could be taken on as an apprentice, the number of years he had to serve and the test of competence he had to pass before being deemed qualified, the number of apprentices which any one master was permitted to take on, and perhaps other stipulations as well. The other matter was the regulation of wages to be paid to workmen employed by a master ('journeymen', from the French *journée* [day]).

Behind the early emergence of these two new functions in the thirteenth century we must presumably see the lone craftsman building up a small workshop as population growth afforded him greater market scope, and simultaneously a growing interest on the part of parents of some modest means in staking out a secure livelihood for their sons, an interest perhaps sharpened to an anxiety as landholdings became more difficult to obtain. Out of this there grew a regular system of apprenticeship. The period of apprenticeship was quite long – seven years was usual in most trades and in few, if any, can so long a time have been necessary in order to acquire the requisite technical skill. Doubtless craftsmen exaggerated the intricacy of their work (the word 'mystery' often used instead of 'craft' is evocative). In some part too apprenticeship was the plebeian counterpart of the aristocratic practice of fostering – having one's children brought up in some other lordly household – and was intended as a general training in citizenship; a boy admitted to an apprenticeship at the age of fourteen would not be mature enough to take an independent place in the world until he was twenty-one or so. But in practice the particular advantage for a master of a long apprenticeship (which was contractually binding on both parties) was that in its later years he had the services of a skilled man available, and at a fairly low wage. Within this period one to three apprentices usually made up the skilled labour force of a master-craftsman. A journeyman or two might also be employed, but before the fifteenth century these were rarely qualified men though in practice many must often have acquired a high degree of competence if they had clung to the one trade. The name reveals their status: day-wage labourers. They were the unskilled urban proletariat. An apprentice once out of his time would normally set up on his own, unless he was waiting to succeed his father as many were. In a society where the average life expectancy was about forty the turnover in craftsmen was fairly rapid, and widening market opportunities in the thirteenth century would have offered early scope in activities where the very modest outlay on tools and a small house was all that was needed to start in business, provided the guild requirements had been met.

The cloth industry

As has been indicated already, there was one craft of pre-eminent importance: the manufacture of woollen cloth. This does not require any special explanation. After food, clothing is man's most important basic need – at least in non-tropical regions. In medieval Europe clothing meant woollen cloth. Linen was too light as outer wear and no other textile material was locally available. Raw wool cannot be converted into cloth in one easy operation. To distinguish only the most important processes: the strands of wool must be carded together to render them suitable for being spun into yarn; the yarn must be woven together to form a meshed material; this material must, usually, be treated to give it thickness and texture (fulling); and taste dictates that the finished product be dyed to give it an attractive appearance. Of these the most labour-consuming are spinning and weaving. Spinning, time out of mind, had been women's work, fitted in with the household chores – with the simple though not very efficient device, the distaff, which could be carried around, a relatively easy business.[1] Weaving, a strenuous affair with a large loom, had become men's work. It is the first occupation which we know of in England, other than the less important working of metals, to give rise to a distinct body of craftsmen. Already at the time of Domesday there were groups of weavers in many places and they seem often to have constituted the nuclei of towns in whose economic life they were destined to play a part. But in every village and hamlet there would have been men at looms catering for their own needs or those of their neighbours. The particular congregations of weavers here and there must have been of those engaged in the manufacture of cloth of a somewhat better than ordinary variety, on account of the higher quality of the wool used and the

---

[1] The spinning-wheel was introduced into England in the late thirteenth or early fourteenth century. It was more productive than the distaff but immobile, and the two coexisted as long as hand-spinning lasted.

superior skill employed, and intended for sale over a wider area than the immediate locality. Considerations of supplies of raw materials and of marketing opportunities, via merchants, of the finished product would be responsible for the tendency to cluster.

As population grew so did the market scope for these men. By the beginning of the thirteenth century we can discern notable bodies of weavers in York, Beverley, Lincoln, Louth, Stamford, Leicester, Northampton, Colchester, London, Oxford, and Winchester, who were clearly producing for quite extensive markets, although lumped together there would be both makers of fine cloth and of coarser cloths for local sale. In at least some instances the cloth industries of these centres were under the effective management of capitalist entrepreneurs who attended to the procurement of the raw materials and the sale of the finished product, and exercised a close control over the intermediary processes: in economic essentials forerunners of the better documented 'clothiers' of later centuries.[1] Some of the cloth even sold overseas, for English cloth enjoyed the advantage of being made from a higher quality wool than was found in quantity elsewhere in northern Europe.

If we pass on another century into the early years of the fourteenth we find a different picture. Oxford, which had had more than sixty weavers in the opening years of the thirteenth century, was reported to have had only fifteen in 1275 and none at all in 1323. So was Lincoln in 1321. In the same year there were said to be only eighty looms in London where formerly there had been 380. In Northampton, which in the second half of the thirteenth century was reputed to have contained 300 looms, cloth manufacture had almost ceased by 1334. Other former centres of the industry could tell a similar story. A story, it may be noted, which while intended to relate a sad decline also reveals in its statistics that we are very far from dealing with an occupation of great proportions relative to economic activity as a whole, or even to the economic life of these particular towns, especially if one discounts those producing cheaper cloths to serve local needs. But while recognising that the manufacture of fine cloth for distant sale was not markedly more than marginally important, the fact of the decline of cloth manufacture sometime around the

---

[1] In these known instances the clothworkers themselves were commonly excluded from membership of the guild merchant and were often confined to working for the 'clothiers'. In such cases this must have been a potent element in the quarrels between weavers' guilds and municipal authorities, briefly referred to earlier.

middle of the thirteenth century in these towns still demands an explanation.

As with almost any interpretative question posed by these centuries, lack of sufficient information precludes dogmatic answers. However, one factor which plainly had a hand in the matter was the intensified competition of Flemish cloth. Drawing, ironically, on fine English wool, Flemish cloth through the thirteenth century won itself an unrivalled reputation for high quality in the markets of northern Europe. It is impossible to say how far down the quality and price range Flemish competition extended. A second contemporary development which may have hit urban English manufacturers towards the cheaper end of the range was the arrival of the fulling-mill, one of the few technological advances of this period. This was a water-powered apparatus for impregnating the cloth with fullers earth and it made for measurably lower fulling costs. It was first seen in England towards the end of the twelfth century but its spread belongs mostly to the second half of the thirteenth. Obviously it could only be located where there was a sufficiently powerful head of water to drive it, by the swiftly moving streams and rivers of rural areas. To some extent it certainly drew cloth manufacture out of the towns into the countryside. There are known instances where urban weavers, prohibited by guild merchant or corporation from sending their cloth out to country mills – a practice which threatened to undo the town fullers – instead took themselves and their looms there, their readiness in some cases to quit the town no doubt heightened by the struggles between their guilds and the town authorities. But it is impossible to assess the overall magnitude of this movement or to calculate its total impact on urban clothmaking centres.

The persistence into the late fifteenth century of ordinances against fulling-mills makes it clear that the older method long remained sufficiently widespread to be worth protecting, while the evidence also makes it plain that rural fulling-mills abounded the most in the more remote counties, Yorkshire, Lancashire, Westmorland, Cumberland, Cornwall, Devon, Somerset, Wiltshire, Gloucestershire. The mountainous or hilly terrain of these counties of course provided innumerable sites carrying the necessary flow of water. But the weavers clustered round them were hardly migrants from the distant cloth towns of the east. Nor is there any evidence from these years to suggest that cloth from the north and west was extensively marketed. Indeed it is difficult to credit that lower fulling costs, which would be little more than marginal when measured against total production costs, could have compensated for the expense on transport involved in selling in eastern and southern markets. It seems more plausible that this spread of fulling-mills in the remoter counties chiefly reflects the population inflow into these formerly very thinly inhabited regions, creating scope for the development of cloth manufacture for local sale, employing a technical aid for which these areas were well suited.

Whatever the causes of the decline of urban cloth manufacture, and acknowledging again that at no time within this period was the specialist production of fine cloth an activity of central economic importance, it yet retains the special interest of being the first instance we can discern, however indistinctly, of an 'exposed' industry – one with a life history which discloses the operation of wider ranging forces than anything which the economy had earlier experienced. More particularly, fine cloth was the first finished manufacture to be extensively distributed as regional variations in costs and quality caused certain centres to secure a competitive advantage. Fine cloth brought, so to speak, a new element of sensitivity and mobility to the economy; it constituted an economic activity liable to fluctuations of fortune which could not be attributed to the universally intelligible works of God or nature: frost, drought, flood, fire, disease; a sector where production was no longer undertaken in response to immediate need, where there was no longer a virtually automatic equality of supply and demand, where the services of a merchant, hazarding his judgment, were needed to ensure that what was made was sold. In a word it meant commercialism.

Non-urban industry

There were of course other industrial activities, apart from rural cloth-making based on fulling-mill locations, which were carried on outside towns and beyond the orbit of guild control. The most important were the mining of iron ore and the smelting and refining of iron. Iron, in small quantities, was needed for many tools and for weapons and armour. Shallow deposits of ore of varying quality were found in many parts of the country but, in the early part of this period, the Forest of Dean in Gloucestershire was the only centre marketing iron on any extensive scale – not only unwrought but articles of iron manufacture as well. The productive unit was small: the ore lay close to the surface and could easily be quarried by one man with the assistance of another to haul it up if a pit of perhaps ten or twenty feet had to be dug. The bloomery in which the ore was smelted could hardly have been simpler – virtually nothing more than a hole in the ground lined and enclosed with stones. Capital played little part in this kind of operation. In the thirteenth century the Weald of Sussex and Kent started to establish itself as the major English iron-producing centre, which it was to remain for another four centuries. The abundance of wood in this extensive forest area yielded plentiful supplies of the charcoal which was required for smelting in as great quantities as the ore itself. Population growth and, though to a very modest extent, the more extensive use of iron stimulated production, which would seem to have led to some advance in metallurgy in a rough empirical way. There was something of a keener appreciation of what was required to obtain good quality pig iron and of what was needed in the refinement of pig to yield satisfactory bar.[1] The thirteenth-century forge in which refining was carried out became a rather more elaborate concern, with perhaps six or eight employees and a water-powered tilt hammer. The forge-master (or the manorial lord who maintained a forge, or several of them if he owned extensive estates) was by way of being a small industrial capitalist; but smelting, which was often a separate under-taking, remained a simple and small-scale affair. And with most native ores being of only indifferent quality high grade metal, either as bars or as artifacts, had to be imported.

Of other metals tin mining and smelting had been carried on in Devon and Cornwall since pre-Roman times. Requirements of the metal were small – it was mostly used with lead to make pewter for drinking and eating vessels of a superior kind; some was alloyed with copper to make bronze for bells and ornaments. But the deposits in the south-west were the most abundant in Europe; and with the growth of European trade output probably rose through the twelfth and thirteenth centuries. To start with all the ore worked was alluvial, found as pebbles and small stones often within a few feet of the surface, and one self-employed individual could both fetch the ore and attend to its smelting in a simple ovenlike affair made of clay or stone. Before

[1] Pig iron is iron which has only been smelted and which will contain impurities: these include carbon, a certain amount of which is desirable for the sake of hardness although it lessens the malleability and resilience of the metal. Bar iron is iron from which the impurities, including excess carbon, have been refined out. Until the eighteenth century refining was carried out by successive heatings and hammerings. Bloomery iron, if made from high grade materials, might need little or no refining, and the terminology employed here with its sharp distinction is actually anachronistic.

the end of the period, however, deeper pits or trenches were being dug
to get at the ore, requiring the coordinated activity of several men,
while smelting was being carried out in more elaborate 'blowing
houses', manned by a regular 'blower' or two. These developments
gave rise to the formation of syndicates amongst the tinworkers, some
of whom had large enough claims to employ hired labour to work
them or to lease them to others – in some cases being members of more
than one syndicate.

Lead, for roofing substantial buildings, for water pipes and for
pewter, was worked extensively in Derbyshire, Yorkshire, Shropshire
and Cumberland; some was exported. Generally it was quite accessible
and was mined by individuals or small self-constituted groups. Smelting
was conducted in a 'bole', analogous to a bloomery. Small quantities
of silver in low yield concentrations occurred in Cumberland and
Devon. By law precious metals belonged to the Crown which leased
the mining rights to capitalist entrepreneurs. Coal was dug out here
and there where it outcropped in various parts of the north of England
by individuals for their own use instead of wood. From the late
twelfth century it was quarried commercially in the vicinity of Newcastle, most notably on the extensive estates of the Bishop of Durham,
who leased the mining rights to small syndicates of miners or to an
individual who would employ a small work force – perhaps no more
than two or three men. In this area it was probably substituted quite
generally for wood as a fuel and ships trading to Newcastle often took
on a cargo of coal rather than sail light; by the end of the thirteenth
century smiths and lime-burners along the East coast were using coal.
Clay suitable for good quality pottery also only occurred in particular
areas and in Staffordshire, at least, its presence gave rise to an industry
whose wares were marketed widely.

Most vital of all these necessarily localised industries was saltmaking.
Inland, salt was obtained from the brine waters in Cheshire and
Worcestershire from where it was marketed quite extensively. Along
the coast it could be had from sea-water and all coastal areas must have
been at least self-sufficient in salt, while the beaches of Lincolnshire,
Norfolk, Kent and Sussex yielded a surplus for wider distribution, some
of which was exported. The technique was simple, consisting merely
of boiling the water until the salt was separated. Such a process needed
neither elaborate equipment nor more than one man to execute it.

Perhaps the most interesting industry of this period in point of the
special kind of organisation it required was large-scale building – not

the building of ordinary wood and plaster houses, which was within the scope of local craftsmen, but the erection of those monumental edifices in stone which are the period's most enduring memorials: cathedrals and castles. Indeed, the thirteenth- and early fourteenth-century cathedrals in the Early English and Decorated styles could fairly be said to be the supreme achievements, both technical and aesthetic, of the period. All the medieval English cathedrals date from these two and a half centuries after Domesday. Along with the castles – that is the elaborately fortified ones of the thirteenth century which replaced the simple keep of the earlier Normans – the cathedrals represent a productive effort unmatched by any other undertakings. This is not to suggest that in proportion to total economic activity they employed a large share of productive resources – we are speaking of the construction of just seventeen English cathedrals and perhaps twenty-five castles of comparable massivity, to which we can add a number of abbey churches which rivalled the cathedrals for size and splendour. At any one time no more than two or three of these were in course of construction simultaneously. But as single projects they were, in simply economic terms, unparalleled. The recruitment of labour, skilled and unskilled, the control and coordination of the work, the procurement of building materials, the financing of the enterprise, posed problems not found elsewhere. The key figure often seems to have been the master mason who apparently, in terms of modern functions, was sometimes simultaneously contractor, engineer and architect. The unskilled labour was doubtless obtained locally. The skilled men must have been largely freelancers, ready to travel to wherever there was work for them. Very possibly they operated, at least periodically, in small syndicates subcontracting with the master mason for a particular part of the work. The master mason may have needed to be something of a capitalist. The disbursements of his employer, king, baron, bishop or abbot, may not have been as regular as the wage payments to the work-people. But of the management of these great constructional enterprises we know regrettably little.

We are similarly ignorant of another industry of a comparable nature in point of organisation though not of scale: shipbuilding. Along the coasts and river estuaries, shipbuilding benefited from the expansion of trade through this period although much of the trade was carried on in foreign ships. The medieval ship, big at a hundred tons, while much smaller than a cathedral was a more considerable and complex affair than a cart, a plough, a pair of gloves, a length of cloth or anything else turned out by a medieval craftsman. The master shipbuilder with his fairly large work force, the quantity of materials needed for a single job, and the lapse of time between order and completion, had to be both manager and capitalist as well as a skilled craftsman. But again we are out on the fringes of the economy. For the great majority of manufacturers, small men, town-based and guild-controlled, problems of management and finance, except of the simplest kind, did not exist.

Agriculture

After this excursion into industry it is salutary to remember that we are still dealing with an economy that was heavily agricultural. Nine-tenths of the population in 1348 lived off the land. Clearly only a fraction of the economic endeavour which that represents was devoted to feeding the other one-tenth. Indeed if we make the initial assumption (realistic enough in a society which knows little of labour-saving devices) of a common degree of labour intensiveness in all productive activities, then only one-ninth of the rural effort expended was so applied. If we further assume that there was no specialisation within agriculture (i.e. that the same things were produced everywhere in the same proportions so that there was no interchange of goods between rural areas – also realistic enough as a preliminary statement), then only the same one-ninth entered into exchange, the remaining eight-ninths being consumed where they were produced. If we then make some allowance for raw materials which come from the land (wool, hides, wood, ores) and say that the value of the finished products made from them consisted half of the value of the materials and half of the labour employed in processing them, then we should add a half of one-ninth to the amount entering into exchange and subtract the same one-eighteenth from that consumed *in situ*. And if we allowed for some rural specialisation (e.g. in wool) we might say that two-ninths of rural output was sold and seven-ninths remained where it was produced. However this assumes an identity of real income *per capita* as between agricultural workers and non-agricultural workers. In fact the average town craftsman in all probability had a higher real income than the average peasant. (The chief effective agent of this discrepancy would have been the manorial lord who deprived the peasant of part of his product, much of which part the lord sold in exchange for industrial goods at a rate of exchange which valued the craftsman's or merchant's labour more highly than the peasant's.) Making some allowance for this and rounding out we could strike a figure of one-third as the proportion marketed outside, the remaining two-thirds remaining where it was produced.

Now this is evidently a highly theoretical exercise and we have no means of checking its conclusions against hard data. But while recognising the spurious pretensions to accuracy of these neat fractions we would be warranted in taking them as a mathematical statement of the general order of things. And if what follows is largely devoted to the more interesting portion which reached the market any appreciation of its importance must be heavily weighted by the consideration that it was the smaller portion.

There is no question but that the proportion of agricultural produce marketed grew within this period. The plainest reason for that has already been given: the particular growth of the larger towns, to which something could be added on account of the probably larger non-agricultural element in the country towns. Additionally, the increased demand from English and, especially from the early thirteenth century, Flemish and Italian cloth manufacturers would have brought about an increase not merely in the amount of wool marketed but also in the amount of foodstuffs, in so far as the wool came from areas devoting themselves to sheep-farming to the point where they did not grow enough cereals for themselves. Such areas would have been few. The bulk of the wool came from sheep grazed on the commons adjoining arable land and there is no indication that any significant quantities of arable were turned over to sheep. But here and there, most notably on the slopes of the Pennines, in the hilly country flanking the Severn and on the moors of the south-west, land which could not bear corn was being more intensively settled by sheep-farmers.

Lastly, there seems to have been a purely social change which had the same consequence. The owners of scattered estates who had formerly, with their households, travelled from one to another consuming their produce as they went, rather in the manner of a swarm of locusts, tended increasingly to remain at the one seat; at first they had the produce of their other estates transported to them but as marketing opportunities grew they came to adopt the more convenient method of having such produce sold and the proceeds remitted to them for the purchase of local supplies. The scant indications are that such a practice was already quite common at the time of Domesday; and, indeed, in a number of instances, had been taken a step further, when great estate owners had farmed out their demesnes (and even perhaps entire manors), i.e. leased them in return for a specified amount of money or produce. ('Farming' seems to have reached its greatest intensity in the middle decades of the twelfth century, when it can plausibly be associated with the civil wars and internal disorders following the death of Henry I (1135) and the consequent difficulty for multimanored lords of maintaining regular communications with their estates. With the restoration of effective royal control under Henry II after 1174, direct exploitation of demesnes through the agency of a bailiff or steward seems to have been generally resumed.) At any time, however, remission either of demesne produce or of 'farm' payment would have been confined to the relative handful of owners of numerous estates: the Crown – pre-eminently, the bishops and greater abbeys, the baronial magnates.

Lords and villagers

At the same time as, and to some degree as a consequence of, the widening of commercial opportunities there emerges into full view what historians have dubbed 'the manorial system'. We have already seen Continental ideas encroaching on English ones. In the twelfth and early thirteenth centuries we see this process come to culmination, without, however, entirely eradicating older English ways. In particular the doctrine of one lord, one piece of land, one man triumphed. Outside the chartered towns, by the early decades of the thirteenth century, little land and few men lay beyond the scope of lordship. The many classes of English society had been transmuted into the two of northern French society: free men and villeins; and most belonged to the latter category to which it was to the advantage of lords to assign them.

Lawyers had evolved precepts and principles which determined a man's status, often in violent collision with his own estimation of himself or with that of the community to which he belonged; he and his neighbours might well remain oblivious of or indifferent to the rules of the law books. In general all obligations which English society had created between peasant and lord were treated as marks of villeinage except where they could be clearly shown to be the subject of a free contract terminable by either party. All land was assumed to have a lord unless the contrary was proven. The burden of proof lay with those claiming freedom. For the lawyers villeinage was a status little above slavery. A villein was not actually the property of his lord, but he was utterly his lord's to command; his labour belonged to his lord; what land he held was his lord's; it followed that the fruit of these was also his lord's – he could call no property his own; it further followed that he could not remove himself from his lord – he was tied to the manor in which he was born, and he was a villein from birth by virtue of villein parentage. So said the law books. But side by side with new law ran old English custom which while it vanished from the courts survived in the villages and in the minds of the villagers. Lords had no legal training; many of them could not read; they were not in the habit of mingling with lawyers. The life of the rural communities in which they lived and of the battlefield was all that many of them knew. Crudely they took as much from the lawyers as suited their interests and could be imposed without goading the peasantry beyond endurance. For the rest, as with the generations they became English themselves, they took their ideas from those immediately around them. Villeinage in practice then was some amalgam of academic law, traditional custom and economic interests. Colloquial attitudes attributed quasi-proprietory rights in land to both lord and villein.

The law liked to assimilate land and occupant: villeins occupied land which owed villein services; freemen occupied land free of such services.[1] But there were villeins who were in occupancy of freeholds and freemen who held some land by villein tenure. And there were smallholdings, quite common in East Anglia, which lay within no manor – apart from larger properties, here and there throughout the country, whose owner acknowledged no lord but was not a lord himself. The urge to reduce one community to a single lordship frequently ran up against conflicting lordly claims. Villages where more than one lord exercised rights over different pieces of land and different villeins remained numerous, especially in East Anglia and the north, as did villeins who were subject to more than one lord. The point was never reached where even the majority of villages with their inhabitants were fully coincident with just one manor. But by the early decades of the thirteenth century the manorial lord who exercised complete and undivided jurisdiction over a whole community was the standard type. More emphatically, the village whose arable land was made up of the individual holdings of the villagers and the demesne land of a lord or lords to whom compulsory labour services were owed by the occupants

---

[1] The reference here is to manorial freeholds, for the law could comprehend a freeholder who rendered agreed services or payments of some kind to a lord but who was yet technically free to detach himself and his land from that lord.

of villein holdings was the characteristic agrarian unit of early thirteenth-century England.

In heavily wooded country, and in much of the Highland zone the widely scattered locations of holdings rendered regular labour services impracticable and the lord commonly took money or produce instead. In East Anglia and Yorkshire, where there was a good deal of freehold land, a lord might frequently have to employ hired labour to work his demesne, which often lay in more than one village. In Kent, which succeeded in preserving much of its distinctive social structure in the face of Normanisation, labour dues were largely unknown – the marketing opportunities afforded by proximity to London and the cross-channel ports may have had something to do with this. Near the Scottish border demesnes were small and the lord received much of his due in kind. Scattered about everywhere were manors with no demesne and where villein dues perforce were usually in cash or kind. Even in the Midlands, where the identity of village and manor was most common, some payments in money or produce generally supplemented labour dues. But, overall, labour services were the most onerous of villein burdens and the most valuable of lordly prerogatives.

Labour was the most readily exactable commodity. Dues in kind presupposed a sufficient surplus over subsistence needs; money payments presupposed not only that but also opportunities for the sale of the surplus. Labour was available from any man in good health irrespective of circumstances. And for the lord with demesne land whose principal economic concern was the provisioning of his household labour was more directly useful than money. Labour dues are characteristic of a subsistence economy. The essence of the 'manorial system' was this reliance on villein labour for farming the demesne and the practical understanding that the villein held his land securely in return for his labour, an arrangement which relieved both parties of any dependence on money and market opportunities.

The extent to which at any time the labour employed on the demesne was actually that of the villein farmers themselves is a question of some obscurity. A lord would rarely have any objection to the work being performed by a hired deputy. As the numbers of cottar/labourers grew with the lag between population growth and the provision of new holdings out of the waste such hired labour became more readily available. When and where this was the case a lord himself might well prefer to employ wage labour directly. Villein labour, grudgingly and resentfully undertaken, was hardly very efficient. The villein indeed had a positive disincentive to undertake it, for each day spent on his lord's land was a day lost on his own. Wage labour where a day's work meant a day's extra pay was apt to be more willingly and efficiently rendered. Both lord and villein then would, where it was possible, be disposed towards a formal 'commutation' – the substitution of an equivalent money payment for labour dues.

Apart from the question of the availability of hired labour, the extent of commutation would in part also be a function of the breadth of market opportunities; the villein obviously needed these if he were to raise the cash to meet his commuted dues. However, increased market opportunities also broadened the scope for demesne farming and at the same time, heightened lords' requirements of labour. Commercial farming, that is to say, might operate either to raise the incidence of labour dues or to diminish it. Whether as we move through the twelfth and the thirteenth centuries the overall balance tips towards more commutation or towards more direct labour services is very difficult to say. It has been very forcefully argued[1] that the middle years of the twelfth century saw a widespread substitution of money payments for labour dues in conjunction with the 'farming' of demesnes, followed from the late twelfth century by a partial reversion to labour services as lords resumed their demesnes to take advantage of the growing possibilities of commercial farming. And even if this view errs in respect of an absolute decline in labour services in the twelfth century, it remains very likely that there was a relative decline as new peasant holdings were created out of the waste without a corresponding extension of the demesne, resulting in holdings which were of necessity free of labour dues and which might quite commonly in fact be constituted as authentic freeholds.

Above all, we are not compelled to look for persistent general trends. Commutation was not necessarily, or even usually, permanent or total. All, or part, of the labour services due might be commuted in one year; the following year labour might again be taken in place of money. At all times it was entirely a matter for the lord's discretion. But, at least from the late thirteenth century onwards, the further we go on in time up to the Black Death the more likely we are to find manors on which labour services had not been directly rendered for many years.

All villeins probably welcomed the change from socially degrading compulsory labour to more honorific money rents but there was a particular advantage for the villein who (like, though on a smaller scale

[1] By Professor M. M. Postan; see Note at the end of this chapter, p. 59.

than, the lord) could produce enough to yield a surplus for sale. To the man whose holding could raise such a surplus if worked intensively enough his own labour was worth more than its commuted money equivalent. That is to say the extra crop he could produce if relieved of the obligation to work on the demesne would fetch more on the market than he paid in rent (i.e. the commuted value of his labour dues). For the man whose holding could not yield more than he needed for himself and his family commutation carried no economic advantage. Labour was all that he could command a surplus of and for that he obviously could obtain no more than he had to pay in rent. Further, commutation introduced him to a new element of insecurity. While his obligation was in labour a fall, for any reason, in the need for labour simply meant a holiday for him. But when he owed a fixed money rent a fall in the need for labour lowered his money income and imperilled his ability to pay the rent. The same applied to the individual who raised just sufficient surplus of produce to meet the rent. A fall in the price of produce or a lower than average yield had the same consequences for him. By the same token it rendered lordly incomes less vulnerable to fluctuation.

Commercial farming

Commutation aggravated existing economic differentiation on the land. The accidents of inheritance would from the beginning have tended to produce inequalities among landholders although the practice where it prevailed of succession by a single son preserved a fairly high degree of uniformity.[1] Wherever commercial opportunities had already existed superior ability, determination or just luck on the part of some would have enabled them to accumulate small sums of capital with which to acquire extra land.[2] The man who had come by enough land to raise a fairly substantial surplus for marketing could weather price falls and poor yields. The man who produced little or no surplus might be

---

[1] There was no formal law of inheritance with regard to villein holdings since the law recorded them as the absolute property of the lord. In practice custom and/or in some degree the personal wish of the deceased occupant commonly prevailed subject to the payment to the lord of a heriot or entry fine by the incoming occupant. However in many parts of England, perhaps most, division of a holding amongst all sons had been the ancient custom and in such areas lords usually sought to check subdivision to the extent that labour dues had to be calculated in fractions.

[2] This might be freehold land or villein land which had reverted to the lord on the failure of a line of succession or villein land bought from the occupying villein and entered into on payment of a fine to the lord.

forced to sell his holding or some part of it in difficult times in order to meet the rent. The distress of one was an opportunity for the other to grow still bigger. The further commercial farming and commutation proceeded the more varied became the size of holdings, though they usually continued to be made up of multiples or simple fractions of virgates (or other standard areas) probably because the lord would only sanction land transfers in such units so that the labour due to him from any one villein, even if commuted for the while, did not have to be calculated in notional amounts. But the range of variation was rarely large. A highly successful peasant might build up a holding of two, two and a half, three virgates but the extent of commercial farming amongst the peasantry did not permit of profit-making sufficient to sustain rapid accumulation (and furthermore in a period when rising population was squeezing the supply of cultivated land popular antipathy to the aggregation of holdings must have been potent).

Commercial farming in the thirteenth century was primarily a matter for lords on their demesnes. In the immediate vicinity of a town, especially a large one, peasants followed their lord's lead (often at a considerable interval in time) although they had, generally, to retain a much larger proportion, if not all, of their crops for their own needs. But beyond a radius of ten miles or so the lack of haulage facilities often debarred the ordinary peasant from access to markets. Even if he had the carts and draught animals for a longer journey, he hardly had the time for it. Additionally, he lacked the storage facilities to enable him to hold on to surplus crops until the time and the market price suited him. The need to pay his rent would also tend to confine him to a quick sale in the nearest town at whatever price he could get. All in all, the lord with his greater command of haulage and storage facilities and of money capital was far better placed to exploit market opportunities, both local and distant. In those parts of the country fairly remote from towns it was usually the demesne crops alone that reached the market. With the total urban population small, peasant farmers at best could only cater for the odds and ends of town needs remaining when demesne supplies had soaked up most of the demand. Probably only in the environs of London were they able to sell all the grain that they could grow and could spare from their own needs. In most cases the likelihood is that it was not grain that the peasant looked to as a principal source of cash income, but wool – especially in the later years of the thirteenth century when Flemish and Italian imports of English wool were mounting rapidly.

Not only was the market for wool more extensive, it was also more accessible, for the market often came to the seller in the case of this commodity. In the case of grain the medieval conscience was outraged by anything that smacked of trafficking for personal profit. The merchant who took his cut from this staple foodstuff was regarded with a special abhorrence and town corporations were fluent in enacting ordinances against 'forestalling' (buying grain at source or on the road to market), 'engrossing' (buying up large quantities of grain with a view to later sale when the price was higher), and 'regrating' (buying in one market and selling in another). The very abundance of such ordinances is evidence that these practices were not uncommon and, indeed, with a commodity that was seasonal and also variable in amount both in time and place they were in some degree essential if supplies were to be available when and where they were wanted. There is a marked element of plain selfishness in the actions of town authorities, anxious to stop grain supplies from their own neighbourhood being diverted elsewhere where the need, and the price, might be greater. But even if the regulations were only partly effective they, especially that prohibiting 'forestalling', did hamper the peasant producer. There were no such restrictions on the freedom of wool merchants. These travelled the country widely and afforded plentiful and readily available outlets for the season's clip. The rich peasant must commonly have been not the man who held fifty acres where his neighbours held only fifteen but the man who grazed thirty sheep where his neighbours grazed ten.

Lords responded to the widening commercial opportunities, as we have seen, both by exacting more villein labour and by commuting such labour for money. At the same time the demesne was extended, perhaps simultaneously with the extension of the arable area of the whole village as rising population necessitated taking in new land from the waste or woods ('assarting'), perhaps by a unilateral encroachment on the commons. The question of commons rights which was to vex another six centuries made its first signal appearance in the Statute of Merton (1235) which recited that a lord was entitled to appropriate the whole commons provided only that he left sufficient grazing for the freeholders, if any, who pastured their animals there. This faithfully reflected the legal dictum that villeins were totally without property rights. Few lords can have attempted to exercise this entitlement to the full – to do so would anyway have been economic nonsense unless the lord proposed to take over both pasture and arable land, for the villein farmers had at least to have grazing for their plough animals.

But if we cannot estimate the extent to which lords took advantage of the statute its mere enactment does tell us that there was a significant amount of lordly interest in the expropriation of the commons. Some of it, especially in the thirteenth century, would have been for the purpose of creating a separate sheep walk but much of it was for the sake of extra arable land. Supplementary arable of this kind was of course made up of one integral area and not of scattered strips and was *enclosed*, separated by a hedge or ditch from the open fields and farmed as a separate unit. The whole demesne in fact might be enclosed by consolidating strips through a process of exchange and then hedging off the consolidated area. The greater ease in working enclosed land is evident and it also left the lord free to use the land in any way he chose: as arable or pasture; under whatever crop he judged the most marketable; fallowed as he thought best. But to consolidate the numerous strips which made up a demesne was a very elaborate undertaking and one liable to occasion much rancour among those who considered they had received worse strips in exchange for those they had surrendered. Partial enclosure of the commons in the thirteenth century was probably quite widespread; enclosure of the arable must have been rare. Partial consolidation of strips through exchange or purchase, however, was general amongst both lords and peasantry whenever suitable opportunities occurred; and newly assarted land was not usually held in strips, although partible inheritance, where it prevailed, might subsequently lead to fragmentation.

More land and more labour were then the principal means whereby the growing population was provisioned. That is to say that the economic response to population change was largely what has earlier been termed a flatly quantitative one. The higher proportion of non-agricultural population was catered for principally by a more extensive use of labour, and perhaps by something of a diversion of foodstuffs from peasantry to townsmen. However, some weight must be given to methods of increasing the productivity of the soil and of the men who worked it. In the thirteenth century in particular, when new readily cultivable land must have been becoming scarce, there was a clear need for such advances, reflected in a rise of about 50 per cent in the prices of agricultural produce over the century, sharpening the commercial incentive.

The most obvious way of extracting more from an existing area of arable land was to use it more often, that is to fallow it less frequently. Increasingly, where land had formerly been fallowed every second year it was now being fallowed only every third year – a transition from a 'two field system' to a 'three field system' – or, more loosely, land was being farmed for longer periods at a stretch. Earlier generations appear to have been unduly cautious in their fallowing practices. The land could often sustain more intensive cultivation, particularly if it were manured more richly; the enlargement of sheep flocks nearly everywhere contributed much to this and use was being made of lime, marl, soot, ashes, town refuse and animals' blood with beneficial effects. Additionally, in many parts of England, especially on the heavy clays of the Midlands, there was much scope for improving the fertility of land by draining away excess water. Stone-paved drainage channels were used with good results. Of a more modest nature there was a greater use of iron for tools and equipment, making for greater working efficiency, especially in the case of the plough whose stronger construction made it possible to use horses in place of oxen[1] and to plough more deeply.

It was naturally on demesnes, and especially on enclosed demesnes, that such practices were most usually adopted. The more extensive markets open to demesne farms provided a keener incentive, and often it was only the lord who could afford to procure artificial manures or to install a drainage system (which anyway could only be installed on consolidated land or by a whole community). Nor should it be thought that this 'high farming' was universal even among manorial lords; as farmers they ranged from keen exponents of the best practices to unimaginative stick-in-the-muds. And, it must be stressed, manorial lords did not necessarily look on their property exclusively, or even primarily, as a source of income. The extent and population of their estates, largely irrespective of the cash yield, defined their social and political status. Money might be the last thing they sought from their manors. Generally speaking the most money-minded lords seem to have been ecclesiastical ones. Bishops, abbots, cathedral chapters and collegiate churches spent lavishly on the construction and embellishment of religious edifices and on benefactions. These undertakings had to be financed largely from their own estates which they, conspicuously, sought to exploit to the full; and the breadth of their connections, both national and international, and their higher standard of literacy helped to keep them more abreast of progress in farming methods and estate management than the average secular lord.

[1] The rather jerky motion of a horse was more than a primitive plough could withstand. Oxen continued to be widely used into the nineteenth century.

It is clear that the extent and depth of 'high farming' was not equal to coping with the pressure on food-producing capacity being exerted by a swollen population in at least some parts of the country as the century reached its last quarter, when evidence starts to accumulate of grave subsistence problems being experienced. But without precise demographic data to serve as a basic term of reference it is not easy to make an intelligible and coherent pattern of the fragmentary and often confusing evidence on the agrarian and subsistence situation through the last seventy years or so of this period. The estate records of these later years yield instances of lords contracting the scale of demesne farming or even abandoning it altogether. In some case this is plainly a result of rising population, generating peasant land hunger and a readiness to pay rents for portions of demesne in excess of the commercial profits which the land could yield. In other cases it seems to point to declining population and consequent market contraction; in others again it appears to be due to soil exhaustion, the land having been overcultivated earlier.[1]

Whatever their causes such retreats from demesne farming necessarily involved the commutation of labour dues wherever these had not already been commuted. And it is these twin phenomena, usually associated most particularly with the population catastrophe following the Black Death, which gives rise to the thesis that the Black Death merely accelerated a change which was in course of taking place anyway.[2] But as yet the available facts from these pre-plague decades do not seem to add up fully to a readily identifiable economic situation. And even if they did the logical sense of defining the Death as a mere accelerator would remain questionable. As long as one accepts, as a matter of historical fact, that the Black Death did have important agrarian consequences, they must be acknowledged as the consequences of a catastrophic fall in population. The 'accelerator' view, then, implies that England had arrived at, or was verging on, a state of critical demographic change of which some other intrinsic factor would have been the agent if the Black Death had not served as such.

[1] Another confusing body of evidence relates to the widespread famine and disease of the years 1315–17. How far are the two related and how far just a cruel coincidence? Are the harvest failures due primarily to weather conditions? Or does the whole situation represent a society brought to the point of collapse by intolerable pressure on food-producing resources and, in effect, finding salvation in a mass loss of life?

[2] In its boldest version, that of Professor Postan (see p. 59n.), the Black Death is not even an accelerator. This thesis, describing an *economic* phenomenon, should not be confused with the superficially similar contention of a vanished generation of historians whose concern was exclusively with the socio-legal history of labour services.

Internal trade

We have seen that the two centuries which succeeded Domesday witnessed a significant though far from sensational rise in the amount of goods, both manufactured and agricultural, entering into exchange – a rise somewhat more than proportionate to the simple increase in the amount of goods produced; and that, while most of this trade took place between towns and the countryside immediately adjoining them, some of it was conducted over greater distances, sometimes over the sea. Merely local trade did of course require the diversion of time, effort and haulage equipment from their normal occupations on the part of buyers or sellers, and to that extent did modify the character of the economy; but such modification was slight. Distant trade had normally a further and much more notable consequence; its conduct required the services of a merchant. A body of merchants is a very distinctive element in any fairly primitive economy. This distinctiveness consists essentially in two things: they produce nothing and the tools of their trade are simply money capital.

We have already seen that the medieval conscience was puzzled by the non-subsistence producer. It found the merchant much more of a moral problem. Again modern notions easily comprehend the situation. The merchant responds to a demand in one place for goods which are supplied in another place. His action confers value on goods by making them available where they are wanted. But for the medieval moralists value was something that was inherent in goods irrespective of where, or even whether, they were wanted. Justice required that the producer should receive this value, which was determined by the amount of labour he had expended. What then remained for the merchant? If he did make a profit was it not either by giving the producer less than value or taking from the customer more than value? Either way was it not an offence against justice? It was a question for which medieval casuistry never found a fully satisfactory answer and trade was always something that seemed tainted with sin.

The other special aspect of a merchant's business, the use of money capital, was liable to give rise to an even clearer occasion of sin: the borrowing and lending of money. A merchant bought goods with his stock of money and sold them again. The more he bought and sold the larger his profits. If he had an opportunity of buying for resale but lacked the money for the purchase he would seek to borrow it, and since its use would profit him would be ready to pay to induce a loan. Conversely if he had money on hand for which he had no immediate trading use he would seek to employ it profitably by lending it to someone who did have a use for it and was, likewise, prepared to pay for it. Once again a modern concept which apprehends capital as a productive agent simply sees in interest the special form of payment appropriate to it. But the medieval mind recognised only labour as a productive agent. Furthermore the most familiar form of borrowing was that to cover an immediate need at a time of personal financial difficulty. Not only, then, was interest a payment for nothing and thus a sin against justice, but it was also very often an exploitation of the misfortune of another and thus, more obnoxiously, a sin against charity. Usury (in medieval usage, the taking of interest, not, as in modern usage, the taking of excessive interest) was condemned absolutely and vehemently by the Church, and by the state which was but the secular and, according to most theologians, subordinate agency of God in the world.

We have no means of determining how far this dubiety as to the morality of trade at all and the much more emphatic anathema on usury hindered mercantile developments. That both trade and money-lending flourished is a matter of historical fact. For supple consciences there were several practices, perfectly legitimate in themselves, which offered ways round the prohibition on interest: it could be concealed under the guise of a penalty for non-repayment of the loan on a stipulated date; land, along with the rent it yielded, could be assigned to the lender for the duration of the loan; produce could be sold for a deferred payment which was in fact higher than its real value; produce could be bought in advance at a sum less than its real value, a favourite device of the great sheep-farming monasteries who needed money for their building programmes and might sell up to five years' wool clip in advance under these terms – indeed among the largest borrowers at effective interest were ecclesiastics, from the Pope downwards, in company with crowned heads who could employ the device of assigning future tax revenue in return for a discounted lump sum. Yet it would be unwise to infer from these lofty examples that the strictures of the theologians went unheeded. The delight in logical niceties which found its fullest expression in scholastic theology may strike us as so much empty formalism, but for its most gifted and saintly exponents, Albert the Great, Bonaventure and Thomas Aquinas, they were vibrant with vital meaning. The practices mentioned above did not fall within the scholastic definitions of usury;[1] They do not necessarily betoken an implicit defiance of what was taught as the law of God. And if the surviving wills of many merchants do witness to an explicit defiance – in their charitable bequests as atonements for the sins incident to trade – by the same token they also witness to prickly consciences. And what records could there be of those who silently refrained from mercantile or credit transactions for conscience's sake?

The use of money as a medium of exchange was not confined to merchants. Given its simple and uniform nature local trade might have been conducted by barter and in particular instances may have been; but all our evidence strongly suggests that even small-scale local trade was very generally undertaken through money and that this had been the case wherever trade occurred in much earlier Anglo-Saxon times. We must be wary then of talking of 'the rise of a money economy'. Like 'the growth of a middle class' it belongs among what Professor Postan[2] has wittily styled the 'residuary' explanations of economic historians – something to fall back on when other explanations fail to account sufficiently for some development and which is always available because always true wherever economic growth takes place. But we must not confuse cause and effect. Money itself is inert – it activates nothing, can cause nothing to happen. The precious metals are a commodity like any other commodity – a rise in their output is an increase in gross wealth as is a rise in the output of anything for which there is a demand. As *commodities* then, the precious metals behave like other goods. As *money* they will be used more intensively when people earn more and spend more: when this happens more money will obviously be required. If there is not enough of the precious metals then people will use other forms of money. The point is that more money is used because expenditure is higher (as opposed to expenditure being higher because there is more money). People spend more when they earn more and earn more when they produce more. An increased use of money is effect not cause. To talk of 'the rise of a money economy' is apt to be misleading: partly because it is historically inaccurate in so far as it suggests a transition from an economy which did not use money to one which did (which obviously occurred sometime but

[1] Two further observations might be made. Most of these practices brought their return by way of capital appreciation, not by way of a running return. The distinction between the two has not been peculiar to scholastic moralists. Secondly for all of their concern with the minutiae of form the greatest of the medieval casuists always insisted that intent was the ultimate determinant of sin – and of that only God could judge.

[2] In 'The rise of a money economy', *Economic History Review*, vol. 14 (1944).

before that time of which we have any clear record); and partly because it seems to assign to money a leading role when it only had a following one. It is perhaps better to use the, admittedly inelegant, word 'commercialisation' when speaking of this aspect of economic change between the late eleventh century and the mid-fourteenth in England – to the extent to which it occurred.

In the country towns commercialisation meant regular markets, once or perhaps twice or even three times a week. Here direct transactions between producer and consumer took place and on occasions an outside merchant or travelling peddlar might appear to buy or sell under the restrictions imposed on him. In the larger towns, especially those with a speciality to offer – most probably cloth but perhaps metalware or earthenware in places close to ore or clay deposits or any manufacture which some chance factor had caused to be particularly cultivated – such visitors would be more common. Town authorities usually required transactions to be effected in the public market so that the appropriate controls could be exercised, and we may assume that not much private dealing took place. But it would appear, in any event, that merchants undertook most of their buying not at town markets but at fairs.

These fairs were a special kind of market held in certain towns once a year, but not under the auspices or control of the town authority. The right to hold such a fair was granted by the Crown – except in the case of some fairs of ancient standing which had a customary right. The grantee was usually a religious institution to whom went the profits of the fair: charges for erecting stalls, tolls on goods, fees and fines paid at the fair court. The usual regulations of the corporation or guild merchant were in abeyance for the duration of the fair: business was open to all and disputes over transactions were settled by reference to the special fair court (commonly known as the Pie Powder court, from the French *pied poudreux*, dusty foot). The code of commercial conduct enforced by this court was empirically evolved and international, being made up of the rules and principles which Western European merchants had worked out in the course of their dealings with one another (the Lex Mercatoria). It owed little or nothing to the theologians, the more especially as the Church tended to treat the merchants as pariahs. It was founded not on abstract concepts of justice but on an experience of the sort of disputes to which trade could give rise and the application to them of a practicable sense of equity. The freedom from artificial restraint was then one of the great points of attraction of a fair for merchants; another was the duration of the fair – instead of the one day of a market it lasted for several days or even several weeks.

Quite apart from these special circumstances the volume of commerce was such that unless goods entering into trade were congregated in a relatively small number of centres to which buyers and sellers customarily resorted, there might not be enough goods or customers at any one place to warrant the time, expense and trouble of a journey. Indeed at the beginning of this period such anciently established fairs as there were may well have been primarily retail in character, supplying directly the special needs of the populace of a region on the annual occasion of a religious festival which drew large numbers to a particular centre. With the growth of population the fairs would have tended more towards wholesale trade between merchants, who from the fairs distributed goods directly or indirectly to the points of final sale – that is they become entrepôt centres of the kind familiar in any regional, national or international economy whenever the volume of trade is not large enough to warrant direct despatch from point of production to point of sale but is large enough to provide profitable employment for a body of merchants. But this is all surmise. Beyond the mere existence of fairs and markets we know almost nothing of the internal trade network nor of the relative importance of roads, rivers and coastal shipping as means of moving goods. In the middle of the thirteenth century fine cloth from as far as York may well have been sold in London, grain from Nottinghamshire doubtless reached Westmorland, iron from Sussex was probably used at Land's End, salt from Cheshire may have ended up in Berkshire and imported goods would have been an exotically conspicuous element at any fair – these are some of the likely instances of extensive distribution of commodities. But of how many hands such goods passed through and of the ways they travelled we are ignorant. All that can be said with any confidence is that to judge from the number of new fairs created between the late eleventh century and the mid-thirteenth, and the lengthening of their duration from days to weeks, they seem to have played an active and important part in the thin countrywide distribution of goods that prevailed.

The wool trade

The commodity which would have been traded in most intensively was wool. But in as much as this was sold for use by English clothmakers the trade would have been largely a local one for there was no

49

part of England where sheep were not kept, and in growing numbers as time went on. Most clothmakers would have used local supplies. But in places, particularly along the Pennines and on the salty flats of the East Anglian coast, more wool would have been raised than there was a local market for; and some centres of cloth manufacture would have found local wool supplies inadequate, in point either of quantity or of quality. Wool therefore should be included among the items entering into distant trade in noteworthy quantities from very early in this period. But it is from about the second quarter of the thirteenth century that the wool trade jumped into very special prominence with the expansion of the Flemish cloth industry. Flanders[1] had been an important European centre of cloth manufacture from as early as the tenth century and had always drawn on the geographically convenient supplies of high quality English wool, but the scanty evidence suggests that the quantities were not really considerable until well into the thirteenth century when the Flemish industry from being one of major importance came to monopolise the market for fine cloth throughout northern Europe, including England, and to depend heavily on imports from England for its raw material. About the same time English wool was also being imported by the industrial towns of northern Italy. There were few parts of England where the consequences of this were not felt. In the first decade of the fourteenth century, when wool exports reached their peak, over half the annual English wool clip may have gone abroad, and from the Midland counties and Lincolnshire which at this time produced most of the finest wool the proportion must have been significantly higher than the national average. We may suppose too that into the fine wool areas were drawn coarser wools from the north, the east below the Wash and Cornwall as local cloth manufacturers found the indigenous variety pricing itself out of consideration.

Although town markets and, more especially, fairs, must have handled notable quantities of wool, the volume of trade was such as to permit of more direct dealings with the growers. The leading export merchants usually bought at first hand from the very large ecclesiastical and secular lords who might keep up to 2,000 sheep on the commons and waste of one manor, and up to 30,000 over all their properties. (Individual flocks of over 5,000 occurred but these were in exceptional cases

[1] Here and elsewhere 'Flanders' is used loosely to describe an area comprising parts of modern Belgium and north-eastern France actually extending beyond the limits of Flanders proper.

of pure sheep ranches in the Pennines area where the wool was hardly of a quality to interest the Flanders market.) These great graziers often acted as agents or intermediaries in the disposal of the five, fifty or a hundred fleeces of lesser local lords and of their own tenants or other peasants whose flocks in sum often exceeded those of their lord's. Where this did not happen travelling dealers operating over a regular beat might buy from the smaller men at source and sell in bulk to the export merchants. But we should not delineate too rigid a scheme of the wool trade. Its regularity and volume certainly tended to produce set commercial patterns and specialist traders, but the ways in which an English fleece reached a Flemish manufacturer must have been many and various, as must the men who handled it.

It was suggested earlier that the rise of specialist centres of fine cloth manufacture in England which was taking place up to about the middle of the thirteenth century was the first development to cause any significant complication of the pattern of economic arrangements; that there radiated from these centres lines of communication which created new sensitivities between the autonomous geographical elements which in aggregate composed the national economy. The lines thrown out by the wool trade as it developed in the thirteenth and early fourteenth centuries were a good deal more ubiquitous and carried a much greater burden. On the flow of wool along these lines came to depend the degree of prosperity of much of the community. For many it was perhaps little more than a marginal factor, but few by the early years of the fourteenth century would have been totally insensitive to it. The net encompassed growers, great and small, travelling wool dealers, local town merchants, exporters in London and the East Anglian ports, specialist wool packers, port workers and sailors, and, by no means least, the Crown, which found in wool exports a readily taxable commodity – the 'maltolte' dates from 1273 and for more than two centuries thereafter was the main regular constituent of tax revenue – and when tax revenue fell short of needs the wool exporters were an easily tapped loan source. Finally, wool exports were the principal means of paying for imports. Wool was the only commodity which England could offer abroad in any quantity.

Overseas trade

The last two sentences explain why there is not much of note to say of English overseas trade before the second half of the thirteenth century. The primary reason is that until the wool trade became of consequence, external commerce was a fringe activity; the secondary and closely linked reason is that until the Crown started to take an interest in it, for financial reasons, and to keep customs records, our sources of information on what trade there was consist of only a few scattered fragments, permitting of no more than a slender survey.

The Vikings, in turn disrupters of trade and then creators of it, had left the east coast ports and Bristol at the time of Domesday with a modest legacy of trade links with Scandinavia and the Baltic region. A handful of Englishmen conducted a regular trade with Norway, carrying out cloth and occasionally corn; in the thirteenth century merchants trading out of Newcastle sometimes supplemented their cargoes with coal. Timber suitable for the masts and spars of ships was virtually all that Norway could offer – although falcons, for aristocratic sport, sometimes figured in return cargoes. Timber of this kind was to be had more abundantly from the regions bordering the Baltic, which also offered other shipbuilding materials, pitch and tar, cordage and sailcloth as well as furs, wax, dried or salted fish and corn from the great north European grain belt at times of bad harvest, but few Englishmen at any time within this period ventured into Baltic waters. Until the early thirteenth century this trade was mostly conducted by merchants of German origin operating from the centrally situated Baltic island of Gotland. Thereafter it fell into the hands of Germans based on Lübeck and other towns on the southern Baltic coasts, who eliminated the tortuous sea route round Denmark by carrying their goods over the land neck from Lübeck to Hamburg and shipping them out from there. First known collectively in England as Easterlings, these Germans by the end of the thirteenth century were commonly described as Hansards – the name by which history styles the mercantile empire which they founded in the Baltic and which was to endure for another three centuries. Neither Gotlanders nor Hansards ever found much in England to bring back to the Baltic and direct Anglo-Baltic trade was at all time sustained by an outward flow of the precious metals from England.

Much earlier established in England were west Germans, who can be discerned even before the Norman Conquest. From the early twelfth century the merchants of Cologne stand out as the most prominent of these, bringing in Rhine wines, fine German linen, the artifacts of the skilled German armourers and, though in tiny quantities, precious metalwares and jewellery coming from the East via Constantinople, the Mediterranean and northern Italy, then across the Alps and down the Rhine. Cloth, wool, hides, salt, tin and lead would have composed their homeward cargoes. In 1281 all Germans trading into England were merged in the one *hanse*, by which time those from the east would have been the dominant element, operating from the east coast ports, London, Ipswich, Yarmouth, Boston, Lynn and Hull. By then also the Germans had become well established in Bruges, the great Flemish mercantile centre, and although once forged it was always the trade via Hamburg and Lübeck which principally occupied the Hansards, they did participate also in that Anglo-Flemish trade which was becoming the major component of England's overseas commerce.

In its early years, before the flow of wool assumed such quantities as to be of real importance to England and of crucial consequence to Flanders, the Anglo-Flemish trade seems to have been principally in the hands of the Flemings themselves. Apart from wool, which at all times would have been England's principal export to Flanders, corn was a commodity of growing importance in the trade as industrialisation in Flanders outran the area's capacity to feed itself. Fine cloth was of course always the main item of importation from Flanders.

Up to the mid-thirteenth century the most considerable single import was Gascon (Bordeaux) wine. At least it certainly was from 1154 when Henry II united in his person the dominion of England and of assorted parts of France which together comprised a block stretching from Normandy to the Pyrenees, creating in economic effect a great free trade area along the Atlantic and Channel coasts. The wine brought to England by Gascon merchants established itself as the normal beverage of everybody of any social standing. The same Gascon merchants commonly also brought salt from the many places along the Bay of Biscay where the flat beaches and warm sun permitted of its cheap and easy production by natural evaporation. The dyestuffs required by the cloth industry were other commodities that generally came from or through the French possessions of the English king. On their return journey the Gascons might take wool, cloth, lead, tin, or corn for a homeland so given over to the vine that it lacked bread-grains. London and, secondarily, Bristol were the main centres of this trade, but all the southern ports participated in it. Bristol too would have commanded the Irish trade, another Viking legacy, though what it consisted of – indeed whether it existed at all – can only be surmise. Particularly after the Norman invasion of Ireland in 1189 fine cloth, weapons, armour, tin and lead probably left Bristol for Waterford and Dublin. Small quantities of gold and gold artifacts may have come back across the Irish Sea. More probably, salted butter and cow hides, for the Irish were great cattle keepers, along with linen and honey, both of which were Irish specialities, came up the Severn to this only port of note on the whole West coast in the eleventh and twelfth centuries.

It is easy when reciting a list of commodities, of the merchants who dealt in them and of the ports through which they traded to create the impression of a great commercial bustle. Only hard statistical information, which is lacking, could set the picture in precise perspective. But the realisation that well into the thirteenth century wine, drunk only by a fraction of the population, was the largest single item of foreign trade may operate as a salutary control to any extravagant notions about the quantities or values involved. In the early thirteenth century maybe some one to two per cent of gross national income was expended on goods of foreign origin, and a like proportion of gross national product sold overseas. In the light of this it should not be necessary to issue a warning against thinking of England at that point in time as occupying a place of any importance in the European economy. It hung on the skirts of the Continent; only its wool and its lack of a native wine invited the attention of Continental merchants. As cloth manufacture in Flanders had grown beyond its own raw material resources and as Gascon wine production had effloresced, the merchants engaged in these areas had come to comprehend England in their sphere of operations. At the cost of some oversimplification we must think of an expanding Europe having reached out to England, rather as some centuries later Europe reached out to Asia. The more particular implication is that it was Continental merchants who came to England, not English merchants who ventured to the Continent; an English merchant in Germany in the twelfth century would have been nearly as bizarre a spectacle as an Indian merchant in England in the eighteenth century. The foreign traders who had been coming to England since the cessation of Viking piratical activity in the tenth century must have been, in the fullest sense of the word, adventurers – of all kinds and types. There may have been Englishmen scattered among these Germans, Flemings and Frenchmen, but only the minor Norwegian and Irish trades which had been inherited from the Vikings afforded much scope for natives.

It was the upsurge in the wool trade which brought newcomers to the scene. The Flemings themselves could not handle the increased quantities of wool which the development of their cloth industry necessitated: they were too busily and profitably employed in attending

54

to the manufacturing side of it to devote much attention to the mercantile side. And although the Hansards did not neglect the opportunities offered they were not prepared to divert much of their capital and energy from their own growing Baltic trades. It was Italians who were the first newcomers to move in. From about the middle of the thirteenth century they were coming to occupy a prominent place in the trade, and by the early fourteenth century the most notable of wool merchants were concerns whose head offices were in Florence and Lucca – companies, not individuals, with branches in Bruges (the great north European entrepôt until supplanted by Antwerp in the later fifteenth century), Paris, London and other centres. These were the most sophisticated commercial institutions of thirteenth- and fourteenth-century Europe. In touch, directly or indirectly, with every part of the continent and of the Mediterranean where trade was of any consequence, they exhibited a sensitivity to fluctuations in supply and demand which no other merchants could match. Should Barcelona inform them of a grain shortage in Catalonia, Bruges could be instructed to direct supplies there; should Paris notify them of the French king's preparations for war, the armourers of northern Italy could be drawn on to profit from it. And if it were not goods but money that was wanted they could supply that too – at a price – for they were international bankers as well; indeed the greatest of them came to devote themselves principally to banking. Loans constituted the major part of their banking business but they would undertake debt collection and, for crowned heads, tax collection as well, remitting the proceeds, not by the expensive and hazardous movement of coin and bullion, but by simple paper instrument, an order on one of their own branches.

It was this function apparently that first brought them to England: to collect and remit 'Peter's Pence', the peculiar English tribute to the Pope; and it was through their dealings with the great ecclesiastics, bishops and abbots, owners of numerous sheep, that, seemingly, they were drawn into the wool trade – providing themselves with locally garnered capital with which to finance their English banking business. But this involvement in banking limited their power of penetrating the wool trade. They were relatively few in number and, increasingly, the money capital of that few was tied up in loans to the king. In gross their share of the wool trade by 1273 was already less than that of Englishmen, operating on a much smaller individual scale, who then had 35 per cent of it as against the Italian 24 per cent, the remainder going to Flemings, Hansards and miscellaneous others. This chance statistic for a particular year may be exceptional but there need be no difficulty in believing that, as the trade swelled, internal native dealers came to venture shipments of their own instead of selling to foreigners in England, or that English merchants on the east coast already engaged in the Norwegian trade often diverted their attention to Flanders. By the closing years of this period the English had plainly secured more of the Flemish wool trade than all the foreigners put together.

The greatest Italians were drawn further into heavy loan commit-ments to the king as his war finance caused him to lean more heavily on them, and his inability to pay his debts contributed signally to their collapse in the 1340s. Other Italians, of more modest means and ambitions, had steered clear of banking and survived, but they were coming to devote themselves more to despatching wool to their own cloth centres as a fresh group of Italians, largely Venetians and some Genoese, from 1314 established a direct sea-link between England and Italy, replacing the former and more laborious and costly route via Bruges, the Rhine and through the Alpine passes. These traders brought the exotic Mediterranean luxuries which previously had only filtered into England in tiny quantities: silk, velvet and cotton goods of both Italian and eastern manufacture; sweet wines and currants from the Levant; precious metals, jewel stones, spices, ivory, brasil (a red dye), which emerging out of an unknown Orient had arrived on Europe's doorstep at the eastern end of the Mediterranean. But at no time could those highly expensive goods command an important market and as early as the mid-fourteenth century they had only a bare toehold in England. Nor did the Italian cloth industry ever consume English wool at the rate that Flanders did up to the end of the fourteenth century. In drawing away from the Flemish trade the Italians were creating a major opening for English merchants. And in the 1330s and 1340s they were being succeeded by Englishmen, not only as wool merchants but also as crown financiers.

It was not only on the Flemish wool trade that Englishmen were encroaching. They were coming also to participate in the Gascon trade. By the early fourteenth century they had a substantial share of it although, naturally enough, the Gascons themselves preserved a larger one. Arising perhaps out of this push into the Bay of Biscay, English-men established a direct route with Spain and Portugal from about the middle of the thirteenth century, providing a supply of iron to supple-ment England's straitened resources of the metal; otherwise the trade was in small quantities of luxuries: olive oil, soap, kermes (a scarlet dye), fine soft leather, figs, dates, raisins, almonds, oranges and lemons. On their way out the ships must often have sailed light. There was no market for wool in a country whose own rivalled English for quality; some tin and lead perhaps commanded a sale; but the outward cargo must often have been silver in coin and bar, and maybe a little gold. The western Atlantic trade as a whole must have been a deficit one; imports of Gascon wine alone would have easily exceeded all English exports to the area. If England was not being drained of her stock of precious metals it was because exports of wool to Flanders handsomely exceeded in value imports of fine cloth from the same area. Given that the one was the only English export of any serious consequence and that the other, along with wine, made up the bulk of imports, England's balance of payments equation in fact would have stood: wool = cloth + wine, with, including other exports, a small surplus for the purchase of a range of relative trifles and for paying foreign shippers who, even after English merchants had started to gain from aliens, continued to carry the great majority of goods entering English trade.

Within this period it seems to have been only on the west coast that English and Welsh shippers came into their own; many of the Englishmen who ventured down the Atlantic coast from the mid-thirteenth century were shipowner merchants working out of Bristol, Chester, Exeter and other smaller Atlantic and Irish Sea ports. These towns were emerging from an earlier obscurity which was almost total. Only Bristol had formerly been a port of any prominence, and between Domesday and the Black Death it grew more rapidly than any other English town, increasing its population perhaps sevenfold, much of this probably in the thirteenth century. This spread of maritime traffic along the western shores should probably be seen as a function of population shift. As the western counties started to fill out we may imagine the trade links with the east becoming stretched and strained and then snapping as the western population broke out on its own more convenient coasts; the west became a semidistinct economic entity with its own overseas and coastal commerce, with Bristol as its London – and the Severn as its Thames facilitating trade between the commercial centre and the hinterland. That it should breed its own merchants and shippers is readily understandable. The Gascony trade already existed; it was merely a matter of adding a new and convenient appendage to it.

The growth of an English mercantile class through the last hundred years or so of this period to the point where native merchants must have nearly wrested their fair share of trade (i.e. a half) from the foreigners who had formerly monopolised it is a phenomenon which merits a little particular attention. There is no real difficulty in crediting that, in general terms, it was simply due to expanding opportunities, seized, in laggardly imitation of foreigners, by Englishmen who enjoyed the advantage of being on the spot. Small personal capitals would have confined initial ventures to a modest scale but, given fairly continuous buoyant trading conditions, profits could be steadily ploughed back to enlarge the scale and cream off fresh opportunities as they arose. In other words, there is no necessity to invoke any special factors to account for the increasing success of English merchants. However, it has sometimes been urged that the policy of the Crown played a particular part in promoting mercantile activity, and Edward I (1273–1307) especially has been portrayed as a chief architect of commercial expansion.

Edward's claim to this distinction is grounded in three measures: the Statute of Acton Burnell (1273), the Statute of Merchants (1275) and the Carta Mercatoria (1303). The first two were concerned with facilitating the recovery of mercantile debts. The prevailing rule was that when a stranger merchant left debts behind him in a town the corporation seized goods of the next fellow-townsman of the debtor who chanced within its jurisdiction, for sale in satisfaction of the debt – a practice which obviously tended to inhibit travel for the sake of trade; Edward's measures provided for a kind of national debt register, and so far as they were operative they would have dissolved that inhibition. But whatever value might be attached to these statutes as encouraging trade there is no question of their conferring any advantage on natives over aliens. The Carta Mercatoria was specifically concerned with the position of aliens. It prescribed that on top of the ordinary duties on exports and imports – by then an established feature of crown finance – aliens should pay extra imports, most weightily a half again of the basic duty. However even the maltolte, the specially high duty on wool, at that time worked out at about only 5 per cent of the selling price, so that the disability conferred on aliens was little more than nominal and was evidently intended by the Crown to be nothing more than a sop to current popular animosity towards foreigners. Indeed the brunt of the Carta Mercatoria was directed towards regularising the legal standing of alien merchants in England and putting them on the same footing as English merchants.

A case emerges for crediting Edward I with a particular interest in trade but, fairly clearly, he was indifferent as to whether it was conducted by his own subjects or by foreigners. More generally it seems doubtful whether anything which could strictly be termed a 'commercial' policy can be attributed to the Crown within this period – that is, whether the promotion of commerce for the sake of the general economic ends which it served can be accounted a motive in decisions of state or fell within the understood range of regalian responsibilities. Apart from the measures mentioned above others could be listed which one way or another had a bearing on trade, but it would be very questionable if in the Crown's reckoning they served any purposes other than fiscal or diplomatic ones. Overseas commerce provided a convenient form of royal revenue and, on occasions, a useful lever in dealing with foreign powers, conspicuously the Hansard towns, which were becoming a political and military force as well as a commercial group, and with Flanders, whose situation on the French frontier gave it a special place in Anglo-French hostilities.

Note (p. 38): Professor Postan presents this argument in 'The chronology of labour services', *Transactions of the Royal Historical Society*, 4th ser., vol. xx (1937) and in 'Medieval agrarian society in its prime. England', his own chapter in *The Cambridge Economic History of Europe* (2nd edition), vol. i (1966), edited by himself. The second of these, in accordance with the convention of the series, is not referenced, and it is difficult for the non-specialist to tell how far it draws on material other than that contained in Professor Postan's 1937 article. It has been observed that the earlier article leans on the evidence of a group of ecclesiastical estates which may be atypical; while it may also be said that discussion of the matter does not always distinguish between 'farming' of the demesne, and commutation of labour services. If the whole demesne were leased to the one 'farmer' there is no reason on the face of it why he should not take over the labour along with the land. For the non-specialist the most remarkable of Professor Postan's assertions is that in the twelfth century more than half the peasant's product commonly went to the lord as *money*. That the average peasant holding was capable of yielding such a surplus, however rendered, is astonishing in itself. That there were cash buyers enough for that quantity would necessitate a total and radical revision of the received version, not only of the medieval agrarian economy, but of the whole of medieval economic structure.

On the particular question of labour services, Professor Postan's representation of the weight of villein money obligations in the mid-twelfth century plainly leaves very little room for dues rendered in labour. From what earlier level of intensity they had fallen he does not indicate. But he does suggest that they reached a peak around the turn of the eleventh and twelfth centuries, and from, implicitly, near extinction were only very partially revived through the late twelfth and the thirteenth centuries before petering out with the onset of agricultural depression in the early fourteenth century. The overall effect then is to reduce the theme of labour services to a very marginal role in medieval agrarian history.

Professor Postan has for some decades been something of a one-man band – one of considerable power and persuasiveness – in searching for an economically articulate arrangement of the facts of English medieval history to replace older compositions which are commonly deficient in economic insight. But it is yet too early to say how far his work will be incorporated into the body of standard scholarship. And on these points where there does seem ground for reservation it seems wiser to lean towards the received version and to employ this rather unsatisfactory device of a very long Note to indicate that an alternative version has been urged by an eminent authority. It may also be pointed out, although this for the most part refers to matter covered in the next chapter, that Professor Postan's fifteenth-century 'Depression' – extended in some degree back into the fourteenth century (see again his chapter in the *Cambridge History* and also his 'The fifteenth century', *Economic History Review*, vol. ix (1938)) – does not figure here. The facts adduced by Professor Postan in this connection will be found here in one context or another but their characterisation as indicators of general 'depression' is not accepted.

On the immediate question of labour services attention is drawn to the only other extensive treatment by a contemporary scholar, Professor R. H. Hilton's long pamphlet, *The Decline of Serfdom in Medieval England* (Macmillan, 1969) – by contrast with the bold clarity of the Postan account cautious almost to the point of obscurity.

Finally, if for the sake of the simplicity of presentation which a general account such as this must strive for, the question is discussed here in fairly clearcut labour services/commutation terms, the overwhelming probability is that in historical fact there were a variety of shadings, ranging from direct labour services, the informal provision of the services of hired deputies, money payments which were clearly acknowledged to be labour substitutes, through to money payments from which all taint of labour dues had vanished.

Three

1348-1475

Demography

The bubonic plague which swept across Europe with devastating rapidity from the early months of 1347 hit England in August 1348. On its arrival the population may have been some 4¾ million; by the end of 1350, after this first and most lethal wave had spent itself, the population had probably been reduced below 4 million.[1] The plague was not a temporary visitor. It raged widely again, though less virulently, in the 1360s, and for another three centuries it lurked continuously, emerging now and then to seize a house, a street, a quarter or a whole town until, having swept through a large part of London and some other scattered areas in 1665 it vanished almost as suddenly as it had first appeared. The fall in English population over the rest of the fourteenth century was of catastrophic proportions. By 1377 it was probably under 3 million and in the early fifteenth century it may have been hovering around 2 million, very possibly dipping below that figure before turning up again from about mid-century. Clearly, the Death was the main agent of this drop in the periods of sharpest fall, but the continuing fall apparently manifested through the last quarter of the century when, as far as can be seen, the Death was only picking up a few stray victims, calls for an additional explanation, especially if one takes the view that what has really to be explained is not merely a falling population but the failure of population to rise (i.e. even if one showed that the plague accounted for the imbalance of deaths over births some explanation would still be necessary on the assumption that the norm is for births to exceed deaths). It is possible that population

[1] On the figures quoted throughout see p. 15n.

61

had already ceased to grow before 1348. But, if so, the most likely reason is pressure of people on resources. The same explanation could not be available for a period when the population was back to what it had been around the first or second quarter of the thirteenth century. Nor could one extend the killing power of the Death by reckoning with the greater vulnerability to other diseases of those enfeebled by it, because the plague killed some 90 per cent of its victims. There is evidence to suggest that in the fourteenth and fifteenth centuries the general death rate became biased against younger people. Had other new diseases of the endemic type intruded which were not fatal in many cases and which conferred a subsequent immunity, creating this kind of mortality pattern? Smallpox is a possible candidate here. Apart from variations in the death rate there is the possibility of a fall in the birth rate, most plausibly as a result of fewer or later marriages. The idea may be entertained that the social or psychological upsets of the Black Death had such a consequence. But where knowledge is lacking speculation can run on interminably – and perhaps pointlessly, for the problem might be just the invention of our faulty demography.

The economic consequences of the drastic drop in population were marked. If the fall in numbers had occurred at the same rate everywhere the structure of the economy might not have been substantially modified although the fact that the amount of land had not diminished with population would have meant that the balance between people and resources would have been materially altered. One can imagine an economy containing two million people functioning much as it had done when it contained close on five million. The number of consumers would have fallen by the same amount as the number of producers; *per capita* consumption and *per capita* production would not be radically different from what they had been; the relative distribution of wealth would be unaltered; organisation and techniques would be the same as formerly. In a purely subsistence economy, even with variations in population fall from area to area, the consequences would have been similarly slight. If then the consequences for the English economy of the population disaster were of a significant order it was because it was not a purely subsistence economy, and because the incidence of the Black Death varied from place to place creating imbalances between supply and demand which could not be readily readjusted.

Lords and villeins

In general nobody felt the impact more than the commercial demesne farming lords. Their economy comprised three human elements: the consumers of their produce, their tenants and their labourers (the latter two distinct only to the extent that commutation had taken place). Their income consisted of the cash yield from the first and second, less their cash outgoings on the third, along with other, usually lesser, costs. Any change in the balance between these elements directly affected their profits. It is clear that from 1348 the national total numbers of customers, tenants and labourers, all fell. But that they all fell at the same rate in the case of any one lord is highly unlikely. Virtually all lords would have been suffering to some degree, either from a shortage of customers relative to productive capacity or a shortage of labour relative to market opportunities. In the face of the first there was nothing to do but to cut down on the scale of demesne farming; where hired labour had been used, to turn it off and where villein labour had been used, to commute it as necessary. In the second case the lord might seek to attract more labour by offering higher wages; where he had been receiving commutation payments he would very possibly try to raise these correspondingly, or he might throw the burden of finding labour back on the villeins, either to render it themselves or to bear the cost of hiring it; or, where he had still been taking labour, he might try to exact more from the survivors.

As far as wage labour was concerned it might seem that the two situations should balance out: that labour would be drawn from the areas where it was unwanted to those where it was short and where high wages were on offer; and that as the number of labourers lured in this manner swelled wages would drop back to their former level. So far as villein services were concerned one might expect that the tendencies for them to be further commuted on the one hand and to be increased on the other would be about even over the whole country and that the net result would simply be more numerous local variations in villeinage. In fact, wages never fell back to pre-1348 standards and the tendency for villein services to be converted into unambiguous rent payments ultimately became dominant everywhere.

The economic determinant here was the supply of cultivable land. With the numerous deaths of occupying tenants, vacant holdings became available. In the short run many lords whose estates had been decimated, and thus lacked both labourers and tenants, sought to fill their unoccupied holdings with those rendering full villein services rather than pay high wages to non-occupant labourers. And the urge, everywhere that there was a shortage of labour, to extend or reimpose villein services, became stronger as wages rose in the years immediately after 1348. But there were too many estates where lords were reducing the scale of demesne farming and instead were looking to rent-paying tenants for an income; these lords were prepared to offer tenancies on advantageous terms which might entirely exclude labour services. They were thus repeopling their estates while others sought strenuously and often vainly to enlarge their stock of villein labour. Economics were on the side of the peasant. There was now land enough for a much larger proportion of them than previously. They could often disdain tenancies on harsh villein terms and select more attractive ones. Labourers could perhaps choose to become farmers if wages were not high enough, and if wages were high those who held land on onerous terms might throw up their holdings and take to well paid labouring instead. Lords who continued to insist on the full range of villein dues were cutting their own throats, failing to get either enough labourers or enough new tenants. But until such lords came to appreciate economic realities and alter their ways, this meant that life for those villeins they did have became steadily grimmer, each gain of freedom by one peasant meant the screw tightened for another. Ultimately the financial pinch compelled all lords to cede to the law of supply and demand, in this case reciting that the supply of land tended to exceed the demand for it and as a consequence, since labourers were potential farmers, the supply of labour tended to fall short of demand. Tenants could only be had on congenial terms and labourers could only be hired for high wages.

The contradictory tendencies regarding villeinage were slow to work themselves out and the final triumph of commutation was long deferred and not necessarily inevitable. For many decades after 1348 the issue was uncertain, and in the immediate aftermath of the plague the balance probably tipped towards heavier labour services. One would certainly not expect a rapid resolution of conflicting economic forces in any economy where social mobility was low: advantageous tenancies in one area might be years in drawing in enough people to produce the same circumstances in another area where local factors operated in the opposite direction. One would expect even less to find a speedy culmination when against the bias of the purely economic forces was set the established political power of the country. The half-century or so that followed the Black Death saw a strenuous attempt through the exercise of legal power to restore the *status quo ante* – to legislate wages back to their former level and to employ the lord's absolute rights over his villeins to prevent them moving in search of better opportunities. Such a policy could ultimately have proved successful and the organisation of fifteenth-century agriculture need not have differed significantly from that of the early fourteenth century. A policy of simple coercion could have controlled and thrust back the economic tide. In the last analysis the policy failed because lords lacked the determination and the discipline to carry it through and the state had not the administrative apparatus to make it effective without their active cooperation.

If such a policy were to stand a chance of success, lords suffering from a shortage of labour or of tenants would have had to resign themselves to the situation for the moment, refrain from offering wages in excess of the legal maximum and rigorously satisfy themselves that a tenant coming from outside was not a runaway villein. But too often the need to get the harvest in or the pinch of a diminished rent roll tempted them to offer an extra halfpenny a day or not to ask too many questions of someone who was willing to take on a vacant holding. Frequently they could break the law with impunity for they might be the very persons who were supposed to enforce it, or men powerful enough in their own neighbourhood to overawe those whose duty that was. (It would probably be more realistic to speak of bailiffs and stewards taking measures which their lords preferred not to know about, and which they could disown if authority was too strong for them.) The Statute of Labourers of 1349 (the legal instrument of wages control, prohibiting wages in excess of those customary before the Black Death) appointed special justices of labourers to execute the measure. The medieval state had no body of bureaucrats from which to staff the countryside with watchdogs; apart from anything else it did not have the financial means to support such a corps. The Statute effectively inaugurated the system, which was to endure for another five centuries, of using the services of local landowners (usually those below the rank of great lords who had other, higher, duties to the Crown) whose property conferred on them both a duty to the king and a vested interest in the maintenance of law and of the established order. Justices of labourers soon became justices of the peace with an infinitely elastic range of responsibilities. The system worked well enough except when there was a clash between the private interests of the justices and the intentions of the law. *Quis custodiet ipsos custodes?* (Who will guard the guards?) Such a clash too often manifested itself at the very commencement of the institution. The attempt to push wages back down to pre-1348 levels was never seriously undertaken, and was formally abandoned by a statute of 1390 which instituted instead the principle of regulating wages according to prices. However we have abundant evidence of justices who were very vigorous, even ruthless, in curbing the demands of labourers – the measure was after all conceived in the general interests of landowners. But numerous as such particular instances were there was not sufficient approach to universality to support and sustain them. And the more the Statute was perceived to be inoperative the stronger the inducement to break it.

It was not only self-interested lords who were active in sabotaging economic policy. The peasantry had minds and aims of their own no less than their lords. And they outnumbered the lords fifty to one. This simple statistical fact may perhaps be the most important of all. Power is a strange thing. It is normally exercised by the few over the many who, with various degrees of readiness, acquiesce in their subordination. But the most formidable of all power is that of a large majority acting in concert. In different parts of the country and to varying extents that power was making itself effective in the England of the later fourteenth century. Wherever justices cut back wages which represented modest affluence to bare subsistence levels, or labour services were reimposed on those who for many years had not known them, or peasant burdens were in other ways made heavier, there was anger and resentment. And here and there such feelings became sufficiently widespread and sufficiently acute to translate themselves into action. Action might take many forms: from the stealthy slaughter of a few lordly sheep by night to the seizure of the manor hall, the destruction of the manorial rolls with their record of villein dues and a mass refusal to render dues or work for wages other than those set by the peasants themselves; occasionally an especially harsh bailiff or justice or lord would have his throat cut. Most lords probably responded by taking reprisals when outside force had been summoned and the peasant mob had dispersed. But after a show of restored authority many would deem it more prudent to ameliorate their former line of conduct rather than hazard a repetition. This was the pattern of many local disturbances throughout the second half of the fourteenth century as it was the pattern of the much more general movement of 1381, the Peasants' Revolt which at its most widespread in Kent and Essex put the peasantry in possession

66

of the capital and would have secured them control of the kingdom had they been organised to exploit their victory. That villein dues rapidly vanished in the fifteenth century and that higher wages had come to stay may have been in the last analysis because the ruling classes had come to take the view that the dubious advantages of trying to frustrate these developments were not worth the struggle with a dangerously hostile peasantry.

The failure of the policy of wages control and enforcement of villein dues conspired with price trends to drive lords from demesne farming, thus ensuring the irrevocable passing of villeinage. Contrary to what one might expect, at a time when the gross demand for foodstuffs was falling as population declined while the supply of land remained the same, the price of foodstuffs continued to rise until about 1375. We must believe that the depressive effect on prices was more than offset by the rising costs of labour; that we have in the second half of the fourteenth century what modern economists have called 'a cost-push inflation', infecting the prices of all goods. But in real terms the profits of commercial farming must have been falling and, obviously, since there were fewer mouths to feed, the amount of land devoted to it was dwindling. While prices went on rising most lords clung to demesne farming, though usually on a reduced scale. They would often in any event have little option: while population continued to fall and with it the demand for land, the only alternative in many cases would have been to abandon the demesne altogether; as long as lords could just manage to break even, or hoped to, they would defer such a course. But when prices ceased to rise and instead started to slide gently down-wards – as they were bound to do if population went on falling for long enough – and wages did not drop with prices, commercial farming of the demesne was becoming just a way of losing money. Land was allowed to fall out of use or, where possible, was rented out. As demesnes ceased to be worked by their owners, labour dues became useless and the money rents which could be substituted for them came to con-stitute the whole of lordly incomes.

It would be absurd to assign a precise date to this transition from farming lord to *rentier* lord. In particular cases it had occurred even before the Black Death. Some lords struggled on long after others had decided the game was not worth the candle. The change in many individual cases was not an abrupt one. But it would be a convenient generalisation to say that the period up to the Peasants' Revolt (1381) saw demesne farming lords endeavouring to contend with adverse circumstances and that thereafter they were steadily succumbing to those circumstances. The decision to switch may not have always been founded on calculations of profit and loss. By the fifteenth century it may sometimes have been a matter of aping a fashionable trend; sometimes of preferring a lower but more certain and trouble-free rent income to farming profits that hung on the vagaries of the weather, the efficiency of a steward or bailiff, decisions as to whether to sink capital in a new barn or drainage system etc.

The withdrawal from demesne farming was often less than total. A home farm would commonly be retained for provisioning the household. Commons grazing might not be given up when the arable was let go, more especially as wool prices were more buoyant than grain prices and pasture farming, with its low labour content, was not as hard hit by high wages. But by 1450 the dependent connection between the farming of demesne land and the occupancy of villein holdings had broken virtually everywhere. With that break came automatically the end of 'the manorial system' – and with that we can drop 'manorial lord' from our vocabulary and start to speak simply of 'landlord'.

The decision to abandon demesne farming was facilitated by the stabilisation of the population in the early fifteenth century, easing the problem of finding tenants for demesne land (there would, save in exceptional cases, be no question of selling it, for no other form of income yielding investment existed).[1] But while it was clearly better to have a tenant than let the land fall completely out of use, this further lowered landlord incomes by adding to the supply of rentable land with the depressive effects on rents and labour supply already mentioned. Landlords were caught in a vicious downward spiral: the more of them there were abandoning demesne farming the more difficult circumstances became for those persisting with it; the more of them there were renting their demesnes the more rent incomes fell. It was not, of course, quite a case of out of the frying pan into the fire because, while money could be actually lost in demesne farming, rents, however small, were at least clear gain. But the first three-quarters of the fifteenth century were ones during which landlords were pinched as they had never been before and as they were never to be again.

[1] The feudal 'entail' which preserved land for the heir would have been a legal barrier had the economic incentive to sell existed.

Peasant farming

The corollary to landlord difficulties was peasant comfort. A plentiful
supply of cheap land and good wages (which remained up even when
prices came down) made of the same period for the mass of the rural
populace the easiest until modern times. The judgment is a relative
one; nobody grew rich on thirty or fifty or even a hundred acres of
land farmed with fifteenth-century methods. We must think in terms
of an easing of strain, of the appearance of a margin between elementary
needs and the means of supplying them, or of the closing of a gap
between those needs and the inability to meet them properly. But we
must remember too that the fifteenth-century peasantry were the
beneficiaries not only of contemporary changes but of the work of
their thirteenth-century predecessors. The land which new farmers were
taking over was land ready for the plough – the task of making it so
had been undertaken for them. Through this period and some way
beyond it English agrarian society was working within the bounds of
cultivation, not, like earlier and later generations, continually up against
them. And, obviously when there was land surplus to current needs, it
was the worst land that reverted to nature. The average peasant holding
was both larger and better.

Average, of course, is not the same thing as typical; an average can
conceal wide variations around an arithmetic mean. But although
evidence is not abundant we can be fairly confident that the fifteenth
century effected a levelling up in peasant landholdings. The large
peasant doubtless grew a little larger but the biggest gainer was the man
who had had to work for wages either because he did not hold enough
land or because he held none. Factual indications to this effect apart, the
same circumstances which drove lords from demesne farming must
have curbed peasant tendencies to expand very much beyond subsistence size. The typical would have tended to approximate to the
average; and the typical was the subsistence holding. The virgate might,
in a sense, be said to have come back into its own, except that a lord's
concern to maintain standard holding sizes as long as they represented
units of labour tended to vanish when they represented practicably
divisible rents; and increasingly oddly sized holdings appeared as
vagaries of testamentary dispositions, and small purchases among
peasants proceeded unchecked by lordly veto.

No more than for any other period can a general statement comprehend the range and variety of agrarian people and we lack the data

for any well-founded mathematical representation. But on circumstantial grounds we could affirm certain broad traits of the mid-fifteenth century. At the extreme those who depended exclusively or very heavily on wages were proportionately fewer than at any time in the preceding four centuries or at any time since. At the other extreme those who farmed holdings which required the regular employment of hired labour would not have been many. In between there were those whose holdings were large enough to yield something of a grain surplus for sale – where, in effect, the occupant costed his own labour at less than its market value so that as long as he, and other members of his family, undertook a large share of the work he was relatively immune to the high labour costs which inhibited commercial farming on a larger scale. Such peasants would have sold anything from a tiny fraction of their grain up to about one half of it. There must have been a good number falling within this category. Otherwise how was the non-agricultural population fed? Shading downwards were those who as farmers hovered around subsistence level, through to those whose holdings were the basic element in their economy but who substantially supplemented their farming yield with wages. The great bulk then belong to the category of subsistence farmers if we mean by that those who, with their families, themselves consumed a large proportion of what they produced and produced on their own holdings a large proportion of what they consumed.

While the passing of the essentially commercial demesne farming lord and the succession of the essentially subsistence peasant farmer constituted a radical change in the organisation of English agriculture, it might be said that the full implications of the divorce of landlords from direct association with the soil only emerged over a much longer period (perhaps three centuries); that the immediate consequences were relatively modest. In particular, to speak of a reversion to subsistence farming can be misleading, partly because it suggests that at some earlier time subsistence farming had ceased to be of major importance; even at the height of the thirteenth-century 'high farming' no more than one-third of foodstuffs can have been raised by essentially commercial farmers. But that is a fairly large slice and its disappearance, or transformation, could warrant emphatic language. The more crucial mistake would be to suggest that there was a large fall in the proportion of foodstuffs sold. Now this could only be true if there was a correspondingly large shift in the balance between agricultural and non-agricultural elements in the population. Our evidence suggests that this was not the case. Given the way we use the words we must speak of the disappearance of commercial farmers but not of the passing of commercial farming. It was the essentially subsistence farmers who took up the market opportunities abandoned by manorial lords. The opportunities were spread thinly among them so that very few emerged as a new class of distinctively commercial farmers. The primary character of peasant farming remained unchanged. The modest edging of any one peasant farmer a little closer to the market could pass unremarked. But the sum of thousands of such inching advances equalled the sum of one-fiftieth of that number of dramatic retreats.

However, if we should not talk of the decline of commercial farming, we should certainly note that the character – and quality – of farming for the market underwent a significant change. For the demesne-farming lord the market had been a central preoccupation; for the small peasant farmers who replaced him it was a supplementary or even marginal consideration; they looked on their land first and foremost as a way of feeding themselves and their families; they probably, as before, regarded sheep as their principal source of cash income. The keen concern which demesne lords, or at least the more advanced of them, had taken in getting the most from the land by way of the use of artificial manures, drainage, an attention to market requirements, etc., was not shared by the average peasant. Or if he had such a concern he commonly lacked the capital to make it effective. When lords quit farming progressive techniques, such as they were, disappeared also. Another two hundred years or so elapsed before the keener sensitivity to general economic and technical developments and the requisite capital with which landlords as a class were endowed once again started to shape decisively the nature of English arable farming. If it is only in a qualified sense that we can speak of the decline of 'commercial farming' in the fifteenth century it is in an absolute sense that we can speak of the decline of 'high farming'.

This change in the nature of commercial farming obviously consisted also in the greater immediacy of contact between farmer and market, as a direct consequence of population fall. A town of 5,000 inhabitants in 1450 could be provisioned from within a narrower radius than the same town in 1347 when it had had a population of some 10,000 or more. The need to invoke supplies from a distance was diminished and, correspondingly, the opportunity for marketing at a distance. The premium on command of haulage and storage facilities was lessened; the element of producers' 'rent' in the profits of conveniently placed farmers contracted.[1] The one tended to even out market opportunities, the other to lessen the incentive to exploit them, and both to provide comfortable scope for the small, unambitious farmer of slender financial resources within easy reach of a town market. One noteworthy consequence then of the population fall was that the economy tended to become even more heavily localised in character than it had been previously.

An important question remains untouched. If these fifteenth-century peasant farmers were not villeins, what was the form of tenure by which they held their land? Quite a number – perhaps a fifth over the country as a whole – were those who in earlier times had eluded the clamps of villeinage – freeholders whose land had always been their own and whose distinctive legal standing might often accompany an economic status of small peasant farmer indistinguishable from that of a villein. But for those emerging or recently emerged from villeinage a new tenure was being evolved – or, more accurately, a radical modification of villein tenure. We have seen that the popular notion that the occupant had fixed, quasiproprietary, rights in his holding had always contrived to coexist with the strict legal view that the lord's rights were total and absolute. This notion derived ultimately from Anglo-Saxon times, but as the memory of these faded the rationalised justification was that the land was held in return for the services rendered, and that at least as long as the services were performed the occupant could not be disturbed – a view which, in certain circumstances, the law was now increasingly disposed to share. As labour services everywhere were commuted into money rents this assumed the form of a perpetual tenancy for which the commuted value of the labour services was due to the landlord; and just as in practice labour services had tended to be customarily fixed, so also were the money rents which now took their place.

Even when labour services had not been commuted the practice had become general by the Black Death of recording them in terms of their money equivalent. When a lord on abandoning his demesne effected a general and permanent commutation of the then useless labour dues it was naturally at this customary rate. If he considered that the rents thus created were unduly low he could compensate himself by requiring high admission fines from those succeeding to holdings or

---

[1] In its technical sense 'rent' means the additional profit secured by more favourably placed or lower cost producers over the minimum profit necessary to induce the worst placed or highest cost producers to engage in production.

acquiring fresh holdings: admission fines were most often not determined by customary valuation since they were conceived of not
essentially as payments for the land but as payments for the lord's
permission to enter on to it which was not susceptible to regular
monetary evaluation. Thus the villein without any change in the
ostensible form of his tenure became in effect a new kind of rent-paying
tenant – styled variously a 'customary tenant' (since the terms were
simply those fixed by custom) or a 'copyholder' (one whose ostensible
title to his holding was a copy of the relevant entry in the manorial
roll). It was a natural and undeliberated evolution – simply a universal
and abiding application of the sporadic commutation of earlier
times.

The extension of this kind of tenure to new incoming tenants was
more artificial because then the terms of occupancy were a matter for
considered decision by both parties and there could be no question of
the newcomer having any traditional rights in the land. Here it was,
presumably, that the essentially contrived device of the copyhold for
life arose: the new tenant was vested with the holding for his lifetime
on the terms customarily attaching to the land; the variable admission
fine would be the point on which bargaining would pivot. It was an
arrangement which in fifteenth-century circumstances suited both
landlord and tenant. The one was pleased enough to have a permanent
occupant for vacant land; the other sought little more than the insurance
against want that a subsistence size holding for life would afford him.
A non-terminable arrangement on invariable terms well met the
interests of both and the copyhold lay ready to hand as a suitable
instrument. The putative security lent by its origin masked its lack of
solid foundation. It was at its flimsiest when the copyhold was of ex-
demesne land to which no customary dues could attach. Then it was
only a form of lease devoid of the proper contractual forms and thus
in effect a mere tenancy at will. Yet for all its legal deficiencies the
copyhold was easily the most common form of tenure in the second
half of the fifteenth century when perhaps rather more than three-
quarters of rented land was held in this manner.

Other kinds of tenure rarely occurred except on ex-demesne land.
A dispirited, lackadaisical lord might allow his demesne to pass to small
copyholders, but most lords commonly sought to retain clear control
over their demesnes by letting them on terms which made explicit their
freedom to resume them at a later date if they wished. Sometimes mere
tenants at will were installed. More usually a formal lease was entered

into. Many leaseholders were in economic status and ambitions the same kind of people as copyholders, as was often reflected in the terms of their leases: the duration of the lease might be the lifetime of the holder or even the lifetimes of himself and one or two successors; and the payment due to the landlord might consist largely of a lump sum paid at commencement, analogous to an admission fine, and a relatively low regular rent.

Small in numbers but holding larger farms were the more distinctive and ultimately typical leaseholders who were actuated by unambiguously commercial motives. Quite often a whole demesne would be taken over by such an individual. They were men who believed they could still make commercial farming on a large scale pay. Often it would be in sheep-farming rather than in arable that they saw the scope for profit, and their readiness to take over large tracts of demesne land was fired by the grazing rights which accompanied them – although the lord might retain these for his own profit; where the demesne was enclosed some of the arable land leased might be converted to sheep pasture. Lessees of this kind usually took over not only demesne land but also all or some of the animals belonging to it. The sheep indeed might often be the principal attraction for a market-minded lessee. The type of lease known as 'stock and land' was then typical of large demesne lettings. (Whether the demesne was let in large parcels to this kind of tenants or in small lots to peasant farmers the draught animals at least would normally go to the new tenants anyway, since the landlord had no further use for them and they would be needed by the incomers.) Leases of this kind were usually of fairly short duration (seven and fourteen years were common periods). The profit-conscious lessee would be reluctant to commit himself to a fixed payment over a longer period, while the landlord who offered such a lease often conceived of it as merely a temporary or tentative arrangement which left him free to resume the demesne himself if circumstances had become more favourable when the lease expired.

Demesne lessees as to type fall into three categories: the former bailiffs of the manors, thoroughly familiar with the circumstances and already working under an arrangement which partially resembled a stock and land lease;[1] the biggest peasant farmers already farming for the market quite extensively and ready to hazard the jump to purely

[1] A bailiff was normally required to secure a specified amount of produce from the demesne; any shortfall he had to make good himself; and, in practice, he probably had a substantial share of any surplus.

commercial farming; outsiders with money made in trade or manufacturing looking for profitable employment for their surplus capital
– the wool merchant, or clothmaker seeking to secure his own wool
supplies, would be a special case of this kind. The huge bulk fell into the
first two categories. Very probably lords who were abandoning their
demesnes first sought lessees of this kind and only turned to small
peasant farmers on lease or copyhold terms as a last resort. But the same
circumstances that induced lords to pull out of demesne farming made
others reluctant to take over, though a bailiff who was threatened with
a loss of livelihood by the withdrawal itself would be less averse than
most. Lords who had clung on until towards the middle of the fifteenth
century, when market opportunities were improving, had most success
in finding large lessees. Those who had earlier let their demesnes go to
small leaseholders or copyholders on easy terms could not readily
detach them again when their market value rose.

The towns

The non-agricultural sectors of the economy experienced something
of the consequences of the Black Death that we have seen working
themselves out on the land. The same disequilibria in local supply and
demand caused disproportionate contractions of the market in some
places and labour shortages in others. But what happened in the towns
and other centres of industry as a result of the plague is to be understood
not primarily as a distinct experience but as a mere part of the agrarian
experience. Agriculture was the heavily preponderant activity. The
course of prices and wages there decisively set the tone for the whole
economy. Incomes derived from the land constituted the huge bulk of
purchasing power. The largest towns – those defined earlier as having
a distinctive urban economic identity – could in a limited way modify
the general pattern according to their own peculiar circumstances.
But the 'country towns' could be nothing but the passive subjects of
the forces abroad in the countryside in which they were economically
immersed. High agricultural wages and the increased chances of
obtaining a subsistence holding reacted on the urban proletariat in the
same way as they did on the rural peasantry. Urban and other industrial
employers found themselves squeezed by rising costs as did manorial
lords.

But the parallel between demesne farming lords and small-scale
manufacturers does not extend very far. The agrarian counterpart of the

urban craftsman was the larger peasant farmer who could absorb rising wages because much of his labour was his own. Few manufacturers in 1348 employed more than two journeymen and many supplemented their own work solely with that of an apprentice or two whose remuneration was largely in kind and who were, in any event, insensitive to rising wages, since their social ambitions precluded them from ordinary labouring. Such tendencies as there may have been during the earlier era of rising population for larger-scale producers to emerge would certainly have been curbed, and the profit margins of all who employed wage labour would have diminished in some degree, but more important than higher wage costs in determining the prosperity of manufacturers was the change in the volume and pattern of expenditure of the agrarian populace. And it is on circumstantially derived inferences relating to the demand for urban produce that we must chiefly lean in any appreciation of town fortunes through this period. The hard data is quite inadequate to yield a direct account. We have abundant evidence of a decline in town populations and of pleas from town corporations that they were unable to support the *firma burgi* fixed at an earlier time. But it would be remarkable if such had not been the case: it would have meant that the plague had shown a curious selectivity in favour of the towns. Obviously, too, the total amount of manufactured goods must have fallen. But the meaningful quantity is the *per capita* not the gross. And *per capita* output would be very largely determined by rural demand.

What we have seen of rural change indicates positively that during the period of transition from lordly farming to peasant farming – that is up to about 1450 – a transfer of incomes was taking place from landlords to peasants. We can also affirm that the concentration on better land as the worst fell out of use and the greater amount of land available to each person would have raised average agrarian incomes. In summary, average agrarian incomes as a whole would have been somewhat higher than formerly but lordly incomes rather lower. It is doubtless true that of the increase in peasant incomes much went on foodstuffs; that is to say peasants with larger holdings devoted them principally to raising their own dietary standard. This would have the effect of lowering the proportion of agrarian incomes spent on manufactured goods, probably to an extent that offset the average rise of such incomes. On balance then, we could say that the volume of agrarian expenditure (*per capita*) on town produce would probably have declined a little – but only a little. It is likely that changes in the patterns of expenditure were more consequential. The slight fall in the volume would have been made up of a fall in purchases by lordly households not fully compensated for by a rise in peasant purchases. It would be a crude truth that landlord purchases would consist more of the fairly expensive products of the specially skilled craftsmen of the larger towns, while peasant purchases would be of coarser or more mundane local wares. The inferences then would be that the 'country towns' would have gained somewhat as a result of agrarian change while the larger towns would have suffered to a slightly greater degree, an inference which the stray scraps of reliable information tend to confirm. This would be the other aspect of the tendency, already noted, for the economy to become rather more heavily localised in character than it had formerly been – for single rural regions each enveloping a small town to close themselves off from outside areas. But the principal brunt of such conclusions as can be inferentially arrived at is that the impact of the Black Death and its economic consequences on the level of industrial activity relative to population cannot, in anything but the short run of immediate dislocations, have been very marked.

This is consonant with numerous and persistent local difficulties in readjusting the number of producers to the reduced scale of gross demand. The uneven incidence of deaths both at the time of the first great wave of plague and during the next half century of population decline would have meant that in many cases the number of producers was more than there was full market scope for, with the corollary that in a roughly equal number of cases the reverse was true – paralleling the situation among agricultural labourers, except that a town craftsman was less mobile than a rural labourer: he would be reluctant to quit the place where he had an established business and a status of modest dignity and the craftsmen of another town where the mortality pattern had had the reverse effect would not be eager to allow a stranger to share their windfall gains. Here and there this kind of situation led master craftsmen to take protective action by using the guild's power of ruling on admissions to mastership in order to keep the number of new entrants down to a level which ensured a decent share for those already established. Once such a practice had been adopted at a time when population and demand were diminishing, it was unlikely to be abandoned when these trends were reversed. The advantage to those already on the inside of keeping others out and of securing for themselves the benefits of an expanding market might not readily be thrown away. We may imagine too that craftsmen in areas where the uneven incidence of deaths had brought them additional business might take similar measures to preserve their increased prosperity as the situation tended to revert to normal. Under this view the population disaster was the solvent of the mass of customary attitudes and ethical standards which had hitherto kept the acquisitive instinct in check. However, it is arguable that this tendency for the guild to be used as an instrument of monopoly on behalf of those who controlled it was one which would anyway have manifested itself with increasing strength in the natural course of events. The history of power is generally the history of its abuse.

The corollary to limiting admissions as masters was that those who had served a full apprenticeship were increasingly required to work as journeymen for the privileged insiders. In many cases they could continue to look forward to becoming masters eventually but the virtually automatic transition from apprentice to independent crafts-man was starting to become a thing of the past, and the prospect of a working life spent entirely in the employ of another man was becoming more of a reality. A gap between employer and employee was begin-ning to open up. The division of industrial society into distinct classes with opposing interests was replacing the older uniform order of small independent producers, brother members of their guild, for whom the interests of the craft and of the craftsmen were of necessity coterminous. Within this period one can only speak of signs of this trend here and there – in some towns, in some crafts. Its full evolution in its multi-farious forms occurs over succeeding centuries. And if retrospectively the incipient cancers which were eventually to destroy the craft guilds can be discerned so early, the fifteenth century yet saw the institution at its most vital, with the developments of the (late) twelfth and thirteenth centuries, described in the previous chapter, coming to full term, con-ferring on the craft guilds a conspicuous dignity and importance in the corporate life of urban communities, and doubtless in many cases winning an authoritative recognition for what had earlier been merely private associations without any kind of formal public standing.

The cloth industry

Cutting across the disturbances caused by the ravagings of death was the revival of the manufacture of fine cloth. Here we tread on the firm ground of solid statistical data. Before the middle of the fourteenth century exports of cloth were small. By the end of the century they were running at the rate of about 40,000 cloths a year (the standard cloth was a piece measuring 72 ft by 4 ft 6 in) – enough to clothe three-quarters of a million people and incorporating the wool of one-and-three-quarter million sheep. There are no usable figures of production for the home market but exports on that scale can only have been achieved by outselling Flemish cloth in overseas markets, compelling the conclusion that English cloth had largely replaced Flemish among home buyers of high quality material. If we assumed that Flemish cloth was ousted from England to the plausible extent of 10,000 cloths a year, that would mean that by the end of the century 50,000 cloths annually were being manufactured in England which in the absence of the revival would have been made in Flanders. Now the process of converting raw wool into a finished cloth probably required something between fifteen and twenty work weeks. Allowing for holidays during the year (of which there were many, apart from Sundays) and striking a convenient round figure, 50,000 cloths annually represents then the labour of about 20,000 people – that is, 20,000 jobs which otherwise would not have existed. In 1400 the total non-agricultural labour force would have been between 100,000 and 150,000 people. On the basis of such figures it seems safe to assert that over the country as a whole the boom in fine cloth manufacture easily offset the slightly depressive consequences of population fall on the level of industrial activity.

This is not to say that every town experienced the stimulating effects of the expanded opportunities for cloth manufacture or that those which did did so in the same degree. Again evidence of sufficient precision is lacking. The ancient major centres of cloth production seem to have recovered something of their former importance, but the more marked trait is the emergence of fine cloth centres in Wiltshire and Gloucestershire, and to a lesser extent in Somerset and Devon, while towns in Suffolk and Essex attained an eminence which they had not enjoyed in the twelfth and early thirteenth centuries. Particularly in the western counties, this upsurge commonly took place in communities which had not the formal status of borough (i.e. had not received a charter) and which often in fact started off as large villages. In some cases the efflorescence spilled over into the countryside merging with the fulling-mill-centred industry of earlier date. But in general the making of fine cloth seems within this period to have been largely confined to towns old or new, although spinning, which occupied more people than weaving, must very often have embraced the surrounding rural areas. Thus many of the older established corporate towns may have suffered a modest decline due to general economic factors, while newer communities prospered on cloth.

The reasons for the rise of fine cloth manufacture in the counties mentioned is not easy to discern. They were quite well placed for supplies of high quality wool but they did not, with the partial exception of Gloucestershire, actually lie in the best wool areas – which were Herefordshire, Shropshire, the Cotswolds and Lincolnshire. A fine balance compounded of proximity to raw materials, accessibility of markets, existing concentrations of population, an established tradition of cloth making along perhaps with greater freedom from lordly control and other factors which evade rational determination must have so decided matters.[1]

The statistics show that after the initial leap of the second half of the fourteenth century exports of cloth, taking one decade with another, stagnated through the first half of the fifteenth. To a large extent this must have been simply because the existing market possibilities had been fully absorbed. The early gains had been scored at the expense of Flemish cloth in what must have been a declining market. They were not sustained by dynamic circumstances creating continuing scope for expansion. Home sales of fine cloth probably behaved in much the same way. As long as rents fell and high wages trimmed profit margins the market for high quality goods cannot have grown any faster than population, if as much. The fine cloth industry thus reached a high plateau around the turn of the fourteenth to the fifteenth century, and rested there until fresh market opportunities, setting in from just about 1475, inaugurated a second vigorous growth phase.

The dramatic upward swing in the output of fine cloth in the later fourteenth century demands an explanation. In one way the explanation is simple; in another way it is elusive. The simple and fully explanatory fact is that English fine cloth enjoyed the clear competitive advantage of locally available and abundant supplies of wool of the requisite quality, the very wool which constituted the raw material of the Flemish industry. Plainly, the difference in transport costs meant that an

---

[1] Dr Joan Thirsk, in 'Industries in the countryside', *Essays in the Economic and Social History of Tudor and Stuart England* (ed. F. J. Fisher, Cambridge University Press, 1961), has drawn attention to the common geographical coincidence between cloth making and subdivision of holdings, suggesting that the reduction of holding size created a special interest in supplementary sources of income. She does not offer the suggestion as anything more than the intelligent and informed piece of speculation which it is. That there is a significant correlation seems likely; the chief difficulty is establishing which of the two factors is cause and which effect.

English manufacturer paid significantly less than a Fleming – even more so after 1275 when the Flemish price had to absorb the export duty as well. The real question then is not why did the English industry establish a dominance in the second half of the fourteenth century, but why had it not done so earlier? The soft answer is: the more efficient organisation and the superior techniques of the Flemish industry. The Flemings certainly had a highly capitalised industry in which a single entrepreneur commonly controlled all stages of manufacture from carding to final dressing and dyeing. But the economies of large-scale production are paltry when they do not arise out of the use of productive equipment, which is at its most economical in large units. If we think of the Flemish 'clothier' as essentially a merchant buying raw materials and selling the finished product in bulk we can appreciate that the element of trading costs in his total expenditure would be lower than that of a small English manufacturer buying materials and selling cloth in piecemeal quantities. But this element is small in proportion to total costs. And, in any event, such 'clothiers' had, as seen, existed in thirteenth-century England. Organisational advantages would not suffice to explain Flemish supremacy. Whether superior techniques would is a more open question.

We do not know how sophisticated Flemish methods were. Contemporaries evidently thought that the Flemings had special skills which the English lacked but they probably exaggerated the subtleties involved. It is certainly a historical fact that the English industry was launched on its upward move shortly after an influx of Flemish weavers in the 1330s and the 1340s, responding to invitations issued by Edward III offering them favourable treatment – in pursuit of a policy of promoting home manufacture followed sporadically since the middle of the thirteenth century, although its elements, banning the export of wool to Flanders, prohibiting the wear of foreign cloth and encouraging the settlement of Flemish clothworkers, cannot be accurately disentangled from a purely diplomatic policy towards Flanders. But to what extent either Flemish skills or royal policy contributed to the development of the English industry can only be a matter for conjecture, as can the degree to which the Flemish industry had drawn a competitive advantage from those skills.

In the lack of compelling reasons to account for greater Flemish efficiency one might toy with the idea that the merchants are the key to the matter; that, as has been seen, it was to begin with European trade, not English, that had expanded outwards, particularly from that area where the North Sea, the Rhine, the Meuse, the Scheldt, and the English Channel converged to make of Flanders a natural centre of mercantile activity and consequently a source of widely dispersed goods. If the Flemish industry grew in response to mercantile pressure, might not the growth of the English industry be regarded as the effect of the rise of a body of English merchants carrying, so to speak, England to Europe whereas formerly Europe had come to England? This view would have it that Flanders grew and prospered because merchants congregated there, sought to carry away convenient native produce in increasing quantities and, as long as the native industry could answer to the need for mercantile profit, found little incentive to look elsewhere; that when the wool trade brought a body of English merchants into existence, in enjoyment of nearly the same geographical advantages as Flanders, they sought more scope than that single commodity provided and, naturally, found it in native cloth.

The incentive to export cloth was perhaps sharpened by the fact that the export duty on cloth came to about 2 per cent of its value while by the mid-fourteenth century that on wool worked out at about 20 per cent. Obviously too the more or less contemporaneous decline of the Flemish industry and rise of the English industry are casually related, and while it is probably true that it is chiefly by way of the Flemish decline being the effect of the English rise, it may be that the Flemish industry was on the decline anyway as a producer of traditional fine cloth. The periodic interruptions to English wool supplies, their higher cost as they bore an increasing tax burden, the civil struggle between those who controlled Flemish economic life and those who were the subjects, or victims, of control which in fluctuating fashion was sustained for the century and a half straddling the horrible and bloody years 1323–28 caused at least temporary drops in output and might have permanently impaired productive capacity even had English cloth not intruded.

Non-urban industry

Of the other non-urban industrial activities enumerated previously something should be briefly said. In ironworking water power was from the early years of this period here and there harnessed to the bellows in bloomeries and forges, with distinct cost advantages, offsetting rising labour charges; however there were many tiny ironworks throughout the country catering for restricted local markets which would not have found the capital cost of water power economical and were protected from more efficient outside competition by high freight costs; and the quality of English iron remained generally low so that for many purposes imported, mostly Spanish, iron continued to be used. Notwithstanding the general European lack of economic buoyancy tinworking prospered and English tin seems to have penetrated further into Europe than it had done in earlier centuries. The same might be true of lead but there are no statistics as there are of tin. Tyneside coal continued to be distributed in modestly increasing quantities to suitable points bordering the North Sea. Saltmaking along the east coast where it had been practised most intensively declined, perhaps as the saltmakers found more remunerative and congenial occupations on the land or in clothmaking; England in this period came to lean more heavily on salt supplies from the Bay of Biscay. There are much fewer large-scale building projects in these years, ecclesiastical and military needs having been largely met in earlier times. Shipbuilding, however, seems to have prospered in at least modest fashion as English merchants and shippers enlarged their share of overseas trade.

If an apology is needed for this summary treatment it must be that existing knowledge does not permit of any satisfactory economic analysis of these activities and that in any event they are by themselves of too little economic weight to merit an extensive account. The justification for singling them out earlier was principally the characteristics they possessed which led to arrangements differing from the organisation of town crafts. But the manufacture of hats and caps, which nobody presumably would consider to warrant special treatment, employed more people than any one of these industries.

Overseas trade

It remains to look more particularly at England's overseas trade within this period. Already by the thirteenth century wool had drawn England tightly into the European orbit and made of foreign commerce a significant element in English economic life. And it was a sector which, as far as the meagre data from the first half of the fourteenth century permit of a judgment, surprisingly fails to show the gross contraction which one would expect as an immediate consequence of the European population catastrophe. For some forty years before the Black Death wool exports had been running a little below the level attained in the first decade of the century, but they showed no further tendency to fall off in the years immediately following the Death. The turning point comes around 1365 with the onset of a more or less unremitting decline of wool exports. There was of course the closely associated compensation of the growth in cloth exports. Graph I.1 is an attempt to integrate the two trends and to indicate, then, the record of English exports in gross.

The long-run decline of wool exports reflects the dwindling of the Flemish cloth industry but the particular sharp drop in total exports through the 1370s and the 1380s may have been due in some measure to the unfavourable course then being taken by the Hundred Years War, including lively commerce raiding by French ships. Certainly in the 1390s, which saw the war petering out until the truce of 1396 brought hostilities formally to a close for seven years, cloth exports soared upwards while wool exports for a while ceased to fall. But wool exports soon started down again and fell with a sickening thud in the 1430s, when they decisively gave way to cloth, after which they bumped along for the remainder of this period at a level only some 30 per cent of that of their heyday. Through the 1440s wool and cloth combined were well below their level of the 1360s. And 1448 ushered in a phase which was to endure until 1475, during which cloth exports were gravely depressed. For this unhappy situation the protracted quarrel with the Hanse, the last disastrous phase of the Hundred Years War and the internal disorder bred of the Wars of the Roses disrupting trade routes and closing markets would seem to have been responsible.

Of the major items of importation cloth fell away to virtually nothing as English made cloth secured a monopoly of the home market. Wine, most of it from Gascony, of all commodities showed the greatest degree of sensitivity to the course of war. Between the destruction or desertion of the Gascon vineyards during military campaigns in the region and attacks on shipping along the exposed route between Bordeaux or Bayonne and the English ports the wine trade suffered severe periodic setbacks, notably in the 1350s, the 1370s, the 1400s, the 1420s and from 1448 to 1475 when the final French assault on Gascony resulted in the fall of Bordeaux and Bayonne (1453) and the sustained obstruction of the Anglo-Gascon trade until the Treaty of Picquigny (1475) restored amity, and free commercial intercourse between England and a France which had by then absorbed all the continental possessions of the English king except Calais.

Of other goods entering into trade it is impossible to say anything with certainty. Exports of tin, lead and pewter very probably rose for

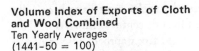

**Volume Index of Exports of Cloth
and Wool Combined**
Ten Yearly Averages
(1441–50 = 100)

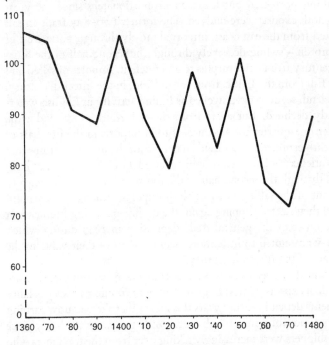

GRAPH I.I

(The customs records register exports of wool and cloth only by quantity and make no kind of distinction between different grades of the two commodities. No really accurate summing of the two, therefore, is possible. The above graph is founded on data and a suggested summing procedure contained in A. R. Bridbury, *Economic Growth, England in the Later Middle Ages* (Allen & Unwin, 1962), pp. 31–2. It can fairly confidently be relied on as a general trend indicator, serving for total exports since those of commodities other than cloth and wool were of only marginal importance.)

a while but would have certainly fallen during the general depression of the third quarter of the fifteenth century. But these along with other lesser items only accounted for about one-twentieth of a trade dominated by wool and cloth. Imports of luxury Mediterranean and eastern produce increased through the fourteenth century, while Venetian and Genoese merchants were widening the all-sea trade channel from Italy, but the limited market scope for such articles must have been fully exploited by the beginning of the fifteenth century. Imports of dye-stuffs, most of which had to be obtained from abroad, rose as native clothmaking prospered but less then proportionately since the great bulk of cloth exports were undyed. The former two-way trade in salt – exported from the east coast, imported mostly through ports west of Southampton – swung decisively through the second half of the four-teenth century from a net surplus to a net deficit. Imports of salted and smoked fish from the Baltic, from Ireland and, in the fifteenth century, from Iceland, seem to have swelled as fishing activity in English waters apparently declined. But apart from these, Flemish cloth, and wine (the latter one-quarter to one-third of total imports in the first half of the fifteenth century), the individual courses of the numerous imported commodities cannot be even roughly charted. Gross imports must have declined through the second half of the fourteenth century, principally on account of the falling away of cloth imports; steadied until around 1435 and then started slipping again, the decline gathering momentum with the onset of the general trade depression in 1449 during which phase they amounted to little more than one-half of their value in the early years of the fifteenth century.

It is plain that over the period as a whole imports contracted more sharply than exports. Unless England had been running a heavy balance of payments deficit in earlier years this means that she was now earning a surplus – possibly quite a substantial one, the more probably since English shippers were increasingly taking over from the foreigners who had formerly carried to and from English ports. However, no great weight need be attached to this fact. It means simply that hoards of the precious metals were being built up, and the only consequence that might be argued to have ultimately flowed from that is that the reserves thus constituted facilitated the great expansion of imports of a later period. More immediately, the acquisition of gold and silver had no significance beyond the fact itself, but it may appropriately be observed here that such accumulation was regarded by contemporaries as a prime object of foreign trade. The disposition to conceive of the precious metals as wealth itself is doubtless older than recorded history. Just when the idea started to root itself that a nation's overseas commerce should be directed towards enlarging its holding of this wealth we cannot say, but certainly by the fifteenth century it was becoming something of a commonplace, and that commercial policy which has been dubbed 'bullionism' had become an evident element in contemporary statecraft. By the sort of tenets that would have been applied at the time, the long-term tendencies of English trade were in the right direction. The precious metals were being garnered and a growing proportion of mercantile profits were being secured by Englishmen. But a more meaningful test would be a calculation of the gains and losses of society as composed of producers and consumers.

We have noted already the record of exports of English produce. We need now to set against their decline the gains of English fine cloth makers at the expense of Flemings in the home market. Taking this at the previously used figure of 10,000 cloths by the end of the fourteenth century, which would be approximately equivalent in value to 15 per cent of total English exports before the onset of the decline in the 1360s, we can set that against the percentage falls suggested by the exports graph, to indicate the net consequences for English producers of the shifts in foreign trade by comparison with the pre-1365 situation. This yields a net loss of 5 per cent by the 1440s and one of 20 per cent during the worst of the phase 1448-75, which (after discounting for population change) is to say that the trend was broadly favourable for producers up to the years of the trade depression, during which, however, it was evidently adverse. But this experience must be set in the perspective of the total productive effort of English society. At the most exports can have accounted for only 3 per cent of English output of goods and services. Thus even the severe setback of the trade depression years could only have been of the most marginal consequence for the economy as a whole. Such a general statement, of course, comprehends everybody from the pure subsistence peasant farmer who would be completely impervious to trading conditions to the overseas merchant who would feel the undiluted effects of commercial fluctuations.

Within this wide range one set of producers merits particular attention: the sheep graziers. Did the new English cloth makers provide a sufficient market for wool to compensate for the decline of the Flemish one? We can only essay an answer on the same assumption of 10,000 English cloths replacing Flemish in the home market by 1400. Into their manufacture would have gone some 2,500 sacks of wool. To this we must add the wool contained in the great addition to former exports of cloth – impossible to calculate precisely since the amount of cloth exported before 1347 is not accurately known – 7,500 extra sacks giving the conveniently round tota l of 10,000 for 1400 would be close to the mark. By then exports of wool itself had fallen by about 13,000 sacks. The net fall in wool sales was then some 3,000 sacks. On the eve of the trade depressi on the fall amounted to about 7,000 sacks and at the very end of the period to about 10,000 (assuming constant home sales of fine cloth after 1400). But the cut represented by the last figure amounts proportionally to rather less than the drop in population. So that even at the most depressed point in the whole period the average sheep farmer cannot have been any worse off than he had been when Flanders was soaking up English wool.

Looking at society as a set of consumers of imported produce the situation can be put quite simply. If Englishmen bought less from abroad it was because they chose to do so, not because diminished resources forced them to do so – and, of course, overriding that, because there were less of them to do so and because at certain times, notably 1448–1475, interference with trade prevented them from doing so. Put another way, there is no evidence to be found of internal depression over the economy as a whole in the reduced volume of imports. Where the lower *per capita* consumption of imported goods cannot be attributed to the sheer impossibility of obtaining them because of political or military obstruction it represents a shift in preferences – most signally from Flemish to English cloth and more generally, with the redistribution of agrarian incomes, from imported luxuries, conspicuously wine, to more mundane domestic produce. Imports anyway were a purely marginal element in the economy not only in the sense that they accounted for only a very small proportion of the total stock of goods available, particularly the case after the elimination of Flemish cloth, but also in that they were dispensable since, as to the great bulk, they consisted neither of basic items of consumption of which England was chronically short, nor of materials vital to English manufacturing activity. Their total cessation would have meant little more than that the wealthy would have been forced to adopt a rather plainer mode of life.

As has been indicated already the set of people most sensitive to variations in foreign trade and whose fortunes contemporaries tended to regard as a test of the usefulness of trade were the overseas merchants themselves. Plainly their prosperity would be a direct function of the volume of trade, which is to say in summary that they experienced, in gross terms, a modest decline until 1448 and a more grievous decline from then until 1475. But within this total picture there are variations in particular elements. The most pertinent distinction is that between English and alien merchants. In the second half of the fourteenth century the promotion of English merchants over foreigners starts to become a clear object of state policy; more generally, in the same period there develops something that could be called a genuine commercial policy as distinct from royal measures which were simply fiscal or diplomatic in their intent. The background to this development, as with most changes in attitudes, defies dogmatic analysis, but it can plausibly be associated with the more active participation of the House of Commons in affairs of state and perhaps with the sharpening of a popular sense of national identity, associated with chauvinistic sentiments engendered by the Hundred Years War. Certainly at its first appearance specifically commercial policy carried that tinge of bellicosity which was to characterise it for centuries until the sweet reasonableness of free trade doctrines came to pervade it in the nineteenth century. International commerce was conceived of as a kind of battleground on which nations contended with one another for possession of the precious metals and for profitable employment for their merchants.

The first beneficiaries of this nationalist attitude towards trade were the English wool merchants. The wool trade, however, did have a rather particular character which owed much to the Crown's special concern with this lucrative source of finance. The very high duty on wool exports meant that even in the mid-fifteenth century, when wool was only about one-sixth of all goods entering into trade, it yielded nearly four-fifths of customs revenue and roughly a quarter of all Crown revenue. It was an administrative convenience for the Crown to have the wool trade closeted among a restricted group of merchants. It was an even greater facility to have all wool exports channelled through one 'staple' town – an arrangement which, provided the town was conveniently situated, also suited the merchants since it made it easier for them to act in concert over prices. On the other hand it militated against the interests of the growers and middlemen, unable to achieve a sellers' union to match that of the merchant buyers. The idea of a staple town was first tried out in 1314 and from then until 1392 the device had a vacillating history. At times the interests of growers and middlemen prevailed and the staple was abolished or several English towns were appointed; at other times a single conveniently located continental town was constituted as the staple, often in association with diplomatic policy which employed the promise of the valuable commerce which it brought to the favoured town as a bargaining counter. In some measure the fluctuations in exports of wool through the fourteenth century might be attributed to the trading difficulties caused by these frequent changes in staple policy.

From 1392 the staple was permanently located at Calais and from then, if not earlier, a fully evolved mercantile organisation controlling the wool trade with northern Europe can be discerned (wool shipped to Italy was normally exempted from the staple provisions and could proceed direct from any English port). This was the Company of the Merchants of the Staple. Its early origins are obscure. It seems likely that in characteristic medieval fashion the English wool merchants had joined in some form of association as soon as there was a fair number of them regularly engaged in the one activity, and that this body came to assume a more formalised character as the Crown interested itself more closely in the trade from the first levying of the maltolte in 1273 and as it became increasingly necessary then to have a representative organisation which could negotiate with the Crown on behalf of the English wool merchants. The functions of price and quality control typical of guild activity were probably also assumed before the fifteenth century when we have clear evidence of the Company acting in this way, although the vagaries of an international market and the independent position of the foreign buyers inevitably meant that control could not be as rigorous as that exercised by a local town guild. Between regulating the business conduct of its members, representing the trade to Crown and Parliament, negotiating with Flemish authorities whose object was to so control matters as to keep wool cheap as it was the Staplers' object to keep it dear, arranging loans from wool merchants for the chronically necessitous king and administering their recovery out of the wool tax, and from 1466, arising out of its increasing involvement in the collection of the tax, formally taking over this duty and providing directly for the Calais garrison out of the proceeds – between these multifarious functions, the Company was almost a state within a state. If its role in English history was not as decisive as, say, that of the later East India Company, this was perhaps because it was involved in a declining trade. If wool exports had maintained their pre-1365 level it would be difficult to imagine Calais detached from English control as easily as it was in the mid-sixteenth century; and it would be tempting to dally further with the conjectural history of a company commanding a prosperous trade in a key commodity enjoying the virtual governance of a fortified town a sea's breadth beyond the immediate power of the Crown. But reverting to actual history, the Company of Merchant Staplers was of its nature an organisation for English nationals only. The commanding position that a combination of circumstances had conferred on it finalised the monopoly by Englishmen of the wool trade – other than the Italian section of it.

By the mid-fifteenth century the Staplers, who as such were purely exporters, handled about 15 per cent of all English trade. At the same time other English merchants handled about 45 per cent so that by then the English were in control of some 60 per cent of their own foreign commerce (i.e. 10 per cent more than would be provided by a strictly proportionate division of the trade among the merchants of all the countries involved). As a trading people they had certainly not yet attained the international status of the Hansards or the Italians, but they had clearly come a long way since the thirteenth and earlier centuries when England had waited on continental mercantile initiatives.

The figures just quoted make it plain that it was not the near monopoly of the declining wool trade that accounted principally for the relatively strong position of English merchants but activity in other commodities of which cloth and wine were the most weighty single items. We have already seen that from about the middle of the thirteenth century Englishmen were pushing down the Atlantic coast and joining in the Gascon and Iberian trades. Although the Italians exploiting the sea route to England which took them past the Spanish and Portuguese coasts encroached much on the latter in the fourteenth and fifteenth centuries, the English share of the much more important Gascon trade continued to grow, a trend which must have owed a lot to the availability of a commodity, cloth, which could be profitably carried on the outward journey. By the beginining of the fifteenth century English merchants had relegated Gascons to a very minor role in the Anglo-Gascon trade and thereafter maintained their supremacy through the fluctuations which that trade experienced.

Of even greater ultimate significance, though probably of less immediate weight, was the intrusion of Englishmen into the Anglo-Flemish trade. Hitherto, so far as England was concerned, this had been a trade *with* Flanders but as the old pattern of wool to and cloth from that region dissolved it became more of a trade *through* Flanders, the established focal point for central European trade. The Flemings themselves were indifferent as to who conducted the international trade which passed along their waterways and through their towns, since they did not aspire to monopolise it themselves. No political or military struggle had to be waged in order to establish a footing in this valuable commerce, though the trade was liable to suffer from the quarrels between the English King and the Duke of Burgundy (who ruled Flanders from 1369 to 1477) which succeeded the Anglo-Burgundian alliance of 1419–35, and the consequent favourable turn which the Hundred Years War had briefly taken. The early history of English activity in this trade is as yet uncharted in detail. It might be conjectured that the wedge was first driven by wool merchants who extended their trading range to other commodities. An alternative view would be that the trade originated independently of wool; that local English dealers in imported produce who had formerly relied on foreign merchants for supplies took to venturing, either in person or by a servant, to the international markets of Flanders to procure their wares themselves; and that those who dealt locally in English made goods, some of which they had formerly sold to foreign merchants, similarly took themselves to Flanders to sell there. We must not categorise as sharply as a knowledge of modern conditions might lead us to do. A conceptual scheme of distinct overseas merchants, wholesalers and retailers in particular commodities, does not fit fourteenth- and fifteenth-century facts.

Many traders could be assigned to all three or any two of these categories, and some could even count as manufacturers as well. This would be particularly the case in the Flemish trade. The proximity of Flanders to eastern ports, the constant presence there of numerous merchants from or trading with all parts of Europe meant that a man might only have to absent himself from his local business for as little as a week or two to effect a year's trading. It is known from as early as the later thirteenth century that Londoners who at home were mercers, drapers,[1] haberdashers, skinners and grocers were trading into Flanders, and that their dealings were not confined to goods proper to their home designation. And though the fragmentary information available from the later fourteenth and the fifteenth century does suggest that the great bulk of wool exports were in the hands of specialist wool merchants it is clear that many who were not principally occupied in the staple trade occasionally dabbled in it and that the specialist wool

[1] Strictly defined, mercers were dealers pure and simple in textiles, most particularly silks; drapers were those who sold cloth, usually woollen, whose manufacture or finishing they had undertaken themselves. In practice the distinction became increasingly blurred.

merchants sometimes dealt in other commodities in other markets. It must be appreciated that, even though an English merchant of the period reckoned to conduct his main business personally, partnerships of a temporary nature for particular ventures or even of a semipermanent kind, the employment of servants or factors at a home or foreign branch, the assignment of goods to a commission agent were all common practices, so that many merchants were simultaneously engaged in more than one trade and where membership of a guild of company was requisite would belong to two or more – there is within this period little of the monopolistic exclusivism that characterised company-controlled trade in the sixteenth and seventeenth centuries.

Those engaged in the general Anglo-Flemish trade were first formally constituted in a company in 1407 although the body for a long time had a Flemish existence only; at home those belonging to it continued as members of the mercers, drapers, etc. or whatever local guild, if any, was appropriate to their domestic business. It was not until 1486 that the company known as the Merchant Adventurers was established in England but, without the capitals, the designation is generally used for all Englishmen trading to northern Europe other than the Merchant Staplers; as seen above, however, the two were not mutually exclusive and even if generally men tended to be either adventurers or Staplers the ease of transition was such that the decline of the trade of the latter simply swelled the ranks of the former.

The customs statistics which are our only abundant source do not reveal the origin of imported or the destination of exported goods, but it is clear that a substantial portion (perhaps something like a quarter) of English cloth was marketed in Flanders, much for further distribution, some of it reaching as far as the banks of the Danube and thence perhaps even to the Black Sea. By the early years of the fifteenth century English adventurers were solidly established in this high potential trade although it had to be shared, perhaps roughly fifty-fifty, with many others. In this great European entrepôt region there was no lack of goods to carry back to England or even, in the case of some, to carry to a third area before making the journey home – the faint lines of a fairly regular triangular England–Flanders–Gascony–England trade can be discerned in the fifteenth century.

Once the taste for the profits of foreign commerce had formed itself Englishmen were drawn to indulge it in regions other than those which offered them easy access. The Baltic with its shipbuilding materials, timber, cordage and sail-cloth (or their raw materials, hemp and flax), pitch and tar, became the more alluring as English ships won carriage from foreign vessels. It offered, also, ashes, of the kind needed in the preliminary scouring of wool and corn to supply local deficiencies. And it proffered a set of established trade routes for the dispersion of English cloth deep into eastern Europe. But these routes and the Baltic which gave access to them and to the materials which its littoral yielded were the creation and the preserve of the Hansard towns. To intrude here was to challenge the most powerful vested mercantile interests in northern Europe. Yet towns which live by trade must always have mixed reactions to outsiders who propose to intensify mercantile activity. There were elements in Danzig, in which English merchants were congregating in the later years of the fourteenth century, who welcomed the newcomers, the more especially as these merchants were not like those who merely commuted periodically to nearby Flanders but were men who came to take up established residence: whether they were the factors of a home merchant adding an offshoot to a main trading artery or principals themselves, the distance from England required that they made Danzig their base of operations, with beneficial results for local craftsmen and dealers – although in so far as they participated in local retail trade as many did or sought to do they were a competitive threat to these men. We cannot follow here the twisted and many-stranded skein of their history in Danzig, made up as it was of the clashing interests of the Danzigers themselves, of the conflicting ambitions of the other Hansard towns whose own privileged position in England was often at issue and of English politics both internal and external cutting across purely economic factors. It can only be said in summary that amid a thicket of problems the English had established a useful position in Danzig by about 1385, maintained it until 1449 when their situation was gravely prejudiced by the piratical assault of their fellow countrymen on the Hansard mercantile fleet in the Bay of Biscay, and that Edward IV completed their discomfiture in the Treaty of Utrecht (1475) when he, in effect, abandoned them as the price of Hansard support for his Yorkist cause against the Lancastrians in that sordid dynastic struggle, the Wars of the Roses. Deprived of the backing of their own government the position of the English in Danzig soon become untenable.

Even in their most prosperous years the English adventurers never made serious inroads into the Hansard hegemony of the Baltic. At best they were a small group of tolerated outsiders hanging on the fringes of this German mercantile empire. And at the same time as some

Englishmen were securing a footing in Danzig their compatriots were being prised out of the ancient Scandinavian trade by the diplomatic pressure which the Hansards could bring to bear on the king of the united Scandinavian countries. Fish were the staple of this trade and denied Scandinavian fish Englishmen turned to Iceland, whose Viking-descended inhabitants had by the end of the fourteenth century been almost entirely forgotten by Europe. From 1412 English fishermen and merchants were coming to Iceland in growing numbers bringing cloth and a wide range of commodities to a land deficient in or totally void of everything except what the sea yielded. In so doing they further endangered their standing in Scandinavia, for Iceland was part of the dominions of the Scandinavian kings and although they would take no steps themselves to provide their Icelandic subjects with the trade so desperately needed, they, with the hostile Hansards jogging their elbow, were averse to allowing the English to remedy their own short-comings. Unable to control effectively comings and goings in distant Iceland they made life still more difficult for the few Englishmen persisting with the Scandinavian trade. Until about 1475 the English enjoyed in practice a virtual monopoly of the trade with Iceland, only to lose it all over the next decade or so when the favoured Hansards decided to take it up. Colourful a story as this is, its real economic importance is highly marginal. Even given its heavy dependence on trade the tiny population of Iceland could not sustain a commerce which, one way or the other, made any weighty difference to English mercantile prosperity.

More important than Iceland was Ireland with whom trade was already well established. Although English rule in Ireland was only very shakily exercised throughout this period and was but an empty form over much of the country, the ports of the east coast remained solidly English in sentiment and attachment and even on the southern and western coasts where the native Irish predominated English merchants were welcome. The Irish themselves were active traders and participated in the trade between Gascony and the west of England but English merchants had at least their fair share of the Anglo-Irish trade which reached unprecedented heights in this period, uninter-rupted by the conflicts, mercantile, political and military, which at one time or another cut across all other trade routes.

There remain only two areas which were in direct contact with England over this period. One, Normandy, had never had much to offer England though it now became a useful market for English cloth for local sale – cloth for wider distribution in France went for the most part via Gascony or Flanders. The indications are that Anglo-Norman trade, such as it was, was mainly in the hands of Englishmen. The other area, the Mediterranean, remained an Italian preserve. The few ventures there by Englishmen belong more to a history of daring deeds than to an economic narrative.

In summary, the virtual takeover of the Anglo-Gascon trade, the entrenched position achieved in the Flemish trade and the consolidation of the staple monopoly dominate the lesser gains and setbacks of English merchants between 1348 and 1475. Within the period these advances were registered mostly before 1400 and probably more than offset the general decline of trade over the last three decades of the fourteenth century as far as English mercantile profits were concerned. Thereafter, on balance, Englishmen probably did little more than hold on to the share of trade already acquired and their fortunes as a body followed pretty closely the graph of total trade.

There is one further distinction which is worth drawing through the gross record of trade. That is between the experience of different ports. The customs accounts cover twenty ports of which eleven stand out clearly from the rest. They are: London; the North Sea ports – Hull, Boston, Lynn, Yarmouth and Ipswich; the Channel ports – Southampton and Sandwich; the western ports – Bristol, Plymouth and Exeter. The most outstanding comparative trait is the virtual extinction by the mid-fifteenth century of Boston – a hundred years earlier exceeded only by London in importance. Out of Boston flowed the fine wools of Lincolnshire and the Midlands to Flanders and few can have felt the decline of the wool trade more acutely than its inhabitants. Merchants who had come for wool had brought in imported goods for distribution to a wide area covering Norfolk, the East Midlands, Lincolnshire and Yorkshire and had often filled out their wool cargoes with cloth. With the withering away of wool this supplementary trade went elsewhere. Hull and Ipswich were also wool ports and shared in part the fate of Boston; but for Hull the effects were mitigated by the need for a port to meet the continuing general needs of Yorkshire and adjoining parts and to handle the cloth of York, Beverley and other centres of the region; Ipswich's decline too was less drastic; possibly shipbuilding with its need for imported materials helped to sustain modest mercantile activity; dyestuffs and ashes for the cloth industry of Suffolk and Essex may also have played a part.

This last reference leads to a particularly significant observation.

Ipswich, notwithstanding its favourable location, did not maintain itself as a cloth port. For a while after the falling away of wool exports cloth did provide a compensation. In 1447 some 8,000 cloths (about one-seventh of total cloth exports) left Ipswich. Thereafter cloth exports ebbed away much more rapidly than the general trade depression would explain and never really recovered. Ipswich had lost its cloth trade to London. Essentially the same fate overtook Lynn and Yarmouth. Only in the case of the unimportant Norwegian trade did these ports continue to conduct the bulk of their own foreign commerce. Even the west was linked to the Baltic and the North Sea almost entirely through London. The main exceptions to London dominance were: the trade of the western ports with the Atlantic coast, Normandy, Ireland, Iceland, and the trade of Southampton and Sandwich – these last apparent rather than real exceptions since their sustained prosperity was due almost entirely to Italian merchants who often preferred to avoid London, partly because of their unpopularity there, partly because the extension of their voyage to the capital was unnecessary since what they principally sought to carry away was the prime quality wool and cloth of the west country which was more accessible from Southampton. But the great bulk of the Mediterranean produce which they brought was sent direct to London – overland from Southampton, by coastal shipping from Sandwich – and virtually all of what they took on at Sandwich had come from London. Thus Sandwich was no more than an outport for London and much of Southampton's trade too depended on London merchants. Allowing for this, something like three-quarters of the goods entering overseas trade were by 1475 passing through the hands of London based merchants. Bristol merchants may have directly handled a tenth and would have been followed in importance by the merchants of Southampton (including Italians resident there) and those of Hull with the rest way down the field.

London was, of course, well favoured by nature: flanking a deep and broad river which reached far towards the west, well sheltered from storms, close to those parts of the continent where trade opportunities were the most abundant. Nothing but human malevolence could have prevented it from being, as it always had been, England's premier port. But something more than nature led to its swallowing up the commerce of other ports which for particular trades were as well or better placed. That something was capital and local market scope. London merchants commanded larger capital resources than those of

97

12

any other town; they had a larger doorstep market. The one meant they could buy in larger quantities; the other meant they could sell in larger quantities. Both of these meant a saving in time and in transport and storage costs. When the gains arising in this way become sufficiently great a large merchant can outbid or outsell a small merchant who possesses a geographical advantage, and a small local merchant can even find it cheaper to buy from a large metropolitan merchant than more directly from source. In essence this was what had been happening in fifteenth-century England. London merchants had been using their advantages of scale to divert through London cloth and wool which had formerly left England through more direct egress points and were buying in bulk imported commodities for redistribution to places which had formerly obtained them more directly in smaller quantities. The same trend, it might be noted, must have been at work within English interregional trade, further swelling London's importance and diminishing that of fairs as distribution centres. One other comment should be made. Probably in all cases the decline of a local port is overstated by the contraction of its foreign trade. With coastal shipping the cheapest form of transport many goods must have continued to pass through ports in transit to or from London but no longer, of course, showing up in the customs accounts.

Four

1475-1640

It is the economic historian's normal experience that the closer he approaches to modern times the more abundant his sources of information become – partly for the evident reason that the chances of contemporary records having survived are higher, and partly because the habits of mind of officials, academic inquirers, the managers of economic enterprises etc. approximate more closely to our own the nearer in time they are to us, and the information they record is more likely to be of the kind which answers twentieth-century-type questions. There is a further particular reason why the period now under consideration is more prolific in yielding information than preceding ones. In 1476 William Caxton set up the first printing press in England. The printed book, produced in quantity, adds a new range to state and estate records as witnesses to the economic life of the times – partly, again, because of the higher survival chances of something reproduced hundreds of times, but more importantly because of the way it induced men to inquire and report the findings of their inquiries or at least to publicise their opinions and such immediately apprehensible facts as sustained or formed those opinions – and the more men observed, thought, wrote and printed, the more others, their minds and imaginations stirred, were prompted to do likewise. The printed page is not only a source of history, it is a major historical event. In the latter respect we will have occasion subsequently to note its effects, in the former the essential difference it makes is that virtually for the first time we can refer to records whose deliberate aim was to acquaint a general public. A curiosity for which merely administrative documents did not seek to cater is being more directly, though still only partially,

99

satisfied. The advantages for posterity vary widely according to the aspect of English society under scrutiny and the student of its economic aspects is less favoured than many; the student of religious thought in this age of religious upheaval is the richest beneficiary. Much of the literature on economic matters is of a polemical nature and while it is invaluable as a record of economic and social ideas, affording an unprecedented insight into intellectual responses to economic environment, it is of doubtful value as a mirror of the material facts. The relatively few publications of a cooler temper written simply to instruct or inform are often revealing, but they almost invariably lack the statistical dimension on which the modern economic historian insists if data are to be usefully evaluated in perspective.

In 1640 we are still standing just short of the age when contemporaries were starting to develop this kind of curiosity. The growing volume of economic literature was still using figures as an essentially rhetorical device – 'hundreds' was just a literary variant on 'many', 'thousands' on 'multitude', and so forth. Particular men for particular private or official purposes of course required accurate figures as they always had done but this *ad hoc* concern had still to translate itself into a felt need for mathematical measurement when men addressed themselves, as increasingly they were doing either as a public responsibility or as a personal interest, to matters of general economic import. Nothing perhaps reveals this more closely than the apparent indifference to what a modern inquirer would consider to be a fundamental term of reference for purposes of economic appraisal: population. Nobody knew or was concerned to know what the population was, whether it was rising or falling or to what extent. One consequence of this lack of interest is that in default of contemporary investigation we are not today well placed to attempt a measurement. There are baptismal and burial registers, other stray pointers as to the direction and degree of change, an official survey of 1545 (in connection with charitable resources) and – one of the great feats of the early age of sociological measurement – a contemporary and largely reliable calculation for 1696 which can crudely be worked backwards and at least operates as some sort of control on estimates for earlier periods.

Demography

Very tentatively an English population of about 2¼ million could be posited for 1475, one of about 5 million for 1640 and midway (in the

1550s), about 3¼ million. Such figures suggest a continuous growth rate of about one-half per cent per annum, but short-run movements were almost certainly of a spasmodic character, typified by sharp setbacks due to epidemics of plague, syphilis, influenza, the mysterious sweating sickness, typhus and smallpox. However there is one demographic trend which seems to exhibit a fairly constant character from about the mid-sixteenth century: the slow but steady urbanisation of the population. Up to then the balance between town and country was probably fairly constant, having indeed changed little since the later thirteenth century when, as has been suggested earlier, about 7 per cent of the population lived in communities of more than 2,000 people. By 1640 the proportion was about 10 per cent and the numbers resident in such centres had increased from about a quarter of a million in 1550 to about half a million. But of this latter figure something like three-quarters belonged to London. The increase in other towns was probably little more rapid than that of population as a whole while London's rate of growth was three or four times faster. This tendency for London to pull ahead was not new. It ran back at least to the early fifteenth century. But it accelerated markedly over these years – in 1640, perhaps, 7–8 per cent of the English populace lived in London; in 1550, maybe 4–5 per cent had done so and in the early fifteenth century, 2–3 per cent.

London

This London of 1640 was not just the old medieval city. Already by the mid-sixteenth century the walls could not contain the population and perhaps half of it lived in a flanking extramural belt with a spillover across the river into Southwark, an eastward ribbon development along the river and a detached outpost around Westminster. The next century or so saw a thickening out of all these surburban parts, but most particularly the creation of a solidly built up area to the west and north-west of the walls about half as large again in extent as the city itself. Altogether, for each Londoner who lived within the walls, three to four by 1640 lived outside them. It is, then, this conurbation which, virtually alone, gave a sharp tilt to the urban–rural balance. That is to say, the factors responsible for the shift are peculiar to London and whatever economic changes were taking place elsewhere in the country, they did not engender significant urban development.

An earlier reason for the particular growth of London has already been seen at the end of the last chapter (London's encroachment on the trade of other ports), but by 1550 London must have engrossed as large a share of foreign trade as it was to have at any time over the next century. The tendency for internal trade to be rerouted via London had probably not yet spent itself but the major reasons for the rapidity of expansion were essentially social and political. Most important among these reasons was the spreading fashion among the owners of great landed estates of maintaining a London residence, and among those of lesser estates of passing some part of the year in London; while there they spent as lavishly as means permitted on entertainment and ostentation as well as making many of their purchases of personal and domestic durables while in London rather than in their local centre. This development, itself a whole chapter in social history to which justice cannot be done here, owes much to the success of the Tudor monarchs in arrogating to themselves the political power which the feudal structure of earlier times had dispersed among the territorial nobility. The castle and the private army were no longer the bases of strength in the land. A man who aspired to national consequence had no course open to him now but to establish himself at court, and so to London he came. And hardly had it destroyed the politico-military system which had imperilled its security for centuries than the Crown was raising up the institution which was later to prove itself an even more formidable opponent – Parliament. This too, with the enlargement of the prestige and opportunities which membership conferred, drew more men to London more often. And as London established a political pre-eminence it acquired too a social pre-eminence. If, by 1640, a man whose fortune could sustain the expenditure did not feel moved himself to make the trip to London, he was very likely prodded into it by his wife and unmarried daughters.

Politicians and socialites were not the only creations of the new order. With government more centralised and attempting to encompass a much wider field of activity than formerly, the number of London-based state servants multiplied. Alongside these officeholders and often seeking to join their ranks were the lawyers. Litigation had largely replaced the more direct methods of settling disputes often favoured in earlier times. The tenurial wrangles of the period and the halting emergence of new concepts of the rights subsisting in land provided lucrative work. The increasing formalisation of the law and the mass of new legislation as both Crown and Parliament sought to extend their area of control made the services of a widely experienced London lawyer more and more necessary.

Now it is not being suggested that these people by themselves account for the huge increment in London's population (of the order of 200,000 between 1550 and 1640). With their families they might amount to 15,000 or 20,000 on the eve of the Civil War. To appreciate their impact on London the social discrepancies in income must be realised. The duke or earl who was master of 40,000 acres might have £10,000 p.a.; the more modest squire of 2,000 acres might have £500 p.a. as would the holder of a good office or a successful lawyer. A shopkeeper or master craftsman would be accounted prosperous on £50 p.a.; an unskilled London labourer could get a shilling a day and a kitchen maid maybe an annual £1 over and above her keep. The London élite can hardly have commanded a gross income of less than £2 million p.a. Allowing for savings and expenditure outside of London, this could have created direct employment for 40,000 working Londoners, who in turn would require the goods and services of others, with cumulative consequences amounting perhaps to employment opportunities for over 120,000 people – and, reckoning in dependants, the means of support for roughly double that number. London, then, from the mid-sixteenth century, has an economic history all its own. In 1640 it was not so much a production centre, or even a distribution centre, as a consumption centre. And one should acknowledge too its role as a refuge. Many of those uprooted by the forces of economic change made their way to London whose obtrusive wealth must often have seemed to offer the prospect of retrieving a wrecked livelihood. The swiftly expanding city doubtless accommodated most of them without difficulty, but in all probability the London of 1640 contained a higher proportion of social flotsam and jetsam than it had done in earlier times.

The special case of London apart, no other marked change in population distribution is discernible. The west, especially the cloth-making areas, probably maintained the long-established trend for that region to comprehend an increasing proportion of the national population without, however, surpassing the midland block stretching from Berkshire and Middlesex to Leicestershire which, in point of population density, further increased the superiority over the coastal block between the Humber and the Thames which it had been steadily building on since the thirteenth century.

Implications of population growth

At some point through this period – perhaps around the turn of the sixteenth to the seventeenth century – the population topped its previous peak. From at least that point it must have been pressing on its resources of readily cultivable land. And given the novel demands being made on land, the pressure on food producing capacity would have been operating from an appreciably earlier date. England was ceasing to live off its thirteenth-century heritage and was having to work to create new sources of supply to feed a growing population. The general consequences of this kind of situation in an agrarian society of a relatively primitive kind have already been considered. Extra economic resources must be employed to extend the cultivable area and, furthermore, some time lag will occur between the need making itself felt and its being satisfied. This lag in a subsistence economy will simply mean shortage. In a commercialised economy it will mean shortage *and* its automatic concomitant, rising prices. Indeed it will only be on account of rising prices that landowners will undertake the expenditure of reclaiming land or of other projects for raising output. Now, if there is a scarcity of the extra resources (principally labour) needed for this undertaking, because existing resources are already fully, or nearly fully, employed, the demand for them will drive up their price (wages in the case of labour). However, if there is a prevailing surplus of resources their price, in real terms, will not rise and, in fact, landowners may not find it profitable to undertake the expenditure unless real costs fall. And the very situation, growing population, which causes prices to rise will also increase the supply of labour and thus tend to depress real wages creating the circumstances in which additional land is most likely to be brought into use.

This, in crude general terms, would be the train of actual causation, but the matter can be viewed another way. The reclamation of land and other output raising projects are a form of capital investment. Now any kind of capital investment must be financed either out of savings (i.e. money which otherwise would not be spent) or by the diversion of money from consumption expenditure.[1] The fall in real wages can

---

[1] This line of analysis cannot be understood unless it is appreciated that 'savings' and 'consumption expenditure' mean the total national amount of each (the two added together give total national income) – not the amount saved or spent by the individuals actually undertaking the investment who may do so with other people's savings or, in effect, by diverting other people's expenditure. What is being undertaken here is a crude

be considered as such a diversion. While the investment is taking place, proportionately less is being spent on foodstuffs themselves and proportionately more on creating extra sources of supply. But if any of the investment is financed from savings (by definition, money which otherwise would not have been spent) then total expenditure is increased, and increased not merely by that amount but by a greater amount, since those who receive it in payment for goods or services supplied (principally labourers receiving wages) will in turn spend it, and so on.[1] Thus total consumption expenditure will increase if the extra amount generated by savings-financed investment exceeds the amount initially diverted from consumption to investment. *Per capita* consumption expenditure might still be lower of course, since population will be rising, but this too would increase if the extent of investment financed by savings was large enough. Whether it will be large enough will depend not only on the balance between savings and diverted consumption expenditure in the amount invested, but, of course, on the size of that amount itself, which may be small or great according as landowners each of them differently circumstanced, respond to rising prices and falling real wages. For some, investment may be a highly expensive matter of draining a swamp; for others, just a question of ploughing up land already well cropped by sheep. Some will take the view that the high prices are merely temporary; others will anticipate a further rise. Some will be unable to find funds; others will have ample past savings of their own or easy access to loans. Some will be content with the windfall gains derived from the existing area of cultivated land; others will be spurred to execute improvements whose profitability had formerly seemed too uncertain and will undertake extensive investment projects.

Furthermore we must look beyond the investment itself to its fruits and ask if it does result in an addition to productive capacity capable of meeting increased needs at the same average cost as the pre-existing sources of supply. This is a question of both quantity and quality. The first will be determined by the amount of investment, which we have just seen to be unpredictable. The second will be determined by the nature of the new land made available or of the improvements effected

---

application of Keynesian analysis to the particular historical situation, directed, fairly evidently, at those not already familiar with this mode of analysis.

[1] This process of repeated expenditure is not infinite since a part of the money received at each stage is saved. The sum in circulation is thus constantly dwindling and ultimately expires.

on old land. The worth of the improvement will be limited by existing technical knowledge which might, of course, permit of increased (i.e. lower cost) yield. The nature of the new land could be supposed to be inferior to that of the old inasmuch as the best land will already have been brought under cultivation. However, there are two possibilities to set against this: one, that under the stimulus of rising prices, some land of high fertility will have been reclaimed whose steep reclamation cost had formerly inhibited the undertaking; two, that some of the old land will have been overworked and that the virgin new land will initially prove superior. If, however, as is probable, the new or improved land is on balance more costly to work, then the rise in prices triggered off by the timelag will be sustained or, at least, prices will not settle back again when supply has adjusted to demand. (Prices will almost certainly not revert to their former level in any event since there will have been something of a prices–wages spiral while population has been rising which will have set a new 'normal' level of prices.) This additional factor making for higher prices will of course further depress real wages and must mean that *per capita* consumption of foodstuffs will be lower then before (except in the improbable event of a large transfer of resources from other productive activities whose output in that case would suffer a diminution in the same proportions). But as long as investment was still going on at an adequate level and if it were being financed out of savings to a sufficient extent, a lower level of *per capita* consumption of foodstuffs could be accompanied by an increase in purchases of other kinds of consumption goods. This would mean that those with very low incomes which had to be spent largely on foodstuffs would be worse off, but that those whose incomes yielded a fair surplus after food needs had been catered for would be better off.

In summary there are three variables in this kind of situation: the level of investment in extra sources of supply; the manner in which this investment is financed; the yield on this investment. The particular combination obtaining in any historical case will determine whether and to what extent economic growth or economic decline would be the consequence. That is to say that it is impossible to predict on *a priori* grounds what would result. A consideration of what were the actual consequences for England within the period 1475 to 1640 can be deferred until the course of agrarian change, which includes important elements other than basically demographic ones, is looked at. It should be observed, however, that the agrarian economy of this period cannot be considered as wholly commercialised – that is, that the analysis outlined above would not be exclusively appropriate but should be weighted with the simpler approach already brought to bear on the twelfth and thirteenth centuries,[1] when little account needed to be taken of the relative movements of prices and wages and communities could be deemed to respond directly to chronic food shortage.

Prices

Prices can be considered here and now. Prices did rise, and real wages did fall, as one would expect under conditions of expanding population. But the question must be posed: is the rise in prices sufficiently accounted for by reference to demographic and supply factors alone? Here we enter on controversial ground involving issues of fact on which there has as yet been insufficient research and issues of theory on which unanimity may never be attained. The very way the question has been stated is a measure of the change in attitudes among economic historians. Until very recently it would have been a novelty to raise a question at all and even then its form would have been: is the price rise sufficiently accounted for by reference to the influx of precious metals? For, previously, economic historians were satisfied that the price rise, which was a European not just an English experience, could be fully explained in the opening up by the Spaniards of the rich reserves of silver and, to a lesser extent, gold, of South and Central America from about 1525. Silver and gold and, in some places, copper, were all that Europe regarded as true money. If other things were accepted as money it was only because they were believed to be convertible into these metals. Money prices were then, in fact or effect, prices in terms of specified quantities of the precious metals. If the quantity of precious metals increased and the quantity of goods and services available for purchase failed to increase in the same proportion, the excess of precious metals could only be soaked up by an increase in prices to the requisite degree. Or, put another way, the extra demand created by the extra money would either have to be met by a corresponding increase in supply or by a rise in prices to the point where the extra demand was stifled. So, anyway, runs the 'monetary' argument which held undisputed sway until a few years ago. And an immensely able American scholar, Earl J. Hamilton, painstakingly compiled data on the flow of American metals to Spain which, with impressive plausibility, he then correlated with the rise in prices.

[1] See pp. 13–15.

Subsequent criticisms have ranged over the measurement of the flow of precious metals; the calculation of the price rise and consequently of the correlation between the two; changing value ratios between the metals; the real monetary role of the metals; the sensitivity of countries other than Spain to the increased supply of the metals; the significance of internal currency depreciations (reductions in the metallic content of the coinage); and the contention that prices were rising anyway. This should serve to indicate the complexity of the question. An adequate discussion of it would have to comprehend much of European, and even American, economic history as well as the conflicting sophistications of monetary theory. It would be grossly excessive to attempt that here, and no happy resolution of the formula, 'on balance it would be safe to conclude that . . . ' could, without naive pretentiousness, be essayed.[1]

It is even difficult to make a pertinent statement about the course of prices since our only abundant data relates to corn prices, which were liable to sharp fluctuations according to the state of the harvest, so that although the long-term tendencies of this, the most important group of commodities, can be clearly discerned, the determination of when these tendencies set in is a matter of imprecision and even of controversy. Thus though prices on average were a little higher over the first two decades of the sixteenth century than over the last quarter of the fifteenth, it is a very open question if the commencement of the long-term price rise is to be located here. The 1520s saw sharp increases but the 1530s and early 1540s brought no further rise on average. The mid-1540s witnessed both very high and quite low prices, still then challenging dogmatism although by then the average was some 75 per cent above that prevailing around 1475. Nobody, however, would contend that the starting point of the general inflation can be put any later than 1551 when corn prices shot up and fairly regularly scored new highs into the 1560s, when they were some three times what they had been around 1475. From the 1580s there was a further spate of irregular price leaps until the closing years of the century when the average level stood at about five times that of 1475. The tendency remained persistently but only moderately upwards through the first three decades of the

[1] For a detailed examination of the question, which yet fails to reach a conclusion, see F. P. Braudel and F. Spooner, 'Prices in Europe from 1450 to 1750', chapter vii in *The Cambridge Economic History of Europe* (2nd edition), vol. iv, *The Economy of Expanding Europe in the 16th and 17th Centuries* (1967). If the matter can be adequately handled in more compressed form, this has been done by Dr A. B. Outhwaite in his pamphlet, *The Price Rise in Tudor and early Stuart England* (Macmillan, 1969).

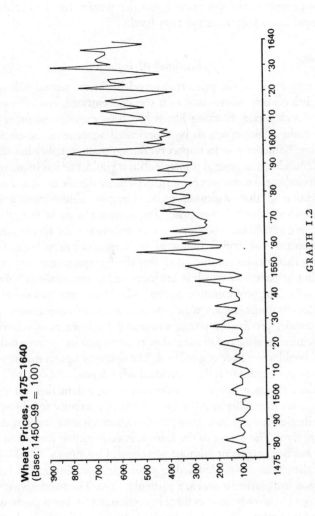

Wheat Prices, 1475–1640
(Base: 1450–99 = 100)

GRAPH 1.2

seventeenth century, but in 1630, a year of very bad harvest, there was a rise to unprecedented heights and although no subsequent year of the 1630s brought such high prices again the average for the decade was some six and a half times the 1475 level.

Implications of inflation

The magnitude of the price rise, especially in the second half of the sixteenth century where most of it was concentrated, gives this period a special character. Nothing like it had been experienced previously. And nothing like it was to be experienced again until the twentieth century. Something of its impact on the agrarian economy has already been considered in general principle. But it could, and has been, argued that its industrial consequences were even more significant. The essential contention is that widening profit margins administered a sharp stimulus to industrial enterprise. The contention is, in fact, that an economic revolution was born out of inflation – the revolution that has been variously styled 'Industrial' or 'Capitalist'; or, at least, if these clumsy rhetoricisms are discarded, that the European economy was set moving in directions which it has more or less continuously followed ever since. The profit motive was unleashed to operate to a degree and with an economic efficacy which the aspirations of subsistence farmers, of parasitic, prestige or power orientated landowners, of merchants whose income arose out of natural price discrepancies between different areas, could never have engendered. The dynamic figure, the argument runs, in any economy is the individual who depends solely on exploiting the difference between production costs and market value; and the greater that difference the greater the opportunity for this special contribution to economic growth. There is much sense and shrewdness in this view. The course of the European economy in recent historical time has been an event without precedent. One cannot just think of a seed planted aeons ago destined in accordance with immutable laws to burgeon in a particular area at a particular time. The acquisitive instinct may not be the only human force in economic play but nobody would accord it anything other than primacy. Any line of analysis, therefore, which points to circumstances particularly favouring the operation of the profit motive must command considerable respect.

Inflation will widen profit margins in two ways. As prices rise faster than wages (which they will almost certainly do, at least to begin with, except under modern conditions of full employment and strong trade unions) sales revenue obviously rises faster than labour costs. Secondly, costs are incurred some time previously to sales so that when inflation sets in, or the rate of inflation increases, profits will initially rise faster than prices. The amount of gain from this latter factor depends on the lapse of time between meeting the costs and selling the goods. In simple production processes where the interval is short it will be negligible. It will be most marked in enterprises using expensive fixed equipment which has a long working life. The gain is more apparent than real since new production, at inflated cost levels, has to be financed from past profits, but where the time interval is long and accounting techniques are not very sophisticated the immediate appearance of high profits will probably have as stimulatory an effect as a more genuine rise in profits. And if an enterprise is financed by borrowing at fixed interest rates there is a real, permanent gain, by the entrepreneur at the expense of the lender whose interest income is declining in real value.

In the last analysis the argument from widening profit margins involves the same considerations as those raised already in connection with agricultural investment: the extent to which entrepreneurs will be induced to lay out capital (which will be determined by a variety of factors, economic, cultural and political, amongst which profit margins may be quite minor, although possibly decisive); the extent to which the investment in extra industrial production is savings financed; and the productivity of the new sources of industrial output. So far as the first of these considerations is concerned one can only look at particular cases and their peculiar circumstances. The same goes largely for the other two considerations as well, but a couple of general comments can usefully be made. A fall in real wages may stimulate profit conscious industrialists but it also means a fall in the expenditure of wage earners, that is, a fall in purchases of mass consumption goods, unless sufficient consumption expenditure is generated by the employ-ment of savings in new investment to offset this; this consideration is then crucial for on it depends whether that which makes for increased investment by widening profit margins is not simultaneously having the reverse effect by narrowing market scope.

The third consideration, productivity, is from a long-term point of view of transcendent importance. Economic growth (an increase in *per capita* output) can be achieved only through a fuller employment of existing resources or through the introduction of methods which increase productivity. There is a rigid limit to the first. Beyond that rigid limit further investment can only switch resources from one sector to another and cause prices to rise, unless means of increasing productivity are devised, creating spare resources for employment in new investment ventures. It is arguable that comfortable profit margins will deaden rather than sharpen interest in innovations; that the most likely circumstance to engender a lively concern with new methods is one of *rising* real wages, pinching profits at the same time as enlarging market scope. However, in any pre-modern economy there would be abundant scope for achieving limited growth, simply by taking up the slack of unemployed resources or by reallocating resources to make optimum use of them (i.e. by an intensification of local, regional and national specialisation). Given that productive equipment was simple and cheap the new enterprises might be small-scale affairs, no different essentially from those of the past; the amount invested in each might be small and might be principally expended on raw materials and wages. That is to say, the development need not give rise to those features which in more recent times are characteristic of industrialism and capitalism. But inasmuch as it consisted in increased specialisation (principally geographical specialisation) it would increase the degree and extent of commercialisation and would necessarily be accompanied by the growth of a mercantile class which would almost certainly be dominated by men commanding relatively large capital sums.

Aware then of the view that there is a connection between inflation and industrial growth to which the general European experience has been summoned to testify, we can approach the history of English industrial change within this period alive to the possibilities of discerning in it features of a wider relevance: and the notion that industrial developments may, in a certain sense, be of more significance than what occurs in the preponderant agricultural sector warrants our starting an examination of the course actually taken by the economy in that quarter.

The woollen industry

There is a more particular reason for looking at industry first. The most eye-catching agrarian change within this period was due directly to industrial development. The extent of sheep-farming was what struck contemporaries most forcefully about the agrarian economy. And behind sheep-farming lay the cloth industry. Exports of cloth rose fairly steadily, from about 45,000 cloths around 1475 to about 125,000

by the middle of the sixteenth century,[1] after which various vicissitudes
kept them bumping up and down at or below that level for the rest of
the period. Taking these exports as consisting entirely of fine cloth
(which would not be quite true) and adding in guestimates for home
sales of fine cloth, total production may have expanded from 65,000 to
160,000 which would have provided full-time employment for something like 50–60,000 people. Taking account of cheaper cloths for
home sale, the total numbers wholly employed in the industry could
have been 130,000 which would be about 7–8 per cent of the total labour
force in the 1550s. Stray scraps of information suggest that this figure is
of the right order, and that the numbers actually employed were rather
higher, since many cloth workers were also partly occupied in agriculture.

We have already seen that the manufacture of coarser cloths had
long been a rural industry and even that the revival of fine cloth manufacture may have been partly rural. Between 1475 and 1550 the fine
cloth industry moved decisively into the countryside. For this the very
rapidity of its expansion was in significant part responsible. Urban
centres could not generate labour fast enough to keep pace. Rising
wages might have drawn new workers in from the country but that
process could be anticipated, and rising wages forestalled, by taking the
work to the country instead. In some towns the employment of rural
labour might lead to trouble with the corporation or with the guilds;
either might be reluctant to see work entrusted to those they could not
control and who very probably had not served a proper apprenticeship. The urban clothworkers who had met the formal apprenticeship
requirements and who conceived their interests to be threatened might
prevail on corporation or guild to intervene on their behalf; where the
men complained against were not a powerful element in municipal
politics simple conservatism would often tell against them. In such cases
those wishing to employ rural labour would probably remove themselves altogether from the towns and their cramping interference.

Even when there was sufficient labour to be had in the towns, rural
labour might be preferred on account of its cheapness. Again, corporation or guild might maintain urban wages above a free market level
or where wages were forced down labour disputes would follow. Rural
labour was more tractable. The workers being scattered, concerted
labour action was more difficult. Rural wages in any event would
almost certainly be lower than town wages because of lower food costs

---

[1] In 1550 itself exports soared to about 150,000 cloths, but this quantity was plainly
excessive to current market requirements.

and a narrower range of habitual material wants; furthermore, many rural workers had smallholdings and so would not depend exclusively on wages – the initiative indeed might not come from the employer but from the peasant who provided himself with a loom (with any aptitude the necessary skill could be acquired fairly easily), set his wife to spinning or used the yarn she spun already for others and, in the intervals between working his own land or that of others for wages, turned out occasional lengths of cloth: his relationship with the 'employer' might really be one of seller to buyer.

It is difficult to find an economic category for the 'clothier', to use the contemporary term for this kind of person who exercised a role falling imprecisely between employer and merchant. The fully evolved clothier controlled every processing stage from the procurement of the wool at source through to fulling and perhaps dressing and dyeing, though these final processes were usually undertaken abroad in the case of exported cloth. Such an evolution may often have been gradual, perhaps extending over more than one generation, perhaps never coming to comprehend the whole range of processes. The clothier's precise function at each stage would often defy definition in terms of modern concepts, and so also would the precise relationship between himself and those actually undertaking the work. They might look like his employees, or like independent operatives charging a fee for their services, or like independent producers selling him their product having, though not necessarily, bought their raw material from him. Some might work exclusively for him, others for several different people or even sometimes on their own account as well. Ideas derived from experience of modern industrial organisation with its fairly clear-cut distinctions, especially that between employer and employed, are a positive hindrance to visualising the scheme of a clothier's operations (which in any event might vary quite widely from one man to another). If one is to apply a simple functional label to the clothier, merchant would in one way be more apposite than producer: that is, one would think of him as buying wool and selling cloth.

This conception is especially pertinent to his use of capital which was essentially mercantile rather than industrial: at any one time his capital was invested in goods which were, after processing, to be sold, at which stage his money capital would be restored – that is, it was circulating capital as distinct from the producer's fixed capital sunk in manufacturing equipment. This is not just a distinction for the sake of distinction – a distinction without a difference; it meant that his position was a more flexible one than that of the industrialist proper: if the market fell off, he reduced his outlay of capital proportionately, holding the residue in money until the market picked up again. The burden of carrying the cost of fixed equipment was borne by the worker who owned his own tools or apparatus. Clothiers did sometimes provide looms but it seems as if these were usually hired out to the weavers who paid a fixed rent for them (such rent was normally deducted from the payment for work done and whatever the formal arrangement in this kind of case the likelihood is that if times were slack and no work was being done, the clothier in practice lost at least some of his loom rent). A clothier too might own his own fulling-mill. This was in fact the only substantial piece of fixed equipment involved in the whole range of processes so that the significance of not having capital tied up in the physical means of production can easily be exaggerated – in any circumstances wages and raw materials would constitute the greater part of costs. The principal saving in capital by contrast with industrialism proper was probably on premises, and even here we must note the existence of 'factories': buildings in which clothworkers in the direct employ of the clothier were housed for work, though these were few and only flourished for a decade or two around the middle of the sixteenth century.

But whether due to the peculiar nature of the organisation of the clothier's trade or to the intrinsic cost structure of the industry, the relatively small element of fixed costs made it fairly easy to commence or extend business. This factor, allied to the breakout from the restraints of town control and migration to country districts where chronic underemployment as a result of the seasonal nature of agricultural work was aggravated by rising population, meant that output could respond rapidly to a rise in demand – indeed that it could easily overrespond and create a temporary glut of cloth, which seems to have happened in the early 1540s and again in the early 1550s. This is the particular hazard of industries producing for distant markets in an age of poor communications. The feedback mechanism from the final points of sale is too slow; production is taking place on the basis of market trends which have changed course well before production has started.

The question presents itself: what is one to make of the clothier as an economic phenomenon? Into what kind of evolutionary scheme, if any, can he be fitted?[1] Broadly speaking there are three possible

[1] This question is raised now in the historical context in which it has most relevance. But thirteenth-century 'clothiers' have already been noted; and while as a general phenomenon

representations. One would have him originating as a small master and would relate his rise to the perversion of guild power in the favour of a privileged few: as a master craftsman was enabled to increase the scale of his output by the suppression of potential rivals he ceased to be a worker himself and became a controller of the work of others; the talents he then required were no longer those of an artisan skilled in a particular task but those of management and organisation; the natural boundaries between one clothmaking craft and another, as particular technical skills, thus dissolved as far as he was concerned and, if he was able and ambitious, he sought to be more than a mere link in a chain, dependent on the links before and after; he sought to construct his own chain. A second approach would represent the clothier as essentially a wool or cloth merchant extending his activities so as to control his own outlets or supply sources. A third, and less simple, approach would treat him as an entirely new kind of individual thrown up by the opportunities created by the rapidly rising demand for fine English cloth from 1475, starting off probably from some point of contact with the industry but developing in response to an esssentially new set of pressures and incentives.

Under this last view, we would regard the clothier as a novel and distinctive kind of economic individual brought into existence by the stretching of links between sources of raw wool, specialised centres of production and distant markets, which the producer and the merchant between them were unable to span; the clothier was an intermediary who coordinated and financed production on an extensive scale. This attitude would imply that the 'domestic system' was not really a new system of *production*; that the unit of production was what it always had been: one man with perhaps two or three assistants; that the move from town to country (which anyway was not total) does not represent a new mode of manufacturing but only an expansion of the old mode to comprehend a larger work force beyond the constraints of guild and corporation regulation, whose dispersed character necessitated a new kind of intermediate functionary.

If the rural clothworker was as such just the small urban master transplanted to the countryside beyond the orbit of guild and corporation, then he cannot be regarded as the clothier's 'employee'. He has to

the clothier is chiefly to be associated with the great rural expansion of the industry through the years now in hand and is analysed here with reference to that development, the terms employed would, with minor modifications, serve for any earlier period in which the phenomenon is discernible.

be considered as an independent producer. But there is no such thing
as complete independence in the world of producers. Every producer
is wholly dependent on the market. Producers can achieve a powerful
position in the face of the market by securing a monopoly or a quasi-
monopoly. So, however, can buyers, and if they do the bargaining
position of the producer becomes weak. Modern experience has
taught us to think of producers as few in number and buyers as many
and disorganised so that the balance of bargaining strength tends to be
tipped in the producers' favour. If we reverse that notion we can think
of the rural clothworker as an 'independent' producer in a disadvantageous position vis-à-vis the clothier. To the extent that a rural
clothworker had land, and could therefore afford not to work on cloth,
to that extent and that only he had a measure of real economic freedom. From his point of view it is entirely academic what economic
category we find for him. Even if he could bypass the clothier by
buying his own wool and dealing direct with a merchant he would be
no better off – a merchant could easily dispense with the output of one
small producer. Most of the cloth sold internally in fact had not been
handled by a clothier but was either marketed direct or distributed by
a merchant; those making these cloths were not any better off than
those working through a clothier. The point is that while one can
certainly speak of the exploitation by capital of labour there is no need
to identify the clothier with the modern industrialist nor the clothworker with a factory labour force in order to do so. Nor is there any
need to postulate a radical change in the system of production to
account for the emergence of capitalism – to represent the domestic
system as a new departure in the depression of the proletariat. If one
considers the extension of markets as being the mainspring behind the
emergence of the clothier, then one can consider the producers themselves as remaining in essentially the same economic situation as before,
while the premium profits of distant sales were absorbed by capitalistic
clothiers and merchants. The small master of the older order of things
would, in this account, be revealed as a proletariat which had lacked
capitalist suzerains because the opportunities of earning a 'surplus'[1]
had not yet presented themselves.

As implied already, the clothiers' activities were largely confined to
fine cloth intended for export. The clothiers of an extensive field of
operations, and of very considerable wealth in some cases, were, then,

[1] The Marxist definition of capitalist profits.

to be found in the area which by the early years of this period had
established a clear pre-eminence as a region of fine cloth manufacture:
the West Country, comprising Wiltshire and adjoining parts of Somerset and Gloucestershire, with odd outposts in Berkshire, Oxfordshire,
Worcestershire and Herefordshire. An important secondary centre
was a region straddling the boundaries of Suffolk and Essex where,
however, the clothier was not quite the dominant figure that he was
in the West Country, presumably because there direct dealings with
London merchants could take place. This area produced more cloth
than the West Country but much of it was of inferior quality. Elsewhere there were scattered towns where fine cloth was manufactured,
but by 1550 or so in relatively small quantities. To complete the geographical picture there were through the sixteenth century two other
principal rural clothmaking regions: Devon with adjoining parts of
Dorset, Somerset and Cornwall making, in general, medium quality
cloth, and the Pennine slopes whose output consisted almost entirely of
coarse cloth.

Most towns throughout the country would have continued to house
the manufacture of cloth of varying qualities, much of it for local sale.
In general these lower grade areas drew on nearby wool supplies,
purchased at source or through a local wool dealer ('brogger') and
when the cloth was not sold direct in a local market centre it was
bought by cloth merchants for wider distribution. The wool dealer and
the cloth merchant were usually distinct individuals and although a
wool dealer might sometimes have his wool spun before selling it
elsewhere as yarn (one weaver used the output of three or four spinners
so that weavers sometimes could not obtain enough yarn locally), and
although a cloth merchant would commonly attend to the fulling,
dressing and dyeing of cloth, these areas did not generally produce
anybody analogous to the full-blown West Country clothier, and when
they did the availability of other channels of wool supply and of other
market outlets prevented such clothiers from establishing a dominant
position.

Some of the lower-grade cloths were sold abroad – south-western
cloth was marketed in Normandy, as was cloth from the Pennines,
which also sold in Germany. Some part of these exports, perhaps the
bulk from the south-west, were shipped from adjacent ports, but much
was despatched to London by the local merchants and there sold to
merchant adventurers who regarded these cloths as useful makeweights
to their major consignments of fine cloth. Both clothiers and local cloth

merchants usually employed a London factor (a broker or commission agent) to negotiate sales to adventurers, or to wholesalers who re-distributed the cloth internally over an extensive area including of course the giant market, London, itself.

Markets and materials

The history of the cloth industry over the years 1475 to 1640 falls, fairly naturally, into three distinct periods. The first runs from the end of the general trade depression in or around 1475 to the early 1550s; the second from then until 1614; and the third from 1614 on through 1640 into the eighteenth century. We could also register a separate period straddling the last two, running from around 1570 onwards. The first is the great period of expansion of cloth exports. The second is a period of general stagnation of exports. The third sees a clear decline in exports of traditional fine cloth, compensated for by the develop-ment of new lines. These new lines comprised two very different kinds of cloth: 'Spanish cloth', made from superlatively fine Spanish wool, a highly expensive luxury fabric; and the 'New Draperies', light, gaily coloured, inexpensive worsteds, whose age of expansion constitutes the fourth, supplementary, period above.

The dominant long-term factor making for stagnation from the mid-1550s was simply repletion – Europe was by then absorbing about as much cloth from England as it had need of or could afford. A secondary factor was the enlargement of native clothmaking capacity in England's European markets, just about creaming off the still grow-ing demand of rising European population which had, in significant measure, been responsible for the earlier growth of English exports. The decline from 1614 can be attributed in the short run to a topical factor and thereafter to a conjuncture of circumstances. The topical event was the attempt to foist dressed and dyed cloth on the Dutch market, from which hitherto the great bulk of English exports of fine cloth had been distributed to northern Europe, having first been finished there. The Merchant Adventurers argued, in vain, that English dressing and dyeing was so poor that the cloth would not sell. James I was captivated by the prospect of creating employment for English dressers and dyers and of adding greatly to England's export earnings (finished cloth fetched up to double the price of unfinished cloth) as well as by the promise of enhanced customs revenue. Against the weight of official opinion, he authorised the necessary breach of the

Merchant Adventurers' legal monopoly of the trade and the creation of a new company to export finished cloth.

Whether the projectors of this new company, of whom the chief was Alderman Cockayne, having persuaded the king of its virtues, ever seriously intended to rely on exports of finished cloth is very doubtful and that this profession was merely a ruse to break the Adventurers' monopoly is correspondingly probable. Certainly exports of finished cloth were negligible, and, between lack of capital and ignorance of the market, exports of unfinished cloth fell drastically also. The Merchant Adventurers as a body, confident that the failure of the scheme must lead to the restoration of their privileges, resisted all blandishments to bring their money and knowledge to the rescue of Cockayne and his associates. Their faith in their own indispensability was rewarded after two years of piteous protests from the fine cloth industry. In 1616 the scheme was abandoned, the new company dissolved and the old Adventurers restored. But exports of traditional fine cloth never fully recovered. In the interim, Dutch and German manufacturers had seized the opportunity to dig themselves into the market, to add to the English difficulties caused by two other apparent long-term changes: a general down-turn of the continental economy from around 1620, associated with falling population (most European countries experienced economic adversities over the rest of the century which in sum have provided historians with the notion of a 'Crisis of the seventeenth century'); and the deterioration in the quality of English cloth as English wool lost the special fineness which had been the basis of the industry's competitive success.

This last was what apparently first led to the use of Spanish wool in the West Country where between the 1620s and the end of the period it largely replaced English wool in the territory flanking the Somerset–Wiltshire border. By 1640 about a tenth by quantity of cloth exports consisted of this new material and by value the proportion might have been double that (part of which, of course, consisted of the value of the imported wool). Even more striking was the rise of the New Draperies. Worsted[1] fabrics had been made in Norfolk from as far back as records

[1] Worsteds, while made of wool, are conventionally distinguished from woollens proper. Woollens are made from short strands of wool which are carded before being woven and then fulled to give them thickness and texture. Worsteds are made from long strands of wool, combed instead of carded, and are usually not fulled, the tightness of the weave being sufficient to produce the necessary consistency. The differences in raw material and processing meant that woollens were relatively heavy and hard-wearing while worsteds were light and fairly easily frayed.

run and small quantities had been exported, but the varieties of worsted which came to enjoy such success appear to have been introduced into England by Dutch and Flemish Protestants, refugees from Spanish rule, principally between about 1560 and about 1585. The lightness of these fabrics made them unsuitable for general wear in cold northern regions, but they were ideal for the warmer Mediterranean area whose opening to English commerce happily coincided with their introduction. The protracted war with Spain (1585–1604) prevented full exploitation of the opportunities for some time, but on its conclusion exports of these cloths increased rapidly; by 1640 they accounted for about a third, by quantity, of all cloth exports. Apart from these commercial openings, their manufacture was stimulated by the changing nature and quality of English wool, due to autonomous agrarian changes, resulting in the short silky wool suitable for fine woollens being replaced by the longer rougher wool used for cheap worsteds; while the contraction of the market for traditional fine cloth further encouraged an interest in alternative products.

In East Anglia the coming of the New Draperies effected a virtual revolution. By 1640 in Suffolk and Essex the manufacture of woollens had been well surpassed in importance by that of worsteds, and in Norfolk, mostly in the countryside around Norwich, the ancient nucleus of the worsted industry had expanded enormously. These were the regions in which the Dutch and Flemish immigrants had principally settled; they were also the regions whose sources of wool were changing most in character. Along with the pre-existence of a worsted industry these factors made it certain that far from declining as the old draperies ran into difficulties, East Anglia was entering the most prosperous era in its history. Devonshire and West Somerset had also largely converted to worsteds by 1640 as had towns on or close to the south coast to which the religious refugees naturally came. The West Country leant on Spanish cloth as compensation for declining sales of the traditional product, but even there a few worsteds were being made by the end of this period. Both Spanish cloth and New Draperies were finished in England and, at least in the case of the former whose marketability would have been destroyed by poor finishing, this does suggest that within a few years of the Cockayne fiasco, English dressing and dyeing methods had greatly improved – indeed that that wretched project may have initiated an advance which it did not survive to benefit from.

Other textiles

Worsted was not the only textile fabric to achieve something of a new economic impact in this period. We become aware of quite an extensive coarse linen manufacture in Lancashire in the sixteenth century, drawing fairly heavily on Irish supplies of flax or yarn through Liverpool and Chester out of which went some linen cloth for coastwise distribution, while more probably went overland to much of northern and midland England. However for fine linen England remained exclusively dependent, and even for coarse linen partially dependent, on imports. Of little immediate consequence but full of portent was an allied industry which can first be discerned in Lancashire around 1600: the making of fustians.[1]

Cotton cloth of eastern origin, fine and expensive, had been known in England as early as the fourteenth century through Italian merchants. European manufacturers were unable to acquire the skill necessary to spin a strong cotton thread and reproduce the eastern cloth. But raw cotton was to be had cheaply in the Levant and the weak coarse thread which Europeans could spin from it served if woven up with a linen warp to provide an inexpensive substitute for the rougher kinds of wholly linen cloth.[2] In Holland and Germany the manufacture of fustians was well established by the end of the sixteenth century. How and why it came to Lancashire is not known, though the pre-existence of something of a linen industry obviously had much to do with it. By 1640 it had become well rooted in and around Oldham, Bury, Bolton and Blackburn, a small area squeezed in between the manufacture of coarse woollens to the north and east and the manufacture of coarse linens to the west, the whole being the southern segment of the most desolate and backward quarter of England. This last observation perhaps affords a clue to these first stirrings of industrial development there. The Lancashire peasant, scratching the barest of livings from the poorest of soils, lay beyond the frontier of a society with a comparatively high standard of material expectations. He would take to working linen or fustians, seeking a lower return for his labour than those within that frontier would do; the cost of the raw materials themselves

---

[1] Coarse twilled cloth with a linen warp and a cotton weft, including corduroy, etc.

[2] Cotton was also sometimes employed with a wool warp, notably for bombasine made in Norfolk from the later years of the sixteenth century; this was a worsted with a cotton weft, used principally for black mourning wear – presumably because its lack of hard wearing quality was not a consideration for that purpose.

being small, the proportion of labour costs in total costs was relatively great so that a low return to labour made for markedly low prices of the finished product. Only another area within the north-western wilderness could match south Lancashire's production costs and south Lancashire being the closest to the 'frontier' had the advantage of lower transport costs in selling to other parts of England.

A textile industry which experienced a radical change within this period was hosiery – the knitting of hose or stockings. At an earlier time it had not been an industry at all, stockings having been knitted by the women of the household or by neighbouring women from yarn supplied by the customer, and into the eighteenth century charity commonly took the form of having a poor widow knit up a pair or two of stockings. But by the early sixteenth century knitting for the market had become a source of supplementary income for numerous families, especially in the north and the east Midlands. But the length of time it took to knit one pair of stockings precluded its developing beyond a sparsely remunerated way of filling in spare hours. Hosiery needed its counterpart to the loom if it were to become a full-blown industry and it was doubtless his experience of the strained earning resources of his poor neighbours in the knitting district of Sherwood in Nottinghamshire that stimulated William Lees to invent a knitting frame in 1589. Popular fear that it would destroy rather than promote employment opportunities for some time frustrated its introduction, which was also hindered by the absence of any established entrepreneurial class within this quasi-industry to finance a device whose relatively elaborate construction put it beyond the means of the cottage knitter. That is to say there was really no ready market for it; but by 1640 it had engaged the attention of men with entrepreneurial flair who were already starting to make of Derby, Nottingham, Leicester and North-ampton the centres of a hosiery industry which they had clearly become by the end of the century. This was a real 'industrial revolution', although given the limited requirements for the product, only a miniature one. The master hosiers who ran the industry were true industrial capitalists in the sense that they provided the essential capital for a machine which the ordinary worker could not afford. It was, to be sure, a very primitive kind of industrialism. There was no reason for master hosiers to go to the expense of building special premises. The frame could be installed in the worker's home and the cost could be sloughed off by charging him a rent for it, nominally payable whether he was working the frame or not. In function the master hosier closely resembled the clothier but as a historical fact he owes his origin to a machine, and the machine owes its introduction to his emergence.

The knitting frame was not the only mechanical innovation in textiles over these years. The gig mill made its appearance in the early sixteenth century, perhaps borrowed from the continent. This was a water-powered device used by a shearer (who trimmed the surface of woollen cloth) to raise the nap. It was not a very large or elaborate piece of equipment but it did require some capital outlay and was perhaps beyond the means of many shearers. But the extent of its cost advantage over hand-raising was probably not great as long as the shearing itself had still to be done by hand. There was sufficient apprehension of loss of employment among shearers to lead to its prohibition in 1551 and again in 1633, but despite the evident flaunting of the law, its economic consequences do not seem to have been marked.

Of greater potential impact was the hand-operated Dutch loom for weaving ribbons, with which one operative could do the work of four. Its name indicates its origin and it seems to have arrived in England early in the seventeenth century. By 1638 its repercussions among ribbon weavers resulted in its being banned and it was not until later in the century that it succeeded in obtaining a secure footing. If one takes note also of the complex water-powered silk-throwing (i.e. spinning) machine devised in Italy in the sixteenth century (although it did not reach England until the eighteenth), it will be appreciated that technical advance in the textile trades was not the perquisite of the eighteenth century, nor of English inventors. If technical progress were the sole mainspring of rapid economic growth, then the only reason why textiles over these years did not have a more dynamic record would be the capricious fact that innovation took place in ancillary activities or industries catering for a fairly small market rather than in central productive processes.

Revolution in textiles?

Can one fit the record of the woollen and other textile industries through this period into a scheme of new economic departures which add up or conduce to 'revolutionary' changes? The question really hangs on the woollen industry. Interesting as developments in other branches of textiles might be, their weight in the total economic complex was too slight for anything much more than academic importance to be attached to them.

Perhaps the first point to be stressed is that the record of the cloth industry up to the middle of the sixteenth century while the great growth in exports was taking place is clearly to be seen as a continuation of a well established pre-existing momentum. The combination of an exploitation of abundant supplies of high quality wool and mercantile initiatives which had carried cloth exports dynamically upwards through the second half of the fourteenth century was reinforced from about 1475 by favourable trading circumstances and rising European population. No other special factor within that period needs to be invoked to account for the expansion of the industry nor does the particular form of capitalism which it engendered require any explanation other than the expansion itself. More particularly, there is no ostensible association between these developments and the great inflation – indeed the most marked period of inflation coincided pretty nearly with the stagnating of cloth exports, although the dramatic leaps in overseas sales of cloth from 1542 to 1551 must be closely connected with the steady debasement of the coinage during those years, which temporarily had the effect of making English prices and costs markedly lower in terms of the precious metals than those prevailing on the continent, that is of widening the profit margins of those organising or disposing of production for continental sales. It can be no mere coincidence that the shortlived cloth 'factories' were most conspicuous in these years.

It is, almost paradoxically, in the later less halcyon years that the signs are more suggestive of new currents running through the economy. The comparative rapidity and resilience with which the industry adapted to changes and difficulties by taking to new lines hints at a fresh sensitivity to profits and to the opportunities for earning them. The men, whether they were merchants, clothiers or small producers with maybe half a dozen journeymen or apprentices, who sought out new openings with Spanish wool or Dutch devised fabrics strike one as alerted to moneymaking possibilities in a way in which earlier generations who had merely cultivated natural homegrown advantages had not been. Capital, perhaps often in very small individual quantities, was evidently seeking profitable employment. Capitalists, which word can denote among others the man with no more than money enough for a couple of looms, evidently believed that investment in novel enterprises could yield worthwhile returns – and those who lacked capital sufficient for their purposes were possibly borrowing or entering into credit arrangements to secure these returns.

Was the disparity between wage costs and prices the particular incentive? Or are we confronted with wider cultural changes, sharpening commercial awareness, which would have prompted the same kind of actions even had the wage/price ratio been less favourable? There is a very respectable body of historical opinion which has perceived a close connection between commercial assiduity and the new religious attitudes.[1] The Protestant ethic, it has been argued, demolished the hesitance of the medieval Church on the morality of incomes which could not be attributed directly to personal labour. With reservations in the name of charity and Christian brotherhood it permitted exploitation of market forces and even positively encouraged the exercise of a talent for harnessing economic circumstances for private profit, sometimes to the point of identifying worldly success with spiritual worth. A variant and less theologically centred analysis would have it that the challenge to received dogmas in itself and the doubt, scepticism and cynicism which it infused, led to a divorce between religion and everyday morality, freeing the acquisitive instinct from the effective inhibition of ecclesiastical doctrine. Were men attempting to make money in a newly conspicuous fashion because there was more money to be made or because their social conditioning was inclining them more in that direction? The historical facts can support either view.

The event itself, whatever its causes, is not in the final economic analysis of profound importance. Neither Spanish cloth nor the New Draperies brought any fundamental changes in organisation or techniques, and so far as total economic effort was concerned they did not do much more than absorb resources rendered surplus by the decline of traditional cloth. But in adverse circumstances the capacity to run in order to stay in the same place is its own kind of progressiveness. If the cloth industry over the later sixteenth century and early seventeenth did not go very far forwards, at least it did not go backwards. Entrepreneurship enabled it to ride out difficulties which in earlier times would probably have marked the beginning of the end. Had the English cloth industry succumbed in the face of change, as for instance the prosperous Italian industry did around this time, the course of subsequent economic development in England must have been very different.

[1] The founding English text is R. H. Tawney, *Religion and the Rise of Capitalism*, Murray, 1926; Penguin, 1969.

The coal industry

In other industrial fields a pattern of change and development can be discerned which, at least chronologically, does closely fit the thesis of an association between inflation and economic growth. The outstanding instance of rapid industrial growth over the period 1540 to 1640 (which can plausibly be regarded as the inflationary century) is that of coal-mining. Output of coal in Britain over those hundred years rose from roughly 200,000 tons to roughly 2 million tons. Put another way, coalmining from being an obscure local activity became an industry which catered for the fuel needs of much of the nation. On the demand side, the factor responsible for this escalation was the growing shortage of wood. The pressure of population on land generated in the twelfth and thirteenth centuries, and now again exerting itself in the sixteenth, had levelled much of the Domesday woods and forests. Constructional needs had taken much besides and little had been replanted to make good the loss. Responsible opinion only awoke to the depletion when, and because, the effects of scarcity were already being felt. From the mid-sixteenth century it was state policy to protect and extend England's woodlands. But the policy was only sporadically and weakly pursued. A vigorously executed scheme of reafforestation was beyond the scope of existing state machinery, and in any event the state's concern was not with the threat to fuel supplies but with that to shipbuilding timber; the burning of wood was, from this point of view, as undesirable as the assarting of woodland.

There was then a market of considerable potential for a cheap alternative fuel for both domestic and industrial purposes. England, above all European countries, had the means of effecting a conversion from wood. In several parts of the country there were extensive coal deposits lying accessibly close to the surface. Of equal importance was the geographical configuration of the country: narrow, elongated and, except along the short Scottish border, flanking the sea on all sides, with the result that coastal areas constituted a considerable part of the whole, while much of the inland area was penetrable by water via three major rivers, Thames, Severn and Trent, and other lesser ones. Without the facilities for water carriage thus afforded, much of the coal from the mining regions would have had to remain in the immediate vicinity. One of the crucial economic facts about coal is the cost of moving it. No other commodity of widespread consumption is so bulky in proportion to its value. Under sixteenth- and seventeenth-century conditions it cost as much to move a consignment of coal two or three miles by land as it did to mine it. The major determinant of price for customers was not production costs but transport costs. Over any distance exceeding ten or twenty miles coal was only competitive with wood (even at scarcity prices) or within the means of most buyers if moved by water. By sea, coal could be transported for thirty miles at much the same cost as one mile of overland transport by wagon; by river the comparable mileage would be rather less because of the smaller capacity of the carrying vessels.

One coal-bearing region in particular enjoyed the double advantage of abundant deposits and proximity to navigable water: the coalfield of Northumberland and Durham. Above Newcastle the Tyne, fairly wide and deep for some distance, literally cut its way through coal which could be loaded direct on to rivergoing 'keels' to be transhipped at Newcastle for coastwise distribution. Coal had moved sporadically in this manner out of Newcastle since the twelfth century, but from about 1540 the traffic was rapidly assuming a regularity founded above all on the supply of increasing quantities of coal to London which could be reached direct by sea. By 1590 Tyneside coal had become the universal fuel amongst London's poor; the better-off, their nostrils offended by the smell, were still buying higher priced wood or more expensive coal from the Firth of Forth which, burning with a clear bright flame, was odourless. But by 1640 the relative cheapness of Tyneside coal had overcome the sensitivity of many and the passage of another thirty years or so saw coal in general use among all classes.

London with its gigantic population dominated the market, but the pattern of its shift from wood to Tyneside coal was repeated along the whole coastal belt from the Scottish border down the North Sea into the Channel as far west as Plymouth, and in wedges driven inland by the Humber, the East Anglian Ouse, the Medway, and the Thames as far as Oxford. But the low cost at which Tyneside was able to serve so extensive a market could not in the nature of things endure unchanged. Transport costs have already been distinguished as a crucial element in the economics of coal. A second fundamental element is that it is an activity doomed to work with a wasting asset. The tendency of coal-mining costs must always be upward as the most favourable seams become exhausted and less favourable ones have to be worked. From as early as about 1565 mines along the banks of the Tyne were having to be pushed to depths of over ninety feet to find more coal. By about 1610, either because the water drainage problems encountered at greater depths were technically insoluble or because the costs of deep mining were rendering it uncompetitive, collieries were being forced to move away from the river and cope with the expense of shifting coal by wagon to the riverside. By 1640 some Tyneside pits were having to absorb the cost of four or five miles land transport, which had permitted Wearside, where the shallow deposits occurred above the navigable reach of the narrow river, to enter Tyneside's external market on competitive terms and to supply about a fifth of the whole north-eastern coalfield's seaborne output. But within this period and well beyond it the great bulk of the rich coal reserves of central and southern Durham were shut out by the lack of water transport from markets beyond the immediate locality.

This was the situation also of what in point of geographical extent was the largest English coalfield: the east Midlands, encompassing roughly a rectangular block having Leeds, Bradford, Derby and Nottingham as its four corners. Only in the extreme south where it touched the Trent could this coalfield cater for distant markets and even there scope was limited; Trent-borne coal could not reach the east coast as cheaply as Tyneside or Wearside coal. But between the belt flanking the Trent, along with the Humber and the Yorkshire Ouse to which it gave access, and the extensive local area itself, east Midlands coal could command a considerable sale and throughout this period it was steadily ousting wood within that region just as north-eastern coal was doing in more widespread markets.

In the west of the country where the erosion of woodlands had not yet proceeded so far as in the Midlands and east, the exploitation of coal resources lagged behind, and the period of most rapid opening up of western coalfields occurred between about 1640 and about 1690. But well before 1640 there was activity in the coalfields of the west. From the mid-sixteenth century the rich South Wales field was being tapped and from its advantageous coastal position was shipping coal up the Severn, around Land's End as far as Southampton and across the Irish Sea to south-eastern Ireland, while Dublin was drawing coal from Flintshire. Towards the source of the Severn the small riverside Shropshire field was sending coal downstream, branching off to go up the Avon to Stratford. Along the sparsely populated north-western coast coal was being distributed in small quantities from the high potential Cumberland field and from a few Lancashire pits lying near the Mersey estuary; while in inland Lancashire the easily worked outcrops scattered over much of the county were being denuded. In the landlocked west

Midlands Staffordshire coal was being worked for local sale and the thick seam of the constricted Warwickshire coalfield was being plundered to meet the needs of metal-workers as well as ordinary domestic users.

All in all, allowing for a few lesser coalfields and minor rivers, there was only two well populated areas of any extent which lay beyond the economic reach of coal: a roughly triangular area comprising those parts of Hampshire, Dorset, Wiltshire, Gloucestershire and Oxfordshire which were too far from the Channel, the Severn or the navigable length of the Thames; and a smaller area in the interior of Suffolk and Essex. 'Economic reach' is, of course, a relative concept – in this case relative to the price of wood, to the means of the labouring classes and, when coal was used as an industrial fuel, to other manufacturing costs and the price of the finished article. That is to say that as far as domestic use was concerned it is a question of whether coal was cheaper than wood; and then, whether the large section of the populace whose income was principally expended on food, clothing, housing and heat could keep themselves warm and cook their food without having to make sacrifices on the other necessities. Certainly over the greater part of the east and Midlands by the end of the sixteenth century and persistently thereafter the market price for wood would have been well in excess of that for coal (although in rural areas there must have been many who never reckoned to buy fuel in the market anyway but relied on foraged brushwood, dried dung, straw, turf, etc., and slept huddled together to preserve body warmth). The indications are too that in normal times coal was cheap enough to be bought by most without necessitating serious economies on other purchases – or, put alternatively, that the extent of poverty and deprivation was not significantly determined by the price of coal – except during particular periods of shortage, which were, however, fairly frequent and, poignantly, often occurred during the worst winter months when the same weather conditions which rendered coal most necessary also interfered the most with the movement of seagoing colliers. But, these bad seasons apart, this could stand as the most notable achievement of the English coal industry over these and subsequent years: that it did supply enough cheap coal to ensure that cold did not become the public menace which it must otherwise have done while wood became steadily scarcer. Forced to choose between chronic lack of warmth and a diversion of resources to costly fuel supplies England, either way, would have experienced a drag on social energies.

Over this period coal prices, in real terms, by and large did resist their natural tendency to rise. For this several factors were probably responsible: falling real wages, modest technical advance in drainage and boring methods, the organisational economies arising out of large-scale production, and the distributional economies of a large regular trade. But it would also appear that rising costs were in significant part absorbed by reduced mining profits. Until towards the end of the sixteenth century colliery operators enjoyed something of a sellers' market as a growing population was converting steadily from wood to coal; the returns on mining investment in these halcyon years were high – high enough to lure many newcomers into the field. By the early seventeenth century the field had become overcrowded, supply was running ahead of demand and competition between rival producers was fining down prices and eating into formerly comfortable profit margins. On Tyneside in 1603 this had led to a protective combination among producers – the first recorded instance of what was to be an intermittently permanent feature of the coal industry thereafter. The difficulty of sustaining the attempt by combination to restrict output (by means of allocating fixed production quotas to each colliery) and thus to maintain prices is indicative of a situation which had already been reached at this early stage in the industry's history, at least on Tyneside, and which was to persist until, in very recent times, the industry passed out of private ownership. The situation was one which along with the high element of transport costs in final price and the inexorably upward tendency of production costs, already noted, makes up a trio of factors which give the economics of coal a very distinctive character; that situation in which the costs of different producers vary widely as the multifarious natural conditions which determine costs differ enormously from pit to pit and from area to area.

In the early days of Tyneside mining, when it was confined to shallow deposits on the edge of the river, conditions were much the same for all producers, but once mining had to go deep and move away from the river, discrepancies opened up with the comparative ease or difficulty of locating underground coal, of penetrating the soil or rock which overlay it, and of pumping away the water which accumulated as mining went below the natural drainage level. All these were governed by, among other things, the depth at which coal was found, as was the cost of winding it to the surface and the distance the coal face should be pushed from the shaft before sinking another one. This in turn determined the cost, capable of being very high, of underground haulage. At the face itself output per man-hour varied with the thickness of the seam being worked; and above ground the distance from the river could make a vast difference to total costs. All in all, even within a very limited area, the discrepancies in producers' costs could reach dimensions utterly unknown to manufacturing industries. This was what always caused producers' combinations eventually to collapse. For a while adverse marketing conditions and poor returns might lead to unanimity on the need to restrain output, but the relatively low cost producers were under the constant temptation to break out of the ring and seek their own salvation by *expanding* their output at prices which their less well placed co-producers could not afford to match.

The inevitable cluster of high cost producers who could only make a profit in fair weather meant that even from early times the coal industry was characterised by a chronic sickness and high dropout rate among its members. It is a crucial fact about the industry that at any level of demand there will be producers who are currently losing money but clinging on in the hope of the modest up-turn in prices which will take them out of the red, or because to cease production will mean even greater losses since fixed capital costs, possibly very high, still have to be covered even in a totally inactive pit. The coal industry is unique in the spectacle it affords, once any substantial development has taken place, of great wealth jostling shoulders with bankruptcy. In these years, 1540 to 1640, as in any others, a low cost coal mine was about the most lucrative investment that capital could find. But finding a low cost mine was analogous to finding the winner of a horse race. A knowledge of the terrain was just about as much use as a knowledge of form is to a racing expert. Not until a mine was in actual operation and the capital involved irrevocably committed could costs be accurately known; and in the lack of a scientific geology much money could be expended on a fruitless search for workable seams.

Competition, then, was the product of this kind of situation as it came into being in the closing years of the sixteenth century – interspersed with periodic attempts at price maintenance; competition from low cost producers seeking to exploit their advantage; competition from those with high fixed costs seeking to spread them over maximised output. The domestic consumer was the principal beneficiary, partly because the domestic consumer would not have had, as the industrial user had, the opportunity of passing on high costs to a further customer, more importantly because the domestic consumer accounted for something like two-thirds of total output. This simple statistical fact should be enough to warn against a chronologically premature association of the expansion of the coal industry with a corresponding expansion of industry at large. We are, after all, simply dealing with a switch from one kind of fuel to another – a switch prompted solely by considerations of price and not by any consideration of technical advantage. There is no reason on the face of it to expect any special further consequences to follow the conversion. Where wood was formerly burned, coal was now being burned. Such economic gain as might accrue would be by comparison with what *would have* happened if relatively cheap coal had not been made available (i.e. not by comparison with what had been the case formerly) and, possibly, by comparison with what *did* happen to countries in economic competition with England which did not effect such a conversion. In fact, with the exception of Belgium, then the Spanish Netherlands, no other European country was, or became, coal using to any noteworthy extent until the nineteenth century.

The particular importance of coal in different industries can be considered as an element in an account of those industries themselves, but the general observation can be made here that just as it has been already suggested that in the domestic field the supreme importance of coal was that it obviated the distressing situation that would have occurred had the mass of the populace had to continue to depend on wood for heat, so also it protected fuel-using industries (in proportion to the incidence of fuel costs in their total costs) from similar difficulties. If it is not to be argued that coal was responsible for important industrial advances at least it could very reasonably be contended that it played a key part in ensuring that there was no recession.

The most striking organisational development engendered by the swift expansion of coal output was within the industry and trade itself, and, above all, in Tyneside and the delivery of coal to London. The consequences of the exhaustion of shallow riverside deposits have already been indicated. The deeper mines that followed necessitated expenditure on exploration and soundings, on the sinking and lining of shafts, on drainage and ventilation equipment, on winding gear and, as pits receded from the river, on horses and wagons which in gross could amount to considerable sums. Such large outlays of initial capital required extensive working if the investment was to be recouped; that is they called for the employment of a large labour force, with consequent high outgoings on wages which could not be recovered until the coal was sold – and with a commodity for which demand was largely a winter one, the interval between production and sale in the summer months could be quite lengthy, during which time money was tied up in stocks, requiring storage space which again had to be paid for. Of these various items of expenditure drainage was often the most burdensome just as it was often the gravest technical problem besetting deep mining, some pits being constantly threatened with total inundation. In such cases drainage equipment might in extreme instances cost up to £5,000 to install and up to £2,500 p.a. to operate when the gross revenue of the enterprise probably did not exceed £5,000 p.a. (roughly equivalent around 1640 to the rental income from a landed estate of 20,000 acres).

Drainage costs of this kind, where they occurred, were a powerful incentive to very large scale operations since one installation could drain several adjoining pits from the deepest of them, to which the water could be channelled from the others. Such giant undertakings could represent in total a capital investment of perhaps £40,000, far exceeding that of any other industrial enterprise of the period and quite beyond the financial scope of any one individual. Mines of that order were financed by syndicates of perhaps a dozen or more persons, one of whom probably attended to the actual operation of the concern while the others were sleeping partners, although some of them would very likely be coal merchants anxious to secure privileged access to supplies. Indeed in the early years of the development of deep mining on Tyneside colliery ownership was almost exclusively confined to members of the Newcastle Company of Hostmen who had the sole right of dealing in coal passing through Newcastle, as all seaborne coal had to, and for a while used that prerogative to debar non-Hostmen from operating collieries for outside sale by refusing to buy from them. However, before the end of this period as colliery profits were squeezed the Hostmen were pulling out of the uncertain business of coal-owning and confining themselves to their original and less hazardous business of just dealing in coal.

Apart from the special case of the Newcastle Hostmen the capital required for these costly undertakings on Tyneside and elsewhere came mostly from the only two sections of society commanding substantial reserves of capital: the landed proprietors and the London merchants. The first, as a rule, confined their involvement in coal mining to deposits on their own estates. Much of the coal-bearing land in the Tyneside area belonged to the Bishop of Durham who, rather foolishly, let it go on a long lease on low terms to the town of Newcastle but elsewhere landowners usually made more of coal lying underneath their property. Sometimes they contented themselves with leasing the mining rights, usually on terms that provided for a fixed cash payment plus a royalty on coal raised. But quite often they worked the coal themselves, employing their own capital as far as it would go and supplementing it where necessary with loans or by taking in partners. Some of them laid the basis of aristocratic fortunes which have lasted to the present day. Others ruined themselves. London mercantile capital was perhaps most often made available as loan funds, at fixed interest and secured on the property itself, but London merchants also weighed in with local interests as risk-bearing partners and experienced the same wide range of fortunes as anyone else who ventured his money in coal.

The importance of large capital in coalmining must not be exaggerated. The circumstances described above were very largely peculiar to certain areas. Tyneside, Wearside, the few Midlands collieries close to the Trent and, mostly in the years following 1640, South Wales, Cumberland, and the Firth of Forth in Scotland – areas enjoying extensive market scope and where, in consequence, the easily worked deposits were fairly quickly exhausted. Outside these areas in regions where production was confined to limited land-sale, rich, readily exploited deposits requiring little capital investment survived into the nineteenth century. But even after allowing all due weight to this consideration coalmining over the later years of the period 1540 to 1640 does present what for all practical purposes is a striking new economic phenomenon: industrial capitalism, a form of enterprise which required the permanent vesting of big sums of risk capital and where, because of the high fixed costs, relatively large-scale production was imperative. Both the risks and the sums required conduced to a spread of the burden of any one undertaking among several entrepreneurs both by way of syndicates or partnerships and by way of what might be termed vertical dispersion: subleasing or subcontracting arrangements of various kinds, from the renting out of a whole mine which had been put in operating order to agreeing with a team of miners, or a 'butty' who employed such a team, for the fetching of a stipulated quantity of coal from one face, payment to be made on final performance of the agreement. On occasions there might stand between a miner and the owner three or four intermediaries, each carrying some part of the capital load through the financing of work in hand or the provision of equipment. Such arrangements often also served the purpose of securing managerial and supervisory functionaries on terms which directly related their remuneration to their competence and diligence. It was to be a couple of centuries before social conditioning created the psychology proper to the salaried manager or foreman.

The coal trade also required its own special structure, although what was new here was the scale rather than the intrinsic nature of the organisation. Of the inland distribution of coal or of coastwise distribution to smaller centres, we know little. Coal was probably handled by general dealers along with other commodities. It is of the Tyneside–London trade, far exceeding in importance any other single trade, that we know most. Within these years it was dominated by two groups, possessed of a legal monopoly, at each end: the Hostmen, already mentioned, and the London Fellowship of Woodmongers, who succeeded in having their ancient craft privilege of carting wood in the city extended to the new fuel and became in effect wholesale stockists.

As the trade grew the liquid capital required to finance it grew correspondingly. The Hostmen, whose turnover was fairly rapid, do not appear to have found this a problem. Their monopolistic position along with the buoyant demand situation of the early years won them high profits capable of financing expansion and of still leaving a surplus for investment in collieries and in associated enterprises, salt, glass and lime manufacture, as well as for general moneylending. By 1640 the dwindling returns on fixed investment were curbing this kind of employment of funds, but the increasing involvement from about 1620 of Hostmen in shipping, mostly in the admittedly small export trade, suggests that they were not being embarrassed by lack of capital – an impression further confirmed by the beginnings around 1640 of an extension of their business into the Thames itself: whereas formerly the Hostmen had sold to merchant shippers in Newcastle they were starting to hire cargo space for their own coal instead, thus appropriating the profit of that stage in the distribution train at the cost of prolonging the length of time for which their capital was tied up in coal stocks (i.e. of increasing the amount of capital necessary to finance any given quantity of coal handled).

At the other end the London Woodmongers do not appear to have been extending their range of business in any similar fashion. As stockists their turnover must have been markedly slower than that of the Hostmen, especially in the winter months since (until the middle of the eighteenth century) from December to February the colliers would not hazard the North Sea so that the Woodmongers had to be stocked up by the end of November with at least three months' supplies, taking the strain on capital which that involved. From about 1660 (to anticipate a little), possibly because of this weakness, they were losing their dominance at the London end to the 'crimps', originally merely lightermen ferrying the coal from ship to shore (there being no docks in the Pool until the end of the eighteenth century), who developed into brokers matching up shippers and Woodmongers and hence into dealers on their own behalf and thus, in effect, relieving the Woodmongers of some of the capital burden of a growing volume of trade. Thus in its developed form this trade necessitated four mercantile intermediaries, including the London retailer, and three water freighters: Tyne keel, seagoing collier and Thames lighter. Small wonder that the London customer paid about five times the Tyneside pit-head price.

The comparatively well recorded spectrum of the Tyneside–London coal trade and the shifts along it are of interest not only with regard to coal itself but also as suggesting something of the complex nature of the internal trade network generally, of which we know very little directly. It shows that there can be no simple model of the development of a distribution chain; that the different functions of dealer, broker, freighter and stockist might simultaneously fuse at one point and fragment at another; that growth in the volume of business might generate capital enough to lead to absorption by one functionary of another or might, on the other hand, cause problems of capital shortage leading to a diffusion of functions; or, more simply, might result in expansion beyond the managerial capacity of one man so that delegation became inevitable – delegation which had to take the form of a total surrender of some part of the business since, as noted already, society had not yet bred the type of salaried employee who could be entrusted with independent responsibility.

The iron industry

Another industry to assume a distinctively capitalistic character over this period was iron-smelting. This was a development which was due to technological innovation. The blast furnace, already known on the continent, reached England in the closing years of the fifteenth century; the first recorded furnace in England dating from 1496. The very biggest of the old style bloomeries might on each charging have yielded 300 lb of iron; an early blast furnace, 15 to 20 feet tall, produced about a ton an hour and could be kept constantly in blast until the internal brick or stone walls needed relining – a 'campaign' could last up to forty weeks. The handling costs per unit of output were therefore markedly lower and, additionally, the blast furnace yielded more metal per unit of ore so that even when the capital costs of a furnace with its attendant water wheel for powering the large bellows had been allowed for, blast furnace smelting was significantly cheaper than bloomery smelting. However, the gain accruing to the final user was relatively slight. The pig iron as it emerged out of a blast furnace was a very impure metal, with a high carbon content, rendering it brittle, and depending on the kind of ore used, containing other substances (silica, phosphorus, etc.) which impaired its usability. For most purposes it had to be further refined into bar iron, a lengthy and expensive process which roughly quadrupled the cost of the metal; and before it finished up as an article of use it had further to bear the cost of a smith's or metalworker's operations. Without corresponding economies in these subsequent activities the ultimate economic impact of the blast furnace could not then have been notable – as, in fact, it was not until the late eighteenth century. Only over the narrow range of articles which were tolerant of its deficiencies and could therefore be made directly from pig iron could the blast furnace yield major economies. This range was severely limited, not only by the unacceptability of pig for most purposes but also by the physical impossibility, on account of its proneness to fracture or splinter, of fashioning it to a desired shape and size. The only way in which the pig could be directly transmuted into an article of use was to remelt it and when molten pour it into a mould of the requisite shape and size, thus producing a cast iron article. But the high viscosity of the molten metal prevented it flowing into small, slender or intricately patterned moulds. The composition of the mould itself also determined castability and the scope of cast iron was gradually extended a little by improvements in mould design; but for the first half century its use was confined solely to the making of cannon and cannon shot.

Until towards the middle of the sixteenth century it appears as if the blast furnace was used only for producing cannon iron, the bloomery continuing to cater for all other needs. Refining techniques had to be adapted to cope with the rather different metal coming from a blast furnace which never yielded as high a quality bar iron as did the bloomery process; the shift from bloomery to blast furnace, when it took place, generally meant a sacrificing of quality for quantity and a dependence on superior foreign iron for many purposes. By 1640 this was just about the position which had been reached. Except in remote, thinly populated districts, principally in the north-west where the small local market could not support the capital costs of a blast furnace and where high transport costs excluded outside competition, the bloomery had been replaced by the blast furnace.[1]

Hard data are almost totally lacking but it seems likely that the new blast furnace capacity considerably exceeded that of the former bloomeries. That is to say that this period, more particularly the century 1540 to 1640, witnessed a marked growth in English iron output. However, as has already been implied, the blast furnace can hardly be distinguished as the prime causal agent of this increase. The slight overall cost fall which it effected doubtless stimulated a modest rise in demand – or, put another way, enabled something of an increase in output to be achieved without a corresponding increase in resources employed. But given the merely marginal economies resulting from it we must suppose that the apparent growth in output would have been largely achieved by an expansion of bloomery smelting anyway. It must be stressed that if the growth record of the iron industry in these years bears any sort of a similarity to that of the 'Industrial Revolution' the two differ fundamentally in that the latter was self-generated through major cost reductions whereas the former must be seen as largely a passive response to an autonomous rise in demand.

Such a rise may be explained as due to general economic growth or to a shift to purchases of iron from purchases of other commodities or to a substitution of English for foreign iron. Much of it is to be attributed to the first of these: simple population increase could be expected to bring about an approximately corresponding increase in the output of iron as in the output of any other commodity. If, furthermore, there was actually an increase in *per capita* wealth, then an increase in *per capita* use of iron would not be surprising. A shift from other commodities to ironwares would, of course, produce the same effect and an important redistribution of wealth which occurred within these years has been considered as making for a change in expenditure patterns which could have resulted in such a shift. It has been suggested[2] that the dissolution of the monasteries and the secularisation of their wealth along with the general stemming in the post-Reformation age of the

---

[1] The bloomery was still also general in the Forest of Dean where the privileged position of the local inhabitants prevented capitalist entrepreneurs intruding.

[2] By J. U. Nef in *Cultural Foundations of Industrial Civilisation* (Harper Torchbooks edn, 1960), pp. 44–53.

flow of wealth to ecclesiastical bodies through pious donations and bequests did cause less to be spent on grandiose edifices, embellishment and decoration, requiring careful individual artistry and relatively more on goods of practical utility susceptible to cheap standardised production methods. If such changes did occur iron would surely be one of the beneficiaries. However it can fairly be questioned if an age which brought forth Nonsuch Palace, Longleat House, Hatfield House, and such artists as Hans Holbein, Inigo Jones, Anthony Van Dyck and others was any less given to costly display and expenditure on the arts than an earlier one of lavish ecclesiastics. The third possible explanation of a growth in iron output – substitution of English for foreign iron – is one which in the lack of trade statistics cannot be verified. There is no reason to suppose that English raw iron would come to be used for purposes for which better quality foreign iron had always been imported but it is within this period that we start to hear more of English made iron (and other metal) artifacts and less of German imports; by the early years of the seventeenth century hardwares seem to have been regularly items of exportation. While the raw iron needed for high quality manufactures was probably imported, the cheaper wares would have been made from local lower grade and lower cost iron.

This quickening of activity in the metal-working trades, notably in the Birmingham region, itself demands a parenthetic explanation. As with cloth manufacture in earlier times so it seems to have been with metal-working – a case of tardy exploitation of opportunities which had always existed, of the inertia of earlier centuries rather than of any especially favourable contemporary circumstance, of the slowness of England in catching up with Europe, or parts of it, in point of industrial inclinations and aptitudes. England up to the sixteenth century could be described as an 'underdeveloped' country in the same sense as could North America in the eighteenth century, Russia in the nineteenth, Brazil or Central Africa today, the economic state of each of which has to be explained in cultural terms rather than in terms of natural resources and opportunities. As was suggested in the case of the cloth industry in the fourteenth-century mercantile initiatives, sharpened in the sixteenth-century environment, may have been what induced the Birmingham region and other centres to extend their metal-working trades to cater for wider markets in England, and, though of less consequence, abroad. Once initiated the plenitude of convenient iron, wood and coal would sustain the development and the ready availability of coal in north Warwickshire, and south Staffordshire may have given that area a competitive edge not merely over other English centres but over foreign ones in whose vicinity wood was also becoming scarce. Certainly the lack of coal was the reason why the Weald, although pre-eminent as an iron-smelting region, did not develop associated manufacturing crafts. The smelters had to cling to dear wood since it was as yet technically impossible to smelt with coal, but the manufacturers could settle near cheap coal.

The Weald could, of course, supply cast iron products: cannon, shot and the handful of other articles that were cast in this period. The first known blast furnace (1496) was set up there for the purpose of casting cannon and there is no record of a blast furnace outside the Weald until the 1560s, by which time there were some fifty in operation in that area, largely employed in supplying cannon and shot to the royal arsenal. Much of the growth in iron output, over the earlier years, consisted of cannon iron. England had been slow to take to cannon. The French had made effective use of it in the closing stages of the Hundred Years War but even in the later Wars of the Roses (1455–85) little use had been made of it in England. Henry VII was the first English monarch properly to appreciate its possibilities, not least that of rendering the castles of his over-mighty subjects untenable, and under him and Henry VIII the first half of the sixteenth century saw a steady building up of royal fire-power, for both land and sea use – the latter of particular note as giving birth to the specifically designed fighting ship which in essentials was to endure for another three centuries. That the production of these cannon and their shot was entrusted to the Weald is readily understandable: not only was it the major iron-producing centre in the country but it was much more advantageously placed than any potential competitor for delivery to the crown armoury at the Tower of London and to the shipbuilding yards of the Thames and south-east coast. The protracted hostilities, official or un-official, with Spain in the second half of the sixteenth century probably kept actively employed the considerable capacity which had by then been developed and probably initiated the blast furnace on the coast of South Wales in the 1560s; when home needs periodically slackened there was a lively export market to be supplied, for English cannon founders had devised a mould whose composition yielded better results than those obtained by their continental counterparts. But the extra furnaces then coming into operation must have been mainly produc-ing pig for conversion into pacifically destined bar and those being erected in the west Midlands and south Yorkshire through the last quarter of the century were almost certainly exclusively so occupied initially.

Through the quieter years of the Stuarts until the Civil War the Wealden and South Wales furnaces must have switched from cannon to pig for bar, the more especially as in the early years of the seventeenth century others, particularly the Swedes, became capable of supplying comparable or superior guns. Through the last quarter of the sixteenth century and onwards, however, the Weald was on the decline, although still the most important producer in 1640 when of a national count of seventy-eight blast furnaces, thirty-nine were in this area alone. This decline is capable of two distinct explanations, between which in the absence of direct data it is difficult to choose: the depletion of the forest and consequent shortage of charcoal; and the reduced demand for cannon and consequent dependence on the demands of metal-workers, congregated in coal-bearing areas, who could be more cheaply supplied from blast furnaces in or adjoining those areas.

The fall off in the armaments market was, of course, only temporary while the decline of the Weald was never arrested, but once blast furnaces had been located in places where a regular market was assured they would possess a permanent and decisive advantage since capacity could be expanded in wartime without creating what would prove to be a ruinous excess when peace returned.

A blast furnace, while nowhere near approaching a deep coal mine in point of cost, necessitated a capital outlay previously unknown in iron smelting, and a large contemporary forge might have represented an investment, spread over a period of time, of similar scale. However, in many cases the need to raise a fairly substantial initial sum did not lead to the immediate appearance of a new kind of entrepreneur. Iron-working from very early had been an estate enterprise. A large land-owner who had always exploited the ore on his property would have little difficulty in financing a conversion to blast furnace smelting and many of the early blast furnaces, along sometimes with associated forges, were so owned; but the ore, and more particularly the charcoal, resources of one estate alone would rarely permit of prolonged opera-tion of a blast furnace, and it would seem that landowners generally ceased to be interested in iron-smelting when there was no longer any integral connection between it and their own landed property. Cer-tainly few would have remained in the industry once the exhaustion of local raw materials compelled migration to a new site.

Even when erecting a blast furnace themselves landowners would generally have committed its operation to an outsider on some agreement ranging from an outright lease of the enterprise to employment of a furnace master on profit sharing terms. Apart from the need, common to all undertakings where ownership was divorced from immediate supervision, to relate remuneration directly to effort there was the especial difficulty of securing the services of a man with the still rare technical knowledge that the direction of blast furnace smelting required – in the early years most furnace masters in England seem to have been French or Flemish. An expert furnace master would command a seller's market and would be unlikely to content himself with a mere wage. The financing and management of sixteenth- and early seventeenth-century blast furnaces still awaits its historian but it would seem that it is not until towards the end of the seventeenth century that a new class of capitalist iron-masters clearly emerged as a distinctive element, and that up to and rather beyond the end of the period at present in question the initiative and finance behind the developments in the industry came largely from the owners of ore-bearing land in association with professionals who eventually came to assume the dominant role as the owners' land became unable to furnish the basic materials.

Not all furnaces had associated forges attached. The advantage of minimising transport costs by moving bar instead of the pig, a third to a half heavier, from which it had been derived was often offset by the cheaper wood available outside the ore-bearing regions in which the furnaces had to be located, while the lack at the one site of sufficient water power to drive both the furnace bellows and the forge bellows and tilt hammer also often enforced separation – a tendency aggravated when, from about 1565, water-powered 'battery' mills were introduced for the making of plate and, from about 1600, rolling and slitting mills for the making of sections. A reluctance or inability to vest the further capital required for these operations may also have dissuaded furnace owners from extending their activities to forging. Forges which were not erected in conjunction with furnaces were usually located as close to manufacturing centres as wood and water facilities permitted. Water was of importance not only as a source of power but also as a means of transporting the bulky material – whether as pig being brought to the forge or as bar being sent out. The Severn and its tributary the Stour exercised a particular attraction, and through the century or so preceding 1640 many forges sprang up on or near their banks, fairly close to the metal workers of the Birmingham region and well placed to draw supplies of pig not only from the furnaces of the region itself, notably in still abundantly wooded Shropshire, but by water from the bloomeries of the Forest of Dean, the furnaces of South Wales and even those of the Weald. Some of these forges with their water-powered equipment must have represented a capital investment exceeding that of a blast furnace but of the men behind them we know next to nothing. Much of the capital, however, may well have come out of the profits of forge-masters who started in a fairly small way and grew up with the industry.

Other metals

Although of little real importance, one concern associated with iron which appeared within these years and which merits particular mention is the Society of Mineral and Battery works. Formed in 1568 it stands amongst the first joint stock companies known in England. It possessed a statutory monopoly of wiremaking and by 1608 had two wiremaking factories in operation, using a special water-powered apparatus, in the Wye valley in Monmouthshire, drawing on local iron and sending wire down river into the Bristol Channel. This appears to have been the only regularly profitable undertaking of the Society which had first been formed primarily to engage in copper and brass manufacture. Despite its success in locating calamine (zinc ore) deposits (alloyed with copper to make brass and whose presence in England was hitherto unknown) it never contrived to make much of this side of its business – in which it was closely associated with another company formed at the same time, the Society of Mines Royal vested with a monopoly of copper mining.

Just as Englishmen had had to look to Frenchmen and Flemings to learn the technique of blast furnace iron-smelting so they had to turn to Germans to learn about copper. In southern Germany copper mining had by the sixteenth century been pushed to depths of over a thousand feet and the manufacture of copper wares was anciently established. The techniques of exploration and mining at depth, borrowed for coalmining no less than copper-mining in England, and the methods of smelting copper ore and fashioning the metal were introduced by Germans brought over by the Society of Mines Royal which included a number of Germans amongst its founding shareholders. Considerable sums were expended, but partly because no really rich deposits were uncovered and partly because of the impossibility of effecting proper managerial and technical control from one London centre the Society steadily lost money although it contrived to show a current profit when it took to using its monopoly (until withdrawn in 1689) to charge a fee for permitting others to work copper. The only copper works of any noteworthy scale of output which the Society itself succeeded in developing was at Keswick, Cumberland, and even this failed to show a profit.

The oldest of English extractive industries, tinworking, evidently experienced something of a boom in the early years of this period. Between the 1470s and the late 1510s output appears to have increased by about two-thirds and then to have roughly maintained that level until the early 1550s, after which it fairly steadily slipped away again so that by the end of the period it was back to what it had been at the beginning. This chronological record, just about the inverse of most other industries, can hardly be accounted for in demand terms. Rising population in England and, much more importantly, in Europe, which presumably had been a principal factor in the early growth in production, should have made for a protracted increase well beyond the middle of the sixteenth century. That it did not was probably due to problems of supply as the easily worked alluvial deposits became less abundant and for the first time it became necessary to sink shafts through the bedrock to get at the lode itself – an exigency which was not paralleled by signal advances in exploration techniques or in boring and drainage methods, although this phase apparently did bring forth the water-powered stamp mill to reduce the large fragments, in which the ore came away from the lode, to suitable proportions for smelting.

No indication of lead output is available, but the industry had no divide to cross such as that between alluvial and lode workings in tin although, as in the case of any established extractive industry, it was progressively having to reach to greater depths. The development of new smelting methods in the 1550s and 1560s suggests vitality. The ancient 'bole' was being replaced either by a low blast furnace or by a new kind of ore hearth, both employing water-powered bellows. Both were small-scale affairs, capable of being worked by two men, and their advantage over the bole apparently consisted in lower fuel consumption. Neither lead nor tin working in this period manifest any marked tendencies towards large-scale capital-dominated concerns. There continued to be scope for the lone independent worker although, in both, syndicates, often including non-working members who employed hired labour, would have accounted for the bulk of output.

Economic revolution?

A keenly sharpened, if not indeed entirely new, interest in exploiting what might be beneath the soil strikes one as a particular characteristic of the later sixteenth and early seventeenth centuries. The intensified working of mineral deposits which had always been exploited can be thought of as a natural response to rising demand, but the widespread probing for coal in new areas and the copper and calamine explorations of the Societies of Mines Royal and Mineral and Battery Works suggest a deliberate profit-minded pursuit of possibilities which earlier centuries had been largely content to stumble on by chance. They seem to speak of a readiness, an alacrity, to lay out money in the speculative hope of making money. Again we touch on a basic issue. Are there forces abroad in these years conducing to a more acute development of the acquisitive instinct? And if the appearances do manifest a genuine change in economic attitudes what was causing the change? Inflation? The new religion? Humanism, with its distinctive belief in man's natural powers and its byproduct, scientific thought and inquiry which aspired through knowledge and understanding to the capture of the physical world to serve man's material needs? In 1620 Francis Bacon, lawyer, politician, scholar and in his spare time according to some, William Shakespeare, no idle dreamer but a thorough man of the world, published *Novum Organum*, the founding text of English science, in which he proclaimed the faith that investigation and analysis of the world of nature was destined to multiply human wealth. In so doing he must have been giving rhetorical and reasoned shape to the half-formed optimism of many others, perhaps prompted in part by the great advances already achieved by scientific method in astronomy. The fact that no economic advance within this period or indeed well beyond it was due to new scientific knowledge need not preclude us from crediting that the confidence associated with this faith may have contributed to a more thorough application of existing knowledge, and a belief, perhaps rather facile, that England possessed stores of potential wealth which only the ignorance and unimaginativeness of earlier generations had prevented from being realised. Might not an age which had discovered new lands across the oceans make discoveries also on its own soil?

Other ventures

Whatever the reason, men do seem to have scrutinised the earth
and its contents more closely than ever before. Apart from the
minerals already mentioned, alum, essential for dyeing and hitherto
mostly imported, was discovered in the opening years of the seventeenth century on the Yorkshire and Durham coasts, convenient for the
delivery of coal which was needed in large quantities, for the lengthy
boiling process by which it was extracted.[1] A little later copperas, used
in the making of black dye and ink and for tanning, was discovered in
Kent on the Thames estuary, again well placed for the coal which was
needed in processing. In several parts of the country brick fields were
being opened up. Some perhaps had been lightly worked in the past
but many must have been virgin since it was not until the closing years
of the sixteenth century and, more especially, the seventeenth that
brick replaced stone or lath and plaster as a normal constructional
material in a number of places, having scarcely been used anywhere
previously, either because the presence of brick clay was not known or
because its possibilities were not appreciated. High fuel costs were an
initial impediment to its use because early coal fired kilns did not produce brick of good quality, but by 1640 careful selection of the type
of coal used enabled the cheap fuel to be fairly generally burnt for
brick-firing.

Behind all these enterprises stood men with capital. Unlike deep
coalmining or blast furnace smelting, the extraction and processing of
these materials could have been on a small scale, but it is indicative of
the kind of initiative that was responsible for their development that
operations were from the beginning conducted on a fairly large scale.
It was not local peasants seizing opportunities for a supplementary or
alternative source of livelihood who brought these new industries into
being, but those with money, often outsiders, seeking profitable
employment for it. So it was also with the revival of the near extinct
manufacture of salt from sea water. From about 1580 the cheap coal
of the north-east was being extensively used for salt manufacture at
the mouth of the Tyne and Wear and at many points further north
where coastal coal occurred. The initiative here often came from
Newcastle Hostmen with capital surplus to their mercantile needs, or
from colliery owners seeking outlets for their coal, the latter especially

[1] See also pp. 159-60.

along the Northumberland coast where the lack of good harbour facilities made it difficult or impossible to ship coal out.

Another capitalistically organised industry which came to have its principal centre on Tyneside was glassmaking. This is an industry which can be said to have been created within this period. Before 1550 glass was used only for windows in churches and in the more sumptuous secular buildings, usually elaborately stained with pictures or colour patterns, and for fine ornaments very largely of foreign manufacture. It was not so much an industry as an art, to be ranked alongside painting and sculpture. Through the second half of the sixteenth century coarser glass for ordinary windows and mundane drinking vessels was being produced in England, but market advance was limited by the need to use expensive charcoal for firing since the impurities given off by coal rendered it unusable for this purpose. Around 1620, however, the difficulties in using coal were overcome following a royal patent granted in 1615 to a prominent naval officer, Sir Robert Mansell, and his associates, conferring on them the exclusive right of glass manufacture in order to enable them to develop a successful coal firing method in a protected market. The patent was still in force in 1640 and while it had served its purpose of promoting cheap glass production it constricted exploitation of the advance; it was not until after the Civil War that glass output on Tyneside and elsewhere experienced any very marked expansion.

A less well documented industry which, like glass, would seem to have created a markedly wider market sphere for itself was soapmaking. A rather exotic product in earlier centuries, it had by the later years of this period become sufficiently commonplace, at least among the better off, to sustain a good number of manufacturing establishments, notably in London and Bristol where the concentrations of population provided not only an immediate market but plentiful supplies from the butchers of the animal fat which was the main ingredient. These two cities were also able to receive coal direct by water, the one from the north-east, the other from South Wales, and the availability of a cheap fuel in an industry where the principal process was prolonged boiling must have had much to do with its growth. There are no known instances of really large concerns in the industry, but the soap manufacturers were clearly of a class and financial weight distinctly superior to that of the small artisan.

Entirely new within this period were the manufacture of paper and of gunpowder. One might readily associate the former with the arrival of the printing press, but in fact throughout this period most of the paper made in England was coarse wrapping paper, the finer kind for writing and printing being largely imported. Water power was used for pulping the rags from which it was made and, particularly from about 1580 (lagging a century and more behind the continent), paper-mills were being erected at suitable sites in the south-east, close to the principal market, London. While of modest enough scale such concerns were clearly the undertakings of men with capital, or at least access to it, and the strong probability is that it was London mercantile capital which initiated most of these ventures. The development of the manufacture of gunpowder was clearly intimately associated with the build-up of the Crown's stock of cannon. The major process involved was the refining of the principal constituent saltpetre, little of which was to be had in England. It was usually imported in a refined state but from about 1550 saltpetre obtained from the encrustations in old buildings and pigeon lofts was being refined in one or two establishments in England by favoured Crown licences.

The range of industries dealt with above, from coal to gunpowder, is symptomatic of what is most strikingly new or even 'modern' about the English economy over this period, especially over the years 1540 to 1640. Development proceeded in ways which, in essentials, are redolent of the great economic advance of the late eighteenth and the nineteenth centuries, and the thesis that we are witnessing in these years the birth of a new economic era is, in the light of this experience, an insistently credible one. The key role of the capitalist entrepreneur, the use of power, the employment of new techniques, the concentration in particular localities of industries catering for a national market and the extensive distribution network thus necessitated: these are features which seem to place the period on this side of the divide which separates medieval from modern. Yet a view of the period which was informed solely by the record of these industries would be a very lopsided one. To preserve a sense of proportion it is necessary to note that total industrial activity by 1640 would have supplied only about a fifth of national income (compared with about a third in the mid-nineteenth century and about a half today), and that the group of industries in question would have contributed but a fraction of that fifth. Nose to the ground in quest of evidence of 'revolutionary' change, one is impressed by its abundance. But standing back to look at the English economy in perspective this abundance rapidly dwindles to detail, modifying but not radically altering the character of the whole. The whole was in course of change but of a nature that is most aptly termed gradualist so that as late as 1640 (or even 1740) much remained both in objective forms and in subjective attitudes which was rooted in a medieval past.

The old order

Within the already established industries the most conspicuous change is the transformation or dissolution of the guilds.[1] The beginnings of this change have already been located in the years after the Black Death, which it has been suggested may have been in some measure responsible for it. The evaporation of guild control over much of the cloth industry has also been considered, along with possible explanations for the emergence of new forms of organisation (which, it was argued, need not betoken substantial changes of any radical order). The use of guild power to serve oligopolist ends on the one hand and the escape of the ambitious entrepreneur beyond guild power on the other have already been pointed to as tendencies making for either the alteration or the extinction of craft guilds. These were, in general, the forces already subverting the old forms. But up to the Civil War they were far from being allowed unrestricted play. Public, parliamentary and state opinion under the Tudors and the early Stuarts still inclined heavily to the belief that the functions of control and regulation in the interest both of customers and producers were proper and necessary. And to the local provisions of corporations and guilds there was added throughout this period a plethora of legislation prescribing, often in minute detail, the manner in which production and trade were to be conducted. For the enforcement of this legislation reliance had often to be placed on the old institutions.

The nature and rate of change in these circumstances varied widely from craft to craft and from town to town. Here a guild is to be found in the mid-seventeenth century functioning just as it had done in the mid-fourteenth; there it has entirely disappeared; somewhere else it has lost its former grip but survives in an attenuated form; elsewhere again it has become the efficient instrument of a tight oligopoly. Nevertheless, certain general statements can be made. Guilds are not found in those new industries which were capitalist-organised from the beginning, or

---

[1] This is a theme which does not lend itself to the chronological divisions adopted generally in this book. What follows covers developments both before 1475 and after 1640.

in old industries which had migrated or expanded into the countryside, such as clothworking or west Midlands nailmaking, where dispersion over a wide area made combination for the benefit of producers or inspection for the benefit of customers impracticable. Where such an industry was still partially carried on in towns uncontrolled, rural competition would render guild regulation largely useless, though the functionless guild probably survived into the later seventeenth century. Of guilds which retained a vitality, the ones to be most drastically altered in character were those where the product came to be marketed widely. The most enterprising masters in such trades would have initially expanded production beyond the scope of their own workshop by employing journeymen in their own homes and then expanded further by buying the output of small masters who were unable, through lack of time and capital, to secure access to distant markets. At that point the distinction between a journeyman working in his own home and a small master was beginning to blur, the more so if the large master/merchant ceased to employ journeymen directly (i.e. ceased to provide them with the raw materials), as he probably would to save himself tying up capital in materials and work in progress and so leave his capital free for the single task of distributing the finished goods. In this way there would emerge, within the guild framework, a dominant class of merchants clearly demarcated from the small masters and the journeymen whom those masters might employ in twos or threes.

As early as the beginning of the fifteenth century this kind of process had gone far in a number of London crafts and the guild was on the point of becoming the livery company with a formal distinction between its superior mercantile membership, alone entitled to wear or able to afford the extravagant livery which was its ostentatious mark, and the working membership: the yeomanry. The yeoman section of the company was, of course, in essence the old craft guild and it could be contended that the economic situation of its members was substantially unchanged. They were now, as they had been formerly, small producers. As opportunities for distant sale had arisen a class of merchants had grown up to exploit those opportunities. In the last analysis it makes little difference whether these merchants emerged from the ranks of producers and retained a formal association with them, or developed quite independently. In either case they discharged a function which the small master was incapable of performing, which, as a *small* master, he could never aspire to perform. Trade was capable of elastic expansion because the only limitation was capital which, given the enterprise, could in time be accumulated. Manufacture in any effort to expand ran up quickly against the limits of exercising supervision over a body of workpeople and against the need to vest capital in premises, with the hazard that fixed investment involved. It is a crude economic truth that fixed investment will only be undertaken when it offers a clear cost advantage or when the nature of production necessitates it. That is to say that wider marketing scope will not in itself normally lead to any great increase in the size of the productive unit, but it will lead to mercantile initiatives, of considerable profit potential, linking the necessarily small producer to his new customers. The point, in this particular context, is that the merchant can reasonably be apprehended as creaming off the profits of the new opportunities rather than as eating into the established earnings of small producers. The relative status of the producer was certainly debased but his income was not necessarily lowered – and indeed there is no evidence that it was. The same point has already been made with regard to the cloth industry in particular. What it comes to is that amid the emergence of new and often wealthy functionaries as the distribution chain became lengthier and more complex, and amid the changing formal nature of guilds, the small producer, the nub of it all, survived unaltered in essential economic character and function.

Outside London there is no clear instance of a guild developing distinct mercantile and manufacturing sections; but both in the provinces and among London crafts which never reached that point of development, there would be numerous particular instances of the rise to positions of wealth and economic dominance of mercantile functionaries: masters transmuted into merchants or shopkeepers with the capital to finance stockholding; masters who remained manufacturers but who distributed the wares of others as well as their own; those who had never been anything other than merchants. Sometimes the key figures might be merchants who supplied the raw materials; where there were several processing stages they might be manufacturer/merchants at an intermediate stage. In any of these cases such individuals might extend their range of operations over several or all of the processing stages like a clothier in the cloth industry. Occasionally an industrial capitalist would play the central role: a forge-master might supply iron to local metalworkers and might furthermore dispose of the finished product. Wherever goods were marketed widely something of this general kind would occur. Viewed from another aspect it is to say that regular distribution channels were taking the place of periodic fairs and itinerant merchants, although it was not until as late as the nineteenth century that internal trade assumed the regularity and volume which enabled it to dispense altogether with these institutions characteristic of slender or sporadic trade.

A craft guild in these circumstances might follow any one of various courses: without the formal distinction of a London livery company it might effectively become divided into a dominant mercantile element and a subordinate manufacturing element – in time it would dissolve as the dominance secured by capital rendered command of guild authority unnecessary for the one element and guild organisation useless for the other;[1] the guild might remain the preserve of the manufacturers and provide the respectable forms of a producers' combination, but if it were powerful the combination could dispense with the guild trappings and if it were not it would eventually collapse under either economic pressure or the probable hostility of the corporation.

Within and outside these broad patterns of change there would be almost as many types of guild history as there were guilds. In the huge majority of cases the guild would still exist in 1640 but the forces undermining it would already be at work, in many cases had been at work for a long time, and all that often remained was an empty shell kept in existence by inertia and a public and official opinion which still credited the institution with a social value.

Many, perhaps most, craft guilds would not have been subject to the peculiarly acid effect of mercantile dominance. Numerous craftsmen went on dealing directly with local customers for generations until as late as the nineteenth or even twentieth century factory production finally made an anachronism of them. But long before that their guilds had vanished. The dissolution of some guilds began with their capture by an exclusivist group, perhaps as early as the fourteenth century, which on occasions led to separate associations of journeymen, for whom the guild had become an instrument of oppression; these associations are most conspicuous in the decades after 1540 when real wages generally were falling. Without legal standing, their efforts to force higher wages from their masters earned them official hostility at a time when public policy sought to prevent wages and thus prices from

---

[1] The London livery companies have of course survived to this day, but as purely honorific and ritualistic bodies whose formal styles give no indication of the actual occupation of their members – a development which was well under way by the end of the seventeenth century.

increasing; prosecution brought about their formal disbandment. Sometimes the impossibility of preserving craft demarcations was the initially erosive factor, although mergers of associated guilds quite often gave the institution an extended lease of life. But even in the absence of specific circumstances like these and despite an unchanged economic context guilds crumbled away – generally over the second half of the seventeenth century and most particularly through the last couple of decades. Much of their economic function passed into other hands. The law and its agents steadily through the sixteenth and seventeenth centuries took over on a national scale much of what had formerly been the responsibility of local institutions. Wages and apprenticeship were the subjects of specific statutes, had been so indeed from the middle of the fourteenth century, although in these earlier times legislation was more a supplement to than a substitute for traditional controls if only because the creation of the administrative and judicial apparatus necessary for effective central control only really started under the Tudors; and even then it long remained the case that without the active cooperation of the crafts themselves wage and apprenticeship laws, along with other statutes regulating the nature and quality of goods, were unenforceable with any regularity. But even while the law's dependence on the guilds might tend to prolong their existence, their reduction to a mere role of economic policemen must have sapped their innate vitality. The common law and equity too encroached increasingly on traditional guild spheres. Incorporating elements of the old *lex mercatoria* they offered alternative means of authoritatively resolving disputes between seller and buyer, though the cumbersomeness and expense of court proceedings, even in the courts of equity supposed to offer cheap and simple law, would have deterred many from resorting to them. More destructive perhaps was the sharpening in the later years of the seventeenth century of the common law hostility towards concerted activity 'in restraint of trade', capable of application to traditional guild practices and tending then to throw the weight of the law against guilds, whereas formerly it had generally been cast in their support. This legalistic development was not, of course, an autonomous one but a mirroring of contemporary political and intellectual changes tending to favour free enterprise and creating a general climate inimical to the survival of guilds. Once this point had been reached, where public policy attributed no social value to guilds and only self-interest sustained them, their extinction was certain and rapid – self-interest survived, but it had to find other forms of expression.

If the decisively fatal switch in public policy was very much an event of the closing years of the seventeenth century, the transformation of the guilds in such a manner as to bring them into disrepute as organisations dedicated to the promotion of their own sectional economic interests above those of society as a whole was much longer in the making. The tendency towards exclusivism has already been noted. But equally subversive of a claim to social usefulness was their loss of cultural function. Craft guilds were introduced in this book with the observation that they are only to be fully understood as a cultural and not just an economic phenomenon. They can be ushered out on the same note for it would be foolish not to credit the possibility that the guilds might have preserved an economic role for themselves had they continued to meet those wider needs of urban society which had first brought them into being. That they did not was partly because the guilds themselves changed in character and partly, too, because the needs changed. Most particularly, perhaps, the religious sensibilities to which they had at one time answered took on different forms or perished entirely; the pieties, the charities, the participation in public religious ceremonials had increasingly less relevance to urban culture from at least the later fifteenth century and with the Reformation they generally ceased altogether.

To speak of the passing of guilds is to speak of the passing of a particular kind of organisation with a formal place in civic life. It is not necessarily to speak of substantial economic change. Nor is it necessarily to speak of the abandonment of the public purposes which guilds had served. Nor, further, does it mean at all that associations amongst men ceased when guilds no longer provided the outward forms. The guild was perhaps unique in providing the form for an association which answered several social objects simultaneously. Its dissolution often meant no more than that associations of a more specific nature and without the quasi-official status of a guild succeeded it. Bodies essentially resembling trade protection associations, employers' associations, trade unions and friendly societies, though leaving no records of their own, flit across the transcripts of court proceedings and other public documents from the later seventeenth century until they clearly emerge in modern guise in the nineteenth century.

What has been said already makes it plain that no simple model can describe the organisation of industrial production and distribution in sixteenth- and seventeenth-century England (a statement which can be extended to cover the eighteenth century, much of the nineteenth and even some of the twentieth). The large heavily capitalised enterprises often reveal complex subleasing and subcontracting arrangements, the small productive units widely varying degrees of dependence on mercantile intermediaries and what little we know of the internal trade network suggests a snarled jungle of wholesalers, retailers, agents, brokers, stockists and hauliers. Small wonder that it is one of the most neglected sectors of English economic history. And one must further confound confusion by touching more particularly on the role of the state in it all. Passing for the moment over the legislative activity of the state, we must note more direct forms of state involvement in industrial affairs.[1]

Patents

Crown association with economic enterprises arose from various motives which while distinct in principle are generally quite inextricable in particular instances. And the particular instances are legion – such that one would not attempt here to mention more than a handful of the more notable or notorious ones. They run from about the 1560s through to the end of the period and the general economic background against which they are to be set is the quickening of interest in economic opportunities, the quest by capital for new fields of employment, the climate of optimism and high pitched expectations as to the country's economic potential which have already been remarked on and which were sometimes founded in a naïveté which cost the holder dear. The government was as much enveloped in this atmosphere as the private individual and in the minds of government men it set off two impulses: one, that as a matter of public responsibility it should promote exploitation of new possiblities; two, that as a matter of private financial necessity it should profit from them.

If the first was chronologically prior, the latter tended increasingly to become the dominant though never the exclusive one. The one motive slid the more easily into the other since commonly the same device was employed for both ends: the patent of monopoly, conferring the exclusive right to undertake a particular activity on the patentee(s).[2] As a means of promoting enterprise its efficacy lay in protecting the operator of a new, untried and possibly expensive

[1] The terminal dates 1475–1640 are here resumed.
[2] It may obviate misunderstanding to say that 'patent' in itself had not today's restricted sense but signified any grant of right, privilege or authorisation by the Crown.

activity until the undertaking was securely established, without the benefit of which protection the risks involved would not be tolerable (in this respect the patent is analogous with the 'infant industry' tariff protection of modern times). Apart from this justification in terms of economic policy, there was also the equitable consideration that those who contributed to the public welfare were entitled to some special return. And behind these *ad hoc* rationalisations, which really follow rather than precede the practice, lay the fact that restriction of an activity was as much the rule as the exception, that it was perfectly normal for an occupation to be confined to those belonging to a formally sanctioned guild or company or vested with a particular authorisation, and that to engage in a trade was as much a privilege as a right. Certainly one must not think of the patent of monopoly as a startling innovation but as an extension, if also at times an abuse, of an anciently established instrument of good governance.

Similarly, one of the ways in which the Crown might privately profit from a patent was also far from new: the sale of charters runs back at least to the twelfth century; in charging a straight fee for a patent, the Crown was certainly not setting a precedent. However this was probably not, in ostensible principle at least, the usual way in which the Crown secured its cut and under Elizabeth, indeed, it seems as if the Crown rarely, if ever, actually obtained cash from a patentee, although doubtless the officials who facilitated the grant of a patent had their pockets lined for their pains according to the custom of the times. The only substantial benefit which Elizabeth's treasury could be said to have drawn from the issue of patents was an indirect one: among the principal recipients of beneficiary patents were Crown servants of one kind or another who otherwise might have had to be remunerated in cash.[1] The other way in which the Crown could make money was by having some portion of the revenue of the enterprise assigned to it. This took several forms, ranging from payment of a stipulated sum annually, distinguishable from a straight fee only in that the payment was spread over the patent's duration, to the Crown's putting up the capital itself and declaring a monopoly in its own favour. Between these two extremes are to be found various degrees of participation by the Crown in association with private entrepreneurs.

---

[1] Patents were only one of the various perquisites of state employment which often constituted the bulk, even the whole, of official remuneration. Such stipends as were attached to posts were sometimes of ancient standing and had been rendered derisory by inflation. There were a few handsomely salaried offices for the well placed, but the huge Cecil fortune, for instance, was not accumulated out of official pay.

The undertakings in which the Crown itself took a hand, although relatively few, are perhaps the most interesting but also the most complicated, and something may be said first of the more straightforward, though also often murky, grants of patent to others. It may be said at the outset that the bulk of them, viewed retrospectively, were of no economic value whatsoever and it is difficult to believe that they ever had any credible pretensions as such. They covered industries to which the patentees had nothing of their own to offer, and many of them related not to manufacturing processes at all but to dealing in or transporting specified commodities. Such claims as these had to be of public benefit usually consisted in abuses or breaches of the law, real or supposed, prevailing in these activities, to which the monopolists were to put a stop. Indeed this kind of patent shades away into the properly distinct kind under which the patentee was merely empowered to search out illegalities and receive, in whole or part, the fines then imposed by the courts, or the associated kind in which, in order to check abuses, certain trades were subjected to a licensing system, the authority to grant a licence being assigned to patentees who retained the fees payable; and these in turn merge into the related kind under which the patentee was granted certain crown dues which the crown itself found it too troublesome to collect. This last might be an ordinary 'farm', employed by the Crown for centuries as a convenient way of gathering revenue; and all of these non-monopoly type patents can clearly be seen to have been, in origin at least, ways of overcoming the chronic difficulty of a shortage of trustworthy officials. They really belong to administrative history and should not intrude at all here.

The difficulty is, however, that, while abstract categorisation would place them aside, in practice all kinds of patent tended to degenerate into the one undifferentiated and unpopular kind: a levy payable to a patentee who did nothing to earn it. The licenser undertook no investigation as long as he received his money, the detective compounded privately and the monopolist never attempted to set up in business on his own but, for a fee, licensed others – principally those already so engaged – to do so. Even in some cases where the industry concerned was a new or insecurely established one in England and the ostensible object of the patent was to enable patentees to develop it under shelter, the undertakers having embarked on their own soon found it more convenient or more profitable to grant licences to others; courtiers found they had not the taste or the aptitude for industrial management or were unable to raise the capital to expand as market scope permitted.

In fact without impugning the element of disinterestedness in the Crown's use of patents as an instrument of economic policy, one need have little hesitation in saying that, in the light of actual events, there is no unambiguous instance of important industrial development as a result of the system.

The best candidate as an advertisement for the public usefulness of the practice would probably be the patent awarded to Sir Robert Mansell for the making of glass. Smelting of glass by coal did pose serious technical problems; it did take time and money to solve them such as might not have been readily expended without special privileges; and it did culminate in success. However, there was an already well-established charcoal smelting industry which doubtless in time would have overcome the difficulties involved in coal smelting and which for twenty-five years was held in check by Mansell's patent. Had it had more luck the Society of Mines Royal might have emerged as a credit. It was hardly its fault that England had little in the way of copper deposits and if any were to be found it could only be through extensive and expensive exploration. The money for such an uncertain venture could scarcely have been forthcoming except under special guarantees. In these remarks the society can be associated with its sister company, the Society of Mineral and Battery Works, of which additionally it could at least be said that it did enjoy a modest but useful success in its wiremaking business and could lay claim to as much reputability as any modern concern which introduces a new device under patent protection. Characteristic of the commendable aims which could be publicly invoked in justification of a monopoly and of the narrow sighted and destructive meanness which could really inspire it was Cockayne's Project. But for all its calamitous consequences it may, as suggested earlier, have actually played some part in the development of an English dyeing and dressing industry.

Something might also be said on behalf of the alum monopoly. A good supply of cheap home-produced alum promised to be of positive assistance to the dyeing industry struggling to put itself on a competitive footing with the Dutch. Large-scale production employing cheap coal held out a prospect of achieving this end if the capital were raised for the essentially new undertaking. Following an earlier failure four patentees received a monopoly in 1607, but six years later, after spending considerable sums of their own and borrowing heavily, they had exhausted their capital resources and the Crown took over the enterprise, laying out in all £70,000 in paying off the creditors and in fresh investment. At least from a financial point of view this was one of the Crown's most successful ventures. Through the 1630s it was receiving on average over £11,000 p.a. from the alum monopoly, but some part of this came from licence fees paid by successful private operators and whether the tribulations of the original patentees are to be attributed to the intrinsic initial difficulties of the undertakings or to their own incompetence is impossible to say. Much earlier, in 1564, the Crown had attempted to launch the large-scale evaporation of salt from sea-water using coal by creating a royal monopoly of the sea salt industry, but the enterprise was a failure and the subsequent vigorous development of the industry proceeded without the benefit, or hindrance, of patent privileges.

The instances cited above, with or without the participation of royal capital, along with other less notable ones, do not add up to a record of impressive achievement, but through the welter of favouritism, failure and financial improvisation which attended them, it is possible to discern the shadowy line of a deliberate state policy of industrial development, particularly the development of natural resources. But this particularisation carries a warning. If one speaks of 'a policy of *industrial development*' this should not be translated into 'a policy of *industrialisation*'. Nothing could have been further from the minds of contemporary statesmen: as the concept, under any verbal guise, did not even exist it evidently could not have entered into anybody's reckoning. There was no question of altering the balance between the agricultural and industrial sectors of the economy, of a general principle that the path of economic progress was by way of a concentration on manufactures, or indeed of any notion of sustained economic progress at all. If some sort of analogy is permissible between the England of these years and the 'underdeveloped' countries of today it consists in the objective facts and not in the goals set by public policy. Although it would be absurd to say that contemporaries did not appreciate the importance of techniques and of technical improvement it would remain a truth, if a somewhat oversimplified one, that they still conceived of the material goods of life as those provided by God or nature, which could be utilised through human agency in greater or less degrees but whose store was limited. The object of policy, such as it was, was to employ this store more fully, not to fashion a new kind of economy.

Interest in new industrial development seems to slacken off over the last two decades or so of the period – perhaps because the most promising opportunities had already been exploited, perhaps because the excessive expectations of the preceding years had bred a reaction of scepticism and caution. Under Charles I grants of monopoly were no less frequent but the most noteworthy were of a novel character, and of a rather confusing character. They were not production monopolies but marketing monopolies, and the motives behind them are not easy to disentangle. They all involved a cut to the Crown – that at least is one plainly comprehensible reason for their creation – but they also carried a claim to social usefulness either in respect of the producers concerned or of the buying public, or both. The best recorded cases are those of the London pinmakers inaugurated in 1635 and the London playing-cardmakers (1637), but what appear to be essentially similar schemes were contrived for a number of other London crafts as well as for the soapmakers of London, Bristol and Bridgwater (conjointly), the North Eastern salt manufacturers, the Newcastle coalowners and the brickmakers catering for the London market, although of these provincial instances only the first operated with any protracted efficacy. The essential feature in all of them was that sales were to be conducted through a crown-appointed agency at fixed prices, with the ostensible object of eliminating the mercantile intermediaries who, so it was contended, were appropriating an inordinate amount of the proceeds of these industries. To what extent, at least initially, the arrangements secured the concurrence of the producers themselves is not clear. In the case of the pinmakers it evidently did. These were small artisans heavily dependent on a dominant merchant group[1] and crown inter-vention on their behalf may be reckoned an instance of Stuart 'pater-nalism', as even more clearly is the case of the playing-cardmakers who petitioned Parliament in 1641 for the continuance of the scheme.

Other producers too may have conceived that they would benefit from a rationalisation of marketing arrangements. But whatever sound reasons may have been adduced in support of the schemes the effective impetus behind the great majority of them doubtless derived from the opportunities of converting them to private advantage: on the one hand that of the Crown which compensated itself for its pains by a fixed levy on the commodities sold; on the other, that of the various patentees who relieved the Crown of the actual task of administering the schemes and who made sure that the margin between buying and selling prices was enough to reward them for their endeavours –

[1] Part, probably most, of the pinmakers' distress was due to Dutch competition and the scheme was accompanied by a prohibition on the importation of Dutch pins.

posessed of a monopoly they were of course well placed to ensure this, the formally prescribed prices being treated in cavalier fashion. These ventures have not so far been investigated in detail as has the Cockayne project but the probability is that such an examination would reveal similar features: a group seeking to muscle in on a profitable market; the support of the Crown secured through a judiciously mixed representation of the public benefits and the augmentation of Crown revenue which would follow; and the whole impaired by insufficient capital to finance sales and a lack of practical familiarity with the market. The soap monopoly which did actually survive from 1627 until the Civil War seems nevertheless to have been unable or unwilling to handle the normal quantities produced; certainly it was vehemently accused of having led to a ruinous reduction in output and it may be that the patentees found it positively more rewarding to sell smaller quantities at scarcity value than the larger amount the market could have absorbed at lower prices.

Effectively similar in principle to these commercial monopolists, although hardly so prejudicial in practice, were the overseas trading companies.[1] Of these the greatest and that which excited the most rancour was the Merchant Adventurers. It is difficult to say just when this body decisively assumed an exclusivist character; just when, from being an organisation serving the interests of those seeking to conduct trade with the Low Countries, it was transmuted into one whose prime object was to keep people out of this trade, to the advantage of those already established in it; just when membership of the company instead of being a normal concomitant of engagement in the trade became a sparingly accorded qualification for entering it. Very probably the Company had exclusivist tendencies from an early date, tendencies which were exacerbated by the contraction of its market with the slump in cloth sales in 1551. Initially approved in general as contributing to the maintenance of cloth prices by eliminating competition amongst overseas merchants, company restriction of trade to a privileged few got swept up with the other forms of monopoly in the assault mounted against them with gathering strength and momentum from the 1590s.

The body of opinion supporting this attack should not be thought of as a homogeneous one informed by a coherent set of economic principles. For many of the assailants monopoly as such was not reprehensible; it was particular instance, particular abuses, particular consequences that excited their denunciations. And alongside the public-

[1] More extensively dealt with, pp. 201–9 *passim*.

spirited were the simple 'outs' – those whose only objection to monopolies was that they were not themselves parties to them. Probably some
of those associated with Cockayne's monopolistic cloth exporting
company had formerly been vocal critics of the Merchant Adventurers
monopoly. William Noy, chief engineer of the soap monopoly, had
earlier distinguished himself as an antimonopolist champion. But if
there were a hundred and one particular or private grievances contributing to the campaign against monopolies there was also a doctrinal
element, perhaps not of very great immediate weight but destined to
survive long after topical passions had subsided. This was the 'free
trade' principle, the assertion as a general truth that all men should be
free to follow whatever legitimate trade or profession they wished,
unhindered by the reservation of certain activities to vested privilege.
Although sometimes reinforced by or merging with arguments of
economic advantage it was not really an economist's doctrine and, if
anything, tended to run counter to the general drift of seventeenth-
century economic thought. Neither, although a little later in the century
drawing some sustenance from the thought of Locke, was it really a
philosophical doctrine. It was above all a lawyer's doctrine and its
evolution occurred within the context of legal and constitutional
history. The ascendancy which it secured in the seventeenth century,
particularly the latter part, is a measure of the force of Common Law
principles (or more accurately what the weight of judicial opinion
pronounced to be Common Law principles) in shaping contemporary
attitudes on a range of public issues, including more than one of economic import.

The antimonopoly wave left three major tidemarks. First the angry
discussion on monopolies in the parliamentary session of 1601, which
prompted a royal undertaking that the whole system of granting
patents would be drastically reformed, accompanied by a winning
declaration from Elizabeth to the assembled Commons: 'I never put
my pen to any grant but that upon pretext and semblance made unto
me that it was both good and beneficial to the subjects in general,
though a private profit to some of my ancient servants who deserved
well.' These were not mere words, and the reforms put in hand were
initially sustained by James I.

Attention shifted to the overseas trading companies and a Commons
Bill of 1604 provided for the throwing open of foreign trade to all. For
reasons which are hidden from us, this Bill was abandoned before going
through the Lords, but all that we know suggests that this was certainly

not on account of any levity of attitude towards the measure. Much discussion, inquiry and strength of feeling had gone into its preparation. The value of company organisation in facilitating trading activities in foreign lands was properly appreciated and the Bill did not contemplate the abolition of the companies but merely the breaking of the grip of the entrenched interests which controlled them. It was evidently intended as a major reform measure and it is puzzling to know why no more was heard of it. Some part of the answer may be that antimonopolist sentiments became once more absorbed with internal abuses as James slid away from the rectitude of the commencement of his reign, for which a chronic budgetary deficit, the importunities of favourites and an obstinate conviction of the soundness of his own economic judgment were variously responsible. Against his exalted sense of prerogative periodic parliamentary protests were largely unavailing, and the monopolies issue was among those which set Crown and Parliament so much at loggerheads that ultimately the sword became the only arbiter.

But the end of James's reign brought temporary accord when in 1624 the king found himself at a serious moral disadvantage in having to ask the Commons to vote taxes for a war with Spain for which over the past four years popular opinion had clamoured and which the king had strenuously sought to avoid. In this brief era of good feelings, or the appearances of them, a comprehensive Monopolies Bill became law and during the same parliamentary session the export of cloth to the area covered by the Adventurers' monopoly was declared by the Crown to be open to all. Here should have been an end to the matter as a major polemical issue but to the general prohibition of monopolies the Act made certain understandable particular exceptions. Patents of monopoly for fourteen years were to be allowed in respect of genuine innovations – the patent law as we understand it today and which has sometimes by outside observers been distinguished as a peculiar contribution to fostering a spirit of inventiveness and thus as promoting technological advance, a judgment on which there might be conflicting opinions. Secondly, it was no part of the intention of the framers of the Act that it should extend to guilds and other bodies controlling crafts whose insistence on certain qualifications for admission to membership and thence the freedom to ply the trade in question was quite in accord with contemporary economic thought (at least, if guilds were believed to be guilty of abuses of power a sweeping measure of this kind was not the place in which to undertake the delicate and invidious task of reforming them). Corporate bodies were therefore exempted from the provisions of the Act. But the power of incorporation rested with the Crown which could by charter make of any collection of individuals a corporate body. Impelled by much the same mixture of motives as his father, though perhaps with rather less sensitivity to the claims of intimates and rather more to preserving at least the forms of public benefit, Charles I made ample use of this gaping loophole in the Act. With no Parliament summoned between 1629 and 1640 the lack of parliamentary taxes heightened the king's anxiety to employ every possible means of raising revenue at the same time as it preserved him from organised criticism. And in 1634 the Merchant Adventurers made it worth his while to restore to them their trading monopoly.

Charles's corporations as a group have little contemporary importance other than as a way of evading the 1624 Act but they were, of course, in the ordinary sense joint stock companies and although this was probably of no more than incidental importance to their members, it does merit some comment in historical retrospect. However, probably the most salutary observation, which may as aptly be made here as elsewhere, is that the history of joint stock organisations has often been accorded an undue prominence in economic narratives and that the leading features of this history are really matter for legal historians. From the narrowly economic point of view the interest of joint stock concerns in any period consists in such indication as they afford of enterprises requiring sums of capital beyond the means of single individuals. From the legal point of view the principal questions raised are two. Did they possess a corporate identity such as would enable them to sue and be sued in a court of law through the person of a principal officer, rather than through the persons of each individual member (clearly in the case of a large concern a cumbersome procedure); and such as would enable the concern to acquire property and other assets and contract debts through the agency of a principal officer?[1] And further to this: were the members of the concern individually and fully liable for its debts should it be unable to meet them out of its own assets? Economic history need only concern itself with these questions to the extent to which the ease of constituting enterprises in which there were several participants hinged on the answers to them – that is to say, to the extent to which ordinary syndicates or

[1] The question of property and debt contraction is less crucial since the ordinary law of agency would cover most likely circumstances whether the officer was acting on behalf of a corporate or of a non-corporate concern.

partnerships, possessing no sort of corporate identity, would not serve, either because the inability to act through a principal officer in legal proceedings was a serious impediment in the conduct of business, or because unlimited liability for debts frustrated the raising of capital. Where these were not practical issues there is no useful economic distinction to be drawn between a corporate concern and a partnership.[1] In the period at present under review, the Society of Mineral and Battery Works or Charles I's corporations are no more significant economic phenomena than the large syndicates to be found in coal-mining.

Legislation

Ranging much more widely than crown finance and royal patents and charters was legislation. Parliamentary opposition to exclusivist privileges and the growing strength of 'free trade' sentiments have been noted but these should not be confused with the 'free trade' doctrines of the nineteenth century. Crown and Parliament might clash on issues of economic policy but the clash was fundamentally one between conflicting financial interests and certainly not one over the propriety of having an economic policy and of using state power to make that policy effective. Indeed an obtrusive feature of English society of the period is the faith in legislation as a means of curing economic ills, or what were conceived to be economic ills. Sometimes the initiative came from the Crown, occasionally in the form of a direct exercise of royal power by proclamation; sometimes from Parliament; sometimes from those seeking protection or the removal of some hindrance by way of petition. Numerous enactments were unconsidered *ad hoc* responses to particular situations introduced without reference to wider consequences and even sometimes conflicting with other measures. Much of it was forgotten or ignored, even by the legislators themselves, almost as soon as it was born but frequently remained unrepealed so that the statute book was like an old minefield, occasionally exploding in the face of the unsuspecting, often detonated by that legal booby-trap, the common informer. Even the elaborations of Tudor central bureaucracy, the Privy Council and its ancillaries such as the courts of Star Chamber and Requests with their efforts to harness the local

---

[1] The phrase 'joint stock company' is an unhappily ambiguous one. Most commonly it designates concerns with a corporate identity but it is often used in a historical context with reference to concerns which raised their capital from the general public but which legally were merely large partnerships.

magistracy more effectively in the service of public policy, could not relieve the law of its heavy dependence for detection of breaches on private self interest: the informers' cut of fines or the similar reward assigned to patentees for the discovery of specified offences. Even with a strong sense of purpose at the centre, law enforcement under these circumstances was necessarily sporadic and often arbitrary.

In the light of this it would be pointless to launch into a recitation of the economic legislation of the period and it would be a rough truth that in anything but the very short run it did not significantly modify the nature or direction of economic change. But as a commentary on contemporary intellectual responses to economic environment the leading principles of the mass of legislation are revealing. It is something of a paradox that this age which saw England move closest to constitutional absolutism also saw public opinion coming to play an unprecedented part in the shaping of state policy. Both Tudors and Stuarts sought total power but once seized of it commonly employed it to give effect to the dominant aims and aspirations of those they governed – with serious reservations on matters touching their purse or their religious beliefs. The printing press and Parliament ensured that monarchs and their advisers were kept well informed of the trend of popular feelings. The statute book then is not a bad mirror of broadly based contemporary attitudes, and if it reveals much muddled and confused thinking, and if it often testifies to the strength of the forces of economic and social conservatism, then that is because society itself was confused and conservative. And it further serves to indicate that economic change often occurred despite, rather than because of, contemporary sentiments.

It might be said that the most pervasive characteristic of this economic legislation is the concern to preserve people in their accustomed employments. At the back of this there seems to lie an essentially medieval vision of the social order. The image of the human body, much used by medieval writers, still seems to have sprung readily to men's minds. Just as the human body had its different members each playing its part in the whole and each drawing its life from the whole, so it was with the body social. Social arrangements were the work of Divine Providence and it should be the aim of the Christian legislator to preserve this work as it issued forth from the hands of its heavenly author. Each to his appointed station then, and to each the rights and duties pertaining to that station. Whatever threatened to disrupt the established pattern was to be resisted. (Before the end of this period the new science was nibbling at the core of this philosophy and a sharpened sense of history was cultivating an erosive awareness of social change in the past. The publication of Thomas Hobbes's *Leviathan* in 1651 marks the definitive arrival in England of a fully formulated counter-thesis of social evolution according to positive laws, converting God into an effective irrelevancy and making frail vanities of human attempts to halt or divert the evolutionary tide.)

On one issue the economic legislation of the period did effect a rupture with the medieval past, though even here the hesitant, back-ward-looking caution exhibited testifies as powerfully to the strength of inherited attitudes as it does to the force of new tendencies. This was the matter of usury. How far the shifting of ground on this issue is to be attributed on the one hand to a change in economic environment specific to this period and, on the other, to a gradual refinement and sophistication of theological analysis of the nature of interest, running well back into the fifteenth century, is difficult to say. It is certainly striking that reform of the usury law took place within that phase, *c.* 1540 to *c.* 1640, through which the evidence accumulates of increased borrowing to sustain both capital investment and lavish consumption expenditure. On the other hand, moral theologians had from much earlier been moving towards a distinction between borrowing for the sake of profit and borrowing out of necessity though the reformer Melanchthon (1497–1560) was the first of weight explicitly to sanction the taking of interest, being followed in this by the much more in-fluential Calvin (1509–64); but neither of these ceded anything to the adherents of the old school in the vehemence of their denunciations of those who preferred profit to charity in lending to the needy. Protes-tant divines were divided among themselves on the question, and while the first venture in the legitimation of interest in England might with some plausibility be associated with Calvinistic influences, the general bias of Anglican teaching abided by the ancient anathema throughout this period. And if the eventually decisive reversal of the law is to be linked with religious trends it must be more by way of the opening up of a gap between secular and ecclesiastical morality than by way of the authority of any particular school of divinity.

The first experiment in legalised interest was initiated in 1545 with a statute which permitted a rate of up to 10 per cent but, on top of criminal penalties, prescribed the total voidance of any loan on which a higher rate was charged. Whatever considerations had prompted the Parliament of 1545 they obviously carried no force with that of 1552 which not only repealed the statute but accompanied its action with a strong denunciation of interest-taking of any kind. There the matter rested until 1571 when the Act was revived in modified form: in addition to the earlier provisions it was specifically recited that although a lender might, without offence, take up to 10 per cent he could not enforce his claim to interest at law. The stigma and penalties of criminality were thus removed from a calculatedly moderate rate of interest without the law conferring any positive sanction on usury. In practice this statute seems to have inaugurated open and widespread lending at straightforward interest. Many borrowers were probably unaware of their legal freedom to default on interest payments – and lenders were hardly at pains to enlighten them – while regular borrowers who did know of their rights hesitated to take advantage of them for fear of being denied further accommodation.

Although interest contracts were finally made enforceable at law in 1623, neither this nor the 1571 measure are to be understood as prompted by a tenderness for lenders. They were enacted by Parliaments in which the borrowing classes, chiefly the landowning class, were heavily preponderant. These legislators were concerned to regularise the exigencies imposed by the facts of economic life in the hope that by drawing a sharp distinction between legal and illegal interest transactions, they would universalise moderate interest rates in the place of the effective 20 per cent and more which had commonly prevailed. If by the closing years of this period the theological content of the debate had vanished everywhere but from the pulpit, the concern that personal misfortune should not be the prey of the usurer was still very much alive. For another two centuries and more public policy was concerned to keep interest rates as low as possible without driving the business underground again. The 1623 measure reduced the legal maximum to 8 per cent. A further statute of 1660 lowered it to 6 per cent and, finally, one of 1715 brought it down to 5 per cent.

The element of protectiveness which even the halting reform of the usury law manifests is unadulteratedly plain in virtually all the other economic legislation of the period: in the banning of the gig mill and Dutch loom;[1] in an Act of as late as 1483 forbidding the use of fulling-mills; in the many interventions both by corporation and state to preserve craft demarcations; in repeated legislation against dealers in various materials who were conceived to be depriving the craftsman of part of his rightful gain; in occasional prohibitions on imported

[1] See p. 124.

goods which could be supplied by Englishmen; in the charters of incorporation granted by James I and Charles I to certain London crafts whose guilds had fallen under mercantile dominance; and in the anti-enclosure legislation.[1]

The Statute of Artificers (or Apprentices) of 1563 is the fullest single exposition of this essential conservatism, although most plainly evidencing its repressive aspects. The Statute, as much a synthesis of old regulations as an enactment of new ones, aimed to subject every man and unmarried woman between the ages of twelve and sixty without independent means to a meticulous national code of industrial discipline, modelled on what was conceived of as the natural economic order unhappily disrupted in recent times. All were to be bred up in a particular vocation – agriculture for most – serving a seven years' apprenticeship, and bound, up to the age of thirty, to take employment in that occupation on yearly engagements. Should employment for those trained in a craft or trade not be available they were to work as agricultural labourers, as were all without any other current occupation; while at harvest time the local magistrates could recruit everybody in or out of employment for work in the fields. Wages for all occupations were to be fixed annually by the magistrates[2] and hours of work were prescribed by the statute to be from 5 a.m. to 7 p.m. or 8 p.m. in the summer and from dawn to dusk in the winter. On completion of a yearly engagement no one was to quit the town or rural parish in which he had been employed without an official certificate that he had finished his term and that further employment was not available. This was the meat of the Statute. Among its other provisions those worth noting are: the requirement that no master was to take on more than two apprentices without employing a journeyman for each extra apprentice – designed to check the practice of using apprentices as cheap labour at the expense of employment opportunities for qualified journeymen – the only clause to attempt to provide such opportunities; and the restriction of apprenticeships in certain occupations to those of parents with a specified minimum income – in the case of all but one of these occupations because they carried a social standing which it was felt should not be available to any Tom, Dick or Harry; the exception was

---

[1] Treated separately on pp. 185 ff.

[2] The Statute only imposed a penalty for giving or taking wages in excess of the official rate – probably to be understood not as a deliberate favouring of employer over employee but as reflecting contemporary concern with inflation. Certainly in subsequent practice the official rates were considered as legal minima.

rural weaving, a far from honorific occupation, with the evident object of severely limiting the numbers of country weavers.

This last rather curious provision affords a revealing clue to a specifically topical object of the Statute, and indeed, it has been suggested, to the official motives behind its enactment as a whole. It is to be associated with the Weavers' Act of 1555, which confined rural weavers to the ownership of one loom and rural clothiers to the ownership of two. Both Acts belong to the aftermath of the sharp falling away of cloth exports from the high peak of 1551 and both might be seen as responses to the consequent high unemployment amongst the numerous clothworkers drawn into the industry by the boom of the 1540s. Certainly it is plain that it was official policy over these particular years to reduce the scale of rural cloth making. Was this essentially a concern to guard against a repetition of the overproduction crisis of 1551? If so, why the exemption of towns from the containment policy? Was it out of regard for the ancient liberties and privileges of urban communities? Or was the curbing of rural industry undertaken primarily in acknowledgement of a prescriptive claim of the urban workers to be secured against the threat to their livelihood posed by rural competition – competition which, beyond the scope of guild control, produced inferior cloth such as current contentions held to be among the principal causes of the decline in overseas sales?

The differences in interpretation expressed by these questions are really only ones of emphasis – between saying that these Acts of 1555 and 1563 were intended to cure current ills by re-enforcing an older and supposedly stabler order of things, and saying that the anxiety to re-establish the ancient ideal was sharpened by topical circumstances. Looked at either way, it is clear that official opinion was unhappy about the great expansion of the cloth industry. The enlargement of cloth exports certainly answered to the objects of commercial policy. But it was currently felt that the price in terms of economic and social disruption was not worth paying. The Statute of Artificers manifests the central economic preoccupation of public policy: subsistence. Tillage was and should be the dominant economic activity of the community. All other activities were subsidiary and admissible only to the extent that they did not interfere with this primary occupation. This was at one and the same time a recognition of a simple truth – the necessity, overriding all others, that the population be fed – and a social blueprint: the land and the subsistence needs it catered for were fixed and constant as must be the nature of a landbound society and as should be the nature of society. Basic economic realities, then, underpinned a scheme of proper social order. The belief that social and economic balance were threatened by undue industrial development explains the Statute's insistence on agricultural employment. And the most disquieting industrial development was cloth manufacture, not only because it directly weaned people from the land, but also because of the encouragement it afforded to pasture farming at the expense of arable. The Statute has a place among the anti-enclosure legislation of the period: and in its concern to pin people down in the one location, it has also a place along with the legislation on poverty and vagabondage, swelling in quantity and coverage from about the 1540s and culminating in the great codification measure of 1601.

No other single piece of legislation of the period, or perhaps of any period, incorporated such an omnibus of aims, and it hardly needs saying that at no time was it enforced in full. The history of the Statute in operation, up to and beyond 1640, can be conveniently summarised here. The direction of labour for which it provided was never generally undertaken, although up to about the end of the seventeenth century, errant individuals who came under the notice of the magistrates might be put to work as the Statute required, and loafers might be rounded up for harvest work. The Statute's assumption that there would be employment in the vicinity was hopelessly unrealistic and nothing short of a national system of labour exchanges and public work projects could have realised the aim of keeping everybody in regular employment. The particular object of confining the under-thirties to a single occupation was similarly impractical, though both this provision and the requirement of a seven-year apprenticeship were often invoked by skilled workers to exclude others from their craft right up to the formal repeal of the Statute in 1813. Whether or not an apprenticeship was served depended at all times not on the dictates of the law but on the craft itself: the strength of the guild (or the working element in it) or some successor organisation and the degree of training really needed. As early as the beginning of the seventeenth century the courts confronted with particular cases were interpreting the statute so as to exclude from it occupations where no technical skill was required, and by the end of the century were seizing every pretext to limit the applicability of the apprenticeship clauses in consonance with the 'free trade' principles by then paramount amongst lawyers.

Wage regulation by the justices was probably the most generally observed section of the Statute. With a history running back to the

Statute of Labourers (1349) this was an established practice, though there had doubtless been much laxity in the past and specific re-enactment in 1563 accompanied by chivying from the Privy Council very probably stimulated magisterial activity. Wage-fixing was never comprehensive, numerous minor occupations were always outside its scope and in a city like London with its multifarious different crafts it would have been a practical impossibility. But in the countryside where the bulk of the populace were employed in one or two unskilled or merely semiskilled occupations wages for these were set annually virtually everywhere until the closing years of the seventeenth century and the practice was not entirely extinct in the middle years of the eighteenth. Of course it is one thing to proclaim a wages schedule and another thing to ensure that it is maintained. On occasions it was just an annual ritual, the official rates unchanged year after year and bearing only a very approximate relationship to those actually paid. But more commonly official and actual wages were closely linked, though it is probable that the practical function of the official rate was to give a formal sanction to existing actual rates and to prevent the exploitation of special circumstances to force sharp changes up or down – amidst inflation up to 1640 or so official weight was much more usually thrown against upward than downward movements but with general price stability in the latter half of the seventeenth century magistrates seem to have become more concerned with using their powers to ensure a living wage and in so doing increasingly fell foul of the growing apprehension that English goods were internationally uncompetitive because of high wage costs.

Of the other elements of the Statute, that requiring certification before quitting town or parish seems to have been quite widely enforced – at least to the extent that forged certificates were the subject of a special Act of 1572 – and eventually merged with the certification required for somewhat different purposes by the Act of Settlement (1662).[1] The attempt to curb rural clothmaking was a total failure; indeed it does not appear that any serious effort was ever made to implement either the Weavers Act or the relevant clause of the Statute of Artificers. More generally, the principle of maintaining a certain balance between different sectors of the economy did not outlast the sixteenth century. Indeed the endeavour embodied in the Statute to mould the entire economy to a desired shape and proportion was never

---

[1] Concerned with preventing the indigent becoming a charge on a parish other than that in which they were normally resident.

again contemplated, let alone attempted. At least subconsciously states-men accepted that there were some limits to the efficacy of legislation and turned from grand designs to patching up the system which events had contrived.

An extensive cloth industry, misgivings as to its desirability put aside, yielding the bulk of England's exports and providing employment for thousands, was the object of special attention. Hardly a session of Parliament passed without fresh legislation aimed at preserving the quality or holding down the price of English cloth, or at impeding foreign competitors. Profuse regulations touching methods of process-ing nominally governed manufacturing techniques. Uncompetitive prices were commonly attributed to unduly high wool costs which were blamed on the multiplicity of wool dealers. Public opinion was long in coming to recognise the middleman, in any trade, as discharging a useful economic function. Right through this period he was conceived of as an intrusion between supplier and user, appropriating an unwar-rantable profit. Following earlier legislation of a more limited kind an Act of 1552 confined wool dealing to clothiers and Staplers. After a history of erratically variable enforcement it was repealed in 1624, not in acknowledgement of the role of the middleman but in response to the clamour of wool growers distressed by the fall in wool prices which had set in in 1620. These were also years of difficulties for cloth export-ers who found the principal cause of their troubles in the growth of cloth industries on the Continent which, it was coming to be generally believed, would be frustrated if they were denied supplies of English wool. A Parliamentary Bill of 1604 had already sought to prohibit wool exports and a royal proclamation of 1614 in association with the Cock-ayne project had temporarily imposed such a ban. A further procla-mation of 1622 inaugurated the prohibition which lasted until 1825 although it was not until 1662 that it assumed permanent form as an Act of Parliament. For good measure the proclamation also covered exports of fuller's earth and wood ashes (for wool-scouring) although England possessed no advantage in point either of abundance of or quality in these items. Indeed it is doubtful if English wool by then any longer enjoyed its former pre-eminence and if deprivation was any real handicap to continental manufacturers; we have already seen that English makers of the finest cloth were themselves turning to Spanish wool.

While between the mid-sixteenth century and the early seventeenth official policy swung from attempting to limit the scale of cloth manufacture to affording it 'pet industry' treatment, concern with the periodic phases of unemployment inevitable in an industry catering so much for volatile foreign markets did not abate. Stuart statesmen found no long-term substitute for the discarded Tudor containment policy. At times of depressed demand merchants were enjoined to keep up purchases of cloth or clothiers were urged to continue to provide work. As short-term measures such expedients had some success but clearly were powerless to relieve protracted difficulties.

This kind of appeal to a sense of public duty in the fact of social distress exemplifies the persistence of 'medieval' values into an age which was experiencing essentially 'modern' problems. The concept of a society whose principle of organisation was a moral one had yet to be supplanted by that of a society held together by a balance of self-interests. The elements of society were still apprehended as having fixed organic functions, not yet as being mobile factors of production. But while society was conceived of as an organic whole in which every member had his proper part it was a steeply hierarchic whole. No other period in English history manifests such a keen sense of social divisions, with its six formalised categories: noblemen, esquires, gentlemen, yeomen, husbandmen and labourers; divisions whose base was essentially economic – in open principle in the case of the last three, the criterion being solely the amount of land held,[1] and effectively so in the case of the higher classes since, at least by the early seventeenth century, the acquisition of sufficient property could almost automatically secure admission to honours while the application of primogeniture both to property and dignity generally ensured the preservation of the connection between the two. The scale only referred properly to those whose income came from the land and was directly related to the amount of land held; it could not be transferred exactly to the more variegated industrial and mercantile classes whose income bore no necessary relationship to real property holding but customary attitudes defined the status of members of these classes by equating them with their landed equivalents in financial terms.

Contemporary sensibilities as to pure rank drew the sharpest line between gentlemen and yeomen (the latter worked with their own hands, the former did not) but under other important aspects the major cleavage ran between the yeoman and the husbandman (whose industrial equivalent was roughly the craftsman without employees). This

[1] In the strictest sense a man had to be a freeholder to qualify for the designation yeoman but it was commonly used to describe any substantial farmer.

was the great economic divide, the recognition of which explicitly or implicitly underlay much of sociopolitical attitudes and theories until the triumph of democracy in the nineteenth century. It was a fundamental distinction between those who produced a surplus and those who did not. Long before any thorough attempt was made to underpin it with a reasoned economic analysis it was apprehended as distinguishing those who made a positive contribution to national wealth, prosperity and strength, from those who merely existed. The one had a claim to be assisted and promoted in their economic pursuits, the other had only the lesser claim to have the means of existence safeguarded to them in their accustomed employments; and that minimum once assured their part in the social order was a strictly subservient one – 'hewers of wood and drawers of water' – any efforts of whom as a class to better their lot could only meet with repression. (Nothing, of course, in public policy precluded an individual from passing from one class to another; then as more recently snobbery and adulation of the self-made man would contend in disclaiming and eulogising such a transition.)

The safeguards which the state sought to extend to the proletariat were the protection of livelihoods, the provision of an adequate money wage and the preservation of the purchasing power of that wage. Sporadic measures to secure the first have already been mentioned and their most pronounced feature is their helplessness in the face of major economic change. Wage regulation too has already been noted. But the threat to living standards through much of this period came not directly from falling wages but from rising prices. Ironically the only means contemporaries could devise to halt sustained inflation was to try to hold down wages. Starting from the relatively high level which they had reached in the fifteenth century wages could absorb cuts in purchasing power without driving the wage-earner below bedrock subsistence level. But the lower real wages fell the more vulnerable the wage-earner became to sudden rises in prices – above all to rises in the price of bread, the basic foodstuff. The ancient assizes of bread appear to have collapsed under the stress of inflation and following casual interventions in earlier years the government attempted to take the matter in hand in regular fashion from 1587, a year of poor harvest. In that year and, throughout this period, in subsequent years of particular shortage and high prices, the Privy Council issued an elaborate set of instructions to magistrates, the 'Book of Orders', requiring them, in summary, to ensure that all grain stocks were made available on the local markets at prices which wage-earners could afford. The efficacy of such a system clearly depended on the zeal and energy of the magistrates on a national scale and, paradoxically, their indifference to high prices in one area could have had the effect of drawing in supplies to that area from another where the magistrates were more strenuous in curbing prices. The evidence is that by and large the magistrates did apply themselves vigorously to their task but it is clearly impossible to attempt any estimate of the real benefit arising from their activity.

Underlying these administrative responses in bad years were the old common law prohibitions on forestalling, engrossing and regrating. In normal times these lay unenforced, recognised as obstructions to the flow of supplies, but occasional prosecutions occurred in support of magisterial activity at times of shortage. Much the same applies to legislation of the period forbidding or limiting the export of grain – hardly implemented in good years, energetic attempts to operate it were undertaken in bad years. But slackly or tightly enforced the mere existence of such legislation indicates the bias of public policy: profitable marketing opportunities for farmers were of secondary importance to the task of feeding the population. This was the paramount economic function of society and on the quantity of grain produced depended above all the wellbeing of the mass of the populace.

Grain and livestock

Throughout this period English land was called on to feed a population which attained unprecedented size as well as to supply the basic raw material for a greatly enlarged cloth industry. The major theoretical implications of population pressure and rising food prices have already been considered in general terms. Sheep-farming beyond a certain point can be considered simply as aggravating this situation: sheep competing with humans for the produce of the soil. This, indeed, along with its lower requirements of labour were the features of pasture farming which most keenly engaged contemporary attention. But to a considerable extent arable and pasture farming were not mutually exclusive. There was still much little used moor, mountain and hillside, woodland, floodland, and coastal saltmarsh which could not be ploughed and therefore, it if was to be of any value at all, could only be grazed by animals. Further, given the right balance, the two forms of farming were complementary. Animal manure enriched the soil and made for higher crop yields. Land had to be fallowed and might as well carry stock while it was otherwise idle. On certain soils a higher output might actually be obtained by reducing the amount of arable and manuring it heavily with the dung from the larger number of animals which could then be kept – or, a variant of the same theme, by putting more animals on the existing grazing land instead of adding to the arable. An extension of that approach was ley farming, incorporating the recognition that some kinds of land would benefit from more prolonged resting than the customery fallowing practice allowed. A ley was a field given over to grass for anything up to twenty years, during which it was used some of the time as pasture and some of the time as meadow, increasing supplies of winter fodder, after which it reverted to arable in reinvigorated condition.

Flexible farming like this could be undertaken most readily on enclosed land, but open fields did not necessarily preclude it. Apart from occasional instances of an entire community agreeing on a ley period for part of the arable, animals could be grazed on ley strips in the midst of crops if they were tethered or if the strips were bounded with hurdles (neither very satisfactory compared with free range grazing). There is evidence of ley farming from the early fifteenth century, but it is within this later period that it first emerges as a relatively widespread practice, though in open-field communities it would have remained exceptional for as long as they survived. Of course if the ley period were long enough no quantity of manure and no benefit from resting would make up for the crops lost during that period. In such a case a conversion from arable to pasture would effectively have occurred even though crops were still grown on the land from time to time. But, while recognising that 'ley farming' might often have been just a discreet masking of reprobated conversion it must be stressed that more animals did not necessarily mean less grain, and up to a point could mean more grain.

The problem of estimating the impact of extended pasture farming on food supplies becomes even more complicated when account is taken of the fact that the wool growers were very far from being the only graziers. After grain wool would almost certainly have been the most important single commodity produced on English land, but it is probable that wool was exceeded in importance by the aggregate of meat products: mutton, beef and pork, not to mention pigeon, poultry and rabbit. It is clear that by the second half of the sixteenth century meat raising was the specialist activity of many commercial farmers. Of the earlier history of this development we are largely ignorant:

whether gradually here and there a shift in emphasis took place from the originally central business of arable farming to the originally ancillary one of livestock farming, or whether it was a more abrupt change, occurring mostly around the middle of the sixteenth century. It would be a plausible conjecture that when the froth went off the wool market after 1551 growers often sought compensation in mutton, killing more frequently than previously, or supplemented reduced sheep flocks with cattle.

What we are speaking of now is distinguishable from the age-old grazing of animals in association with arable farming, not necessarily in that it involved a conversion from arable to pasture but in its deliberate market orientation and its conscious concern to get as much edible weight as possible on to animals. This last is a matter of breeding and feeding. Breeding in the full sense of establishing a particular strain was little practised if at all as it was generally believed that environment not heredity was the basic determinant of physical characteristics. But there is every reason to suppose that the best rams, bulls and boars were selected for building up herds. However it would be true that in the sixteenth and seventeenth centuries the best animal was the best fed rather than the best bred, and in particular the animal which had been best fed in the few months immediately before it went to the butcher. Rough grazing in summer and hay in winter would suffice in early life but the big profits were made from the richer feed supplied as the beast neared its end. This meant good natural grassland, supplemented by extra artificial feeding. Often this involved migration: animals reared in indifferent country were moved to richer pasture lands for fattening. And such movements might be over considerable distances. From throughout the Highland Zone and even from Ireland store animals were driven south and east to the lusher lowlands.

Many of the specialist fattening centres lay in fen and estuarine land, bearing rich grass crops, but unsuitable for ploughing. But the damp clays of the Midlands also offered good grass and if the plough remained paramount here the press of animals on ancient pasture was nearly everywhere increasing throughout this period. More wool was the principal object of this enlargement of the animal population but meat for the market was no mean object. This meant not only or even necessarily ley farming (where it did not mean outright conversion) for the sake of the better grass that the ploughland would yield,[1] but also the

---

[1] Better inasmuch as the best land would originally have been selected for cultivation. Ploughing in itself would not make for better grass although if as arable the land had been

cultivation of arable crops for animal fodder instead of human food-stuffs. Much of what was raised to feed to animals both in the Midlands and elsewhere was indeed capable of being used for human consumption so that a planned switch to animal fodder was usually not irrevoc-able – if the bread-grain harvest was poor, high prices or popular or magisterial pressure might induce the grazier to divert feed from his beasts to the grain market; and in some cases such crops would simply be grown for cash, the balance of supply and demand in the open market determining their ultimate destination.

Of such multipurpose crops barley was the most extensively culti-vated – in fact the most extensively cultivated of all crops. Though pig and poultry keepers made much use of it, in general it was grown not purposefully for the trough but primarily for ale or beer and second-arily for bread or some form of cake or biscuit. With oats the bias was reversed. Over much of the north they were the basis of the human diet, but elsewhere people would only eat oaten foods as a last resort in times of grave shortage and the oat crop normally went entirely to animals of all kinds. The same was even more true of peas and beans. Nowhere were they a major item in the human diet, but they were extensively cultivated for feeding to pigs, sheep, pigeons and horses. Of fodder crops grown under the plough in any quantity vetch was the only one which could not be converted to human use. In the south of England it was fed to cattle either in the trough or on the ground, after which it was ploughed in as a green manure. In the closing years of the sixteenth century turnips and carrots make their first signal appearance, initially in market gardens close to London, grown as a table vegetable, but quickly, though not apparently widely, adopted as animal feed. The quantities were small and they were probably grown in separate gardens tilled with the spade; a proper appreciation of their usefulness as a major arable crop does not seem to have been achieved until later in the seventeenth century.

Thus the raiser of fat stock might continue to work within the tradi-tional pattern of balance between grazing and ploughland and his transition from primarily a producer of bread grain to primarily a producer of meat might be almost imperceptible, and capable of reversal within a single year.

To a very modest extent pressure on ploughland was relieved by advances in grassland management in the later years of this period.

intensively manured it would for a while prove superior grassland to existing pasture of the same innate quality.

From the early seventeenth century – and before that for all we know – it was appreciated in some quarters that permanent grassland, whether pasture or meadow, could be improved by the deliberate growing of selected 'artificial' grasses, clover most notably among several such; but there is no clear evidence before the 1650s of the use of artificial grasses for leys or as part of the regular crop rotation on the arable. Also from the early seventeenth-century date artificial water meadows, an extension of the age-old appreciation of the lush grass to be had on ground subject to winter flooding. By means of a dam and timberlined channels higher ground was put under water through the winter with the same beneficial results – indeed with superior results because after the water had been drained off in mid-March the tall grass could be grazed down by sheep and the land briefly flooded again for hay; the hay mown the process could if desired be repeated twice more before the end of September. The construction of the dam and channels was an expensive business and within this period there are only a few instances of 'floated' meadows, in Wiltshire and Herefordshire where the technique was apparently originated by Rowland Vaughan, who published his methods in 1610. It is interesting to note that some of these instances are of whole communities undertaking and financing the operation in concert, though most, as would be expected, relate to enclosed land.

Easily the biggest contribution to grass yield was the reclamation of a great tract of the East Anglian Fens. Of approximately 700,000 acres of marsh, the recovery of nearly 400,000 was put in hand from 1607, the great bulk of the work, planned by the Dutch engineer Cornelius Vermuyden, being executed between 1634 and 1652. The heavy costs were borne by a mixed group of local landowners, courtiers, London financiers and the Crown. The undertaking was not a total and enduring success: the technical problems of preventing gradual reflooding were scantily appreciated and a certain amount of land was subsequently lost again, but at least in the immediate aftermath the gain was considerable. It was supplemented by that of other reclamation projects, though these were few in number and of modest extent.

It would seem that, all in all, the increased emphasis on meat was not a serious menace to grain supplies. Doubtless in numerous places it went beyond the point where manure and resting compensated for the lesser amount of land under crops, but of the animals destined for the market many, perhaps most, were reared in parts of the Highland Zone where arable farming was difficult or impossible and were fattened on land which was either too heavily wooded or too wet for ploughing. And in areas suitable for the cultivation of arable crops meat production commonly did not lose all touch with the original business of supplying bread stuffs; between its use of multipurpose crops and ley farming it was flexible enough to be able to respond, at least partially, both to the short-term needs posed by a bad bread-grain harvest and to a longer-term deficiency occasioned by the devotion of too much land to grass. Of course it would only respond to a stimulus; and though both in the short and the longer terms official coercion played a part the most potent stimulus was commercial. Those farming for the market who had a real option as to the use to which they put their land produced what the market required – whatever there was the greatest effective demand for. The shift towards meat reflects changes in the dietary habits of the comfortably off and a swelling of the ranks of this class, whose mode of life at all levels from the prosperous yeoman up to the resplendent duke took on a new sumptuousness through the sixteenth century, especially the second half. If grain production failed to keep pace fully with population increase it was principally because the gross income of those for whom bread was the staple foodstuff likewise failed to keep pace.

The available price data would be consistent with the interpretation that a marked extension of meat-eating was initially prompted by the abundance of livestock in the early 1550s when wool growers found themselves with surplus flocks or grassland;[1] that by the early 1580s meat raising responding to this development in taste had overreached itself and that from the 1590s there was something of a swing back to bread-grains until in the late 1610s a rough equilibrium was achieved which was maintained through the rest of the period. This equilibrium position was better calculated to provide the prosperous minority with a lavish and varied table than to fill the stomachs of the multitude, but if many of the latter were often hungry they did not, except in the most isolated communities at times of especially bad harvest, actually perish from want of nourishment – or, rather, when some of the penniless did so perish it was not because bread was unavailable but because they had somehow slipped through the net of private charity and public relief

---

[1] It is difficult to say how much weight should be attached to England's conversion to Protestantism in explaining the rise in meat consumption. The medieval Church had prescribed some 140 days in the year on which meat was not to be taken – a prohibition which seems to have been generally observed. The Church of England continued to recommend abstinence as a worthy practice and under Elizabeth a 'political Lent' was enjoined in order to sustain fishing, a militarily valuable nursery of seamen.

which should have sustained them. In a phrase, over the country as a whole there was probably no year in which there was not enough bread to go round, although poor communications or lack of individual means might cause local or personal privation to the point of starvation. By no means is this to say that in bad years life was not bitterly harsh for the mass of the populace. In such years there was enough bread for all only if it was rationed and, official attempts to the contrary notwithstanding, the effective instrument of rationing was price. Within this period as a whole the harvests of the years 1481–82, 1502, 1520–21, 1527–29, 1531–32, 1535, 1545, 1549–51, 1555–56, 1562, 1573, 1585–1586, 1594–97, 1608, 1612–13, 1621–22, 1630 and 1637 could be said to have been such that the average wage earner with a family to support can have had little left over after buying bread.

The bad years enumerated above amount to thirty-two in all, an average of about one in five over the whole period, but it can be seen that they are not evenly distributed: one in ten over the first fifty years; one in three and a half over the next seventy-five; and one in six over the last forty. And these three periods might be summarily categorised as: pre-livestock intensification; rapid development of livestock farming, first for wool and then for meat; and readjustment to overdevelopment of livestock. Very tentatively then, since both the identification of bad years and the chronology of livestock farming rest on inadequate data and to the considerable extent that both are founded on the same set of price data tend necessarily to establish a relationship, we might say that the differences in the frequency of seriously defective harvests do reflect the varying extent of the encroachment of animals on breadgrain.[1]

[1] The whole of the above two paragraphs should be considered as conjectural. Little as yet is known about conditions of life for the mass of the English populace in this period and more research may necessitate a revision of the general picture outlined here. It may also be that a more detailed knowledge of the course of climatic variations over the period would yield a purely meteorological explanation of the incidence of bad harvests, though the length of the periods dealt with above would seem to be sufficient to eliminate discrepancies due to ordinary random weather changes. It should further be pointed out that the concept of 'enough' food is not a simple objective one. Between the amount necessary to sustain full health and vigour and the bare amount necessary to prevent a person dying purely of lack of nourishment there is an enormous range, within which a large proportion, perhaps the majority, of the English populace must have lived perpetually, as indeed does the greater part of the world today. Between the top and bottom of this range there is a steadily increasing likelihood of dying of whatever diseases are prevalent, the degree of likelihood determined not only by food intake over a period of particular shortage such as that between successive harvests, but also by normal long-run intake. This without taking any account of variations in individual needs and the importance of a balanced diet and of vitamins and mineral elements.

Conversion, engrossment and tenures

Meat was at least food, and to some extent the more meat that the better-off ate the less bread they ate and to that extent bread was released for consumption by those who could afford little else. (But the crucial fact must not be forgotten that much more land is needed to raise a given quantity of meat than to raise the nutritive equivalent in bread.) The same cannot be said of wool. When grain was lost because a wool grower had invaded the arable, the only food compensation was the tough mutton of worn-out sheep and, occasionally, better meat from animals which had met a premature death. And certainly, at least up to the middle of the sixteenth century, wool was a graver threat to grain supplies than meat. As cloth exports bounded upwards from 1475 so did the need for more grazing land. Waste, understocked pasture, and short leys permitted of much expansion without cutting into grain output. But growers often coveted the arable as rich permanent pasture and meadow with the prospect of securing three and four pound fleeces at a clip instead of the one or two pounds they were accustomed to get.[1] And there were areas where no more pasture land, good or bad, was to be had; where the wilderness had vanished and every acre of usable land was already doing maximum service; where – bar technical advance – more of any one thing could only be produced at the cost of something else. This was the nub of the agrarian problem that so passionately occupied the attention of contemporaries and which constitutes the centrepiece of most historical accounts of sixteenth-century agriculture. It is usually called the 'Enclosure movement'. It might more usefully be styled 'What happened when the frontier started to vanish'. Because over much of the most densely populated part of rural England, the Midlands, this was what occurred. Sooner or later it happens everywhere and when it does it could warrantably be regarded as a major watershed in the history of any society. It happened earlier than it need have done in these parts of England because of the great acceleration in the demand for wool and meat; and wool, since that time itself, has been accorded a unique prominence as the agent of the event. 'Sheep trample down men', a contemporary's comment, has become a kind of epitaph. But this terse judgment, though it does express a real historical truth, can be gravely misleading if left unamplified.

[1] But in so doing forfeited the short silky wool which was the basis of the traditional broadcloth industry. Wool from the heavier fleeces was generally only suitable for worsteds.

Conversion was the tip of the iceberg. Arable became pasture because there was no other way of obtaining additional pasture; and this happened at a time when the arable itself was in need of extension. Conversion could equally well have been the other way round: from pasture to arable. Relative prices were the determinant and the defective purchasing power of the bread-eating populace meant that the price ratio favoured animals, especially in the central Midlands where the absence of navigable water made grain freightage relatively expensive, whereas animals could be moved out on the hoof. This bias towards animals in the Midlands was often no more than a marginal event, but here the margin no longer consisted of spare land. A thousand extra sheep in say Leicestershire might mean a local revolution when 10,000 more in say Herefordshire could be quietly absorbed.

Although there was probably no county in England in which there were not instances of conversion for the sake of richer grassland the situation in the Midlands was a distinctive one: it was here, and only here, that it constituted a major social problem. The area in question can be defined more precisely as consisting of northern and western Lincolnshire, Leicestershire, southern Warwickshire, Northampton-shire, Bedfordshire and northern Buckinghamshire; to these there might be added substantial parts of Nottinghamshire, Hutingdonshire, Norfolk, southern Buckinghamshire, Berkshire and Oxfordshire. It was to the redressment of the situation in this region that were designed Acts of Parliament of 1489, 1515, 1533, 1536, 1549, 1552, 1556, 1563, 1597; and commisions to enforce them of 1517, 1548, 1565, 1607 and 1630. These are what in sum are styled the anti-enclosure measures – a convenient but unhappy designation. Convenient, because anti-conversion would not fully describe them – some of them were directed also against engrossment, and enclosure commonly accompanied either. Unhappy, because they were not directed against enclosure as such.

The observation has often been made that contemporaries did not distinguish clearly between enclosure for pasture and enclosure for arable or between harmful and beneficial enclosure. Certainly in the rhetoric of the day and sometimes even in the wording of statutes 'enclosure' is used very freely, but there is no reason to suppose that contemporaries were not clear in their own minds what they meant, and equally what they did not mean. There was a clear recognition that the consolidation and enclosure of open field strips was always desirable or at least harmless provided that the land remained arable, that the number of farms was not reduced and that equitable agreement was reached with those who lost stubble grazing rights; nor was there any hostility towards equitable partition of commons among users. The age was conservative in its public attitudes but not blindly and unreasoningly attached to existing institutions for their own sake nor so stupid as automatically to identify a hedge with public danger.

The 'anti-enclosure' measures were intended to secure two particular ends which we have already noted as principal objects of public policy: the protection of food supplies and the preservation of livelihoods. Conversion of arable land to sheep pasture was a particular menace to both: to food supplies for evident reasons already dwelt on; to livelihoods because land needed far fewer hands when grazed by animals than when planted with crops. Depopulation was the most vivid and most heart-wrenching consequence of extensive conversion; there are many instances of small communities of up to a hundred persons being eliminated entirely in this way and numerous others of village population heavily reduced. Quite apart from the appeal to social conscience and human pity evoked by such happenings, no Tudor or early Stuart statesman could in cold prudent policy remain oblivious to those thus deprived of means of support. A dynasty whose only real title to the throne in its earlier days was the sword, and whose religious policy, whatever it was, at any time after the 1530s was bound to be unpopular in some quarter or another, could not afford to let the ranks of the disaffected be swollen by the footloose victims of conversion. The momentarily dangerous northern rebellion of 1536 (the Pilgrimage of Grace) while primarily religious in motivation had a distinct element of agrarian discontent to it. The scattered risings of 1549 of which Kett's Rebellion in Norfolk was the most signal were also often fired by agrarian grievances. And the Midlands Revolt of 1607 was a peasant movement of classical type. No wonder then that the government brought to the prosecution of the anti-enclosure measures a vigour which was largely lacking in the implementation of other economic legislation.

Simple conversion was only one of the symptoms of the new pressures on land resources. Overstocking of the commons was a more frequent and widespread one. From a narrowly economic point of view this was certainly undesirable, but it had an even more disturbing social aspect when, as was often the case, it was a matter of the large grazier crowding out the small men. The landlord was frequently the oppressor here. Although the courts were increasingly taking cognisance of customary rights, the Statute of Merton was by no means a dead letter and lords might well usurp the commons under colour of law. Or it might be that there was not even any customary definition or limitation of commons rights, it not having been a practical issue in the past, so that there was no ready redress against a member of the community, or possibly even an outsider, who thronged the common pasture with his animals. The chief sufferer in these circumstances was very generally the labourer/cottager with little or no land of his own whose personal economy leant heavily on his having adequate grazing for an animal or two. He was also the victim when conversion resulted in unemployment and he probably sustained the greatest harm when the commons were enclosed, whether this was done by the landlord to create new farms or by agreement among the community so as to substitute individual holdings for shared grazing right, with the advantage to keen graziers of reducing the risk of infection of their own stock by the animals of others. The question of entitlement to compensation for lost pasture is a thorny one, but such rights as might be recognised were usually related to arable holding. The man who held no arable in the open fields, whatever effective grazing rights he had formerly enjoyed, was very likely to be ignored when the commons were enclosed.

Portentous of much more devastating social disruption was enclosure of the arable when this was a preliminary to conversion. Although strips did not preclude a shift from arable to pasture profitable grazing on any large scale was clearly impossible if the flock or herd had to be divided up amongst several separate pieces of land – if only because of the diseconomy of employing several herdsmen to tend numbers that one could manage if grazed together. Consolidation of strips was imperative; and as tethering or hurdling could not serve for large numbers of animals, so was a permanent hedge or fence. An enclosed pasture farm might be built up within open arable fields by a process of exchange and purchase of strips, culminating in agreed compensation to the other members of the community for their loss of stubble-grazing and for the grazier's withdrawal from participation in communal ploughing and other farming operations; and if the farm were not large only a minimal loss of employment opportunities might result. But the difficulties at each stage were such that a painless transition of this kind would be rare. And it would be rare for another telling reason: pasture farming, because of the labour economies it offers, is competitive only on a fairly large scale (or on a very small scale, when the owner is his own cheap labour force). It would perhaps be somewhere near the truth to say that under the conditions of this period, it would not be worth while converting from arable to pasture on less than a hundred acres and that the lowest unit costs would be achieved on pasture farms of several hundred acres. Farms of this size could hardly be built up piecemeal from arable strips. They had to be created by the landlord, repossessing himself of several holdings, consolidating and then enclosing them (or, of course, by enclosing the commonland or some extensive part of it). This was to perpetrate the other cardinal agrarian offence of the age: engrossment.

This sin could be committed otherwise than in association with enclosure for pasture. An engrossed farm might remain under the plough in which case it need not necessarily be enclosed: the consolidated block might lie in the open fields still subject to general stubble-grazing and communal farming discipline. Or engrossment might be a matter of throwing together several already enclosed small farms. Even so contemporary sentiments remained inflexibly hostile. There was now only one farm and one farmer where before there had been several. The vanished farmers might conceivably be the dead and heirless or rather more plausibly those who had sold out at market value. But the bulk were men whose tenancies had been unilaterally terminated or who had been refused entry to holdings to which they regarded themselves as the successors. Even when no specifiable individual had been harmed the fact remained that holdings which could have accommodated and sustained somebody had been extinguished. Very likely there was little fall in the numbers finding employment on the land if it remained arable – a former occupant would probably still be required as a labourer – and in the immediate aftermath of an enclosure hedging and ditching might lead to an actual increase in the demand for labour. But although contemporary opinion was presumably aware of this it found engrossment none the less heinous, even when it had no further consequences. A holding of his own was still thought of as the normal, natural and socially desirable vocation of the countryman. Land was not just an economic resource to be used in the most productive manner, it was the solid indestructible base of homesteads and livings. Labouring would always be the lot of some, but a knowing and avoidable inflation of their numbers could only be repugnant and reprehensible to a society which cherished stability as a prime social value.

The ease with which landlords could create engrossed holdings was in inverse ratio to the security of tenure of occupants. Here was an issue on which law and custom met, wrangled and then mingled, so that gradually a new synthesis whose principles were common to lawyer, landlord and occupant can be said to have established itself. A synthesis which took from legal doctrine the concept of single outright owner- ship of land, extinguishing more primitive notions of divided rights or claims in land, and construed all modes of occupancy as a contractual cession by the owner of the use or enjoyment of the land under specified terms to a tenant. And into this scheme it fitted customary modes of occupancy which were not the subject of a formal contract. Already well before the opening of the period the copyhold grounded in ancient prescript had gained a solid footing in the courts of law. But it by no means followed that all those who held under customary modes of tenure and who conceived themselves to be rooted in their holdings were able to recruit the law on their behalf when threatened with eviction or deprivation of commons rights.

This is not the place to enter into an account of the tortuous and indeed obscure evolution of juristic attitudes towards those who held by customary tenure, but among the obstacles to be overcome before the protection of the courts could be successfully invoked were: proof that the plaintiff was in truth a copyholder and not merely a tenant-at- will (without an actual copy of the relevant entry in the manorial roll a claim to copyhold tenure would be difficult to establish and to many the demand for documentary evidence would come as a novel require- ment); proof that the holding was not on ex-demesne land if it were contended by the landlord that it was; proof that the customs of the particular manor afforded the sought after protection (the courts would undertake to do no more than enforce what had been the ancient practice in each individual manor); where a copyhold had been shown to exist, proof from a plaintiff heir that it was a copyhold of inheritance and not merely one for life, and even then an heir might be excluded by the requirement of an impossibly high admission fine unless it could be demonstrated that the fine was customarily regulated, which most commonly it was not. Overshadowing all this was ignor- ance of the possibilities of legal action or lack of the means to employ a lawyer and to enable both plaintiff and witnesses on his behalf to make the trip to London, where the case was very likely to conclude even if it did not start there. A whole community or a large group would strenuously contest an infringement of what they conceived to be their rights, but stray individuals, especially in the more remote parts of the country, might be crushed without exciting anything more formidable than a deep sense of grievance.

No general statement, then, can cover the position of customary tenants. According to the particular circumstances a landlord bent on engrossment might find them the easiest or the most difficult people to clear from the land. Of other occupants, those who were unambiguously tenants-at-will could of course be got rid of without difficulty. Legal ingenuity might find defects in leases enabling their holders to be dismissed prematurely; otherwise the holdings could be repossessed on expiry of the lease, though that might mean a long wait if leases ran up to ninety-nine years or three lives as not a few did, and the landlord might prefer to buy the unexpired portion of leases on land that blocked an intended engrossment, as he might do of course with secure copyholds or with freeholds. But if occupants on terminable tenancies recognised that the landlord was only doing what he had a full legal right to do, it does not follow that they were not often just as embittered as evicted customary tenants. For many of them the fact that their tenure was terminable must have signified no more than that their rent was subject to periodic revision or that a fine was periodically payable – loss of their holdings had not entered into their practical reckoning. Tenants-at-will and leaseholders were thickest on ex-demesne land and for the landlord termination or non-renewal of their tenancies might be a perfectly proper and fully defensible resumption of his own. Indeed in the early years of this period, when the land in some instances had been demesne within living memory, all parties concerned might consider resumption an unreprehensible proceeding – although feelings amongst the dispossessed must have been aroused if the land was then converted to pasture or let out again in larger farms.

The extent of landlord farming for the market in this period has not yet been investigated but it seems clear that there was something of a swingback to it – in some cases, of course, it had never been given up even through the worst of the fifteenth century and in others the interruption had been only a brief expedient. But there were perhaps more cases where it had been given up so long ago that its recommencement is really to be thought of as a new departure – a departure prompted most especially by the opportunities in sheep grazing. A landlord with superior rights in commons and a retrievable demesne, very possibly taken out of the open fields at some time in the past, was well placed to embark on this alluringly profitable venture. For those with other preoccupations, sheep-grazing had the further advantage of needing little close control or supervision and one hears less of landlord farming generally after the wool market slumped in mid-century, although it is plain that some continued to draw a substantial part of their income from farming. But at any time landlord appropriation of the commons and engrossment of holdings was probably more often with a view to creating farms for letting rather than for direct exploitation.

Even in the Midlands, however, where the temptations were greatest, the landlord who coveted his tenant's land was probably the exception rather than the rule. The much more common challenge to tenant security came from landlords who wanted only higher rents; who having beaten down a tenant's claim to copyhold tenure were content to leave him in possession at the increased rent that they were then free to require, or perhaps only to substitute a tenancy-at-will or a short lease leaving them future room for manoeuvre. The landlords of the time may have been an unusually rapacious body of men – they certainly were if a good deal of contemporary pulpit and pamphlet literature is to be credited. But there is no evidence of that in their patent anxiety to enlarge their rent rolls while inflation proceeded. As prices rose, the maintenance of customary rents would have reduced many of them to beggary. If their living standards were to be preserved they had to slacken the noose of custom. Uncertain entry fines could of course go a long way towards compensating for invariable rents and many of the instances of seemingly exorbitant fines must be understood as the procurement of no more than value for land on which an artificially low regular rent was being paid.[1] For a landlord who counted his tenants by the hundred this method of raising his income probably served well enough. But the smaller proprietor who could not depend on a fairly regular succession of deaths or expiries might be bankrupt before the opportunity of recouping himself from fines presented itself (the law of averages can only be relied on if the sample is sufficiently large).

The scanty evidence so far available suggests that over the period as a whole, landlord incomes rose no more rapidly than grain prices. Or put another way, that the increase in rents and fines about matched the increase in farming profits. But even accepting this as a broad truth –

---

[1] This is to view the matter in modern fashion, treating the increment in the money value of the land as legitimately belonging to the 'owner'. But contemporaries, even disinterested ones, would not necessarily view it in the same way. The universal use of the emotive term 'rackrent' for what we would consider as market price is revealing.

and the subject does require much more investigation – it would comprehend widely discrepant individual circumstances. With prices escalating so rapidly over the last hundred years of the period, with sharp changes occurring in the relative profitability of different kinds of farming, with greatly varying conditions of tenure, the average landlord can only be an unreal abstraction. A more useful general statement might indeed be that however landlord income rose landlord expenditure tended to rise faster, and that by the end of the period a sizeable fraction of the revenue from landed property was going to the moneylenders.

To return to the mass of the agrarian populace: in summary, legislation, to the not insignificant extent to which it was enforced, protected them against engrossment and the effects of conversion; the courts of law might protect those pleading customary rights against eviction, rent increases and loss of commons grazing. But this edifice of law was pitted with loop-holes. The government was ready to take direct action where a legal remedy did not exist or even where one did. *Droit administratif*, extinguished in England by the Great Rebellion, was a powerful instrument of state action in Tudor and early Stuart England, though even under Elizabeth the lawyers were inveighing against it. This was the principle that a man's liberty to do as he pleased was subject to curtailment not only by the law but by considerations of public policy which the law did not embrace and, further, that in the case of a seeming breach of law, the Crown need not await a judicial determination but could itself proceed directly to enforcement. Cases of eviction, appropriation of the commons, overcrowding of the commons by large graziers, rackrenting, etc. were assured of a sympathetic hearing in the royal council or, more commonly, in its subcommittees, the Court of Star Chamber and the Court of Requests. These state organs did not necessarily wait for plaintiffs to bring their suit before them but would act on their own initiative on report reaching them of local incidents of such a kind, the more especially if accompanied by disturbances of the peace. Where and when it took place this direct state intervention, brooking little of the evasion and delays that could be practised in the rule-bound courts of law, was extremely effective, and on occasions, doubtless, unjust. But it could not be much more than a matter of making an example of a haphazard selection of cases. The council had a hundred and one other questions of state to concern itself with. Its offshoots would have needed to be multiplied several times over to provide it with the elaborate bureaucracy necessary for comprehensive action in all the fields in which it aspired to act. And such a bureaucracy would have had to extend itself into the countryside, supplanting the magistrates on whom the council had largely to depend for information and sustained enforcement of its policy – magistrates who varied widely in point of assiduity and who might at times be the very offenders themselves.

One final observation may be made on public policy in the face of agrarian change. In so far as such change bore onerously on the peasantry, and to the extent to which they could have been relieved by simple fiat, the measures essayed by the state contain one conspicuous omission: no attempt was ever made to protect by statute rights of common and customary tenures, though the clear drift of both juridical and administrative attitudes was in this direction and, indeed, the Duke of Somerset, effective head of state as Lord Protector during the early part of the minority of Edward VI, had such a statute enacted in respect of his own tenants. Such a measure would not only have directly safeguarded many of those threatened with eviction or less of commons grazing, but by hindering engrossment would also have tended to check conversion. But perhaps even to pose the hypothesis is to be guilty of an anachronistic approach. For the age, property rights were defined and guaranteed by the Common Law on which even Tudor and Stuart absolutism, royal or parliamentary, could not trespass. It would, at least, have been in the eyes of contemporaries a radical step and impressed as they were with the gravity of agrarian dislocation many perhaps would not have considered the situation so serious as to warrant such an extreme measure.

So serious? How serious? The only strictly objective answer would be a mathematical one: how many holdings extinguished; how many deprived of commons grazing; how many unemployed as a result of conversion? And the data does not exist to reply to these questions with any degree of precision.[1] What we have is mostly a set of double impressions: the impressions of partially informed contemporaries put into words, usually with polemical intent, from which historians in turn have formed their impressions, supplemented by the hard knowledge of certain Midlands communities devastated by reorganisation of the land and the manifestly contrasting experience of other regions.

[1] The reports of the various Enclosure Commissions do contain statistical data and have in the past been drawn on by economic historians but the judgment of recent scholarship is that they are too fragmentary and their basis of compilation too uncertain for any useful conclusions to be founded on them.

The most pertinent available comment is perhaps the one already made: that it is seriously to misunderstand the nature of the agrarian situation through these difficult years if the encroachment of large scale sheep-farming or general livestock-farming on smaller scale arable farming is treated of in isolation; if the social distress of the period is attributed peculiarly to this development; or to consider that a determination, were it possible, of the extent of conversion would provide a measure of the deterioration in the conditions of life of the mass of the populace. Transcending the pressure of animals on land was the pressure of people on land, and this is to be apprehended in the last analysis not only as a problem of providing holdings and employment for the peasantry but even more fundamentally as a problem of feeding the nation at large.

Farming efficiency

To some extent the solutions to these two distinct problems may have been mutually exclusive: more holdings could be created by subdivision of existing ones but a more efficient use of land possibly required engrossment. Here we tread on very uncertain ground: uncertain as to the actual changes in size of holdings; uncertain as to the possible gains to be derived from engrossed arable farms. To consider the latter point first. We must be very wary of transferring simpliste notions about economies of scale derived from modern experience to sixteenth- and seventeenth-century farming. Only up to a very limited point could larger units have yielded economic advantages in respect of installations and equipment; and indeed the semicommunalism of traditional small-scale farming might plausibly be considered as securing such advantages as there were through a form of collectivisation which the larger farmer operating on his own could not surpass, or perhaps even equal. Likewise the economies to be obtained by matching the regular labour force more exactly to the size of farm would be slight or non-existent by comparison with the flexibility of labour achieved in communities where the labourer/smallholder was a significant element in the population; and the supervisory problems involved in the employment of a large labour force might positively tell against it. Pasture farming offered distinct economies of scale in the use of labour, and in that kind of mixed farming which made for optimum use of the arable the same quantity of foodstuffs could be produced with a smaller labour force as the size of the individual farm, up to a point, was increased.[1] But in all probability the advantage of the large arable farm, such as it may have been, from the national point of view, consisted not in intrinsic economies of scale but in the differences in mentality between the small farmer and the large one, and in the incidental fact that the small farm was apt to be an open field one while the large one was more probably enclosed.

It would be a gross caricature to represent the small farmers of England as dull, unimaginative, custom-bound men, content as long as their land yielded enough for their own subsistence needs; in contrast with the large farmers, lively minded, enterprising, well-informed, continually on the alert for new ways of improving their yield. It would be an equal distortion of the truth automatically to identify backwardness with open field farming and progressiveness with enclosed farming. But it would be a matter of caricaturing and distorting not one of basic falsehoods. Certainly, there were many small farmers keenly alive to commercial opportunities and to making the most of them, and there were large farmers who clung myopically to unrewarding routines. Certainly, strips were not an absolute block to progressive farming. Both *prima facie* grounds and actual scraps of hard facts from the period indicate this. Whole communities might act in concert to raise the level of efficiency. But the likelihood of securing a sufficient consensus of opinion and readiness was plainly small. More probable would be the assent of the community, in return for some form of compensation, to an individual withdrawal of strips from communal ploughing and stubble-grazing so that they could be employed in whatever way the occupant pleased. But there still remained the evident drawbacks of managing a farm dispersed in fragments over an extensive area, the difficulties posed if some of the strips were to be used as pasture in the midst of crops, the problem of keeping the strips clean if the rest of the community did not maintain a tight weeding discipline and, if the occupant had it in mind, the impossibility of draining his land on his own.

The enclosed farmer was relieved of these handicaps as well as from the inhibitions and initial impediments that were likely to surround a member of an open field community. That he had more favourable opportunities is very far from meaning that he necessarily exploited

[1] Since the question of farming efficiency is actually being discussed here in the context of the problem of feeding a growing population from an inelastic land supply, the references to labour economies are properly speaking irrelevant. What matters is getting more per unit of land, not per unit of labour; the latter, of course, is only of benefit to the farmer himself unless the labour released can be absorbed elsewhere.

them; but manifestly the average level of enclosed farming must have been superior to the average of open field farming. Similarly the man with more means was that much more likely to move about in the world, to have received a broader education, to be literate or to read more and to that extent to be more open to new ideas; to be more money conscious and thus more sensitive to opportunities of making more money; with larger money reserves to be readier to hazard an experiment. Again, of course, this is no matter of necessity, merely one of greater probability. And, in any event, a fundamental question has been begged. This hypothetical 'progressive' farmer, large or small, enclosed or open field, what was he likely to be doing that his backward counterparts were not doing? More particularly in this present context by what means, if at all, was he raising more breadstuffs?

Straight away one must say that he was almost certainly doing nothing that was in any strict sense new. There is no question of any important breakthrough in arable farming methods as such in this period. It would be almost entirely a matter of doing things which previously had only been done by a few, or had been confined to particular localities, or had been the practice on the best demesne farms before their break up in the fourteenth and fifteenth centuries and which had been half-forgotten since. Indeed it may well be the case that throughout the whole of this period, 1475 to 1640, the average level of commercial arable farming practices was below that attained in the thirteenth century. It is not until the last twenty years or so of the period that indications of improvement-conscious farming practices on arable land become at all abundant, and it would seem to be a rough truth that up to then the enterprising farmer looked to livestock as the way of getting more out of his land. It may be, in fact, that it was devotion of formerly arable to permanent pasture or leys and the use of the arable for growing animal fodder that initiated a questioning of traditional crop courses; that when men edged back to raising bread-grains they did not necessarily return to the ancient rotations but implemented the new lessons learned about the soil and its possibilities, or at least having broken with the past once were not afraid of doing so again. In any case a keener appreciation of the possibilities of different crop cycles is one of the characteristics of the best arable farming by the end of the period, as is a livelier awareness of the different varieties of particular crops and their appositeness under different conditions of soil and climate. One might conjecture too that having come to cherish manure on the arable, the better farmers were more alive to the fertilising qualities of other additives such as town refuse, marl, soot, lime and chalk. Other characteristics of the best arable farming in the later years are a greater attention to drainage on over-wet land and the use of ploughs and other tools of improved design and construction, doubtless to be associated in part with the contemporary advances in metallurgy.

To be classed under a different head really, but conveniently to be brought in here, is the introduction of completely new crops. Of these the most extensively cultivated were hops. Arriving from Holland, apparently sometime around 1520, they were by the end of the period widely grown throughout the south-east. The first English tobacco crop is dated from 1571. Although officialdom frowned on it, once the crown colony of Virginia started to export it in the 1620s there were many home growers, particularly in Gloucestershire. From the later years of the sixteenth century fields of coleseed became common in East Anglia, Dutch immigration probably being the responsible agency. Grown for its oil it had the particular advantage that after harvesting it could be ploughed back into the land as a green manure. More or less at the same time East Anglia also became the scene of extensive cultivation of the dyestuff, saffron. This along with weld (yellow) in Kent, and woad (blue) more generally, is of course to be associated with the upsurge in English dyed worsteds, but the growth of these dye crops, though greatly extended, was not entirely new. In any event, hops, tobacco, coleseed, and dyes, though their adoption may say something for the readiness of English farmers, or some of them, to take to novelties, were no contribution to relieving subsistence difficulties and, indeed, by trespassing on cornland positively aggravated them. Artificial grasses, turnips and carrots have already been mentioned as new fodder crops. Only one new crop was capable of an important contribution to the task of feeding the human population: the potato. Introduced from America about 1585 it never within this period, nor indeed for long after, graduated beyond the status of an exotic garden vegetable.

One beneficial technique theoretically available to the progressive farmer was omitted above: dibbing (i.e. placing seed at regular intervals in prepared holes in the ground instead of sowing broadcast) – omitted because it seems highly unlikely that it was ever employed other than by amateur experimenters. The laboriousness of the task would have precluded its being undertaken by hand and though the patent registers of the last two decades of the period record designs for mechanical seed drills, there is no evidence that a practicable one was ever constructed.

It is only mentioned here for the sake of making a point that applies to progressive methods generally. We know from the contemporary instructional works on farming practices that the potential advantages of dibbing were appreciated, and in general our knowledge of the best farming of the times is founded heavily on the recommendations contained in this literature. What we have no means of estimating with any pretensions to accuracy is the extent to which the best methods were actually employed in practice. We can be sure that the numbers who worked their land as fully as contemporary knowledge permitted were an insignificant minority. Between full enlightenment and, say, a hesitant trial of a different strain of oats there are numerous degrees of progressiveness, and we cannot say how the numbers falling somewhere within this range would have compared with 'your mouldy old leavened husbandmen who themselves and their forefathers have been accustomed to such a course of husbandry as they will practise and no other; whose resolution is so fixed no issue or events whatsoever shall change them'.[1]

Plainly there was no dramatic upswing in the productivity of English land: the majority of small farmers over most of the country farmed much as they always had done in the past and as they were to do for another century or two. However, economic history rarely deals in revolutions but rather discusses marginal increments. There may have been enough being done on English land over the concluding part of this period to make for an appreciable, though slight, alleviation of the problem of subsistence as the pressure of population on resources continued to mount. To the extent that farming methods did improve the printed word must be credited with some, albeit uncertain, part in it. The first known farming manual printed in English is John Fitzherbert's *Boke of Husbandrye* published in 1523. But the age of the literary agriculturalist really begins in the last decade of the sixteenth century, and from then on those with a taste for this kind of reading had an ample choice. The author was often a gentleman farmer who might report on trials and experiments carried out on his own land. Sometimes he was a professional scribbler plagiarising bits of other books, padding them out with stray scraps of information and gossip which came his way, all of which he might be quite incompetent to evaluate. Deprecatory hands have often been raised at the failure of the English farmer to heed the good counsel extended to him. What is less often com-

---

[1] Walter Blith, *The English Improver Improved* (1649).

mented on is the appalling amount of bad advice that was showered on him. The scepticism of the son of the soil in the face of book learning was grounded not only in the instinctive contempt of the practical man for the theorist but in a history of dangerous nonsense in print. Good and bad could only be distinguished by trial, and to hazard part of next season's crop on the outcome was understandably more than many small farmers, at any time, were prepared for. Inevitably until the days of research stations, the pioneer had to be the large farmer who could tolerate the consequences of failure, or even more aptly the gentleman farmer for whom it was only a hobby.

Probably the most useful kind of literature, when it was founded on detailed observation, was that which recounted or drew on the established practice of particular regions or of continental countries and thus helped to break down the semi-isolation of localities which might mean the persistence of inferior practices when for years something better had been available just across the county boundary. However, although works of all kinds on agriculture obviously commanded a reading public, it is impossible to know to what extent this consisted of practising farmers anxious to keep themselves well informed; of such the gentry may have constituted the bulk, and many buyers may well have been the merely curious in an age when the choice of entertaining reading matter was not wide.

If it is to the large enclosed farm that one would look especially for an implementation of the best advice, it would be helpful to know something in detail of the structure of English landholdings. As observed already such detail is lacking. We have seen that public sentiment was averse to engrossment on social grounds but the very frequency of denunciations, along with a certain amount of hard data, seems to indicate positively that the tendency, such as it was, was towards larger rather than smaller farms.[1] Even if we could say no more, this in itself would be a noteworthy fact when contrasted with the record of many other preponderantly agricultural societies at times of population pressure when an increasing subdivision has occurred. Many of the large units were of course pasture farms and it may be that side by side with this development went a reduction in the size of basically arable farms, but there is no general indication of this and one might toy with the speculative paradox that it was the very weight of

---

[1] A clear exception to this is to be found in those areas, notably in East Anglia and Yorkshire, where there was a good deal of freehold land and the practice of gavelling prevailed.

feeling against engrossment that checked subdivision; the resolution of the paradox hingeing on the consideration that landlords themselves tend to dislike numerous small tenants on account of the administrative difficulties and general untidiness they occasion; that fractionalisation is usually the work of a large intermediary lessee who at times of land hunger finds it more profitable to sublet than to farm himself, and thus, that the discountenancing of large lessees would prevent this development. Whatever the worth of this suggestion it can provide the occasion for commenting on the fact that the middleman, a ubiquitous figure in many agrarian societies, has always been largely unknown in England and that his absence is particularly remarkable at this time when circumstances would seem to have favoured his appearance: a landlord class especially anxious to enlarge its rent-roll in an age when the dissolution of feudalism had attenuated the intimacy of the connection between landlord and estate, when the attractions of society and politics might have disinclined owners to busy themselves with the management of their property, and when a determined profiteer could have made much of the shortage of holdings for the small peasant. If English agriculture did not go very far forward in this period, at least it did not get itself enmeshed in a tangle of intermediaries and smallholdings which would have snarled up advance at a later date.

Overseas trade

It remains to say something in particular of overseas trade. The record of cloth exports, easily the most important element, has already been substantially discussed. Of their more or less continuous rise from 1475 to 1551 it need only be added that the greater part of this increase was handled by the English Merchant Adventurers trading through Antwerp, whence the cloth was distributed over an extensive area. The Hansards, however, preserved their monopoly of the direct Baltic trade during that time and even nudged in on the Antwerp trade – becoming of greater consequence as cloth for southern Europe abandoned the all sea route and travelled instead via the Low Countries. The Mediterranean, trafficked by the Venetians and Genoese, had been the major artery of distribution for the south but from the mid-fifteenth century the Levantine end of this Italian trade was being subjected to regular harassment by the swelling power on land and sea of the Ottoman Turks. By the 1470s the Turks were in the Adriatic. By the 1480s they were rounding the toe of Italy. By the 1530s they were established on the North African coast and from 1534[1] regular commercial contact by sea between England and Italy was broken. Occasional vessels still hazarded the passage of the Mediterranean but for safety's sake it was necessary to turn back two centuries, to the route via the Rhine and the Alpine passes; Antwerp became what Bruges had once been, the entrepôt for the whole of Europe.

If, then, through these efflorescent years up to 1551 one hears little of English merchants pushing into new territories as they had been doing in the fourteenth and early fifteenth centuries, it was because there was no necessity for them to do so. They needed to go no further than Antwerp and there wait for Europe to come to them. But the slump of 1551 was followed by other adversities and things were never quite the same again. The immediate cause of the slump was a movement of foreign exchanges raising the price of the pound in terms of continental currencies and thus the price of English cloth. This was deliberately engineered by the Crown financier Sir Thomas Gresham to facilitate the repayment by the Crown of loans raised in Flemish guilders from continental bankers. The effect of Gresham's operations was of course shortlived but English cloth was, at least momentarily, heavily oversold and a sharp check was in any event inevitable. To general factors already mentioned[2] holding down cloth exports to northern Europe may be added the particular difficulties of the Merchant Adventurers as religious feeling in Spanish-ruled Antwerp threw obstacles in their way and required them to trade through other towns which lacked the established commercial patterns of Antwerp. Antwerp, in any event, abruptly and decisively lost its importance when in 1585 the Dutch, having revolted against Spanish rule, blockaded the Scheldt which gave access to the city. It was not until 1611 that the Merchant Adventurers finally settled in a new base at Hamburg, in the meanwhile having operated from various towns with inevitably disturbing effects on trade.

Their hardening into a tight monopoly has already been noted but the extent to which this frustrated sales of English cloth, or other produce, was perhaps slight or even nil. The scope for a significant

---

[1] The date given in English sources. F. Braudel, *La Mediterranée et le monde Mediterranéen* (1949), p. 482, quotes a Venetian source to show that the galleys continued to sail regularly until 1571. More generally, Braudel argues, not altogether convincingly, that Turkish naval activity had little effect on Anglo-Mediterranean trade. Nobody has yet reappraised the question from the English end, although J. H. Parry, 'Transport and trade routes', in *The Cambridge Economic History of Europe*, 2nd edition, vol. iv, *The Economy of Expanding Europe in the Sixteenth and Seventeenth Centuries* (1967) has followed Braudel's account.

[2] See pp. 119–20.

extension of the market just did not exist – indeed, it would seem to have been precisely a contraction of the market that was in some part responsible for an intensified exclusiveness. Nor would it appear that monopoly resulted in damagingly high prices of English cloth in the Adventurers' markets; as a rule they did not look to exports as their source of profit but to imports, content to cover their costs on sales of English produce and make their turn on the foreign goods bought with the proceeds – such goods were doubtless as a result somewhat more expensive than they would have been in a completely open market but as they were mostly luxuries and semi-luxuries that was a matter of small consequence. In any event the Adventurers in practice were far from enjoying a total monopoly. Their trade abounded in unauthorised interlopers, some perhaps who would have joined the Company were it disposed to admit them, more perhaps who saw little point in paying high membership fees when they could conduct an illicit trade with little fear of apprehension.

If the Adventurers' trade through the last ninety years of this period lacks the ebullience of the first seventy-five, and if for colour and vitality one must look to other areas, it should not for a moment be forgotten that up to and well beyond 1640 it was along the traditional way through the Low Countries and Germany that the great preponderance of English exports continued to travel.

Before turning to the new endeavours a terse epitaph should be uttered on the Merchant Staplers. Although the body sustained a formal existence into the twentieth century it can as an overseas trading organisation be ignored after the mid-sixteenth, by which time wool exports had all but ceased; and, as already seen, from 1622 it was actually forbidden to send wool out of the country.

The commercial push into new areas must be related to two general background features: the stagnancy of the major traditional markets for English cloth; and the geographical discoveries of the age. Columbus reached America in 1492; Vasco da Gama, following a steady deliberated inching down the African coast by earlier Portuguese since 1481, rounded the Cape and struck out across the Indian Ocean to reach Calcutta in 1498. Portugal was quick to exploit the opportunities pioneered by da Gama and with an early established position and command of the intermediary points was able to preserve a monopoly of the route for virtually a century – a route which enabled East Indian spices to be brought to northern Europe with much greater facility than the ancient one through the Levant.

But the pickings of this trade were enticingly rich and the semi-fabulous Cathay still remained an open and alluring prize.[1] Other nations aspired to contend with the Portuguese by taking the East from the rear. Indeed even before da Gama brought the Indies into direct sea contact with Europe by sailing eastwards men had dreamed of doing so by sailing westwards. Columbus was the first among them to raise a landfall in the attempt. Not for fifteen years after did the conviction start to become general that it was not the extremities of the Indies that Columbus had reached but a New World; and while Spain turned to making the most of her non-Indies others tested out their belief that America did not stretch in a solid block from north to south but could be breached to gain the East by uninterrupted sea journey.

John and Sebastian Cabot, Genoese, but sailing under the aegis of the English Crown in 1497 and 1498, were not the first to set out from Bristol in the hope of striking land across the Atlantic; but they were the first to do so knowing of Columbus's discovery and believing that if he had not in fact reached Asia that he had merely lighted on an island straddling his path there. Their discovery of the 'New Found Lands', barren and desolate, while a blow to the high expectations of winning through to the East, stimulated further eagerness, an eagerness which petered out as later ventures brought neither the East nor the promise of wealth such as the Spaniards had been favoured with. Through the second and third decades of the sixteenth century it was Portuguese probing southwards and Spaniards probing northwards who demonstrated the intimidating extent of the new continent and helped to foster in the minds of Englishmen the idea of a third way to Cathay, over the roof of Europe. If the Portuguese commanded the way round Africa; if a North-West passage around America was not to be had, then there remained the possibility of a North-East passage.

The sharp contraction of the European market in 1551 lent a particular edge to mercantile interest in exploration and in 1552 a company including merchants, landed proprietors and courtiers was formed to finance and organise an expedition to open up a North-East passage. The following year three ships set out under the command of Sir Hugh Willoughby. The Arctic seas overwhelmed two of them and the third, under Richard Chancellor, abandoned the attempt to push eastwards

---

[1] The first Portuguese reached China by sea in 1507 but it was not until 1557 that they established a trading post at Macao.

through the ice. But Chancellor did turn into the White Sea to find safe anchorage at Archangel and, resolved to salvage something from the wreckage, thence made his way overland to Moscow to initiate negotiations with the Tsar with a view to opening up a direct Anglo-Russian trade.[1] This eventuated in the founding of the Muscovy Company in 1555, chartered by the English Crown to control and regulate the trade and recognised and privileged by the Tsar. Although some individuals seemed to have plied their own trade in the manner of the Merchant Adventurers, distance and the lack of great commercial centres in Russia meant that the time devoted to the business might be disproportionate to its returns and its volume was not such as to make it worth while for an individual merchant to employ a permanent factor there. The device of the partnership was therefore extended to comprehend all members of the Company, a capital sum being raised among them for the purchase of a stock of goods consigned to factors employed by the Company in Russia, who used the proceeds on their sale to buy Russian goods for despatch to England, the money realised on their sale then being used to finance another venture and so on perhaps through several round trips before the final proceeds were distributed amongst the members in proportion to their subscription to the sum originally raised. Such a system especially recommeneded itself to Merchant Adventurers, or other merchants, who wished merely to spread their risks a little or to employ capital surplus to the immediate requirements of their own trade. Its drawback was that the scope for extending the trade was less likely to be exploited by hired employees than by merchants on the spot in pursuit of profit and when Dutch merchants began to push in from the 1580s, their greater vigour enabled them to win business from the Company, even in English goods. Their success in ingratiating themselves with the Tsar was a major element in the expulsion of the English from Russia in 1649.

Although, at least for the first three decades or so, handsome profits were made in the trade, Russia was too backward economically for it ever to become a market of real consequence for English goods, of which cloth of course made the most important contribution to the trade, supplemented by metal goods of various kinds, among which cannon, small-arms and munitions were those which most interested

---

[1] Russia (or more precisely Muscovy) did not as yet border the Baltic and such Anglo-Russian trade as there had been was conducted through various intermediaries. Russia did not establish herself permanently on the Baltic until 1718, although Narva was briefly held from 1558 to 1581.

a ruler whose shifting western frontier ran with technically more advanced nations than his own. The trade in fact was a classic little model of that between developed and underdeveloped countries. In return for manufactured goods Russia supplied primary produce: fish oil, furs, wax, potash, timber, tar, hemp and cordage – the final quartet comprising the 'naval stores', vital to maritime strength, mercantile or military. But at no time were these Russian supplies more than a marginal alternative to those obtainable from other regions flanking the Baltic. Indeed there was more than one respect in which the Russian trade was only a secondary substitute for other channels: in the 1560s and 1570s one of the principal elements in the Muscovy Company's business was a trade with Persia conducted overland through the dominions of the tsar. Once Englishmen penetrated the Baltic and the Mediterranean such interest as there was in the Russian trade was bound to diminish. And both these things were happening within a few years of the foundation of the Muscovy Company.

In the Baltic the power of the Hanse, riven by internal disputes, was on the wane by the middle of the sixteenth century. English merchants were quick to exploit the opportunities offered by the break-up of the Hansard monopoly and by the 1560s had assumed a dominant position in the Anglo-Baltic trade. In 1579 the Eastland Company was chartered to regulate the trade and act on behalf of the merchants engaged in it. But the Dutch, in Baltic waters since the late fifteenth century, were dangerous competitors and by the early years of the seventeenth century had gained the upper hand, importing white cloth from England, finishing it in Holland and underselling cloth brought direct to the Baltic from England; then shipping Baltic produce, conspicuously naval stores, to England at rates which Englishmen could hardly match. Dutch rivalry was a formidable obstacle to English mercantile expansion in most of the known seas of the world from the closing years of the sixteenth century but nowhere more so than in the Baltic, where to such superiority in aptitudes and policy as they possessed they added a clear technical asset in point of ship design.

It would be a fine task to say to what degree the Dutch drew advantage from such factors as greater enterprise in seeking out markets and sources of supply, toleration of lesser profit margins, freedom from the controls and monopolistic tendencies of company organised trade, more vigorous military and diplomatic support from their government. Doubtless these played their varying parts but alongside such imponderables were the measurable economies of the *fluyt*. The typical

English ship was a multipurpose vessel, designed to sail in any sea and to serve as a fighting ship if need be. The *fluyt* was tailormade for the Baltic and aspired to be nothing other than a freighter. Broadbottomed, of frail construction and sparsely rigged, it was unable to weather an Atlantic storm, to provide a gun platform or to command any speed or manoeuvrability, but the same characteristics yielded maximum cargo space at minimum cost. It was cheap to build – a third to a half cheaper than an English ship of the same carrying capacity. And it was cheap to operate – a conventional 200-ton ship required a crew of twenty-five to thirty, a *fluyt* sailed with nine or ten.

On top of the intrinsic economies of the *fluyt*, Dutch ships generally enjoyed a further cost advantage on the return leg of a Baltic voyage: they had carried a full payload on the outward journey, whereas English ships had usually sailed part empty or even in ballast and consequently had to cover much or all of their costs on the homeward run. Exports of cloth and scanty other miscellanea fell short in value, and even more in bulk, of imports in the Anglo-Baltic trade. The Dutch could as readily sell English cloth as the English themselves – even more readily since what they sold was probably better finished. But cloth, the English staple, was only one of several cargoes for the Dutch. For filling a hold there was always herring: the shoals had moved out of the Baltic into the North Sea in the late fifteenth century, and were caught in abundance by Dutch fishermen, cured in Holland and consumed in quantity in the regions where its former proximity had made of it a basic foodstuff. Good Dutch beer was a useful makeweight. And when Dutch produce was lacking Amsterdam could almost certainly yield a cargo of foreign goods of some kind, for with the closure of the Scheldt (1585) Amsterdam had taken the place of Antwerp as entrepôt for Europe – increasingly for a wider area as Asian and American commodities sought European markets.

One must not, of course, confuse English shippers with English merchants or Dutch shippers with Dutch merchants. The Dutch share of the Anglo-Baltic freight business was almost certainly much larger than their share of the strict mercantile profits of the trade. But although the pure merchant/shipowner was a figure of the distant past the two functions were still often closely related. Ships were commonly owned in parts and conspicuous amongst the owners of ship shares (usually sixty-four to a ship) were merchants. Such merchants perhaps regarded shipowning primarily as a way of diversifying employment of their capital in a field where their professional contacts and knowledge were useful and where fractionalisation of the asset permitted the risks to be spread. But, whatever the motives prompting mercantile investment in shipping, merchants in practice would often, from reasons of convenience or reasons of finance, consign goods to ships in which they themselves had an interest. And, in any event, difficulties of communications, language and national prejudice would tend to make it easier for an English merchant to find cargo space in an English ship than in a foreign one. The inferiority of the native mercantile marine must certainly have handicapped English merchants in some measure. However it was as Baltic carriers more than as Baltic traders that the Dutch were a particular object of jealousy and fear.

Fear, because Dutch supremacy in this field had more than purely commercial implications. The fewer English mercantile vessels afloat the less the potential strength of the English navy. This was partly a matter of ships; armed merchant vessels could be a useful supplement to fighting ships proper in time of war. But it was much more a matter of sailors; with no standing navy experienced seamen to man warships could only be recruited from the crews of merchant and fishing vessels (within this period this applied even to the 'officers' who handled the ship). Of even greater weight was the consideration that without Baltic naval stores there could be no ships at all and that to become dependent on a foreign power for the carriage of such stores was to tie the country to a lifeline which might snap on the outbreak of hostilities. It was in the years just outside this period that this situation hatched out most of its clutch of military, diplomatic and legislative consequences, but as early as 1622 an Act of Parliament essayed the sweeping measure of prohibiting Baltic imports except those carried in English ships. The effects of this ambitious fiat would almost certainly have been the very reverse of those intended – the sudden and drastic cut in the provision of shipbuilding materials would have crippled the English mercantile marine – and this appears to have been implicitly recognised in the subsequent non-enforcement of the Act. And indeed the Act itself tacitly admitted the necessity of the Dutch in making an exception in favour of corn, imported from the Baltic at times of deficient harvest, such as 1622 itself.

If it was the dissolution of the Hanse which opened the Baltic to Englishmen, it was the decline of Venice and Genoa which created room for newcomers in the Mediterranean. But the Turks who were eroding the power of the Italians were an equal menace to other Europeans. English ventures into the Mediterranean which had become more numerous in the first half of the sixteenth century appear to have ceased altogether after 1552. The first major setback to Turkish sea-power was the crushing defeat sustained by the Ottoman fleet at Lepanto in 1571. This was far from sweeping the Turks from the sea; they remained the dominant naval power in the eastern Mediterranean until towards the middle of the following century and only ceased to be a danger in the west some three decades after Lepanto when their depredations on shipping were succeeded by those of the Barbary corsairs – curbed by Dutch, English and French naval expeditions, beginning with the Dutch one of 1617 but not finally extirpated until the 1820s. Nevertheless Lepanto can be said to have initiated the ebbing of the Turkish tide. By demonstrating the potential of European fighting power, it impressed on the Ottoman régime the necessity in realistic prudence to modify the strategy of conquest with the tactics of co-existence. And although to the end of its days the Empire regarded infidels with disdain, it now was prepared to enter into limited relationships with them. The English were among the first beneficiaries of this attitude,[1] for the Ottomans were keenly interested in the tin which the English could offer more abundantly than any other available source and which was required for the making of bronze cannon. A trade once established, the Levant Company was formed in 1581. The diplomatic functions of an overseas trading company were peculiarly necessary in this trade, while, to begin with, the distance and the slender volume of business, as in the case of the Russian trade, rendered joint stock trading through Company factors the most suitable methods of conducting it.

The quantities of tin required, even for the considerable Turkish arsenal, were inevitably small and could never have sustained a commerce worth speaking of. Nor in a Mediterranean region was there much of a market for the traditional heavy cloth on which the trade with northern Europe was founded. The metal utensils, whose manufacture was currently developing in England, enjoyed some sale, but the only English commodity which could command an extensive market was the 'new draperies' for which there was scope alongside the local cotton and wool textiles. These were sold not only within the Empire but also in Persia, now more cheaply reached through the Mediterranean than via the route of the Muscovy Company. Swelling

[1] The English had, however, been preceded by the French. As early as 1536 France had concluded an alliance with the Ottoman Empire, outraging the conscience of Christian Europe; and into our own times the French preserved a special position in the Levantine world.

sales of these cloths had by the 1600s made it worth while for merchants to venture individual cargoes of their own, and Company conducted trade petered out. Levant merchants were of course legally required to be members of the Company but increasingly in practice this requirement was ignored, much to the disgruntlement of those who had paid their Company dues but who were unable to place any serious check on the activities of interlopers. Back from the Levant were brought currants, sweet wines, cotton (raw and cloth), silks and, for a decade or so around the turn of the sixteenth to the seventeenth century, the spices which had previously been diverted by the Portuguese but which briefly reverted to the Levantine route when in 1594 Portugal, then effectively incorporated into Spain, closed Lisbon to the Dutch and English. Before long, however, the Dutch had opened up their own sea route to the East and England was getting its spices from Amsterdam. With or without imports of spices English trade with the Levant was generally a deficit one and the inability to sell as much as was bought may be attributed to the ubiquitous Dutch. There was almost certainly sale enough for light worsteds to amply cover purchases of currants etc. But the Dutch were the original fabricators of the 'new draperies' and although they were at something of a competitive disadvantage in respect of wool supplies and labour costs, they seem within this period to have been able largely to compensate for this through superior techniques and perhaps more vigorous selling and lower freight costs, though the clear advantages of the *fluyt* were not available in the Levantine trade.

Dutch competition was equally strenuous in the western Mediterranean where the 'new draperies' could command a lively sale, especially in Spain and Italy; the anciently established industry of the northern Italian cities failed to adjust to the competition of these cheap cloths and succumbed. Tin and hardwares also sold on both the European and African coasts. There was an extensive market for cured fish and some part of the catch of English fishermen from both the North Sea and the Newfoundland Banks found its way here, although in much smaller quantities than that taken by the Dutch in European waters and that taken by the French and Portuguese off the North American coast. Naval stores from the Baltic could sell on the African shore but inevitably that opportunity was engrossed by the Dutch although the English had anticipated them on the Barbary coast (western Morocco) with which a fairly regular though slender trade had been conducted from the 1550s. Barbary supplies of saltpetre had initiated this but became of less importance as England improvised her own sources or drew on Amsterdam; and sugar which had also figured fell away too as cheaper Brazilian sugar became available through Lisbon and Amsterdam. However the bellicose Barbary states would pay gold for shipbuilding materials and armaments – which no good Christian of course should have supplied to Muslims, least of all when their likely use was to fit out a slave-hunting corsair. England, for a period, could offer the best cannon in Europe, but small arms in any quantity had to come from elsewhere. In the early seventeenth century the Dutch became general purveyors of armaments to most of the known world. What they did not manufacture themselves they bought in Germany or Sweden or elsewhere and redistributed as wars and rumours of war brought their messages of alarm and exigency to the great nerve centre, Amsterdam. Such arms as English ships now carried were intended for their own use, and the new draperies took the place of cannon in the Barbary trade.

This western Mediterranean region had no major staples to offer to balance exports of cloth. Return cargoes might have to consist of a miscellanea of items ranging from Venetian glass to Barbary monkeys. The problem of covering homeward costs in a highly competitive trade was met by various expedients. One was to sail on to the eastern end and, illicitly, take on a Levant cargo. A variation on that theme was to try to pick up Levantine goods at an intermediary point. Through the last quarter of the sixteenth century Leghorn (Livorno) established itself as such a centre into which were drawn commodities from the whole Mediterranean littoral. Once fixed as a commercial centre outward cargoes could be taken direct there and merchants conducting a large regular business maintained factors at Leghorn alongside Englishmen of various origins who conducted their own entrepôt business. Before Leghorn came to provide a focal point for the trade its ramifications had often necessitated tramping from port to port to raise a payload home subventing the itinerary by undertaking local freighting in the course of it. In some cases this became a principal activity, ships remaining for years or even permanently to ply a trade between Mediterranean ports. Other English vessels in these waters found piracy the most rewarding occupation.

Pirates, English or otherwise, were not of course peculiar to the Mediterranean. In their own home waters the English suffered from the savaging of coastal shipping by the Dunkirk pirates, especially during periods of hostility with Spain when the pirates became more honorific privateers, as did their English counterparts who menaced the Spanish trade routes from Cadiz to the Pacific or patrolled the French Atlantic coast in seach of easier if less lucrative prey, crossing trails with Bretons engaged in the same game. In Far Eastern waters trade rivalry was conducted by gun and sword as readily as by more orthodox mercantile methods. Piracy in fact, with or without some form of official licence, was by the economic lights of the times the logical extension of trade in the same sense as war has been said to be the logical extension of diplomacy; and a dressment of the balance of trade should really include the gains and losses resulting from it. Lacking statistical data we must be content with the impression that the English were better pirates than most.

Almost parenthetically, two remaining parts of the Old World should be touched on: France and Ireland. The course of Anglo-French trade over this period as yet lacks a historian. It has not the drama of other trades and the absence of collated statistics after 1547 means that the bare bones of it cannot be readily reconstructed beyond that date; and even up to that point one can only chart one side of the trade: imports of wine. These picked up sharply in 1476 after the long years of depression; had reattained their earlier level by the turn of the century; but showed no further tendency to rise. Over the years after 1547 they may have fallen off as a taste developed for Spanish, Portuguese and other southern wines while the spread of Puritanism perhaps made for a reduction in average consumption. Certainly the apparently scant attention given by contemporaries to the Bordeaux trade does suggest a declining importance. An alternative explanation might be that some significant proportion of it had from the closing years of the sixteenth century been diverted to Amsterdam. The Dutch certainly came to handle the French wine trade for north-eastern Europe in general and English merchants trading into the Low Countries may have picked up consignments from Dutch stocks. However a direct trade with Bordeaux certainly continued and the earlier tendency for it to become engrossed by Englishmen was finalised in the sixteenth century. These wine merchants doubtless carried out cloth. The French Wars of Religion (1562–98) had damaging effects on the native cloth industry which only fully recovered after the middle of the seventeenth century and France throughout this period was an important market for the whole range of English cloths, especially the cheaper woollens of the south-west – which were, however, despatched largely through Norman and Breton ports.

Anglo-Irish trade in absolute terms may have held its own but it showed no expansive tendencies through this period. Neither old nor new draperies commanded much of a market in a still half-wild country with its own traditional coarse woollen and linen industries; nor did the gradual extension of English rule, attaining completeness in the early seventeenth century, bring any significant commercial consequences in its train. For the handful of merchants and shippers in Chester, Liverpool and some tiny Welsh ports, traffic across the Irish Sea was of real consequence and it remained of weight in the commercial life of Bristol. But set against the dynamic trends which English trade in gross was experiencing in one direction or another through these years, it dwindles into insignificance.

There remain the lands beyond the great oceans. It should be stressed at the outset that these years saw little more than the basis laid by England for the great extension of her extra-European commerce through the later seventeenth and the eighteenth century. We have seen already that early English probes across the Atlantic had ended in disappointment. The first attempt to open up a North-East passage had got no further than the White Sea, and subsequent expeditions of 1556 and 1580 decisively disclosed the impossibility of the undertaking, while a revived interest in the North-West passage engendered the three journeys of Martin Frobisher (1576–78) and the three of John Davis (1585–87), which although not destructive of hope of final success also failed of their object. With all evident opportunities usurped by the Spanish or Portuguese, other nations had for the while to content themselves with the scavengings, the Dutch with the terminal end of the spice trade to northern Europe, the English with the spoils of voyages of plunder, especially the major ones mounted against the Spanish treasure ships and organised and financed, in peace or war, as business enterprises – extremely profitable in the 1570s and 1580s but abandoned in the 1590s as the Spaniards strengthened their defences. But while Spain was consolidating her hold on the Americas, her satellite, Portugal, was losing hers in the East as domestic troubles drained away energy and finance from the spice trade, aggravated by the foolish closure of Lisbon to the Dutch in 1594, wrecking the established northern distribution network without being able to construct one to replace it.

Dutch and English raced neck and neck to supplant the languishing Portuguese. The English had a head start: their first trading expedition to the Indies sailed in 1591 but ended disastrously while a Dutch voyage mounted in 1595 was conspicuously successful. Before that returned, however, a more elaborate English venture was being organised. Prominent among its promoters were Levant Company merchants eager to retain an interest in the spices which they were temporarily handling. In 1599 the 216 subscribers to the capital sum raised for the undertaking were incorporated as the East India Company with exclusive rights to English trade with the East. In 1602 the Dutch East India Company was formed. Neither side then had a built-in advantage, yet within a quarter of a century the English had withdrawn ignominiously from the spice islands and, Portuguese remnants apart, the Dutch had appropriated the entire trade. Commercial factors, such as a command through Amsterdam of a much larger home market and of a wider range of goods to bring out to the East, or of more abundant stocks of the precious metals with which the trade had to be largely conducted – these factors played some part in this striking Dutch triumph. But its completeness was the result of military superiority. As a state the Dutch Republic was dedicated to the pursuit of profit as no other European country was. Where other governments were bent on the acquisition of territory or prestige or the support of their coreligionists that of Holland sought commercial advantage and, when necessary, employed its resources to that end with a singlemindedness with which the diffuseness of the policy of others could not contend.

In the East both the government and the Company were prepared for whatever level of military expenditure was necessary in order to secure the spice trade. The English Company had at the best only the good wishes of its government and not always even that – nor were its members themselves prepared to finance regular warfare. The differences in financial arrangements between the two Companies epitomise the difference in attitudes and largely explain the difference in fortunes. The Dutch Company began life with a considerable permanent capital for investment not only in trade but in ships of both a freighting and a fighting capacity for the job they were to undertake and in land bases which were simultaneously trading posts and fortresses. The English Company was modelled on its Muscovy and Levant predecessors. Apart from the relatively small sum raised in membership fees it had as such no capital – individual subscriptions to each venture were liquidated on completion.[1] The consequences of its military weakness were,

[1] Liquidation sometimes took place at the end of a single voyage, sometimes after a series of voyages and sometimes on the expiry of a stipulated period of time.

after two decades of much adversity, made chillingly apparent by the massacre by the Dutch of British merchants at Amboyna, in the Moluccas, in 1623 and the Company retreated to the Indian mainland where the Dutch did not consider the trade worth contending for. The English Company had maintained a trading post at Surat, on the west coast, since 1608 but of the spices which had brought it to the East only low quality pepper was available there. This tricked out with indigo, silks and fine cotton cloth (calico) and a trade with Persia, yielded a quite profitable business but one of very slender dimensions in the context of total English trade, the more especially as it was almost entirely a one way affair. Even the light new draperies could make little market headway against native Indian silk and cotton textiles. A few metalwares and other odds and ends were sold, but the great bulk of outward cargoes consisted of bullion.

On the other side of the world the beginnings of a trade of very different character were slowly taking shape. The densely forested shores of northern America with their thinly dispersed population of savages had offered no readymade prospects of commerce. But their very bleakness by failing to attract the Spanish left them wide open to penetration by others who, *faute de mieux*, might attempt to make something of them. They could at least provide land and thus a basis for civilised communities who after meeting their own fundamental needs, food, warmth and shelter, might raise a surplus of primary products to exchange for manufactured goods from the Old World. Every European country was experiencing the problem of accommodating a rising population, and most too contained elements – political or religious dissidents or other undesirables, including common malefactors – who, in their own judgment or that of authority, would be better resident in another world. These were the considerations, mixed in varying proportions, which gave rise to the idea of plantations or colonies.

But founding a viable settlement was a much more arduous and uncertain affair than establishing a trade with an already developed region. Heavy financial subvention was needed to clear the land and provide the settlers with the means of livelihood until they became self-sufficient. Accustomed agricultural practices would not necessarily serve under strange conditions of soil and weather. The severity of the climate and the hostility of the native inhabitants might menace life itself. Even without physical hazards the psychological effects of isolation in an alien wilderness thousands of miles from the nearest of their kind could be destructive of a small community; in the actual event lack of a strong community spirit or inspiring leadership often proved fatal. And, as a background to such consideration, the unfamiliarity with any precedent for an attempt to create tolerable conditions of life from the utterly raw. We need not wonder that the idea itself was slow to form and that even then there was a long lapse between conception and successful realisation.

The French were the first to essay the experiment, as early as the 1540s when a community was planted on the banks of the St Lawrence, but the survivors were soon repatriated and it was not until 1608 that the first enduring French settlement was established in Canada. In England the notion of colonisation seems to have been initially aired in the 1560s, and in 1585 Sir Walter Raleigh under crown patent despatched the first English group to attempt to make a home in the New World. A year later they took the earliest opportunity of returning to England. Raleigh's second group, sent out in 1587, had to wait longer for a ship home – too long: when a vessel called with supplies in 1590 the entire community of over a hundred persons had vanished. This experience was not exactly encouraging and nearly twenty years passed before a fresh effort was made. Raleigh's ventures had failed amongst other reasons for lack of appreciation of the difficulties to be overcome and of the cost of nursing a settlement through its infancy.

The ventures of 1606 were also founded in overoptimism but they were rather more businesslike. Two companies were chartered, one operating from London, the other from Plymouth, each with substantial financial backing, much of it mercantile. The Plymouth company sent its settlers to Maine, but the New England winter was too much for them; the settlement was soon abandoned and the company dissolved. The Londoners went to Virginia, loyally styling their settlement Jamestown. The first year nearly undid it; the community was within an ace of perishing from starvation when supplies arrived from England. But it held on to inaugurate the peopling of North America by the British race. Whatever wider importance might be attached to that historical curiosity the event of most profound economic significance was the decision, taken locally in 1612, to edge away from a subsistence agriculture and cultivate tobacco. In 1614 the first tobacco consignment was shipped to England and thereafter exports increased fairly steadily, although even by 1640 the tobacco crop was not large enough to figure weightily in England's import bill nor to destroy the primacy of food crops in the Virginian economy – nor did it save the Virginia Company from bankruptcy; in 1625 the colony was taken over by the Crown.

Investment in colonial settlement rarely proved remunerative, except for those who took themselves as well as their capital across the Atlantic. For this two general reasons can be assigned: the difficulty of exercising effective financial control from the other side of the ocean; and the expectation of quicker returns than could in fact be achieved in virgin territory under unfamiliar or even hostile conditions. The men who put their money into plantations were used to commercial enterprises where capital was recovered within two or three years at the most. Colonial investment required not only readiness to commit money capital for an indefinite term, to which at least the owners or real property were accustomed, but also preparedness to earn nothing on that money for a considerable while, and, very likely, to send more money after it to make it fructify. Disappointed in their highpitched expectations, colonial investors commonly declined to send good money after bad. Yet it is a useful comment on the attitudes of the times that the money to launch plantations was in fact forthcoming, and that within this period all the English settlements were the work of private enterprise, the Crown conferring no more than its blessing and the necessary grant of lands over which it exercised nominal sovereignty. The colonies were born out of that same mixture of a recital of public benefits and a calculation of private profit which attended the domestic monopolies of such ill repute. For even the Pilgrim Fathers needed the assistance of a group of financiers; only Maryland started life independent of home-based capitalists looking for their money back.

The Pilgrim Fathers who landed at Plymouth Rock, Massachusetts, in 1620 are of course the most famous of the early settlers, but they need occupy little space here. Until well beyond this period their settlement remained of diminutive proportions, in near isolation economically both from the other American communities and from Europe; only a trickle of furs, timber and maize enabled them to purchase some slender means of relieving the rigours of their austere life. Their co-religionists, nestling in the bosom of Massachusetts Bay from 1628, enjoyed both more support from home through the New England (later the Massachusetts Bay) Company which financed the settlement and from more favourable natural conditions, with good fishing waters and better corn land, from both of which they could supplement exports of furs and timber, although the total sum was still insignificant in England's commerce and insufficient to pay for much needed imports. Nevertheless, 20,000 English puritans between 1630 and 1643, considered it on balance superior enough to home to emigrate there, and thence to spread southwards towards the Dutch settlements at the mouth of the Hudson (dating from 1613), creating the nuclei of New Hampshire, Connecticut and Rhode Island.

Maryland, founded by the Roman Catholic Lord Baltimore in 1633, also offered a haven for tender consciences. The early entrepreneurs were mostly Catholic gentry who sold up at home and transferred entirely to the colony. With the Virginian lesson to hand they often started their new life as tobacco planters, while cultivating enough corn to meet local needs. In terms of personal profit at least Maryland was probably the most successful of the trans-Atlantic settlements of these years. Beyond the mainland that title might have been disputed by Barbados had it not been for the clash between Sir William Courteen, who initially settled the uninhabited island in 1626, and the Earl of Carlisle, who had an antedated patent in vague terms for the colonisation of the Caribbean – of which he had made little use. After a flourishing start the island was crippled for some years by the cessation of regular supplies from England while the two rivals jockeyed for a favourable royal determination of their conflicting claims. Carlisle eventually won and by 1640 the settlement had resumed its economic growth, founded on tobacco, cotton and indigo, the last two borrowed from India.

The story of the development of European trade and navigation over this period is one above all of the prowess of the Dutch. Even though good and cogent reasons can be assigned for the commercial achievements of this small country endowed with no natural advantages other than its geographical situation, its remarkable rise, through a time when it was fighting for independence from the greatest military power in Europe, will always perhaps stand as one of the 'economic miracles' of historical times. Wherever we have had occasion to note the mercantile activity of Englishmen there also were the Dutch, usually with a clear edge on the English. But if the Dutch were easily first the English were second. The Germans were disappearing from the Baltic; the Italians no longer ventured north and were only one amongst many in the Mediterranean which they had once dominated; the pioneering

Portuguese had entered into a pathetic decline; French commerce was only struggling back on to its feet after a generation of civil war; Spain lorded it over central America but what she reaped in treasure she sowed in blood rather than trade.

This league table type of evaluation is one to be used with caution. We should avoid the contemporary error of identifying the weakness of one national economy with the strength of another and the even more dangerous premise on which that canon rests: that economic wellbeing is to be measured by the volume and profitability of overseas trade. Nevertheless, even if it only served to demonstrate England's economic status in the eyes of the times the classification would have some historical value. And it does do something more than that. Merchants and shippers were part of the population, even if a very small part, and their prosperity was an element in total prosperity. To that limited extent then the larger the share of trade in English hands the better off England was. More important, there was bound to be a close correlation between the fortunes of English merchants and shippers and the sale of English goods abroad as well as with the availability of foreign goods in England. In a modern age of swift and comprehensive international communications trade can almost be said to conduct itself – the pattern of world trade is effectively determined by relative cost structures. But at any earlier time markets and sources of supply had to be 'discovered' and kept open by merchants. Plainly, English merchants were more likely to do this for England than were foreigners, the more especially as merchants often considered their outward consignments as the most convenient form of financing their purchases abroad or, in other cases, their inward consignments as a way of remitting the proceeds of export sales,[1] and, either way, goods might be included in a consignment just for the sake of spreading shipping and other fixed costs. Even with the keen-eyed Dutch hovering in the vicinity English exports and imports must certainly have been lower had English traders been less active.

The importance of exports to the cloth industry needs no stressing and although it was only the relatively tiny tin industry that also leant heavily on exports, the growth of metal manufactures owed something to an extension of overseas markets and that of hosiery perhaps even

---

[1] Transmission of the precious metals was hazardous and usually illegal. Quite elaborate facilities for international settlements by paper instrument had existed from at least the thirteenth century and in this period Antwerp and then, pre-eminently, Amsterdam were major centres of international banking activities, but the network was far from universal.

more, while foreign sales were of some marginal consequence for Tyneside coal owners, salt-manufacturers, leatherworkers, the makers of gloves, caps, hats, fustians and a dozen and one other things. All in all, probably about five per cent of gross national income was derived from foreign trade. A similar proportion was of course expended on imports. As earlier, these were mostly consumer goods of a fairly expensive variety. Naval stores were the principal exception to this generalisation – their importance is not to be measured by their money value which was not considerable in the total import bill. The only other 'necessary' imports of any weight were dyestuffs and, erratically, corn. Even with the eye-catching developments that took place through the whole of these 165 years, the extent to which England in 1640 was geared to an international economy was still slight.

Advance or decline?

That concluding sentence on overseas trade can serve as a further reminder that what leaps most prominently into retrospective view, what most stirs the historical imagination, and, indeed, what has received most attention in this account is not necessarily what is most important in strict economic analysis. The final term of reference of that analysis is a hard quantitative one: the change, if any, in *per capita* enjoyment of goods and services. The general considerations determining that were outlined at the beginning of this section. What attempt can we now make after considering in some practical detail the course and nature of the economy between 1475 and 1640 to answer the questions there posed in abstract? No true cliometrician would make any such attempt. An answer with any pretensions to precision would require statistical data that does not exist and which no amount of intelligent imagination can supply. We do not know and never will know whether the standard of living rose or fell over this period. That between the two terminal dates gross national product rose is transparently true; whether that rise offset the rise in population is quite indeterminable. But, paradoxically, that very uncertainty hints at a kind of certainty. The lack of any clear indication as to 'up' or 'down' points positively to a situation falling within imaginable limits – say thirty per cent either way. Our sources of information are sufficient to show up any movement in excess of those limits. We could, then, rest with the negative assertion that whatever change there was it was not a momentous one. But it would be valid to venture further than that. A historian may, and even ought, to pursue lines of inquiry as far as they can be taken even when starting with the knowledge that they cannot be pushed to a conclusion. And we are not totally without hard data. There is a great deal of contemporary prices and wages material and though it does not permit of absolutely exact mathematical statements it is enough to make the kind of statement that would satisfy anybody who is not in love with figures for their own sake provided that it is not used to make general judgments about changes over short periods.

TABLE I.I. *Wage rates in southern England and their purchasing power*

| | AGRICULTURAL LABOURER | | | BUILDING CRAFTSMAN |
Decade	Money wage rate	'Cost of living'	Purchasing power of wage rate	Purchasing power of wage rate
1450–59	101	96	105	104
1460–69	101	101	100	100
1470–79	101	97	104	103
1480–89	95	111	86	93
1490–99	101	97	104	103
1500–09	101	104	97	96
1510–19	101	114	89	88
1520–29	106	133	80	76
1530–39	110	138	80	68
1540–49	118	167	71	70
1550–59	160	271	59	51
1560–69	177	269	66	62
1570–79	207	298	69	64
1580–89	203	154	57	57
1590–99	219	443	49	47
1600–09	219	439	50	46
1610–19	228	514	44	39
1620–29	253	511	50	38
1630–39	287	609	47	—
1640–49	304	609	50	49

Reproduced from P. Bowden, 'Agricultural prices, farm profits and rents', *The Agrarian History of England and Wales*, vol. iv, ed. J. Thirsk, p. 865.

Table I.1 tells its own story – a story whose long-term burden would not differ if the figures contained say a twenty per cent margin of error. To that statistically based story we can add the unambiguous pointers to a growth in the numbers of poor and destitute: the contemporary references, general and particular, to the problem of poverty; the steady legislative move towards a comprehensive and effective system of poor relief. There can be no doubt that below some real income line there was both an absolute and a relative increase in numbers. Where that line should be drawn is a matter of less exactitude. Even with much more information than we have it would be practically impossible to make any useful calculation as to what proportion of the population were wage-earners, partly because so many who did earn wages also had landholdings, and partly because of the large numbers who straddled the shadowy line of distinction between employee and independent craftsman. Furthermore, although the existence of the new poor is manifest we do not know who they were: contemporaries sometimes suggested that they were in particular the footloose victims of conversion or engrossment, or clothworkers out of employment in bad times, and later writers have tended to accept this identification. But although many such individuals must have figured among those in need of relief the composition of this class was probably more variegated than such accounts imply. In particular the question arises of the extent to which it consisted on the one hand of those severed from their livelihoods by economic disaster and on the other those whose wages in real terms had become so chronically low that they could not maintain themselves and their dependants. The distinction is overstated for the sake of brevity; the important point is that inasmuch as the new poor tended to belong to the latter category what we are looking at is simply another aspect of falling real wages – the other evidences of poverty add nothing to the picture presented by a wages graph and bring us back to the unresolvable question of the total impact of lower wages. Thus while we can confidently speak of a decline in living standards towards the bottom of the income scale, we can have no useful notion of what degree of increase further up the scale could have so offset this as to produce an overall rise in average incomes.

That there were countervailing income tendencies of some weight seems evident. But here we are without benefit of direct statistical data. The evidence is that of expenditure patterns – indirect, fragmentary and very often open to misinterpretation. The sumptuousness of upper-class London life is a piece of it. Suggestive of higher incomes over a wider social range is the rise in meat consumption. Similarly broad is the greater elegance and comfort of houses, with their furnishings and fittings. This is less a matter of a Hatfield or a Longleat than it is of the numerous unpalatial but very commodious Elizabethan and Jacobean manor houses; some of these survive, and there is plenty of evidence of others which have perished, as there is of town houses of considerable dignity, nearly all of which have vanished as a result of later urban development. But most impressive perhaps as witnesses to rising living standards are the farm houses. In its architectural aspect, rural England was transformed, notably over the period *c.* 1570 to *c.* 1640. The sparsely utilitarian wooden structure that served to provide a bare, earth-floored, windowless hall for living, cooking and sleeping, with a storage shed and an animal byre, was being replaced by houses built of stone, or occasionally brick, with paved floors, glazed windows and several separate rooms; plain enough in design as a rule but usually with some sensitivity to aesthetic effect and, at least, generally quite distinct from the other farm buildings. From all these residences, Lord Burleigh's downwards, we have relics of the cupboards, chests, tables, chairs, beds, bed-coverings, floor-coverings, wall-hangings, pots, pans, crockery, cutlery etc. with which they were fitted; but much more telling is the evidence of wills and inventories which speak clearly of a great increase in stocks of such household impedimenta through this period.

Current knowledge does not allow of the translation of this information into useful statistics: the proportionate numbers manifesting such evidences of wealth; the income range to which they belonged. But *prima facie* there was a group who must have done very well out of the movements of prices and wages: those with holdings large enough to require hired labour and who were protected against rent increases by a freehold, a proven copyhold or a long lease. Inasmuch as it was those so circumstanced who owned the solid comfortable farmhouses and their range of domestic equipment, we are just witnessing a transfer of wealth from labourers and landowners to a fortunate class of farmers. More generally, lower wages certainly meant, in some degree, higher employer incomes all round. That is to say that more generous expenditures higher up the scale might be no more than, nor even as much as, the obverse of diminished incomes lower down the scale. Furthermore, although it is very difficult to resist the impression of a marked increase in wealth from the middling range upwards, we must take account of other possible explanations of the appearances of more lavish spending. A mere reshuffling of objects of expenditure could be deceptive.

It seemes hardly credible that we could be gravely misled this way – it is not easy to imagine things on which much less might have been spent in order to finance expenditure on both the ostentation and the comfort which we have remarked. But a couple of particulars warrant comment. In the highest reaches private expenditure on the means of warfare must certainly have fallen off under the Tudors. Lower down, the use of stone and brick as building materials must in some part be just a reflection of the scarcity of wood; and glazed windows result from the cheap glass formerly unavailable (the latter a real economic gain). Consonant with our knowledge of bankruptcies and heavy mortgages among landed proprietors over the later years of the period is the suggestion that a high level of expenditure by that class was sustained by drawing on savings, both by way of depleting capital accumulated in the past and by reducing the proportion of current income saved.

We are now verging on the question of investment levels – the analytical key to the issue of economic growth. In its immediate outcome a reduction of savings has the same effect as increased investment; in both cases money which otherwise would have been idle is being spent, and in both the effect is multiplied as the increased expenditure circulates through the economy. The important difference between lesser savings and greater investment is that the latter is intended to increase production capacity, and will usually do so to an amount at least equivalent to the sum invested. Higher consumption expenditure unaccompanied by investment will of itself only elicit greater production to the extent that extra capacity is already in existence but is not currently being employed. Clearly this will only be the case to a limited extent; without new investment higher expenditure will just burn itself out in inflation. However an upward shift in consumption will prompt new investment in some degree and may even be the initiating factor in economic growth. If doubts about this possibility arise in the present context it is because the very class we are now suspecting of eating into savings was the one in which we would expect to find agricultural investors.

The two activities are not mutually exclusive. For one thing, all members of the same class do not necessarily behave in the same way. For another, a man may simultaneously increase his consumption expenditure *and* his investment expenditure, borrowing if his own resources cannot sustain it. Nevertheless a general ambience of conspicuous consumption is not the social climate most likely to foster long-term investment, though it might positively promote outlay in undertakings from which a quick return was expected. And indeed in considering the changes taking place on English land, we had little occasion to note large investment projects. Engrossment, expropriation of commons, pasture farming and the dissolution of customary tenures are the most manifest ways in which landlords sought to increase their incomes. But this kind of impressionism is not very reliable. Engrossment etc. obtrude because they were lively public issues. A massive undertaking like the Fens' reclamation also catches the attention. The laying out of mere tens of hundreds of pounds on the clearance of wood and scrub, drainage trenches, roadways, farm buildings, tools and equipment – these are not going to be matters of notoriety. All that one can say is that we do not hear of this kind of activity in the same way as we do in, say, the eighteenth century. But historians have already pushed the improvement-conscious landlord as a type further back in time than the received account had it and more research in estate records may bring to light evidence of significant landlord investment within this period. Until such time we must abide by the strong impression that the level of agricultural investment was low and that such as there was must in effect have been sustained largely by depressing the consumption standards of wage earners.

It would follow that if the general level of investment were such as to make for a higher average rate of consumption, it would have been principally on account of capital activity in the industrial sector. That there was a noteworthy amount of such activity has been seen. That its importance in the overall economic context lends itself easily to exaggeration has been pointed out. Little more than this can usefully be said. But the fact that industrial prices rose much less steeply than agricultural prices is interesting. It points less to cost-reducing techniques than it does to a ready adjustment of supply to demand, even perhaps to a tendency for supply to run ahead of demand. And this implies investment. Not only, or even principally, great outlays in coal and iron etc., but modest unobtrusive ones in thousands of small workshops all over the country. To this should be added the increased investment in shipping, haulage equipment and mercantile stocks corresponding with the extension of trade, inland, coastal and overseas. To none of these, of course, can we assign even a vague mathematical quantity. The approach by way of considering the mechanism of economic growth

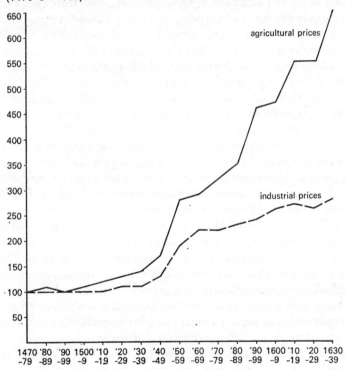

Relative Movements of Agricultural and Industrial Produce, 1470-9 – 1630-9 (1470–9 = 100)

agricultural prices

industrial prices

1470 -79	'80 -89	'90 -99	1500 -9	'10 -19	'20 -29	'30 -39	'40 -49	'50 -59	'60 -69	'70 -79	'80 -89	'90 -99	1600 -9	'10 -19	'20 -29	1630 -39

GRAPH I.3

(or decline) is in fact even less suggestive of an answer to the question of 'up' or 'down' than that by way of the face appearance. But it is suggestive of a kind of explanation of what the face appearances imply: lowered living standards towards the base of the social pyramid, heightened standards further up. We do seem to be confronted with such an investment level resting effectively in some part on diminished wages and in other part on savings as was earlier posed as a hypothetical possibility creating this kind of situation.[1] And the scanty indications are that it was an increase in industrial and commercial investment that was the distinctive instrument of this.

One final observation: the issue of overall advance or regression has been considered without reference to specific time periods. It is highly improbable that such movement as took place was evenly spread over the whole hundred and sixty-five years. It is a moral certainty that it was not a matter of a single abrupt jerk at one particular period. But since we cannot even determine the direction of the movement, it would be plainly ridiculous to try to plot its fluctuations in time. There would be some ground for a general tripartite division of the whole period. The records of prices and cloth exports would tend to establish a marker point at or towards the middle of the sixteenth century (within that division a submarker might be located in the 1520s); prices again and the evidences of new departures would lend themselves to an identification of a second division running into the first or second decades of the seventeenth century (this period might be inaugurated in the early 1570s, leaving the 1550s and 1560s in a kind of economic limbo); this would yield a residual period covering the two or three decades up to the Civil War. Of this last period it should be said that there is a tendency among economic historians to regard it as a time of adversity and to associate it with the contemporary onset of the 'Crisis of the seventeenth century' with which term the evidences of economic setback on the continent have been endowed. But although the periodic trading difficulties of these years have been made abundantly plain, we are not really in a position to make an effective comparison with earlier (or later) times, in which also tribulations were certainly not absent;[2] and in any event the vicissitudes of overseas trade were not necessarily very closely correlated with the course of the economy as a whole.

[1] P. 106, end of first paragraph.

[2] The implied reference is principally to B. E. Supple, *Commercial Crisis and Change in England 1600–1642* (Cambridge University Press, 1959) which offers a detailed chronological account of the obstacles to exports. Although traces of Dr Supple's work can be

found elsewhere in this book, the opportunity which it presents of providing something of an analytical narrative of those years has not been taken for the reason intimated above: that in a general account there seems little point in picking up a theme which cannot be sustained.

Five

1640-1740

The hundred years which succeed the outbreak of the Civil War are perhaps the most decisive of all in English political, or at least constitutional, history. But under the economic aspect the period has left behind a general impression of anonymity. Anglo-Dutch trade rivalry and new ventures in finance bring a dash of excitement but, at least in the midst of a general account, it has to be largely treated as a relatively quiet interlude, most of the dramatic content either having been absorbed by the earlier period or being reserved for succeeding ones.

The Civil War with which the period is launched might be thought to lend some vibrancy to an economic narrative. And, indeed, the virtual omission of any reference to the background to the war in the previous section may have seemed strange to some, especially those acquainted with the 'gentry controversy' whose blend of acrimony and scholarship attracted an audience ranging well beyond specialists in the field. The smoke of that battle has now settled and the opinion of judicious men seems to be that the origins of the Civil War are not susceptible to an economic interpretation or, at least, not to one whose lines are immediately apparent – except for the evident part played by the use of the royal power in connection with patents, charters and extraordinary revenue and by the opposition thus excited.

The war, of course, was not entirely without economic effects. It stands as the most considerable military struggle ever waged on English soil. But the scale of hostilities was small. At no one time were there more than about 60,000 men under arms throughout the entire country. The New Model Army, that paradigm of regular forces, had a strength of 22,000. There was no continuous battlefront, no extensive tract of territory torn up by the collision of armies, no subjection of large areas to military control. Looting was not uncommon but there was no widespread destruction of property or of crops. The civilian populace was nowhere treated as the enemy, as it was, say, on the continent during the contemporary Thirty Years War. Long-distance trade inland must have been subject to some interruption, but with one side, Parliament, in undisputed command of the seas, maritime commerce was largely unaffected. The economic life of those large towns which experienced fairly protracted sieges, Bristol, Gloucester, York, Hull, Newcastle, must during that time have been badly disrupted but London suffered no military harassment the whole length of the war. The general atmosphere of uncertainty as to the future engendered by the war and by the later inability to fashion an enduring political settlement did not conduce to long-term investment projects and evidences of new ventures are conspicuously absent until the Restoration. Those engaged in the manufacture and supply of armaments must have enjoyed something of a boom; and, no doubt, in many different ways the shifting times made the fortunes of some and ruined others; but no particular economic interest emerged clearly as either a gainer or a loser from the hostilities themselves or from the Parliamentary victory. One collection of individuals did pay heavily for backing the wrong side. The landed estates of royalists shrank under outright confiscation or sales enforced by swingeing fines. The new owners, however, belonged generally to the same socio-economic class as the dispossessed, although some well-placed individuals were able to acquire property of an extent to which in normal times they could not have aspired.

The English economy then came out of the Civil War and the Interregnum in essentially the same shape as it had gone in. In the light of that it is not to be expected that the other great political turnabout of the period, the Revolution of 1688, briefly and bloodlessly effected, would be marked by signal economic consequences, although it can be argued that it did have effects in the field of economic policy.

Demography

No more than from political or military events can major economic change be looked for as a result of demographic factors, which have earlier been distinguished as prime agents. Over the whole hundred years the population of England rose from perhaps five million to probably a little over five and a half million. The first figure is subject to a wide margin of error, but by 1740 we are within the ambit of sound statistical method and although precision remains unattainable until the first national census of 1801 (even until 1821, since the administration of the first two censuses was faulty) the figure obtainable for that date can be worked back with tolerable accuracy using baptismal and burial registers.

Retrogressive calculation in this manner has been carried back to 1701, at which point it can link hands with the contemporary estimate of Gregory King made for 1696 on the basis of the hearth tax returns, each tending to confirm the other. These suggest that over the last half of the period the population on balance was almost stable so that if five million for 1640 is correct the modest rise that there was occurred mostly in the first half. Note, however, that if the 1640 figure were 10 per cent too low, and there is no guarantee that it is not, there would be no net change over the whole period, and if it were 10 per cent too high the rate of population increase in the following half-century would be commensurate with that of the preceding couple of centuries.[1] The best guess seems to be that sometime within a couple of decades either side of 1640 the rate of population growth slackened, that this deceleration became more marked as the eighteenth century was reached and, more confidently, that over the last two decades of the period population actually fell off a little.

This pattern, or any other which is consistent with the available data, is puzzling, particularly in the light of the great increase in population over the rest of the eighteenth century. The period's most striking feature of demographic relevance is the passing of the plague after its final frightful onslaught of 1665–66. The disappearance of this killer could, above anything else, be expected to initiate a phase of especial population growth. But the evidence points in the other direction. At least, if there were a marked increase in population after 1666 it was very soon overtaken by some other adverse factor. Indications of a greater prevalence of other diseases from around this time are not lacking. Most notable is the intensification of smallpox, marked particularly by the outbreak of 1667–68 and by a series of waves between 1677 and 1685 – the disease seems to have attained its most virulent phase between the early 1710s and the early 1740s. The very bad typhus epidemic of

[1] That is, it would suggest that the long-run growth rate over the whole stretch c. 1450–c. 1690 was a fairly constant two-fifths per cent p.a. It would also suggest that the population did not top its pre-Black Death peak until the middle of the seventeenth century – i.e. on the basis of the figures already quoted for earlier centuries, themselves of even more dubious reliability.

1685–86 appears to mark a new chapter in the story of that disease although it has a well recorded earlier history of sporadic deadliness. Summer diarrhoea of infants – until into the twentieth century responsible for more deaths among babies than any other illness – manifested itself with particular viciousness in 1669, while its worst protracted period seems to have been roughly 1720–40, suggestively coincident with the years of apparent population decline. Whether these manifestations of aggravated threats to life add up to a counterweight to the vanished plague is impossible to say – and they would have to do rather more than that to account for the contrast between the demographic pattern of this period and the more vigorous one of preceding times. Even if their mortality rate were sufficient to account for the contrast there would still remain the problem of explaining this new killing power – which could hardly be divorced from social and economic factors.

Two principal possibilities offer themselves to account for such a deterioration in the quality of life as might make for enfeebled constitutions and greater vulnerability to disease. The one is a decline in the standard of living among the lower income groups; or, put another way, the failure of grain output to keep pace with population. The scrappy indications are that this situation was worsening until about 1660 and easing off thereafter. But the effects of serious undernourishment say between 1640 and 1660 might manifest themselves particularly in the generation born over these years as they came to adulthood through the following two or three decades. It would not be very plausible, however, to extend this line of reasoning much beyond the 1690s. Historians have pointed to bad harvest in 1660–61, 1673–74, 1691–93, 1696–97, 1708–10, 1725–29 and 1739–40, giving a frequency over the last eighty years of the period of about one every four years. This is certainly high, and the particular cluster in the 1690s could be expected to have specially deleterious effects in both the short and long terms. On the other hand the indications are that overall these same eighty years yielded a comparative plenitude of grain – from 1697 figures for external trade in corn are available and these show that between then and 1740 in all but two years, 1728 and 1729, England was a net exporter of grain. Taken together with evidences of the enhanced purchasing power of wage earners this does not accord very well with a picture of a population experiencing grave subsistence problems. The impression is of a more generally favourable situation than that prevailing over the period of similar length, 1520–1600, when the population notably increased. To the uncertain extent that nutrition levels can be invoked in explanation of the population pattern they would apply, of course, not only to the diseases specifically mentioned but to all forms of illness, both those caused by organisms and, even more pertinently, to deficiency diseases such as rickets; and, further, though more speculatively, to fecundity so that a lower birth rate might reinforce the demographic effects of a higher death rate.

The second possible explanation of a degradation of conditions of life is as a matter of historical fact free of ambiguity. The spread of gin drinking is notorious. Starting in the 1690s the habit was at its height between 1720 and 1740, which years a large section of lower London society seems to have passed in a state of more or less continual inebriation. But the total demographic impact of the practice is difficult to estimate and has perhaps been exaggerated in the past. Certain heart, liver and kidney conditions can be caused or gravely aggravated by heavy drinking, and there must have been cases of outright alcoholic poisoning. But the direct bearing of gin drinking on the incidence of the common diseases would be very slight; its significant repercussions would more probably be by way of the human consequences of frequent drunkenness and excessive expenditure on gin: neglect of oneself and one's children, inadequate food, warmth, clothing and housing. But gin was cheap and the living conditions of the poor were very bad anyway. Furthermore the gin-soaked masses are a phenomenon largely peculiar to London and one hears nothing of gin drinking in the countryside which contained the bulk of the population.

If the domestic situation does not yield any very evident explanation of the course of population, what of migration? The population of the trans-Atlantic colonies, excluding natives and Negro slaves, has been estimated at roughly 300,000 in 1698 and at about 375,000 in 1714. Plainly if these numbers (less the relatively small amount of pre-1640 inhabitants) are transferred back to England one has then a population pattern for this period roughly consonant with the preceding one. But although there would be some legitimacy in this procedure as long as a large proportion of the colonists were of English birth, allowance would have to be made for a lower mortality rate under the better living conditions as well as for the presence of a certain number of colonists of other national origins, principally the Dutch in New York. Furthermore, this was a time not only of emigration but of immigration into England. Following the revocation of the Edict of Nantes (1685) 15,000 French Huguenots were numbered in England in 1687 and there was a steady flow of them right through this period. To them can be added some Jews, principally Spanish and Portuguese, after they were readmitted by Cromwell in 1655, and Rhineland Germans, several thousand of whom sought religious refuge in England in the early eighteenth century. Scots and Irish immigration must also be reckoned with, though the latter only seems to have started to assume its later extent at the very end of the period. On balance the flow of migrants was certainly outwards over the whole period and is thus a positive contribution towards an explanation of its demography but one which, all things considered, seems to fall short of completeness. Future research will doubtless throw more light on the matter but at least in the interim the population history of this period must remain something of a puzzle.

A prices graph for the period would exhibit some relationship with the apparent course of population. The tendency remained upwards through the 1640s, wobbled through the 1650s and in 1662 started gently downwards until the bad harvests of the 1690s sharply reversed the movement. On recovery in 1700 prices remained about stable for the next three decades; a tendency to fall off in the 1720s was checked by the run of defective harvests, 1725–29, but made itself felt in the 1730s. The course of prices then, like population, was not such as to initiate important movements in the economy.

If quietness is the economic keynote of the times that is not to be confused with retrogression or even with stagnation. All the indications from about 1660 onwards are of a modest increase in real wealth. And indeed that is just about what one would expect on *prima facie* grounds. No disaster or profound upheaval occurred to undo the improvements, such as they were, already effected in the means of satisfying material wants nor to check their gradual extension; and, now, gains in productivity were not likely to be eaten up by rising population. Nothing evidences this better than the course of agriculture. With the Restoration could be conveniently dated the beginning of that very slow but steady raising of farming efficiency which was to work itself out on English land over the next couple of centuries or so.

Agriculture

The overall balance as between grain and livestock had been broadly settled by the early years of the seventeenth century, and no development of these years seriously altered it. But within that general pattern of stability a good deal of internal reshuffling was taking place as larger commercial farmers adapted their kind of farming to the land they occupied. There would be many particular local instances of this sort of change but the two general regional tendencies that stand out most clearly are the shift from pasture to arable on the light sandy soils of East Anglia and the reverse shift on the heavy wet clays of the Midlands. In East Anglia this arose out of a growing recognition that the thin permanent pastures which for centuries had carried sheep could be converted into excellent cornland if treated in the right manner. (What they required was additional nitrogen although it was not understood in these terms until the nineteenth century.) The key to putting the land into fertile condition was the use of root crops and artificial grasses. The full potentialities of these were perhaps gradually realised as a result of the experience of those who were already using the former as animal fodder and of those who were sowing the latter on permanent grassland; perhaps their developed use in conjunction with grain crops was borrowed direct from the Dutch, who pioneered the method. Either way, by the end of this period after local trials and experiments of which we have only hints the standard Norfolk four-course rotation had been fully evolved, although even in that county which was the most advanced in East Anglia the practice was not yet universal. It was a four-year crop cycle: a root crop (usually turnips); barley or oats; clover (or some other artificial grass) or rye; wheat. (The third element varied according as it was judged whether or not the land should be made to bear three successive grain crops after turnips.) The whole was commonly assisted by an initial marling of the land.

The outstanding feature of this cropping course is the elimination of a fallow year, the roots or grasses not merely serving as a substitute but making for positively greater grain yields in subsequent years. Much of the benefit of the method would of course be lost if there were not a profitable outlet for the roots and grasses raised in quantity. The encroachment on pasture did not mean at all that livestock were wholly abandoned, if only because of the need for their manure. It was a mixed farming system, but one in which the optimum balance was tilted away from livestock so that it could only be fully implemented if there were an outside market for the fodder crops grown; and, therefore, one not very well suited to the essentially subsistence farmer who had no ready access to distant markets. It was most profitably adopted by large commercial farmers with enclosed pasture which could easily be partially converted to arable; and, though we have as yet little positive knowledge on this point, its adoption can plausibly be related to the contemporary movement away from arable in the Midlands, creating a market there for fodder crops. But there was also plenty of scope for exploiting the system on the spot by shifting from the rearing of beasts to finishing animals brought in from the north and west, and this was certainly the consequence that most caught contemporary attention. Here too, however, the small man was at a disadvantage. The same problem of access to markets arose with respect to buying in store animals, intensified by the need for liquid capital to finance the purchase as well as by the general diseconomies of small scale livestock farming.

The agricultural movement in the Midlands was neither as novel nor as progressive as that in East Anglia. Conversion from arable to pasture had been conspicuous there in earlier times. Its continuation after the passing of the particular incentives of those times is in general to be attributed to negative factors: the difficulty of moving grain because of poor transport facilities, and the high cost or technical problems of draining land which in its primitive wet state was more suited to grass than to corn. Other than in the extended use of artificial grasses for pasture and meadow – and in appropriate places, the introduction of water meadows – it was not a swing that was accompanied by any advance in farming techniques although the keener discernment as to alternative forms of farming which it manifests is a mark of progressiveness of a kind.

The patterns of change most evident in East Anglia and the Midlands were repeated elsewhere in less pronounced or less extensive fashion. In many parts of southern England root crops and artificial grasses were here and there being incorporated into arable courses. Over the last three decades or so of the period their use became regular on the chalk soils of Wiltshire, Oxfordshire, Berkshire and Buckinghamshire, where, as in East Anglia, they were employed to convert permanent pasture into cornland. The Midlands pattern was to be found also in the Wealden region of Sussex and Kent, where land assarted from the forest was, after varying periods under the plough, given over more and more to livestock.

Turnips and clover were easily the most important contribution of the period to agricultural productivity. Hymns to their praise were on the lips of every progressive speaker and filled the pages of the abundant farming literature. In other directions there seems to have been little advance. The use of various artificial manures was doubtless extended, but the tendency to switch to pasture on wet land probably deadened the interest in drainage. There was some progress in tool and equipment design but the two devices particularly associated with the most memorable propagandist of the times, Jethro Tull, were not to emerge from the experimental stage within this period. Tull's *Horse Houghing Husbandry* published in 1731 was based on over thirty years' experience of farming his own land. It was a strange mixture of farfetched theory and close practical observation and some of its exhortations were very wisely ignored. The starting point of Tull's approach to arable farming was not, in principle, new: dibbing instead of broadcast sowing. But Tull went further than earlier experimenters. In the first place he designed and constructed a workable seed drill which nobody previously seems to have been able to do, and without which dibbing could remain only a beautiful idea. In the second place dibbing for Tull was not merely a matter of preventing waste of seed but also of creating straight paths through rows of growing corn along which a horse-drawn hoe could pass to break up the soil and thus promote growth. Even by the end of the eighteenth century, however, the seed drill and the horse hoe had not become standard pieces of agricultural equipment.

The relationship between advanced farming practices, large farms and enclosure has already been discussed,[1] and all that need be reiterated here is the danger of appraising English farming as a whole by reference to its highest levels. Enclosure went on steadily through the period. Sometimes, particularly in connection with enclosure of the commons, it resulted from a community initiative. More often perhaps it was the work of a landlord, in which case it might be accompanied by engrossment and, in the Midlands, by conversion from arable to pasture. The indications are that the rate of enclosure was more rapid in this period than in the preceding one. Yet there was none of the public furore with which earlier enclosures had been attended. For this two principal reasons can be assigned: one, that much of the earlier distress associated by contemporaries with enclosure had been due to rising population; two, that establishment opinion through this period swung decisively to the view that enclosure was positively beneficial. This attitude in turn can be run back to two grounds: a keener appreciation of the gross economic advantages of enclosure, and a dulling of the sense of public responsibility for the deprived in an age which attributed a particular sacrosanctity to property rights and which tended increasingly to conceive of the propertyless as so many adjustable units of labour. The same sharp sense of property rights, however,

[1] See pp. 194–6.

tended to operate also to check enclosure since often, especially in the case of commons, such rights could not be clearly determined. The Statute of Merton was by now a total dead letter, buried under the earlier wave of anti-enclosure sentiment – and, in any event, commonly inapplicable since lordship of a manor had often become an empty style voided of any rights of real ownership. The legal complications thus posed were usually met by securing the forms of agreement from those parties who could be conceived to have legal rights in the land and registering this agreement in the Court of Chancery. But the validity of this procedure was not unquestionable, the more especially as it was sometimes accompanied by various kinds of chicanery. An absolutely unchallengeable procedure was needed if enclosure were not to be impeded by legal difficulties. Against an Act of Parliament there could be no appeal and from the early years of the eighteenth century some landlords were cutting through the legalistic thicket by obtaining a private Act legitimising an enclosure, though even by 1740 this procedure was still largely confined to those enjoying Parliamentary influence.

The enclosing landlord was no longer an object of public contumely. Nor was the engrossing landlord. From at least the early years of the eighteenth century there was a clear if slow drift towards larger farms, both arable and pasture, not only on enclosed land but in open fields as well. As earlier, an engrossment-minded landlord often found himself obstructed by copyholds – tenures which, certainly by the early eighteenth century, had shed the ambiguities and uncertainties which had earlier pervaded them and had become the subject of comprehensive and secure definition by the common law, so that their extinction had usually to be a long-drawn-out affair, waiting on deaths or the expiry of lines of inheritance, unless copyholders could be induced to sell out.

The extirpation of copyholds was far from being invariably a prelude to engrossment. More often than not it merely reflected a landlord's concern to secure more flexible control over his property. For the extinguished copyhold a tenancy-at-will would commonly be substituted, the net result being that regular, but variable, rents took the place of irregular entry fines. Where engrossment did take place the newly created larger farms might be held on lease, the sort of business-like tenant whom the landlord wanted being reluctant to expose himself to abrupt rent increases. But leases for very long periods or for lives became less common – seven, fourteen and twenty-one years were normal and the bias amongst landlords appears to have been steadily towards as short terms as were consonant with sustaining the lessees' interest in conserving the land. Enlightened opinion was evolving an ideal type of landlord who brought to the management of his property the close careful watchfulness of the businessman rather than the comfortable indolence of the *rentier*; who nursed his estate so that it yielded steady returns rather than plundered it for occasional large sums. The best management extended to control of tenant farming practices with the landlord's own home farm serving as a trial ground for new methods. By the end of this period tenant contracts in Norfolk commonly contained detailed specifications as to farming routines and when the landlord was ready to vest abundant capital in farm buildings, roadways, fences etc. the tenant had almost become a mere intermediary through whom the landlord farmed his property. But as with farmers so with landlords: the average fell well short of the best. Contemporary with the most advanced Norfolk estate owners were all sorts of proprietors: those whose land under copyhold and long lease was quite beyond their control or concern; 'posterity be damned' rackrenters; amiable but ignorant squires; great graziers who found sheep less troublesome than tenants; and so on. There can be no warrant for speaking of the typical English landlord through these years. But the kind of landlord who appreciated that his own prosperity was best served by promoting that of his tenants was becoming more and more common. Landlord initiative must be credited with some significant part in enhancing the productivity of English agriculture over this period.

That enhancement seems to have gone to the point that when population growth was checked in the 1720s and '30s English agriculture found itself experiencing a crisis of overproduction.[1] The years 1725–40 were ones of agricultural depression. The fundamental nature of the depression was masked over the first five of those years by a run of bad harvests, when many farmers found their yield too low to secure them a decent return, but the good harvests of the 1730s took them out of the frying-pan into the fire. Their land was now yielding too much. Produce could only be sold at prices which often did not enable them to cover their rents, and landlords were sometimes forced to share the distress of their tenants. Although exports rose steeply, overseas markets could not absorb the surplus, and, indeed, the established policy of

---

[1] Perhaps better styled a crisis of imbalanced income distribution. There were still plenty of people with empty stomachs but who, even at low bread prices, lacked the money to fill them.

encouraging exports of grain was in some measure responsible for over-production.

TABLE 1.2. *Wheat exports: annual averages in 000 qtrs*

1700–09	1710–19	1720–29	1730–39
105	109	116	296

After trial measures in 1663, 1670 and 1673, the decisive reversal of the earlier antagonism towards grain exports had taken place with the Corn Law of 1689 which granted a bounty of 5 shillings a quarter on exports of wheat as long as the home price was below 48 shillings a quarter (that price was regularly exceeded in the 1690s but only infrequently thereafter). Below 53s 4d a quarter imports of wheat were subject to a duty of 16s a quarter; below 80s a quarter to one of 8s; and above 80s one of 5s 4d. Similar regulations governed external trade in barley, oats and rye. The justification for these privileges was threefold. They tended to redress the fiscal bias against landowners arising out of the land tax.[1] They compensated the agricultural interests for the ban on wool exports. And by promoting the cultivation of grain they softened the effects on consumers of bad harvests – at the cost of rather higher prices during ordinary years.

One set of farmers prospered during the depression years: the dairy farmers. Evidences of specialist dairy farming are manifest from the very beginning of the seventeenth century. Within this period an extensive area comprising adjoining parts of Wiltshire, Gloucestershire and Somerset, became a major production centre of cheese and butter, its supplies supplemented from lesser centres in Suffolk, Essex, Cheshire, Warwickshire and Yorkshire. The taste for dairy produce appears to have developed steadily through these years and while the suppliers of meat and grain were suffering from languishing demand, the dairy farmers were still in course of catching up with expanding market opportunities. But the difficulties of the producers of basic foodstuffs were, in the long term view, a healthier portent. Their surplus capacity was a cushion against the shock of population explosion in succeeding years.

[1] Bias, because there was no income tax and land was the only income-yielding asset which bore tax.

Industry and science

The record of industry is in very broad terms similar to that of agriculture. But in no important field was there a technical advance comparable with that effected by the introduction of root crops and artificial grasses into arable rotations. This is perhaps all the more remarkable when one considers that the early part of this period witnessed the rapid spread in enlightened circles of the Baconian faith in the capacity of scientific inquiry to promote technological and, thus, economic progress; when one remembers that these are the years of the great seminal achievements in physics, chemistry and mathematics of Descartes, Torricelli, Boyle, Leibniz and Newton. The Royal Society at its foundation in 1660 was imbued with the conviction that science was the handmaid of technology. Yet as early as the end of the seventeenth century science had lost interest in industry and industry had been given little reason to look for assistance to the laboratories and the tomes of the natural philosophers. Newton lived and died without giving a thought to possible practical applications of his work. The task of disclosing the fundamental laws which governed the physical universe had proved much more formidable than the early optimists had supposed and few were prepared to leave this grand project in abeyance while seeking more limited ends which might tend to close the gap between pure and real. Furthermore, an element indispensable in bridging that gap in most fields was lacking: there was no body of engineers to translate the theoretical concepts of scientists into practicable productive techniques. This is something of a chicken and egg matter: such a corps was unlikely to appear until it had something substantial to work on; science was unlikely to take a sharp practical turn without a close association with men who combined a technical competence with a theoretical understanding. When later an engineering profession started to constitute itself, it was not science which provided the fillip and it was many years before a fruitful intimacy was established between the two.

The period did engender one distinctly useful technical advance which originated in pure science, and it would be convenient to start with the industry which was its principal beneficiary. The work of the Italian, Torricelli, around the middle of the seventeenth century on atmospheric pressure and vacuum led eventually to the construction in 1705 by Thomas Newcomen of a workable engine in which a piston moved up and down inside a cylinder, the top of the piston being

attached to one end of a pivoted beam which therefore see-sawed with
the movement of the piston. The downward strike of the piston was
caused by evacuating the cylinder, the upward stroke by readmitting
the atmosphere at the bottom of the cylinder so that a weight suspended
from the opposite end of the beam was enabled to pull that end down
and the piston up again. Evacuation of the cylinder was effected by
first filling it with steam through a valve which was then closed rendering the cylinder airtight when the steam was condensed by pouring
cold water on the outside of the cylinder.[1] The full theoretical power
potential of the Newcomen engine was, of course, limited to the force
of atmospheric pressure but in practice the telling limitation was not
posed by the engine itself but by the absence of any attachment to
convert its straight up and down motion into more widely usable rotary
motion. The development of such a device would not in itself have
presented any serious engineering problem – knife-grinders already
used one obscurely. But nobody for many years was to make the
imaginative leap towards envisaging an engine as a general prime
mover; fundamentally, perhaps, because there was not enough machinery currently in use and susceptible to being powered to excite such
a project, nor, as a consequence, sufficient engineers likely to turn their
minds in this direction. The Newcomen engine was designed specifically
as a pumping engine and a pumping engine it remained. As such it had
uses in various fields: the delivery of municipal water supplies; the
prevention of reflooding in reclaimed fenland; the building up of a
reservoir for use in dry periods by water powered enterprises; and above
all the drainage of deep mines. It may have been with Cornish tin and
copper mines in mind that Newcomen first constructed the engine but
from the beginning it was most widely used in the much more important coal industry.

The coal industry

Early technical difficulties retarded the introduction of the Newcomen
engine, but from about 1720 it was steadily replacing water, animal or
wind powered pumps in collieries operating below the natural drainage
level. Its impact in economic terms is impossible to estimate with any
kind of precision. Certainly without it the deepest mines at the end of

---

[1] This brief explanation is given principally for the sake of making the point that while
steam was used, it was only for the purpose of creating a vacuum. There was no use of
steam *power*.

this period could not have been worked at all – in Tyneside, for instance, it enabled collieries to move back towards the river bank to work deep seams which earlier had had to be passed over. But the proportion of gross British coal supplies coming from such depths was slight. In the less intensively worked areas (those less well placed for delivery to large markets) there would still have been numerous mines needing no pumping equipment and even where a Newcomen engine was substituted for an earlier source of power the economies effected may often have been merely marginal, indeed in many cases were perhaps only available because the coal for the engine was being used at the point of production. And drainage costs were only one element in total costs, although a very considerable element in some mines. On an overall balance the engine must have made for some reduction in coal prices, probably more by way of permitting the exploitation of deep deposits near to navigable water and thus lowering land haulage costs than by way of direct cost reductions in existing mines.

Haulage from pit-head to water was itself the subject of improvement by the laying of 'dramways', two lines of parallel wooden planks (their first recorded use dates from the 1590s), sometimes on an artificial causeway. In some pits by the end of the period dramways were also in use underground, between the coalface and the bottom of the shaft. In particular cases the resulting economies in labour, animals and equipment employed in haulage may have been considerable.

By and large it was in the north-eastern coalfield where the need was greatest that Newcomen engines and dramways were mostly in evidence. At the beginning of the period Tyneside alone accounted for approaching a quarter of total British output but even by then its rate of expansion had greatly slackened and although Wearside and the Northumberland coast maintained a high growth rate until towards the end of the seventeenth century the principal scene of the rapidly escalating activity which had characterised the previous century shifted to the west, where development had earlier been slower. South Wales and Cumberland in particular effected a marked upsurge in output through the first fifty years or so of this period. Both areas were well placed for delivery to Ireland, and Cumberland, a virtual monopoly of the Lowther family, leant very heavily on the Dublin market, being too far removed from other major population centres to be able to compete effectively with the north-east, or with South Wales, which sold up the Severn and round the coast to Southampton. London, the most valuable prize of all, continued to draw exclusively on the north-east, thus ensuring the sustained primacy of that region and checking further growth in the west.

If one takes account of development in south Lancashire, Staffordshire, Warwickshire and other scattered western coalfields, the record of the west along with continuing though decelerating growth in the north-east and the east Midlands would permit the first great phase of exploitation of British coal resources, starting around 1540, to be run through to about 1690. Its continuation into the first half of this period would seem to have been founded principally on rising population and the completion of the shift from wood to coal as a domestic fuel, especially in western areas. Industrial users, accounting for about a third of total output, similarly finalised conversion in fields where the process was already under way. New as coal users were those saltmakers using the natural brine waters of Cheshire and Worcestershire who had continued to burn wood until about 1670, and the maltsters who had hitherto found the fumes in coal-fired kilns intolerable. The device of first coking the coal was introduced around Burton-on-Trent in the mid-seventeenth century and was considered by some actually to improve the flavour of the beer. Iron-smelters also experimented with coke but apart from Abraham Darby at Coalbrookdale, Shropshire, who succeeded in producing acceptable quality pig, some time between 1709 and 1717, the results were hopelessly unsatisfactory and within this period the secret of Darby's technique seems to have remained closeted in Coalbrookdale. Some tin, lead and copper smelters were using coal from around the end of the seventeenth century, but for the while the major extension of markets ceased and over the last half of this period the level of coal output cannot have run much ahead of the graph of population.

The metallurgical industries

One of the most eye-catching developments of the period is the continuing and probably accelerated growth of metal working in Birmingham and a wide surrounding area. By 1740 one could consider north Warwickshire, south Staffordshire and east Worcestershire as constituting an industrial region, though Birmingham would provide the only conspicuous instance of urban development; outside that town, work, most notably nailmaking was scattered throughout the countryside.

In some measure the expansion of metal manufactures here was probably only the obverse of contraction elsewhere as, despite transport costs, wares from this region ousted local products in many parts of England. In some part too it was probably a matter of replacing foreign articles on the British market. Export opportunities had a hand in it also, most especially in the trans-Atlantic colonies whose growing populations leant heavily on the mother country for supplies of tools, utensils, weapons, etc. Birmingham did an especially lively trade in muskets and pistols. In wartime the British government was, of course, an outstanding customer but even in peacetime the colonists, the East India Company and the slave-traders who bartered cheap muskets for their human cargoes provided a regular market. Furthermore metal goods from this burgeoning region were not only filling markets but creating them through the cultivation of novel cheap wares which excited the contempt and anger of older crafts elsewhere, particularly in the field of decorative and ornamental articles; buttons and shoe buckles in imitation silver were lines that came to sell especially well.

Although through the later years of this period copper and brass were figuring prominently, the hardware trades of Birmingham and region were above all ironworking trades, and it was a fine balance of supplies of iron and coal and accessibility to markets that gave the area its competitive strength. By 1720, the first year for which estimates of output are available, the west Midlands had become the leading bar iron producing region in the country accounting for some 6,000 tons out of a national total of about 13,500. This west Midlands area extended beyond the manufacturing region which constituted its market comprising in addition north Staffordshire and, most importantly, Shropshire. The latter smelted more iron than any other district in the country, some being refined in the immediate vicinity, some being sent as pig across the Severn. But even with Shropshire to draw on to supplement the output of local furnaces the forge-masters of Warwickshire, Staffordshire and Worcestershire had to look further afield for supplies of pig. The great bulk of the output of the Forest of Dean, under pressure of demand largely converted now from bloomery to blast furnace, came up the Severn to them, along with shipments from South Wales. Thus reinforced the west Midlands may have been about self-sufficient in bar iron. But if so the shortfall in the rest of the country was enormous.

Against the 7,500 tons or so of bar produced elsewhere in Great Britain, there was being imported around 1720 about 20,000 tons, nearly all of it from Sweden. A considerable proportion of this was used in London, easily the most important centre of the manufacture of fine, expensive wares. Not only did many craftsmen positively require the better quality iron which Sweden with its high grade ore and charcoal could supply, but the relative Swedish plenitude of charcoal, which in Britain accounted for a larger part of smelting costs than did ore, along with direct access by sea, meant that much of the eastern seaboard area could obtain its raw iron more cheaply from Sweden than from any home centre, and although ingenuity, specialisation and cheap coal might give the Birmingham area an advantage over a wide range of manufactured articles, many continued to be the work of local smiths who bought their iron where it was cheapest. And the most considerable of all contemporary ironworking concerns, that of Ambrose Crowley, founded at Winlaton on the Tyne in 1691, had been deliberately located in the north-east for the sake of local coal and convenient deliveries of Swedish iron.

The 1720 data yield a good picture of the British iron industry at that point in time. But the lack of similar information for any other date within or even close to this period means that it is a still picture, incapable of being run forwards or backwards. Whether it is one of an advancing industry or of a declining industry is difficult to say. Counts of the number of blast furnaces made in 1640 and 1717 amount to seventy-eight and sixty-one respectively but it is improbable that either was exhaustive and, even if both had been, the strong probability that the average furnace of 1717 had a higher capacity than the one of 1640 would preclude any clear inference being drawn. But in the lack of anything else, this slender indication must sustain the tentative judgment that domestic output remained much the same over those seventy-seven years. Imports of iron, for which figures are continuously available from 1697, rose fairly steadily from about 16,000 tons around that date to about 25,000 tons over the concluding years of the period. If the increase in domestic output were commensurate with this, it would signify a growth rate in the iron-using trades of 58 per cent over forty-odd years – an impressive rate considering the course of population change over those years but not an utterly incredible one. A more modest view of the likely change in iron consumption could start with the given estimate for 1720 of a domestic pig output of 25,000 tons of which some three-quarters were refined yielding about 13,500 tons of bar, leaving, in conveniently rounded figures, 6,500 tons of cast when the total content of iron goods divides about evenly between home and foreign iron (20,000 tons each). If then the domestic output of raw iron had remained the same from 1697 onwards the increase in imports would signify a consumption growth of 25 per cent (about ½ per cent p.a.) which would be quite consonant with the general impression one has of the record of metal manufactures through the years concerned. Any lower rate of consumption growth would signify an actual decline in the activity of British blast furnaces.

The history of particular regions is in broad terms clearer than that of the country as a whole. Output of pig in the west Midlands (including therein Gloucestershire) grew through the period. The decline of the Wealden industry proceeded unchecked. South Wales, already a major producer in 1640, at least maintained its level of production; towards the end of the seventeenth century its furnaces probably turned out more pig than any other region in the country, though thereafter the west Midlands outstripped it. It was in the north, with its better preserved woods, that development was most vigorous, in a strictly mathematical sense. The furnace counts of 1640 and 1717 yield seven and twelve respectively for the northern counties, indicating a growth from 9 per cent of national capacity to 20 per cent, but the furnaces were scattered over a wide area comprising Derbyshire, Yorkshire, Durham, Cumberland and Lancashire, some of them located in very remote spots, and only as a matter of literary convenience can they be grouped together.

In addition to the geographical movement two other internal shifts within the industry as a whole warrant a comment apiece. The one is the edging out of the old type of estate owner, exploiting his own ore-bearing land, by the authentic 'iron-master', simultaneously capitalist, manager and technologist, although the two types sometimes continued to coexist in association with one another as, most prominently, in the case of the affiliated ore pits, charcoal woods, furnaces, forges and manufacturing establishments, scattered through Monmouthshire, the Forest of Dean, the Stour valley and north Staffordshire which in the late seventeenth and early eighteenth centuries were loosely held together by the common participation of the landed Foley family. The second shift is the edging away from bar iron towards the cast iron for which the generally mediocre quality British pig was more suitable, or, at least, less unsuitable. The obverse to this was of course a correspondingly increasing dependence on foreign sources of bar, principally Sweden, supplemented over the last couple of decades of the period by Russia and North America.

To some extent then British and foreign iron were not competitive but complementary. As indicated above, about a quarter of British pig by 1720 was transmuted directly into cast iron articles, constituting in all about one-sixth of British iron manufactures, and though lack of statistical data precludes any strict comparison with earlier times, it appears as if a fairly steady attention was being given by iron-masters to extending the scope of cast iron by new casting techniques and, possibly, by modifications in smelting so as to produce a less viscous material. A more conspicuous technical breakthrough in ironworking was achieved in the 1690s when the art of tinplating, producing a rust-free material for saucepans and other utensils and long known in Germany was mastered in south Wales. From about 1710 imported tinplate was being steadily replaced by the south Wales article. All in all then while the record of the British iron industry over these hundred years may not be one of signal growth it exhibits enough evidence of continuing enterprise to render the word, stagnation, inappropriate.

The impact of tinplating, continental and domestic, also seems to show up clearly in the statistics of Cornish tin output and exports, with production increasing about three-fold over the period as a whole, about nine-tenths of which went abroad. A dip in output registered in the 1690s may in some part reflect economic adversities in western Europe generally due to the peculiarly bad run of harvests of that decade, but is probably to be more closely associated with the arrival of Siamese tin on the European market, brought in by the Dutch at a price only some two-thirds that of Cornish tin, though the quantities shipped were never enough to oust Cornwall from its position of premier European supplier.

It was in the opening years of the eighteenth century, after earlier experimentation, that the smelting of tin with coal was successfully effected in conjunction with the development of a reverbatory furnace. The lack of local coal deposits limited the advantages to be gained from the technique. And though coal could be had fairly cheaply by sea from South Wales the method offered no marked cost advantage over charcoal or peat smelting in the simpler and cheaper blowing house; moreover it produced tin of a slightly inferior quality, so that even by the end of the period most tin was still smelted with the traditional fuels. The reverberatory furnace was only one of a number of technical improvements realised both in smelting and the preliminary dressing of the ore through the years from about 1670 onwards, which were characterised by a marked quickening of inventiveness and imaginative-ness in the industry, perhaps to be associated with the intrusion of outside entrepreneurs equipped with a wider acquaintance of mineralogy and metallurgy than the local miner, wedded to traditional methods. However, the fact that only one Newcomen engine is known to have been installed in this period suggests that as yet large capital sums were not being vested in deep mining while the fragmentary price data available indicates that technical progress was doing no more than offset rising costs as the poorer ores surviving in relatively shallow deposits had to be worked.

Signs of technical progress are as plain in lead working as in tin, and indeed the lead industry was the more forward in the introduction of the Newcomen engine to permit of deep mining: the first recorded installation dates from 1720 and several were in use by the end of the period. A reverberatory furnace capable of coal smelting was perfected about 1690 and over the next fifty years came to be widely used in Derbyshire and north Wales where coal was locally available. Else-where the mixture of fuels, wood, charcoal, peat, cinders, traditionally employed, continued in use.

Prominent in the introduction of both the reverberatory furnace and the Newcomen engine was the London Lead Company, whose foundation in 1702 could conveniently be said to date the decisive transition from the epoch of the free miner to that of the capitalistic concern in the industry. Indeed as a historical phenomenon the Company could be made to bear a significance of much wider import since it was one of the first large-scale industrial enterprises successfully to operate on a basis of such a widely dispersed share ownership that it had itself a distinct impersonal existence which hung on the competence of a succession of salaried executives. By 1721 it was working mines in north Wales, Derbyshire, Cumberland, Durham and Scotland and although it did not show a regular working profit until 1743 the mere fact that it had survived until then is a measure of the efficiency of its direction. Most of the original shareholders were Quakers, as were its chief officers, and one can readily credit that it was the cool, prudent and patient realism which these men brought to bear that granted it a history contrasting sharply with that of the numerous contemporary fly-by-night joint stock ventures launched on a wave of lunatic opti-mism. Its durability and ultimate profitability can be attributed to three factors: professional expertise among its directors; the vigilant watch kept on its scattered undertakings by means of frequent personal visits from the directors, along with a careful selection of local managers; and the ability to raise fresh capital to support original investment which had not yet paid off. The Quaker reputation for honesty doubtless helped here although the company was not above the customary practice of paying dividends out of new capital in order to sustain credit.

In a sense the London Lead Company was only an extension of a long-established form of organisation, familiar in both tin and lead mining on account of the uncertain life of enterprises excavating ores of very slight lateral extent and therefore prone to vanish abruptly. The prudent investor in tin or lead spread his risks by taking shares in several local syndicates. The Company simply offered a much wider spread, though it differed fairly radically from the local groupings in offering it to those who had no association with the industry and in relieving them of any personal involvement in its management. Other smaller joint stock type concerns were also formed around the same time but, notwithstanding the pre-eminent position of the Company from 1702, the great bulk of British lead was still produced by enterprises in which ownership and management remained intimately associated: syndicates containing both working and non-working members; mines conducted by the wealthier owners of ore-bearing land; and even the diminutive diggings of independent miners. Of the course of gross output from these multifarious units we are ignorant but the figures for lead exports – available from 1697 and more or less the same thoughout – do not suggest any marked change.

Copper-working already had its counterpart to the London Lead Company in the Society of Mines Royal. But this, after the closure of its Keswick works during the Civil War, undertook no further ventures of any consequence. Indeed its continuing statutory monopoly of copper-working, along with the corresponding monopoly of brass manufacture enjoyed by the closely associated Society of Mineral and Battery Works, would appear to have been a positive hindrance to development in these fields. Certainly, it was in the three decades or so following the withdrawal in 1684 of these monopoly privileges that English brassmakers mastered the techniques which enabled the country largely to dispense with imported brasswares and provided the almost extinct copper industry with an important domestic market.[1] The copper mines of Cornwall and Devon, which little had been made of under the Society of Mines Royal, sprang into life, and copper might have displaced tin as the chief metallurgical activity of the region had

---

[1] Private ventures, technically illegal, in copper and brass antedate 1689. The abolition of the monopolies is probably to be thought of as the removal of an embarrassing impediment to continued development rather than as an instigator of new enterprise.

it not been that while the tin ore was smelted locally the copper ore moved out raw.

While tin markets lay largely overseas and the comparative economics of freighting ore and freighting metal over considerable distances told decisively in favour of on the spot smelting, copper markets consisted principally of the home makers of brass goods, situated chiefly in London, Bristol, Gloucester and, increasingly, Birmingham; a complex balancing of the distance from copper ore, calamine, fuel[1] and markets, and the need of abundant water power, scattered copper-smelting over a number of localities, among which south Wales and the Bristol region were the most important. The resulting need to coordinate activities on an extensive geographical scale had a further particular consequence. The powered equipment used in smelting and in rolling and slitting copper or brass plates necessitated capitalist organisation in any event. But the span of control which had to be exercised placed a particular premium on large-scale operations and virtually from the beginning smelting and the immediately associated processes were concentrated in a handful of concerns which were among the largest industrial enterprises of their day, and which exercised a dominant position in the face of the copper miners in one direction and of the makers of brass and copper artifacts in the other.

The newer industries

The use of bricks as a building material was greatly extended through this period, before the end of which it had become standard for all but the grandest (stone) and the humblest (mud) edifices throughout most of lowland England. This was of course associated with a great increase of activity in brickfields and kilns. But caution must be exercised in employing this as an indicator of economic progress. The main agent of the swing to brick in these as in earlier years was the diminishing supply and consequently rising price of timber. The availability of brick and the enterprise that made it available ensured that no universal deterioration occurred in standards of housing, and inasmuch as a good brick built house would be more durable and healthier than a wood and plaster one the conversion would constitute a welfare gain. But could the mere wage-earner or small farmer afford a *good* brick built house or cottage, particularly in areas distant from brickfields where high transport costs would add substantially to brick prices? In particular

---

[1] A fully practicable method of coal smelting was evolved in the 1690s.

districts at least many must have had to make do with homes constructed of low grade materials and/or smaller dwellings than those their predecessors had inhabited. And those who did occupy better homes may often have had to expend a higher proportion of their income on them than their ancestors had expended on theirs at a time when timber was still comparatively cheap.

Of two other industries, glass and soap making, earlier noted as developing before 1640, one cannot say a great deal for this period. The clear indications are that glass manufacture, released from the constraints of Mansell's patent, effected a vigorous expansion through the second half of the seventeenth century in coal-bearing areas, conspicuously Tyneside, the Birmingham region and St Helens. This expansion must have been founded very largely on relatively cheap glass for fairly general use as windows, bottles, jars and drinking vessels, but the manufacture of expensive ornamental wares of the kind which had been an Italian and a French speciality may have benefited somewhat from Huguenot immigration after 1685.

Marketing opportunities for the soapmakers were almost certainly extended with the disappearance of the monopoly instituted by Charles I, but whether subsequently the English took to washing more often is uncertain until excise figures become available in 1713; between then and the closing years of this period they indicate a growth in output of 8 per cent, suggesting a marginal raising of standards of cleanliness.

Two further industries lend themselves to a mathematical appraisal from the late seventeenth century, through the availability of excise statistics. One of these can easily stand as the period's record holder for rate of growth. Between the late 1680s and the early 1740s, when the peak was reached, the output of spirits (gin and whisky – much the same thing at this time) rose by 1500 per cent, representing at the height an annual consumption of about ten and a half pints of excised spirits per head of the population.[1] Over the same period the brewing industry contracted: annual *per capita* consumption of duty paid beer dropped from about 350 pints to about 250 pints, which is to say that net alcoholic intake does not seem to have changed very much.

Excise figures also indicate the record of the paper industry from 1713 onwards, revealing a growth of about 20 per cent through the first decade or so after that date and stability thereafter. Other sources make it clear that the statistics pick up the industry at the end of a

[1] The next peak was achieved in 1901 when *per capita* consumption was about seven and a half pints.

phase of very lusty development, getting under way in the 1660s. This followed a period during which the industry had been unable to extend the wrapping paper market which it had captured from foreign suppliers through the later sixteenth and early seventeenth centuries. Attempts to produce printing and writing papers which were competitive with those of the French, the Dutch and the Italians had been uniform failures, but allied with the technical lessons learned from experience and from immigrant Huguenots the obstacles posed to imports between 1666 and 1714 gave British manufacturers the opportunity to break into the fine paper field. Wars with two of the exporting countries, Holland and France, were through these years barriers to imported supplies, but intermittent ones. More enduring was the tariff wall steadily built up from 1690, when the duty on most imported papers stood at 5 per cent, to 1714 when it was raised from the 20 per cent which it had then reached to 30 per cent. Only the best quality foreign paper could leap that barrier, and behind it English paper manufacturers snugly enjoyed about three-quarters (by quantity, less by value) of the home market.

Tariff shelter also assisted the silk industry to achieve a modest advance. Here was another quality trade in which England had always lagged behind France and Italy and whose tardy development can in some measure be associated with Huguenot immigration. The industry was not unknown in England in 1685 – in 1621 there were reputed, probably with some exaggeration, to be seven or eight thousand people engaged in it in London – but its early history has not yet been probed and it is only with the closing years of the seventeenth century that it arrests attention. From then, rising tariffs and, in 1701, the absolute prohibition of the use or wear of Indian silks in England secured English weavers, congregated in the Spitalfields district of London, the major share of the home market.

The inescapably high cost of the raw material necessarily confined silk goods to a limited luxury sale, and the same factor also accounts in part for the fact that from the earliest glimpses we have of it the industry was of capitalist organisation. Raw silk was beyond the economic reach of the working throwster (spinner), as silk yarn was beyond that of the weaver; and either, whether working at home or in a rudimentary factory, was unambiguously in the service of an employer, though a journeyman weaver possessed of his own loom and skilled in the making of the more elaborate fabrics which might take a month or six weeks to complete could be in the nature of a commission worker, operating for different employers at different times. Capital was required not only to command supplies of silk but also to acquire equipment. A silk loom was more complicated and costly than the looms used in other textile trades and while many weavers did own their own looms, others could only hire them and others again worked in a factory on their employer's looms. These weaving factories were small – very few housed more than twenty looms and many no more than half a dozen –and a thrifty journeyman weaver in regular employment might accumulate sufficient capital to get a tiny business of his own going. The scale of a master throwster's operations was much greater. The centrepiece of his enterprise was the throwing machine of Italian origin, spinning dozens of lengths of yarn simultaneously. In the seventeenth century these were probably all hand operated but at least by the early years of the eighteenth century they were sometimes being turned by horses and, in one instance recorded in 1714, by a water wheel. Such a device plainly represented a fair capital outlay but the greatest financial burden was imposed by the large numbers who had to be employed in the initial winding of the raw silk on to the bobbins which were then fixed to the machine. Some employers had a labour force, virtually all women and children, of up to a thousand persons, the great majority employed in winding, usually in their own homes.

The first establishment in which several hundred operatives were housed in the one factory was that of the Lombe brothers, Thomas and John, which about 1721 set up business in Derby with some 300 employees. The water-powered throwing machines installed by the Lombes were of a far more sophisticated kind that anything used previously in England, being a direct copy of the apparatus long established in Italy but hitherto only known in England in a much simplified form. Its distinctive contribution was to make available at home a good quality warp thread, whereas previously weavers had had to use French and Italian imports or make do with the inferior English yarn, only really suitable for sewing thread, ribbons, handkerchiefs, and suchlike small pieces. The capacity of the Lombe mill, however, does not seem to have been such as to make any signal dent in yarn imports and the Lombes' patent rights in the machine prevented other English suppliers entering the field until 1732 when the patent expired, after which its history is rather obscure. The Lombe concern started to lose money and disappeared, and no successful followers made an appearance until the 1750s. Possibly, costs in the long run proved higher than anticipated and uncompetitive with those of the more strongly rooted French and

Italian industries. Possibly, English engineering skills were not adequate to the task of making and maintaining machines said to incorporate 97,746 components each. Even behind its tariff wall the English silk industry, both throwing and weaving sections of it, failed to find complete security against foreign competition within this period, or indeed at any later period.

The manufacture of fine linen makes a quartet, along with glass, paper and silk, of industries which had a field cleared for them in the home market by tariffs on imports and which in some degree were helped to exploit this field by an infusion of Huguenot skills. But in the case of linen it was Irish and Scottish manufacturers, rather than English, who grasped these opportunities. Over the last fifty years of this period Belfast and Glasgow became the mercantile centres of rural linen industries far exceeding in output that of the only English region of weight, Lancashire. It was, overwhelmingly, cloth from Ireland and Scotland which with growing success contended with Dutch-finished German linen for the English market. Lancashire was not languishing and, indeed, the general indications are that the production of linen yarn there was slowly but fairly steadily increasing throughout this period, and that the manufacture of the coarser kinds of linen material was at least holding its own. But Lancashire was doing more than this. Through the seventeenth century it was using a growing proportion of its linen yarn for the manufacture of fustians, ousting Dutch, German and other Continental cloths of that kind from the English market and even exporting small quantities. And from the turn of the century it was venturing into new fields, using cotton weft with a linen warp to make a material which was lighter than fustian and more closely resembled pure cotton cloth, with which, in the form of Indian calico, England was by then thoroughly familiar.

Not only was England acquainted with calico but English women were delighted with it, above all with the varieties painted or printed in colourful patterns. From about 1660 the East India Company had been building up a regular and voluminous calico trade. By 1690 the taste for calico had so developed that the manufacturers of woollen cloth conceived themselves to be menaced by it. Their strident protestations eventuated in an Act of 1701 prohibiting the use or wear in England of Indian coloured calicos, but not extending to white Indian calico printed in England. This omission gave an enormous boost to English cloth-printing, which had been slowly developing in London from the 1670s in imitation of Indian work, but using printing blocks, more economical though cruder than the hand-printing usually favoured in India. The woollen interests now bent themselves to stopping this loop-hole and an Act of 1721 comprehensively forbade the use of any coloured cloth made in whole or part of cotton, with, however, an exception in favour of fustians.

In the long run it was the Lancashire cotton using industry rather than the woollen cloth industry, at whose behest they were passed, that was the major beneficiary of the Calico Acts. The 1721 Act explicitly though only incidentally gave it a privileged position – a privilege which in practice extended beyond that conferred by a strict interpretation of the statute for under the name of 'fustians' Lancashire cultivated the production of the lighter cotton-linens which, properly speaking, were a distinct kind of material; a clarifiying Act of 1736 put their legality when made for printing beyond question. The position with regard to checked and striped cloths of this material, pattern woven using dyed yarn, was rather different. These were an imitation of calico checks and stripes which, while never as popular in England as painted or printed calico, had also sold quite well. Fustian, always woven white, could not as a designation be stretched to cover them but it appears that, as long as they were fairly readily distinguishable from calico, authority took the view that they were not in breach of the spirit of the Act, although they did offend against its letter, and the classification of them as linens preserved appearances. They were not, of course, illegal under the 1701 Act and between that date and 1721 the established taste for Indian checks and stripes presented a market opportunity for a homemade substitute, but Lancashire cotton-linens were not as yet fine enough to take much advantage of that opening, which was principally filled by mixed silk and cotton cloths of Dutch and Spitalfields origins. The development of cotton-linens, whether white for printing or in checks and stripes, seems to have proceeded only slowly until towards the very end of this period. But from the mid-1730s Lancashire and lesser centres, such as Weymouth and Spitalfields, were offering a material which, while it could hardly be mistaken for calico, was selling at home for purposes which Indian cottons had once served and was securing a foothold in open competition with Indian cloth in the trans-Atlantic colonies and in the markets of the English slave-traders in West Africa. The rougher fustians had from much earlier won a modest position in New England on which, however, they were not able to improve through the last half of this period, possibly because Irish and Scottish linen was creaming off the market. At home, sales of fustians appear to have fairly steadily expanded until the late 1710s by when they had probably fully absorbed the limited demand for this material.

The bulk of the textiles so far mentioned ended up as garments, but of this final stage there is little one can say. In its essentials tailoring, whether of these or of woollen fabrics, continued to be, as it had been for centuries, conducted mostly by independent tailors working on materials supplied by the customer, perhaps with the help of an apprentice or two and maybe a journeyman working for wages. In London, however, the master tailor who no longer occupied a workbench himself but confined his activity to the management of employees, numbering up to a dozen or more, and held stocks of materials for the customer to choose from had, by the early eighteenth century at least, become a common type in the fashionable trade. Women's clothes and household draperies, when they were not made up at home, were the work of individual seamstresses.

There were, however, three minor textile-using trades which did not lend themselves to custom working: haberdashery, lacemaking, and hosiery. In the first of these the Dutch loom for weaving ribbons, tapes and similar smallwares had by the end of the seventeenth century overridden the bitter and at times violent enmity of the London weavers and was solidly established in two principal centres: London and Manchester, the former devoting itself particularly to silk articles, the latter driving a more general trade using worsted, silk, linen and cotton but naturally biased towards the last two. Capable of weaving up to twenty-four lengths simultaneously the loom was a fairly expensive piece of equipment – not so costly as to necessitate a class of capitalist entrepreneurs but sufficiently so as to confine it in Manchester to those who started out with a modest patrimony or by frugality accumulated the necessary capital while working as journeymen for others who had prospered to the point where they could install extra looms and who in particular cases might effectively be running a small factory containing as many as twelve or fourteen looms. With its well enforced seven-year apprenticeship requirement the Dutch loom business in Manchester was in fact a re-creation of medieval craft conditions. Its products were marketed widely, but those who handled the trade do not seem to have achieved the dominant position vis-à-vis the weavers as they had done in Lancashire's other textile industries, where conditions closely resembled those prevailing in the West of England woollen cloth industry. In London the position of the Dutch loom weaver was the debased one common to the great majority of artisans in that city and most of them probably worked on the premises of merchant-manufacturers who controlled the business.

Lacemaking first forces itself into view towards the end of the seventeenth century as a cottage industry employing a large number of women, particularly in Buckinghamshire, Dorset and Devonshire. Like all industries leaning on female labour it was miserably paid. Activity fluctuated sharply with the vagaries of fashion, and imported Flemish lace was always apt to be more popular. The men who controlled it, supplying the raw materials and distributing the finished product were hardly exclusively so occupied but conducted this trade as a variable adjunct to others.

A stocking industry organised and dominated by a class of master hosiers who procured the materials, supplied the knitting frames and marketed the goods was already in course of development by 1640. The next eighty years or so saw it come to full growth in the east Midlands, building up a considerable export trade, notably with southern Europe. Silk, linen and cotton were used but the great bulk of stockings were made of worsted yarn. And this can lead us finally to what was still easily the most important, not merely of English textile industries but of all English industries.

The woollen industry

However appraised – by numbers employed, by capital involved, by worth of output, by value of exports – the woollen industry in 1740, as in 1640, as in 1540, transcended all others. If what one has to say of it through this period seems disproportionately little by comparison with the attention given to some other industries of much slighter consequence, that must stand as a measure of its success in retaining the commanding position which it had already established, undisturbed by serious adversities. And if it cannot exhibit a growth rate comparable with that achieved in certain industries which started from a low base, such as glass, paper or silk, the absolute value of the increment to output over the whole hundred years exceeded that of any other industry. On the basis of the fragmentary information available it would be plausible to contend that between the beginning and the end of this period the production of woollen goods about doubled, and that taking one decade with another this growth took place at a more or less even pace throughout.

The main lines of advance were those already laid down earlier: a movement away from woollens, which could only sell in quantity in the stagnant northern European market, to worsteds, with their high selling potential in other areas. By about 1720 the manufacture of woollens was virtually extinct throughout East Anglia while only small quantities were still being made in the south-west. The cloth industries of Wiltshire and adjoining areas continued further along the twin paths being followed in the couple of decades before 1640: on the one hand switching from traditional broadcloth to Spanish cloth; on the other abandoning woollens and going over to worsteds, though this latter tendency never became very pronounced and the region always remained principally devoted to woollens, and even to broadcloths, since the very costly Spanish cloth could never command an extensive market. Hardest hit by, and slowest in adjusting to, marketing difficulties in northern Europe was the Pennines industry. The expansion of native cloth-making industries on the Continent, often, especially from the mid-seventeenth century, a matter of deliberate state policy and aided by tariffs on imported cloths, in general proceeded furthest with lower grade materials, partly because these did not set such a high premium on operative skills, partly because duties levied by quantity bore relatively more heavily on cheap cloth than on expensive ones. The Pennines industry at first edged towards better quality woollens in an endeavour to preserve its European markets, but the dwindling of supplies of good quality short staple wool from Lincolnshire curbed this development and forced back on poor quality local wool and supplies of equally indifferent short staple wool from Scotland and Ireland the Pennines industry by the 1660s was in an impasse from which it could only break out by following the example of other cloth-making areas and taking to worsteds. But the experience in this branch of manufacture and the command of markets already achieved by East Anglia and the worsted makers of the west blocked any rapid advance in this direction and it was probably not until the mid-1720s, by when southern European population was launched on a phase of rapid increase, that the swing to worsteds in the West Riding of Yorkshire really got under way in the manner that was ultimately to carry that district to the premiership of the English cloth industry.

It was, above all, the Iberian and Mediterranean markets, along with population growth at home, which enabled the industry to maintain a solid if undramatic growth rate. But although little was to be feared from the competition of local cloth industries in these regions, the field had to be disputed with other exporters. Dutch rivalry, while at no time negligible, was of lessening potency from the 1660s onwards. Production costs had always been higher in the Netherlands and the compensating advantages of lower freight costs and better dyeing techniques were being eroded. But the French industry, developing in its protected home market and with cheap and easy access to the area through its Mediterranean ports, was a power to be reckoned with from about 1700 onwards. Abundant supplies of low-cost long-staple wool ensured English producers a competitive edge, but the margin of advantage was never overwhelming and the commercial need to maintain a high level of productive efficiency must be reckoned a factor in the continuing vitality of the English industry. It could of course count on whatever help government measures were able to afford it. The Navigation Acts conferred a clear advantage in colonial markets, still of marginal but growing importance – about a tenth of cloth exports by the end of the period went across the Atlantic. The prohibition on wool exports, despite a fair amount of smuggling, hampered foreign rivals, especially the Dutch. The industry was truly the darling of public policy. We have already seen how its claims to special protection overrode the interests of the politically powerful East India Company in the passage of the Calico Acts of 1701 and 1721, the latter of which, in form at least, was prepared to put down the English cotton-linen industry on behalf of the woollen manufacturers. An earlier Act of 1698 had crippled the promising Irish woollen industry by forbidding it to export except to England, thus at a stroke of the pen eliminating a strong competitor in overseas markets – perhaps the most blatant instance of economic imperialism which history can offer. There were few lengths to which Englishmen were not prepared to go to preserve and promote an industry whose wellbeing was widely held to be synonymous with that of the nation at large.

Viewed in total perspective the leading trait of English industrial history through this period is, perhaps, the virtual finalisation of that slow process, originating around the middle of the sixteenth century, of bringing England to a position of parity with the most advanced of continental industrial countires. By 1740 there were only two industrial activities of any great weight in which Britain was invidiously retrograde: iron production and silk manufacture,[1] and in the first of these

[1] To which cotton manufacture could be added if the comparison were extended to extra-European countries.

it was the innately inferior quality of native raw materials which placed her at a disadvantage. While in the current state of historical knowledge it cannot be much more than a matter of general impressions, there does seem to be a good case for regarding the phase *c.* 1690–*c.* 1720 as particularly decisive in the achievement of this position, a phase which also contains within its bounds much of the development in other economic sectors with which the rest of this chapter must deal.

The infrastructure

In retrospective view perhaps the most noteworthy developments of these years were in what may be termed the economic infrastructure – that complex of communications and financial agencies which while not themselves productive yet promote or facilitate production, and which become of gathering consequence as different productive activities come to be concentrated in particular centres and in larger units.

A statement of this kind can carry implications of which one certainly ought to be very wary. To focus attention on developments which in a later extended form were of central importance is to run the hazard of a historically premature attribution of that importance and of an exaggeration of the contemporary extent of the development in question. So, if one discerns economic trends in this period which appear to prefigure some of those of that complex of events loosely styled the 'Industrial Revolution' one must at the same time be careful to preserve them in their historical context and to avoid anachronistic perspectives by speaking, or seeming to speak, of bases being laid, of avenues being opened up, of preparatory steps being taken – not because such retrospective observations would be untrue: they would not – but because this retrospective view had no part in determining the developments themselves.

Of the two trends referred to, regional specialisation and larger production units, the first is much the more pronounced through these years. The more important of its specific manifestations both in agriculture and in industry have already been noted. The infrastructure elements whose development accompanied this trend, both as cause and effect, were the transport, credit and remittance facilities required as the distribution pattern of goods became more complex and more farflung.

Transport

Improved transport meant above all an extension of water transport. Only by water could goods whose value was low in proportion to their bulk reach a distant destination without so adding to costs as to price them out of any popular market. Coal occupied a unique position in this category, being of very low value/bulk ratio and much of it produced at a considerable distance from markets. Grain, in this kind of classification, would rank second; it was a more important commodity than coal but of higher value/bulk ratio and for the most part not having far to go to market – only London would have regularly drawn large supplies from places more than, say, fifty miles distant. Pig iron too would figure quite high, saved from vying with coal because the customer was usually closer to the producer. Iron in its other forms, bar and fabricated, would descend this scale as processing increased its value, though transport costs would still be of weight in the final selling price of the widely distributed cheap wares of Birmingham and region. Salt, fodder crops, dairy products, artificial fertilisers, the coarser kinds of cloth, bricks and timber would all be items whose marketability would be determined in significant though different degrees by transport costs, and whose production for one reason or another was, to varying extents, concentrated in particular regions. Such regions often commanded extensive markets by virtue of natural amenities – it has already been seen that coal could penetrate into the greater part of the kingdom. Nothing that man did through these years came anywhere near equalling what nature had provided. The relative contributions of the two can in fact be stated mathematically. To the 2,350 miles of coastline can be added the 685 miles of river estimated to have been navigable in 1662: a total of 3,035 miles of natural waterway (properly a little less since a small amount of river improvement had already taken place); human effort during this period added about 500 miles. But, although only about a seventh of the total, that represents a considerable increment when contrasted with the achievement of earlier generations, which in net terms was probably less than nil, the little work that had been undertaken having been offset by losses due to silting up. It is the more impressive when one realises that most of it was concentrated in three short spates of activity: 1662-65, 1697-1700, 1719-21 (the dates refer to the initiation of projects; work to completion stretched over longer periods).

As feats of technique or imagination these undertakings have little claim to distinction, consisting as they did of little more than the widening and deepening of rivers so as to prolong their navigable length or to make them capable of taking larger boats, merging indistinguishably at one extreme with ordinary maintenance work, although at the other incorporating features of truly artificial waterways: locks, 'cuts' to straighten out the line of rivers, and reservoirs to maintain the water level; nothing, however, ever came of the well-aired schemes, prompted especially by Dutch and French achievements, for the construction of genuine canals, mostly with a view to linking up the existing river system.

On a strict cost appraisal the results of river improvement could be striking: the substitution of water for land carriage could be guaranteed to at least halve transport costs and often to effect much more sensational results. But since in the majority of instances it was merely a matter of completing a haul the greater part of which had always been undertaken by water anyway, the overall economies were commonly of a more marginal nature; it could hardly be said that any important productive activity had its market greatly expanded, or that any nationally significant new centre of production was called into being, as a result of river improvement. But dramatic leaps are only exceptionally the stuff of economic history; most of the time it is at the margin that it plays itself out.

If a case could be made for any extensive area as a major beneficiary of river improvement it would probably be the West Riding of Yorkshire. Leeds, for instance, had stood more than twenty miles from navigable water and Sheffield forty. The Aire and Calder Navigation (1699)[1] with its two branches from Leeds and Wakefield converging to join the Humber put those cloth-market towns in direct water contact with Hull and must be reckoned a factor in the development of the West Riding cloth industry. The Don Navigation (1726) by doing the same for Sheffield was of benefit to the local cutlers. And both permitted collieries on the north-eastern edge of the East Midlands coalfield to break clear of the constricting land sale limits hitherto frustrating them and enter into effective competition with Tyneside, Wearside and Trentside coal in York and the Humber estuary.

The Mersey estuary also experienced a quickening of traffic with the Mersey and Irwell Navigation (1720) letting into it from Manchester, and the Weaver Navigation (1720) from the Cheshire salt pits. The

[1] The bracketed dates are of the Acts of Parliament authorising the undertakings which would not have been completed for some years.

sum effect of many lesser schemes was to put the interiors of Wiltshire, Hampshire, Suffolk and Essex in direct touch with the sea and to extend the navigability of the Severn, Thames and Trent watersheds.

These river improvement projects have the further particular interest that they necessitated large capital outlays: the costliest undertakings ran to over £50,000 and, although there are one or two early instances of a single 'adventurer' embarking on a project, in general the sums required had to be drawn from many pockets. In legal status rivers hovered uncertainly between being public highways and being private property and to some extent this distinction was reflected in the manner of river improvement, sometimes undertaken by public authorities, sometimes by private entrepreneurs, and sometimes by bodies who could not be categorically assigned to either class. Both before and in the early decades of this period a little work was done by Commissioners of Sewers, bodies in each county of ancient standing and crown appointment, whose proper concern was drainage and flood prevention; but the clearance of obstructions, dredging and embanking undertaken in discharge of these functions also facilitated navigation and in some instances comissioners executed work in which navigation was a prime object. But this hardly amounted to much more than maintenance work and its legality in any event was open to question – the commissioner's powers in this direction were in fact questioned by those who bore the cost of the work: the landowners compelled to undertake it in respect of stretches passing through their property: the county at large charged with rates.

More important was the work of town corporations, seized of clear powers over rivers within the bounds of boroughs and securing special powers over further stretches by Act of Parliament. Rates again sometimes provided the finance but projects of any extent had to be loan financed, the loans secured on the authorised tolls to be levied on the users of the improved river. Such loan funds might emanate from a variety of sources but most commonly from local individuals of means, prompted by a mixture of considerations: civic mindedness, eagerness to find a profitable use for surplus wealth in an age which did not provide many such opportunities, contemplation of the benefits likely to accrue to their own businesses from improved local transport facilities. But most important of all were private associations armed by Act of Parliament with the necessary compulsory purchase and toll levying powers. Some of these were in the nature of a trust – *ad hoc* public authorities, constituted of the same sort of people just described as the principal source of corporation loans – but these fade into pure profit-making concerns, composed of individuals ready to hazard their capital against the hope or expectation of enough traffic to yield a handsome return.

Thus the history of river improvement over this period provides in itself a conspectus of virtually the whole range of possible ways of providing and financing public utilities. The clear drift is steadily towards private enterprise and risk capital – not, it should perhaps be said, on docrinaire grounds of any kind – Parliament, if anything retained a positive preference for corporations in granting the necessary powers – but because the structure of English government, central and local, did not make for widespread public initiative. At the centre, action was confined to the merely permissive, partly because the bureaucratic apparatus to control provincial undertakings was lacking, partly because a government whose revenue and expenditure was continually subject to jealous parliamentary scrutiny neither would nor could extend the range of its habitual activities. At the local level many of the town corporations were already sunk in that moribund and sometimes corrupt condition to which they were to become increasingly victim until rudely restored to life by the Municipal Reform Act of 1835; in the counties, and that includes many non-chartered towns, among them Birmingham and Manchester, not much could be expected of the part-time, amateur, gentleman magistracy, already charged with a wide range of responsibilities. That France joined the Mediterranean to the Atlantic by the Canal du Midi while England confined itself to modest river improvement schemes was because of fundamental differences in the nature of government in the two countries.

Much, perhaps most, river traffic was concerned only with movements between points on the same river system. This was specially true of the longest rivers and their tributaries: the carriage of agricultural produce to London was the principal business of the Thames; Trent-borne coal did not usually pass out of the Humber; intraregional distribution of iron and coal was the leading function of the Severn, counting the south Wales coast as part of the Severn estuary. But the rivers must also be seen as extensions, long inlets, of the sea, with the fairly important proviso that seagoing vessels drew too much water to venture very far up any river and the shallow draught river boats could not weather the open sea so that goods entering a river from the sea, or vice versa, had to be transhipped and thus incur further handling costs. Coastal traffic and river traffic were, in some measure, the same thing and to speak of the one is implicitly to speak of the other. Perhaps then the best pointer to the growth in river carriage over these years is the increase in the volume of coastal shipping for which some kind of statistical indication is available, although its scrappy nature and dubious reliability preclude its yielding an exact record. Its burden in crude terms is, however, unmistakable. Its course throughout was pretty steadily upwards, and by the end of the period the tonnage of coastal vessels had perhaps doubled. As an indicator of the quantity of goods entering into interregional commerce this is subject to certain qualifications. One is that to some extent it just reflects the ousting of Dutch ships from the English coastal trade – itself, of course, an event of some note. More important, it is heavily weighted by the trade in one commodity, coal. Colliers, by the end of the seventeenth century, accounted for about three-fifths of all coastal shipping and in the years up to that point the rapid growth of the western seaborne coal trade had much to do with the increase in numbers of vessels, although thereafter other kinds of coastal trade probably expanded faster.

Only a very marginal importance need be attached to road improvement over these years. Goods which were at all sensitive to transport costs only moved for short distances by road, becoming shorter as river navigation was extended. There was in any event very little road improvement. Roads were the responsibility of each parish in respect of the stretches within its bounds. As long as its condition was adequate for local purposes a parish straddling a main road was little disposed to spend money on providing a good all-weather surface for through traffic, more concerned with ease and rapidity of passage. Occasionally the county magistrates might, as they were empowered to do, levy a fine on a parish for its negligence and apply the fine to the improvement of the offending stretch of road, but until the financial onus was squarely transferred to central funds or to road users, any improvement was bound to be spasmodic and poorly sustained.

As with inland waterways, centralism, such as obtained in France, yielded much better trunk roads than England had at any time within this period. And in making a comparison between England and France (and with the other continental countries which adopted Colbertian style *dirigisme*) in respect of internal communications it would be a crude truth that whereas in the one improvement followed on general economic growth in the other it was intended to induce such growth. The English mode of awaiting initiatives and then on parliamentary approval granting the necessary powers did achieve some results in these years, but worth mentioning only as the first instances of a method which was later to be quite widely employed. In the late seventeenth century magistrates in a few cases were authorised to levy tolls on road users to raise a maintenance fund but from about 1710 toll powers, when conferred, were granted to a self-constituted trust of the kind already noted as sometimes responsible for river improvement; and such turnpike trusts in time became almost the sole agency of main road maintenance.

Banking

However it moved, merchandise entering into interregional trade posed payment problems: two problems essentially, one a function of distance, the other a function of time. The first arose out of the simple fact that buyers and sellers were not in immediate contact, so that money due had to be transmitted from one to the other; and the physical transfer of coin or bullion was both costly and risky. The second stemmed from the fact that the cost of goods had to be borne for some interval of time between production and receipt of payment from the final consumer. Neither problem was in any sense new, and in particular the second could be said to be an eternal and universal one since goods can never be sold in the very instant of incurring costs of production. The introduction of an explicit reference to these particular aspects of trade at this stage rather than at some earlier stage is justified principally on the grounds that it is within this period that there emerge in England distinct institutions amongst whose specific functions were the provision of the remittance and credit facilities which producers, consumers or mercantile intermediaries had formerly contrived for themselves. And, while this phenomenon is certainly to be associated both as cause and effect, with an increase in interregional trade, there is no need to see it as marking any dramatic upsurge, nor as a revolutionary or epoch-making event. This the more especially since the banks or quasi-banks established during these years were often little concerned with trade, and when they were it was commonly with overseas rather than internal trade.

The first institutions which can be discerned as discharging clear banking-type functions grew out of goldsmiths' businesses. Possibly from a very early time London goldsmiths had extended the security precautions which they themselves took to protect their precious stock in trade to provide safe deposit facilities for customers' cash and valuables and had issued receipts in acknowledgement of such deposits. From the 1630s there is plain evidence that these receipts had assumed a stereotyped form and were being issued in batches made out for convenient sums so that a depositor wishing to make a payment to someone else could do so simply by paying receipts to the appropriate amount, thus transferring title to that amount lodged with the goldsmith. Once there was a fairly widespread familiarity with these receipts and with the reputation and good standing of the goldsmith who issued them, so that it was his credit-worthiness rather than that of the depositor which rendered them acceptable, they could change hands repeatedly in settlement of debts without being brought back to the goldsmith for encashment. They had, that is to say, become bank notes, and the goldsmith had become a bank of note issue. Men of means appreciated the convenience of making any but petty payments in this form, as well as that afforded by the safe custody of wealth for which they had no immediate use, and were prepared to pay for these facilities.

Goldsmiths could have halted their evolution as bankers at this point, confining their banking functions to safe deposit and note issue. But the more widely acceptable the notes became the less they returned for encashment and the longer deposits remained in the goldsmiths' hands, i.e. the more cash they had in their possession at any one time; inert, idle cash which could be out at loan earning interest until such time as its owners wanted it back. From safe deposit and note issue it was but a short step to lending other people's money and from there to waiving charges in order to acquire more deposits and thence sometimes to a small interest payment on deposits. So long as the goldsmith banker kept himself sufficiently liquid – that is so long as he kept enough cash in hand to meet withdrawals by depositors and encashment of notes, and made loans on such terms as enabled him to call money in again to replenish his cash reserves should they fall dangerously low – he could convert deposits to his own profit while keeping depositors fully satisfied. By the 1660s, if not earlier, the volume of this kind of business as conducted by a handful of individuals had grown to such an extent that they had shed their goldsmith origins and had become bankers pure and simple. But the spanner in their particular works was the financial character of the biggest borrower, the Crown.

Not only did a great deal of bank money go directly as loans to the Crown, but a considerable amount also was employed in the discounting of exchequer bills or tallies – liens on future crown revenue, payable at a specified date out of a specified item of revenue, assigned to crown creditors, usually contractors and suppliers, though such devices were sometimes used as loan securities as well. The creditor who did not want to wait for his money could discount the bill or tally for cash, if he could find a taker, and bankers looking for employment for their funds were the most apt takers. In the twelve years following the Restoration the Crown continuously covered a chronic deficit by borrowing and each fresh loan added its burden of interest to the deficit. Borrowing snowballed. By 1672 the bankers could lend no more and the whole process of borrowing from Peter to pay Paul came to an abrupt halt. Forced to chose between drastic economies and declining to meet its debts, the Crown elected for the latter. It did not take the extreme step of disowning its obligations entirely. Soon afterwards it resumed interest payments on the outstanding debt but the principal was never repaid and became in effect the basis of the permanent National Debt. Those who were not thereby deprived of needed capital were not really hurt by the arrangements, but the bankers, under the imperative necessity of keeping their position liquid, could not easily withstand the blow, the more especially as many depositors fearing for their money now sought its return, while note-holders sought to convert their paper into cash, thus providing the first clear English instance of the ironic law to which bankers are subject: the harder it is for them to meet their liabilities the more likely they are to be called on to do so. A number of the largest bankers crashed but the institution survived the shock, although for the next couple of decades or so London banks warily avoided lending to the government and confined themselves to private loans.

In 1694, with war finance straining its credit resources, the government raised up for itself a new and considerable lender. The by now well rooted London banking habit afforded scope for a much larger concern than those existing already, launched with only the personal wealth of an individual or two as founding capital; and in those 1690s years when joint stock was widely believed to be the open sesame to a fortune there was no lack of money ready and willing to participate in such a concern, especially one baited with the suggestion of monopoly privileges. A royal charter created the Bank of England,[1] and 1,300

---

[1] The charter did not specifically confer any exclusive privilege on the Bank but its grant did carry the suggestion that no other corporate body would be created by charter to engage in the same kind of business. Under legislation of 1697 and 1709 the bank became effectively possessed of a monopoly of joint stock banking in England.

founding shareholders raised a capital of £1,200,000 which was immediately lent to the government at 8 per cent, secured on a number of specified taxes and duties. Customers' deposits of course provided funds for engaging in general banking business, including further lending to the government, both long and short term, but the Bank extended its lending capacity by making much of its capital do double duty: payment, including payment of the original loan to the government, was, where possible, made not in cash or bullion but in bills and notes, secured on the Bank's assets. Since the bulk of its assets consisted of loans to the government, and since the government's capacity to pay its creditors depended in significant measure on its ability to borrow from the Bank, the credit standing of the two was from the beginning founded on a large measure of reciprocal dependence. The whole set-up was in fact an enormous confidence trick. Its justification was that it worked.

Of course it might not have worked. The paper issued by the Bank might at any time have come back to be exchanged for 'real' money in such quantities that the gold and silver held by the Bank would have been insufficient to meet the demand. In such circumstances the supposed assets behind its paper would have proved incapable of realisation. This very situation did in fact threaten to overtake the Bank at one point, but not until more than a hundred years after its foundation and by then (1797) Bank paper had so established itself in the public confidence that the Bank was able to suspend cash payments without causing more than a momentary flutter of alarm. But in its early years refusal to pay cash would have been fatal to the Bank[1] and acutely embarrassing to the government whose gain from this credit cornucopia can be meassured by the fairly steady fall from the 8 per cent it had to pay for money in the 1690s to the 3 per cent at which it could borrow by the end of this period. Even by the 1720s, within a generation, the rate on government loans had not only shed its risk premium but had become the groundfloor rate, at around 4 per cent, for the money market at large.

This enhancement of the state's credit owed much to the effective transfer of financial control from an irresponsible monarchy to ministers answerable to a parliament in which the fundholding interest was well represented. But the concern of these ministers that the state should be seen to be an honourable and reliable debtor under the stress of heavy

---

[1] Through 1696–97 the bank was forced to limit, but not to suspend, cash payments, by the general shortage of coin occasioned by the Mint's calling in for reminting the numerous shortweight coins then in circulation.

war expenditure up to 1714 would of itself have achieved little without the readily available resources of the Bank to sustain credit at times of difficulty, in particular through its constant willingness and capacity to discount Exchequer bills, thus ensuring that through years of unprecedentedly high outgoings the government was never forced to any measure resembling the 'stop' of the Exchequer of 1672 and in this way contributing also towards the maintenance of the stability of the London banking and credit system as a whole. In fact, it might be argued that it was precisely the precarious interdependence of government, bankers and the men of means who, both personally and through a great corporate concern like the East India Company, lent to the one and deposited their money with the other which guaranteed the solidity of the whole paper structure. A refusal by one to accept the paper of the other could bring about the collapse of all. This truth was hardly perceived with total clarity at the time – indeed a full century and a half later Walter Bagehot was trenchantly berating the Bank of England for failing to acknowledge it – but a limited perception of it in the course of person to person contact within the small circle of interested parties, of the 'you scratch my back, I'll scratch yours' variety, could be said in effect to have achieved the same end. Central to this argument would be the sense of a community of interests amongst those concerned: statesmen, upper middle class, landed aristocracy and greater gentry. It would posit, in one very useful word, an establishment – an élite group whose individual members might differ in political loyalties, might not frequent the same drawing-rooms, might hold different religious tenets, but who were not so divided that on the things which mattered disunion and disarray would be permitted to engender private and public calamity.

That such a concert of power was both the instrument and the creation of the Revolution of 1688 could, with some plausibility, be contended. And that much of subsequent British history in comparison with that of many Continental countries through the eighteenth and nineteenth centuries is explicable by reference to such a thesis could further be urged if one were bent on a grand theme of that order. But in this particular context it is being called on only for the modest task of explaining the survival of the Bank of England, launched on the same wave of high optimism in the 1690s, that excited dozens of nonsensical ventures, initiated by the same sort of people and in somewhat similar circumstances as the derisible South Sea Company (1710–20), created at a time when paper money had still to establish itself firmly with the general public, preceding by two decades the fiasco of an attempt to

float a French state bank on a paper currency. Looking back there is
little to be seen in contemporary circumstances to assure its survival.
And if it is argued that it survived because too many important people
could not afford to let it fail, it should also be allowed that it was
blessed with a handsome share of sheer luck.

The Bank of England, as seen, was principally engaged in government business: lending to the government, remitting money for the
government by means of bills on itself which commanded a general
acceptability not only in Great Britain but in the financial centres of
Europe as well. The extent to which it became a government bank had
not originally been envisaged: the initial loan of its founding capital to
the government had been conceived of as a jumping off point for
engagement in general banking business. But as the cost of the War
of the Spanish Succession mounted, the press of government needs
squeezed its capacity for transacting private business; straightforward
lending, of its nature usually of a relatively long term variety, was
almost wholly abandoned and the discounting of trade bills, whose term
to maturity rarely exceeded six months, was considerably curtailed.
This heavy bias towards government finance persisted right through to
the end of this period. Thus the role of the Bank of England in the
economy at large was a very modest one, except for the part played
by its notes in increasing the volume of the circulating medium, and
thus easing the strain on the internal stock of the precious metals. Even
in this respect its contribution was limited; its notes circulated very
little outside London and within London they made their headway at
the expense of the notes of the other banks who by the 1720s had
largely given up issuing their own notes in the face of an insistent
preference by their customers for the more widely acceptable ones of
the Bank of England.

Notes, in any event, while an excellent substitute for gold and silver
in hand-to-hand payments, could not serve for the settlement of distant
transactions such as arose out of interregional commerce; the cost of
transmitting notes was of course much less than the cost of moving
cash or bullion, but the hazards of theft or loss were even greater. The
London banks made little or no direct contribution towards supplying
suitable instruments for distant payment. A few bank bills or drafts
may have been created, but in general the banks did no more than
discount the trade bills of London merchants – that is they went no
further than to provide cash against the bills of others and even then
only those others whom they could contact directly and with whose

financial standing they were familiar. Inasmuch as the provision of this facility enhanced the acceptability of such bills it promoted their circulation as money by enabling a bill to pass more freely than formerly through several hands before, on maturity, returning for encashment to the merchant who had issued[1] it against a consignment of goods (whose value constituted the bill's security). Although it was not entirely new to the function, the good London trade bill in this period firmly established itself as the principal medium of both provincial and metropolitan mercantile dealings. That is not to suggest that the existence of discount facilities in London was crucial to this development. Indeed since the provincial merchant had no ready access to these facilities they cannot have been a major factor in its spread outside London. Nor was it as if the London banks played any part in the dissemination of trade bills. A bill once discounted by a bank was normally held until maturity, and bill-broking was not among the usual functions of London banks. The specific contribution of these banks towards commercial expansion was not the provision of remittance facilities, nor even the provision of a nationally available fund of mercantile credit, but the more limited one of an extension of the credit resources open to London merchants – and inasmuch as the bulk of the nation's overseas commerce and a good proportion of internal commerce passed through London, that was a contribution of some weight.

The question arises: if the London banks were not the agency responsible for the circulation of London trade bills in the provinces, who undertook their dissemination, discounting and eventual representation to the issuers? The only simple answer is a negative one. There was no clear institutional provision for the discharge of these functions. No country banks emerged within this period. Plainly, however, there must have been individuals who in the course of their principal business were providing banking-type services. The bulk of London bills in provincial circulation probably emanated from purchases by London merchants from provincial suppliers and in turn passed on by such suppliers in settlement of debts, eventually ending up with someone who had a London creditor to whom he despatched the bill, when it could be discounted or, if mature, presented again to the issuer. The most likely sort of person to be regularly in the position of making payments to London was the shopkeeper, wholesaler or merchant procuring supplies from the capital, who would be positively glad of London bills with which he could conveniently pay his supplier(s); if corresponding

[1] The more intelligible 'issue' is here preferred to the technically correct 'accept'.

regularly with a London mercantile concern, he might employ bills for which he had no immediate use by transmitting them to his London correspondent to be credited against a future debt; and might, further, proceed from receiving such bills in settlement from his creditors to using his line to London for transmitting the bills of others, paying cash against them himself. Once he had become known as a man who regularly received London bills, those in the vicinity who themselves wished to make a London payment might apply to him for bills for the purpose, and should he be short of them he might request his London correspondent to obtain them for him, debiting his account accordingly. A local tax collector needing to remit sums periodically to London could develop along similar lines. There is clear if very patchy evidence of this sort of thing happening, but right through this period the ways in which a London bill in the provinces passed from somebody in receipt of one to somebody who wanted one remained in many cases informal and haphazard.

As implied already, only a relatively small part of London bank funds was employed in financing trade. And certain banks had little or nothing to do with merchants. These were the 'gentlemen's' or West End banks, accounting in the 1720s for about a half of London banks and, by then, clearly distinguished from the 'merchants'' or City banks. Even the latter, while confining their dealings with individuals very largely to making advances to merchants or, more commonly, discounting merchants' bills, invested a good deal of their money in the readily marketable stock of the Bank of England, the East India Company and, after its formation, the South Sea Company, along with that of a few other smaller corporate bodies and in the relatively small quantities of government stock at that time available to the general public (much of the government's funded debt being in the hands of the three companies just named). The West End banks likewise invested in these securities, but their private business was largely limited to those of ample private means of whom they sought to constitute their clientele. A copious rent roll, or possibly a handsome income from the funds, was normally necessary to open an account at these establishments, which valued the relative stability of the balances on such accounts by contrast with the sharp fluctuations to which mercantile accounts were liable. Clients who lived beyond their incomes could receive loan accommodation on mortgaging a parcel of their estates or lodging a holding in the funds as collateral. The same security was sometimes employed to obtain capital for the improvement of landed property but within this period most advances from these banks were essentially consumption loans.

Thus the role of London banks as sources of capital needs to be set in fairly careful perspective. The Bank of England was principally engaged in lending to the government. The private loans of the City banks were mostly devoted to the financing of foreign trade and those of the West End banks to personal extravagance. (Stock purchases by banks were very largely of old securities so that the bank funds thereby released might have been employed for any purpose.) One clear negative warrants insistence: very little bank money was directly employed in productive investment and not a great deal either in the financing of internal commerce. Furthermore, although the number of London banks and the volume of bank deposits was fairly steadily increasing throughout this period, so that by the end of it very little money among the class of people who composed the banking public would have been held in private hoards, that class was a constricted one. Banks were only interested in fairly large accounts (say, those of individuals with clear incomes of £500 p.a. and upwards at a time when pretensions to gentility could be borne on £100 p.a.) and could cater only for those permanently or semipermanently resident in London. That was one limitation, though given the steeply raked distribution of wealth and the concentration of men of wealth in London hardly a pinchingly severe one, on the gross size of bank funds. More restrictive was the fact that a substantial proportion of these funds lay idle. The prudent banker, and only the prudent survived, kept himself liquid: probably between a quarter and a half of his assets consisted of cash (least, presumably in the case of the City banker with his holding of short-term and fairly negotiable trade bills, most in the case of the West End banker).

Against these cautions on the role of bank credit in the economy at large must be set the fact that, for whatever purpose, banks did recirculate a significant amount of money which otherwise would have been inert; they eased, so to speak, the grip of the dead hand of savings on economic activity and to that extent invoked the employment of resources which otherwise would have gone unused and unremunerated. And, if the great bulk of bank credit was directly applied only to certain limited purposes, by relieving the strain on personal capital in those sectors it in some degree released it for employment over a wider field.

Savings and investment

Those last words invite a further question. In what wider fields would surplus personal wealth be employed? In ranging over English industry we have had little occasion to note concerns of such a size as to necessitate the participation of outside capital on an extensive scale. The two principal sources of large private fortunes were of course land and trade. And land itself was the sponge which soaked up much of the savings of large estate owners and prosperous merchants. But one man's investment in acquisitions of landed property was just another man's disinvestment. Land purchase was limited to the amount of land coming on to the market. Emulatory ostentation from at least the mid-sixteenth century was an important factor making for enforced sales, and up to about 1640 the disgorgement by the Crown under budgetary pressure of expropriated monastic land had also contributed significantly to the supply. But as long as land remained the only asset which could fairly confidently be relied on to yield a steady return with minimal personal attention, the flow of land on to the market had to be made up largely of distress sales; and even these were inhibited by the same lack of alternative income-yielding assets: the marketability of an estate was often impeded by the charges on it stemming from marriage portions and provisions for younger sons, unmarried daughters and widows (estates with handsome rentals which yielded little or nothing for the actual owner were not uncommon). An entail on an estate might also prevent an embarrassed owner from selling to raise cash although, as the feudal conditions which had given rise to the device receded into distant history, the courts were coming to adopt a highly permissive attitude towards the fictions invented by lawyers to allow of the effective sale of tied estates while preserving the forms of entail.

Apart from land, opportunities for investment had tended to be a matter of chance. The landowner who happened to light on minerals under his property could vest money in their exploitation and, perhaps, in ancillary enterprises. The lottery of personal contacts, social or commercial, could introduce capital to an undertaking requiring finance or to a personal need accompanied by good security. Some element of the haphazard about such encounters was removed from at least the early seventeenth century by which time scriveners, legal specialists in the drawing up of contracts including those regarding loans, were sometimes acting as loan brokers as well. The right sort of personal contacts had offered opportunities for participation in the various monopolies of the later sixteenth and the seventeenth centuries including the joint stock trading and colonisation companies. But for many persons of wealth land was the only accessible way of employing spare funds and for all it was the only way which afforded a high degree of security. The inelasticity of the supply of land was perhaps already a factor in inducing an interest in new capitalist ventures as early as the sixteenth century. It must certainly be reckoned a main factor in the emergence of new openings for capital outlays through this period and in the two particular outbursts of such activity of 1690-94 and 1719-20. But that inelasticity is only one side of the investment equation. The other side is the volume of savings seeking profitable employment. It is impossible to resist the inference that through the years from about 1670 onwards this swelled considerably.

In some measure this growth was simply the obverse of a shrinkage in private hoards of the precious metals. The development of the banking habit had much to do with this but one should possibly reckon also with something of a change in the psychology of wealth – away from a conception of it as a store representing solidity and security towards an apprehension of its accumulation as a measure of estimable achievement. (It might be argued that the particularly dynamic motivation behind the acquisitive instinct is not the desire for material well-being but what has been called the spirit of pecuniary emulation,[1] which in certain societies has come to replace the urge to exhibit prowess in war or the hunt or in other forms of honorific activity as a principal manifestation of competitive egotism; and that this substitution is to be closely associated with the economic progressiveness of societies in which it is effected, in contrast with the economic stagnancy of those in which it is not. If one did toy with a thesis of this kind the sixteenth and seventeenth centuries might be identified as the crucial period of transition in England.) However a shift from hoarding to investing could hardly have accounted for more than a minor element of the extra funds in search of a return through the years in question. The major element must have been an increase in gross savings. There is no reason to suppose that within any income range there was an increased propensity to save. Larger incomes must be the explanation

---

[1] The phrase and the thesis are those of Thorstein Veblen, *The Theory of the Leisure Class* (1899) and other writings. An American thinker of great originality with a gift for devastating irony, Veblen's lack of rigour in the historical and sociological application of his psychological insights has limited his influence.

– not necessarily larger incomes all round but merely among those who provided the bulk of national savings, the wealthiest two or three per cent of the population. It is the especial enlargement of incomes in this thin top stratum that stands out as the responsible agent.

In some part this enlargement was the result of a transfer of incomes through one of the new lending opportunities itself: government loans, the interest on which was paid out of the revenue from an increasingly regressive tax system.[1] By the end of this period about 4 per cent of gross national income was being transferred in this manner every year, the bulk of it to individuals of considerable wealth and most of it from persons of more modest means. Possibly by that time this item alone was equivalent to the increase in annual savings over the period; and to the large extent that it was transferred from spenders to savers would actually have constituted a weighty part of that increase. Perhaps by then as much as a half of the increase in savings derived in effect from this source. But that of course would still leave a large proportion unaccounted for and would further beg the question of where the loan funds had originally come from to build up a government debt of that order.

Contemporaries singled out one particular group of people as experiencing a signal increase in wealth through the years in question: the overseas merchants, in particular those engaged in the importation and re-exportation of extra-European produce which sprang into prominence over the last three or four decades of the seventeenth century. The quasimonopolistic position which a command of capital, an established footing with suppliers and in markets, and in some cases legal privileges, secured for these men ensured them handsome profit margins. While the volume of trade was expanding rapidly the major part of these profits went back into financing it, but when the rate of growth slackened, as it did from about 1690 through to the early 1720s, merchants found themselves with large sums which they could not employ in their own business; and as a class they were particularly wedded to the doctrine that money should make money. It is almost certainly these men above all, with their eagerness to find profitable

[1] Over the five years 1688–92 direct taxes provided 38 per cent of revenue, customs and excise duties 50 per cent. By 1736–40 these proportions were 21 per cent and 78 per cent. The former were roughly proportionate to income. The latter fell proportionately more heavily on low income groups, who expended a larger fraction of their incomes than high income groups. Given the nature of dutiable commodities the middle income groups (say £50 to £300 p.a.) were probably the section who paid away the greatest fraction of their incomes in taxes.

outlets for their funds, who were responsible for the especial upsurge in large-scale borrowing and capital-hungry projects of those three decades. And over the wider period from, say, 1670 onwards it was that portion of their profits which was not ploughed back into trade which made a major contribution to swelling the volume of gross savings. To these English merchants may be added their Dutch counterparts who, notably from c. 1710 onwards, were finding difficulty in employing their funds at home and were turning to the developing London securities market for investment opportunities.

Of the institutions or concerns which absorbed the enlarged stock of capital the most important have already been mentioned in one connection or another. Three dominated the public investment scene: the government, the Bank of England and the East India Company. To these might be added the Royal African Company with a chequered history running back to 1553 and reconstituted in its final form in 1672; it was a great devourer of capital but only briefly enjoyed any financial success. However, while the commercial concerns mentioned did on particular occasions raise substantial capital sums from the investing public, they were not resorting constantly to the money market as was the government, directly or indirectly – principally in the post-Restoration years and during the mountingly expensive phases of war finance, 1693–97 and 1706–12. And of the sums raised by the commercial concerns much was in fact raised on behalf of the government. Of the £9 million paid up capital of the Bank of England in 1722 nearly £7½ million had been applied directly to the National Debt, without speaking of the sums lent to the government out of banking deposits and retained profits. Of the nominal capital of £3·2 million of the East India Company on its reconstitution in 1709 all of it consisted of the sum due in respect of two loans made to the government in 1698 and 1708; the Company in fact traded with funds borrowed on bonds, amounting at that time to £1·7 million. (The government, however, had never attempted to borrow on the dubious credit of the Royal African Company, whose paid up capital of £1 million was in 1712 written down to a nominal value of £100,000.)

The role of these concerns, then, in the investment market was chiefly exercised through the stock of existing shares which they had created in sufficient number to make for regular dealings – that is, to provide a mechanism by which efforts to invest in these enterprises could be readily matched with efforts to disinvest on the part of those who wished to recover their capital for other purposes. Once initiated on a substantial scale these concerns played relatively little further part in absorbing *net* savings. (But it should be allowed that by providing for a freer flow of capital they released money which might otherwise have been hoarded or have got locked up in ventures of dubious worth. And the East India Company did continue to employ net savings by borrowing on bonds while the Bank of England in its banking capacity provided a home for deposit funds wishing to keep liquid, although of the Royal African Company after the 1680s, it could only be said that it gave scope for those looking for a speculative stock exchange flutter.)

As a continuously substantial employer of net savings, then, we come back to the government, which between 1690 and 1740 increased the total of its outstanding debt by some £45 million. Through the same years total net savings may have amounted to something of the general order of £150 million. Since much of this would have been devoted to covering depreciation of the savers' own stocks of physical capital and to meeting their own investment needs, it is quite likely that government borrowing absorbed more 'questing' savings than all other projects put together, so that while these other projects certainly claim attention it was the froth, albeit a very effervescent froth, which they skimmed off from the barrel of national savings.

Implicitly the line being taken in this account is that capital-necessitous projects, over the years when they are most prominent, were essentially prompted by the relative abundance of savings seeking employment rather than by spontaneous entrepreneurial decisions, reversing the analysis normally brought to bear on investment undertakings. There is no need to pose a sharp antithesis. Just as one would allow in our own times that decisions to invest, which in pure theory are treated as 'autonomous', will in practice be influenced by the state of the capital market so, in the historical instance in question, one would not argue that the promotions concerned were indifferent to authentic economic prospects – although there can be little doubt that this would be true of many of the flotations of the bizarre 1719-20 phase. We must think of 'adventurers' initiating projects which at other times would never have been contemplated because of inability to attract the funds needed to finance them; which in the majority of cases, on any rational economic appraisal, never ought to have been contemplated; and whose flimsy prospects of commercial success only allured funds because those funds could find nowhere else to go.

It is from about 1670 that enterprises seeking to raise capital on a broad base begin to manifest themselves in some number. The early

ones included a couple of fishing ventures (the ousting of the Dutch from
the fisheries had long been a sporadically and ineffectually pursued aim
of national policy), some municipal water supply undertakings, a few
other miscellaneous concerns and two foreign trading companies: the
Royal African Company (1672) and the Hudson's Bay Company (1670)
– a fur trading venture which in its early decades could make little
headway against the French, already established in Canada, which never
had a part of any weight in English overseas trade, but which did
eventually become a concern of some consequence in Canadian economic life, as it is to this day.

From 1690 the number of joint stock enterprises started to multiply
prodigiously. At the beginning of that year there were perhaps twenty
joint stock companies[1] in England. At the end of 1694 there were
around a hundred. Five years later again the number was probably back
to twenty or so, and some of these had no more than a paper existence.
Indeed it is doubtful if anything more than a very small percentage of
the companies formed between 1690 and 1694 ever got beyond raising
a fraction of their proposed capital to engage in the business for which
they were formed. The companies of this phase included wreck recovery
ventures, prompted by the retrieval in 1687 of a quarter of a million
pounds from a Spanish treasure ship which had foundered off His-
paniola; more fishing and water-supply concerns; companies for the
manufacture of armaments, paper and glass; mining and metallurgical
concerns; and, mostly after the boom in other promotions had spent
itself, banking organisations. The handful which went on to lead useful
commercial lives consisted, along with one or two other uncertain cases,
of the Bank of England and some lead and copper working companies.

One product of the promotional wave of 1690–94 which merits at
least parenthetic notice is the London stock exchange. It was not a
development which responsible opinion applauded. A parliamentary
commission of 1696 recited that 'the pernicious art of stock-jobbing
hath of late so perverted the end and design of companies and corporations erected for the introducing or carrying on of manufactures to the
private profit of the first projectors, that the privileges granted to them
have commonly been made no other use of by the first procurers and
subscribers but to sell them with advantage to ignorant men drawn in
by the reputation, falsely raised and artfully spread, concerning the
thriving state of their stock'. Thus is described the first English stock

[1] 'Joint stock company' is not used here with any precision of definition. See p. 166
n.

exchange boom: a speculatively fired market in overvalued shares, eventually engendering its own collapse. And while the logic of the Report quoted would seem to indict the company promoters rather than the opprobriated stock-jobbers it was the latter who were the subjects of legislation of 1697 which instituted a licensing and control system for their business.

In the short run it was probably the experience of financial losses sustained and of the failure of most of the companies launched along with the generally unsavoury reputation attaching to the whole episode which prevented any hasty repetition of the 1690–94 surge of company promotions. In the longer run the role of government borrowing in soaking up savings was probably the decisive agency, but it is noteworthy that the Peace of Ryswick (1697) and the consequent tapering off of government borrowing did not initiate any new ventures which were the subject of stock exchange activity, although the interlude of peace which lasted until 1701 did witness a spate of river improvement undertakings, whose financing appears to have been locally controlled and which in general were more soundly founded or, at least, of more authentic economic benefit than the earlier run of assorted ventures.

It was not until 1719 that enthusiasm for joint stock undertakings reappeared on any extensive scale. In the interim there were two new ventures which command attention: a reorganisation of the East India trade and the foundation of the South Sea Company. These two have much in common. Both were foreign trading enterprises. Neither actually gave rise to anything worth speaking of in the way of fresh trading initiatives. And both derived their primary impetus from the financial needs of the state. The one commenced in 1698 with the cancellation of the exclusive privileges of the East India Company – a move which had more of party politics in it than anything else, the Whigs being currently in the parliamentary saddle and the Court of Governors of the Company being of a strong Tory colouring. This was not, however, a preliminary to a general emancipation of the East India trade. Participation in the trade was reserved to those who subscribed to a simultaneously floated £2 million government loan, subscribers to the loan being entitled to carry annually to the East goods or money to the value of their subscriptions. The 'Old Company', as it now became known, subscribed £315,000. Its opponents, who had engineered the scheme, assembled all but a tiny fraction of the other subscribers into the 'New Company'. The situation then was that one organisation in possession of trading stations, forts, locally resident agents, established relations with native rulers and, in brief, a general competence to undertake the trade was legally entitled to less than one-sixth of it, and the organisation vested with the legal right to the huge bulk was ill-qualified to exercise it. Such a situation evidently could not last. But it was not until 1709 that it was brought to an end by the merger of 'Old' and 'New' companies, parliamentary sanction for the move being facilitated by the douceur of a further £1·2 million loan to the government. All that effectively happened in the eventual outcome was that the capital and share structure of a monopolistic East India Company had been fairly radically modified.

Hitching government loans to participation in a commercial enter-prise had in the instances of the Bank of England and the East India Company shown itself to be a popular method of state finance. And the purely private venture of the 'Million Bank', founded in 1695, had enjoyed a similar success. This had raised much of its capital in holdings in the Million Lottery Loan of 1694,[1] investors being lured by the prospects of continuous participation in profits in place of the fixed and terminable payment to which they were entitled under the terms of the loan, while the bank proposed to employ the interest payments on the holdings as working capital. In the event the company did not remain long in banking although it survived until 1796 after it had redeployed its income to the purchase of annuities. Another company – one with a weirdly varied history – to raise capital in the form of government debts was the Sword Blade Company which, having forsaken its original sword making business, in 1702 invited subscrip-tions of Army Debentures (bills payable by the War Department) with which it proposed to purchase landed estates in Ireland expropriated by the government from Irish Jacobites. Legal difficulties in securing a proper title to the estates brought this venture to an end and the concern, reconstituted as a partnership, now took to banking, at which point it joined hands with the South Sea Company, whose banker it became.

---

[1] A loan of a million pounds, the subscribers receiving varying rates of interest, rising from 10 per cent p.a., according to their luck in the lottery. Interest payments ceased after sixteen years and the loan was not repayable. Other than money raised on bills and tallies most of the government loans of this period which were obtained direct from the general public contained an element of gamble, being either of a lottery type or of an annuity type, payment in the case of the latter being made for the duration of a named life or lives. In neither case was the principal repaid – or, more accurately, the element of capital repayment was incorporated in the interest or annuity payments.

It may well have been the men behind the Sword Blade Bank who initiated the proposal made in 1711 to the holders of £10 million of government bills, tallies and bonds, that they should exchange their claims on the government for shares in a newly chartered company to trade into the South Seas, i.e. Spanish America, the company to receive 6 per cent interest on government debts thus acquired – a rate below the average that the government was currently paying on the miscellaneous body of debts involved, with the further attraction from the point of view of the Treasury of relieving it of any immediate need to repay these debts. The facts that it had been standing Spanish policy to exclude foreigners from the trade of their empire and that the war which Europe had now been waging for a decade to settle the succession to the Spanish throne was still unconcluded seem to have dulled little of the glitter of the fabulous wealth of the Indies. Conversion was optional, but nearly all of the designated debt was exchanged for South Sea shares.

The Spanish concession under the Treaty of Utrecht (1713) of the right to despatch one ship annually to America[1] was hardly what the most optimistic had anticipated, but it was enough to keep the stock exchange price of South Sea shares moving around par into 1720, even though it was not until 1717 that the Company first sent a ship to America – and not until 1723 that it sent another. (It sent eight in all before the arrangement was cancelled by mutual agreement in 1750. It should be remembered that whatever its trading profits the company had a guaranteed income on its holding of government debt.) Public estimation of the Company's prospects was certainly still buoyant enough to permit of the notion of repeating, on a larger scale, the conversion operation of 1711. In January 1720 the proposal was formally made in the House of Commons to convert all outstanding obligations of the state, other than those held by the Bank of England and the East India Company, into shares of the South Sea Company at a capitalised value of nearly £31 million, less £3 million which the Company was to cancel, interest on the total government debt then held by the Company to be at 5 per cent up to 1727 and at 4 per cent thereafter, with an immediate saving to National Debt charges of about

---

[1] The Company also secured the Asiento, the contract for the supply of slaves to the Spanish colonies. However it subcontracted this, first to the Royal African Company and then to private traders. Most of the Spanish American slave trade seems to have been conducted, illegally, outside the Asiento, which was never an important source of income to the South Sea Company.

£150,000 p.a. and one of about £550,000 p.a. after 1727. (Government expenditure at the time was running at about £6 million p.a.)

By January 1720 a wave of company promotion, of 1690–94 character, was already in course of formation. Since September 1719 at least fifteen new companies had been floated, the endemic fishing itch accounting for five of them and various kinds of insurance undertakings for eight.[1] Surplus funds were once again in search of fresh outlets. Such a phenomenon might be expected to have manifested itself in the immediate wake of the Treaty of Utrecht with a return to balanced budgets, but, in the first place, the country remained on a part war footing, for some while, necessitated by fears of France and an attempted restoration of the Stuarts, by difficulties with Sweden in the Baltic and by open, though limited, warfare with Spain. However government borrowing certainly did drop off. The figures in Table I.3 suggest a further reason why it was not until late 1719 that the signs start to show again of money in search of employment.

TABLE I.3. *Gross value of English foreign trade 1710–22 (exports plus imports) (in £m)*

1710	1711	1712	1713	1714	1715	1716	1717	1718	1719	1720	1721	1722
8·7	8·7	n.a.	10·3	11·5	10·7	10·6	11·7	11·0	9·9	10·7	10·4	11·7

These illustrate the upsurge in trade following the end of the war and the sharp setback of 1719, with implicit contraction of scope for mercantile funds; this was more or less coincident with the return to peacetime finance on the part of the state and, very possibly, with an inflow of Dutch money, now that the new Hanoverian dynasty seemed securely seated.

Given then that a stock exchange boom was in course of getting under way in any event, what was the role of South Sea stock in it? How far was it just the market leader in a natural bulls' market, and how far were the particular terms of the conversion responsible for the extraordinary behaviour of its stock exchange valuation over the

---

[1] These and other figures cited in this general connection are derived from W. R. Scott, *The Constitution and Finance of English, Scottish and Irish Joint-Stock Companies to 1720* (1911). It is unlikely that Scott's enumerations are exhaustive.

following months? Passing over the complicated details of the conversion the key feature for the purpose of explaining the 'bubble'[1] is that for each amount of government debt converted an equivalent amount of South Sea stock *at its par valuation* could be created. But in effecting the exchange the Company had complete discretion as to what amount of South Sea stock it actually supplied against converted government debt: it needed to offer no more than was required to induce conversion. In other words it had to offer no more, or only a little more, than the equivalent in South Sea stock *at its current market valuation*, which was of course perfectly fair and reasonable: there was no reason why the holders of government debt should be given the opportunity of acquiring South Sea stock on privileged terms. For example, if the market price of South Sea stock (with a par value of £100) were £400, it would have been grossly inequitable if the holder of government debt to the value of £100 could acquire it for that amount when the buyer in the market had to pay the market price; and since the market valuation of South Sea stock was bound to vary with judgments as to the Company's future, there could be no question of fixing a conversion value for the stock. Nor, at first glance, was there anything improper in allowing the Company to create stock to the par equivalent of the government debt converted. Indeed the alternative of providing for stock creation only to the amount actually supplied would have given rise to the anomalous-looking situation in which varying amounts of stock would have been created against identical amounts of government debt, which would have seemed at least to offend against the founding notion of a straightforward uniform exchange. And after all, one might say, the number of stock units in a concern is an utterly arbitrary matter; all that signifies is the sum of the real assets of the concern and the number of nominal units among which those real assets are formally distributed is of no consequence. One must not jump too hastily to the conclusion that the manipulative possibilities of the operation were from the start foreseen and intended.

The manipulative possibilities arose in the following way. As long as the stock stood above par (100) more stock could be created than was exchanged in conversion. The Company in fact effected eight block conversions, six of which included an element of cash payment

---

[1] The attention given here to this ephemeral incident is really disproportionately great. But a reader might reasonably expect to find some adequately detailed account of what is perhaps the most sensational and most bewildering single episode in English economic history.

for the debt acquired. The last of the eight, which was the simplest, can serve as an example. Under this a quantity of government bonds, issued and repayable at £100 each, to a total amount of £14,393,788, were converted into South Sea stock. As a sweetener the bonds were valued by the Company at £105 and its own stock at 800, as against a current market price of around 900. Thus, for each bond 105/800 of a unit of stock was given, meaning that the bond holders for an asset of a face value of £100 received one with a current market value of about £118. More importantly, the Company had parted with stock of a par value of £1,889,185 but had created stock to a par value of £14,393,788, so that it had on hand unissued stock of a par value of £12,504,603, and of a current market value of about nine times that amount. Over the whole eight conversions, undertaken between May and August of 1720, the Company created nearly £27 million of stock of which less than £6 million were issued against converted debt, leaving some £21 million in the Company's hands, which at the time of the last conversion had a gross market valuation of about £190 million. Looked at in this way, the Company had assets of about £190 million. Since the total issued capital (including earlier issues) was then £21 million (par value: the identity with the £21 million then in the Company's hands is pure coincidence) a market price of 900 for stock of 100 par was, represented in this delusive fashion, fully justified.

The effect had been a geometric one. The higher the market price of stock, the more the Company could retain on conversion and, simultaneously, the greater the valuation of each unit of retained stock; the larger this multiplied value of the retained stock, the more considerable the Company's so-called assets, and the higher still the market price could go, until conversion was completed and capacity to create new stock exhausted. The geometric effect could, of course, work equally potently in reverse even while conversion was still proceeding. If the price started moving down, the less new stock could the Company retain on conversion and the less its unit value; below a certain price this would mean an actual fall in its asset valuation, initiating a cumulative fall in market price. In a word, the chief determinant of the market price of South Sea stock was the market price of South Sea stock! (A floor was of course set by the government debt held by the Company: the market valuation of the total issued stock would not fall below the value of the Company's holding of this debt.)

As indicated already, it is impossible to say just when the directors of the Company resolved on a deliberate attempt to keep the price of its stock moving continuously upwards. And in any event such an attempt would have been hopeless in the absence of autonomously buoyant market conditions. Through late 1719 and January 1720 South Sea stock had been benefiting from the first ripples of a gathering enthusiasm for joint stock investment. Then, in the first week of February the stock leaped to 161, as against a previous high of 136. In March it was hovering around 350 but made no further advance until mid-May when the first block of debt conversion was effected. However, ebullience was by no means peculiar to the South Sea Company. Between 22 January, when the conversion scheme was publicly proposed, and the time of the first conversion operation, at least sixty-three other joint stock flotations had taken place, while among existing concerns, East India stock had risen to 250 and that of the Bank of England to 200. The early rise in South Sea stock may then have owed little to any immediate appreciation of the special effects of the conversion arrangement or to any manoeuvring on the part of the directors. The credibly vast potential of the South Sea trade and the huge 'fund of credit' which it would command, may have been enough in themselves to attract particularly keen attention in a phase of investment eagerness. However, from mid-May onwards the market in the Company's stock was plainly in the play of special forces: the speciously plausible belief that the higher the price went the further still it was bound to go; the manipulations of the directors to check any slippage which might throw the mighty engine into reverse.

The chief device used by the directors was to take collateral in the form of South Sea stock against loans for the purchase of more stock in the market – which had the simultaneous effects of withdrawing stock from the public, thus constricting its supply, and of increasing the demand for it. At the same time delivery of stock against conversion was held up, preventing potential profit-takers from selling. On 24 June the market price reached 1,050 and although that level was not held, the stock was kept at around 900 until mid-August. Yet, despite the implications of that degree of appreciation, the South Sea Company was still far from monopolising investors', or speculators', attention. There are twenty-two recorded instances of stocks which sold at more than the ten and a half times par which South Sea fetched at its peak. Between 18 May and 24 June when South Sea stock went from 352 to 1,050 another one hundred enterprises sought funds from the general public, sixty-eight being recorded in the single week 6 June to 11 June. That week was in fact the dizzy plateau of the boom which may be said to have extended overall from September 1719 to September 1720 but which was mostly compressed into the five months mid-January to mid-June 1720. Over the whole stretch 190 invitations to subscribe funds have been counted; and the total capital nominally sought was about £250 million, equivalent to some five years total national income. It must be doubtful if even a twenty-fifth of this was ever raised; and quite evidently in many cases there was never any intention of calling up the declared capital. The enterprises of the early months seem generally to have settled on capitals which bore some sort of relationship to what they might ultimately require if their ambitions were to be realised, but increasingly the sums announced were just the conventional millions which 'bubble' protocol demanded. Two, three, and four million became customary, and a company for dealing in brushes and mops airily estimated that it would need 'some millions sterling'. Likewise, if the promotions of the early months were commonly founded in a good deal of naïveté they do seem to have been inspired by a genuine intention to engage in business; but there can be little doubt that a growing number of the promotions appearing from February onwards sought to do nothing more than attach some sort of reputable sounding description to scrip which might then be floated to value on a tide of indiscriminating and, indeed, uncaring stock market ignorance; it is not much more difficult to find buyers for paper which is worth nothing than it is to find buyers for paper worth only a fraction of the price paid, so long as the buyers have no intention of holding the paper for any longer than it takes to make a profit on its resale. For this kind of purpose an initial payment of some diminutive proportion of the nominal value of the share would suffice to give it the right sort of character. Even authentic undertakings rarely required more than an eighth to be paid on first subscription, the remainder to be called up as the businesses got under way: The speculating 'bull', of course, reckoned to have sold again before any further calls were made.

If, then, an analysis of the various declared purposes for which companies were formed has any interest it is perhaps more as a measure of what kind of activities commanded the requisite degree of public respect than as a measure of genuine entrepreneurial judgments as to the profit potential or capital needs of different sectors of the economy, and certainly not as any sort of objective measure of the useful contemporary scope for capital. There was in fact very considerable bunching. Of the 190 promotions, 131 can be assigned to 9 fairly narrowly defined fields and 69 of these to 3 of those fields (Table I.4).

TABLE 1.4. *Joint stock promotions, 1719–20*

Textiles	Insurance	Foreign trade	Money lending and banking services	Metallurgy
23	23	23	16	13

Colonial settlement and development	Fishing	Land improvement	Urban property development
11	10	7	5

Plainly, South Sea stock was not without company in the market. In fact it had to compete for attention to an extent that the South Sea directors, anxious to build up a powerful head of demand for their stock, found highly uncomfortable. They resolved on using their considerable parliamentary influence to sweep rival seekers after the public's money from the field. (According to a contemporary calculation, 122 peers and 462 M.P.s held South Sea stock at one time or another through the spring and summer of 1720, all of them presumably interested in removing any obstruction to the appreciation of their holdings, without speaking of the thirty or more, including members of the government, who were in receipt of bribes from the Company.)

An Act of Parliament, publicly proclaimed on 11 June, declared illegal any company which was not vested with an official charter, or which was acting under a charter originally granted for some other purpose, or which had at any time ceased to conduct business. The first provision caught the vast majority of the recent promotions, though some sought to take advantage of certain obscurities in the Act to carry on and there were even some further unchartered promotions. The purpose of the other two provisions was to eliminate certain concerns, including some of the largest, which were acting under an earlier obtained charter but which had changed the original nature of their business or had recently revived a business which had been allowed to lapse. The Act, then, did drive most of the rabble from the field straightaway and was immediately followed by a great upward leap in the price of South Sea stock – accompanied, however, by a similar movement on the part of other stocks which remained in the market. For the while, the Company rested content with its immediate gain but as soon as the last conversion was completed on 12 August and the prospect of further stock creation ceased, the price started to slide.

The Company was now at the end of its financial tether. No funds were available for further substantial loan support of the market. The directors made their last throw. On 18 August they instituted legal proceedings, on the grounds of change or previous lapse of business, against four of the companies operating under charter whose stock was amongst the most actively dealt in. The move was successful in so far as the Company's plea was upheld in respect of three of the concerns, whose stock then vanished from the market, while, as intended, a shadow of grave doubt was thrown over a number of other chartered enterprises and their stocks. But as a means of drawing market demand on to South Sea stock, the move was an unmitigated disaster. It was not only South Sea stock which had been bought on credit of one kind or another. The whole market was so sustained. Now the stocks which had been looked to to cover obligations and realise a profit had the ground cut from under them. Creditors started to close in. Speculators had to sell on a falling market. And prominent among the stock sold was that held in the greatest quantity, South Sea stock, with its peculiar capacity to multiply any price trend, up or down. By 6 September it had already slipped to 770. From that point it dropped like a stone and on 28 September it stood at 150.

The meretricious 'surplus' stock had not yet lost all its magic. A resurgence of buying momentarily carried the stock back over 300; through October and November it oscillated steeply around 200 and until the 'surplus' was incorporated into the issued stock early in 1721, the price remained very mobile. But in December it was moving around the 150 or so which was the floor established by the Company's interest income on its holding of government debt. The bubble was over. It remained only to air a lot of dirty washing and make some sort of arrangement for those government debtors who had converted at South Sea prices of 375 and 800 and had therefore sustained a considerable loss of income – only partially restored by the subsequent provisions made by Parliament. The one enduring consequence of the whole episode was the Act restricting the formation of joint stock companies – the 'Bubble Act' as it is known to history. Introduced to facilitate the operations of the South Sea Company, it was preserved as a safeguard against the repetition of such operations.

Looking finally at the three-hundred-odd companies promoted over the whole half century c. 1670–1720, one can almost dismiss them all as having been founded in folly and finishing in failure. The only significant exceptions to this sweeping generalisation would appear to be the lead and copper concerns referred to earlier as survivors of the 1690–94 boom, along with some water-supply ventures, most of which raised their capital locally, and the similarly financed river improvement undertakings; to which should be added the Bank of England, whose legal monopoly it was perhaps which prevented the appearance of successful imitators, and three insurance companies, the Sun Fire Office (1706), the Royal Exchange (1717), and the London Assurance (1719) – the last two, marine and fire concerns – all of them deriving the evident advantages of scale arising out of the spread of risks. Of the numerous life insurance ventures only one, the Amicable Society (1706) is known to have enjoyed a prolonged existence but this, like most enterprises in the field, was a mutual society not a joint stock company in the ordinary sense.

The question that remains is: what became of the flow of funds which had supported the 1719–20 boom? Part of the answer is that, in the immediate aftermath, they almost literally evaporated. Paper instruments of credit had provided the form for much of the money which had been in play – without speaking of the various 'option' and other devices which permitted of a succession of stock exchange sales without the employment of money in any form. In the general alarm which followed the crash, much of this lost all currency. No estimate of the total money supply is possible but the figures shown in Table I.5 are indicative of the general trend.

TABLE I.5. *Bank of England state as at 31 August (in £m)*

Year	Notes in circulation	Drawing accounts	Total
1720	2·5	1·6	4·1
1721	1·9	1·1	3·0
1722	2·8	1·2	4·0

(The validity of reckoning Drawing Accounts as money is questionable since the extent of their transferability via 'cheques' is unclear but was certainly limited.)

In the short run too the damage to confidence doubtless led to wealth being hoarded and in the longer run the 'Bubble Act' must have played some part in stopping up possible outlets for funds. This would indicate that investment, and with it general economic activity, was kept at a lower level than otherwise would have been maintained. The general impression left by the last two decades of this period is not inconsistent with such an effect, although it would be erroneous to suggest that any significant amount of potentially productive investment was neglected for lack of ability to organise the requisite capital. The nature and history of the companies of the two main promotional phases makes it clear that few contemporary fields of productive endeavour had either any need of large capitals or the capacity to employ them efficiently; such authentically economic significance as these investment phases had lies largely in the way that they lured savings out into circulation to play a part in sustaining the level of demand.

Over and above these probably rather marginal considerations in accounting for the flow of investible funds after 1720, there stands the strong recovery of overseas trade and its need of mercantile finance.

TABLE 1.6. *Gross value of English foreign trade 1721–25 (exports plus imports) (in £m)*

1721	1722	1723	1724	1725
10·4	11·7	11·2	12·5	12·8

Overseas trade

Unquestionably foreign commerce was the sector in which capital fructified the most through this period as a whole. It was the dynamic quarter of the economy *par excellence*. But it should be stressed at the outset that the extent to which this dynamism was imparted to the rest of the economy was relatively modest. Exports of English produce rather more than doubled over the whole hundred years. That was a noteworthy achievement (although its expression as an annual growth rate, 0·7 per cent, robs it of something of its rhetorical impact). But to be appreciated in full perspective it needs to be set against the fact that at the beginning of the period only some 5 per cent of national income was earned from exports so that the *per capita* increase in wealth directly attributable to this growth would have been of the order of that 5 per cent over the entire period.

The most sensational record was that of merchandise which was very largely insulated from the domestic economy: re-exports, the produce of other countries which merely passed through England on their way to market leaving behind them only the profit return to English merchants and the payment made in respect of carriage and handling, though these items were not inconsiderable. Utterly negligible in 1640 or even in 1660 the value of re-exports by 1740 was equal to about two-fifths of that of all home-produced goods sold abroad.[1] And, since both average profit margins and the proportions of English shipping space occupied were distinctly larger in the case of re-exports than of domestic exports and retained imports, perhaps close on a half of the mercantile and shipping incomes derived from overseas trade were by then obtained from this entrepôt commerce.[2] If one also reckons in earnings in the slave trade; in the intra-Asiatic trade of the East India Company and of its servants; and in participation in trans-Atlantic intercolonial trade, it would certainly be true that external trade in English produce and in goods for English consumption would have accounted for the lesser fraction of the profits of foreign commerce by the end of this period.

The intense attention given to extra-European trade from the late seventeenth century is not then to be accounted for in terms of its overall economic importance, which was comparatively slight, but in terms of its importance to certain interests which for one reason or another commanded a special place in public affairs. But before enlarging on that theme, we should detail more closely the record of this entrepôt trade. Chronologically three phases may be distinguished: c. 1665–c. 1690; c. 1690–1721; 1721–44; the first covers the very rapid build up of the trade, the second a levelling off tendency and the third a clear, though less momentous, resumption of growth. The first phase was founded very much in three commodities: tobacco, sugar and calico.

[1] Although there are full trade statistics available from 1697 onwards a precise comparison between re-exports and domestic exports is not possible. Both were nominally valued at their worth on leaving England so that the valuation of re-exports included all costs incurred since leaving the point of origin. At these valuations re-exports were equivalent to 56 per cent of domestic exports over the years 1738–41. All official valuations, however, are subject to a further and more serious qualification: after 1700 goods, with a few minor exceptions, were valued according to fixed rates drawn up in that year on the basis of then prevailing prices; no account thereafter was taken of subsequent price variations. At any remove from 1700 then the official figures are useless as a measure of true values. But the fixity of valuation means that in the case of any one commodity the official series is in effect a record of changes in quantity. And as long as there is no great shift in the price ratios between the important commodities entering into trade (i.e. no great variation in the factor cost of any one of them) the composite series for domestic exports, re-exports and imports can be treated as measures of changes in volume.

[2] In the case of shipping arising not only from the fact that foreign ships were almost wholly excluded from the carriage of imports destined for re-export but also from the much greater length of the average haul of these commodities.

The English settlements in the southern part of the North American mainland, most especially Virginia, had early taken to the commercial cultivation of tobacco. The heavy cost of initially clearing and preparing the land once covered, the techniques of successful cultivation learned, a plentiful supply of slave labour secured, full and regular employment for ships engaged in the trade assured, and what had initially been an exotic luxury became cheap enough to command a mass market, first in England itself and then over much of the Continent, which had only limited sources other than the English possessions to draw on for supplies. Sugar had an essentially similar history but here English possessions accounted for only a fraction of European supply sources. French, Portuguese, Spanish and Dutch colonies in the Caribbean and on the South American mainland did not leave much market room for Barbados, Jamaica (captured from Spain in 1655) and the other smaller English islands. Sugar, however, sold in much larger quantities than tobacco so that even with a much smaller share of the market, sugar re-exports did not in this first phase lag very far behind those of tobacco, and retained imports of sugar easily outweighed tobacco. In the case of calico it was not of course a matter of establishing its production – the Indian calico industry was old before the first English ship nosed out of home waters – but of cultivating a European market for it. The significant event here seems to have been the re-organisation of the East India Company in 1657 when it raised a permanent capital, supplemented at need by short-term borrowing on bonds, to replace the self-dissolving capitals with which successive voyages had been financed up to this time. With regular and continuously functioning trading stations maintained in India, the Company was much better placed to tap internal industries. The small quantities of calico which it had hitherto imported had always sold well and now it was able greatly to enlarge these for sale not only at home, but in Europe, America and West Africa. Carried more or less on the tail of these three commodities were other odds and ends including indigo, from India and the West Indies, ginger, raw cotton and various woodstuff dyes from across the Atlantic, pepper and silks from the East.

Growth was of course bound to decelerate somewhat as market limits were approached, but more particular impediments were also encountered from around the turn of the two centuries. Re-exports of sugar were meeting intensifying competition from the French colony, Saint Domingue, whose considerable potential as a cheap sugar producer was now being more fully exploited than had been the case up to

1697 when it was under Spanish rule. And European sales of calico were hit by the adoption of prohibitory measures in continental countries analogous to the English Calico Acts, a sharp decline in this trade only being prevented by continuing growth in American and West African markets. Tobacco experienced no serious check, although with the Act of Union (1707) English merchants and shippers had increasingly to share the trade with Scots, who were starting to make of Glasgow a major tobacco entrepôt. Tobacco it was too which led the fresh spurt in the re-export trade from the 1720s (probably founded in the spread of the smoking habit in eastern Europe). Sugar and calico still maintained their position as the next important items of re-exportation, although sugar could make no new headway in foreign markets. Coffee was now figuring quite prominently. The East India Company, drawing principally on Near Eastern supplies, had already a useful home market, the English taste for coffee at moneyed levels having spread from about the middle of the seventeenth century. But it was on the Continent that the popularity of the beverage was particularly marked and although the Dutch could very largely cater for continental demand, its growth afforded scope for a considerable expansion of re-exports from England through the 1710s and 1720s. Tea, starting to vie with coffee as a socially distinguished drink from the late seventeenth century, also attained a modest importance as an item of re-export in the 1720s, but the great bulk of tea imports were retained for home consumption.

Roughly hand in hand with the record of trade in extra-European produce went that of a re-export trade in the reverse direction. The East required little from Europe, but the settlements across the Atlantic were heavily dependent on the Old World for an enormous range of goods. A variety of articles of continental origin were imported into England for remission to the colonies, most notable amongst them wine and German linen. The trade in Indian calicoes has already been noted – almost wholly extra-European at both terminals in the later years of this period. And England was also the effective centre of the slave trade. Although cargoes of slaves never touched English shores and so, technically, formed no part of the English re-export trade, they were bought with English money, carried in English ships and returned a profit to English merchants. The growth of the slave trade was of course in close correspondence with the growth of the tobacco and sugar trades. Indeed it was integrated with these trades not only in that it supplied the necessary plantation labour, but also in that it provided a means of closing the payments gap on the trans-Atlantic trade. In the absence of an adjusting item bullion would have had to have been found by English merchants to cover the excess of imports from the Americas over exports. Slaves, if one may be forgiven the clinical tone about such a filthy traffic, provided that adjusting item. On delivery across the Atlantic, slaves were paid for in bills on the home agents of local plantation owners and merchants, which in England were set against moneys due on consignments of sugar, tobacco etc. This payments triangle obviated the need for bullion flows.

A second triangle pivoted on New England whose external trading position was the reverse of that of the more southerly colonies: with very little to offer to Europe it yet had to draw on Europe for a variety of wants. From New England went corn, fish, salted meat, timber, and a few other odds and ends to the southern mainland and to the Caribbean, both to English and other possessions. The proceeds on these goods financed the purchase of commodities for sale in England and thus imports back to New England. However, through the eighteenth century this becomes more and more a part of American rather than English economic history as New England shippers themselves appropriated the trade.

This widely flung and fairly complex trade network was the subject of meticulous legislative control in the form of the Navigation Acts which prescribed among other things that: (1) all the major items of colonial produce (the 'enumerated commodities'[1]) could be directly exported only to England or to another English colony; (2) European produce could not be imported by the colonies other than via England – in both cases the goods to be carried in English or colonial ships; (3) goods from outside Europe imported into England or the colonies likewise had to be carried in English or colonial ships. The first two evidently assured English participation in the great bulk of colonial trade both outward and inward. The third could be said to have ensured that calico, tea and other Asiatic commodities imported into England and the colonies came from the areas within the East India Company's orbit rather than from the areas of control or influence of other European powers. That however would be to misrepresent the real purpose of the provision at the time of its enactment and even in the case of the other two their original object was not precisely that which they ultimately came to serve. These provisions must be set along with

[1] Initially: tobacco, sugar, indigo, ginger, cotton, dyewoods; various others were subsequently added.

the others of which the Navigation system consisted and the whole set in the contemporary context of its enactment. These other, rather complex, provisions may be resumed as: (4) nearly all imports from outside Europe along with some from Europe were to come directly from their place of origin or normal point of shipment; (5) most major imports from Europe were to be carried in English, including colonial, ships, or ships of the country of origin or shipment of the goods.

The fundaments of this system were contained in legislation of 1651, modified and extended at points by further legislation of 1660, 1673 and 1696. The first point to note then is that this apparatus of control was created before extra-European trade was of any real consequence to England. And the second is that it was concerned very particularly with shipping. Its supreme object was to ensure as far as English legislation could reasonably do so that all goods entering trade were carried in English or colonial ships rather than those of any other nation, and especially that they should not be carried in Dutch ships. Construed in that sense the first provision as given above can be restated as: colonial produce could not be sent to Amsterdam for final distribution in Dutch vessels. And the other four can be summarily restated as: imports into England or the colonies should not be carried by the Dutch, neither into an English port nor into Amsterdam for transshipment to an English vessel. The Navigation Acts then, at least in origin, are not to be understood as part of a programme defining the economic relationships between England and her incipient overseas empire but as a culmination of the century old Anglo-Dutch maritime rivalry in which hitherto the Dutch had made all the running.

The English concern to overthrow the Dutch as third-party carriers can in some measure be attributed to specific politico-military considerations: a concern to maintain a strong English mercantile fleet as a training ground for sailors against a need for them in wartime; and an aversion to dependence on the Dutch for Baltic naval stores, vital to fighting strength. But since over the years in question the Dutch themselves were the most probable enemy, and since war with the Dutch would be war over trade, this line of analysis tends to become circular. Nor is the anti-Dutch policy to be explained largely in simple bullionist terms. There was of course an element of shipping earnings and mercantile profit which earned precious metals for the Dutch which could have been secured for England. But the balance on goods themselves was a much more important element and the enfeeblement of Dutch producers was not an object of the Navigation Acts. Obviously, too, English shippers and merchants stood to gain personally from the ousting of the Dutch, but they constituted only a tiny fraction of the population.

Now there was, of course, some weight in all these considerations – military, bullionist and personal; in sum perhaps quite enough weight to explain the Navigation Acts. What does not seem to be explained satisfactorily by simple recitation of these factors is the enormous importance attached to the navigation system, the administrative energy devoted to its elaboration and enforcement, and the intensity of Anglo-Dutch hostility which gave rise not only to the Navigation Acts but to three wars between the two countries (1652–53, 1665–67, 1672–74), remarkable, in objective retrospect, only for their pointlessness and futility. All this becomes comprehensible only on the assumption that commerce in itself was something particularly prized and deemed especially worth contending for, the more especially when its amount was apprehended as predetermined so that knocking out a rival contender was the only way to secure a larger portion for oneself. An increase of commerce – the handling, carrying and disposal of goods – understood in this way is analogous to territorial aggrandisement, the extension of religious creeds, the furtherance of ideological systems, the exercise of power over others or any of the other objects which through history states have set themselves as proper and honorific ends in themselves of political and military activity. There was in a phrase a mystique about international commercial achievement which transcended practical calculations of gain and advantage, or at least elevated them above the common calculus of the marketplace.

Not only the Navigation Acts but establishment attitudes generally towards foreign trade – in which the criteria, as observed already, did not necessarily have reference to its overall economic importance – have to be understood against this sort of background. And although one is here drifting into sociologico-cultural fields, it is perhaps desirable to essay a brief, and necessarily very crude, analysis of this phenomenon. It may be observed first that the period now under review is nothing like so fertile in state interventions in the purely domestic economy as that dealt with in the last chapter. In some part this is to be explained in the realisation, bred of earlier attempts, of the great difficulties involved in exercising close control over the multiple and variegated activities which made up the internal economy; and the concentration on external aspects of the economy is due in part to the greater ease and efficacy with which these could be subjected to control. But this shift as between the two broad areas of state economic activity must also be seen as reflecting shifts in political power. The Tudor and early Stuart monarchies evaded the embraces of any particular economic interest. The state, so to speak, stood above the economy. This aloofness was never recovered after the Civil War. Thereafter state economic policy took its colouring and orientation from economic interests with which it was closely involved.

The most obvious aspect in which this can be seen is the increased power of the House of Commons, composed of men with private interests to serve and a sense of values conditioned by those interests. It is true that only a distinct minority of these men had a large direct interest in foreign trade. A mere handful of merchants and shipowners had seats in Parliament. Even at the end of the period the number of absentee West Indian plantation owners and of members of the Court of Governors of the East India Company who sat there was small. If one counts in those with close relatives engaged in trade and those with shareholdings in the East India Company – from amongst the landed proprietors who composed the bulk of the House – the numbers with some sort of personal commercial connections would be considerably increased. But it is not only or even principally by way of a mathematical summing that the weight of the 'commercial interest' is to be gauged. For one thing the 'landed interest' had no important economic ends of its own to pursue and was at least indifferent to questions of commercial policy. When such were the subject of debate in Parliament attendance was low and the number of members speaking lower still. A small group closely bound together by a common economic concern could exercise an influence quite disproportionate to its numbers and could set the tone for the whole assembly. There was no other economic interest represented by sufficient members of Parliament with which the commercial men had to share the stage. Production, as we have seen, did not give rise to large personal fortunes on the scale that commerce did, and only wealth, or the accidents of birth, secured an entrée to Parliament. The interests of labour or of ordinary consumers were without representation. The voice of commerce was commonly the only one heard on economic issues.

Less manifest but probably more telling was the influence exerted by the commercial interest at a particularly sensitive pressure point: state finance. Both tax revenue, leaning heavily on custom duties, and loan revenue were drawn in significant part from 'the City', to use an anachronistic term to describe conveniently the mercantile/financial coterie of the capital. Again this is not necessarily a matter of crude quantities. For instance the sums borrowed from the Bank of England and the East India Company may not have constituted a huge proportion of state revenue, but when they could be had on the mere nod of an individual or two those individuals obviously commanded a standing in the eyes of government which could not be matched by the faceless thousands dealt with through the impersonal machinery of state. And more generally, the 'City' men, tightly knit, stationed on the government's doorstep, able to mobilise wealth rapidly, had inevitably a place in the councils of state of which the constitution knew nothing. And since state finance, through the interest on the National Debt, that great income-generating engine, increasingly involved the wealthy of all kinds in its functioning, influence exerted at this point had ramifications beyond the closets of cabinet ministers. In the crudest sense this is to say that the merchant/financier class could not be handled in the cavalier fashion sometimes characteristic of feudal or absolutist states since the interests of too many others of political weight were bound up in the financial system in which that class had a key part.

What is urged here is not merely that the commercial interest constituted a powerful political lobby – a group able to secure the passage of measures of its own devising – but also that in a more subtle and more pervasive way this interest secured a hegemony of economic thought and suffused contemporary culture, at the establishment level, with its own values. It is to this phenomenon that the much battered word 'mercantilist' is perhaps most aptly to be applied, not to any particular set of economic doctrines or modes of economic analysis but to the generalised disposition to assess national achievement by reference to commercial performance.

The Navigation Acts did succeed in their primary objective of expelling the Dutch from English trades. They did not succeed overnight. Between the problems of enforcing the code, legal loop-holes and under the earlier legislation, stipulated exceptions, the Dutch continued to do a good deal of English carrying through most of the remainder of the seventeenth century, especially in the Baltic, which remained very much a Dutch sea. This was to a considerable extent inevitable. England did not have the ships to replace the Dutch with any rapidity. And when, around the turn of the two centuries, the Dutch were being effectively displaced, it did not constitute a rout for them since there was plenty of business for them in other waters. Indeed the fairly rapid dissolution of anti-Dutch venom from the closing years of the seventeenth century was largely due to the fact that the two nations were no longer crowding each other. The great growth of extra-European trade afforded plenty of room for both; and Dutch manpower resources were fully stretched in handling their share. English trade could grow without cutting Dutch throats.

Increasingly redundant through the eighteenth century as an anti-Dutch instrument the Navigation Acts assumed a more specifically imperial character. And with a mercantile fleet, British and colonial, capable of holding its own in the Atlantic the importance of the pro-visions regulating colonial trade now consisted less in the protection conferred on shipping than in the guarantee that Britain should serve as entrepôt to the trade. But even in this respect the importance of the navigation system is dubious. In the first place the bulk of colonial imports were of British or colonial origin anyway. A considerable proportion of colonial exports were retained in Britain – over the later years of the period about five-sixths of the sugar, though with tobacco a like proportion was re-exported – and in no imaginable circumstances would these retained imports have gone any way other than direct to Britain. Thus only the lesser part of colonial trade might conceivably have bypassed Britain if the law had permitted it. But by virtue of its own character the trade between the Americas and the continent of Europe was bound to hinge largely on an entrepôt centre. As between the colonies and the several regions of Europe there was not in many cases a sufficient twoway volume of trade to justify the maintenance of direct links. Purely commercial considerations would inevitably have caused a great deal of colonial trade to merge with some other more voluminous trade.

Would that other more voluminous trade have been England's with or without the Navigation Laws? Personal connections and a common language would have exerted a strong impulse in that direction, but it is not improbable at the time when the colonial trade was starting to become of consequence that it would have been captured by Amsterdam had purely economic factors been allowed free play. The extensive Dutch mercantile network would at that time have offered more advantageous distribution facilities than England could command, and in the event Amsterdam did serve as a secondary entrepôt in connection with eastern Europe. But the trade once based on Britain it is very unlikely that at any time after the end of the seventeenth century it would have been lost again. With the important East Indian trade by then well developed and a substantial non-entrepôt trade established with the colonies there could have been no reason for the entrepôt trade to move elsewhere, i.e. no reason for the considerable part of it which was bound to be channelled through one focal point or other. A certain amount of the tobacco trade would certainly have been lost, in particular a direct Franco-American trade would have sooner or later been founded. There could, however, have been no point in the diversion of any significant quantity of the sugar trade; separate arrangements for the fraction destined for the continent would have been quite impractical. Indeed in the case of the West Indies the balance of advantage in the tie with Britain lay very much with the colonies. Preferential tariffs in the British market assured them sales which they could never have commanded in open competition with other sugar producers. Of course the 'West Indians' who derived the major benefit from this were British absentee plantation owners or those who aspired to return home eventually. They have already been noted as an element of the 'commercial interest' in British public life; a powerful element which in 1733 secured an Act of Parliament (the Molasses Act) requiring the mainland colonies to levy a discriminatory duty on sugar from other West Indian islands. The same 'West Indians', rather later,[1] were decisive in ensuring that Guadeloupe, captured during the Seven Years War, was restored to France on the conclusion of peace in 1763. They had no wish to see the British Empire making room for another sugar producer.

The Caribbean colonies, then, had no quarrel with an imperial economic policy in whose shaping they enjoyed an influential part. The same is not true of those mainland colonies which eventually became the United States of America. The Molasses Act was rancorously resented there, so much so that it proved impossible to enforce it, and in a revived form as the Sugar Act of 1764 it was hastily and substantially modified in 1766. Another, and more imperious, measure of 1750 relating to North American iron production perhaps excited less anger because of less widespread effect but it proved similarly difficult of execution. This sweepingly prohibited the erection of any new works for the manufacture of finished or semifinished iron goods, accompanied by compensation in the form of duty-free admission of North American raw iron into Britain.

The underlying conception of the economic relationship between the mother country and her colonies which this measure plainly

---

[1] For convenience' sake, some of what follows transgresses the strict chronological bounds of this chapter.

manifests was of a complementary one between secondary producer and primary producer. However it must be stressed that the general conception was the expression, less of a deliberate strategy than of the actual facts of the situation. North America had as yet little disposition to alter the overwhelmingly agrarian character of its economy. If issues of economic, as distinct from fiscal, policy had any hand in the final revolt of the mainland colonies it was much more by way of an apprehension as to the course of the future than by way of frustrations currently experienced. And the Navigation Acts, to return to the particular point of departure, taken as a whole, were not a source of grievance to the Americans. For one thing, one or two likely causes of particularly acute exasperation were the subject of special exemptions from the general terms of the code. Wine could be imported direct from Madeira and the Azores; the fisheries of New England and Newfoundland could draw their salt supplies direct from Europe; under licence, rice (an 'enumerated' commodity from 1705) could be sent direct to southern Europe after 1730, as could sugar after 1739. More weightily, if the colonies were the subjects of many of the restrictions of the system their ships were also amongst the beneficiaries. New England in particular not only built up its important carrying trade within the shelter of the Acts but its shipyards drew the benefit of certain provisions of the navigation code which either required an English ship to be English built or conferred a preferential advantage on English built ships – and 'English' for these purposes comprehended the colonies. With cheap and abundant local materials available, New England shipbuilders from at least the early decades of the eighteenth century were constructing not only the growing fleets of Boston, New York, etc., but meeting also an increasing number of English orders. It is not without significance that in the 1770s, as events moved towards a rupture with Britain, mercantile and shipping interests, while as forward as any in declaiming against the British government's pretensions to tax the colonists, were among those who showed great reluctance in proceeding to the final and total severance proclaimed by the Declaration of Independence.

The re-export trade aside, English commerce with the Americas, the Indies and Africa, for all its growth, for all the attention devoted to it, and for all the personal wealth which it generated, was not, even at the end of the period, of much more than subsidiary weight in a gross context. The Old World (the continent of Europe, Ireland and the Ottoman Empire) still took some four-fifths of English domestic exports and still supplied rather more than a half of English imports, of which the great bulk were retained in England for domestic consumption while of the somewhat lesser amount which came from more distant parts perhaps something like a half was re-exported again. If relatively little is said here of this, the preponderant sector of English overseas trade, it is because its pattern underwent comparatively little change throughout this period. The 'narrow seas' remained, as they had done for centuries, England's principal commercial artery. Over the closing years of the period more than a third of all goods leaving English waters still went no further by sea than to the facing ports of the Low Countries and Germany, above all to Amsterdam and Hamburg. However, the markets tapped in this way were increasingly markets for re-exports and as buyers of English produce such regions had by the early eighteenth century ceded place to the countries of southern Europe.

Other centuries-old features persisted. The Baltic trade continued to harass bullion-conscious thinkers and statesmen, its deficit growing as the expansion of English navigation necessitated increasing supplies of naval stores, as the shortcomings of English iron led to steadily heavier leaning on Swedish bar, as swelling output of linen materials involved recourse to Baltic flax – and none of this compensated for by a long-run rise in exports to the region: better markets for cloth were found there in the decades immediately following the Restoration; and around the turn of the centuries the monopoly of supplying tobacco to Russia was briefly held. But various circumstances, including the development of a Swedish cloth industry behind high tariff walls, resulted in ground being lost early in the eighteenth century which was not recovered until the 1760s. It should be said that the sale enjoyed in the Baltic by goods from England cannot be measured with certainty since much that was consigned to Holland found its final destination there. Although the Navigation Acts did steadily drive Dutch ships from the direct Anglo-Baltic trade Holland continued right through and beyond this period to conduct a very considerable entrepôt commerce with the Baltic; it was not until as late as 1775 that more British vessels than Dutch were recorded through the Sound. (An internal shift in the Baltic trade, worth a parting parenthetic comment, resulted from the Russian acquisition of a Baltic port when Peter the Great secured effective control of the Gulf of Riga in 1710, giving rise to a much more active involvement of Russia in the supply of Baltic produce to England.)

Another constant is the continuing predominance of woollen textiles among domestic exports. At the beginning of the period they accounted for perhaps four-fifths of the total, at the end for something over three-fifths, of a total which had more than doubled;[1] and while over the early decades this relative slippage was due to more rapid growth on the part of other, miscellaneous, manufactures, from the closing years of the seventeenth century it reflects nothing more than the development of an export trade in grain, accounting in certain bumper harvest years during the 1730s for as much as a quarter of total domestic exports. Expressed as a proportion of English manufactures exported, woollen textiles through much of the first four decades of the eighteenth century were little below the level obtaining around 1640. However, beneath this overall consistency lies a persistence of the trend which had been operating since the later sixteenth century: the substitution of worsteds, marketed mainly in the south, for woollens, marketed mainly in the north.

Such shifts as there were in the structure of trade with the Old World were not, then, of a particularly bold or dramatic character and such closer details as do claim attention demand little more than a few words apiece here.

Anglo-Irish trade would seem to have reached a nadir in the decades following the outbreak of the Civil War. On Irish soil the war fed on racial and religious passions which gave it a viciousness and a destructiveness which it never knew in England. And, while the mere appearance of William's army in England had sufficed to consummate the 1688 Revolution there, it was only after a nationwide campaign that Ireland was brought to heel in 1691. Nor, despite an increasing flow of Irish linen yarn and wool to the northern textile industries, had the interlude between Restoration and Revolution brought much encouragement to commerce between the two nations. On the contrary, by a series of measures between 1663 and 1681 England had closed her doors to the cattle and animal produce which were Ireland's principal exports and much Irish trade was diverted to France and the Low Countries. The policy of repressing any Irish activity which vied with an English one reached its culmination in 1698 when Ireland was forbidden to export

---

[1] Expressed as a proportion of *total* exports – not really a very meaningful procedure since re-exports and domestic exports are very different things – the share of woollen textiles would of course be shown as falling much more.

woollen textiles other than to England, where they had to bear heavy duties. At the same time, however, Irish linen manufacture was deliberately promoted and it was on the basis of this that Anglo-Irish trade started to grow again from the early years of the eighteenth century.

Repression was very much the keynote of commercial thought and policy through the second half of the seventeenth century; and if it assumed its ugliest forms in the employment of English power in Ireland to enforce subordination of the economic interests of the subject country to those of the master, the most thoroughly repressive results were achieved in the case of the Anglo-French trade – an outcome to which the measures of both countries contributed in about equal degree, it being as much French policy to exclude English woollens as it was English policy to exclude French produce. The grounds of concern, however, were rather different as between the two countries. France's chief endeavour was to protect her own woollen industry; England's was to remedy the overall deficit on the Anglo-French trade balance, which, through the 'sixties and 'seventies especially, affronted bullionist principles even more grievously than did the Anglo-Baltic deficit, for, while Baltic imports were more or less essential, French imports all came under the head of luxuries: wine, brandy, silks, fine linens, high grade paper and glassware. The Revolution of 1688, replacing the Francophile Stuarts with that inveterate enemy of France, William of Orange, set the final seal on the growing body of anti-French sentiment. Between 1689 and 1697 imports from France were totally prohibited, as they were again between 1703 and 1710.[1] In the interim and subsequent years a generally high tariff schedule along with special discriminatory duties on French goods kept officially recorded imports from France down to very low levels. (The qualification is very necessary: the Straits of Dover were a smugglers' highway; and the quantities of claret, brandy and French silks reaching England handsomely exceeded those showing up in the customs' registers.) As evidenced by the official records, the bullion drain was reversed. But exports to France must have been kept down to some extent by the rebound effect of curbing imports from France, as well as by the high French tariffs on English textiles. Certainly, considering its proximity,

[1] England was at war with France throughout these phases. But while this lent a particular edge to the anti-French policy it does not wholly explain the prohibition since warfare, into the nineteenth century, did not normally preclude commerce between belligerents – although it had, of course, to be undertaken in neutral ships.

population and relative prosperity, France was a poor market for English manufactures.

Obversely correlated to Anglo-French trade was Anglo-Iberian trade. Portugal, with not much more than a tenth of the population of France, was, over the closing decades of this period, taking three to four times as many English goods. (The comparison is based on the customs accounts which only record the foreign country to which exports were directly consigned. Since English goods also went to France via the Low Countries and Germany, and goods finding their ultimate sale in Brazil were despatched to Portugal, the comparison is somewhat overdrawn, but still striking.) Portugal had been an important market for English worsteds since the late sixteenth century, but it was the particular development of the Anglo-Portuguese wine trade through the years c. 1690–c. 1720 which supplied an especial stimulus to Portuguese purchases from England. (Although its application is not in the least peculiar to Anglo-Portuguese trade the point may be explicitly stressed here that into the ninteenth century international trade preserved much of its old bilateral character. The trade in one direction between any two countries was a function of trade in the opposite direction, for three distinguishable reasons: shippers sought to balance inward and outward freights; trade had to be conducted by merchants personally, so that once on the spot they sought to extend their business in both directions; there was not a fully multilateral international payments system, permitting of a general offsetting of external surpluses and deficits.) Port came to replace claret in English cellars as official policy threw obstacles in the way of French wines and, under the Methuen Treaty (1703), gave preferential tariff treatment to those of Portugal.

The generally lighter Spanish wines were already well established in England but they too drew further advantage from Anglo-French hostility. And wine was weightily supplemented by wool amongst Spanish exports to England. Trade in the reverse direction grew very rapidly between c. 1710 and c. 1735. Norwich stuffs (a variety of worsted cloth) greatly broadened the Spanish market for the lighter English woollen textiles while hosiery and, in certain years, grain also made notable incursions.

Iberian expansiveness was counteracted in some degree by market difficulties in the central and eastern Mediterranean where English textiles from around the turn of the sixteenth to the seventeenth century were encountering increasingly stiff competition from the greatly developed cloth industry of southern France, with its convenient outlet through Marseilles and the advantage held in the Levant through the specially favourable diplomatic standing which France had for long enjoyed at the court of the Sultan.

Finally, there is enough published statistical data from which to construct a summary representation of the shifts in the geographical structure of markets for English exports through this period, though it should be stressed that the data is not as precise as Table I.7 might suggest and most of the figures are founded on a measure of approximation; the first column, in particular, can purport to be nothing other than an indication of the general orders of magnitude involved.

TABLE I.7. *Markets for exports 1640–1740*

Market	1640 Domestic exports	c. 1665 Domestic exports	1701–5 Total exports	1701–5 Domestic exports	1736–40 Total exports	1736–40 Domestic exports
Low Countries	⎫	⎫	35	⎫	23	⎫
Germany	⎬ 60	⎬ 57	15	⎬ 44	12	⎬ 32
France	⎪	⎪	negligible	⎭	6	⎭
Baltic and Scandinavia	⎭	⎭	6	6	3	4
Portugal	⎫	⎫	10	⎫	12	⎫
Spain	⎪	⎪	2	⎪	7	⎪
Barbary Coast	⎬ 35	⎬ 33	5	⎬ 33	5	⎬ 40
Italy	⎪	⎪	3	⎪	2	⎪
Levant	⎭	⎭	3	⎭	2	⎭
Ireland		3	4	3	7	5
North America	⎫ 5	⎫ 7	4	6	8	8
British West Indies	⎭	⎭	5	5	5	5
Asia	⎫	1	2	2	3	4
Africa	⎭	negligible	2	2	2	1

(The table refers to the location of the ports to which goods were initially despatched. 'Germany' comprehends only German North Sea ports, other German ports occurring under 'Baltic'.)

There remain three subsidiary themes pertaining to foreign trade which should be briefly mentioned: the fate of the Companies; the emergence of a protective tariff schedule; and the experience of different ports.

Early 'free trade' sentiments have already been noted in the previous chapter. Their final triumph can legitimately be associated with the Revolution of 1688: in some measure, because it was the same principle of law which favoured free trade as was opposed to that exercise of royal prerogative which had precipitated the Revolution; more specifically, because the Revolution decisively transferred in effect the power of regulating commercial affairs from Crown to Parliament. However this last is not to say that exclusivism in trade was integrally linked with absolutism, and openness in trade integrally linked with constitutionalism. Rather is it a cruder matter of the Crown having in the past, for purely financial reasons, been prepared to sell monopoly privileges to those prepared to pay for them. As far as disinterested, or if one likes, ideological, considerations bore on the question they were increasingly telling in favour of free trade anyway and would doubtless have brought the issue to the same conclusion, if more tardily, even without the benefit of James's expulsion from the throne. By the closing decades of the seventeenth century few voices, other than those of the beneficiaries, were being raised on behalf of company-controlled trade, except where the nature of the trade required the diplomatic and military services of a company. Indeed the dismantling process had commenced even before the Revolution. In 1673 the Eastland Company's privileges had been reduced to the inner Baltic area when it was deprived of its monopoly in respect of Scandinavia, and, furthermore, had been compelled to admit aspirants to the Baltic trade on payment of two pounds, which effectively threw it open to all serious participants. However it was the new régime which in 1689 took the major step of throwing open to all comers the massive trade with the Low Countries and Germany, the preserve of the Merchant Adventurers. Since trade with western and southern Europe and with the Americas was already free,[1] this action in itself formally emancipated the great bulk of English trade.

Four trades then remained in exclusivist hands and of these the

---

[1] Apart from the original plantation patents, trade with the Americas had never been reserved. A French company which had been formed in 1611 disappeared during the Interregnum, and a Spanish company had existed between 1577 and 1606; but neither of these appears to have been very effective.

Russia trade was effectively opened in 1699 when membership of the Company became available to all on payment of five pounds. The other trades were of that special character conferred by the political situation in the areas concerned. The Africa trade depended on the maintenance of fortified stations along the slave coast and the Company of 1672 had incurred considerable costs in the provision of these, only to find the trade itself being stolen from it by interlopers whom it could not control. The matter was settled in 1698 when the trade was formally thrown open, subject to the payment to the Company of a levy of ten per cent on all goods exported to Africa, the money thus raised to be applied to the maintenance of the forts. The situation of the Levant Company was somewhat similar, its diplomatic role being peculiarly necessary to the safety of merchants trading with the territories under the control of the Sultan. But under its umbrella many traded who had never paid their Company dues. Over the closing decades of this period, however, interloping activity seems to have fallen off, as the Levant trade declined and more attractive opportunities offered themselves in Spain and Portugal. (The Company retained its monopoly until as late as 1825, having been substantially reformed in 1754.)

By the end of the period the only trade of weight which was still reserved was that of the East India Company. This was a trade of unique peculiarity on more than one count. It was very much an import trade. Its conduct depended on the commercial network established in India by the Company and on the political control which it exercised, originally sought in support of its commercial activities, but by the end of this period starting to become an object in itself. (It was in the immediately succeeding decades that this transformation was rapidly completed, culminating in the India Act of 1784 which effectively converted the Company into a political agent of the British government and confined the Company's shareholders to a fixed annual payment.) The distance and hazards of the voyage to India necessitated ships of a class and cost quite unknown in other trades, while the distance again required the venturing of capital for much longer periods than in any other trade, so that few private individuals would have wished to engage in it anyway. And, finally, participation in the profits of the Company was open to anyone who cared to pay the price of a share on the stock exchange. It was only in the greatly changed conditions of the nineteenth century that any clamour was raised for the dissolution of the Company's trading monopoly.

The emergence of protective tariffs is a theme which has already been attended to in connection with those industries which were the chief beneficiaries: silk, linen, paper and glass. All that need be spelt out here is the chronology and motivation of the development. The one in fact implies the other. Between 1690 and 1704 the general level of import duties was raised fourfold. Revenue, to sustain the long and costly struggle with France, was the object. But many of the duties thus heightened in the cause of war finance were not subsequently lowered on the return of peace. Fiscal considerations had led to their imposition. Commercial considerations prompted their retention. The War of the League of Augsburg and its successor, the War of the Spanish Succession, were decisive in making of the customs system an instrument of economic policy, where before it had been simply an administratively convenient way of raising tax revenue. The assumption by the customs system of this additional role was given a particular clarity of purpose by Sir Robert Walpole's reforms of 1722. With surplus revenue in prospect Walpole preserved most of the high import duties but abolished over a hundred export duties – fiscally, just as serviceable as import duties but plainly a competitive impediment in foreign markets – and started a whittling away of duties on imported raw or semiprocessed materials, with the burden they placed on home producers of the relevant finished goods, thus initiating a programme which was to persist, whenever the state of the revenue permitted, for close on another century and a half. The commonly received impression that there is some radical difference between eighteenth- and nineteenth-century tariff policies, or between something called 'mercantilist' policy and something called 'free trade' policy, is largely due to the intervention of the Revolutionary and Napoleonic Wars which necessitated a long suspension and, indeed, reversal of the trend referred to here – a trend which could proceed much more rapidly in the war-free decades after 1815 than had been possible in the bellicose eighteenth century.[1] Any appreciation of tariff policy from the early eighteenth century onwards must keep constantly in view the fact that it had to balance two fundamentally opposing aims. The full realisation of the commercial aims, extinction of all obstructive duties and the raising of all protective duties to the point where competing imports were entirely excluded, would have annihilated customs revenue, in an era when political and administrative considerations made it impossible to transfer the fiscal burden wholly, or even very substantially, to other forms of taxation.

[1] This theme is resumed and expanded in Part II, pp. 627-31.

The final theme with which we are concerned – the record of different ports – poses a problem of treatment. How does one measure the business of a port? From the point of view of mercantile profits the value of the goods handled is the major element. From the point of view of the income of port workers the volume of goods is the chief consideration. From the point of view of shipping earnings it is an amalgam of value and volume multiplied by the distance over which the goods are carried which is the determinant; and the ultimate impact of this last kind of income depends on where the ship is built, provisioned, and repaired, where the sailors who man it are normally resident and where its owners live and spend their profits. Clearly then no single set of figures is going to provide a measure of the income generated in different ports by their seagoing trade. Indeed the complications involved in a quantification of the question are such that it is really something of a relief that the base data from this period is far too defective to permit of attempting it.

Even without the benefits of accurate quantification there is no doubt of London's clear primacy amongst English ports. In an earlier chapter London was seen to have encroached greatly on the overseas trade of other ports through the fifteenth and early sixteenth centuries. London probably held the position then reached until the onset around 1680 of the re-export upsurge which in its first phase further increased London's lead, the merchants and shippers of the capital engrossing the bulk of these fresh opportunities in the early years. From the last decade or so of the seventeenth century, however, western, Atlantic facing, ports were moving in on the African and American trades. The business of Bristol, ideally located for the triangular Africa–America–England trade, grew rapidly up to the 1730s. Liverpool, little more than a fishing village at the beginning of the period, grew more rapidly still and by the close was vying with Bristol in importance, both in the Atlantic trade specifically and in gross trade. Liverpool's early opportunities had occurred in the Anglo-Irish trade as the silting up of the Dee gradually closed down Chester and diverted to the Mersey the linen yarn and the wool (raw or yarn) which the northern textiles industries drew from Ireland. These were growing industries, particularly over the last couple of decades of this period, during which Liverpool constituted itself as the maritime hub not only of this growth and of the general development which it engendered, but also of the supply of colonial produce to its own hinterland, including North Wales and the north Midlands. The latter activity was greatly facilitated by the

Weaver Navigation which had the even more important consequence of making Liverpool the head port for the trade in Cheshire salt, a commodity of relatively little value but of considerable bulk, and therefore a great employer of ships. The Anglo-Irish trade which had given it birth was also expanding through these years but in this Liverpool was now overshadowed by Whitehaven.

Whitehaven's foundations as a port lay in the Anglo-Irish coal trade. From the closing decades of the seventeenth century Ireland was a steadily growing market for Cumberland coal; and while these coal exports formed only a very small fraction of national coal output and a diminutive one of total exports (by value), they did require a large collier fleet. By the turn of the century a greater tonnage of foreign-going shipping was clearing Whitehaven annually than left any other English port bar London. By then Whitehaven had also moved into the North American trade and had become a major tobacco re-export centre; and although after 1707 it quickly lost much of this to Glasgow and a good deal of Irish-bound tobacco, under the Navigation Laws, continued to come to Whitehaven, which contrived to sustain something of a general Anglo-Irish–American trade on a base of coal and tobacco.

We have just seen what a staple bulk cargo could do for a port. That which, in their varying degrees, coal did for Whitehaven and salt for Liverpool, grain did also for East Anglian ports, most particularly Yarmouth, enabling them for some six or seven decades extending into the 1760s to recover something of the distinction they had once enjoyed as wool ports. Further up the east coast Hull participated actively in fetching back the Scandinavian and Baltic commodities which were needed in notably increasing amounts over the last half or so of this period. Thus a date in or around 1690 serves very handily to mark a turning point in the London *versus* the outports story. From about 1660 up to that point London was increasing its share of foreign-going trade. Beyond that point, although London's trade continued to grow and its primacy remained unchallenged by any other single port, the outports grew rather faster still.

While there are particular reasons for the development of particular outports there is at least a chronological plausibility in associating this relative sluggishness of London with the break up of company monopolies. Membership of the trading companies had in practice been largely confined to Londoners and while, as seen, many interlopers figured in these reserved trades legal barriers had certainly played some part in constricting the activity of provincial merchants and shippers.

One substantial element has been omitted from this review of English ports. The theme has been taken up in the context of overseas trade, to the neglect of coastal trade which employed a third or more of the ships engaged in English waters. And while miscellaneous coastal commerce was perhaps shared amongst the different ports in much the same proportions as foreign commerce, this was not true of that sector which accounted for more coastal freightage than all other branches put together: coal carriage. If Whitehaven is to be allowed a leading place amongst English ports on the strength of the coal it shipped across the Irish Sea, Newcastle and Sunderland cannot be excluded just because the great bulk of their coal shipments never left home waters. In terms of laden tonnage cleared these were in fact the first and second ports of England, with Newcastle clearing perhaps four times London's tonnage and Sunderland, by the end of the period, perhaps twice London's. Of course many of these clearances showed up again as London entries and in any appreciation of their relative standing the fact that the trade of these coal ports was very much a one way affair should be weighed along with the low unit value of the cargoes and the relatively short distances they moved. But a reminder of the enormous burden thrown on transport resources by this one commodity is not a bad note on which to leave the trade and shipping of a period which attached so much importance to activity in these fields.

Tailpiece

In concluding a coverage of some six and a half centuries of English economic history a few bold sentences of summary survey might seem to be called for. They are not offered here. If they are sought, something of the kind will be found in the opening paragraphs of Part II which, designed to set the scene for what follows, are necessarily a digest of what has gone before, or at least of the leading consequences of what has gone before. However if there is one refrain which can serve as a signature to the centuries which have come under our view it must be that throughout, in 1740 as in 1086, we have been dealing with a society which, under an economic aspect, was primarily dedicated to the task of feeding itself. That is the persistent and fundamental truth which must inform and control any overall appraisal of the English economy at any point in time through these centuries. A narrative account must always devote most attention to the element of change. An insistence on a primary continuity is perhaps then as good a last word as any.

PART II

1740–1970

One

1740-1785

The Economy in 1740

In 1740 Great Britain, measured by any contemporary gauge, was a prosperous country. It was not a flamboyant or obtrusive prosperity. Few continentals would have thought immediately of Britain as an outstanding exemplar of high economic achievement. Holland was still the model of such appraisals and in terms of gross wealth France would have been rated more highly than Britain. And it was in gross terms that contemporaries usually evaluated economic standing. The welfare criteria which are usual terms of reference today would not have been included in the critical apparatus of an early eighteenth-century observer. More precisely: above a certain minimum level the enhancement of the standard of living of the mass of the populace did not constitute an economic objective. The opinion of the majority of men who considered such questions was that a wage level which just ensured the minimum necessities of life and no more was the one best calculated to promote the national economic interest. This was based on the thesis: low wages = low production costs = competitive strength as against rival foreign producers, supplemented in some cases by the attitude to which Arthur Young gave pungent expression: 'Every one but an idiot knows that the lower classes must be kept poor or they will never be industrious.'[1]

This attitude clearly subsumed the desirability of full employment of the working population but equally evidently not out of a central concern with social welfare but rather out of a fear that productive resources would go unused and the might of the country be thereby

[1] *Farmer's Tour through the East of England* (1771).

impaired. One says 'might' advisedly because although the concept of national wealth was not yet a closely analysed one and different men meant different things when employing it, there generally lurked within it the notion of military power. A nation was wealthy in proportion to its capacity to outfight other nations, and fighting strength was in the last analysis a matter of gross quantities of men and materials. Not until the Seven Years War (1756–63) had demonstrated Britain's potent military capacity did foreign observers generally turn with interest and a touch of envy to contemplate the British economy.

But the situation in the 1760s was not very different from that of the 1740s. In either decade the element of central economic importance was the state of British agriculture, accounting as it did for close on two-thirds of all incomes derived from production (and about two-fifths of total incomes, including those derived from commercial, financial, and personal services). A comparison with most parts of Europe would have disclosed two particularly distinctive features. First, British land on the whole was rather more efficiently worked, partly because of the more widespread use of superior techniques, partly and probably most importantly because of more intensive local specialisation. Secondly, a greater proportion of agrarian wealth was in the hands of a middling class of farmers. These were not those extremes to one or other of which much of Europe tended: on the one hand, general fragmentation of land amongst subsistence peasants; on the other, great estates worked by servile or wage labour. A special importance of this second feature was that it provided a relatively large body of customers for manufactured articles of a non-essential but fairly inexpensive kind; while the comparative efficiency of British agriculture permitted a relatively large proportion of labour and capital to be devoted to such manufactures without creating an intolerable shortage of essential agricultural produce.

Supporting this flexibility in the apportionment of productive resources was a favourable balance between population and the supply of good land. The respite that Britain had enjoyed from sustained population rise for some decades before 1740 afforded room for economic manoeuvre which would not have been available had continuing demographic pressure created chronically grave problems of subsistence, as it was doing in parts of Europe by the early years of this period. The state of agriculture then not only governed dietary standards, which for most people were the dominant component of general living standards, but also by its bearing on demand and supply determined in significant measure the level of industrial activity. Enterprise, technical accomplishments, an infrastructure of mercantile, financial and transport facilities, a state revenue system which was increasingly being shaped in the interests of manufacturers, foreign markets, absorbing about a quarter of manufactured goods – all these were elements in making industry much more than a fringe activity in the British economy of 1740, but the most important single factor was a fundamentally healthy agrarian base.

Britain in 1740 was not, in any useful sense of the term, an industrial country, but the strong probability is that by then in no other country did manufacturing activity account for as large a proportion of national income. The content of Britain's external trade is some indication of her international position in this respect: 85 per cent of domestic exports were finished (or nearly finished) manufactures, only 20 per cent of imports had undergone major processing before arrival:[1] iron and textile yarns, both for subsequent working up into articles of use, accounting for about a half of the latter, while silk cloth, the only fully finished manufacture of any note, even allowing for smuggling, hardly represented more than 1 per cent of imports retained for home consumption. Britain, then, had gone much further in the development of manufactures than had the great majority of countries with which she traded. However, only in one commodity, woollen goods (constituting some 60 per cent of domestic exports), did Britain enjoy anything of an international eminence, and these goods went very largely to relatively backward regions rather than to Britain's economic peers – a group of economically self-sufficient countries which along with Britain itself included the Low Countries, France, and certain of the German and Italian states. The single, though important, case of woollen goods aside, the prosperity of British manufacturers rested heavily on command of their home market – and thus on the purchasing power of that market, determined above all by the level of agrarian incomes.

The weight of industry in the British economy is partially discernible in the demographic geography of the country. The prime determinant of population concentration was the quality of the land. For the most part people abounded where corn was the most intensively cultivated, and in many places industry merely thickened out a naturally dense population. But certain areas stand out as maintaining populations well in excess of meagre local agricultural capacity: central Devonshire,

[1] The percentages are derived from the available printed material (E. B. Schumpeter, *English Overseas Trade Statistics 1697–1808*, Oxford University Press, 1960) where nearly all exports are separately enumerated but only about a half of imports; the figure for the latter is based on the assumption that a breakdown of the unenumerated articles would yield the same proportion of processed items as that for the enumerated ones.

supported by woollen manufactures; the West Riding of Yorkshire, similarly sustained and drawing some support also from coal mining and, in the Sheffield district, from metal working; south Lancashire, leaning heavily on linen, cotton and woollen materials; Tyneside and Wearside living off coal and associated industries, notably glass and salt. Less obvious because they were situated in what were also fair to good agricultural regions are the woollen cloth manufacturing which occupied much of the population of Wiltshire, Somerset and Gloucestershire and the hardware trades which, supplemented by coal mining, were the economic base of those parts of Warwickshire, Worcestershire and Staffordshire lying within twenty-five miles or so of Birmingham. The counties of Norfolk, Suffolk and Essex with their mixture of very good and very poor land would have borne a fairly considerable population in any circumstances, but that they were as densely populated as the more uniformly fertile counties on their western flank was in part due to the large numbers employed there in the worsted industry with its copious export sales. Leicestershire, heavily given over to pasture farming which required little labour, along with the neighbouring counties of Derbyshire and Nottinghamshire maintained many thousands of people in the hosiery industry. And apart from these extensive regions there were numerous industrial pockets, sometimes dominating a locality, sometimes only an adjunct to agriculture: necessarily localised industries, coal mining; iron, lead, tin and copper mining and smelting; saltmaking; glass manufacture; shipbuilding. Dotting the countryside here and there were paper mills. Brick kilns abounded throughout the lowlands. Lacemaking, sailmaking and ropemaking were important cottage industries providing female employment in a number of localities. There were in fact few parts of England of any extent where some form of industrial activity was not of appreciable consequence to the local economy.

On the other hand there were even fewer parts where a substantial proportion of the population had lost all contact with the land. It would seem to be true that the male industrial worker by 1740 did not usually hold land – other than, perhaps, a quarter of an acre or so of garden – but many women workers were the wives and daughters of agricultural labourers and small farmers; and even when no member of the household was principally occupied on the land, an animal or two was probably grazed on the village commons and at harvest time industrial workers, especially the women, would commonly take to employment in the fields. Total severance of large numbers from the soil was the peculiar achievement of a handful of urban agglomerations – eight to be precise if one defines 15,000 people or more as a large number. These (with rough estimates of their population) were: London (675,000), Edinburgh (40,000), Norwich (30,000), Bristol (30,000), Birmingham (25,000), Glasgow (15,000), Liverpool (15,000), Manchester (15,000), constituting in sum around 12 per cent of the population. There were about twenty-five more towns in the 5,000–15,000 range, totalling some 3 per cent of the population, while towns in the 2,000 to 5,000 bracket probably made up about 2 per cent. The remaining 80–85 per cent of the populace lived in the countryside, which accounted for some two-thirds of industrial output.

Of the eight large towns only three could be said to have been industrial centres in the sense that their economic base was the manufacturing of goods for extensive marketing: Norwich, making worsteds; Birmingham, hardwares; Manchester, assorted textiles largely of cotton and linen. In all three cases they were not exclusively production centres but marketing and distribution centres for rural manufacturers whose output exceeded their own. Of the remaining five large towns three were essentially ports: Bristol, Glasgow and Liverpool – although Glasgow also owed much to its linen manufacture. All eight towns of course housed large numbers engaged in production to serve local needs; garment and leather workers, building workers, furniture workers, soapmakers, candlemakers, butchers, bakers, brewers, distillers and others whose trades had little or no tendency to become concentrated in specialist centres. And in addition to these there were the numerous individuals employed in rendering domestic, retail and other services to the inhabitants. Urban economic life was in fact highly self-centred – most conspicuously so in Edinburgh and London.

Very little of Edinburgh's economic activity was directed to meeting the needs of other areas. Its economic *raison d'être* lay in its role as Scotland's capital – since the Union, no longer a political capital but still the centre of residence or resort of Scotland's social élite, still the seat of the Scottish judicature, still a base of civil and military administration, still the country's ecclesiastical and academic capital. The consumption expenditure of the rentiers, lawyers, officials, etc. congregated there sustained it as the second largest city in Britain.

On a much vaster scale London is to be explained in the same terms – not fully explained, because London was also a great port and internal entrepôt centre, handling perhaps ten times the trade of Bristol, and was also something of a national industrial centre, principally in luxury articles: silks, fine metalwares both base and precious, jewellery, clocks, watches, optical instruments, high quality furniture, books, engravings and so on – but its predominance in these fields was basically due to the concentration of customers for such articles in the metropolis. By 1740, however, that concentration was no longer intensifying. The social and political trends which from the mid-sixteenth century had been drawing an increasing number of the well-to-do to the capital had reached a point of culmination by the early years of the eighteenth century, and as a mercantile centre London was no longer increasing its share of national trade as it had been doing through the second half of the seventeenth. As a consequence the earlier absorption by London of a growing proportion of gross population had ceased. In 1700 some 10 per cent of the British (some 12 per cent of the English) population had lived in London. Neither in 1740 nor in 1785 was that proportion appreciably higher and the probability is that it was fractionally lower. But it was already of course a massive proportion. Paris, second to London amongst European cities, contained no more than $2\frac{1}{2}$ per cent of the French population. Only Amsterdam so dominated a major state as London did Great Britain, where the rest of the urban population all put together would only have three-quarters filled the metropolis. But even with monstrous London, Britain was no more urbanised than western Europe generally – much less so than Holland and to about the same extent as France where Lyons, Marseilles, Bordeaux, Lille and Rouen well exceeded in size any British city bar London.

If the weight of industry in the economy of 1740 is only very partially reflected in the degree of urbanisation it is hardly disclosed at all by the presence of a class of industrialists. Indeed the word 'industrialist' had not yet been coined, nor did the concept under any verbal guise even exist distinctly in the minds of contemporaries, so small were the numbers of individuals who would have answered to the modern notion of an industrialist. Men could speak adequately of the structure of the economy using the terms 'merchant', 'dealer', 'artisan', 'craftsman', 'master' – the last in certain contexts approximating to modern 'industrialist' (e.g. ironmaster) but more often simply denoting an independent skilled craftsman who might or might not employ others in his trade. Where in particular cases the standard vocabulary would not serve a specific designation might exist – notably 'clothier' in the woollen cloth industry. And if one is looking for the 'industrialists' of the times

the clothiers and those discharging a similar function in other industries would be the largest body lending themselves to the identification,
inasmuch as they financed the cost of raw materials, of work in
progress and of carrying stocks of the finished product until first
disposal.

On the other hand they could not be said to have 'owned' a business;
they possessed neither manufacturing premises nor, as a general rule,
productive equipment. The premises were the workers' own homes and
the tools or apparatus also the workers' own – except of course if the
'worker' were a master with an employee, or even as many as a dozen
employees, perhaps dubbed 'apprentices', working along with him in
his house or workshop, using his equipment. Who then was the 'industrialist'? And what if the 'worker' dealt sometimes with one
'clothier' type functionary and sometimes with another and sometimes
again with another . . . ? And what of the 'worker' who himself 'put
out' some of his work such as a weaver who employed neighbouring
women to spin his yarn?

Certainly in branches of the textile and hardware trades especially
there were individuals who, while owning none of the physical means
of production, exercised a crucial and dominant role through their
provision of liquid capital and coordination of the elements of production and sale – some combination of the cost of raw materials, the distance from which they had to be brought, the number of different skills
and the length of time required for production, the breadth and volume
of the market for the finished product and the accidents of history so
determining matters. In such cases the producers themselves were a fully
depressed proletariat. But even when producers did have to rely on an
intermediary agency for the supply of raw materials and disposal of the
finished product they often retained a measure of real independence –
or, more pertinently put, retained some part of the profits of production, which could be ploughed back to build up small businesses employing additional labour. In many industrial fields a 'medieval' fluidity
of transition from artisan to small master was still commonplace. The
relative plenitude of such small masters ensured a competitive situation
which kept profit margins narrow; the 'surplus' derived from a master's
labour force was no more than an adjunct to the return on his own
labour. A great fortune could not be mustered in this way – 'captains
of industry' were not bred out of this kind of business.

Only within a comparatively small industrial sector did the need for
fixed capital investment create a distinctive class of owners of enterprises

who were clearly marked off from their workpeople. This sector comprised the smelting and refining branches of the iron industry, papermills, saltworks, glassworks, many coalmines, most lead, tin and copper works, a few London breweries and some other miscellaneous enterprises. Command of capital conferred a quasimonopolistic advantage on a relatively small group of entrepreneurs and here there was real concentration of economic power. But, generally speaking, such concentration was not sought if it could be avoided: subleasing and subcontracting arrangements to relieve the strain on capital and managerial capacity were widely resorted to. Indeed if one single feature could be insisted on as pervasively characteristic of British industry in its various forms at the outset of this period, it would be the diffusion of the functions of capital provision and operational control – the functions, that is, of the 'industrialist'.

Demography

The extent to which the British economy of 1785 was recognisably different from that of 1740 is open to discussion, but there was one obvious respect in which an appreciable change had taken place: population. In 1740 there were about 7 million people living in Great Britain; in 1785 there were about $9\frac{1}{4}$ million – and this was only the beginning of a growth that was to be sustained at an accelerated rate throughout the nineteenth century and in attenuated form is still with us. This persistence and the continuity it establishes with modern times give the demographic upsurge getting under way in this period a special character and have made of it one of the most intensively studied and keenly debated aspects of British economic history. Neither the study nor the debate are yet concluded and no definitive answers are available to the questions posed by the phenomenon. Indeed one is not even sure what questions should be raised. The yearly growth rate over this particular period was about 0·6 per cent. Now that is not 'abnormal' – such a rate had almost certainly been sustained over periods of similar length in previous centuries. One could argue that it is the sort of rate to be expected in the absence of special or unusual factors, so that the demographic record of these particular years need not present any special question. The inquiry shifts from these years to the preceding period of demographic stagnancy – only of course to shift back again. If what is at issue is some special factor (or factors) keeping population down in the decades before 1740 then it (or they) must be identified as having ceased to operate or operated less vigorously after 1740.

Smallpox offers itself for identification as such a factor. The evidence points to a marked intensification of this disease from the late 1660s, reaching a crescendo *c.* 1710–*c.* 1745 and falling away erratically thereafter. Although it remained one of the principal epidemic diseases until towards the end of the century, the reduction in smallpox mortality from the mid-1740s onwards might have been just about enough to have brought about a return to a 'normal' balance between deaths and births. On much scantier evidence a somewhat similar chronology as for smallpox can possibly be traced for the major infantile disease, summer diarrhoea. Deaths from it remained at a very high level until into the twentieth century but there may have been something of a drop from a summit, attained *c.* 1720–*c.* 1740, which could be thrown in as a makeweight with the smallpox record to account for the resumption of population growth from the early years of this period. If there was a fall in diarrhoea mortality there is no reason which can be assigned for it other than the development of a certain degree of natural immunity. In the case of smallpox, while a process of natural immunisation may also have been taking place, there is an artificial check to the disease which can be pointed to: inoculation.[1] Introduced into England about 1720 the practice after a good deal of hostility spread, especially from about the middle of the century, and though neither its extent nor its efficacy can be measured, its adoption on an appreciable scale lends a particular credibility to the fragmentary statistical indications of a significant fall in smallpox mortality.

The essence of the approach so far adopted here is that three roughly distinct demographic periods are to be defined: *c.* 1670(?)–*c.* 1740; *c.* 1740–*c.* 1785 and *c.*–1785–*c.* 1880,[2] to be crudely characterised as 'abnormal' (low), 'normal' and 'abnormal' (high) respectively. The crucial turning point in the long-term view appears as occurring around 1785. That is to say that the search for exceptional explanations need not be commenced until around the date from which an exceptional rise

---

[1] Not to be confused with later vaccination. Inoculation establishes immunity by means of a controlled dose of smallpox itself; vaccination by means of a dose of the allied but much milder disease, cowpox.

[2] Too little is known of seventeenth-century population to enable an initial date to the first period to be assigned with any certainty. Possibly the whole period *c.* 1620–*c.* 1740 should be treated as demographically uniform; possibly the much shorter period *c.* 1700–*c.* 1740 should be regarded as having a distinct character: *c.* 1880 marks the onset of modern conditions; from then both birth and death rates were falling.

in population took place. From that date one must find peculiar grounds to account either for a marked rise in the birth rate or a marked fall in the death rate. Before that date one is not under that necessity – whatever special circumstances are adduced in explanation of the unprecedented tidal wave of population growth on which Britain swept into modern times they do not, on this view, have to be valid for any preceding period. If that is insisted on some, though by no means all, the difficulties involved in explaining one of history's most signal phenomena can be overcome. It is less daunting to have to explain a massive upsurge in British population dating from *c.* 1785 than one dating from *c.* 1740.

TABLE II.I. *Average annual rate of population increase,
England and Wales*

	%			%
1740–50	0·38		1790–95	1·05
1750–60	0·64		1795–1800	1·14
1760–70	0·67		1801–21	1·34
1770–80	0·65		1821–31	1·47
1780–85	0·63		1831–81	1·22
1785–90	0·99		(Great Britain)	

(Up to 1800 the rates are derived from the estimates of G. T. Griffith as reprinted in B. R. Mitchell and P. Deane, *Abstract of British Historical Statistics* (Cambridge University Press, 1962). The censuses of 1801 and 1811 are known to have been defective. For 1801–21, then, Griffith's corrected 1801 figure and the census 1821 figure have been used. Thereafter the census figures have been used.)

The basic questions proposed then by this approach are: why was population change 'unnaturally' sluggish in the decades before 1740? Why did it revert to a 'natural' growth from *c.* 1740? Why did it accelerate startlingly from *c.* 1785? An alternative approach would see in the acceleration simply an accentuation of whatever factors were making for growth from *c.* 1740; would not draw any sharp distinction between pre-1785 and post-1785 growth: and would ask essentially the same question of both phases. It would not accept the smallpox record (possibly reinforced by that of summer diarrhoea of infants) as largely sufficing to explain pre-1785 population increase, but would combine it with other factors to account in roughly uniform fashion for the long-run course of population change from *c.* 1740 onwards. To appreciate this point of view we must push beyond the period 1740–85 and cover the course of population through the period otherwise reserved for the next chapter (1785–1830).

As far as the very imperfect statistical evidence of birth and death rates over the whole stretch 1740–1830 is of any help it permits of only two categoric statements: that taking one decade with another there was neither a notable fall in the birth rate nor a notable rise in the death rate. Put another way, one could argue for more births as the principal factor making for population growth, or for fewer deaths as the chief agency, or for the roughly even importance of each, without fear of clear statistical refutation – but also without hope of firm statistical confirmation. Any examination of the question must at a very early stage cut loose from statistical moorings and float in a sea of circumstantial evidence.

An upward turn in population is most probably explicable by a fall in the death rate, as a result of a spontaneous ebbing of serious disease, or of improved methods of curing or preventing disease, or of a general increase in standards of living making for greater resistance or immunity to disease. In our particular case there is only one specific disease that was plainly on the wane through the period in question: smallpox. We have already seen that its decline must at least be reckoned a factor in population growth up to 1785. That decline proceeded further through the closing years of the eighteenth century and the first decade of the nineteenth, after which smallpox mortality remained at about the same absolute level, by then very low, for another thirty years or so. But by the last decade or two of the eighteenth century mortality had already been so reduced that the further fall can have had little bearing on the accelerated rate of population growth then being maintained.[1] (One particular implication of the smallpox chronology is that, within this period at least, vaccination, publicised by Dr Edward Jenner in 1798 following his experiments with the technique, played relatively little part in controlling the disease – or, rather, if it did it was not signally more effective than earlier inoculation.)

There is no positive indication of a dwindling on the part of any other disease – apart, that is, from summer diarrhoea, already mentioned. Nor are there medical grounds for supposing that deaths from any other particular illness declined. Inoculation and vaccination

---

[1] The demographic argument about smallpox mortality turns on the level attributed to it at the *beginning* of the period.

aside, the age effected no advance whatsoever in either the prevention or the treatment of disease. In the large towns and cities it was something of an age of hospital building but in the lack of disinfectant measures the consequences of herding the sick together was almost certainly to increase mortality. To postulate a significant fall in the death rate, then, one is forced back on the thesis of a general rise in living standards – people on the whole were better fed, more adequately clad, cleaner, better housed, provided with improved sanitary facilities. To some extent such an advance might be looked for as a result of public authority initiatives in the field of social welfare and communal amenities. There are particular instances of municipal activity in respect of water supply and sewage disposal systems but they hardly add up to a general movement. In any event the population at the beginning of the period was heavily rural and thus quite untouched by such undertakings, while there can be no doubt that in the later years of rapid urbanisation the provision of sanitary facilities hopelessly failed to keep pace with expanding town populations. And neither authority nor philanthropy were to concern themselves with working-class housing for many years to come.

So far as direct relief of poverty was concerned, England (not Scotland) already had at the beginning of the period a more or less comprehensively efficacious system for the prevention of utter want – it aspired no higher than that and in particular cases not always even as high. Although with the widespread introduction of the Speenhamland System (1795)[1] it took on a more lavish appearance, it was not with the professed object of raising minimal living standards but merely that of preserving the existing ones in the face of cruelly high bread prices. However it may be allowed that the greater readiness to grant extra-institutional relief and the formalised scaling of relief according to bread prices and family size did tend to ensure a bare adequacy for some who formerly might have been denied it – that it effected something of a levelling up to minimal standards. But it is plain that any case for generally improved living standards must rest heavily on positing an enhanced purchasing power of the working masses – on the contention that they could themselves afford to buy more and better food and other goods.

[1] Introduced originally in the county of Berkshire, this was a mode of assessing poor relief which was soon adopted in many other rural areas. Its key feature was the provision of cash relief on a fixed scale according to family size, bread prices and, in the case of employed persons, wages.

Towards resolving this issue there is available a fair amount of information about wages, especially over the later years of the period. But no unambiguous trend emerges. The behaviour of wages was far from uniform in different occupations and in different parts of the country. Furthermore, to obtain a measure of purchasing power wages must be related to prices, and though changes in these can be measured with a fairly high degree of precision there are decided variations in the price movements of different commodities. What selection of commodities, weighted in what way, is to be used to determine real wage movements? No one 'shopping basket' would be accurately representative for all parts of the country and for each level within the fairly wide range of wage incomes. Again, during a period of economic change one has to reckon with shifts in the relative numbers employed in different occupations and with the emergence of new occupations. One must take account also of payments in kind and of changes in average periods of unemployment. These refinements might be consigned to the province of specialist students concerned with pinpoint precision if the raw wages data itself spelt out a bold obvious record. But its margins of uncertainty are such that no assertion could be made as to whether average real wages rose or fell without a determination of these other factors – and the means for effecting such a determination do not exist. Investigators in this area – one might say arena because it was until very recently the most passionately controverted ground in the whole of British economic history, on which the historical objectivity of the disputants tended to be coloured by contemporary ideological quarrels – moved away from wage data as a means of resolving the question and endeavoured instead to derive a definitive answer from consumption data. But this too has failed, principally because there is not enough information about consumption. For the whole period 1754–1830 tea and sugar are the only commodities of mass consumption for which runs of figures are available, and these did not root themselves as popular habits before the end of the eighteenth century, so that even the limited value which tea and sugar statistics have as indicators of mass purchasing power pertains only to the closing years of the period in question.[1] And in any event they too fail to yield any clear pointer before the 1840s.

The position then is that the evidence is inconclusive and, given that

[1] The 'standard of living' debate in the context of which these figures were first used related to the period 1780–1850, for which they have more relevance. This controversy was concerned with the impact of the Industrial Revolution on working-class living standards, rather than as here with the possible demographic implications of those standards, however occasioned.

it is not altogether meagre, its inconclusiveness creates the inference, the near-certainty, that living standards neither fell nor rose to any very significant extent. The greater abundance of data and the more intensive research in the years after 1780 mean that the situation in the earlier years is more open to question, but on face appearances the record of living standards 1740–1830 is all much of a piece. There is thus no evident warrant for positing a lower death rate as a result of an improvement in the conditions of life of the mass of the populace.

And so one is driven to consider the possibility of a higher birth rate as an explanation of rising population. This is a much less attractive idea. Most major demographic changes in history whose causes can be ascertained are attributable to fluctuations in death rates. There is a fairly wide range of simple hypotheses available to account for diminished mortality. But there are no external agencies which could have an evidently direct effect on birth rates, with the single exception of acute malnutrition which will depress or even entirely suppress fecundity. Above a certain very low level there is no known relationship between dietary standards and fertility. One may toy vaguely with ideas about self-exercised controls on family size but that involves highly speculative and uncertain theories as to both motivation and means.

This approach has been aired in connection with the later years of this period, invoking two contemporary circumstances: the Speenhamland System and child labour in factories. A relaxation of putative family control is suggested to have been occasioned by the cash allowance in respect of additional children granted by the one, and the opportunities for remunerative employment at an early age provided by the other. But even if the very dubious premise is allowed, the effect of Speenhamland relief on parental attitudes remains questionable, partly because Speenhamland was to some extent only a formalisation of existing Poor Law practices, partly because even with relief an extra child was still a drain on family income. The child labour thesis is even more flimsy since it is far from certain that over the country as a whole there was any increase in employment of children, whose services always had been used wherever practicable. The implication in some versions of this thesis that parents deliberately bred large families for the sake of child incomes can only be described as fantastic. In summary, if the argument from intensified procreation cannot be positively refuted it is perhaps because it deals in conjectures that belong only in the higher flights of imagination where all fancies are equal.

There remains the possibility of more *extensive* procreation, resulting from more or earlier marriages or sexual unions. But this is not to move a great deal closer to credibility. A change in matrimonial habits, while there are well authenticated instances of it in history, cannot readily be correlated with any hypothetical change in social or economic circumstances. A theory which has been in vogue is that an older insistence on trade or craft apprenticeship now crumbled and men became free to marry younger than hitherto. It is a theory open to several historical objections: at no time had the majority of working males served a formal apprenticeship; there is no reason for singling out this period as one of a particular decay of apprenticeship; and few indentures ran on to the age at which men began to contemplate matrimony. But historical criticism is unnecessary. The age at which *men* married is irrelevant. The determining factor is the age at which *women* married, and this was not affected by apprenticeship.

There is one further notion that bears examination: that other things being equal the more highly urbanised a population, the higher its marriage rate. The truth inherent in this assertion is a purely mathematical one, contingent on the laws of probability. On average there is an approximate balance between men and women in a population. But the degree to which the average corresponds with the actual depends on the size of the sample: the smaller the sample the greater the likelihood of a departure from average. When a population is dispersed in small communities there will in any community be a greater likelihood of an imbalance between the sexes than when the population is concentrated in large communities and thus more individuals unable to find marriage partners within easy reach. Given that the later years in particular of the period in question were ones of rapid urbanisation this is superficially a useful looking notion. But unless one starts with very small communities (under a hundred persons) the effect is very slight. Under English conditions of the time it might have produced an increase of 1 per cent in the marriage rate, which would have yielded an increase in the percentage growth rate of population of about 0·03, whereas what one is trying to explain is an increase which eventually touched 1·5 per cent, or at least an increment of about 0·8 per cent, i.e. the excess of the peak growth rate over the pre-1785 rate.

Unable to discern any factors which stand out as evident agents of population growth must we resort to the belief that it was due to a chance conjecture of a number of different circumstances, none of which were of great weight in themselves? To credit that it was all the result of a haphazard coincidence is to stretch credulity to an almost intolerable extent, the more especially because of the insistent feeling that there must be a causal connection between the population upsurge and its contemporary, that pronounced upswing of the economy which we call the Industrial Revolution, and that ultimately research in this busily worked field will disclose what that connection was. Given that the onset of the Industrial Revolution, considered as an economic phenomenon, can hardly be dated much before 1785, this of course is to slip back into the view that the pre-1785 growth is 'normal' (to be explained largely if not entirely by the passing of smallpox) and that the post-1785 growth is that 'normal' growth reinforced by some special consequence of the processes of marked economic change then under way. One might guess that this 'special consequence' was one operating to raise the birth rate rather than to lower the death rate – partly for the rather sorry reason that the factors governing birth and marriage rates are more mysterious than those governing death rates and therefore leave more room for groundless speculation; partly because if one starts from a point where the population is already growing steadily, such as 1785, then the prevailing birth rate is higher than the prevailing death rate and a change in the birth rate will have a greater effect on population growth than a proportionate change in the death rate.

At the same time, one is not compelled to see some special agency at work from c. 1785. If the upturn in population from c. 1740 was substantially due to a rising birth rate (rather than to a significant decline in smallpox mortality or some other factor bearing on the death rate) then, other things being equal, this would engender a further 'echo effect' on the birth rate a generation later, through the particular increase that would have then occurred in the numbers within the childbearing age range. Indeed, at the moment of writing it is towards such an explanation that much current scholarly opinion is tentatively inclined. But in a field where favoured theories have fluctuated almost as frequently as the length of the hemline it would be unwise in a book of this kind to conclude on any very assertive note. In prudence, the question must be left standing as one of the most thoroughly explored and still one of the least understood aspects of British economic history.

From a strictly economic viewpoint the fact of population rise, rather than its causes, is what matters. Not that gross quantities, whether of people or of goods, are of much significance in themselves. The fundamentally important characteristics of an economy are not defined by mere size, but by the *balance* between population and production. As long as any given balance is maintained, no significant change can be said to have taken place simply because of variations in the gross quantities involved. An increase in population is at one and the same time an increase in the need for goods and services and an increase in the labour power for the production of such goods and services. However it by no means follows that an equilibrium is automatically maintained under conditions of rising population. For one thing the increase in the labour force may not correspond with the increase in population. Indeed this, to some extent, will almost certainly be the case.

If population growth is due to a higher birth rate the proportion of those below working age will increase and if growth is due to a lower death rate the proportion beyond working age will increase. Nevertheless the extent to which a shifting workers/non-workers ratio should be reckoned with here may be slight. Under eighteenth-century conditions the enormous bulk of the non-workers were those below working age (20–30 per cent of the population as compared with the 2–3 per cent who were beyond working age) so that if the growth of population, 1740–85, was principally on account of a falling death rate (and if there were no especial decrease in infantile mortality) it would have been among the old that the proportionate increase of non-workers largely occurred – and since the old were so few in number they might increase markedly more rapidly than population as a whole without imposing any notable extra burden on labour resources. Of course if the increase in population were to any appreciable extent due to a rising birth rate (or falling infantile mortality rate) the impact on the workers/non-workers ratio would have been sharp (if a rising birth rate had been wholly responsible the proportionate percentage of non-workers would have increased by about 5). And this indeed is perhaps the most plausible causal connection to posit between population growth and the Industrial Revolution: that demand grew faster than labour power, prompting a special interest in ways of economising on labour.

But since we are here essentially concerned with the pre-Revolution phase we must ask: might economic disequilibria result in other ways from rising population? Conceivably, from lack of the enterprise requisite to organise the extra labour to meet the extra demand. But only the most inertia-ridden economy could fail to respond adequately to an annual increase in demand of the order of 0·6 per cent. Conceivably too, because the extra needs could not translate themselves into effective demand. At first sight we might seem to be faced with a vicious circle: the extra people could only buy more if they were employed; they would only be employed if more was being bought. But, unless the economy were already in an advanced state of exhaustion and current purchasing power already fully absorbed, savings, credit and charity would be drawn on initially to finance the extra purchases and thus set the wheel of growth in motion.

What of the raw materials and physical resources needed for extra production? In this context this is almost exclusively a question of farm-land. The mineral resources to meet industrial requirements existed in abundance and were readily capable of increased exploitation, given the necessary labour and enterprise (it is after all in the very nature of ex-tractive industries to be continually pushing into new ground as long as demand does not cease altogether). But in agriculture the supply factors are notoriously inelastic. It takes time to raise extra crops, to rear extra animals. More important, extra land needs to be prepared for use. More important still, extra land of good quality may not exist in any quantity.

Agriculture

Britain is not an extensive country, the more particularly if barren heath, moor and mountain is excluded. By 1750, indeed by half a century or more earlier, nearly all the reasonably fertile land, actual or potential, was already in use – only certain tracts of drowned ground, principally in the Fens, and smaller areas of wood-land still awaited reclamation. By 1785 the need for agricultural produce had risen by some 30 per cent. The area of good farmland was incapable of being extended in the same proportion. This was the most profound economic implication of rising population: that it threatened to extinguish the margin of reserve food-producing capacity and generate a growing deficiency of the staples of life.

For most of this period that threat was not an imminent one. Britain entered the 1740s with a modest but comfortable surplus capacity in agriculture. Over the preceding decades the adoption of improved techniques and a more discriminating use of land on the one hand and stagnant or declining population on the other had resulted in something of an excess of supply over home demand, not entirely absorbed by foreign sales. For perhaps the first twenty-five years after 1740 rising demand could be catered for simply by taking up the existing slack in the agrarian economy and by diverting exports to the home market. But by the late 1760s the gap had closed. From then until the end of the period Britain teetered on the edge of self-sufficiency in bread grains – in years of good harvests still able to export tiny quantities, in years of poor harvest compelled to import, sometimes in considerable amounts, though even in the worst years imported supplies were only about 2 per cent of home produce. One might say then that on the first lap of the race with population British agriculture lost the lead with which it had started and entered the second lap a little behind. It was of crucial consequence that it should not fall much further behind as population continued to rise. It is impossible to state with precision just what did happen. Certainly the distance lost in earlier years was not recovered. Equally certainly farm output did not stand still. The scanty indications available suggest that when the crunch came in the later 1760s the response of British agriculture was sluggish, that it was not until the mid-1770s that its pace notably quickened, but that over the last decade or so of this period the output of foodstuffs did keep roughly in step with population growth.

One would not expect agriculture to exhibit great resilience; it is of its nature an activity which cannot adapt rapidly to increased demand. Instinctively conservative, farmers would be slow in taking to improved methods. Capital if needed for projects to increase production might not be readily procurable, and the projects themselves might take time to put into execution. And the whole was just the sum of myriad individual initiatives prompted only by considerations of self-interest. There was, needless to say, no question of a national plan. Although in hindsight it may appear a matter of national exigency, in fact the impulse to raise output exerted itself solely in the form of enhanced profit opportunities for farmers and landowners through higher food prices. Agriculturalists were well accustomed to price fluctuations. The upward turn in prices of the mid-1760s would not have been regarded as initiating a new higher regular level until it had been established for some years. Contemporaries had no reason to suppose that a steady increase in demand had started. The population rise was unknown to them – indeed it was widely believed that population was falling. Thus, in summary, the need for increased output would have been slow in communicating itself and even when the need had become manifest, under the guise of sustained high prices, British agriculture as a whole could not be expected to have responded with alacrity.

That response had to be by way of improvement in farming efficiency, a raising of the output per acre – both to swell the yield from existing arable land and to render hitherto unworked land economically cultivable. It required, that is to say, an acceleration of the beneficial changes already being slowly effected on British land: the use of root crops and artificial grasses in conjunction with suitable crop cycles; the employment of appropriate fertilisers; better tools and equipment; superior strains of seed; seed-drilling instead of broadcast sowing; more intensive hoeing and weeding among growing crops; drainage of over-wet land; good roadways, fences and farm buildings. And, although open fields and small farms were not an absolute bar to better farming, in practice the rate of improvement would be closely related to the rate of enclosure and engrossment. Advance in these general directions was maintained and, over the closing years of the period, speeded up. But research in this field does not yet permit of any precision regarding the rate of improvement in different directions and in different geographical regions. Turnips and clover had been the most signal improvement in earlier years and these by 1785 had probably completed their conquest of chalky and sandy soils in East Anglia, substantial parts of Wiltshire and Berkshire, and patches of Hampshire, Oxfordshire, Yorkshire, Durham, Northumberland and southern Scotland. On the other hand, little headway was made in drainage methods; arable farming in the Midlands, wherever it had not been wholly abandoned in favour of livestock, remained bogged down in its heavy clays. Of the use of fertilisers, implements, seed selection, sowing methods and the attention given to growing crops one can only say vaguely that while there was improvement there was also much backwardness.

The credit for such improvement as there was in any direction may be attributed in some part to British landlords. It was through these years that it became socially fashionable, almost obligatory, for a landed gentleman to take an interest in farming. Members of Parliament were more concerned, or affected to be more concerned, with their turnips than with affairs of state. Cabinet ministers were reputed, by their friends rather than by their enemies, to open letters from their estate stewards before turning to official correspondence. A mad king gloried in the title 'Farmer George'. Much of this sort of thing was doubtless drawingroom froth, but to the extent that it was genuine it served one very useful function: the salons, the balls, the seasons at Bath and London, the assizes, the parliamentary sessions, acted as clearing houses for the dissemination of farming knowledge gleaned from trials and experience in various parts of the country. Transplanted to landlords' home farms sound practices might eventually spread amongst their tenants, sometimes by way of specific stipulations written into leases. In this way one of the chief obstacles to the diffusion of better methods, the semi-isolation of farming regions, was partially overcome. Gentlemen enthusiasts probably also made up the bulk of the clientele for the varied farming literature of the times, among which Arthur Young's meticulous reports in his *Tours* (*Southern Counties* (1768), *North* (1770), *East* (1771)) and his later *Annals of Agriculture* (1784–1809) were probably the most valuable – again by helping to pool knowledge derived from manifold experiences.

But the most apparent contribution of landlords to agricultural advance was the enclosure of open fields and the engrossment of small farms. Some two and a half centuries of steady enclosing led up to 1740. By then probably only about a quarter of British agricultural land (excluding rough pasture) still lay open, most of it in a thick midland belt running from north Berkshire to south Yorkshire, including much of the best, or potentially the best, soil in the country. This quarter was the intractable core which had defied earlier enclosure through the implacability of its occupants, wedded to ancient and sometimes advantageous ways or jealous lest an untangling of their jumbled holdings and rights would result in inequitable reallocation. Only a vigorous determination to override such sentiments could write the last chapter in the history of the enclosure movement. And now, landlords whose predecessors had been frustrated by peasant obduracy found themselves an irresistible ally – Parliament. Enclosure by private Act of Parliament was already an established though scantily used procedure in 1740, and for some little while longer it remained a rarity. But from about 1760 the volume of petitions for enclosure Acts swelled enormously and the virtual totality of such petitions were granted.

Parliament adopted as a general principle an automatic readiness to pass the necessary Act as long as the owner(s) of four-fifths of the land and the owner(s) of the ecclesiastical tithe supported the petition. The views of copyholders, current leaseholders and even of small freeholders (unless there were a large number of them) were ignored and their existing holdings and rights were transmuted into single consolidated farms of supposedly equivalent value by the commissioners appointed under the Act. There is no solid ground for supposing that commissioners did not set about their invidious task in a spirit of equity and that discrepancies on reallocation were any greater than was inevitable when an extensive area comprising different qualities of land was involved. Such conspicuous injustices as did result from an enclosure were in the case of individuals who held no arable land but occupied a cottage and grazed a few animals and gathered fuel on the commons. Such individuals often found it difficult to establish a claim to any compensation when the commons were enclosed. Indeed establishment opinion inclined to the view that the possibilities afforded by commons of tricking out a living without regular employment bred idleness and delinquency; and that one of the arguments in favour of enclosure was that such persons would be compelled to take to full-time labouring, with beneficial consequences for both their own moral character and for society at large. Unless they could prove customary rights the mere cottagers seem to have received short shrift from commissioners in these years, though from the 1790s onwards there is evidence of a more sympathetic attitude towards them and of awards of patches of a couple of acres or so against extinction of commons' freedom.

The small farmer, even though he received full compensation, might also suffer from enclosure. His consolidated holding was more valuable than his old dispersed one but now he might be compelled to bear the cost of a plough and team himself where formerly it had been shared with his neighbours, and in other ways he might lose the benefit of the economies of semicommunal farming, such as tending of animals, free stubble grazing, maintenance of hedges, walls, drainage or irrigation channels.[1] But the gravest threat, if he were a tenant, lay in the very enhancement of the value of his farm. At best that meant an increase in his rent – virtually immediately if he were a tenant-at-will, on expiry if he held by lease. At worst it spelt out the end of his tenancy, for, increasingly, enclosure was but a preliminary to engrossment. The drift towards larger farms was gathering pace. With prices picking up sharply from the mid-1760s there were successful, thrifty, enterprising farmers anxious to expand and prepared to pay good rents for enclosed farms of ample scope – higher rents per acre than the small man with marketing difficulties, and often inferior techniques, might be able to pay. Nevertheless the small man had his own competitive strength: he was often content with a lower net yield per acre than would be commercially acceptable, in effect being prepared to pay to keep himself out of the labouring ranks; he was not necessarily technically backward and if he were industrious he got more value out of his own labour and the closely supervised work of perhaps one or two employees than did the

[1] The extent to which some degree of communalism still prevailed on open fields is obscure. Scattered strips, making particularly for communal farming practices, were not necessarily characteristic of open fields, within which the elements of a holding might, in whole or part, be consolidated although not enclosed.

bigger man out of his larger labour force; and a sitting occupant had the advantage of goodwill in dealing with landlords who as a class prided themselves on their humanity towards their tenants – a humanity which might be paid for in a much lower level of landlord expenditure on farm buildings etc. than a businesslike large farmer would tolerate. It is proper then to use phrases such as 'a drift gathering pace', rather than to suggest rapid or revolutionary change in the increase in farm size. Yet, if enclosure were not invariably a prelude to engrossment an intended engrossment of open field farms was usually preceded by an enclosure. And when landlords bought up small copyholds and freeholds, as they were commonly doing when suitable opportunities occurred, it was generally with at least an eye to the ultimate creation of larger farms.

The legal and parliamentary expenses attendant on an enclosure Act, the cost of the subsequent fencing or hedging, the purchase of small-holdings, the provision of roadways and buildings appropriate to business farm units – these added up to what might be an improvement-minded landlord's most considerable contribution to agricultural advance: the provision of capital. A thorough reform of say a 10,000 acre estate might involve an outlay of up to £100,000, perhaps raising rental income from £2,000–£3,000 p.a. to £7,000–£8,000 p.a. But expenditure of that or even much lesser proportions would usually be spread over a number of years, even decades.

With social canons enforcing a high rate of consumption expenditure few landed proprietors had the necessary surplus funds to put in hand a rapid reorganisation of an estate made up of small undercapitalised farms, perhaps scattered in open field strips, perhaps intermingled with the property of others. Initiatives of this kind had often to be a continuation of the work of predecessors or a process to be handed on to heirs. Even a landlord with ample capital might be reluctant to employ it on his estate. The readily negotiable and reliable stocks of the government, the Bank of England, the East India Company and others offered an attractive alternative – the mounting government debt soaked up much money which might have been productively employed in other ways. Funds not immediately required would be invested in stock and a subsequent fall in stock prices would often deter landowners from liquidating their capital for estate investment until their stockholding had recovered its market value. Protracted low stock prices invariably accompanied the fairly frequent periods of warfare throughout the eighteenth and early nineteenth centuries when heavy government borrowing drove interest rates up and stock prices down.[1]

There was, it is true, a certain degree of capital mobility helping to sustain the rate of investment in land. Smaller estates capable of improvement were bought by large landowners with capital to spare. Landed proprietors could anticipate future revenue by borrowing on mortgage either privately or from banks and, occasionally, insurance companies. But the prospective return on agricultural investment was often not high enough to warrant the interest payment on loan funds, especially at high wartime rates; and if the rate went above 5 per cent, the limit imposed by the usury laws on ordinary borrowing, loan funds for private purposes dried up almost entirely since lenders then switched to government stock, exempt from the usury laws, or to old securities.[2]

In summary then, while landlord investment must be plainly distinguished as one of the chief agents of agricultural advance it must be equally emphatically observed that the fairly slow rate of such investment goes a long way towards explaining the sluggishness of that advance. And, posing the matter to comprehend all the elements involved in increasing the output of foodstuffs, what we witness through these years and indeed for half a century and more after is no more than a modest quickening of the tempo of change already under way. What has, rather unhappily, been termed the 'Agricultural Revolution' was anything but revolutionary in its pace.

Having said that, one notable technical breakthrough which belongs to the later years of this period merits attention: selective breeding. Apart from a certain amount of progress in grassland management, and, more or less incidentally, through the availability of quantities of root crops as animal fodder, the techniques of rearing livestock had stood still while arable farming methods were being steadily improved. Animals were better fed, more animals could be maintained on any given area of land. But their capacity to convert feed into meat was unenhanced. They remained a very wasteful way of applying soil fertility to human nourishment. What Robert Bakewell appreciated

[1] For example, a £100 unit of stock issued at 3 per cent would sell for only £50 if the prevailing interest rate went to 6 per cent.

[2] Fixed interest securities, other than those of the government, could not be issued at a rate above 5 per cent, but a subsequent purchase of them at a depressed price such that the effective return exceeded 5 per cent was not in breach of the usury laws. Bank of England and East India Company stock although in practice maintaining a very regular payment entitled the holder only to a proportionate share in the profits if any and were therefore outsied the scope of the usury laws.

was that some animals transformed fodder into edible flesh more efficiently than others, and that if this characteristic could be established as a hereditary trait high meat yielding breeds could be created (or breeds with other desirable characteristics). He may not have been unique in this perception but he was unique in the deliberation with which he set about realising it. His outstanding success was with sheep. His Leicester sheep, developed by the 1760s, became in subsequent decades, the basis of all flocks where quantity of mutton was the prime objective. And if his beef cattle and draught horses were later superseded, it was by beasts developed along the lines which he had pioneered.

Of course the economic importance of selective breeding lies almost entirely outside this period. It took time and a readiness to accept failure to establish new breeds and, like any agricultural improvements, both the technique and the superior animals resulting from it were slow in spreading, though the pace of progress in pasture farming once initiated was more rapid than that of arable farming. Graziers, by and large, operated on a bigger scale than arable farmers; were more businesslike, more alert to profitable opportunities; while markets in livestock, both in store animals and in finished animals, were wider ranging than grain markets so that advance in one area reacted more quickly on other areas. By about 1820 the quality of British livestock had been thoroughly reformed, though there was still plenty of scope for further progress.

However, even the marked raising of the efficiency of livestock farming which was ultimately achieved was a scant contribution towards meeting mass consumption needs. For most people meat, into the twentieth century, remained too expensive to constitute a major part of their diet. The principal benefit to general dietary standards was possibly an indirect one: with less land needed to raise any given quantity of meat relatively more was available for the cultivation of cheaper food-stuffs. In this context cheaper foodstuffs means above all bread and other cereal foods, but to these one other item of still limited but growing importance can be added: the potato. Strangely neglected in nearly every part of Europe since its introduction in the late sixteenth century, it was, as the Irish experience showed, the most effective answer of all to population pressure. Very possibly it was through Irish immigrants that it came to make a regular appearance on the ordinary dinner table in Lancashire through this period, as it did also in the Scottish Highlands, though it was not until about the 1830s that it could be said to have become an important element in the national diet. But the fact that it yielded much more nutrition per acre than grain means that even through these years it must be credited with at least a marginal role in easing the strain exerted on inelastic food supplies by a swelling population.

Ultimately the answer to persistent population rise was to be found in the massive importation of foodstuffs but that lay far in the future. No settled area as yet had a great grain surplus available for export. Nor in any event could Britain in this period have financed the purchase from abroad of any substantial proportion of its corn requirements – or, at least, it could only have done so at the cost of foregoing other imported supplies such as sugar, tea and tobacco. That is to say there was not the scope for any signal expansion of exports of British manufactured goods, until towards the very end of the period, when British cottons started to carve out new opportunities. British exports had already reached the stage where, fresh technical initiatives apart, only population growth in their market areas could make for continuing expansion. More precisely, British woollen goods, the only commodity capable of commanding an extensive international market, had more or less fully penetrated all regions where they could be expected to sell.

The Woollen Industry

Population growth in certain of the woollen industry's markets did permit a vigorous growth rate to be maintained until the early 1760s, when exports of woollen goods were running some 40 per cent higher than they had been around 1740. Southern Europe was still in course of the powerful demographic upthrust which had commenced earlier in the century. Portugal, Spain and, of lesser consequence, Italy, were through these two decades exuberant markets for British exports. Across the Atlantic, the colonies which were to become the United States of America were developing lustily. Already taking about a tenth of woollen exports in 1740, they were taking about a fifth in 1760. And, of particular note, the American market took as many woollens as worsteds, being largely responsible for the partial reversal of that pronounced shift from woollens to worsteds which had been taking place in the British industry since the later sixteenth century. But 1760 marked a peak which was not to be gained again for more than thirty years. As a market for worsteds the Mediterranean region lost much of its expansive momentum as the rate of population growth there slackened off, and

342

as a market for woollens it steadily shrank for reasons which are obscure.[1] The high growth potential of the American market was vitiated by the dispute between the colonies and Britain. And useful markets for cheaper cloths in Prussia, Poland and Russia were lost as these countries developed coarse cloth manufactures of their own. The nadir was reached with the military and diplomatic adversities of the years 1778–81; but even in 1785, with international amity restored, woollen exports were only some three-quarters of what they had been around 1760, although still fractionally greater than at the beginning of the period.

Steady population growth at home must have brought about an approximately corresponding increase in domestic sales, though towards the end of the period some of the lighter cloths were probably losing ground to cottons. The British woollen industry was somewhat larger in 1785 than it had been in 1740, but the modest increase in size was among the less noteworthy changes which the industry had experienced through the period. Of greater import were geographical and technical changes. The outstanding feature was the momentum of development in the West Riding of Yorkshire where output may have tripled while total national production hardly increased by more than a fifth. In the space of these years the West Riding transformed itself from a distinctly secondary centre of woollen manufacture into the main seat of it, and a steady contraction of the industry in the West Country and in East Anglia had set in.

The West Country was the first of the two to start on a downward slide – from as early as about 1720. The Devon worsted industry led the fall, and though the cultivation of worsteds in the West Riding probably played some part in it the main agent was Norwich and vicinity, whose stuffs won new markets at the expense of Devon serges and by 1760 accounted for about a third of all cloth exports. By then West Country woollens were also feeling a cold breeze – in this case clearly blowing from the North. The superfine cloth of the Frome–Bradford region in Wiltshire and Somerset was secure against it but some of the medium quality woollens made elsewhere in these counties and in Gloucestershire were being displaced by West Riding cloth, notably in the growing American market. And at the same time West Riding bays (worsted) were ousting those of Suffolk and Essex, while

---

[1] The course of the wine trade and the flow of Brazilian gold appear to have been important variables in the determination of the external purchasing power of southern Europe, but it is not clear how closely these factors are to be correlated with the fluctuations of British exports to the region.

West Riding serges were aggravating the plight of the Devon manufacturers. As long as markets were buoyant this several-pronged thrust of the West Riding could perhaps be borne without grave harm in other centres, but the continuing and indeed accelerated growth in Yorkshire after 1760 while markets contracted could only mean recession – and sharp recession – elsewhere. Even Norwich, which by 1760 had attained an unprecedented prosperity, now started to feel the edge of Yorkshire competition in the cheaper varieties of stuffs. By the end of the period the West Riding had almost wholly appropriated the manufacture of lower grade worsteds, had converted its former dominance in the field of coarse woollens into a virtual monopoly, and had amply compensated for the shrinkage in foreign sales of this kind of cloth by extending its range of woollens to cover everything but the highest quality material.

How is one to account for this usurpation by the West Riding of the long held preserves of others? More particularly, can it be associated with the technical advances being affected in the industry through this period? Three particular innovations may be distinguished: the flying shuttle, the spinning jenny and the carding machine. The first was devised by John Kay and patented by him in 1733. It was an attachment fitted to a loom which when actuated by the weaver caused the shuttle carrying the weft thread to pass forwards and backwards between the warp threads – designed, then, to replace the hand-thrown shuttle. It enabled a single weaver to accelerate his rate of work, and in the weaving of broad cloth it allowed the second person required to catch and return the hand-thrown shuttle to be dispensed with. In its early form it was far from satisfactory, being liable to break the warp threads unless very skilfully operated and it required many years of modification of the device and adaptation of weavers' methods before it was at all widely employed. It first took root in Bury, Kay's home town, in the East Lancashire woollen area and from there it spread into the adjoining cotton districts where it made rather more rapid headway, cotton, a stronger fibre than wool, being more tolerant of its deficiencies. Its diffusion in the woollen industry was much slower and varied according to the kind of yarn being used. Outside East Lancashire it does not appear to have been employed before the 1760s, when it was introduced into the bays' manufacture in Leeds. The tougher worsted yarn lent itself more readily to flying-shuttle weaving than woollen yarn but even by the end of this period some Yorkshire worsteds, at least, were still woven using the hand-thrown shuttle while in the woollens manufacture everywhere, as in that of worsteds outside of the West Riding, little use, if any, could as yet be made of the flying shuttle.

The big breakthrough in spinning was initiated by the jenny, invented by James Hargreaves in the mid-1760s. In inspiration this was a spinning wheel with multiple spindles so that several lengths of yarn could be spun simultaneously by one spinner. In construction it was to all intents and purposes a radically new device and, though entirely hand-driven, there was a sufficient degree of automation in its mode of operation to warrant one's calling it a machine. It was designed specifically for spinning cotton, which could better withstand the strain imposed on the fibres by the apparatus if at all clumsily handled than could wool. The chronology of its introduction into the woollen industry is obscure. Again the West Riding seems to have been more forward than other woollen areas. Its spread there perhaps dates from the mid-1770s and it would appear to have taken it some two decades to drive out the spinning wheel and distaff, by which time it was apparently only starting to intrude in the West Country and East Anglia.

The carding machine has the particular distinction of representing the first application of power to the woollen manufacture (other than the centuries old fulling-mill). The device had a complex genealogy. Patents for powered cotton-carding machines of differing design were taken out in 1748 by Daniel Bourn and Lewis Paul. In the hands of the patentees neither of these machines were fully successful but they gave rise to further trials and modifications and by the mid-1770s practicable methods of powered carding were in widespread use in the Lancashire cotton industry. The earliest evidence of powered carding for the preparation of woollens[1] yarn in the West Riding dates from around the same time but within this period it evidently remained in the experimental stage and little economic significance can be attached to it.

Certain basic facts which emerge from the chronology of technical innovation may be stressed. One, the extent to which the woollen industry waited on cotton initiatives; even in the case of the flying shuttle, originally designed for woollen weaving, it seems to have been its successful employment for weaving cottons which supplied the principal fillip to its adoption in the West Riding. Two, the technical forwardness of the West Riding by comparison with the other woollen areas. Three, the relatively late date by which technical advance can be supposed to have had an important bearing on the course of the woollen

[1] Wool for worsteds was not carded but combed before being spun. This remained a hand process for more than another half-century.

industry. Amplification of the first point may be reserved for treatment of the cotton industry. As to the second and third they offer with one hand what is taken away with the other: an explanation of the success of the West Riding in winning markets from other centres, a phenomenon which is quite manifest by 1760 at the latest while technical progressiveness could hardly be reckoned to have secured any clear competitive edge for the West Riding before the 1780s. If its greater responsiveness to new technical opportunities and its commercial achievements are to be linked it must initially be not as cause and effect but as twin effects of the same underlying cause.

Before examining that notion we should acknowledge what is superficially at least the most obvious explanation of the greater rapidity with which the West Riding took to new techniques: mere proximity to Lancashire in which the practicability of these techniques was first plainly demonstrated. At a time when distant travel was arduous and newspapers had only a restricted circulation, men in Leeds, Bradford, Halifax etc. must have had a much more lively impression of what was being done in Manchester, Bolton, Oldham etc. and were much better placed to acquire the appropriate equipment and expertise than those in East Anglian and south-western counties. Taking this view one could argue that there were really two quite distinct phases, overlapping perhaps through the 1770s and 1780s, in the history of the rise of the West Riding cloth industry – two phases which have the misleading appearance of continuity and causal connection; the one merely bringing the West Riding to the position of *primus inter pares* amongst British cloth industries, permitting other regions to preserve a strong if reduced position; the other conferring a formidable competitive advantage on the West Riding as it established a clear technical lead. One might then attempt to explain the first phase as a fairly natural development, tardily put in motion. The plenitude of fast moving rivers and streams for operating fulling-mills and the abundance of coal for heating water for scouring and dyeing could be pointed to as assets which while certainly not conferring an overwhelming advantage should at least have made the region fully competitive with other centres. The difficulties in obtaining the outside wool supplies necessary for marked expansion of output could be adduced in explanation of earlier retardation and the opening of the Aire and Calder Navigation in the early eighteenth century could be considered as contributing significantly to the resolution of this problem as well as lowering the costs of moving cloth out.

If one wanted to insist more positively on a connection between pre- and post-technical revolution growth, the emphasis might be thrown on the entrepreneurial function. In any event that must be allowed some role in the early development of the West Riding industry. Natural advantages do not automatically engender their own exploitation. And the requisite human initiatives in this case needed to be of a particularly dogged and determined kind. The inculcation of the unfamiliar skills needed for the successful imitation of West Country and East Anglian cloths, and the sapping of the entrenched market position of these other producers, required time, patience and the readiness on the part of entrepreneurs to see little or no return on their money and effort for quite a while. One could go further and contend that it was such entre- preneurial virtues in themselves which constituted a significant part of the West Riding's competitive strength, through a willingness to accept lower profit margins, a greater vigour in probing markets, a more assiduous attention to standards of workmanship and then as new tech- nical possibilities offered themselves a keener alertness to these and a greater readiness to bear the cost and trouble of proving them. To lend credibility to such a thesis one could air notions about the psychological inertia bred of established success by contrast with the lively questing attitudes of those trying to break through; notions which might be shored up by commenting on the differences in organisational structure between the West Riding and the other main centres.

In East Anglia and the West Country the dominant local figure was the clothier, although in neither area did this entirely preclude the exist- ence of small manufacturing establishments run by a master weaver, a few of which operated on a large enough scale to be able to bypass the clothier, and in the West Country the clothier himself was often in a position of effective dependence on a London 'factor'.[1] But, with qualifying shades, a picture of the industry in these two areas may be painted with the actual producers, in their own homes using their own equipment, reduced to the status of virtual employees of the clothiers – with the important reservation that the disposal of their time was at their own discretion: the need to earn enough to meet their wants was the only discipline to which they were subject. Under this kind of set-up

[1] These factors had originally been mere agents of the clothiers in dealings with London export or wholesale merchants but in the course of the seventeenth century they had developed into principals trading on their own behalf and sometimes financed the clothiers, thus reversing in effect the former relationship between the two. In East Anglia greater proximity to London or direct shipping from local ports generally preserved the clothier from this kind of dependence.

there was no obvious point at which a very sharp incentive to adopt labour-saving methods could operate. For the clothier to install apparatus would be to move outside his accustomed sphere of action, to freeze liquid capital in fixed investment. And to what end would he be taking this repugnant step? So that his work-people could reduce their hours of labour? The belief was widespread – and it was apparently to some extent true – that the labouring classes would put in no more work than was necessary to secure them a modest subsistence. To cut the rates for work done proportionately to the estimated saving in time would at the very best involve a great deal of trouble and uncertainty in the calculation of rates for a long initial phase when the operatives, dispersed in their own homes, were endeavouring to master the new techniques required; and, anyway, radical interference with the rates, to which customary attitudes imputed a fixity such that even ordinary modifications prompted by price movements had often to be effected indirectly,[1] would almost certainly provoke widespread anger culminating in rioting and violence. For a clothier to resolve these problems at one stroke by turning factory owner would be to transform utterly the nature of his business; it would be to venture further along the hazardous path of fixed investment, and it would be a transformation which in any event he might not be competent to effect since clothiers were quite often wholly ignorant of the techniques of cloth manufacture.

Turning to the producers themselves, it can be envisaged that the more forward amongst them who might learn of and contemplate the use of flying shuttle or spinning jenny would be apt to be intimidated by the apprehension that increasing their output would only result in inciting the clothiers to lower the rate of payment correspondingly and by the fear of the hostility of their fellow workers towards a threat to employment. Powered machinery was of course quite beyond their financial resources and if it were to be introduced at all had to be the work of clothiers prepared to take the plunge into factory ownership.

All in all it can perhaps be allowed that the 'domestic system' created a psychological climate inimical to the spontaneous adoption of signal technical improvements and that an organisational structure in which profit scope and control of production were more intimately associated would conduce more in that direction. The West Riding industry,

[1] For example, by varying the valuation of payments made in kind or by altering the dimensions of the 'piece' for which the rate was paid. It is a revealing comment on contemporary proletarian attitudes that demonstrations against high prices of necessities were much more common than demonstrations against low wage rates.

though not wholly distinct from those of the West Country and East Anglia, did perhaps answer to this requirement. The contrast was sharpest in the woollens branch. Here the small independent productive unit was paramount in the West Riding. The key figure was the master weaver who bought his own wool, had it carded and spun by his own womenfolk or neighbouring women and, probably with the help of sons, apprentices or journeymen, wove it and (in the case of cheap cloth) dyed it. He then paid to have it fulled at a local mill and took it along to the nearest cloth town to sell in the open market. Enterprises of this kind sloped upwards from family concerns to ones in which twenty or thirty workers were employed on the premises and beyond that to businesses in which outworkers were also employed; but the great bulk did not run beyond two employees. Here the only obstacle to the adoption of cheap devices like the flying shuttle and the jenny was that of adjusting operative techniques. One may imagine that the larger enterprises, better cushioned financially against initial losses caused by inefficient workmanship, acted as a trial ground and that the requisite lessons learned passed on to the smaller concerns. It was doubtless, too, such larger enterprises which bought or built water mills to operate the first carding machines.

Worsteds, more of an artificial plantation and less of a gradual growth in the West Riding than woollens, were generally the province of larger entrepreneurs, the nature of whose business more closely resembled that of West Country and East Anglia clothiers. But beneath the objective resemblance lay perhaps a subjective difference. Whereas in these other areas the clothiers historically were an outgrowth from an established industry the West Riding worsted masters were historically the founders of an industry. Although their spinners and weavers usually worked in their own homes they were perhaps more unambiguously in the direct employ of the masters, many of whom maintained a work force on their own premises for the initial scouring, combing and dyeing of the wool (worsted was generally dyed in the wool). The West Riding worsted masters might, then, be considered as owners of productive enterprises in a way in which the large clothiers elsewhere were not and thus as more responsive to opportunities of enhancing productional efficiency. But this is to verge on special pleading. The fact of West Riding gain both in woollens and worsteds throughout this period is plain; its reasons defy dogmatic elucidation.

The cotton industry

It has been seen that the technological history of the woollen industry is closely interwoven with that of the cotton industry, even that the technological history of the woollen industry is but a pale imitation of that of the cotton industry. We have also seen that over the last twenty-five years or so of this period the woollen industry was in something of a rut. Over those same twenty-five years the consumption of raw cotton rose about sevenfold. It is plain that we are entering an era of remarkable development in this particular industry. Graph II.1 traces the chronology of this development more precisely. (In the absence of anything but very vague estimates of the output of cotton goods, retained imports [total imports *less* re-exports] of the raw material are the best available indicator.)

The story is not of a steady upward thrust but of marked growth from the mid-1740s to the mid-1750s, followed by something of a recession until the resumption of growth in the mid-1760s, abruptly and sensationally gathering momentum in 1782 and rocketing upwards in astonishing fashion in the very last year of the period. Clearly no single simple explanation could cover this jagged record. One need of course have no hesitation in ascribing the extraordinary course of the final few years to technical developments. Nothing but signal cost reductions resulting from major technical advance could account for such an expansion of output. To the flying shuttle, the jenny and the carding machine, already mentioned, must be added the water frame.

The water frame, like the jenny, was a spinning machine, but it differed from the jenny in two very important respects. It could spin a warp thread, which the jenny could not,[1] and it was powered, which the jenny was not. The first difference has a particularly profound implication. It virtually created a genuine *cotton* industry where before there had been a mixed cotton-linen industry. Pure cotton articles were not previously altogether unknown in the British industry. Small all-cotton articles, such as handkerchiefs, ribbons etc. may have been made from the seventeenth century, and before the middle of the eighteenth garment fabrics of pure cotton resembling Indian calico had been attempted, but the ability of British spinners to produce the necessary

---

[1] Towards the end of this period modified jennies were spinning warps but these do not seem to have compared in quality with water-frame warps.

strong fine yarn was very variable and these materials were unable to obtain a regular market footing. More successful were heavy cotton velvets for which a thicker warp could be used. By the 1760s their manufacture was well established in Manchester and the velvet makers were the earliest users of water-frame spun yarn, which enabled them success-

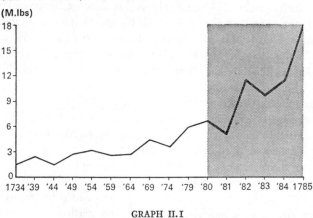

Retained Imports of Raw Cotton
Annual Averages for Five Yearly Periods; 1730-1779
Annual Amounts, 1780-1785

GRAPH II.I

fully to extend their range to lighter velvets. But if the water frame cannot quite be said to have originated the manufacture in Britain of pure cotton articles, it remains the case that without it (or the later mule) the British industry would have been confined to fabrics of limited use and marketability. It is this fact rather than its direct impact on costs which gives the machine its especial significance. Jenny spun yarn was actually cheaper. The two machines, virtual contemporaries, in fact complemented one another. The jenny spun cheap weft for pure cottons and mixed materials, the water frame spun rather more expensive cotton warps.

Thus through to and a little way beyond the end of this period not only did two different techniques coexist in cotton spinning but two different forms of organisation as well. The jenny, simple, cheap, hand-operated, usually just took the place of the spinning wheel in the homes of domestic spinners. The water frame, needing a water wheel to drive it and at its most economical when several frames were geared to one wheel which could also power attendant carding machines, meant of necessity factories: fixed investment in premises and plant, total fusion of the functions of capital provision and production control, a labour force which was unambiguously in the direct employ of and subject to the industrial discipline imposed by the capitalist owner. This distinction between jenny and water frame in terms of organisational structure is not an absolute one. From at least the mid-1770s jenny factories did exist whose essential nucleus was a water-powered carding machine, or several such machines. The jennies housed in these establishments often had fifty or a hundred spindles – outside the means of domestic spinners whose jennies did not usually run beyond two dozen spindles. However it does not appear that any marked advantage derived from the use of giant jennies like these and more common were carding establishments from which the machine carded cotton was 'put out' to domestic spinners, unable to accelerate their own carding to keep pace with their enhanced rate of spinning – indeed it would seem as if it were this problem rather than the expectation of lowering carding costs which prompted the development of carding machinery.

Water frame factories were only just beginning to multiply in 1785, though the patent for the machine dated from 1769 and the first factory to house it from 1771. For this the character of its patentee, Richard Arkwright, was responsible. One uses the particular designation, patentee, advisedly, for the part played by any inventiveness of Arkwright's is very dubious. The most apt comment on Arkwright is perhaps that of his great contemporary, James Watt:

As to Mr Arkwright, he is, to say no worse, one of the most self-sufficient, ignorant men I have ever met with, yet, by all I can learn, he is certainly a man of merit in his way, and one to whom Britain is much indebted, and whom she should honour and reward, for whoever invented the spinning machine, Arkwright certainly had the merit of performing the most difficult part, which was the making it useful.

Something of a measure of the achievement credited to Arkwright by Watt is the history of a slightly earlier attempt at powered spinning, that of John Wyatt and Lewis Paul whose machines, although radically different from the water frame in a number of important respects embodied the same fundamental principle: a series of rollers moving at successively greater speeds in order to stretch the cotton fibres, which along with twisting the stretched lengths is what spinning essentially consists of. Patented in 1738 the Wyatt and Paul machine proved perfectly workable but the inevitably intricate construction of any powered spinning machine gave rise to problems of operation and maintenance which only a great deal of patience, determination, thoughtfulness and money could overcome. Within some twenty years the struggle to put it on an economic footing had been wholly abandoned.

Just why Arkwright succeeded where others using the Wyatt and Paul machine had failed, one cannot positively say. The water frame may have been an innately superior apparatus although it required about five years of trials and modifications before its commercial feasibility was fully demonstrated. Perhaps the water frame would have proved itself in the hands of any reasonably competent and resolute individual. But if exceptional personal qualities were required Arkwright certainly had them. He possessed that intense singlemindedness which is sometimes the strength of limited intellects. His enormous self-confidence supplied his initial lack of capital by prevailing on shrewd business men to part with theirs to get the water frame launched. To the management of his enterprises he brought a crucially sharp awareness of the special need to maintain a high level of labour productivity when the fixed costs of expensive equipment had to be borne whatever the rate of output (a cost phenomenon with which the economy at large had as yet little familiarity); and he accompanied this awareness with a judicious feel for mingling stick and carrot as instruments of labour discipline.

Although without any inclination to dissipate money and energy by dabbling in several fields of activity – the undoing of more than one innovater – Arkwright had no hesitation in moving into the weaving side of the cotton business when, satisfied himself with the quality of his yarn, he found others slow to take advantage of it to make pure cotton cloth. This was a move which he would probably have made in any event since it was not in his nature to allow profit to others when he considered that he could appropriate it for himself. His instincts were those of a pirate. In all probability he had filched the design of the water frame from one John Kay (there certainly seems to be no doubt that Kay's name should at the very least rank equally with Arkwright's as the inventor of the machine though Kay himself evidently had the idea of roller spinning from one Thomas Highs). In 1775 he attempted to seize the prerogative of using the powered carding machine (to which, personally or vicariously, he had contributed some useful modifications) by taking out a patent cast in such vague terms as to comprehend almost any variant of this well known machine. At the same time he took out a further patent for the water frame, supposedly to cover substantial modifications of the original design. A court case of 1781 defeated his effort to monopolise the carding machine and after vainly petitioning Parliament in 1782 and 1783 for an extension of his original water frame patent (due to expire in 1783) he fell back on the 1775 patent to preserve his exclusive rights in this machine. A further court case of 1785 finally ended Arkwright's reign as monarch of powered spinning – although he was of course as capable as anybody of holding his own in open competition.

This disquisition on Richard Arkwright has been entered into for several reasons. First, he affords some insight into the talents, with or without his peculiar rapacity, which successful factory management required. This is an element in a theme, to be touched on again later, which becomes of gathering consequence as we move further into an age during which the modes of organising the forces of production were undergoing radical transformation. Secondly, there is a distinct likelihood that powered spinning would have been much longer in establishing itself had Arkwright not so abundantly demonstrated its practicability; a comparison with the later rate of introduction of powered weaving is perhaps suggestive. Thirdly, and almost contradictorily, Arkwright's graspingness explains why the big boom in powered spinning did not come until 1785 instead of five or ten years earlier. Until the final dissolution of Arkwright's patent only his own factories and those licensed by him could employ the water frame. His own personal rate of business growth was indeed remarkable, much of it achieved by coalescing with carefully selected partners in various parts of Lancashire and in a few other scattered localities. But clearly the time, energy and capital available to any one man placed a distinct limit on the possible rate of spread of the machine through his direct agency and Arkwright only sparingly granted licences to others; when he did it was for fees which few were prepared to pay. Thus the history of powered spinning 1769–85 is very much the history of one man's business empire. And the astonishing upward surge of the cotton industry in 1785 itself is to be understood largely as a sudden mushrooming of water frame factories in that year.

The chronology of the other technical innovations in the cotton industry may be briefly summarised: the spread of the flying shuttle can be assigned to the late 1750s and the 1760s; the jenny was rapidly supplanting the spinning wheel in the early 1770s; and the carding machine was perfected through the 1770s, though hand carding for fine yarns outlasted this period. The principal query then hangs around the interconnection between the innovations themselves and between them and the overall development of the industry.

Clearly no significant relationship exists between major technical advance and the first growth phase, from the mid-1740s to the mid-1750s. This phase may be seen as the culmination of minor improvements in technique directed towards producing cotton-linen materials which could stand some sort of comparison with genuine Indian calico and thus fill the void created by the total denial of calico to the British public after 1721. Home demand for these materials was supplemented by opportunities in West Africa, in the West Indies and in the southern colonies of the American mainland during the long period (1744–63) of internal disturbance in India, whose authentic cottons were normally preferred to the British imitations in these markets. Delivery to distant markets was impeded by the Seven Years War (1756–63) and, more importantly, supplies of raw cotton, principally drawn from the West Indies, were interrupted.

The return of peace enabled the prewar level of production to be resumed and raised. Although some allowance must be made for population increase both at home and overseas, as a growth factor the adoption of the flying shuttle, lowering weaving costs and thus making for lower selling prices, was also a significant element now. This acceleration of the rate of weaving aggravated a chronic difficulty, common to all textile industries in periods of expansion: the recruitment of spinners to keep the weavers supplied with yarn; even without the flying shuttle three or four spinners had been needed to maintain one weaver. The arrival of the jenny was well timed, relieving the industry in its main centre, South Lancashire, of the growing necessity to go further afield to get its cotton spun, bearing the cost and inconvenience of carrying raw cotton and yarn to and fro over quite considerable distances. But it was the way that it slashed spinning costs which gave the jenny its principal economic importance, the more especially when reinforced by the carding machine. In the dozen years or so that followed the end of the Seven Years War the British industry effected technical changes which permitted it to offer a range of mixed cotton and linen materials and all cotton velvets at prices which enabled these fabrics to outsell linen and woollen cloth for certain purposes and in overseas markets to undercut similar foreign fabrics and even sometimes, by virtue of their cheapness, to win sales from genuine Indian calicos – although these, with the effective return of peace in India, were now recovering markets, especially in West Africa, formerly lost in part to British materials. Yarn from Arkwright's water frames added to the variety of good quality low cost velvets which could be offered and over the last decade of this period it was these which made the biggest dent in foreign markets. Calico type materials were still only feeling their way into the industry. As seen already, it was Arkwright himself who initiated their manufacture in Great Britain, having in 1774 secured the repeal of the 1721 Act which prohibited them, but for the while the great bulk of manufacturers found plenty of business in the extended markets for familiar materials – and, in any event, until Arkwright's monopoly was broken, the supply of the requisite yarn for calico was limited.

Revolutionary? Is this an apt epithet for the cotton industry in this period? Certainly it is difficult to evade it in speaking of the record of the final two decades and especially of the last three or four years. Soaring output, profound technical change, the movement of a notable part of the industry into factories, one great fortune already made and others in course of being made, such as that of the Peels, destined to spawn a Prime Minister – the industry was humming with a quite unprecedented exuberance. And already a further wave of technical advance was in the making, though as yet it was hardly even lapping the skirts of the industry. Samuel Crompton had constructed his first mule in 1779; in 1785 Edmund Cartwright patented the power loom; and a steam engine was already in existence capable of driving textile machinery. Such an immensity of change still lay in the future that that in itself is a strong caution against the expenditure of superlatives on development up to 1785; verbal energy must be conserved for later developments. Nor should the role of modest improvements, in no way 'revolutionary', be lost sight of. The enhancement of the quality of British cotton-linens without assistance of new devices has been noted as the principal factor in the industry's growth in the early part of this period. And the marketability of these materials benefited considerably throughout the period from improvements in printing and dyeing methods, so that it was not only their cheapness but their attractive appearance which lent them consumer allure.

But, most particularly, it is needful to set the cotton industry in total economic perspective. Even at the escalated level of 1785 the industry's contribution to national income was about 1·5 per cent of the total – roughly a third of that of the woollen industry, while the value of cotton exports was perhaps a sixth of the value of woollen exports. The impact of recent developments in cotton manufacture on the economy at large was appreciable but far from sensational.

The low base from which it started may well serve to explain in some part the dynamism of the cotton industry. Any industry of course stands to benefit to some extent from cost reductions, but particularly one seeking to encroach on the established preserves of others. And this was the situation of the cotton industry in these years. The potential range of cotton materials offered scope for capturing markets from all the other textile fabrics: at the one extreme fine muslin could contend with silk and at the other velvets and other heavy cottons could compete with woollen cloth, while linen, of course, was especially open to cotton rivalry. And beyond this scope for effecting more or less direct substitution the possibility of printing on cotton fabrics offered opportunities of creating new fashions in women's clothes. While these remarks only apply fully to pure cottons they have relevance also to the cotton-linens which even at the end of this period were still the industry's principal product. One could plausibly argue, then, that the initial impetus towards technical innovation was supplied by these standing opportunities, that the specific triggering incentive was not so much the promise of cost reduction as the prospect of expanding output much more readily and rapidly than could be effected by the recruitment of new hands. Through measures first adopted simply to take an increased share in a more or less static textile market, it followed that lowered costs then made for both the stimulation of that market and the appropriation of a still larger share of it.

By throwing the emphasis on the output expansion rather than the cost reduction function of technical innovation one can put the situations of the cotton and woollen industries into significantly contrasting relief – the one with abundant scope for growth, the other, its worlds already conquered, with little or none. And this line of approach has the further advantage that the technical progressiveness of the cotton industry can then be explained without having to invoke especially buoyant general economic conditions to get the industry moving.

We are touching now, of course, on a theme of enormous and pervasive importance. Whether or not we consider the pre-1785 record of the cotton industry as 'revolutionary' there can be no doubt that at some point in time it merged with and constituted a very important part of that complex of economic phenomena which we know as the Industrial Revolution. This is a theme which must be treated of in its own right later on. But in it technical innovation is a principal element; and in chronological sequence the batch of new devices in the cotton industry which we have looked at constitute the first wave. What launched that wave? Indeed is 'wave' anything more than a literary convenience for a number of inventions which fortuitously occurred around the same time?

One might start by disposing of one naïveté which sometimes lurks about attempts to answer these questions: that all inventions are to be ascribed to some special need for them; that their timing is always to be explained by some special stimulus currently operating. This is a particularly insidious notion because if the invention is useful and is adopted – and history takes little notice of those that are not – it will very probably result in increased output, to be represented by sleight of mind as increased demand prompting the invention. A list of some of the textile inventions of earlier centuries – the fulling mill (twelfth), the spinning wheel (thirteenth), the gig mill (sixteenth), the knitting frame (sixteenth), the Dutch loom (seventeenth) – may suffice, if not to destroy the notion entirely, at least to reduce it to such a flabbiness as to deprive it of any usefulness as an interpretative instrument. Inventiveness is plainly a basic human aptitude though like, say, artistic creativity, it plays more freely in some environments than in others; and it is of course cumulative – a neolithic genius could not have invented the atomic bomb. But while certain preconditions must exist there need not be, and often is not, any very specific relationship between economic circumstances and inventions. Not only may inventions lag well behind insistent need but they may amply anticipate it.

Technical innovation, then, can be an independent variable in an economy and the answer to our question – 'what instigated the inventions?' – could be 'nothing in particular'. And indeed the first of the textile inventions with which we are concerned seems to require this sort of explanation – or non-explanation. The flying shuttle, considering that it was introduced for use in the woollen industry, cannot be related to any particular need – the plainest proof of that being its very slow rate of adoption. Whether Hargreaves and Arkwright were responding to novel pressure on spinning capacity could also be questioned. Certainly by the time their machines had started to operate on a significant scale the accelerated rate of weaving was causing bottlenecks, but slipping back the few years to the first blueprint in the minds of these men one loses the clear appearance of a connection, and the suspicion that there was no connection is reinforced by knowledge of the Wyatt and Paul machine, some twenty-five years beforehand in conception, itself originally intended for spinning wool though never apparently used for anything but cotton. Only the carding machine lends itself easily to identification as the effect of a specific cause – enhanced spinning capacity. On the other hand it is of course impossible to credit that the number of independent attempts at spinning machines, including unsuccessful ones of which we catch only passing glimpses and, doubtless, several entirely lost to historical sight, represent no more than an extraordinary coincidence. But strained spinning capacity was an old, even an ancient, pheonomenon – particularly in regions where weaving was the principal male occupation with the result that the women of the area were insufficient in number to keep the men supplied with yarn. And women with other demands on their time and energy could not be counted on to maintain a regular level of output. Designs for spinning machines antedate this period. Perhaps what was new then was not the felt need for more productive spinning devices but confidence in the feasibility of such projects, and confidence in their desirability.

To touch on this point of desirability first: it is today a commonplace that enhanced productivity is a good thing: better methods – lower costs – lower prices (or higher producers' incomes) – higher demand– more wealth all round. But for most people in the early eighteenth century the predictable result of increasing one worker's output would be a corresponding reduction in the output of others. Some individuals would profit but there would be no net social gain. Conventional opinion only applauded mechanical production devices when they answered certain particular ends: if they rendered possible what had formerly been impossible – the Newcomen pumping engine or the silk throwing machine introduced by the Lombes would be good cases in point: if they were to be used wholly or largely in production for export when those rendered redundant would be foreigners; if they were part of 'a project for setting the poor on to work' by way of the simplification of productive operations so that they could be performed by the unskilled or the weak and infirm – often used as a blanket justification especially when the 'projector' was seeking state support. It can, then, be urged that in a generally inimical climate of feeling the inventive flair would be effectively inhibited in some degree, and moreover that the hostility of those threatened by innovation would draw extra strength from consciousness of their rectitude even to the point where the local magistracy might actively connive at industrial sabotage. In the present context the question is not just whether the discipline of public opinion had in the past stemmed mechanical advance but, more importantly, whether during the years in question a significant change in opinion was taking place – or, rather, taking place amongst those whose opinion was esteemed. Undoubtedly ruling attitudes on this issue by the end of the eighteenth century were quite different from what they had been at the beginning but it would be a fine point whether mechanisation, by demonstration of its usefulness, had changed attitudes or whether changed attitudes had facilitated mechanisation.

Much of the same sort of ambivalent comment must be passed on the idea that the eighteenth century brought heightened expectations as to the practicability of mechanical artifices. The circumstance most likely to engender this kind of optimism would be proven success in some noteworthy field. However, the cumulative effect of many minor technical improvements, most of them hardly 'inventions', might, once apprehended, be to create a new atmosphere of confidence. That such a process of improvement had been going on fairly steadily since the sixteenth century seems evident, though inevitably we get only occasional sights of it. There are indications to support the view that as we get into the eighteenth century these discrete and modest advances were being consciously summed by inquiring and observant contemporaries and being represented as a general movement, capable of going further in the future.

In very crude summary there are three main lines of approach to the themes of technical revolution in the cotton industry and of its interconnections with the Industrial Revolution at large. First, that eighteenth-century circumstances conduced to the development of new techniques in general; that these circumstances acted first on the textile industries because as a group they were the largest and most important sector of the industrial economy; that development centred particularly on spinning because the need here had been longest felt, and more particularly still on cotton spinning because growth opportunities were greatest there and because cotton lent itself more readily to mechanical handling. In this account the cotton industry's primacy is merely chronological. A second approach would shift the emphasis and distinguish the special growth opportunities of the cotton industry as a uniquely important stimulus and would have that industry as a prime agent of major advance elsewhere in the economy, both through the direct impetus which its rapid growth supplied to the level of demand and through the example, technological and organisational, which it set for other industries. A third approach would in effect dismiss the notion of an industrial revolution with its implication of some sort of unitary experience by accounting for the special development of certain sectors of the economy in terms peculiar to each (that is to say, the Industrial Revolution was a fortuitous conjuncture of autonomous developments, though of course only in its initial stages: the interplay between different sectors would soon make for reciprocal reinforcement of growth tendencies). Intimately involved in these issues is the question whether changes in the cultural environment or changes in the more strictly economic environment are to be distinguished as the primary initiating forces; whether shifts in the moral and intellectual ambience or new market opportunities were what set the wheels of innovation rolling.

Reverting momentarily to the more particular theme of the extent of change and development in the cotton industry through the period 1740–85 we may leave it with one final reminder: that even in the very last year of the period it was still primarily a cotton-linen industry; and that if we are warranted in speaking of a 'revolution' within it, it was not much more than half of a revolution – the preparation and spinning of linen yarn being as yet untouched by major technical advance.

Other textiles

The linen industry itself is for much of this period to be accounted among the fastest growing of British industries. Indeed it is an industry which historians have, rather unfairly, allowed to be upstaged by the cotton industry. The fact of the matter is that right through to the last couple of years of this period the value of linen exports of British manufacture[1] exceeded that of cotton exports; and although no gross figures are available there can be little doubt that the total output of the British linen industry continued to exceed that of the cotton industry into the late 1780s. It was, of course, the eventual development of good, cheap all-cotton goods which stayed the extension of the linen industry's market; but up to c. 1770 the industry had been making considerable headway at the expense of Continental, particularly German, fabrics in

[1] Excluding the considerable quantities of Irish linen exported through Great Britain.

both domestic and trans-Atlantic markets – in the latter case assisted by the state bounties granted on exports of linen cloth from 1743. In Scotland, where the industry was already very widely established, being in fact that country's only industry of weight, output of cloth for sale[1] increased nearly threefold between 1740 and 1770. In England, where hitherto the industry had had only a very restricted footing, growth was plainly of a much greater order, conspicuously in west Lancashire and in the West Riding of Yorkshire and adjoining parts of Lincolnshire – much of it founded on yarn imported from Ireland and eastern Europe where domestic female labour could be had at a price which would have been unthinkably low in England. From the early 1770s, however, the impossibility of adapting the jenny (or later cotton-spinning machines) to flax spinning told increasingly against all linen cloth in price terms; and continuing encroachment on Continental linens did not do a great deal more than offset losses to British cotton-linen and all cotton fabrics.

Silk had a more continuously expansive record. The earlier success of the Lombe brothers in introducing the water-powered Italian throwing[2] machine was not rapidly followed up, but in the mid-'fifties throwing mills were being established in some number in Derby, in an area on the Cheshire–Staffordshire border comprising Macclesfield, Congleton, Sandbach and Leek, and in one or two other scattered localities – the Derby ones being principally occupied in supplying the region's hosiers, the others in catering for the weavers of Spitalfields (London), Essex and the Norwich area who hitherto had largely used imported yarn (only gradually and never entirely, supplanted by the homemade product). A total prohibition on imports of silk cloth in 1765 was of evident assistance to British weavers, although smuggling was widespread. At any time, however, the high cost of the raw material placed stringent limits on market scope; and even in the early 'eighties, with considerable growth behind it, the industry's output (including the value of imported raw silk and yarn) was, notwithstanding its much higher unit value, probably less than that of the cotton industry and perhaps a quarter of that of the woollen industry.

* * *

[1] Excluding cloth made for household consumption (estimated at a third of the total in the 1750s).
[2] Silk throwing is analogous to spinning other textile fibres.

In dealing with the textiles industries one has already dealt with a half or a little more of total industrial activity. To set the multifarious range of non-textile industries in total perspective we must appreciate that in sum they supplied only about a fifth of goods in use through this period and, therefore, that no single one of them was an element of any real weight in the economy as a whole. Viewed historically certain developments in these industries may be credited with a considerable importance but that must not be equated with a considerable contribution to contemporary material welfare.

The iron industry

Both in historical retrospect and in point of contemporary importance primacy of place amongst the non-textile industries can be assigned to the iron making and iron using industries. Their approximate record over these years can be stated statistically: pig output in 1740 was probably about 25,000 tons; in 1785 it was probably about 50,000 tons. Allowing for the refinement of some part and the direct casting of some other part of the pig these figures might represent 20,000 tons and 43,000 tons respectively of usable iron.[1] For the same dates comparable figures for imports are 26,000 tons and 47,000 tons so that national use of iron over this period perhaps rose from 47,000 tons to 90,000 tons. Exports of iron goods by weight increased from 5,000 tons to 14,000 tons. Net domestic consumption of iron then would have risen from 42,000 tons to 76,000 tons. Expressed per head of the population this represents a consumption growth of a third over forty-five years – a proportion which is certainly too large to be dismissed as insignificant but equally certainly too small to warrant any talk of radically important new departures in the use of iron. In fact it suggests a growth rate of much the same order as that sustained over the previous two centuries or so.

No single factor stands out as responsible for this maintenance of

---

[1] A whole series of questionable assumptions underlies these figures. First, the closest dates for which actual estimates of pig output, themselves of uncertain reliability, are available are 1720 (25,000) and 1788 (68,000). For the assumptions of no growth 1720–40 and very rapid growth 1785–88, see Part I, pp. 245–6 and Part II, p. 441. Secondly, it is assumed that about one-quarter of output was being directly cast around 1740 and about two-fifths around 1785. Thirdly, it is assumed that a quarter of the pig was lost in refinement.

growth. The new textile machines and their associated water-power equipment, both of largely wooden construction, can only be credited with a very marginal role and even less importance can be attached to the Newcomen and Watt engines, also partly of wooden construction and too few in numbers to constitute a significant market. However combined with dozens of other similarly modest new or extended uses of iron these add up to a notable if undramatic advance on a broad front. Some of these new uses, although of little contemporary import, catch the eye on account of later developments: the first recorded use of iron rails for colliery track in 1767; the first iron bridge in 1779. But more often than not it was just a mattter of the use of more iron than formerly for familiar tools, instruments, utensils, etc., or the use of iron for ornamental and decorative articles. That there was a keen interest in and a lively appreciation of the potential range of usefulness of iron is apparent. But its extension was subject to a serious limitation. For the great majority of purposes bar iron was used; and bar iron, requiring costly refinement, was expensive – expensive relative to other materials (principally wood but also for certain purposes, clay and lead) which would often serve instead of it, and expensive relative to the purchasing power of the buyers of mass consumption goods. As techniques stood for almost the whole of this period the greatest scope for expansion lay in the constricted field of cast iron, about a third the cost of bar.

Two factors impeded the use of relatively cheap cast: its brittleness and its high viscosity, the latter making it impossible to cast a number of articles even where the brittleness was not a consideration. Castability could be extended by increasing the fluidity of the molten metal and by improvements in mould design; and, indeed, it seems as if cast iron had been edging forward in these ways for some two centuries already. Within these years, however, this movement received a particular impetus. Coke was substituted for charcoal in the blast furnace; after decades of trial and failure this last rampart of dear wood was breached by cheap coal. It was a gain secured at a price. British pig had never yielded good quality bar. Coke-smelted pig was even less suitable for refinement. Substantial advantage could only be derived from the economies of coke smelting by widening the range of cast iron articles. On the basis of the figures already quoted, output of cast iron in Britain would have tripled over this period while output of bar iron would have increased by little more than a half. But even so it would have been the case at the end of the period that over three-quarters of British iron goods were still made of bar.

The limited applicability of coke-smelted iron goes a long way towards explaining two phenomena which otherwise would be puzzling in the light of the economies then capable of being achieved in British blast furnaces: the retarded spread of coke smelting, and the big rise in imports of iron through this period. Abraham Darby at Coalbrookdale, Shropshire, appears to have smelted successfully with coke sometime between 1709 and 1717 and yet it was not until around the middle of the century that coke even started steadily to supplant charcoal in the blast furnace. Darby himself was very reticent about his achievement. He took out no patent and in no way publicised his use of coke (probably less out of an anxiety to preserve the benefit of it for himself than out of an apprehension that it would impair the marketability of his iron, previous failures with coal smelting having given it a bad name). In any event it evidently took some time to evolve a standardised technique which could be guaranteed to yield acceptable quality pig regularly. Just what were the crucial features of Darby's technique cannot be determined. The initial coking of the coal was certainly vital but others before Darby had tried coke and failed. In some measure the explanation of these contrasting results lies in the superior nature of Coalbrookdale coal which had excellent coking qualities; but it is very probable that Darby's success was also due in part to his raising a higher temperature in the blast furnace than was usual for charcoal smelting – and that this not only produced the right melt but by making for a higher degree of fluidity enhanced its castability (indeed there is some reason to suspect that Darby's experiments were initially directed towards this end rather than towards the substitution of coal for wood).

Even with established and known success at Coalbrookdale it could not be expected that coke smelting would spread rapidly amongst other ironmasters. The Darby technique would have to be modified according to the particular kind of ore and coal being used – and some coals could not be used at all. (It is important to bear in mind that apart from a few rough rules of thumb nothing resembling chemical analysis was available, so that success often only followed, if at all, on an arduous succession of trials and errors; a good result might fortuitously be obtained but without an identification of the constituents of success it might not be repeatable.) But all these factors combined could hardly account for the seventy-odd years which elapsed between Darby's initial success and the fairly general adoption of coke smelting in Great Britain. Coke smelting could only be adopted in the measure in which coke-smelted iron was capable of being used. The substitution of hydraulic pumps for water-powered bellows in raising a blast – first constructed by John Smeaton in 1761 for the Carron iron works in Stirlingshire – by increasing the temperature not only enhanced the fluidity and thus the castability of the melt but also burnt out more of the impurities and thus yielded a better quality pig. But, notwithstanding this and other modest improvements in refining methods, it is an approximate truth that the economies of coke were achieved at the cost of an increased dependence on foreign supplies for good quality bar. (From the 1720s, at the instigation of Peter the Great, Russia was launched on a programme of exploitation of her rich ore and wood resources and by the mid-1760s had surpassed Sweden as a supplier of bar iron to Great Britain.)

The fact must be emphasised that lower production costs had only a minor role in engendering the noteworthy growth in iron consumption of this period; an autonomous upward shift in demand was the principal agent, though a significant role must also be allowed to lowered transport costs through the construction of canals of which the iron industry was a leading beneficiary. It is particularly needful to stress this here, because by proroguing the story in 1785 we stop on the very threshold of an age in which slashed production costs through the realisation of the full potentialities of cheap coal in iron-making were to have effects of a sensational order.

Two things were necessary to achieve this end: a refining technique capable of converting coke-smelted pig into acceptable bar; and the complete substitution of coal for wood in the refining processes. Over the latter years of this period a sharp attention was being given to these possibilities in ironworks all over the country, and in certain instances, with particular kinds of coal and ore or for particular kinds of bar, satisfactory results were being obtained. Undoubtedly a gradual advance was being effected which through decades would have culminated in the total triumph of coal. But that halting progress was transmuted into a sudden and decisive breakthrough by Henry Cort who, drawing in some uncertain degree on these earlier trials, in 1783 patented his puddling process, periodic raking and stirring of the pig in a reverberatory furnace in which the heat from a coal fire was reflected on to the iron, thus preserving the two from direct contact; and in 1784 patented his rolling method for expunging the impurities remaining in the puddled iron. In combination puddling and rolling not only answered to the objects of producing satisfactory bar from coke-smelted pig and of permitting of the exclusive use of coal but, the saving in fuel costs apart, also made for significant labour economies as against existing refining processes. With the advent of cheap bar the ultimate horizons of the British iron industry were stretched beyond sight.

Almost contemporary with puddling and rolling, such that its principal impact falls just outside this period rather than within it, was the use of steam power in the iron industry – the first industry to take extensively to this form of power other than for pumping water. The story of the development of steam power is specifically the story of one man of genius and two others of faith: James Watt, John Roebuck and Matthew Boulton. Its chronology may be briefly summarised here. In 1764 Watt, working on the improvement of the Newcomen 'atmospheric' engine, conceived of the principle of using steam as a driving force instead of merely as an agent of evacuation. A rapidly constructed working model demonstrated the practicability of his inspiration. But between success on a miniature scale and the development of a reliable engine for heavy work there stretched a great gap – two gaps really: one needing money to bridge it, money to support the fortuneless Watt himself through years of experimentation and to procure the materials and labour for trial designs; the other a technical gap. Whereas existing skills had largely sufficed for the crude simple parts of which a Newcomen engine was composed, for the more sophisticated steam engine with its intolerance of imprecisions in its relatively numerous components, new crafts were a precondition of efficient operation. Without capital and an extensive engineering workshop, Watt's brainchild would have died in infancy.

It was John Roebuck, a principal partner in the Carron concern in Stirlingshire, who in 1767 initially supplied these wants. Many people might have provided the money but few had a great iron works at their disposal as Roebuck had. In 1769 Carron's men built the first steam engine to be put to work – for draining a colliery owned by Roebuck near Edinburgh. But Carron's own field of activity was heavy castings and forgings and it could not readily yield the fineness of workmanship Watt required before producing engines for outside sale. Invaluable as Roebuck's part had been in promoting basic development, there was an ironical blessing in his bankrupting himself – he was an imprudent dabbler in several fields – and, in settlement of one of his many debts, assigning his rights in the steam engine to Matthew Boulton. Dubbed 'the first manufacturer in England', Boulton, at his Soho works in Birmingham, produced a great range of decorative and ornamental articles from materials of all kinds for sale throughout Europe and for these purposes employed a large labour force habituated to working to exacting standards. Soho was not an iron works. It could not itself supply, as Carron could, the basic materials for a steam engine but it could supply, as Carron could not, the requisite precision in fashioning the minor components. In 1774 Watt started work at Soho, and the following year the first steam engine sold was installed to drain Bloomfield colliery near Birmingham. Along with the skills of Soho those of another great contemporary concern, the ironworks of John Wilkinson, played a crucial part in this eventual success. By a happy coincidence Wilkinson had in 1774 devised an improved method of boring cannon barrels – a method readily adapted to boring cylinders with the exactitude needed for efficient working of the steam engine.

It was Wilkinson also who first employed a steam engine as something other than a water pump when he harnessed an engine to a blast furnace air pump. However the advantages of an early steam-powered pump over a hydraulic one do not appear to have been great and, in fact, of the few Watt pumping engines used in the iron industry by the end of this period some were employed, like the Newcomen engine before them, simply to build up a reservoir to ensure a constant supply of water. But by then a Watt engine existed capable of more than just powering an up-and-down pumping action – which, it must be appreciated, was all that it could do in its original form, its advantage over the Newcomen engine consisting solely in its greater power and in its more economical use of fuel. The possibilities of converting the direct linear action of the steam engine into multipurpose rotary action had early engaged Watt's attention – as indeed it had that of others, in connection not only with the Watt but also with the Newcomen engine, which in principle was equally susceptible to such adaptation. All prudent considerations conspired to induce Watt and his associates to concentrate their resources of money and workmanship on the task of developing an engine for which a market already existed, and only when the pumping engine was soundly established did Watt turn to the practical development of rotary action. Just as with the engine itself, a rotary attachment demanded exceptional standards of precision and it was not until 1781 that the first rotary acting engine was sold – again to John Wilkinson, to power a forge hammer; by 1786 Wilkinson himself had modified this engine to operate a rolling and slitting mill, though no engine was specifically constructed for this latter purpose until 1788. Several hammer engines were in use in various ironworks over the country by 1785, and though the direct cost economies offered to iron-masters by Watt are small by comparison with those originating with Darby and Cort the opportunities created through the latter two could only have been very partially realised if the iron industry had been confined to the restricted power potential of Britain's rivers. In the decade or two succeeding this period the steam engine could be said to have emancipated the British iron industry from the constrictions of topography.

Although it is in that following decade or so that, in step with the storming expansion of the iron industry as a whole, the growth in unit size is particularly marked, even within these quieter years some concerns attained a stature which, relative to the characteristics of the economy at large, was considerable. Ever since the coming of the blast furnace iron-smelting had been the preserve of a fully evolved industrial capitalism sometimes comprehending, beyond the smelting works itself, orefields, woodlands, forges, rolling and slitting mills and even manufacturing establishments, though these elements were rarely, and never on any large scale, operationally integrated in one centralised undertaking. Interlocking partnerships, subleasing of particular units, subcontracting of particular tasks diffused the burden of capital and management. In speaking now of a growth in unit size one is not speaking of a widening of heterogeneous sprawls of this kind but of an increase in the capacity of distinct operational units under centralised control: businesses which were essentially smelting and casting concerns but which might also forge and fashion some part of their pig output. It is in Shropshire that development of this kind is most manifest during this period, and it was Shropshire among all iron districts where gross output swelled the most.

Higher temperatures for coke-smelting meant taller furnaces and taller furnaces meant heavier investment and larger capacity. Shropshire, the pioneer in coke-smelting, naturally led the way. The Darby business at Coalbrookdale, the closely associated Reynolds enterprise, and the works of John Wilkinson, although these last were scattered over more than one county, were the greatest of Shropshire concerns. Outside that county, the Walkers at Rotherham in Yorkshire and Carron Mills in Scotland were of similar stature. Carron Mills, in fact, was the largest of them all: by the close of this period it incorporated capital of perhaps £200,000, employed around 1,500 persons, and constituted in itself virtually the whole of the Scottish iron smelting industry. Carron had the further distinction of being planned from the start as a large-scale concern with the founding capital drawn from several pockets whereas the others mentioned, more typically, were essentially family concerns growing through generations. These businesses stand out plainly from the general ruck – the average concern may not have been one-tenth the size of Carron – but, particularly in Shropshire where furnace capacity was roughly tripled, the clear trend through this period is towards larger smelting units.

The same trend is not so apparent with refining and forging establishments, except those which were integrated with smelting concerns; the technical pressure towards enlarged capacity in this field only exerted itself strongly with Cort. Of subsequent processing stages only tin-plating, concentrated in South Wales, manifests any marked development. The substitution in the early years of this period of rolling for hammering in applying the tin plate, yielding a superior product, gave rise to rather larger tinplate mills but in general these did not compare in size with blast furnace establishments and even so the millowners commonly relieved themselves of financial and managerial strains by subcontracting the work itself to professional tinplaters. More generally, the manifold trades engaged in the manufacture of iron artifacts experienced neither technical nor organisational change of any note. The handworking artisan remained the fundamental unit of production, working perhaps on his own, perhaps in the shop of a small master whom he could reasonably aspire to emulate one day, perhaps in some state of effective dependence on a mercantile intermediary for the supply of his raw materials or the disposal of his finished product – in extreme cases, as in west Midlands' nailmaking, indistinguishable in economic status from the West Country clothweaver.

Matthew Boulton's Soho works was *sui generis* both in the variety of its products – iron was only one of the many materials used – and in its concentration of a large work force in the one premises. And in a formal sense Soho was not one concern but several which shared the same buildings. Different sections of the enterprise were owned by different partnerships, though Boulton and his associate John Fothergill were the chief partners in each and exercised an immediate control over all of them. The device seems to have been a way of raising supplementary capital without breaching the legal prohibition on more than six partners to an enterprise, and also of associating the foreman in charge of branches with the profitability of their sections. Boulton and Watt was a truly distinct concern but within this period was only a firm of consultant engineers. The engines were erected on site from materials procured, to Watt's specifications, by the customers themselves.

The coal industry

Some of what has just been said in connection with the iron industry has a bearing also on the coal industry. On the demand side, the conversion from charcoal to coke in iron-smelting, the occasional use of coal in iron-refining and the increased coal consumption of metalworkers roughly proportionate to the increase in iron production were factors in raising the output of coal over this period. In 1750 total output was probably between 3 and 4 million tons. By 1770 it may have been running at about 6 million and by the end of the period it was probably over 8 million. On the supply side, pumping engines played a considerable part in rendering this increased output possible as mining depths increasingly went beyond the capacity of older drainage methods. The already established Newcomen engine multiplied in numbers in all the principal coalmining regions, and here and there over the last decade of the period Watt pumping engines were being installed, though their higher initial cost told against them at sites where coal was at its cheapest and fuel economies therefore of little weight.

As mines went deeper the sinking of new shafts to minimise the distance between coal face and shaft bottom became more expensive and shafts had to be more widely spaced, heightening the incentive to improve underground haulage methods by means of more spacious galleries and more even roadways to permit of larger wheeled carrying vehicles, often drawn by pit ponies, in a few instances along flanged cast iron rails – around the very end of the period vehicles which could be lifted directly by the shaft winding gear were introduced, effecting a useful economy by eliminating the handling stage at the shaft bottom. The winding gear itself was the subject of minor improvements, and in the very last years of the period a few rotary acting steam engines were in use for this purpose. But at best these advances did little more than stave off rising costs as the coal became less and less accessible. Over the last couple of decades of this period, when the increase in coal output was most pronounced, it was neither technical improvement within the collieries nor autonomous shifts in demand which were the main agency of growth, but signal reductions in the cost of moving coal from producer to consumer.

The stimulus administered to the coal industry by the canals of these years was unique. Indeed the first canals were built with no other object in view and in particular instances achieved reductions of more than a half in delivered coal prices. It was not only a matter of slashing costs along established supply channels but also of putting hitherto landbound collieries within economic reach of wider markets – collieries which because of limited sale scope had not previously been intensively mined and therefore preserved deposits which were cheap to work. Within the areas principally affected the whole range of coal users, domestic and industrial, responded exuberantly to cheap coal. However, this experience was far from universal. Canal transport was not as cheap as either sea transport or good river transport; much of the country was already well served by nature and thus stood to gain little or nothing from manmade waterways. Within this period the benefits of canals were confined almost exclusively to the coalfields of south Lancashire and the west Midlands. But as these were the very areas in which population and economic activity were expanding the most rapidly their importance in a national context was considerable; and the transformation of large tracts of these areas into cheap coal regions must stand as one of the most signal economic phenomena of the closing decades of this period. It was a phenomenon manifested not only or even principally in novel departures like the use of coal in iron-smelting and refining, let alone the embryonic use of steam power, but in the expansion of established coal using activities: saltmaking, glassmaking, brickmaking, pottery, hardwares, dyeing, brewing; and, of equal importance, the provision of domestic heat as population congestion outgrew local fuel supplies.

Other metallurgical industries

Of other mineral industries the record of tin can be stated statistically. Cornish output rose through the period from about 1,600 tons to about 2,800 tons, the bulk of it, as always, exported although an increasing proportion was retained at home for the developing South Wales tinplate industry. This notably enhanced output following several decades of stagnancy reflects the decisive breakthrough into deep mining of the lode, after some two centuries of hesitancy while alluvial deposits had become scarcer and scarcer. Outside capital and mining expertise definitively supplanted the traditional local syndicates as the dominant elements in the industry, though in point of organisation many of the ancient features survived. The concerns which opened up deep mines were loose associations of individuals who commonly had interests in more than one such concern. These concerns, having borne the cost of opening the mine and installing the requisite fixed equipment, did not then operate it themselves but leased small workings in it, generally for short periods and for agreed proportions of the ore raised, either to syndicates of miners or to individual entrepreneurs who employed the necessary labour.

As in all deep mining, drainage was the chief problem. Lack of the requisite technical knowledgeability and of capital among the old fashioned parochial groupings had retarded deep mining in the past. The intrusion of outside finance was marked by a rash of Newcomen engines and over the last decade of the period the tinmine concerns were the most forward in adopting Watt pumping engines; with their coal having to bear the cost of the haul from South Wales the fuel economies offered by Watt were especially attractive to them.

Of leadworking there is little that can be said. The only available figures are for exports – showing no significant change over this period which at a time of growing population in market areas suggests an inability to expand output or achieve important economies. Newcomen engines for mine drainage and coal-fired smelting furnaces were already quite widely used at the beginning of the period; but a number of lead mines were too remote from coal sources to find it economical to abandon older methods. Organisationally there seems to have been no marked development either. Concerns still ranged from the London Lead Company with its manifold undertakings right down to the lone free miner.

The copper mines of the south-west were also important early customers to Boulton and Watt, a fact whose most theatrical consequence was the involvement of Matthew Boulton in copper politics and his confrontation with Thomas Williams – a man to be ranked along with Boulton himself and Richard Arkwright as a prototype tycoon, and denied a place among the stock folk-heroes of British economic history only because he operated in a relatively minor industry.[1] It is probably true that no one personality has ever so filled a particular industrial scene as Williams did that of British copperworking through the last three decades of the eighteenth century. A local attorney, he

[1] Williams and his business operations are the subject of a full-length study by J. R. Harris, *The Copper King* (1964).

quickly made himself effective master of the voluminous copper deposits found in Anglesey in 1768 and wasted little time in founding or acquiring smelting and manufacturing establishments elsewhere in order to free himself of dependence on the closeknit group of smelting concerns which had hitherto dominated the industry.

Even more shaken than the established smelters by the meteoric rise of Anglesey and its associated enterprises were the ore miners of the south-west. However, in a period of rising demand for copper, Anglesey could not at the most supply more than two-fifths of the market. The south-west was presented, not with the threat of extinction, but with the more tortuous if less appalling necessity of adjusting output and prices to the levels dictated by Anglesey competition. Only concerted action could achieve this and in 1785 the Cornish Metal Company was formed, largely at the instigation of Matthew Boulton,[1] comprehending the producers of some seven-eighths of south-western ore. The Company was a marketing cartel, its constituent concerns preserving a complete independence as producers. This independence, in fact, was fatal to the Company. Compelled to buy all that its members chose to produce it rapidly built up excessive stocks. In 1787 it was forced to accept terms proposed by Williams under which he undertook to dispose of the surplus on behalf of the Company, in return for the Company's undertaking to employ him as agent in the sale of all their copper over the next five years. And in 1790 the Company, having failed to secure the output discipline amongst its members which was really essential to its functioning, was wound up.

By then the Anglesey bonanza was running down and the bias of Williams's business was shifting towards the smelting and manufacturing side. Effectively a return was taking place to the earlier state of affairs in which the south-west, while supplying the huge bulk of the industry's ore, was too riven by the varying interests of producers with widely differing cost and output positions to be able to offer an organised front to the more compact and homogeneously constituted smelters. However, the smelters never recovered the whole of their former commercial strength. Towards the other end of the processing train the small masters of the Birmingham brassware trades had revolted against the dominance of the large smelting concerns by forming their own

[1] Boulton's concern arose out of the terms of sale of the steam engine. The material costs of an engine were usually met directly by the customer. Boulton and Watt's charges for design, supervision and patent rights consisted of one-third of the calculated fuel savings as against a Newcomen engine, payable throughout the lifetime of the patent: if a customer's business closed down Boulton and Watt got nothing more.

company for the conversion of copper into brass: the Birmingham Metal Company (1780). In 1790 another, closely associated, Birmingham concern was founded to further extend the control of the brassware makers over their own supplies: the Birmingham Mining and Copper Company, primarily engaged in copper-smelting at a works in South Wales, but also involved in ore mining through the purchase of shares in a number of Cornish mining concerns.

As stated already, the impact of Anglesey on the south-west was deadened by rising demand for copper. Indeed the growth of consumption of copper far transcended that of any other metal, being of the order of tenfold over the period. The ingenuity of Birmingham craftsmen in finding novel and varied uses for the metal was one major factor here; and another, its impact dating from the 1770s, was the development of a method of sheathing ships' keels with copper, thus permitting vessels to remain longer at sea and eagerly adopted by the Admiralty.

Overall industrial development

There is no call to dwell on other industrial activities in any detail. While some effected modest but useful technical improvements none achieved advances of major import and in some centrally important fields such as garment-making and building there was no change whatsoever. Nor was there any really significant development in forms of organisation, though there are some pointers to an increase in the average size of concerns in fields where factory-type production was already the rule. The productive capacity of the typical glassworks and papermill was appreciably though not dramatically enlarged. Some London brewers, enjoying a mass doorstep market, grew very markedly in size – to the point in fact where they became the first manufacturers as a class to command enough wealth to secure an entrée to high society and to take seats in Parliament along with the squirearchy, the scions of nobility, the City merchants, the 'nabobs' and the 'West Indians'. The extent to which this development was paralleled in the provinces is not clear and certainly in country districts the ale-house keeper who did his own brewing was still universal. The Staffordshire pottery industry threw up the magnificent figure of Josiah Wedgwood whose Etruria works were opened in 1769 and whose business employed some 250 persons at the end of the period. But Etruria, like Matthew Boulton's Soho works, was essentially the creation of an egregious grandeur of imagination and ambition rather than a commercial response to econo-mic environment and the general growth of capitalistic concerns in the Potteries really belongs just outside this period.

It is, parenthetically, a curious truth that these two concerns, Etruria and Soho, the most outstanding of particular contemporary enterprises, were principally engaged in the production, not of cheap goods for a mass market, but of works of craftsmanship and artistry designed for those with cultivated tastes, or at least pretensions thereto, and with the money to indulge their luxuriated sensibilities. Indeed Wedgwood and Boulton stood the normal law of economic growth on its head: in their cases growth did not so much succeed enlarged market scope as precede it. Having set themselves to engender great businesses they had then to contrive customers and, given the nature of their products, custom in sufficient volume to sustain their grandiose projects could not be had in Great Britain alone – they had to create European markets for them-selves and, under that necessity, added to their historical reputations that of being pioneers in international salesmanship. In an overall historical appreciation, however, Wedgwood and Boulton do not have the portentous significance of a Richard Arkwright. They were not like Arkwright forerunners of a new economic order[1] so much as tardy English imitators of the French state concern, Les Gobelins, with its range of fineries – furniture, tapestries, gold and silverwork, statuary – and the porcelain works at Sèvres, whose economic rationale was the standard of excellence which could be maintained through the congre-gation in constant employment of a body of talented designers and skilled artisans. They were virtually art factories whose prototypes might be seen in the workshops of the masters of the Italian Renais-sance. Etruria and Soho are to be placed more meaningfully in a social history of aestheticism than in an economic narrative. The most per-tinent economic comment they offer is on that distributional structure of wealth which afforded more scope to such undertakings than to a mass provision for more mundane wants.

One can comprehend in the same manner those contemporary London furniture concerns which with workshops housing thirty and forty artisans mark a clear break with the type of master joiner of the past. The names of Chippendale and Hepplewhite belong to this period.[2]

---

[1] Except in the important sense that the management of all large-scale enterprises, whatever the nature of the product, posed similar problems.

[2] Neither of them actually the largest, or even the most distinguished, furniture makers of their days. Their reputations derive from their published design books – posthumous in

Here again size of concern has little or nothing to do with cost economics but has a great deal to do with a standardisation of elegance and a consciousness of fashion.

These marginal observations aside, the polyglot group of 'other industries' can be apprehended as the passive subjects of economic trends rather than as prime agents of them. Their record is more a measure of autonomous changes in demand than of variations in supply factors. Such being the case, the statistical performance of those for which rather arbitrarily the data is available may usefully be stated, without particular amplification, as an indicator of the course of gross domestic demand for industrial goods through this period. Comparable figures for some of the industries already dealt with are also shown in Table II.2.[1]

TABLE II.2. *Industrial growth rates, 1740–85: average annual percentage[2] (to nearest 0·25%)*

Industry	Throughout period	Pre-1763	Post-1763
Leather	0·50	0·50	0·25
Beer	0·25	0·25	0·25
Candles	0·75	0·75	0·25
Soap	0·75	0·50	1·00
Paper	2·00	2·50	1·50
Glass	1·00	3·00	−0·50
Cotton (home consumption)	3·50	0·50	7·00
Iron (home consumption)	1·25	?(1·25)	?(1·25)
Coal (uncertain)	?(2·00)	?(1·75)	?(2·25)
Population	0·6	0·6	0·6

Hepplewhite's case. The third and somewhat later great name in furniture, Sheraton, is that of a cabinetmaker who abandoned his trade to devote himself wholly to the publication of his designs.

[1] Since the Table seeks to measure home consumption the base figures used ought to be of home production *plus* imports *less* exports. However in the case of leather, beer, candles, soap and coal, foreign commerce was negligible. Paper and glass are referred to in the text. Appropriate base estimates have been used for cotton and iron.

[2] It should be said that a certain degree of oversimplification enters into this table, both in the resolution of certain problems posed by the basic data and in the division of the period into two equal phases, the phases not, in fact, having quite the same dates in the case of each commodity (hence the deliberately loose headings to the individual columns). Since a good deal is made of the phase distinction in the following paragraphs it would be

The figures for paper given in the table somewhat overstate the increase in consumption, particularly in the first half of the period, as some of the growth was due to the substitution of home-produced for imported supplies. By the end of the period, imports of paper were negligible in quantity; and this final achievement by the British industry of a virtually total dominance of its own market is in itself noteworthy. The record of the glass industry is also probably open to the same kind of comment. Especially if allowance is made for this substitution factor, the overall figures give rise to two general observations. First, that after discounting for population increase, no manifest rise in consumption standards is revealed – this the more emphatically when it is appreciated that leather and beer would have grossly outweighed the other commodities in importance. Second, that absolute growth was sensibly greater in the first half of the period than in the last half. One should, of course, be very cautious in resting any general conclusions on such extremely partial evidence; but these stray figures do carry about them an order of uniformity which must, at the very least, bear a serious warning against making comprehensive judgments on the course of the British industrial economy through these years by reference only to its most colourful members.

If one does accept the inference that there was a range of consumer industries, achieving no signal cost economies, which did little more than keep pace with population growth and in some cases, perhaps most cases in the latter part of the period, not even that, then towards what conclusions regarding the economy as a whole does this point? Dullness, stagnancy or even decline over a broad sector of consumer goods is of course fully compatible with buoyant demand trends in the economy at large. Consumer preferences may have been shifting – and through these years certainly were shifting in some degree. Tea and

---

proper to indicate an apparent contradiction between the general burden of these paragraphs and that of the much longer, and important, article of D. E. C. Eversley, 'The home market and economic growth in England, 1750–1780', in E. L. Jones and G. E. Mingay, eds, *Land, Labour and Population in the Industrial Revolution* (1967). The general contention of Dr Eversley's article is that there was a build-up to 'take off' into industrial Revolution over the years 1750–80, on the basis of a firm domestic consumer demand. The specific contention in what follows in these pages is, ostensibly, more or less the reverse. However, on a careful reading Dr Eversley's article can be seen to embody the recognition that the later years of this period did witness something of a weakening of consumer demand trends; and it is no part of the general intention of this chapter to suggest that a relatively high minimal level of consumer demand was anything other than an indispensable precondition of 'revolution' – a condition by no means incompatible with a certain sagging of that level in the immediate pre-Revolution phase.

sugar stand out as commodities which were being purchased in increasing amounts although here again tailing off in the later years is very evident. Cheap cotton goods very probably enlarged the proportion

TABLE II.3. *Tea and sugar: average annual percentage increase in real expenditure*

	Throughout period	Pre-1763	Post-1763
Tea[1]	2·25	4·75	0·50
Sugar	1·75	2·25	1·00

of average income spent on textiles and cheap cast iron wares very likely had the same effect in the domestic utensils field. A hypothetical increment to personal income might then have been largely or entirely absorbed in these ways, leaving little or nothing to spare for enhanced expenditure in other directions.

Even if one took the view, as perhaps one should, that on balance composite personal expenditure per head increased only slightly in the earlier years of the period and not at all in the later years, that would still leave room for postulating general industrial growth by way of increased capital expenditure and increased expenditure on armaments, though this of course would be economic growth devoid of any direct or positive welfare content. The figures for iron (already quoted) and for imports of timber might be used as crude indicators of activity

TABLE II.4. *Timber imports: average annual percentage increase*

Throughout period	Pre-1763	Post-1763
1·5	1·5	1·5

in these areas – very crude indicators since proportions of these commodities went more or less directly to satisfying consumption wants.

[1] The data used for tea is drawn from that for the years between 1745 and 1784, so as to exclude the special effects of the cuts in duty of those two years. Additionally, the quantities derived from the base data have been adjusted proportionately to the interim changes in effective rates of duty, so that the result is a notional measure of expenditure on duty-paid tea at constant pre-duty prices.

However their tendency to exceed those for pure consumption industries is suggestive, as is the more evident fact that they do not exhibit that falling away over the latter part of the period which characterises the consumer industries data. (Although the figures for iron cannot be sub-distinguished it is highly improbable that the increase in the use of iron slackened off in the later years.)

Military expenditure can with certainty be assigned an important part here. Both in peace and war it rose distinctly throughout the period. As to the course of capital expenditure on industrial goods, one can only be rather vague. The question threatens a vicious circle. Capital expenditure by industrial producers is obviously in considerable part a function, both as cause and effect, of the level of industrial activity. We can hardly then treat it as a wholly independent variable in trying to estimate that level.[1] Nevertheless we can acknowledge certain possibilities: of new technological opportunities giving rise to extra investment which might not result in a proportionate or even any increase in output, but principally or even solely in a diminution of labour or raw material requirements; of extra investment in capital goods industries themselves – this should of course ultimately result in an increase in the output of the consumer industries catered for by those capital industries but an economy can run on for a very long time accumulating productive capacity before releasing that capacity to meet consumer wants. Both these situations, especially the second, are likely to occur while an economy is in course of industrial growth. There will be a period during which growth is only partially or not at all reflected in enhanced consumption standards – even when consumption standards will be actually depressed. Within this period investment in cotton manufacture, which very possibly did not result in a proportionate addition to total textiles output; in west Midlands and south Lancashire coalmining, in respect of which the canals can be treated as a new technological opportunity prompting investment in previously lightly worked seams; in iron works, in the form of new coke smelting furnaces and new forging equipment, with some part of the extra iron produced going back into the industry for the new apparatus – these are conspicuously forms of investment which in varying measures were initiated independently of shifts in demand and where investment was

---

[1] Under normal circumstances capital expenditure and consumer expenditure will move in close sympathy. What follows is an indication of contemporary circumstances which might have given rise to increased capital expenditure unmatched by an increase in consumer expenditure.

not fully translated into more consumer goods. In this context the extent to which they were concentrated in the latter part of the period is of particular interest.

Outside industrial investment there remain the possibilities of investment in agriculture and transport, but it must be realised that this would largely have taken the form of expenditure on labour for reclamation of land, excavation of canal channels etc., rather than capital expenditure on industrial goods such as we have been discussing. However, if only by way of purchase of tools, investment in agriculture and transport would have had some impact on industrial activity. Again it is plain that expenditure on both agriculture and transport developments was higher in the second part of this period than in the first.

In overall summary it seems improbable that in the earlier years of the period capital and military expenditure made for any higher rate of industrial growth than that suggested by the consumer data – around 0·5 per cent p.a. *per capita*. In the later years, when consumer demand ceased to grow or even declined a little, capital and military expenditure may have served to check the rate of deceleration, possibly even prevented deceleration but almost certainly were insufficient to engender any acceleration of industrial growth.

It remains to suggest some reason why consumer demand should have lost momentum – particularly as the direct evidence of this is not conclusive. In the light of the tendencies just cited one obvious explanation is that a transference of purchasing power was taking place – from wage earners and small artisans, with their high propensity to consume, to profit makers and rentiers via a depression of real wages and to the state via higher taxation. The burden of taxation certainly increased and as much of it was found from taxes on goods rather than on incomes it must have been borne preponderantly by the lower income groups, since the rich usually expend a smaller proportion of their incomes. Whether income transference was taking place within the private sectors of the economy is impossible to say but the slender evidence does not tell against the thesis. More plainly, the export setback experienced by the woollen industry, not fully compensated for by export growth in other directions, would have had depressive effects on incomes generally.[1] But, what is probably a much more potent explanation of the course of consumer demand in the later years of the

[1] Expressed per head of the population total domestic exports (official values, England and Wales) were: 1762–64, £1·50; 1772–74, £1·36; 1783–85, £1·33.

period is the sharp elevation of corn prices in the mid-1760s, so that thereafter they were running about fifty per cent higher than previously. After meeting their basic food requirements the mass of the populace had less to spare for other commodities. Industrial growth was indissolubly wedded to agricultural efficiency.

Transport

Reference has already been made more than once to the canal building of this period and something should be said of its chronology and organisation. In conception there was nothing new about canals. Holland and France had early demonstrated their possibilities. Canal projects had been aired in England from time to time since the later seventeenth century. Their essential features already existed in improved riverways as 'cuts', locks and water reservoirs. Some of the artificial watercourses constructed for the drainage of the Fens were navigable. The degree of continuity between the canals proper and earlier developments is in fact exemplified in the first artificial waterway of the canal era: the Sankey Brook Navigation, started in 1755 and opened in stages from 1757 to 1763, by when it linked St Helens and the collieries of the neighbourhood to the Mersey and thus to Liverpool (seven land miles from the nearest coal source) and, via the Weaver Navigation (an improved river), to the intensive coal-using saltpits of inland Cheshire. Ostensibly this was just an improvement of the Sankey. Actually it had only the most tenuous connection with this miserable stream and was to all intents and purposes a genuine canal over the whole twelve miles or so of its length. But the notion had been initiated as a river improvement scheme of the familiar kind and only when a technical survey of the Sankey had revealed the impossibility of rendering it navigable was it converted effectively into a canal scheme – and even then it was thought prudent not to disquiet investors and Parliament by advertising the intention to embark on an unfamiliar project. This transmutation of river improvement scheme into pioneer canal was really no more than a historical accident, happily serviceable as a symbol of the fusion of the two kinds of inland waterway; the almost contemporary and much more renowned Bridgewater Canal was a canal project from the start – built by James Brindley for the Duke of Bridgewater to connect the Duke's Worsley colliery with Manchester, it was begun in 1759 and opened in 1761.

The more important sense in which river improvement may be

understood as the progenitor of canals is that which can be termed penetration. A prime object of earlier river improvement had been to push navigable water deeper into the interior of the country – to lengthen inward reaching tentacles of the sea. The last major spate of river improvement, in the early 1720s, had effected this extension as far as it could usefully be stretched in this manner. If it were to go further it could only be by way of artificial waterways picking up where navigable river expired, culminating in a network of cross links straddling watersheds and connecting sea to sea. That some four decades elapsed before this impetus did spill over into canals is most obviously explicable by the slackening of economic pressure with the cessation of population growth for a quarter of a century or so from about 1720.

It was in the developing areas of south Lancashire and the west Midlands that renewed pressure first made itself felt. In these regions two needs coalesced: a localised need for cheap short haul transport, above all for coal carriage, although in the west Midlands the movement of iron from one processing stage to another was of considerable importance also; and an outward going need for better links with remoter markets and with sources of raw materials and of food for swollen populations – a need felt particularly by Lancashire's cotton industry, by the iron-masters and metal manufacturers of the west Midlands, by the pottery-makers of north Staffordshire and the salt manufacturers of Cheshire. If it was the economies to be effected on local freights of five, ten and twenty miles which in gross were probably the greater and provided the sharper stimulus to financing construction and the more revenue on completion, the initial inspiration and the line of the major canals were governed by the long haul possibilities extended. Severn, Trent and Mersey were the bases of the canal network laid down in these years.

The extension of the Bridgewater Canal from Manchester to the Mersey was the first big step, initiated in 1762. A year before its completion in 1767, the Staffordshire and Worcestershire Canal was started off from the Severn eventually to link up with the Grand Trunk Canal, commenced in the same year to connect the Trent with the Mersey. The opening of the Grand Trunk in 1777 effectively marks the end of this first phase of canal building, lent an especial unity by the fact that the chief engineer of all three canals just enumerated was James Brindley who above anybody can be credited with the welding of the local and particular interests of the promoters into a single great transport project. These three canals were the arteries of a system of which nearly all the other lesser undertakings of these years were the veins.

In point of finance and organisation these canals were unambiguously the heirs of earlier river improvement projects, although the capital sums required were commonly appreciably greater – the Grand Trunk, the most expensive, needed £130,000 – and the number of participants correspondingly larger. But these participants were, as before, local men of means – the most active were those whose own businesses would directly benefit, supported by others pleased to find a way of conveniently employing spare funds or considering it socially requisite to play their part in enhancing local amenities.

Much, perhaps most, of the money subscribed was not share capital but loan capital carrying only an entitlement to a fixed interest payment.[1] The holders of the bulk of the share capital were probably the chief instigators of the projects, interested not so much in their financial profitability as in the advantages conferred on their own individual enterprises. Indeed, the canals inherited shades of the public highway concept attaching to rivers: their profit potential was limited by toll maxima laid down in the Acts of Parliament authorising them, although in practice these maxima were generally found to exceed the optimum commercial rates. This situation had two noteworthy consequences. First, the high 'gearing' meant that if the canal operated at a comfortable profit – and generally the canals of this phase did – the return to the shareholders could be very high; this fact is of some importance in explaining the enthusiasm of the general investing public for further canal projects a little later. Second, the heavy leaning on loan funds rendered canal projects sensitive to fluctuations in the rate of interest, not so much perhaps because the need to pay one or two per cent more for money would seriously inhibit the promoters, but because many prospective subscribers would already have their money in stocks and would be reluctant to sell at depressed prices to realise funds; and more tellingly, because if the return on government stock and on

[1] This is to translate the matter into modern terms. 'Shares' usually had a fixed rate payment attached to them as well. Although this would commonly be described as 'interest', strictly speaking it represented an agreement amongst the shareholders to make this a first claim on profits. Such a practice was general amongst both large joint stock type concerns and small private partnerships. Contemporary accounts usually show 'interest' on owners' capital as a cost item, charged before calculating 'profits', which were commonly retained in the business and distributed only when accumulated capital was safely surplus to likely requirements. Obviously such 'interest' could only be paid if equivalent profits were made and, equally obviously, its rate did not have to conform to the usury laws since it was money paid by people to themselves.

old securities were approaching five per cent, the usury laws prevented the canal promoters competing by offering more. This second consequence explains the almost total cessation of canal building in the last years of this period when heavy government borrowing for the American War put loan funds out of reach.

Geographically of more extensive effect than canals in this period was the improvement of the road system. However, it may be said straightaway that the strictly economic benefits of this could never be of a really major order. Important production centres clung close to navigable water and few goods moved any great distance by road. In particular agricultural localities road improvement could make for significantly easier access to markets; but even in these cases the gain might not be considerable, as the worst feature of bad roads was commonly their impassable state when reduced to winter mud, whereas most agricultural produce moved in the dryer months. In certain instances the crucial issue was not the cost of moving goods but whether or not they could be moved at all. Mining enterprises were those most likely to be confronted with this question and as an integral part of their operations they had to provide some sort of an all weather road. In some mountainous districts wheeled vehicles could replace packhorses only after much levelling work had been undertaken. But by and large the principal gains arising from road improvement were not by way of important reductions in freight costs but of a kind not readily susceptible to economic evaluation: the greater speed at which people and mail could journey when roads were capable of carrying coaches specially designed for rapid travel. That men could attend to their business affairs in person or by post, that money could be remitted, that samples could be sent, that these things could be effected more speedily and more surely, was clear economic gain but gain of a rather marginal order. That people (of the middle class and upward, coach travel being beyond the means of ordinary folk) could more easily indulge their taste for a change of scene and company may be counted a welfare gain, but not one to which a price tag can be put.

In any event, such gains as did arise out of road improvement were only available over certain routes. Even at the very end of this period the British road system judged by the best Continental standards was still distinctly backward. The main roads between London and provincial centres were by then generally good, as were some others, but numerous major regional roads knew little or no improvement, and minor country roads preserved their centuries-old state. However, the position had been reached where, roughly speaking, the maintenance attention given to a road was proportionate to the amount of traffic it bore. While local roads remained a local responsibility, the upkeep of through roads was increasingly being made a charge on the users through the agency of turnpike trusts – formed in some instances for the construction of entirely new roads, more commonly to rehabilitate those already in existence.

These trusts were not commercial concerns and must be understood as special organs of local government of a distinctively English kind, self constituted and vested with the appropriate authority by private Act of Parliament. The king's highway could not be the subject of personal profit. (In much attenuated form the same principle, as has been seen, held good for canals also.) Amongst other things this meant that the zeal which the trustees brought to bear was often determined more by their sense of public responsibility, apt to be very variable, than by self-interest. Self-interest was commonly not altogether absent, partly because the trustees were local men of consequence whose personal comfort or prosperity might be involved, partly because the trustees were usually among the largest providers of initial loan funds to the trust and were at least concerned that interest payments should be covered. However in the latter connection, any road enjoys a quasi-monopoly, and toll levying powers once secured, the financial incentive to spend generously on maintenance might not be sharp. Furthermore, with occupations of their own to attend to, the trustees frequently divested themselves of as much immediate responsibility as possible: toll collection was subcontracted to toll 'farmers' whose profit turn had to be met out of revenue, often of exorbitant amount since the professional toll farmers operated 'rings' amongst themselves; maintenance also was subcontracted. The net revenue available for keeping a road in good condition was often negligible. But even good administration and ample funds were no guarantee of good roads. Road engineers through this period were still groping towards solutions to the problems of adequate drainage, firm foundations and durable surfaces in varying terrains, and the requisite lessons had often to be learned from expensive blunders. But road engineering was gradually securing a sound technical footing; and out of its trials and errors there were to emerge a little later the matured techniques of McAdam and Telford.

We have seen that as direct stimulants to productive activity the roads of this period do not have the importance of the canals. But irrespective of the ends ultimately served, the work itself was as significant a form of economic activity in the one case as in the other. The point has already been made that expenditure on improved transport media in this period did not usually involve large purchases of materials. But it did involve large outlays on labour. Particularly in the years 1764–77, between the Seven Years War and the intensification of the American War, while interest rates were low, investment in transport – and in agriculture which shared the characteristics of labour intensiveness and sensitivity to interest rates – made an important contribution towards sustaining consumer demand. And since, as already noted, such demand was losing the modest impetus of earlier years, it does not seem too much to say that investment in transport was crucial[1] in ensuring that these were not actually years of recession; rather more speculatively, to go even further and say that had the 'sixties and 'seventies seen purchasing power eroded by dearer food without any counteracting factor brought into play, it is difficult to conceive of the economy being launched into a powerful growth phase in the later 'eighties. The Industrial Revolution, that is to say, would have lacked its springboard.

Money and banking

The major canal projects of these years, of course, required the mobilisation of capital on a scale for which there were few precedents. Contrary to what might be surmised, this did not necessitate special financial institutions. Personal contacts, public promotional meetings, notices in the local press, sufficed to cast a wide enough net. This observation has a particular negative intent here: that though these years were fertile of provincial or country banks such institutions played no special part in the provision of canal finance. Bankers were often amongst those local dignitaries who subscribed to canal projects but, though the distinction is not wholly valid, they may be conceived to have done so out of their personal wealth rather than out of bank funds. Banks of course often served as the depositories of canal funds and temporary overdraft accommodation for small amounts might sometimes be afforded; they were also useful as local collection points of subscriptions for ultimate remittance to a central agency. In fact, putting country banks in total perspective, the provision of remittance and payments facilities was

---

[1] 'Crucial' not of course because demand generated by transport investment had some special potency which demand emanating from other sources lacked but because, of the principal variables involved, investment in transport media was the one least dependent on the demand situation itself – other, that is, than export demand which was wholly autonomous.

their chief, in some cases almost exclusive, role in the contemporary economy. What we witness through this period is the coming to full term of an institution perceptible in embryonic form in earlier years: those provincial merchants and others who had handled London bills for a local clientele now emerge clearly as country bankers, supplying and discounting bills not now as an ancillary but as a primary activity.

To a certain extent deposit banking could grow directly out of this kind of business – money payable on bills discounted might not be taken in cash but left in the hands of the banker. Deposits could arise in other ways. Over periods, bills supplied would often not match bills discounted and the banker's personal wealth might be strained in covering the gap, prompting him to invite interest-bearing deposits to supplement his banking capital. And anybody who believed he could make a profit turn on money received at interest and who could induce others to place funds with him might in theory set up as a deposit banker. In contemporary circumstances the scope for this was very limited. In a country district the wealthier gentry, in most cases the largest potential source of deposits, would probably already have an account at a London bank and would see little reason to transfer it. Others wanting to find profitable employment for spare funds would usually seek more promising security than that offered by the personal credit standing of a banker. Of the few country banks which were essentially deposit banks the most common were those of industrialists looking for capital for their own businesses, which provided the tangible appearances of security. A handful of country banks also grew out of the practice of entrusting money to an individual, usually an attorney, for safe keeping or for informed investment.

One further way in which a banker, however originating, might acquire other people's money for his own use was to exchange his own notes for it. In many cases, particularly in early years, such notes were just receipts issued against deposits – probably interest-bearing and possibly non-transferable. Notes which were functionally receipts obviously played no part in creating deposits; they were a consequence of deposits. But banknotes might be positively sought for their own sake. They were more convenient to carry about than coin; and coin furthermore might not be available – throughout this period the Mint was unable to maintain an adequate supply of coin. A bank then could do business by supplying notes against coin and by changing bills which served for the largeish transactions of wholesale trade into smaller units as required for retail trade, wage payments and so on when sufficient coin could not be had for these purposes.[1] Having issued his own notes against some other form of money the banker then had that money at his disposal, to the extent to which he could count on the notes remaining in circulation (that is, on their not being presented for re-exchange into 'real' money). In practice this extent was slight. The notes would filter out of the locality and outsiders, unfamiliar with the banker's name and reputation, would fairly promptly return them for payment. Even within the locality there would be many who would be dubious about their worth and who would hasten to convert them into coin on receiving them.

Of course, the longer a bank had issued notes and had preserved a record of prompt payment the greater was the likelihood of its notes remaining in circulation and thus the more freedom the banker had in the employment of funds received. But such a record was only acquired through the maintenance of high liquidity ratios in the first place. A well established country banker in the later years of this period might be able to keep only a very small proportion of his notes covering assets in 'dead' money – coin, Bank of England notes, non-earning deposits with a London agent.[2] The difference, or the great bulk of it, would be held in readily negotiable form – good bills, Government securities and perhaps those of the Bank of England or the East India Company. Between income received on such assets and charges made for supplying notes,[3] note issuing in itself might be quite profitable for the banker, though in many cases printing costs and the expense of returning notes from a distance, which had to be borne by the issuer, left little or no gain on balance and a banker might issue notes only because the provision of such a facility was necessary to secure custom or because circulation of his notes constituted a useful form of advertising; but (and this is the essential point in the present context) note issuing created no more than a negligible amount of funds for general lending.

In summary, the various forms taken by country banking in these years did not give rise to large accumulations of capital for investment in productive enterprises. However, it would be a rough truth that the

[1] The formal distinction implied here between 'discounting' and 'changing' a bill is not necessarily one which would have clearly obtained in contemporary practice. It is a question of the extent to which the bill was effectively money and not merely a promise to pay, which would vary from locality to locality and from person to person.

[2] Country bank notes were usually payable either at the issuing bank itself or at the London bank which acted as metropolitan agent. The London bank would require such a deposit as would cover all likely demands for cash originating with the country bank.

[3] Whether or not a charge was made would depend on the circumstances – in effect whether the customer positively wanted notes or was merely prepared to take them.

further on in time one goes the greater the funds at the disposal of country banks, as the institution, despite fairly numerous failures, threw down roots and as the air of novelty gave way to one of familiarity. But at all times the crucial factor in public estimation was not the general reputation of the institution but the particular reputations of individual bankers. Some banks, probably not very many, did achieve a measure of success in wooing the small saver (the sort of person whose savings were counted in tens of pounds rather than hundreds and thousands, but not the working man putting together shillings and pence). Some attracted deposits from municipal corporations, canal companies, turnpike trusts, harbour boards and similar local concerns who had raised money in advance of projected expenditure. Some again secured the running accounts of local clergy whose stipends would commonly not be required immediately for personal expenditure or those of the few other individuals in a locality who might similarly be in receipt of relatively large salaries or professional incomes; but within this period, farmers, shopkeepers and manufacturers seem very generally to have kept their cash receipts by them.

More important than these miscellaneous deposits would have been monies arising out of bill and remittance business: out of an increasing tendency on the part of those regularly discounting bills to run a bill account with the bank to be drawn on at need; the growing practice amongst London resident landowners of having their rents paid into a local bank for convenient transmission to the capital; and the similar use of banks for the remission of tax revenue. But these were transitory funds and a banker had to exercise considerable prudence in lending them out again lest he be caught short when their owners wished to withdraw them. Overdraft and short-term loan accommodation on bill and other accounts into which funds were normally paid fairly regularly was the most sensible form of straightforward lending; above all, bankers preferred to use idle money in the bill discounting business which was for most of them their original and principal activity.

The good trade bill was a banker's ideal security: it arose out of a transaction in commodities which themselves underwrote it; the single signature of the acceptor might well be that of a merchant of known soundness; if it had already been in circulation it would have accumulated a number of other signatures, each of them a further guarantee that it would be paid. Only a general trade slump or credit crisis menaced it then. And with an original term to maturity, in most cases, of only two or three months, it was highly liquid. The banker in a busy trading centre, between mercantile advances and bill dealing, could conduct a kind of business which was well geared to the nature of his accounts. It was not risk-free business: it was intimately bound up with the local economy. A brief commercial setback which might shake local merchants and manufacturers could destroy local bankers. Poor judgment of the credit-worthiness of borrowers or the soundness of bills could ruin a banker; and, perhaps a graver hazard, the established banker's ability to 'create' money – unbacked notes, fictitious bills[1] – provided a standing temptation to lend what he did not have at the time but merely hoped to have when payment in 'real' money was demanded.

More uncertain was the situation of the banker in a locality where there was not normally a heavy flow of trade providing him simultaneously with funds and suitable ways of employing them. Here grave problems of fundamental policy could present themselves. With funds acquired from assorted sources it could be very difficult to determine what kind of liquidity position should be maintained and which of the random opportunities of employing money locally should be selected. Here retrospective generalisation collapses altogether. Some banks conducted a very limited business, providing no more than notes and remittance facilities, and deriving their banking income simply from charges. At an opposite extreme were banks whose funds were largely employed in some other enterprise of the bankers. These were perhaps the commonest instances of imprudent investment of bank funds. Bankers were usually less optimistic as to the ease with which money could be recovered when tied up in other people's undertakings. But, when the yield on government and other gilt-edged securities was only the normal $3-3\frac{1}{2}$ per cent of peacetime, when insufficient good bills were coming their way, such country bankers as had spare funds would be tempted to venture them at 5 per cent to local entrepreneurs under circumstances which often imperilled their liquidity and even their fundamental soundness. Such investments were not of necessity erroneous. A bank with ample funds could safely carry a portfolio which included an element of what in effect, if not in name, were long-term loans. But ironically it was the banks whose deposits were made up of strays and scraps which were the most likely to hazard this course.

---

[1] Bills issued by the banker himself drawn on non-existent persons. These were not necessarily fraudulent. The banker having endorsed them was liable for them and might well intend and be able to meet them. The important difference between such bills and genuine trade bills was that no actual consignment of goods lay behind them.

Those banks which were sustained by a pretty steady flow of mercantile money had, as already seen, little need to try it.

Although, then, country bank money might on occasions be applied in a variety of ways, its most appropriate and most usual employment was in trade and in the securities of the government, the East India Company and the Bank of England. In the latter category most acquisitions would have been of old securities, so that to this extent country bank funds could be said to have contributed to the freeing of capital for all kinds of purposes. But if any degree of crucial importance is to be attached to the institution it can only be on account of the way in which it facilitated the execution of commercial transactions. And in significant part this was a matter of providing the *instruments* of payment: bills, notes, bank drafts. The principal use of these last was the transference of funds from the provinces to the capital via a country bank and its London agent, though as country bankers established themselves securely and became familiar with one another *ad hoc* clearing arrangements sometimes permitted drafts to be used for interregional transferences; they were specifically devices for transferring money from place to place, not from person to person, and never figured very much in trade transactions.

No clearcut distinction can be made between the role of country banks in making available these payment facilities and their role as suppliers of mercantile credit. Since, in those provincial regions where mercantile activity was most intense, the trade bill often circulated as money, one cannot really say in many cases whether a banker in discounting a bill was simply exchanging one form of money for another or whether he was effectively advancing money against security. A certain degree of caution is needful in evaluating the importance of country banks as sources of mercantile credit. (Or, put another way: caution as to the extent to which trade needed credit financing when it is allowed that the first sale of goods to a merchant could itself create the necessary money in the form of the bill issued[1] to the seller by that merchant.) Between mercantile advances on other kinds of security and the element of real lending involved in bill-discounting, the quantity of credit supplied to trade by country banks was far from negligible; but it might be true that the more valuable service provided was that of enabling payments to be effected with comparative ease where, otherwise, awkward difficulties would have intervened. This way of

[1] As in Part I, the more intelligible 'issue' is here preferred to the technically correct 'accept'.

apprehending the special contribution of country banking to the national economy has the particular value of rendering more comprehensible the fact that the institution had clearly evolved (although much growth still lay in front of it) *before* any marked acceleration of commercial activity set in. It can, that is to say, be understood as a response to a long felt want rather than one to any especially novel pressure.

This evolution was far from being an even, steady process. It was very much a matter of convulsive spasms – in this period three spasms: the early 1750s, the mid-1760s and, most prolific, the early 1770s. To set against these gestatory spasms were the mortality years: 1756–7, 1759, 1772, 1778–79, 1781–85, winnowing out weaker members born in the good times when trade was buoyant and bills and notes circulated freely. Here was the chief structural weakness of the institution: the fluctuations in acceptability of the paper money in which it dealt, fluctuations for which the banking system itself was only very partially responsible. Basically, the trouble lay in the fact that commercial transactions at their normal level could only be effected through the extensive use of paper money but that in the last analysis this paper was generally apprehended as money only in so far as it was believed to be capable of conversion into 'real' money: gold and silver. There was nothing bankers could do to guard against a sudden preference for 'real' over 'substitute' money. Even a relatively slight initial swing in preferences could initiate a powerful chain reaction: debtors pressed to pay in gold and silver would attempt to realise the paper they held; banks would be required to pay in precious metal against notes and bills,[1] the word once abroad that a bank was paying out an unusual amount of gold and silver and holders of its notes were likely to encash them promptly for fear of their proving unpayable or unacceptable to others; depositors also might become anxious about their funds and withdraw them; finally, banks not directly affected to start with could get caught up in a general panic triggered off by the public failure of others to meet their obligations.

And failures there were bound to be in such circumstances. Many banks would be unable to realise their own assets fast enough to keep pace with the demand for gold and silver. This not only or even at all because their liquidity arrangements had not been geared to such

---

[1] One should of course distinguish between notes and bills in this context. A bank was obliged to pay cash against its own notes. It could refuse to discount bills. But for various reasons – a slowness in reading the danger signs, an unwillingness to offend valuable customers – it might well discount more freely than was prudent.

unanticipated pressure but because the circumstances themselves tended to freeze normally liquid assets. Money sometimes just could not be had for even the most unimpeachable securities and bills, or cash buyers could not be found by merchants for goods against which bills, now matured, had been issued. Indeed, in this period the ultimate brunt of this kind of pressure fell perhaps not so much on banks as on merchants. Certainly the gross nominal value of trade bills in circulation for which merchants were liable would have exceeded that of bank notes and the few bills created by banks.

Banks stood out as the weakest point in the system for several reasons. Their notes were payable on demand which meant that this was the first sort of paper to seek conversion and that note-issuing banks had the least opportunity of readjusting to menacing circumstances. Furthermore, country bank notes were the most novel form of paper in general circulation and thus the least trusted once apprehension started to spread. They circulated largely among those not formerly accustomed to paper money: wage earners and others whose economic activities were of a purely local character. Such people were especially prone to be frightened into rushing for 'real' money, not only from unfamiliarity with notes but also and perhaps more potently because they felt no solidarity with the banker who had issued them – no sense that their interests and his were bound up together. Merchants and large producers, on the other hand, had a keen, though not necessarily fully explicit, awareness that their wellbeing was crucially dependent on maintaining paper as money, since gold and silver was neither abundant enough nor suitable for their kind of business. Either on a purely person to person basis or by concerted local agreements, merchants' bills would be allowed to run beyond maturity or credit accommodation would be lengthened until the crisis had passed; and, of course, the more of this sort of thing there was the more rapidly the crisis did pass – partly because the rot was stopped directly in sectors where such action was taken and partly because the cash resources of those sectors were thereby released to sustain other sectors. On occasions banks, also, enjoyed the specific protection of local interests – merchants, shopkeepers etc. making a common public declaration of their readiness to accept the bank's notes.

It was this kind of rallying round which ensured that none of the periodic crises of confidence, both of these and of later years, ever got to the point of bringing about the collapse of the whole structure of paper credit along with the seizing-up of the economy which that would have occasioned. But although ultimate disaster was always averted the casualty list could be high. High, most significantly, in terms of the retardation of trade and hence of economic activity generally due to the shortage of acceptable means of payment. High also in the number of banks driven out of existence through inability to meet their cash obligations promptly. In some cases unsound lending was thereby exposed and claims on the bank could not be met in full. In other cases, after final realisation of all assets, creditors were fully satisfied although the destruction of the bank's reputation prevented it from resuming business. In others again, however, it meant no more than that the bank had had for a while to close its doors while it called in sufficient cash to meet demands.

Various factors could make for such a shift in preferences as between paper and metallic money as would initiate an accumulating crisis of the kind just described. The most probable was a seriously adverse external balance of payments, that is to say, a situation in which many foreign creditors required payment in gold and silver.[1] A classic instance of this kind occurred in 1772. A big jump in imports of tea and sugar coincided with a sharp dip in exports of woollen textiles, and to an upset balance of trade was added the consequences of a financial crash in Amsterdam. A good deal of Dutch money was regularly held in London securities; much of it was now temporarily repatriated to meet the domestic pressure for cash. The ultimate repercussions on the economy at large were grave. It was not until well into 1774 that it recovered from the depression which ensued. The banking system took a severe shock, right on the heels of a couple of years during which it had grown with marked rapidity. Indeed it may be that it was the very extension of banking facilities which was partially responsible for the setback. The relative plenitude of paper money may have stimulated speculative dealings in tea, sugar and other commodities for which markets did not actually exist, with the twin effects of disturbing the external balance of trade and of creating a stock of trade bills on which payment could not be made on maturity. Defaulting on bills could in itself, of course, lead to a general crisis.

Of the other occasions on which the ranks of bankers were thinned 1778–79 was of much the same nature as 1772, although here the causation was not economic in origin. The entry of France into the American War in 1778, succeeded by that of Spain in the following year, caused a

---

[1] Since a fully multilateral system of international settlements did not exist an outflow of precious metals could occur even when external payments balanced or were in surplus.

loss of markets which tilted the balance of trade unfavourably. (Imports obviously fell off as well as exports but the Continent was more important as a buyer than as a seller.) However, the seepage of gold resulting from this was less consequential than the panic flight into the precious metals on the French declaration of war. Foreign, especially Dutch, anxiety to recover invested funds would have contributed substantially to the rush, but much of it was purely domestic in character – an instinctive dash to the security of gold and silver when trouble and uncertainty threatened, followed by a gradual re-emergence from cover as it became evident that catastrophe was not imminent. The same phenomenon had attended the outbreak of the Seven Years War in 1756 with similar consequences, stretching into 1757. The distinct crisis of 1759 is probably to be attributed to the outflow of gold consequent on the decision of 1758 to support Britain's only major ally, Prussia, with a large money subsidy.

The more persistent attrition amongst bankers through the later years of the American War and its aftermath (1781–85) is to be largely explained in different terms. The root cause here was heavy government borrowing. In some measure this told on bankers by drawing off bank deposits, but a much more grievous consequence was the depreciation of undated government and other negotiable securities, an important class of bank assets, as the rate of interest rose. Banks which were forced to liquidate such assets were unable to realise them at the value of the liabilities they were supposed to cover and might as a result be driven to a suspension of payments and ultimate extinction. On the other hand, bankers who were not under such pressure might do very well out of the situation by switching to these securities and holding on to them until the withdrawal of the government from the money market brought interest rates down and security prices up again, as started to happen from the spring of 1785 – delayed until two years after the end of the war by the accumulated volume of short-term government debt which had to be funded.

One further factor which might be conceived to have played a part in some of these episodes was the state of the harvest. A very bad harvest coincided with the commencement of the Seven Years War; 1772 was also a year of poor harvest; and the long period of strain 1781–85 included a run of bad harvests, 1782–85. On the other hand, the extremely poor pair of years 1766–67 does not appear to have unduly disturbed the banking system, while recovery was effected from the 1772 banking crisis through the worse harvests of 1773 and 1774. Empirically, then, the evidence for a correlation between low harvest yields and periods of severe pressure on banks is not at all conclusive.

Grounds for positing such a correlation are twofold: that a shortfall in the domestic harvest would necessitate imports of corn and thus lead to an outflow of gold; and that high bread prices would squeeze purchasing power and thus lead to a general contraction of trade. So far as the first of these is concerned it cannot be treated in isolation but only in conjunction with concurrent, and usually much weightier, factors governing the balance of payments situation, and with the contemporary state of the cash and bullion reserves of the banking system – also highly variable elements. That is to say its weight can only be appraised in the context of particular cases, and in the particular cases in question it does not stand out as a principal factor.

On immediate inspection the second ground appears highly questionable. If people are spending more in gross on bread are not bread producers' incomes raised by that amount? Is not the fall in bread consumers' expenditure on other items exactly matched by a rise in bread producers' expenditure? In fact the answer to these rhetorical questions is: no – or at least, not entirely. Some part of the additional expenditure on bread would go on imported grain and thus be lost (although it might eventually return in the form of an increased demand for exports). Furthermore, the bread producers being on average in a higher income group than the bread consumers, and thus having a higher general propensity to save, would not in fact expend as much extra on other items as would match the fall in such expenditure on the part of consumers. However, even in the very worst years, through this period, extra imports were only a very marginal addition to total grain supplies; and the difference in saving habits, given the preponderance of small to medium farmers amongst bread suppliers, cannot have been really great. The overall level of domestic demand for items other than bread must have fallen at times of bad harvest but it can only have been a fall of fractional magnitude. And, to get back to the particular question at issue, a contraction in trade unless it were severe enough to cause widespread defaulting on debts would not imperil the stability of banks. Bankers' profits like those of most other people would tend to diminish but a simple reduction in the volume of business, in itself, involved no threat to a bank's existence.

(Since some of the more general implications of a bad harvest have been touched on here they may, parenthetically, be enlarged on a little. A bad harvest was unambiguously a bad thing. It meant less bread, as

397

well as less beer, less gin, less whisky, less starch. And, however analysed, less of anything in an economy, if a readily acceptable substitute cannot be provided, is real economic loss in the most fundamental way. This particular loss was one which bore most heavily on the lower income groups. Bad harvest years were years in which the poor emphatically got poorer while some of the rich got richer. The low income producer was hit as badly as the low income consumer. A small farmer's cash income might vanish entirely when a poor yield left him with no surplus for sale after meeting his own household's needs, while his bigger neighbour grew fat on scarcity prices. And of course there were other variations in fortunes: as between localities according to regional differences in the quality of the harvest; as between producers of other goods according as their clientele was a high income or a low income one.

One further parenthetic point may be stressed. In terms of their total implications there is a very big difference between temporary high bread prices as a result of a bad harvest and persistent high prices as a result of a chronic pressure of demand on supply factors. The latter situation will involve a much more significant net fall in domestic demand for other goods since in this case the whole of the extra expenditure on bread does not constitute windfall profit for producers; a part of it is absorbed in meeting the higher costs of cultivating marginal land – and in the long run most of the extra return to intramarginal producers will be appropriated in higher rents by landlords with their relatively high propensity to save.

There are two groups of banks to which specific reference has not yet been made and which must in some degree be distinguished from the country banks dealt with above. These are the London banks and the Scottish banks. Scotland differed most specifically from England in one important respect. There was no legal prohibition there on the formation of joint stock banks. In 1740 there were two formally constituted banks in Scotland, both joint stock: the Bank of Scotland (1695) and the Royal Bank of Scotland (1727). Established in Edinburgh, both were by then doing a lively business there, based on note-issuing, interest-bearing deposits and general lending, a distinctive feature of the latter by contrast with English banking, being the amount advanced on personal securities. Large founding capitals, especially in the case of the Royal, and the device of the optional note[1] gave them a standing and

[1] Payable either on demand or six months later with interest, at the option of the bank.

security comparable to that enjoyed south of the border by the Bank of England alone.

This sound base was reinforced and extended with the development of the banking business of the British Linen Company (1746). In origin this was essentially a marketing agency, handling a considerable proportion of the Scottish linen output, the widely spread producers being paid by provincial agents with notes drawn on the Company. Since coin was scarce and the notes of the two existing banks only circulated erratically at any distance from Edinburgh these linen notes quickly established themselves as a very useful form of cash in many areas, enabling the Company's agents to use the notes to discount bills locally. The Company very soon found itself conducting a profitable note-issuing and discounting business and by 1763 had entirely abandoned the linen trade, having become the first effective branch bank in the British Isles and its substantial capital having been reallocated to general banking business. Like the two senior banks, the Linen Company's business in its evolved form consisted very much of receiving deposits and lending on personal security, accompanied by a large note circulation.

By that time these three leading Edinburgh based banks were flanked by other joint stock concerns founded in Glasgow, Aberdeen, Perth and Dundee conducting business of a similar nature. Between head offices, branches and agencies, all but the most sparsely populated parts of Scotland were by c. 1770 comprehended within this banking system, which, by contrast with the rather peripheral nature of English provincial banking, operated at the centre of Scottish economic life. Bank notes which in provincial England were just a supplement, though an increasingly important one, to coin and bills were in Scotland almost the only medium of exchange. The limited nature of Scottish commerce until into this period had prevented the trade bill establishing itself as a familiar instrument, and the same factor probably explains the extreme scarcity of the precious metals in Scotland. Joint stock enabled a relatively large circulation of notes to be achieved from the very foundation of a bank and thus an extensive public could be rapidly habituated to them, whereas an English banker, even if he wanted to, could only very gradually extend his note circulation beyond an immediate locality.

A situation in which, by comparison with provincial England, banking business was in the hands of a small number of relatively large banks facilitated note issue in other ways too: fewer varieties of bank notes meant that the public could more readily become familiar with each, and with familiarity would come confidence and less likelihood of their being exchanged. There was a greater probability that the notes of a bank, when they were presented for payment, would be paid in at a branch of that bank rather than at some other bank, so that the cost of return for payment did not have to be borne. Furthermore, given the greater prevalence of deposits, notes paid in were more likely to be to the credit of the payer's account and not for cash. In fact, all three principal elements of this Scottish banking reinforced one another. Personal lending, by way of creating a drawing account for the borrower, was apt to give rise to deposit accounts, and such accounts, as just indicated, enabled the bank to economise on cash. Lending was also a principal way of getting notes into circulation, and notes in circulation played their part in attracting deposits, partly by way of simple advertisement, partly because people who had come to trust a bank's notes were more easily induced to trust it as a depository for their wealth. And the more notes a bank could keep out in circulation and the lower the proportion of cash it needed to retain against them, the more funds it had at its disposal for lending.

Scottish circumstances, then, conspired to make note issue an element of key importance both in economic life generally and in banking life specifically. The volume of its note issue determined the size of Scottish bank's business to a degree unknown in England. Indeed, the differences between English and Scottish banking are largely contained in the fact that, in Scotland, notes issued by the banks themselves took the part played in England by bills which originated outside the banking system. English banking hung on the skirts of trade: the trade bill was its principal investment and money left with bankers when bills were discounted provided it with much of its funds. Scottish banking created its own investment outlets and its own sources of funds. Able to maintain lower liquidity ratios against its notes and other liabilities, and attracting money which in England would either have been hoarded or would have taken advantage of the suitable investment opportunities in London, Scottish banks could and did lend for a much wider range of purposes than was safe and normal in England. Mistakes of course were made. Liquidity considerations could not be ignored altogether and the extent of lending on purely personal security necessarily carried risks. The firm of Douglas, Heron and Co., founded fairly specifically as an investment bank in 1769, demonstrated that lending had limits. When it crashed in 1773 its very substantial backers had to find over £600,000 out of their own pockets to meet its debts. (The sum itself is a revealing comment on Scottish banking: other than the

Bank of England there would hardly have been any contemporary English bank which could have commanded proprietors' capital of that order.)

There was a group of Scottish concerns which more closely resembled English banks, particularly the London 'City' banks: non note-issuing and confining themselves largely or exclusively to dealings in trade bills. The rise of Glasgow as a major mercantile centre created a need for this kind of speciality. Although the ordinary banks did include the discounting of domestic bills amongst their business, they looked on foreign bills as outside their sphere of action. Stemming from various origins – merchant, broker, factor etc. – and often continuing to conduct other kinds of business, a number of individuals emerged through this period as specialist bill-dealers, and in most cases never passed beyond this to become general bankers. They did not normally receive deposits. Money might be left in their hands when bills were discounted. Otherwise, their funds consisted of payments made for bills supplied; and when these were insufficient to meet discounts they fell back on the credit resources of the banks proper. These Scottish bill dealers were an adjunct or complement to the banking system, rather than, as with many of their English provincial counterparts, bankers in embryo. The gradual evolution through an extension of functions which was the characteristic manner of formation of English banks was not a Scottish phenomenon.

The London banking system was already fully evolved by the beginning of this period, and in terms of amount of business transacted would still at the end of the period have outweighed English provincial banking in importance. The larger personal fortunes were heavily concentrated in the hands of those who lived permanently or seasonally in London and kept their money there. A great deal of the nation's commerce was effected in London, using the discount facilities of London banks. And much of the considerable financial business of the government was conducted through the Bank of England. Moreover, the growth of country banking itself brought more funds to London banks as they became the metropolitan agents for provincial concerns.

More securely established amongst a clientele by now thoroughly familiarised with the banking habit, the London banks, although by no means fully immune to the disturbances described earlier, were more durable than their country cousins. The fact that they had very largely abandoned note-issuing also contributed towards greater stability since it meant that their liabilities were to their regular customers who, by very virtue of the fact that they had entrusted their money to the bank in the first place, were less likely to be alarmed into encashing their claims (deposits) than the Toms, Dicks and Harrys who might come by the notes of a bank of issue. And the notes of the Bank of England, (which had supplanted those of the private London banks) if not at the beginning of this period, at least during it, so rooted themselves in the London region that they were virtually as good as gold in the metropolitan eye.

It might be said indeed that the Bank of England was in course of developing into a central bank. This was far from being a rapid development – it was to take another century and more to finalise it. Throughout this period and well beyond it, one particularly vital element of the office of a central bank was lacking: a readiness on the part of the Bank of England to acknowledge its key role and the public responsibilities thereby devolving on it; a readiness, that is, to *act* as a central bank. For a long time to come, the Bank was regularly to take the view of itself that it was a commercial concern, in essentials no different from any other bank, primarily dedicated to the cause of maximising its own profits in good times and ensuring its own security in bad. More precisely then, the Bank of England was in course of acquiring that degree of effective control over the monetary system at large which would have enabled it to function as a central bank if it had chosen to do so and which, willy-nilly, meant that its actions did have extensive and decisive repercussions on particular occasions.

This crucial position of the Bank was simply a function of size; the only joint stock bank in England, initially launched with a very considerable capital, deriving a special prestige from its close working association with the government, it was a giant amongst pygmies. The particularly significant aspects of its size were three: the Bank was by far the largest single repository of gold and silver in the country; its notes circulated in greater number and commanded a greater acceptability than those of any other bank; its bill business was larger than that of any other institution. This last was perhaps the most significant of all and it is to be accounted a development of outstanding importance that the Bank, which through the earlier years of the eighteenth century had come to devote itself heavily to purely Government business, did from *c.* 1745, and especially from *c.* 1760, greatly increase its bill discounting. (The obverse of this is the relatively, though not absolutely, lesser extent to which the government leant on the Bank of England for credit, as a result of increasing accommodation from the private banks and the general investing public, both through direct subscription to funded loans and through discounting of government bills.) Had it not been for this development the Bank would have been largely isolated from the rest of the financial community and the degree of reciprocal sensitivity much less. As the Bank came to deal more freely in bills this became a principal channel along which its notes – and other claims on it – went into public circulation. The supply of Bank notes, that is to say, became in significant measure a function of the general level of economic activity. And this not only in the sense that a higher (or lower) level generated a greater (or lesser) quantity of Bank notes,[1] but also in the sense that an autonomous alteration by the Bank of the volume of its discounting could appreciably influence the intensity of economic activity, in some part directly through varying the quantity of acceptable means of effecting cash transactions, in more important part indirectly through varying the liquidity ratios of the other London banks whose liquid assets increasingly consisted of their claims on the Bank of England (notes and deposits with the Bank).

It must, however, be stressed that within these years this particular ambience of the Bank was not a nationally pervasive one. Bank of England notes did not circulate widely outside London. Country banks did not maintain deposits with the Bank of England. A change in the Bank's volume of discounting could not have had any notable impact on day to day provincial liquidity. But Bank notes had more than an intrinsic importance. They, along with other claims on the Bank, were in practice the usual means of securing access to large quantities of the precious metals. This carried two implications: first, that the volume of the Bank's discounting was a major determinant of the volume of effective entitlement to the precious metals, further underlining the importance of the Bank's bill business; and second, that any sizeable flow of gold and silver either out of the country or into private hoards necessarily took the form of a drain on the Bank's bullion stock. Country banks with insufficient cash in the till – in common with everyone else wanting gold – supplemented their metallic reserves, in effect, by securing claims on the Bank of England and encashing them. Thus the Bank was becoming in practice reserve bank to the whole national credit structure, without, however, exercising any continuous control over

---

[1] Important, in that it was, obviously, much more desirable that the supply of notes be geared to the state of commercial activity than to the volume of government business conducted by the Bank.

more than a particular, though very considerable, sector – the metropolis. Ultimately, the course of action available to the Bank to defend itself when threatened by an intolerable gold drain did have national repercussions. That action was to curb, perhaps severely, its discounting and thus shrink the volume of claims against it. Those looking for its gold would eventually find their way barred through lack of access to it. London holdings of Bank money (notes and deposits) already created would hardly, in such circumstances, be made available to others against less liquid or less reputable assets, while, as seen, little Bank money was normally to be found in the provinces.

The essence of the situation, then, was that the behaviour of the Bank of England did in fairly flexible fashion govern credit creation in the metropolitan area through the direct control that the Bank enjoyed over the cash supply in that area, but that all it could present the provinces with was gold starvation, at those times when gold was most urgently needed. Or, looked at from a different aspect: the provinces at normal times operated with money which was to a large extent goods backed rather than gold backed;[1] they operated largely independently of London and its gold store in Threadneedle Street. Only in abnormal times when gold was wanted (for money which had not originated in gold) were provincial banks thrown on to London – London with its own normally fairly self-contained monetary system, geared, though not rigidly, to the Bank of England's gold reserves; and not fashioned to take the strain of meeting the provinces' occasional and exceptional requirements for gold.

The Bank of England as a source of ordinary everyday cash – very largely in relation to London; the Bank of England as a central gold holder; and the Bank's bill discounting as the principal way through which in these two roles it was linked with the financial world at large[2] – these are the features insisted on in the account above. One further feature needs drawing out. The aspect of the Bank's bill business emphasised so far was, at least from the point of view of the Bank itself, an incidental one. The Bank discounted because it was a profitable business; because it had large funds and wished to employ them. It is probably true that the most important way in which the Bank's discounting governed the level of trade is that already touched on: the

[1] Essentially a variant way of putting the point made earlier: that country banks dealt in instruments of exchange rather than credit.

[2] The purchase of government and other securities in the open market and straightforward lending were other links; but the Bank obtained the huge bulk of its securities on issue and did very little personal lending.

effect on cash ratios. But the higher echelons of the mercantile community were to a significant degree insensitive to changes in the cash supply. Their money was the trade bill; its currency was in part determined by the ease or difficulty with which it could be discounted,[1] and that in turn was to a very appreciable extent determined by the Bank of England. As the largest concern in the discounting business, any change in the Bank's volume of discounts necessarily had a sensible and direct impact on the currency of trade bills. If the Bank was discounting freely, trade bills could be drawn readily. If the Bank was curbing its discounts, trade bills became less negotiable and therefore less acceptable. And on the freedom with which trade bills could be created depended very largely the volume of trade. In this way also, then, as well as via the diminished cash ratios of the London banks, a dangerous fall in the Bank's bullion stock was liable to bring about a contraction of trade. Contrariwise, increased discounting by the Bank could encourage unsound speculation in commodities. (The great defect in a goods-backed currency is, of course, the possibility that the goods may ultimately prove unsaleable, or fetch less than the nominal value of the bills drawn against them.)

Much, then, depended on the Bank's discount policy, and this cannot be said to have observed any consistent principle. Like any other banker, the Bank was concerned to blend profitability and safety as happily as possible. But what criteria of safety were to be adopted? Was it to have principal regard to its own bullion state or to the soundness of the bills it dealt in? Was it to take the view that at times of gold drain its safety lay in keeping up its discounting, so as to prevent general alarm setting in, or in cutting discounting so as to protect itself against an insupportable demand for gold? Should it acknowledge its own fairly extensive powers in the commercial and financial world and gauge its discount policy so as to prevent overextended credit positions being established with the menace which that would bring to bear on its own gold store? And lurking behind these particular questions the pervasive general one: how should it apprehend its own liabilities since, while they were claims

---

[1] One might argue that this is hair-splitting: bills would be discounted according as cash was available, so that one comes back to the question of cash ratios. In the last analysis this is true. But it misses the point that within the mercantile community itself a bill's value was accorded by the goods behind it and that it could circulate within that community irrespective of cash states. It was the possible need to release it from this closed goods-conscious circle to a wider cash-conscious circle which qualified its acceptability according to the cash supply situation. But in the first instance it was simply a matter of acceptability, not of cashability.

on its gold, they were also in practice a widely acceptable form of money?

Whether or not raised in such explicit terms these were questions to which in effect answers had to be given. They were difficult questions, to be resolved not just according to abstract principles but according to the circumstances of each particular occasion. To say that no consistent principle was observed is not a criticism. Rather would there be grounds for criticism if the Bank had, for example, adhered to a rigid gold ratio rule and ignored all other considerations. The records of the Bank of England do not permit us to determine just what discount policy the Bank did follow through successive shifts of circumstances; how far a lavish policy in good times contributed to boom, and from boom to crisis, or how far a tight policy contributed to converting crisis into depression; how far the Bank followed commercial trends and how far it set them. One can only observe the Bank was powerful enough to have so mismanaged its affairs as not only to have ruined itself but to have caused fearful economic dislocation generally. That at least it did not do that may stand as a negative appreciation of its conduct.

Foreign trade

One principal area of economic activity has not yet been specifically dealt with: overseas trade. However, in treating of the woollen industry we have already comprehended a major part of this theme. Right through to the end of this period, woollen textiles figured so prominently among exports that their individual performance largely determined the record of foreign trade generally. The account already given of woollen exports – vigorous growth into the early 1750s and a falling away thereafter – needs only to be modified somewhat to stand for total exports.

One commodity of some marginal importance which moved in approximately the same direction as woollen textiles was corn. Ignoring sharp annual fluctuations, corn exports increased up to the early 1750s, then started to fall off, while from the late 1760s the adverse gap between imports and exports was fairly steadily widening. Reinforcing the growth tendencies of the earlier years, and just about offsetting the downward trend of the later years, were two particular groups of commodities: other textiles (cotton, linen, silk), and metal goods, both crude and fabricated. Between them these made up the bulk of exports apart from woollen goods, which, accounting for about three-fifths of total domestic exports at the beginning of the period, had slipped to about one-third by the close. To be closely associated with this shift in relative importance as amongst commodities is a similar shift as amongst markets. The Continent, which took some three-quarters of British exports at the commencement of the period, was taking only about two-fifths at the end, having in absolute terms grown vigorously as a market up to the early 1760s and, thereafter, having fallen back to about its original level. It was, then, markets which had been of only modest importance in the early years of this period which ensured that, instead of painfully slithering down the other side of a peak, British exports maintained themselves on a rough plateau, cut across by the depression of the later years of the American War, over the last couple of decades.

The principal markets in question may be grouped as four: the United States of America (as founded in 1783), Ireland, the British West Indies, and Asia, with West Africa and post-1783 British North America as subsidiary markets belonging in the same category. As a crude generalisation these regions could be characterized as having economies which were complementary to, rather than competitive with, that of Great Britain, and whose economic development therefore conduced towards an expansion of trade with Britain rather than towards increasing self-sufficiency as was, generally speaking, the case with Europe. This observation would apply especially pertinently to the West Indies and the southern states of the USA, given over as they were to the cultivation of a few staple crops commanding mass foreign markets, and almost totally dependent on outside sources of supply for everything else. Their growing populations and increasing sales of sugar, tobacco, coffee, cotton, rice etc. had as virtually automatic consequences increased imports from Britain of, most notably, cotton and linen textiles and metal artifacts of all kinds. Even the more northerly American settlements, although with great staples to lean on and thus having to contrive more variegated and complex economic expedients, were as yet only on the threshold of industrialisation and consequently still clients to British manufacturers of nearly every sort within the bounds of their fairly limited external purchasing power.

In the case of Ireland also, under-industrialisation combined with a marked growth in population from about mid-century afforded market scope for British manufacturers. However, the degree of under-industrialisation was only partial and it was two particular commodities which really made the Irish market of noteworthy consequence. One was coal. Although the mass of the rural populace burned peat the towns of the eastern seaboard, above all Dublin, leant heavily on British coal as both a domestic and an industrial fuel. Ireland, in fact, was the coal industry's only export market of any weight. The other commodity was the mixed cotton and linen textiles of Lancashire. Especially from the mid-1760s onwards, their cheapness won them large sales in a country where that was a prime consideration.

Ireland's capacity to step up her purchases of coal, cottons and a miscellany of other goods, particularly rapid through the 1760s, was consequent on a big increase in Irish exports to Britain and the trans-Atlantic colonies, to be attributed in some part to a relaxation of the brute policy hitherto followed by English government in Ireland of denying Irish producers any access to markets where they might compete with their English counterparts. Dairy produce and tallow were chief among Irish products admitted to the British market by concessions of 1758 while the colonial markets were fully thrown open to the Irish in 1780. But apart from the wool, raw or yarn, which had long been a principal and unrestricted Irish export to Britain, linen, the manufacture of which had been positively assisted as some compensation for repression in other fields, was Ireland's biggest external earner. Exports of linen cloth to Britain, much of it for subsequent re-exportation, grew steadily into the early 1770s and when this trend recoiled under the competition of cheap British cotton-linens that circumstance itself provided compensation in the demand for Irish linen yarn to match with the cotton yarn streaming off the jennies. In more than one way, then, Irish economic growth, such as it was, redounded to the benefit of British producers – who were not, however, sufficiently impressed by this experience to refrain from howling down the proposals of 1785 for the establishment of free trade between Britain and Ireland which, they swore, would lead to their being undone by cheap Irish labour.

The fourth principal region keeping British exports buoyant, Asia, is a designation of convenience rather than precision. A kind of unity is lent to this trade by the fact that virtually all the goods entering into it were carried out from Britain by the East India Company, but they were ultimately dispersed over a very wide area along a variety of channels and although their increasing penetration was certainly of importance to the British economy their sale relative to the full market potential of Asia was diminutive. They were a very mixed bag of goods, by no means inconsiderable in gross but even in the case of metalwares, the most prominent constituent, of no more than marginal consequence either to the British industries concerned or to the communities in which they sold. Nor did they suffice to pay for much more than a half of the goods brought back by the Company from the East.

As implied already the growth of exports to these extra-Continental regions was closely correlated with a growth in imports from the same regions; enhanced external earnings by these territories enabled them to expand their purchases from Britain. Paralleling their increased importance as markets, therefore, was an increased importance as sources of supply. In gross from providing about a half of Britain's imports they came to provide some three-fifths through these years. As the figures indicate, they were already important suppliers at the outset of the period – with the exception of Ireland whose development as an exporter has been sketched above. But if the figures also suggest that as sources of imports their growth was less marked than as markets for exports (from one-quarter of the total to three-fifths), this is only because total British imports grew more rapidly than total domestic exports. On the face of it this implies that Britain's balance of trade was worsening. This was certainly the case to some extent after the early 1760s when imports continued to increase while domestic exports in sum stagnated but it was partially offset by the fact that, from then until the outbreak of the American War, a growing proportion of imports was being re-exported – not only recovering the money expended on them but earning a comfortable surplus in the form of mercantile profit and handling and shipping charges. The huge bulk of these re-exports were obtained from across the Atlantic and from Asia, and were despatched to Europe and to Ireland. Thus through the years when Britain was failing to sell an increased amount of her own goods to Europe she was succeeding in selling increasing quantities of American and Asiatic produce there. And the surplus earned by Britain on these transactions made a substantial contribution towards financing a continuing expansion of imports from the Continent.

Of the commodities re-exported to the Continent, tobacco came to hold a place of supreme importance up to the American War, outweighing in fact any domestic export bar woollen goods. It was followed by coffee whose cultivation in the West Indies was greatly extended through this period enabling Britain to vie with Holland, drawing on East Indian supplies, as a purveyor of coffee to Europe. West Indian sugar and Indian and China tea were other items which figured conspicuously in this trade, and they were backed up by a host of articles of less individual weight, such as Asiatic silks, dyestuffs from various quarters, American rice, West Indian rum and cotton.

In varying degrees these commodities were also imported for domestic consumption. Of the very large imports of tobacco only a small fraction needed to be retained to meet home demand and a similar fraction of the coffee sufficed for a country where it had never won much more than a certain modishness. The British taste for sugar, on the other hand, spread greatly through the first three decades or so of this period and re-exports, notable as they were, consisted of little more than the crumbs remaining from the huge quantities brought in for British delectation – far surpassing in value any other imported commodity and accounting alone for about one-sixth of all imports. Tea-drinking was also a spreading habit and, though even at the end of the period it had yet to root itself as a truly national beverage, much the greater part of tea imports were retained in Britain. Cotton for home use was also becoming of accelerating consequence over the last couple of decades of the period.

Two further items originating outside Europe may conveniently be mentioned here, though sold neither in Europe nor in Britain: Indian calico and slaves: the one merely touching British shores for transhipment, the other never coming within a thousand miles of Britain but essentially a British trade nonetheless. They were closely interconnected trades. Calico was a principal item brought out to West Africa to exchange for slaves, while its only other important market was in the slave-owning territories across the Atlantic. Both, then, depended on the prosperity of these regions, and their record through these years can be largely identified with that of sugar and tobacco, though calico was prevented from sharing fully in the expansion of the plantations by competition from British cotton-linen materials. Tea through this period came to supplant calico as the principal element in the East India Company's trade.

The sustained growth of imports from Europe was compounded of two contrary tendencies: a decline in imports of manufactured goods and a more than countervailing increase in imports of raw or semi-processed produce. Already by the beginning of this period imports of European manufactures had been reduced to very slight proportions and these years saw the virtual finalisation of that process. Under essentially fiscal, rather than commercial, pressure the tariff structure took on an even more intensely protective aspect. British-made linen and silk cloth, paper, glass and assorted other lesser items came to usurp practically all such market corners as had remained to French, Dutch, Italian and other Continental manufacturers, though in the case of silk cloth it took the outright prohibition of 1766 to secure the British product against European competition.

The progress of the native silk industry automatically brought in its train more imported raw silk and silk yarn, most of it from the Mediterranean region, although Asiatic supplies were of gathering consequence. Even in an unfinished state it was a highly expensive commodity and, in fact, only sugar loomed larger in the total import bill. The growth of the linen industry, both pure and mixed, had a similar effect. Whether intended for re-export to Ireland or for use at home, flax was required in increasing quantities, the amount grown in the British Isles being quite inadequate. The eastern Baltic was the supply source here. The multiplication of British ships trafficking the Baltic was in fact comparable with their proliferation in the Atlantic. They were there to carry away not only flax but, more important still, bar iron from both Sweden and Russia, while in particular years over the last couple of decades of the period, Prussian and Polish grain cargoes provided their principal employment. And the overall increase in the volume of total British trade, particularly in the long-haul extra-European trades, meant a steady increase in imports of the 'naval stores' which, for centuries, had given the Baltic a very special importance. In gross, British imports from the Baltic region roughly tripled between 1740 and 1785 while, on balance, imports from the rest of Europe hardly altered.

Given its nature this great growth in the Baltic trade – which was very much a one way affair – serves very handily to indicate a crucial characteristic of the British economy of these years: the extent to which even quite modest growth could generate a sharp increase in imports. And this characteristic may be set along with another already noted: that, as things then stood, increased exports to the regions which offered the best prospects of market expansion depended largely on a propensity to import increased quantities of the handful of consumer commodities that these regions supplied. Although it is to reduce a fairly complex situation to two somewhat oversimplified fundamentals, it would perhaps be acceptably close to the truth to say that, in combination, these external features of Britain's economic situation over the final twenty years or so of this period were conspiring to impose impassable limits to continuing development. And one may bracket this with two other interconnected phenomena touched on earlier – the laggardliness of agriculture and the deceleration of consumer demand – to suggest very forcibly that the intrinsic momentum of the central economic trends of the later 'sixties, the 'seventies and the early 'eighties, far from being a cumulative building up to revolutionary force, was a wasting decline into stagnancy. It was only at the margins of the contemporary economy that autonomous factors were shaping developments destined to transform this situation, first by making available a commodity, cotton textiles, which would break export markets wide open again, and secondly by opening up a way of industrial advance founded on the exploitation of Britain's own natural resources of coal and iron rather than on imported materials.

In the meantime, Britain paid her way externally by enlarging her entrepôt dealings in other countries' goods. But the American War blew a big hole in this trade which was only partially repaired after the war. It was not, of course, only the re-export trade which was affected by the war itself. The directly accessible American market contracted overnight to the tiny area under effective British control ; and although a fair amount of British exports continued to get through to America over the long Canadian border imports from America virtually ceased. The entry of France into the war in 1778 was not in itself of major commercial consequence, but when Spain joined France in 1779 not only was an important market lost but a near stranglehold gripped the Straits of Gibraltar, and trade with the Mediterranean region plummeted downwards. The Baltic powers' League of Armed Neutrality in 1780 was a gesture of hostility which, while stopping short of actual war, had depressive though not destructive effects on the important trade with that region. And the general stretching of Britain's naval resources denied adequate protection to the vessels plying both the West and East Indian trades – in the case of the former the effects aggravated by the actual loss of some of the lesser British islands to the French. All in all, by comparison with the years 1774–75, the decline through the worst years 1780–82 was: imports, 20 per cent; domestic exports, 17 per cent; re-exports, 38 per cent.

The particularly high figure for the fall in re-exports reflects above all the almost total cessation of the tobacco trade. And the tobacco trade it was too which was the victim of American independence. Freed of the constraints of the Navigation Acts, American tobacco, unique in the degree to which its natural distribution pattern had been artificially warped, could now bypass Britain on its way to European markets. Not all of it did so. Minor markets were still most conveniently reached through Britain; but in the years immediately after the war, tobacco re-exports were only about a quarter of what they had formerly been and were to fall off even more as the Americans established solid commercial contacts of their own. Glasgow, which had contrived under the Navigation System to secure as much as a half of the valuable re-export trade in tobacco, was reduced straight away to the relatively tiny quantities smoked in Scotland itself, the very important French market which it had catered for passing immediately into direct contact with the USA. As for re-exports in sum, the siphoning off of the tobacco trade meant that it was not until the fortuitous closure of Amsterdam in 1794 brought a fresh flow of goods to Britain that they again attained their prewar level. But by then re-exports were, so as to speak, a jam trade; Britain's own textile goods were ensuring that she was having no difficulty in earning her bread and butter.

Two

1785–1830

Revolution?

'Industrial Revolution': the phrase and the concepts underlying it have quite a history of their own. When about a century ago the historical course of economic change in Britain first started to receive fairly close and deliberate attention, historians were struck by a batch of technical innovations clustered in the later years of the eighteenth century and apprehended these as utterly transforming the nature of the economy in the course of a few decades. Industrial capitalism, exploiting these innovations, was seen as creating entirely new modes of production. A massive transfer of resources was observed to take place, to industrial activities in which Britain led the world. And these resources were necessarily transferred principally from agriculture whose own response, the 'Agricultural Revolution' enabled it to go on provisioning a rapidly industrialising population. About half a century ago historians started to become more vividly aware that developments of the kind regarded as peculiarly characteristic of the 'Industrial Revolution' period had been taking place much earlier – from as early as the mid-sixteenth century. And about the same time they were becoming more conscious of large areas of economic activity which had remained 'un-revolution-ised' through the 'revolutionary' years – in some cases were still un-revolutionised in their own time. The sharp edges delimiting the In-dustrial Revolution were becoming blurred at both ends. Instead of an abrupt transformation occurring between 1760 and 1830 (which had become the classical Revolution period) a drawn-out, accumulating process was starting to present itself and historians were coming to question the usefulness of the 'Industrial Revolution' concept. But even before this attitude started to filter into the pages of the school textbook, that final repository of historical learning, the 'revolutionary' view, in modified form, has reasserted itself.

The school of economic history which now holds the field was not founded in a determination to reinstate the Industrial Revolution; and, indeed, its essentially distinctive character consists not in its conclusions but in its methods. What it found wanting in the older historiography was a lack of proper discrimination in selection of the elements with which an overall picture was built up, and a lack of scientific rigour in plotting the relationships between these elements. In place of a patch-work of random events it has sought to present an integrated whole whose elements stand in an objectively given relationship to one another. It has been an attempt to apply the laws of dynamic economics to data stripped of all shreds of value judgment: pure statistical data. While the endeavour to comprehend all available quantitative pheno-mena within models of the processes of economic change has not yet approached finality, and may well be ultimately abandoned, its essential preliminary, the collation of statistical series, has within the last fifteen years or so given us a measure for determining, not with pinpoint pre-cision but within pretty narrow limits, the timing and extent of gross economic changes in Britain from the early eighteenth century onwards. One may still very properly gib at some of the implications of the phrase 'Industrial Revolution', and even more at 'Agricultural Revolu-tion', but there can be no doubt that within the 1780s the British eco-nomy, quite suddenly, took off on a course of unprecedented develop-ment. Indeed in some ways the phenomenon now appears as even more revolutionary than it did to the classical historians. Preoccupied as they were with its technological aspects they saw it gathering momentum over some decades. Viewed under a gross quantitative aspect it seems to burst forth altogether unheralded. One recent historian[1] in place of the seventy years classically assigned to it has compressed it into the span 1783–1802, taking the view that by the later date it had created its own built-in dynamic and had then become self-sustaining.

Let us bare the statistical bones of the event by extending the series given in Table II.2 (p. 377) into the two decades succeeding 1785:

[1] W. W. Rostow, *The Stages of Economic Growth*, Cambridge University Press, 1960.

A HISTORY OF THE BRITISH ECONOMY

TABLE II.5. *Industrial growth rates 1785–1830: average annual percentage*

Industry	1785–95	1795–1805	(1785–1830)
Leather	1·50	0·25	0·75
Beer	1·75	0·00	0·50
Candles	1·00	2·00	1·75
Soap	3·00	2·00	2·50
Paper	2·00	2·00	2·50
Glass	2·50	1·25	2·00
Bricks (not available before 1785)	3·25	2·75	1·75
Cotton (production)*	5·25	8·50	6·25
Pig iron (production)*	8·00	7·00	5·50
Coal (uncertain)	?(2·00)	?(2·00)	?(2·25)
Population	1·0	1·1	1·3

* Not strictly comparable with the figures on p. 377 which relate to domestic consumption. The figures for cotton (production) would be 1740–85: 4; pre-1763: 1·75; post-1763: 6·5; and for pig iron (production) 1740–85: 1·75.

Much stress must be laid on the leather and beer figures, indicators that, after the initial decade, the participation of the working masses in the benefits of Revolution was minimal, even negative.[1] But despite this heavy qualification it may be said that the upper figures are in a way the most striking. With these commodities there is no question of important changes in technique. The conditions which their performance reflects were not peculiar to themselves but common to the economy at large. It is these figures, then, as much as the cotton and iron prodigies with their special explanations which afford the most valuable indication of abrupt and decisive development in the economy as a whole. Their absolute magnitude may not seem to some to warrant the epithet 'revolutionary'. They are, after all, certainly no better than any humdrum 'modern' economy achieves year in, year out. In a sense they vindicate the 'de-revolutionist' case. There is no sudden massive incre-

[1] More detailed figures would show that after the initial spurt consumption of leather and beer did not again exhibit any persistent increase until 1823.

ment revealed here. But what is revealed is the sudden onset of a steady unremitting overall annual growth of 2 per cent *plus*. That is the Revolution. Admittedly the analogy implied with political revolutions is very misleading; there was no immediate or even rapid substitution of one kind of economic regime for another. But at least if forced to choose between the words 'revolution' and 'evolution' the statistical evidence compels us to opt for 'revolution'. Three features in combination insist on this: the new growth rate, while not sensational, was almost certainly higher than that maintained through even the space of a single year at any earlier time; except for odd stretches, that growth rate was thereafter sustained for over a century; and its commencement followed on some two decades in which economic momentum was probably being lost.

On the other hand, concern to emphasise the special character of the course of economic development from *c*. 1785 should not lure one into drawing excessively bold boundary lines. The notion of a relatively short period during which the economy became so constituted that growth thereafter was 'self-sustaining' is central to any understanding of the process of continuous growth; without that notion we are forced to postulate a fantastic freak of chance: a succession of autonomous 'revolutions'. That saving notion, crudely represented, demonstrates to us an initial expansion phase building up to 'full' employment[1] and a high level of demand, impelling further productive investment, in turn jacking up the level of demand and exerting additional pressure on resources and so on indefinitely. This kind of account does show how investment, a key economic variable, is kept constantly in play once ample opportunities for it have been initially afforded. What it does not purport to show is how the level of technical knowhow is continuously raised to provide ever fresh opportunities for productive investment – or, put another way, how rising demand can, under 'full' employment conditions, be steadily met with rising output instead of being left to burn itself out in inflation.

The specific discipline of the economists, subsuming developments in productive techniques, can single out the couple of decades or so from *c*. 1785 as being of a peculiarly decisive character and can regard

[1] Not in the literal sense of every employable person being in employment but in the sense that many employers find it difficult to recruit extra labour – a situation compatible with a high unemployment rate, especially in conditions of low labour mobility, occupational or geographical. And, given the cyclic character of free enterprise economies, it is not a matter of permanent 'full' employment but of a fairly regular succession of 'full' employment situations.

the general direction taken by the economy thereafter as given; but the course of technical advance, obviously of more accidental and uncertain character, requires one to think in terms of a series of jerks, denying an utterly distinctive nature to any one phase and denying also an absolute inevitability to the path of nineteenth- and twentieth-century economic growth. In historical progression these jerks were similar to those by which a motor car is propelled, merging to make for fairly smooth uniform motion. While one must allow something to mere coincidence this is rather what one would expect, both because of the cumulative character of technical advance and because of the evident relationship between investment and demand levels and technical progress. More obviously, the technical side of the growth process requires the years, the decades and the centuries preceding the Revolution to be admitted within its pale. Nobody would pretend that it emerged out of a technological and cultural wilderness.

This last point brings us indeed to the verge of a near contradiction. We have already urged that it is in the contrast with the dullness of the previous couple of decades, among other things, that the record of these years stakes its claim to revolution. Yet it was in those same dull decades that much of the basis of revolution was laid. In fact, apprehended as a set of inventions the Revolution was already in being at the outset of this period. As seen in the last chapter the textile machinery, the iron-making techniques, the rotary acting steam engine, in their essentials were already on the scene. And, extending the scope a bit, much had already been effected towards the elaboration of a national network and a greatly improved internal transport system while the size of the mercantile fleet had been substantially enlarged. Agriculture had also started to show signs of responding effectively to the needs of a growing population. What now happened that this potential, which hitherto had probably not even been able to keep pace with population, suddenly precipitated itself into a wave of unprecedented growth? A fine sweeping question seeking a fine sweeping answer. We must start soon to climb down from the comfortable grandeur of generalisation. But although a complete answer to the question can only be looked for in many particular quarters we may briefly continue to take a bird's eye view.

Certain factors stand out prominently. Most specifically, as the figures already cited suggest, the tremendous development of the cotton and iron industries played a very considerable part, both directly, by making available important classes of goods at greatly lowered real costs (meaning that more of these goods could be enjoyed or more of other goods could be bought with the purchasing power thus released), and indirectly, through the impact of investment in these rapidly expanding industries on the general level of demand; the more they grew the more sensible their impact. More generally, from the return to normal peace-time conditions in 1785 to the outbreak of war with France in 1793, low interest rates, undisturbed international trading conditions, the absence of serious financial crises and a run of good harvests conspired to create a sequence of favourably circumstanced years such as had not been enjoyed since before the Seven Years War. Even the early stages of the French Wars, after a sharp but short financial panic, had scant economic consequences until the desperately bad harvest of 1795 and the mounting scale of the war brought new and, in certain respects, difficult circumstances into operation. Twinning these two sets of factors – technological revolution in the cotton and iron industries and a generally auspicious economic climate – we are confronted with a fortuitous conjuncture which could warrant singling out 1785 for special mention in a way which the fluid nature of economic processes rarely permits. In that year the government substantially completed funding the debts incurred during the American War and interest rates started decisively downwards. In the same year Richard Arkwright lost his tenacious hold on the water frame. And 1785 was the year succeeding Henry Cort's patenting of his rolling process, itself coming on the heels of his own puddling method and the provision of a rotary acting steam engine which in combination constituted the revolution in the production of bar iron.

We must, however, get closer to the grass-roots if the course of economic change both in its revolutionary aspects and in its staider aspects is to be seen in proper perspective. The cotton industry virtually selects itself as the first sector to be scrutinised more closely.

The cotton industry

Cotton's growth rate over the first two decades has already been stated but the record of the initial few years is worth registering in more detail. Table II.6 spells out the astonishing momentum with which the industry developed through the second half of the 1780s. These were the years in which the industry was essentially transformed from one supplying mixed cotton and linen materials into one providing pure cotton articles – a transformation to be attributed to the proliferation of water frames, exploiting the avenues already pioneered so profitably by Arkwright, and to the rapid spread of Samuel Crompton's mule. The mule, like the water frame, spun good quality warp thread. In fact it could spin an even finer thread than the water frame – fine enough for the industry to extend its range to muslins hitherto beyond the

TABLE II.6. *Consumption of raw cotton 1784–92*[1] *(000,000 lb)*

1784	1785	1786	1787	1788	1789	1790	1791	1792
11	18	19	22	20	32	31	28	33

scope of any British manufacturer. A very extensive range of materials could then be offered, woven from yarn whose low costs enabled these materials both to mount a devastating invasion of the market areas of other textiles and, most particularly towards the cheaper end of the range, to create entirely new sales opportunities.

The huge preponderance of the output of these early years was actually concentrated at this cheaper end. Not only did weaving techniques have to be adapted to produce marketable muslins of high quality but, more important, raw cotton of the kind required for such work was hard to come by – West Indian cotton being fairly coarse. Thus the mule's potential could not be fully exploited yet and it is impossible to say which of the two spinning machines contributed the most to the tremendous initial upthrust. The evident fact that the two coexisted for some years would indicate a rough cost parity between them. However, effective comparison, either contemporary or retrospective, would be difficult. Crompton's machine was hand-driven. It could replace the jenny in the homes of spinners just as the jenny itself had earlier replaced the spinning-wheel; and although it was more elaborate than the jenny it still did not necessitate a heavy capital outlay. The costs of domestic mule spinning, that is to say, consisted very largely of labour and materials. Water frame costs on the other hand included substantial fixed elements: the machinery itself, the motive water-power equipment, the factory premises. At a time when cost accounting techniques were only rudimentary, the calculation of unit costs was bound to be somewhat arbitrary. In all probability, a water frame factory pushed in scale

[1] Strictly, imports less re-exports – i.e. no account is taken of changes in stock levels, which largely explains the wobbling 1789–92.

to the limits of increasing returns operated at lower unit costs than domestic mule spinning. But few if any concerns had yet developed to that extent. And further factors complicate strict cost comparison. The two machines were not frozen in design. Minor modifications were continually improving them, especially by increasing the number of spindles. Again, at a time when profit opportunities were opening up so rapidly, a 'manufacturer'[1] could reap the whirlwind much more expeditiously by converting an existing domestically based enterprise from jennies to mules than by establishing a water frame business, with the delays and problems of labour recruitment which that would involve.

And these were only some of the deterrents to founding a factory concern. The difficulties posed in labour recruitment have further implications. Domestic spinning was integrated with a household economy; no time was lost travelling to and from work; the task could be taken up and put down as inclination or other commitments dictated. Even when domestic spinners had been induced, or compelled by financial necessity, to take to factory employment the work rhythm of generations was not readily broken. Absenteeism, irregular timekeeping, the lack of a suitably conditioned class of supervisors could mean crippling losses when valuable plant was underemployed. (Widespread resort was had, notoriously, to children whose care had fallen on the Poor Law authorities. The parishes were pleased to get them off their hands – the fiction that they were being put out to apprenticeships preserved the legal forms – and factory owners welcomed a labour force which was theirs to mould as they willed.)

If labour was one horn on which the early factory owner was apt to be impaled then fixed capital was the other. This was perhaps less a question of raising the requisite initial sum than of the hazards of sinking it in plant. Given that few of the factories were as yet very large, the man who started off in a small way was not uncompetitive. A hundred pounds of his own, supplemented by funds from friends or business acquaintances, might get him started, possibly in a converted corn mill which he only rented – to mention only one of the various expedients by which initial capital was economised. But, superadded to inexperience in the management of this kind of enterprise, was the danger of a recession during which the factory owner had to go on covering his fixed costs while his domestic counterpart could adjust costs as necessary

---

[1] In contemporary usage the equivalent in the cotton industry of the 'clothier' in the woollen industry, although in other contexts it more usually denoted the actual workers.

by cutting down on the numbers of spinners employed and on the amount of raw material purchased. Such a recession early struck the booming industry. The figures quoted in Table II.6 pinpoint it: 1788, the first clearcut historical instance of a crisis of overproduction. In the headlong rush to exploit the bonanza, the market had become temporarily glutted. Although there is no positive evidence on this point it is not improbable that the manufacturers running domestic enterprises came through this shakeout in better shape than the factory owners.

All in all, the wonder is not that domestic spinning continued for some while to coexist vigorously with factory spinning, but that factory spinning advanced as rapidly as it did. The 'nineties, especially the later 'nineties, saw the factories virtually sweep the board. The technical problems involved in powering the mule were overcome. Powered mules of a hundred, two hundred and even three and four hundred spindles became practicable. The economies of scale started to tell. Although pockets of domestic spinning survived into the 1820s, by the opening of the nineteenth century, a technological revolution, imposing a corresponding social revolution, had been substantially completed in what was by then a major sector of British industry.

The velocity of growth, which had slackened through the mid-'nineties, had been fully resumed and was maintained through the first decade of the new century. On top of the fresh wave of cost economies initiated by powered mule spinning, the industry was drawing substantial benefit from three other circumstances. From the later 1790s both the quantity and quality of raw cotton supplies were greatly enhanced by the large-scale cotton plantation in South Carolina and Georgia (followed at various intervals by Virginia, North Carolina, Tennessee, Louisiana, Alabama and Mississippi, all important suppliers by 1820). This in turn was stimulated in significant part by the development of the cotton gin, a mechanical device for separating the cotton from its seeds. Not only was the price of raw cotton materially reduced but the muslin spinners could now obtain as much fine cotton as they wanted. At the other end of the long processing train chlorine bleach supplanted natural bleaching effected by months of exposure to the sun, which was costly in terms of the capital tied up and of the acres required as bleach fields. The St Rollox works, near Glasgow, founded in 1799 to pioneer the commercial manufacture of chlorine powder, could be said to have launched the British chemical industry. Advances in manufacturing methods kept the price of bleach moving continually downwards through the remainder of this period.

Thirdly, operative right from the beginning of the period, was the considerable gain derived from the substitution of roller printing for plate printing in this final and expensive process. This was the most outstanding of many modifications in finishing (printing or dyeing) techniques whose importance in sum was perhaps not so much the economies effected as the improvements in quality and range of the colour patterns which were such an important selling point with cotton fabrics, intended as so many of them were for a feminine market spanning the whole income spectrum. These were specialist functions and one should not overlook the growth, alongside of the spinning factories, of printing and dyeing works, some of them representing very substantial capital investments. Textile printing, from its very beginning in the late seventeenth century, had been the first branch of the industry to be organised in 'factory' fashion and to experience the peculiar demands of capital intensiveness. Through the early years of this period its centre shifted decisively from London to Manchester where it preceded manufacturing proper as an important element in the storming growth of that town.

On the demand side the continuing growth of the 1790s and, more marked, of the 1800s was increasingly sustained by foreign markets. Graph II.2 illustrates the limited importance of overseas sales in the escalation of the later 'eighties. While total output nearly tripled, exports increased by less than a half and shared only proportionately in the general expansion of external trade. It was home demand for textiles of a novel cheapness which supplied the powerful initial boost. But the economy as a whole was not developing anything like so rapidly as the cotton industry. If left to depend on home demand the momentum of growth would soon have started to fall off and might very well have ceased altogether, with distinctly deadening effects on the growth tendencies of the economy at large. The graph shows export demand quickening in the early 'nineties and streaking upwards from the closing years of the century – shots in the arm for the British economy whose vital value it would be difficult to exaggerate. Between 1789 and 1802, by contrast with the initial phase, although total output did not quite double itself, exports increased sevenfold; and between 1802 and 1810, while output again just failed to double, exports increased some two and a half times. Since by 1802 exports may have accounted for over three-fifths of output, it is possible that the increased output of this last-mentioned period went entirely to foreign markets while home demand stood still, which it had perhaps been doing ever since the later 1790s.

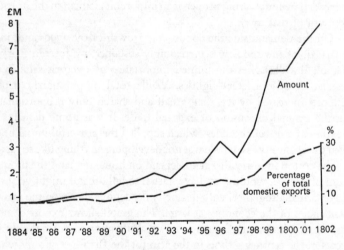

Exports of Cotton Goods

£M

Amount

Percentage
of total
domestic exports

1884 '85 '86 '87 '88 '89 '90 '91 '92 '93 '94 '95 '96 '97 '98 '99 1800 '01 1802

GRAPH II.2.

The exuberance of exports in the course of this phase enabled the cotton industry to arrive successively at two prominent landmarks, first out-stripping the woollen industry as Britain's leading exporter and then surpassing the same industry as Britain's leading manufacturer. On the dizzy peak of 1810, where it temporarily rested, the industry accounted for about 8 per cent of total national income and about a half of total domestic exports.

As might be expected, foreign buyers were found the most readily across the Atlantic where Indian calicoes and British cotton-linens had already prepared the market. Despite its much larger population, Europe took rather fewer cottons through these years of soaring exports. Ireland was early an important buyer but it was only from 1797 that substantial penetration of Continental markets commenced. From then on, ignoring for the moment setbacks occasioned by military and diplomatic vicissitudes, Continental sales were of gathering importance. And success on the Continent was a much more telling measure of the achievement of the British industry than success in trans-Atlantic regions which at best were only just embarking on the development of manufactures of their own. It checked, and then reversed, the dangerous tendency for Britain to become increasingly dependent externally on extra-European areas whose importing capacities for varying reasons – small populations, underdevelopment, difficulty of access – were as yet subject to fairly strict limits.

The cotton industry shared in the general difficulties experienced by the economy through the troubled decade 1811–21 and it was not until that latter year that output again started to climb beyond the point reached in 1810. In some degree the loss of growth momentum on the part of the cotton industry through this generally dull phase is to be explained by circumstances peculiar to itself. There was no further windfall gain from lowered raw material prices once United States supplies had swung into their stride. The potentialities of powered mule spinning and of new techniques in the final processes had been largely exploited. But there remained two wide paths of advance along which only a few hesitant steps had so far been taken: power-weaving and the use of the steam engine. Edmund Cartwright had produced an embryonic power loom in 1785. Steam power had first been applied to spinning machinery in the same year. Yet as late as 1820 the bulk of cotton cloth was still handwoven and the powered equipment in most spinning factories, bleaching, printing and dyeing works and such power loom concerns as there were was still driven by waterwheels. With 240,000 hand-loom weavers the industry employed well over half as many people again in purely manual operations as it did in tending powered ones.

Although there are more particular reasons, to be touched on, for the slow headway of the power loom and the steam engine, one general circumstance retarding their introduction was undoubtedly the slack conditions of the 1810s during which the industry had a great deal of surplus production capacity on hand; such may even have been the case from the very early years of the century notwithstanding the vigorous demand trend of the first decade – the years 1798–1803 had witnessed a tremendous mushrooming of new enterprises and enlargement of old ones. Unable to employ current resources fully, and with narrowed and often extinguished profit margins, entrepreneurs felt little incentive to invest in enhanced productivity. This, for quite specific reasons in the cases in question. If the situation worsened, hand-loom weavers could simply be turned off, but power looms one was stuck with in bad times; as for the steam engine, its economies grew, or only became effective, as its power was increased. Who was going to enlarge his output to accommodate a steam engine when he did not even sell as much as he could already produce with his existing equipment?

This last factor even under continuously buoyant market conditions would have inhibited the introduction of the steam engine. Lancashire and the Glasgow region were well endowed with good riverside sites for watermills. Up to quite a high point on the production scale, the large initial outlay and the fuel costs rendered a steam engine, comparatively speaking, uneconomic. And several circumstances conspired to limit severely the numbers of concerns developing beyond that point. Retained profits were for many the principal source of investment capital; they could grow no faster than their profits grew. Even where access could be had to adequate capital to sustain forced growth there would be apprehension lest a suddenly enlarged output might not find markets. There was safety in growing with the market rather than anticipating it when the consequence of misjudgment was not only unsold stocks but expensive equipment rusting idle. There would be problems of labour recruitment and indoctrination to be contended with. Something of a chicken and egg issue lurks here: rapid growth of large-scale concerns required a large standing pool of conditioned labour; such a pool was the creation of concentrations of large-scale concerns. All three points enumerated run back to the same ground: concern growth tended very much to be an organic function of general growth. Some concerns did break the ranks to forge away on their own. But among the numerous casualties of these early decades were not only small undercapitalised concerns falling victim to technical obsolescence but large steam-powered businesses which paid the penalty of trying to run before they could walk.

More specifically technical factors played a big part in holding up the introduction of the power loom. In design and construction the

early looms were crude, clumsy and difficult to operate without breaking the yarn. Cartwright's original model was no more than a monstrous
curiosity of no commercial value. Although it was fairly soon improved
on and from the 1790s some power-weaving concerns were being
established, it was not until about 1815 that the technical problems were
really satisfactorily overcome and even then a quarter of a century and
more elapsed before the hand loom had been largely displaced.

That Cartwright's loom had not gone the way of many similarly
ingenious but impracticable contrivances of earlier times, to conclude
its history in the footnotes of antiquarian treatises, is itself a measure of
a changed economic and technological milieu. On the other hand, its
very laggardly intrusion into the industry even when improved is plain
evidence that there was no acute need of it. There was entrepreneurial
progressiveness enough to sustain an interest in it. More importantly
perhaps, there was a steady accumulation of practical experience and
skills in the specific field of textile engineering, such that technical
progress less and less depended on individual visionaries and more and
more on the continuous build-up of the work of everyday mechanics.
Ideas which in former times might have perished for want of competent
attention to points of detail could be kept alive until fully translated
into practicability. The power loom was then, so to speak, kept ticking
over until a favourable conjuncture of circumstances galvanised it into
thrustful activity.

One could not attempt to say how the technical difficulties involved
in powering the loom compared with those involved in powering the
mule. But there can be little doubt that a comparison of the sixty-odd
years elapsing between Cartwright's invention and generalised power-
weaving with the twenty years or so between Crompton's inventions
and generalised powered spinning would greatly exaggerate the purely
technical issue. Even with better versions of the power loom becoming
available, the incentive to take to it was much less sharp than had been the
case with the powered mule. Even potentially, powered weaving had
not anything like the cost advantage over hand-weaving that powered
spinning had over hand-spinning. The fact can be crudely understood in
this way: in the case of spinning, power both speeded up the operation
and multiplied the number of lengths of yarn spun simultaneously; in
the case of weaving, power could do no more than speed up the operation of weaving a single piece of cloth of standard width. Given the
capital cost of the looms and of the motive equipment power-weaving
did not necessarily work out any cheaper than hand-weaving. And as

costs gradually fell with the modification of the power loom and the growth of power-weaving concerns to the point where they started to enjoy significant economies of scale, particularly in respect of the steam engine, hand loom weavers contrived to remain competitive by tolerating slow wage erosion. Hand-spinning, drastically undercut, had a relatively quick and painless death. Hand-weaving was murdered with the refinement of the practised torturer.

One uses such terms deliberately. For several decades the continuously deteriorating living standards of the hand loom weavers was a vile running sore in a society which was accumulating wealth as never before. And by a savage irony the hand loom weavers had briefly been the aristocrats of labour. The great upsurge of the later 'eighties had exerted tremendous pressure on weaving capacity. Wages had spiralled upwards to lure weavers from other textiles and people of all kinds from other occupations in order that the commercial opportunities presented by cheap cotton yarn might be exploited. The movement bred its own reaction. With growth temporarily tapering off in the mid-'nineties the numbers by then drawn into cotton weaving were more than adequate and wages slumped back to or below normal levels. What is curious is that from then on weavers' wages far from recovering in subsequent boom phases steadily fell through good times and bad.

This is one of the most puzzling phenomena thrown up by the Industrial Revolution. From c. 1820 one may invoke the power loom as a prime factor. But the trend is manifest from 1793 – long before power can be cited as an agent. Through a quarter of a century of falling wages the numbers of hand loom weavers grew – proof positive that the power loom was not engendering redundancy. It further follows that not only do we have the question: why did wages fall while the demand for labour rose? But also: why did so many continue for so long to enter into and endure a life of such degradation? Even in the later years when power-weaving was making rapid headway, this question still poses itself, for it was not until the early 1830s that the numbers of hand loom weavers actually started to decline. Clearly we are confronted with a form of occupational immobility and of a hopelessly weak bargaining position. Equally clearly it is not of a simple, straightforward kind, not a case of men grown too old in one trade to turn to another. In some part of course it reflects the lack of alternative occupations in the cotton districts, given over heavily as they were to the one activity. In some part too it possibly reflects the extent of employment opportunities for women and children in cotton; a man might better himself by moving elsewhere but total family income might suffer from the move. The intense competitiveness within the industry once the first wave of cost reductions had broken open new markets might also explain a peculiar determination on the part of 'manufacturers' to cut wage costs, though this implicitly involves a total rejection of the supply and demand theory of wages when applied to long-run wage movements. Irish immigrants, accustomed to lower living standards, could be allowed some role in facilitating the establishment of lower wage norms.

But this is all very conjectural and, in any event, is to drift away from the central theme here. From a clinically commercial point of view, it did not matter in the short run whether weaving costs were cut by taking to power or by reducing weavers to beggarliness. In the long run it did matter. Depressed wages meant depressed demand. Foreign markets could be captured by wage economies but sustained growth ultimately depended on increased purchasing power at home, that is on raising the productivity of labour, not on squeezing its reward. It mattered in another sense too. As long as hand-weaving remained competitive the incentive to develop the potential of the power loom was dulled and advance was slower than it need have been.

Under a technological aspect two fairly distinct 'revolutions' can, then, be plotted in the cotton industry through this period: the one founded on spinning machinery, water power and on advances in the final processes; the other founded on the steam engine and power-weaving. And this delineation can be fitted quite closely with the statistically given picture of two long-run growth phases separated by the years 1811-21. This staging meant that the cotton industry did not expend its peculiar dynamic in one burst. It was not until *c*. 1845 that its 'super' growth rate (6 per cent *plus* p.a.) became a merely 'normal' one (2-3 per cent p.a.).[1] Put another, and rather oversimplified, way: it was not until *c*. 1845 that the cotton industry from being a leading agent of general economic growth became a mere participant in it.

The second 'revolution' begins with the strong general recovery in 1821 from the postwar difficulties. The years 1821-25 witnessed a level of investment expenditure in cotton to which there had been no sort of precedent since 1798-1803. The most significant outcome of this wave of investment was an appreciable growth in concern size – not so much at the very top of the scale where there were already to be found a few

[1] Amongst other things, this is to say that the terminal date chosen for this period generally, 1830, has no particular significance for the cotton industry.

egregious giants with over a thousand employees, but in the 200–800 employee range which thickened out while smaller concerns were vanishing, or becoming larger. In this range steam was an economic proposition. Existing water-powered concerns which shied at the initial costs of steam, and which had effectively written off their capital costs, still had plenty of life in them. But they were condemning themselves to ultimate extinction by refusing to convert, or by failing to grow to the point where it was economic to convert. The newly founded concerns of these years were almost entirely steam-powered, and housed in specially designed premises; and it was to them and to those established concerns which had taken the plunge, scrapping not only motive plant but often unsuitable premises as well, that the future belonged. Gone were the days when an enterprising fellow might take over an old corn mill with three men and a boy and hope to prosper. The general economic setback of 1825–26, shortlived as it was, probably wreaked much havoc among those concerns which had not modernised over the preceding four years or so. Although it was not until c. 1840 that these closely interwoven trends – concern growth and adoption of steam-power – could be said to have finalised themselves, it would already have been difficult to recognise in the industry of 1830 that of 1820.

The number of powered weaving factories would have been one of the most striking changes. Although, as indicated already, there were still as many domestic hand-weavers at the end of the 1820s as there were at the beginning, the whole of the increase in cloth output was, in effect, achieved with power looms. ('In effect', because hand loom weavers increased their output of finer cloths for which the power loom was least suitable, but lost coarser work to the factories.) No direct measure is available, but it is probably approximately correct to say that at the beginning of the decade a third of cotton cloth was power-woven; and that at the end two-thirds, of a doubled amount, was power-woven.

The multiplication of powered weaving establishments is of course to be closely associated with the invasion of the industry by steam and the growing predominance of larger production units. In many cases the association was especially intimate. Large steam-powered spinning concerns extended their activities to weaving. We lack sufficiently detailed information, but it may well have been by way of this kind of vertical expansion rather than by the transformation of domestically based enterprises into factory ones that power made most headway. However, it would certainly be wrong to present any stereotype. Some spinning concerns were already employers of out-weavers. There always had been a few hand loom 'factories'. And many power-weaving concerns were entirely fresh creations, though among their founders were owners of spinning or finishing factories, hand-weaving 'manufacturers', cloth and yarn merchants as well as those who had no previous connection with the industry. Although the repeal of the Bubble Act in 1825 removed any legal necessity to employ the device of interlocking partnerships, which had earlier given rise to great ramified undertakings like those of the Arkwrights and the Peels, unitary ownership of several distinct works by an individual or a company remained uncommon. The industrialist who had one enterprise of his own and was a partner in several others did not overnight become a rarity, but it would probably be true that at any time the typical cotton works was a one man or one family affair with, particularly in the case of larger ones, one or two employees of managerial status sometimes admitted as partners.

The cost economies achieved through this last decade had somewhat similar effects to those of the years immediately succeeding 1785. Although the new wave of economies was not quite as remarkable as the earlier one and did not engender the same extraordinary spurt in domestic purchases, the 'twenties did see home demand growing strongly for the first time since the previous century and this accounted about equally with foreign demand for the enlarged output of the decade. Exports, having taken as much as four-fifths of output in the rather unreal circumstances following the end of the war, had dropped back to a little over a half by 1821. Of these perhaps a half were now going to Europe and a rather lesser fraction across the Atlantic, where the United States had started to meet part of her own requirements in the coarser kinds of cottons, while the rate of economic growth in the West Indies was slackening off. In absolute terms, however, sales to the United States and to the West Indies still showed an upward tendency and were powerfully supplemented by opportunities in Latin America. Asia, through the 'twenties, was also becoming a market of some marginal weight. Between well diversified markets and the commercial strength of the new style larger concerns, and with the relatively heavy capital outlay of 1821–25 behind it, the cotton industry as a whole, from the restoration of normal conditions after the general depression of 1825–26 through to the grave crisis of 1847, enjoyed what were probably the happiest years of its life in terms of the profit return to capital.

One final consequence of the decisive intrusion of steam should be touched on. The industry from its earliest times had had a very strong regional character. Although odd outposts had been located elsewhere it had always been heavily concentrated in south-east Lancashire. In the 1760s, however, the need for more hands had caused the spinning side of it to extend into northern Lancashire, part of Westmorland and, more especially, into Cheshire, Derbyshire, Nottinghamshire and Flintshire. In these areas too were located quite a number of the water-powered mills, suitable riverside sites being as frequent as in the original core area, though proximity to Liverpool made that area specially attractive. Steam rapidly reconcentrated the industry in its homelands, fortuitously situated in or on the edges of the south Lancashire coalfield. In fact steam led to even more intensive bunching. Factories which had been strung out along watercourses, often in the open countryside, could now cluster entirely in towns with their better commercial facilities and easier labour situation.

An essentially similar history was that of a secondary cotton region which had only been in its infancy at the beginning of this period. In the Glasgow region cotton had been mixed with a little of the linen which was its staple product from the late 1760s. The freeing of the water frame in 1785 led to swift development of a pure cotton industry. Widely scattered through Lanarkshire and Renfrewshire and even more distant counties through the water-power era, it fell back on Clydeside at the same time as the English industry was pulling its outriders back into south-east Lancashire, though Dundee, drawing on sea-borne coal, remained quite an important centre.

In quitting the industry for the while in 1830 then, we are leaving it well defined, though not yet completely, by those broad features of technique, organisation and geography by which it is best known.

The woollen industry

We have earlier noted that in the opening years of the nineteenth century the industrial premiership of Britain passed from wool to cotton. And to some extent the history of one was bound to be the obverse of the history of the other. They were in part competing in the same game in which if one gained ground the other must have lost it. Cotton also contended in fields both at home and abroad where wool had no place, and won sales at the expense of linen and silk or of foreign cotton manufacturers – notably the Indian calico makers; and there was a considerable further extent to which the success of cotton was due to the creation of entirely new markets as it slashed costs. Nevertheless there is a plain causal connection between the fact that the cotton industry increased its output some fourteenfold over this period and the fact that the woollen industry was only about three-quarters larger again in 1830 than it had been in 1785. After discounting for population growth, this means that *per capita* output had hardly increased at all, notwithstanding forty-five years of progress. The woollen industry had had to do a good deal of running just to stay in the same place.

The pace of technical change in the woollen industry certainly did not rival that of its dynamic cotton rival. As in earlier years, this is to be largely explained by the fact that wool was less suitable for mechanical handling and by the much more restricted market scope of an industry which had already fully penetrated potential sales areas. In the latter respect this is to say again that limited growth prospects were cause as well as consequence of relatively slow technical advance. Indeed, most of the broad characteristics of the industry's history through these years remain those already dwelt on in the previous chapter: modest overall growth; largely stagnant overseas sales; laggardly technical imitation of the cotton industry; gain of the West Riding over other centres, associated with greater technical progressiveness there. A fairly brief summary of the features and developments peculiar to these years will therefore suffice to carry the industry through to 1830, when it could be said to have been on the verge of breaking into new ground.

On the demand side the most favourable factor was the recovery of the United States market after the American War. Throughout this period the nascent American industry was badly handicapped by the lack of good native wool. With the restoration of normal commercial intercourse the USA had immediately established itself as the biggest single importer of British woollen goods and while in the southern states it was soon British cottons which were making the most headway, the more rapidly growing northern states ensured that roughly a third of all British woollen exports regularly found an American market through the whole of this period – the years of Anglo-American hostilities aside. The big spurt in American sales had by the 1790s thrust woollen exports back up to the level attained in 1760 but after reaching a peak in 1801 they slipped back a bit and thereafter ran only fractionally above their earlier high tide mark, so that such further growth as the industry achieved was entirely on the basis of home demand.

The West Riding was the principal beneficiary of the reopening of the American market which along with the generally auspicious economic climate must be reckoned a chief factor in what would seem to have been a fairly intensive phase of retooling in Yorkshire through the first fifteen years or so of this period. The flying shuttle very soon finalised its conquest of worsteds weaving and once initiated into woollens weaving rapidly took over in that field also. The jenny likewise soon displaced such spinning wheels and distaffs as were still in use. Powered carding for woollens yarn established itself, enabling this processing stage to keep pace with jenny spinning. (But attempts at powered combing, for worsteds yarn, made little headway.) An intermediary bottleneck between these two stages was overcome in the 1790s with the slubbing billy.[1] Towards the other end of the manufacturing train mechanical shearing (trimming the surface of the woven cloth), dating from the early 1790s, was taking over from the skilled and keenly craft-conscious hand shearers.

All in all, the West Riding industry had by the opening years of the nineteenth century undergone a fairly radical technical transformation; and it could be said that up to that point in time the rate of technical change, given that it was rather later in getting under way, had roughly vied with that achieved in the cotton industry. But thereafter advance proceeded much more slowly and the development gap between Lancashire and Yorkshire textiles grew steadily wider. It was in the use of power that the two differed most markedly. Powered spinning, first experimented with in the late 1780s, was not yet in universal use in 1830 even for the more manageable worsteds yarn. The first attempts at powered weaving date from the 1790s but the great bulk of worsteds and virtually all woollens were still being hand woven by the end of the period. And while Lancashire through the 1820s was swinging decisively to steam, such power as was used in the West Riding remained very largely water-generated.

One distinctive consequence of this halting and limited technological record was that the organisational structure of the West Riding industry remained a very mixed and varied one through the whole of this period, containing elements of the 'factory system', the 'small master system' and the 'clothier system', both independently of one another and interlocked with one another. At one extreme there was Benjamin Gott's Bean Ing Mill (near Leeds) set up in 1792 and at the end of the period employing more than a thousand workers on the premises, using powered equipment over the whole range of processes in the manufac-

[1] Slubbing is a loose spinning process preparatory to spinning proper.

ture of both woollens and worsteds. But even Bean Ing undertook a form of work which was very characteristic of the mixed nature of the West Riding industry as a whole: commission work for small independent manufacturers – in this case shearing and fulling their cloth. Commission fulling was of course an anciently established practice and many of the early carding mills conducted a similar kind of business. Sometimes these water-powered fulling and carding undertakings constituted the nuclei of more extensive manufacturing establishments as power slowly spread to other processes. On the other hand 'factories' could precede power: the industry had always known establishments in which a manual labour force was employed on the master's premises.

Towards the end of the period the normal type of factory was one whose central activity was powered spinning, along with powered carding in the less common case of woollens spinning. But in earlier years such factories as there were were of a very variegated nature. Some did commission work. Apart from carding and fulling concerns, specialist bleaching and dyeing establishments were particular types becoming more common as techniques in these fields became more sophisticated. Some undertook preliminary processes on materials which might then be 'put out' to domestic workers or might be sold outright; and some reversed this order, undertaking later processes on materials which had first been 'put out' or were simply purchased in a semiprocessed state. Some again combined these different kinds of operations in various ways. Even the spinning factories of the later years were not at all uniform in the nature of their business. Some maintained looms – hand or power operated – on the premises to weave up their own yarn. Bean Ing, as seen, provides a rare instance of a fully integrated concern. More probably employed outworkers on their yarn. Others again just sold the yarn, perhaps to weaving factories, perhaps to masters employing a force of outworkers, perhaps to independent weavers.

To essay much more than this summary survey of the West Riding industry would be to get lost in a welter of multifarious detail. It will really suffice if it leaves an impression of an industry alive to new technical opportunities but denied such market prospects as to prompt a truly revolutionary rate of response, of an industry feeling rather than forging its way towards profound reorganisation. Most of the major problems encountered along that path have already been touched on earlier in one context or another: the nature of the raw material, questions of labour and of capital, the issues involved in a growth in concern size. They need not be repeated here. But, while insisting that the most significant difference between the circumstances of the cotton and woollen industries was that of potential markets, two further respects in which the woollen industry was at a comparative disadvantage should be pointed out. First, as a much older and more deeply rooted industry the weight of human resistance to technical and organisational change was much greater, whether as simple conservative attachment to established habits or, more potently, as fear of loss of livelihoods. (In the latter respect one comes back eventually to the question of potential markets. With its rate of expansion, the cotton industry required many more hands even while effecting substantial labour economies: the woollen industry had not the remotest prospect of achieving a comparable growth rate.) These sentiments played particularly vigorously in an industry accustomed to the tender care and attention of the state. For some two centuries any cry of distress from woollen-cloth workers had been assured of a sympathetic hearing in the highest councils of the kingdom. The clothworkers deceived themselves, however, in looking for state support in the changing economic conditions of these years. Their petitions went unheeded, and when they invoked the Elizabethan Statute of Artificers in their defence Parliament responded by repealing it (1812, 1813).

The second point at which the woollen industry was disadvantageously placed by comparison with the cotton industry was that of raw material supply. The woollen industry, by contrast with the cotton industry, depended heavily on home supplies, obviously incapable of elastic expansion in the manner of American cotton, the more particularly at a time when rising population was exerting competing pressures on agricultural resources. By the end of the period about a fifth of wool requirements were being met by imports (compared with about a fiftieth at the beginning); but the enormous bulk of these were coming from Europe whose own capacity as a wool producer was subject to the same sort of limitations as obtained in Britain. Australian supplies had started to figure but were as yet of marginal importance. (It could of course be argued with some plausibility that had the British woollen industry grown more rapidly Australian sheep farming would have developed more rapidly also – i.e. that the condition would have engendered its own cure.)

It remains to say something of the shifting balance between the West Riding and the other woollen cloth centres. Between 1785 and 1800, already distinguished as a phase of rapid technical change in the

Yorkshire industry, West Riding output perhaps doubled. Over the same period total national output may have increased by a little more than a half, possibly not as much. This probably signifies that in absolute terms the other areas combined succeeded in holding their own and even experienced slight overall growth. But that aggregate record would seem to have been compounded of a real loss to Yorkshire on the part of the worsted manufacturers of Norwich, of Suffolk and Essex and of Devonshire and quite a marked recovery by the woollens manufacturers, especially those of Gloucestershire who from the 1790s were particularly forward in imitating West Riding use of carding machinery, jennies, flying shuttles and shearing machines. Even in woollens, however, the West Riding was pulling away, and by 1800 it must certainly have surpassed any other single county, while its output of worsteds exceeded that of the rest of the country put together. Over the next couple of decades, while gross national output remained more or less static, the West Riding continued to enlarge its share of the worsteds trade but made no further serious inroads into the fields of the West Country woollens makers, who through these years established a rough technical parity with their Yorkshire rivals. The better market conditions of the 1820s brought a further spurt ahead by the West Riding but Gloucestershire at least maintained a strong competitive position, concentrating on the better quality cloths and keeping in step with the West Riding in the cautious introduction of powered spinning for high grade woollens yarns.

At the end of the period, then, West Country woollens though reduced to a decidedly secondary role were by no means on the point of exhaustion, thus contrasting sharply with the situation of worsted manufacturers everywhere outside Yorkshire who had never in any number succeeded in shortening the technical lead early established by the West Riding in this field and, principally through the 1820s, steadily built on through the adoption of power for spinning.

Other textiles

The linen industry took its first step towards technological revolution in 1787 when John Kendrew and Thomas Porthouse, jointly, devised a powered machine for flax spinning, which was quickly taken up in the Leeds district, notably by John Marshall whose business soon became not only the biggest in the linen industry but one of the most considerable of all contemporary enterprises. But the Marshall concern, like nearby Bean Ing in the woollen industry, was exceptional rather than characteristic. The Kendrew and Porthouse machine could only spin the coarsest of yarns; and the modest overall growth of the industry, at the expense of imported linen, continued for some three decades to depend heavily on cheap hand-spun Irish and Continental yarn. From the late 1810s, however, new methods of preparing the flax and modifications of the spinning machine were enabling the range of powered spinning to be gradually extended to finer yarns; and although the fragility of linen yarn continued to defy all but experimental efforts at powered weaving, the quantity of linen cloth exported,[1] much of it to the USA, more than doubled between 1816 and 1830, when linen exports were equivalent to about one-ninth of cotton exports. The crude indications are that over the same years linen, in relative terms, won back parts of the home market earlier lost to cotton. One side effect of the progress in powered spinning unparalleled in weaving was the reversal of the yarn flow across the Irish Sea, cheap machine-spun yarn, mostly from the West Riding, now travelling to the low wage domestic hand weavers of Ireland – and, for a while, to those of Scotland, which was a little laggardly in adopting mechanical spinning.

For much of this period the silk industry only edged forward. But the powerful general economic upsurge of the 1820s and the return it yielded to the better off engendered growth of 'revolutionary' dimensions: between 1819 and 1830 the output of the British silk industry would seem to have increased some two and a half times (representing an annual average growth rate of *c.* 8 per cent). It was a moneyed market which provided the base for this advance. Cost reduction had little hand in it. Throwing had already been revolutionised and only a few hardy experimenters tried weaving silk fabrics on power looms. However, technological transformation quite plainly did play an important part in winning new custom. In 1820 the Jacquard machine (a French invention of 1801) was introduced into England. This was perhaps the most sophisticated of all of the new pieces of technology of this inventive age, and it is not without significance that it was of French rather than British origin. It can be described as the first – and very precocious – instance of automation. It was an apparatus, working on a punched card principle, for attachment to a loom. By initial selection of the appropriate cards, a weaver, using variously coloured yarns, could, while operating his loom in the ordinary way, produce any pre-

---

[1] Including exports of Irish cloth, which between 1816 and 1825 accounted for about a third of the total (no information available for later years).

designed pattern. Its contribution was to make practicable an intricacy and variety of design which hitherto could not have been contemplated,[1] and thus to add greatly to the customer allure of silk goods.

It was in these 1820s years that the silk industry made something of a move northwards. Spitalfields retained the market for the most luxurious fabrics. (The repeal, in 1826, of the prohibition on imports partially re-exposed it to foreign, particularly French, competition but tariffs continued to afford a substantial measure of protection.) The plainer, but still of course expensive, silk goods were, however, increasingly being taken up in the established throwing centres in Derby and Macclesfield and adjoining towns; Manchester was cultivating a silk industry as a minor adjunct to cotton; and Coventry was building up quite a substantial business in ribbons and the like.

If we come to assess the overall welfare gain deriving directly from progress in the textile industries through this period, it is needful to keep certain considerations in mind. One is that the last process of all remained quite unchanged. No cost economies were brought to bear on the tailoring and dressmaking trades. The reduction in price to the final user was not wholly proportionate to the reduction in the cost of cloth. Secondly, and more important, the benefits arising from cheap cotton cloth were only available for certain kinds of fabric use. Given the British climate, wool, achieving much less marked cost reductions, remained essential for many purposes. Indeed in terms of money expenditure, wool continued to hold the leading position in the home market. Very approximately, the ratios of domestic spending on the principal textiles moved as follows:

	Wool	Cotton (incl. cotton-linens)	Linen	Silk
c. 1785	6	3	3	1
c. 1830	6	4	3	2

This mode of representation, of course, obscures the great increase in

[1] Figured weaving had always been possible by dint of re-setting the loom. But its laboriousness had usually confined it to fairly simple patterns. The Jacquard machine could of course be used with any fabric. But in practice its expense restricted it to high value fabrics.

the amount of cotton cloth that could be purchased for any given sum, but it does draw out the extent of that sector of the textiles market which cotton could never aspire to secure. Nevertheless, even when some of the more dramatic implications of the momentous record of the cotton industry are discounted by these considerations, it still remains evident that this period engendered a signal improvement in mass clothing standards. The proportion of national income expended on textiles perhaps rose from about 12 per cent to around 18 per cent. In technical terms, the demand for cloth was obviously elastic, in more everyday terms, a large section of the populace which previously had had to make do with hand-downs, secondhand clothing, worn and tattered garments, once given the opportunity to clothe itself cheaply and decently, seized it eagerly. We are confronted not just with a simple substitution of new clothes for old but with a substantial shift in consumer preferences, a recomposition of the basic elements of popular living standards. The 'revolution' with which we have just dealt was no less a consumers' revolution than a producers' one.

If we move from the textile industries to the metallurgical industries, we are drawing away from the consumer. The departure is by no means total. We are still in an age when a significant proportion of metal output ended up in the household in the form of utensils and ornaments. But a greater proportion went into producers' goods, and it was that proportion which increased with especial rapidity through these years. The direct benefit of cost reduction in the shape of cheaper pots and pans etc. was not negligible, but if any crucial importance is to be attached to metallurgical advance it is of a much more diffuse kind, filtered to the consumer through such a variety of channels that he would be little aware of it. And in some fields the consumer gains were only of a long-term nature; while the military advantages might be said to have had no welfare value at all. In terms of their immediate consequences, then, there is a big difference between the two truly 'revolutionary' industries of this period: cotton and iron.

The iron industry

The last chapter brought iron to the very threshold of revolution – a revolution which is largely contained in the one word: coal. The implications of puddling and rolling in conjunction with coke smelting and the use of steam power have already been spelt out. They are translated into statistical achievement in Table II.7.

TABLE II.7. *Pig iron output, 1788–1830 (000 tons)*

1788	1796	1806	1823	1830
68	125	244	455	677

Over the whole period this yields a growth remarkably similar to that achieved by the cotton industry: about thirteenfold[1] compared with cotton's fourteenfold. And in broad terms the rhythm of growth is also similar: astonishing momentum in the very early years; a duller phase (the lack of data between 1806 and 1823 makes it impossible to locate this precisely, the probability is that a high growth rate was sustained until 1815, followed by quite a severe setback); and a very vigorous participation in the general economic upsurge from 1821 onwards. Thus the impact on the economy at large of investment in these two pace-setting industries was very closely coupled; coupled, particularly in the early years, not so much by common circumstances, as by the mere coincidence of simultaneous opportunities supplied by major technological breakthroughs.

This close resemblance between the behaviour patterns of the two industries hides an important difference. The cotton industry, as seen, was sustained by a succession of distinct cost-reducing phenomena, strung out along the course of the years and fairly continuously re-moulding the organisation of the industry. In its essentials the shape of the iron industry in 1830, and indeed even in 1860, was that which had already been fashioned in the first decade or two of this period with the introduction of Cort's equipment into forges, the accelerated conversion of blast furnaces to coke smelting and the application of steam power to blast generation, rolling, hammering, slitting and other ancillary operations. These developments could be effected the more easily since the organisational structure of the industry did not have to be adapted to accommodate them; in this sector, which had long since inclined to relatively large and heavily capitalised units of production, there was no problem of transition from domestic to factory enterprises, such as the textile industries had to contend with.

There were of course numerous subsequent modifications of basic techniques whose worth in sum was far from negligible and there was too a fairly steady growth in concern size – a tendency controlled by

[1] On the reasonable assumption that growth 1785–88 was at the same rate as 1788–96.

the very particular dangers of overdeveloped capacity in an industry where fixed costs loomed so large. It would certainly be an absurd exaggeration to say that having once introduced a batch of major cost-reducing methods and reaped their immediate benefits, the iron industry thereafter sat back and passively waited for new markets to emerge. But it would be an exaggeration incorporating a significant measure of truth. After the initial revolution, further growth was more quantitative than qualitative, waiting on user decisions to convert from foreign to British iron or from other materials to ferrous ones, or on the appearance of entirely new uses for iron. Whereas a continuing 'super' growth rate in the cotton industry rested on a series of changes in supply factors, the same phenomenon in the iron industry rested largely on a series of changes in demand factors.

Just beyond the bounds of this period lies the most consequential of these demand agencies: the railways, serving to support revolutionary expansion on into the 1870s. Within this period it was less a matter of novelties than of substitutions – not forgetting, of course, that in the initial phase it was very much a matter of direct stimulation of the existing market by way of price reduction. Such substitutions would not be rapidly effected. The suitability of the new cheap bar in place of proven charcoal iron could not be immediately apparent. There would be much reluctance to hazard its use until it had been tried by the more venturesome, and such trials sometimes told against the new metal. If it were a question of substituting cheap bar for wood or other non-ferrous materials, which still remained cheaper, it had to be established that the iron paid for itself in terms of a longer working life or greater efficiency, proofs which of necessity were some time in the making.

The statistics for iron imports reveal this timelag in operation particularly clearly. It is not until 1803 that they turn decisively downwards – that a general substitution of British for foreign iron got under way. (The downturn when it came was very abrupt, clearly attributable to the Admiralty's ceasing to insist on Swedish iron in naval contracts, directly reducing imports for this big wartime user and a powerful encouragement to others to convert.) Imports of charcoal iron never entirely ceased. They remained necessary for steel and certain other special purpose irons. At their nadir, 1815–21, however, they accounted for only 3–4 per cent of British iron use, as against about a half in 1785. Thereafter, in absolute amounts, they edged up again as general economic growth led to increased use in their special fields.

Fairly evidently the substitution of cheap bar for non-ferrous materials cannot be measured with the same kind of exactitude. It did not involve imported goods whose record would show up in the customs statistics, and it was of a much more multifarious nature: in some instances the use of more iron for articles already made partially of iron; in others the use of iron for the cheaper as well as the dearer varieties. For some purposes the technical desirability of iron had always been evident; in others it was an imaginative and, initially, experimental innovation. Thus both in its particular forms and in its timing this development was of a multiple and widely differentiated variety. All that one can aspire to do here is to indicate some of the instances which for one reason or another catch the attention. Before doing so it would be convenient to refer to another fish which can handily be caught in the same net: cast iron. Puddling and rolling greatly lowered bar iron costs, but cast iron still enjoyed a marked price advantage. The user incentive to extend the employment of cast iron was no longer quite as sharp, but it had not ceased to exist. In any event nobody was going to use bar iron if cast iron would serve. A summary view of examples of iron substitution in this period can compound both species – the more particularly since one cannot always be sure which of the two was in fact being used – in a number of cases both were used for different parts of the same article and in other cases there was a shifting about as the cheapness of one was weighed against the toughness of the other.

A particular instance of substitution which merits prominent attention is machinery. Above all this means textile machinery and the machinery used in the iron industry itself, but other general categories of some weight would include grinding machinery in flour and sugar mills, haulage and drainage machinery in mines, assorted and generally simple, small-scale machines in some metalworking trades and machinery in paper, glass, soap, chemical and printing works. Refusing the difficult and tedious task of a detailed examination of the use of iron over this polyglot range, one can in general terms speak confidently of the extensive use of wood for machines at the beginning of the period pretty rapidly giving way to iron over the next couple of decades, as far as new installations were concerned, with a very widespread use of all-iron machinery by the end of the period. Steam engines underwent a somewhat similar change in composition but many of their components were of iron to begin with. Demand from these quarters would have been felt most intensely by the iron industry in the years after 1821, when mechanisation and power were going forward with the greatest momentum, and it will perhaps be noted that as a principal user of machines and steam engines the iron industry was one of its own best customers.

As a constructional material, iron made some headway through these years. A few iron bridges were built and industrial buildings with an inner frame of iron girders were particularly favoured in Lancashire in the 1820s. Above all, iron proved its worth for colliery tracks – and for the pioneering steam locomotives which sometimes ran on them.

Lastly, though important because of the extent of the market, the extended use of iron for agricultural implements, among them the first all-iron ploughs, should be specially noted.

All in all, by the closing years of this period the bulk of sales of British iron must have been for purposes for which it had not hitherto been employed. This proliferation of uses was probably at its most intense in the years after 1815. Until then much of the growth of the industry would have been founded on an extension of the more traditional market, particularly, from the outbreak of the French wars in 1793, of the armaments market. But if the years of the Peninsular campaign and of Waterloo stretched the industry to exceptional heights of output, the early years of peace brought it to unfamiliar depths of depression when the abrupt cessation of military demand left it stranded with much idle and expensive capacity. 1816 and 1817 were grim years for the iron-masters. More than one splendid fortune turned to dust as Hobson's choices were made between blowing out furnaces and accepting a nil return on costly investment, on the one hand, and, on the other, tolerating a running loss at slashed prices in the endeavour to sustain sales. (The fairly tight price discipline which, through formal or informal agreements, the iron men habitually maintained among themselves largely collapsed in these circumstances.) But this profitless aftermath of war was, perhaps, also a seed-time as drastically lowered prices stimulated fresh user interest in the material. One price series shows bar falling from £13.5s. a ton in 1815 to £8.15s. in 1817. A jump back to £13 in 1818 strongly suggests that the slack in the industry was fairly quickly taken up; and the 455,000 tons recorded output of 1823 must have been handsomely in excess of the wartime peak.

In its general nature the pattern of demand response in overseas markets was roughly the same as that in the home market. But it differed quite markedly both in degree and timing. Although the technological lead over other countries established in iron production was just as great as that secured in cotton manufactures, that pre-eminence never within this period engendered the massive export demand which cottons enjoyed. For this three factors were responsible. Freight costs were much higher for iron so that by the time British iron had reached foreign markets its price advantage over a local product would often have withered away. Even where it retained a price advantage it frequently suffered in quality comparison. British iron was certainly cheap but it was not very good. Home users, operating for the most part in a keenly competitive market, were sooner or later driven to hazard it. But in most areas abroad where the pace of economic life was more sluggish and where poor transport facilities often created local quasi-monopolies, the incentive to risk quality deterioration for the sake of cost economies was commonly less sharp. (This same factor also inhibited foreign adoption of British production methods, even in regions with the requisite coal supplies.) Thirdly, whereas cotton cloth catered for a single basic universal want, iron served a multiplicity of needs, old and new, some of which, conspicuously that for machine parts, did not exist to anything like the same extent in other countries as in Britain itself. All this meant that the value of cotton exports, once they had established themselves, was of the order of twenty times that of exports of *raw* iron (pig, cast and bar)[1] and that the British iron industry, for all its international stature, was only exporting about one-fifth of its output at the end of this period.

That fifth, of course, in gross terms represented a considerable advance from the beginning of the period, when the industry exported nothing but small quantities of cast iron, constituting about a fiftieth of its total output. Ireland had figured early as a buyer, its own diminutive charcoal industry rapidly succumbing to cross-channel competition, but discounting Irish demand (and after 1801 Ireland was not, properly speaking, a foreign market, though for the purpose of official statistics it continued to be treated as such until 1826), it was not until well into the first decade of the nineteenth century that British bar prices started to engage foreign attention, while it took the sharp postwar price fall to stimulate it to the point where exports could be said to have had any material bearing on the industry's performance. However much of the

---

[1] The implied distinction between 'raw' and 'manufactured' is inevitably rather arbitrary. Here and elsewhere I have in effect drawn a line separating the output of smelting, founding and refining enterprises from that of other kinds of enterprises making articles of use (whole or components) from iron, treating the former as the 'iron industry' and the latter as part of the general metalwares or engineering industry. Towards the extremes the distinction is an obviously necessary one but there is a good deal of overlapping in the middle and it gives rise to anomalies like classing cast iron articles for use and, later on, iron rails as 'raw' rather than 'manufactured'.

foreign marketing of the immediate postwar years was probably in the nature of 'dumping'. With the recovery of home demand from 1818 onwards, supplies were redirected to meet domestic requirements and it was not until the boom broke in 1824 that exports started upwards again. Thus the laying of a firm base for foreign sales is very much an achievement of the last five years of this period.

All the principal iron producing regions shared in some degree in the general expansion of this period, though its early years did bring about the extinction of the handful of furnaces scattered through the woodlands of the far north and of the already run down industry of the Weald. Two regions in particular, however, developed with breathtaking momentum: south Staffordshire (the 'Black Country') and south Wales; two regions which could stand along, although on a lesser scale, with south-east Lancashire as physical and human testimonies to the impact of revolutionary economic change. The Black Country by night became one of the show pieces of Europe, with its lurid spectacle of giant red and orange tongues of flame from a hundred open-top furnaces fiercely licking the dark sky on every horizon. (The mountain-walled valleys which housed the industry in south Wales denied that region a comparable theatricality.)

These two regions enjoyed to an unrivalled degree the occurrence in close proximity of abundant deposits of coal and ore. Shropshire, the premier smelting district at the beginning of the period, was constricted by limited local coal supplies and, although output there more than tripled, it was providing only 11 per cent of the national gross by 1830 as compared with about 35 per cent in 1785. An area comprising adjoining parts of Yorkshire, Derbyshire and Nottinghamshire, which over the preceding decades had thrust itself forward through the exploitation of plentiful local coal for the production of cast iron, contrived now to increase its output fivefold, but was prevented from vying with the two giants by its dependence on outside supplies of ore to supplement its own scanty resources. On the coastal edge of the Durham and Northumberland coalfield spasmodic ventures had been made in the past in the field of iron artifacts (for which coal had always been usable), employing imported raw iron. Over the closing years of this period the smelting of imported ores got soundly launched, but the relatively high cost of these necessarily confined the industry to limited local scale and a diminutive fraction of national output. In Scotland, the great Carron concern scaled new heights, and over the first couple of decades of the period was joined by several others in both the eastern and western coalfields, but shortage of usable ores limited further growth. The rich but curious blackband ores of Clydeside had been discovered in 1801 but their exploitation had to await the invention of the hot-blast furnace (1828) and belongs just outside this period. Finally, the only other smelting district of any weight, north Staffordshire, was held in check by the meagreness of local coal measures although its ability to draw cheap canal-borne coal either from the south of the county or from Lancashire enabled it to maintain a modest growth. Altogether, between 1788 and 1830 the lesser districts combined nearly quadrupled their output, an impressive record by any but the standards being con-currently set elsewhere in the country. In south Wales output rose from 12,500 tons (18 per cent of national output) to 278,000 tons (41 per cent) and in south Staffordshire from 2,400 tons (3 per cent) to c. 200,000 tons (c. 30 per cent).

Other metallurgical activities

Of the other basic metallurgical industries there is little warrant for saying much in detail. It is not that they declined but that the limited serviceability of non-ferrous metals made them of increasingly marginal importance as multipurpose iron busily broadened its field of use. Hereafter they must disappear under the umbrella of 'other industries', too numerous to receive individual mention in a book of this kind. Tin largely gets lost with the ironworking trades since increasingly it was used principally for the making of tinplate, mostly composed of iron. However, since this was ultimately to become one of the chief branches of the iron industry a considerable retrospective importance can be attached to its continuing development in South Wales through these years on the basis of tin supplies from Cornwall, where output rose modestly from about 3,000 tons to about 4,400 tons. It was even-tually to reach a peak of around 10,000 tons in the 1860s and '70s, after which the tinplaters drew more and more heavily on foreign supplies. Lead was not associated with any particularly expansive sector of the economy and, although no figures are available, it is doubtful if it showed any noteworthy growth tendency. Copper enjoyed something of a wartime boom with Admiralty purchases for sheathing ships' keels, and in peacetime the by now well established Birmingham brassware trades provided quite a substantial market; but in the absence of signifi-cant cost economies at any processing stage, output at most does not appear to have done any more than keep pace with population growth.

Reference has already been made several times to metal artifacts. Hitherto it has been convenient and reasonable to treat of these as branches or extensions of the basic metal industries and of their achievement as being largely determined by the cost and supply position of those basic industries, from which in some cases they are, in any event, inseparable. But we have now entered a historical era in which an autonomous character must be allowed to what are conventionally called the engineering industries.

Engineering is one of the loosest words in the English language. If for the moment we exclude from its scope what is normally styled civil engineering, we can intend it to cover the manufacture of engines and machines. But although 'engine', in the modern sense of the word, has a fairly precise meaning, 'machine' fades into 'tool' and the simpler kind of tools are distinguishable from many other artifacts only in the use to which they are eventually put and not in their intrinsic construction. Thus while at one end of the range the engineering industries have a fairly sharply delimited definition, at the other end they shade away into metal manufactures generally.

There were already well before 1785 a certain number of distinct activities which could, with some plausibility, be comprehended in the phrase, engineering industries. In the textiles regions looms, spinning wheels and knitting frames were commonly the work of specialists. Everywhere, and of very ancient standing, there were millwrights, versed in the construction of water power and wind power apparatus for flourmills, and whose skills could be drawn on in particular cases for the erection of motive equipment for other powered enterprises. Another sophisticated 'engineering' operation would have been the construction of silk-throwing machines. There were too few of these to give rise to a specialist craft, but somebody within, or commissioned by, individual throwing concerns must have masterminded the operation, effected by having the component parts made by local craftsmen who attempted to turn their various habitual skills to the necessary tasks, the whole then being assembled on site. Newcomen engines, the early water frames and other relatively complicated apparatus such as that used in papermills would have been erected on the same order and assemble basis. But the working efficiency of such equipment must often have been gravely impaired by the faultiness and inexactitude of the parts. Although a ransacking of history would probably throw up instances of early nineteenth-century engineering concerns with a genealogy running back to loom-makers, millwrights or other traditional wood or metal craftsmen, this miscellaneous collection of crude forerunners and makeshift expedients could not really be represented as an engineering industry in embryo.

One industry could however be allowed a special role in this context: the iron industry, long accustomed to providing its own blast equipment, powered hammers, rolling and slitting mills. Not the least of the reasons why the iron industry was a pioneer in the use of steam power was that it, above any other, already had in large measure the human and physical resources needed for the manufacture of steam engines. At an opposite extreme on the industrial scale, clock and watch making might be distinguished as an important training ground in the precision techniques characteristic of authentic engineering operations; so too might the manufacture of firearms. And a field which while not concerned with manufacturing operations was yet fruitful in breeding 'engineers' was deep mining. Problems of boring, drainage, ventilation and haulage engendered technical research and an accumulating body of technical knowledge which, if it resulted primarily in the special discipline of mining engineering, carried also a useful overlap into other more general kinds of engineering. It is not just coincidence that the first great railway engineer, George Stephenson, came out of the coalpits of the north-east. Finally, the specific contribution of one concern, referred to earlier, should be given its due weight again here: the Soho Works which gave birth to the partnership of Boulton and Watt. But the real point is that an engineering industry emerged, not essentially by way of the evolution of any particular industry or group of industries, but by way of the coalescing of techniques, knowledge and habits of mind drawn from disparate fields to answer new needs.

The extent of an engineering industry is a simple function of the extent of the market for its products. In the context of this period this means that there were only two branches of the engineering industry producing on a sufficient scale to warrant particular mention here: textile engineering and steam engineering. And while the first of these by the end of the period certainly held a prominent place amongst the metalworking trades, the second was only just beginning to emerge from early infancy. Although in 1830 one great power-using industry, the iron industry, was virtually entirely converted to steam, and another, the cotton industry, was using more steam than water, these two stood quite on their own. The coal industry generally employed steam for its powered operations but many of its operations, including the central one, coalcutting, were not powered at all. The other textile industries, to the extent that they used power, still preferred water to steam, as did the flourmillers, the papermakers and certain other miscellaneous power users, some of whom such as lead and tin mining enterprises at distances from coal used improved versions of the hydraulic engine, cheaper for them than steam engines. And there remained, as there did for many decades to come, vast tracts of the economy which knew only muscle power: agriculture and transport of course (although the first was dabbling with steam-powered thresh-ing machines and pioneering steam locomotives and steamships were to be found in the second); building, garmentmaking, brewing and distilling, leatherworking, shipbuilding, soapboiling, candlemaking, furniture manufacture, etc. and, ironically, the huge bulk of the metal-working trades, including the engineering industries themselves.

This limited range of use of what on the face of it was an enormous technological asset is subject to different explanations according to cases. In some it was a matter of concern size not having been pushed to the point where steam power offered cost economies. In others it was that sufficient concentration in coal-bearing areas had not occurred, so that geographical location meant that other forms of power remained cheaper. This in turn was for varying reasons: sometimes simple inertia; sometimes that other cost considerations, proximity to materials or to markets, told against migration; and, in the case of extractive activities, the obvious impossibility of movement. Even weightier than this run of explanations in cost terms were technological reasons: many hand operations did not lend themselves readily to mechanisation and power; in some instances because of the difficulty of reproducing mechanically a complex human action; in others because, while such mechanical re-production was possible, only a small application of power would be needed – and a steam engine (or a water wheel) can only supply power economically in fairly large doses; steam power is neither capable of being packed in light mobile units nor of being 'piped' over distances from a central station. These technical considerations serve also, of course, to indicate why the use of even non-powered machinery remained fairly constricted in an age which had been made vividly aware of the potential benefits of mechanisation. The flexibility of human faculties acting in sensitively controlled concert was not some-thing that mechanical ingenuity could readily improve on.

No wonder, then, that even half a century after the invention of the rotary acting steam engine we find only a handful of concerns engaged in steam engineering. Indeed it was not until 1795 that the most famous of them actually started making steam engines. Boulton and Watt, in their early days, merely designed engines and supervised their assembly, leaving the procurement of the component parts to the customer. The firm sold only expertise and legal privilege, under a patent specially extended by Parliament until 1800. With the expiry date in sight in 1795 they had to start to offer something more substantial. But the shift in the nature of the business was not a radical one. Neither Boulton and Watt nor subsequent steam engine concerns ever made every part, or even most parts, of their engines. The essential change was simply the transfer of responsibility for the procurement of components from the customer to the firm. And this, then or at any later time, was, and is, a characteristic of engineering industries generally. An engine or a machine was an assemblage of the products of various enterprises, few of whom were principally occupied in that field. Unless one confines the term strictly to final assemblers, 'engineering industries' is a rather artificial abstraction from a complex of general metalworking trades. And in this period – and beyond it – the business of making steam engines was to be found above all embedded amongst the metalworking crafts of the Birmingham region.

Lancashire too had a certain number of steam engine concerns; some of them had supplied pirated versions of the Watt engine before the patent lapsed in 1800. But Lancashire had its own engineering pre-eminence as alongside the cotton factories there grew up concerns specialising in the manufacture of cotton machinery. The early jennies, of simple wooden construction, had been the work of local domestic craftsmen. But the larger, more complex, water frames and powered mules, increasingly iron-built, were beyond the scope of such men. In the lack of existing concerns to cater for this need, some of the larger spinning factories took to making their own machinery, and to selling machines to other enterprises who could not, or did not, run their own engineering workshops. This, however, was no more than an interim phase, at its most conspicuous in the 1790s. In some cases, specialist machinemakers may have developed out of spinning concerns who came to concentrate on what had originally been an ancillary activity; but the origins of the early textile engineers are obscure and were doubtless manifold. All that can be asserted is that by the later years of this period cotton textile engineering had come fully into its own as a distinct activity and constituted an element of some modest weight in the Lancashire economy. Ironically, it was already starting to do its bit towards enfeebling the competitive strength abroad of the industry which had given it birth. At the end of the period exports of machinery (of which much must have been textile machinery) were running at a rate of about £300,000 worth a year, although as yet that was pretty trivial set against approximately £18 million-worth of cotton exports.

Other textile regions bred machinemakers in rough proportion to the extent of mechanisation. In the early years, the Scottish cotton industry leant heavily on Lancashire machines, but Glasgow, especially through the 1820s, was developing an industry capable of meeting local requirements, including those for the limited amount of machinery used in linen manufacture. The West Riding had a somewhat similar history, initially using Lancashire machines, adapted for woollens and worsted spinning; by the end of the period Leeds had a textile engineering industry of some note which probably supplied not only the West Riding but the other woollen cloth regions as well, and, like Glasgow, also produced linen machinery.

The growth of an engineering industry was essentially engendered by demand. It emerged in response to a novel need, and thereafter grew with that need, achieving little itself to stimulate fresh custom. Doubtless, as workers became habituated to new tasks, as operational experience was acquired, certain cost economies were achieved but the industry itself drew little benefit from the technological aids with which it was equipping others. Machinery and steam power played an insignificant part in its operations. It was of course a 'factory' industry, at least in the sense that the final assemblage of the finished product was undertaken in a central workshop. But such engineering factories commonly employed no more than thirty or forty persons, in most cases engaged in hand-controlled operations. Many of these tasks necessitated a high degree of precision and though instruments were being devised for some purposes which reduced or eliminated the margin of operative error – elementary machine tools – engineering craftsmen in general were something of an aristocracy of labour by virtue of the special hand skills which their vocation required.

The technologically primitive state of the engineering industry was common to the metalworking trades at large. The iron users, of course, benefited from the lowered price of their raw material; but the final price of many iron goods was determined more by manufacturing costs than by material costs and the inability to effect any significant reduction in the former limited the gains to be derived from the latter. In speaking of such a polyglot group, any general statement must admit of particular exceptions but it is broadly true that the metalworking trades remained through this period a relatively high cost and rather 'unrevolutionary' sector of the economy. Some statistical indication of this, in the lack of any more apt measurement, is afforded by comparing the rates of population growth in the cotton county, Lancashire, in Monmouthshire, a county devoted industrially to the basic iron processes, and in Warwickshire given over to the later metal manufacturing processes.

TABLE II.8. *Decennial rates of population growth, 1801–31* (*as per census-returns*)

Lancashire	Monmouthshire	Warwickshire	Great Britain
26%	29%	18%	16%

* * *

General accounts of the Industrial Revolution often associate coal with cotton and iron to form a linked trio, within which powerful growth forces reciprocated and sustained one another: cotton required iron for its productive equipment; iron in turn required coal; coal reciprocated by requiring iron for its plant, and was further linked directly to cotton by that industry's requirement of steam power:

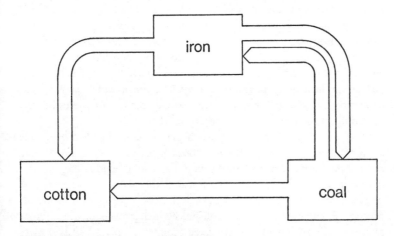

The evident measure of truth in this kind of representation makes it particularly needful to try to get the proportions into proper perspective. The statistical data for a comprehensive mathematically exact input-output analysis does not exist, but some notion of the general order of things may be obtained.

It can be estimated that of the total value of British cotton goods in 1830 (c. £32 million) about a quarter (c. £8 million) was accounted for by expenditure on goods other than the basic raw material, among which iron for productive equipment would have figured prominently. At the same time the output of finished iron goods in the country was in the vicinity of £16 million in value (the iron itself being around £4·5 million). To proceed from these fairly well founded figures to an estimate of the fraction of iron output used by the cotton industry is to embark on guesses as to the weight of machinery etc. in the 'other costs' of the cotton industry, and the value added by subsequent manufacturing operations to the raw iron used for these purposes; but it would seem to be within any likely margins of error to say that not less than one-tenth and not more than one-quarter of British iron ended up as plant in the cotton industry. Even the lower figure is not negligible and one would appear to be fully justified in speaking of a significant linkage between cotton and iron. A similar calculation for the linkage between coal and iron, however, could not, at the very most, show more than three per cent of iron output assuming the final form of colliery track, winding gear etc.

The direct linkage between cotton and coal by 1830 can be approximately assessed on the basis of the following tolerably accurate data: steam power used in spinning and weaving: probably a little over 20,000 horsepower; annual coal consumption of steam engines: about 7 tons per horsepower. This would yield something like 150,000 tons annual coal use. Even after allowing for coal used, both for heat and power, in bleaching, printing and dyeing, the industry as a whole obviously accounted for only a very small fraction of the estimated 22·5 million tons national coal output of 1830.

In summary, while cotton's growth may be considered to have had an appreciable bearing on the development of the iron industry (or, put another way, that cheap iron was of measurable advantage to the cotton industry) the bonds between iron and coal (as a consumer) and between coal (as a producer) and cotton were too slight to be worth distinguishing amongst the multiple links which interrelate the different sectors of any reasonably sophisticated economy. This is to imply that, under the aspects so far considered, coal's participation in the especially dynamic trends of this period was not of any particular note; that the industry does not stand out from the general ruck.

The coal industry

As well as they can be estimated the figures for national coal output are given in Table II.9.

TABLE II.9. *Coal output, 1785–1830 (mil. tons)*

1785	1800	1815	1830
8·5	11·0	16·0	22·5

These give a fairly steady annual growth of about 2·25 per cent, much the same as that of the industrial economy at large. Yet coal as a producer was closely linked to the dynamic iron industry. Coal was the very basis of the iron revolution; and of the coal output of 1830 about a fifth was burned by the ironmaking and ironworking trades, far more than any other single industry group and, indeed, perhaps nearly as much as a half of that burned by all other industries put together. Of the estimated 14 million tons increment to output over these years about 4 million was accounted for by the iron industries alone. This means that without its special relationship with iron the coal industry would have been found along with the duller industries of this period, down towards the bottom of the growth table instead of comfortably in the middle.

Plainly the coal industry itself achieved little to stimulate consumer interest. Indeed it is clear that in some fields *per capita* demand for coal must actually have been depressed. It seems very possible that coal use for domestic heat failed to keep pace fully with population growth – and at the beginning of the period domestic use would have accounted for over a half of total consumption.

This is no worse than what one would expect once overexcited assumptions about coal's role in the early industrial revolution are curbed. Rising costs are part of the natural law for the coal industry, and nothing that was done through this period had any powerful tendency to reverse the operation of that law. In real terms production costs must have increased fairly steadily in most mining areas despite

455

(in some pits, in some regions) improved underground haulage, winding and drainage techniques, including the use of steam power for the latter two purposes. However in many cases genuine economies were effected in delivery costs by the laying of iron tracks for surface haulage, permitting much greater loads to be pulled per unit of tractive power. Although pioneering experiments in the use of steam locomotives through the early years of the nineteenth century foundered on the inability of cast iron rails to withstand the weight of the locomotives, stationary steam engines hauling wagon trains by cable could usefully replace horses on short steeply inclined runs. Bar iron rails, which could have stood up to a locomotive, remained uneconomic as long as they had to be forged into shape. The successful development of cheap direct rolling methods in the 1820s was therefore a valuable advance for collieries distant from navigable water who were thus enabled to employ steam traction to move their coal from pit-head to wharf.

The extent of the gain arising, whether from rails in themselves or from rails plus steam power, obviously depended on the length of the overland haul concerned; and since by the 1820s canals had already pushed deep into most mining regions, it was only in a relatively few particular localities that any very substantial price fall followed. Not until railways cut loose from water routes and struck out across country to link collieries directly with markets could they have significant effects on a national scale. And capital expenditure of that order could only make economic sense with a high rate of track usage – higher than that which any single colliery would provide. As long as railways were just elements of individual colliery businesses they had only a very limited future as feeder routes to water.

As a primary transport medium railways had at least to be the undertakings of colliery consortia and, better than that, general public carriers spreading their fixed cost burden over all sorts of goods. In other words, original entrepreneurial initiatives were required and it is something of a comment on the economic climate of the times that such initiatives were soon forthcoming. In 1825 twenty-five miles of track were opened to carry coal between Stockton and Darlington by steam-drawn train; and the combined coal interests who promoted the venture made their track available to independent contractors for general horse carriage. In 1829, with track and locomotive designed by the colliery engineer George Stephenson, the Liverpool and Manchester Railway Company commenced business as the first autonomous, fully integrated, steam-powered, public carrier – from where on railways became a part of general transport history.

If the impact of railways on coal costs falls mostly in the years beyond this period, much of the impact of canals falls in the years preceding it. Comparatively little of the canal construction of these years had the consequences for collieries and their customers which that of the 1760s and 1770s had contrived in the west Midlands and in south Lancashire. By 1785 most coalmining areas were already directly linked to their principal markets by water routes, natural or artificial. The next fifteen years or so did see a spawning of tributary canals in the areas already provided with an arterial system, including the east Midlands where the canals fed into the Trent, the Aire and Calder, the Don, the Ouse, the Humber and other improved rivers, sufficing to meet local pressure on coal in the region (where industrial development was less intense than in the areas to its west) but incapable of putting its rich coalfield on a competitive footing with the north-eastern collieries in the London and home counties market, even after 1814 when the Grand Union Canal directly linked Trent and Thames.

The same years saw canals come to the mining valleys of south Wales, running down them five, ten and fifteen miles to the sea and making of this the only coal-bearing region which could be said to have signally benefited from the post-1785 canal phase. Although delivery to the region's own metallurgical enterprises was a principal function of the south Wales canals, coal shipments out rose from less than 100,000 tons in 1785 to about half a million by 1810 and to around a million by the end of the period, the great bulk selling in south-western and Irish markets supplanting, variously, Severn-borne coal from Shropshire and seaborne coal from the north-east and from Cumberland. Cumberland output, in fact, dwindled to relatively trivial amounts as canals permitted coal from south Wales and Lancashire to take over on the coasts of the Irish Sea.

The north-east, on the other hand, was affected only at the very fringe of its extensive market area by competition from south Wales, and indeed no development of these years seriously threatened its primacy amongst British coal-mining regions. But that primacy arose from its advantageous coastal and riverside situation; consequently, there was only very limited scope for it or its customers to draw further benefit from contemporary transport improvements. The region had always been to the fore in improving pit-head to wharf haulage and was now pre-eminent in taking to iron rails and steam traction, but the evidence of London coal prices is that this was quite insufficient to offset rising mining costs. Nor was the north-east well placed geographically to take advantage of the special demands of the ironmakers. Thus by contrast with the galloping record of the south Wales coal ports, that of the two chief north-eastern ones, Newcastle and Sunderland, is a little dull: from about 1,850,000 tons around 1785 shipments out rose to about 3,500,000 tons by the end of this period – or, put alternatively, fell from over 20 per cent of gross national supplies to 15 per cent.

Scotland resembled south Wales in that canal construction in its coalfields did not get properly under way until after 1785; but the results here were less striking. The Monkland Canal, opened in 1790 and penetrating deep into the Lanarkshire coalfield, was certainly of appreciable benefit to the citizens of Glasgow. But in general the relatively limited development of the Scottish iron industry through this period and the remoteness from outside markets of any size precluded progress as rapid as that effected in south Wales, despite comparability in point of the extent of coal measures and proximity to the sea.

Pottery

There remains one industry of weight with a claim to a place in the revolutionary firmament: pottery. The great difficulty in offering a useful account of this industry is the almost total lack of statistical data relating to it. However, its claim does not really rest on its gross output – at no time did pottery constitute an element of great weight in the economy as a whole. And the prominence commonly accorded to it is due as much to its possession of the flamboyant figure of Josiah Wedgwood as to anything else. Nevertheless, if the essence of 'revolution' be radical technical and organisational change, pottery experienced as authentic a revolution as any industry. With Wedgwood as the chief, and rather precocious, pioneer, an industry which around the middle of the eighteenth century had still been organised in small workshops, the largest of which might have run to twenty employees, was by the end of this period, in the constricted 'five towns' area which was its chief centre, characterised by factories numbering their labour forces in hundreds. The application of steam power to the basic flint grinding operation – Wedgwood installed a Watt engine as early as 1782 – was an important factor in making for this growth in concern size, but it owed much too to a greatly intensified subdivision of labour to ensure the uniform quality of product which much more than cost reduction was the basis of the industry's market strength.

At this juncture we could profitably pause and take interim stock. We have looked at the textile industries, the metallurgical industries, coal-mining and pottery, a collection on which classically the case for speaking of an Industrial Revolution was rested. But on inspection we have seen that the collection must be separated into three broad categories: (1) those activities which were the subject of radical and throughgoing technical change, e.g. cotton spinning; (2) those activities which were the subject of significant but only partial or incomplete technical change, e.g. woollen spinning; (3) those activities which experienced little or no technical change and only qualify for inclusion by virtue of their close association with the others, e.g. coalmining. There is of course endless room for debate as to the precise definition of any particular 'activity' and as to which of the three broad categories such an 'activity' should be assigned; but in very crude terms the net outputs of the three groups by 1830, expressed as fractions of total net industrial output, might be estimated as being of the order of: (1) one-eighth; (2) one-eighth; (3) one-quarter – admitting for these purposes technical changes effected in the years before 1785. This kind of statement, based on money values, understates the achievement of the most 'revolutionised' activities where the significant effect was precisely a reduction in the money value of the commodities produced; but even allowing for this, and for the overall crudity of the calculation, the statement is useful in getting the 'Industrial Revolution' into some kind of total economic perspective.

Among other things it indicates that the industries treated of specifically here constituted just about a half of total industrial activity, and only about a sixth of total economic activity. Passing references have been made to some of the industries making up the other half. Chief among them, in order of importance, were: garment-making (including homemade clothing), building, brewing and distilling, shoemaking and other leather trades, flour-milling and baking, shipbuilding – which between them must have constituted something like a third of industrial activity. Although in different ways and in varying degrees all these would have felt something of the wind of change blowing from the dynamic quarters of the industrial economy, their leading

common characteristic is the almost total inertia of their own production methods – and it will perhaps be noted that of the six mentioned,
five were concerned with supplying basic consumer necessities.

Agriculture

Although the products of industry as a whole had surpassed in value
those of agriculture within the years 1818–20, and by the end of the
period supplied about a third of national income as against about a
quarter coming from agriculture, agriculture still ranked well above any
single industry. Indeed the value of grain products alone, at something
over £50 million, well outstripped the most important class of industrial products, cotton goods, then running a little above £30 million;
and while virtually all the grain was produced for home consumption,
only about £15 million of the cotton goods went to the home market.
As caterers to domestic wants the corn growers were still of pre-
eminent importance; and the most signal fact to record about British
agriculture through this period is that it did, by and large, keep pace
with the swollen wants of a population grown from about $9\frac{1}{4}$ million
to 15 million. Although it did no more than that, and thus in an
important sense compares unfavourably with most industries, which
achieved a real *per capita* growth, it did so under a condition with which
industry, generally speaking, did not have to contend: a highly inelastic
supply of a basic factor of production, land. There is a certain comparability between the situations of agriculture and of the iron industry.
In the latter revolution consisted, in significant part, in the release
effected from the limitations imposed by inelastic supplies of charcoal
and, less stringently, of water power. But, in general, industry's growth
prospects lay in enhancing the productivity of labour; for agriculture,
that alone offered only the prospect of increasing the profits of individual farmers and, ultimately, landlord rentals. An increase in gross
output depended largely on enhancing the productivity of land. The
same yardstick should not then be applied to agriculture's performance
as serves for measuring industry's achievements.

It is far from being the case that labour economies in agriculture
were unimportant; that the demands being exerted upon land by
growing population would have been adequately met in increasing the
yield per acre, regardless of increases in the amount of labour employed.
This for two reasons. First, that if a clear profit incentive did not exist
better methods, however potentially beneficial they might be to the

community at large, would not be adopted by farmers; or more precisely, would only be adopted when the community's needs had manifested themselves in the shape of such higher prices as created a profit margin. That is to say, scarcity would not be forestalled by greater efficiency but would be awaited until the community's distress provided the farmers' profit opportunities. Turnip cultivation is a good case in point here; its slow spread is, among other things, to be attributed to its high labour costs which often might not be fully compensated for in improved crop yields; and even improved drainage systems or artificial manures might not be readily taken to as long as the labour costs of handling the resulting higher yields simply rose proportionately, so that the extra profit was only minimal. In practice there was bound to be a correlation between the adoption of fertility-raising techniques and the availability of labour-saving methods.

The second importance to be attached to labour is that the more of it agriculture required the less was available for other sectors of the economy; most significantly, the less was available for sectors of high growth potential. Put another way, until such time as abundant foodstuff imports were available, the possible rate of industrial growth was controlled by the efficiency of agricultural labour.

Nevertheless, recitation of these points is only to say that much of the benefit from ways of enhancing the productivity of land would be dulled in the lack of means of enhancing the productivity of labour. The important truth stands: with an inelastic supply of land, and massive imports unprocurable, British agriculture was under the imperative necessity of getting more out of the average acre.

One way of increasing yields was to plough up rough grazing land and convert from an easygoing, inexpensive kind of pasture farming to an intensive, high labour cost, mixed farming, in which human foodstuffs were grown on land which had hitherto supported only beasts, but on which the same weight of animals as formerly could be kept on leys of artificial grasses (convertible farming) or on rotation fodder crops (alternate farming). But, virtually by definition, the land still open to this kind of treatment was usually poor land. Even with the animal manure available to enrich it, it would probably need a good deal of costly artificial manuring and still might not yield good crops. Furthermore, the root crops which offered a better prospect of commercial success than ley farming could only be cultivated on well drained soils. The sandy and chalky land which lent themselves best to the transformation had for the most part already been submitted to it through the previous hundred years or so. And, of course, where there was still useful scope for this kind of thing it involved an imaginative break with accustomed routines – indeed a daring break since much higher costs were to be incurred without the certainty of correspondingly higher returns; while in some cases there existed the absolute bar of lack of the ready cash to sustain the endeavour. Unusually high corn prices were obviously the particular circumstances most likely to prompt the exercise and a good deal of what there is to be seen of it occurred over the years 1795–1814 when wartime impediments to imports and general inflation drove prices exuberantly upwards, permitting the cultivation of marginal land which had to run back to rough pasture when prices came down again – in some cases would have had to revert whatever became of prices since all that had been done was to squeeze a few grain crops out of land which no serious attempt had been made to refurbish.

Although, the wartime froth apart, there was a fair amount of well planned permanent adoption of grazing land to more productive mixed farming, much, perhaps most, of the increase in grain output came from land which was already under the plough. Little that was really new within these years had a hand in this. It was very largely a matter of extending practices already in use in varying degrees: the substitution of root crops for fallows on some of the not so wet clays (the swede, taken to in the early years of the period, facilitated this, being less liable to rot than the traditional turnip); more abundant use of artificial manures (the construction of canals in agricultural regions was helpful in lowering the cost to farmers of these bulky substances which, however, were of limited benefit on poorly drained lands being liable to be washed off the surface by rainfall); an accelerated adoption of the seed-drill, but confined almost entirely to the free draining lands, it being virtually unworkable in sticky soils. The practicability of this last device was greatly enhanced by improvements in design and construction, and this period generally is characterised by a big step forward in the standards of tools and equipment, to be associated closely with the advent of cheap iron, of which the all-iron plough was perhaps the most important consequence, making for more thorough turning of the soil and for speedier, cheaper, ploughing; but once again, it was on the more easily worked light soils that the gains were most marked. Portentous of an entirely new era was the powered threshing machine, invented in 1786 and in quite widespread use on larger farms by the end of the period; but while it effected useful cost economies in this laborious operation, it did not contribute anything directly to increasing yields.

Even though between one thing and another British farming effected a noteworthy increase in grain output within the constrictions of limited agricultural acreage, it is probably true that bread consumption lagged increasingly, though only slightly, behind population rise through this period. During the wartime years, imported grain supplies to make good the domestic shortfall were often difficult to secure, and after 1815 the Corn Laws deliberately rendered them unobtainable or prohibitively expensive in normal times. But British agriculture did do something else to sustain and perhaps even improve nutrition standards: it grew increasing quantities of potatoes. Although there was a widely entertained repugnance towards the potato as being fit only for pigs and Irish, it had become an important element in the diet of the labouring class throughout the country by the end of this period. The extension of the commercial scope for potato cultivation carried an extra benefit for farming generally by permitting greater variety in the root-crop phases of non-fallow rotations and thus helping to preserve soil fertility. But the labour costs of harvesting were a deterrent to substituting the potato for turnips and other crops which could be eaten off the ground by animals, while its liability to damage in transit also told against its commercial cultivation. A significant fraction of the potatoes raised were grown as a subsistence crop, often by rural labourers on quarter-acre plots.

Approached simply as a question of preserving nutrition standards, the problem of limited acreage could have been most simply resolved by devoting less to foodstuffs which were relatively costly in terms of land used and more to foodstuffs which were relatively cheap in such terms – i.e. by a swing from livestock to arable crops. Even in abstract, however, such a strategy would create problems: the loss of manure would endanger soil fertility; the rise in manpower requirements would imperil the labour situation elsewhere in the economy. In actuality the issue of land use never posed itself in these terms. It was apprehended solely as a question of farming profits. The balance between the human need for grain and potatoes and that for meat and dairy produce was one thing. The balance between the effective market demands for the two categories was quite different. And it was the latter which determined land use. In brief, while there was, as earlier, a good deal of internal reshuffling of pasture and arable, including an increasing amount of mixed farming of one kind or another, there was certainly no overall move away from livestock to arable products; indeed, output of meat and dairy produce almost certainly rose more rapidly than that of grain and potatoes.

It may very well be that the increase in animal products was achieved without enlarging the acreage under grass. Of all agricultural developments through the eighteenth and nineteenth centuries that with the best title to the epithet 'revolutionary' would be selective breeding, if one has prime regard to the rapidity and breadth of its adoption, which could easily stand comparison with industrial counterparts such as the use of the power loom or the steam engine, whereas, say, root crops or seed-drilling could not. As a result, the capacity of British livestock to turn forage into edible flesh was undoubtedly improved to a very appreciable extent through these years, perhaps to the extent that the extra meat actually came from less fodder.

Of all the developments which this period inherited from its predecessors, that which, in a certain sense, was pushed forward most decisively was enclosure. By 1820 only a negligible fraction of ploughland consisted of open fields. Virtually all of it lay consolidated within hedges or fences, in the exclusive occupancy of individual farmers. Only certain grazing lands, constituting about a tenth of total pasture, still gave evident testimony to the collectivity which had once marked British agriculture.

The bulk of the enclosing activity which this represented was of course the work of many previous generations; but no one generation had achieved as much as did that spanning the first thirty years of this period, during which probably more land was enclosed than over any earlier hundred-year stretch. Doubtless the rate of enclosure would have accelerated in any event, but the movement was accorded a special impetus by the high agricultural prices of the war years. With the abnormal profits to be made from farming through those years, the rent differential between open and enclosed land hardly permitted owners of unenclosed property to neglect the opportunity of so handsomely increasing their incomes, whatever the initial cost and difficulty; and the more enclosed farms there were for letting, the harder it was to get good rents for the dwindling number lying in open fields. Proprietors who could not, or would not, seize their chances were likely to yield to attractive purchase offers from those who had the necessary means and resolution to effect an enclosure. It was a cumulative trend, reaching a crescendo of intensity in the last five years of the war, such that the setback occasioned by the sharp drop in prices with the coming of peace was of little consequence, for the work by then had practically all been done.

The postwar slither of prices brought many to grief. Having averaged 107s a quarter over the five years 1809–13, wheat averaged 80s a quarter in the years 1814–18 and slumped to 59s on an average of the years 1819–23. Other agricultural prices moved in much the same fashion, although livestock products which had not risen quite so steeply during the war did not now fall quite so sickeningly and, indeed, contrived to remain above the prewar level when the secular deflation brought grain prices below it, reflecting the enhancement of the superior purchasing power of the meat-eating classes as against the bread-eating classes.

Tenant farmers as a class were the worst sufferers. Those holding by leases contracted at high wartime rents could not hope to show a profit at these prices, nor often even after the abatements allowed by many landlords. Rents on tenancies-at-will could be more readily adjusted, but even these did not move downwards with the rapidity of prices. Many landlords themselves were feeling the pinch: those who had only recently bought estates at inflationary values and who were threatened with seeing the return on their investment reduced to a derisory percentage if they allowed rents to follow prices; those who had borrowed at fixed interest to finance purchases, enclosures, new buildings or other improvements at escalated costs and were thus burdened with irreducible outgoings. On the whole, however, the state of landlords was hardly as piteous as their publicists painted it at the time. Most were anciently seated in their property; and not all by any means were in the grip of the moneylenders. In real terms, the majority were probably better off, rents only slowly subsiding towards the continuously lower general price level; though many, not given to doing standard-of-living sums, were doubtless convinced that with lower money incomes they must be worse off, even if their household budgets somehow continued to balance.

One type of landowner who was apt to suffer particularly in the postwar period was the owner-occupier who had burdened himself with loan obligations during the inflationary years. Commanding particular mention is the freeholder farmer who had been involved in an enclosure during those years. It was the small freeholder who was most likely to find enclosing costs onerous, though in normal circumstances even he would probably benefit in the long run, and there are instances where the pressure to enclose came from owner-occupiers in the face of landlord reluctance. The relatively higher cost to a small proprietor of enclosing is a simple matter of geometry: the cost of fencing increases only as the square root of the factor by which the area to be fenced is increased (which, *inter alia*, provided an incentive for a landlord to engross at the same time as he enclosed). Quite often the small proprietor would lack the ready cash to finance fencing or hedging (or other improvements); the proliferation of banks in rural areas through the years in question facilitated the procurement of loan funds for the undertaking, and their charge might become intolerable when money income fell with the postwar deflation. The owner-occupier lacked that cushion of sluggishly responding rents which, at least partially, inured the landlord against price falls.

Nineteenth-century critics who concerned themselves about the quality of rural life often bemoaned an imagined thinning of the ranks of freehold farmers: the sturdy independent yeomen, the backbone of England, the salt of the earth, the fibre and sinew of society – the rhetoric abounds. Such commentators, and later historians, commonly associated this putative phenomenon with enclosure. But it is not only nineteenth-century literature which carries the lament: it can be found in plenty in the eighteenth, the seventeenth, the sixteenth. Either, somewhere along the line of the centuries there was gross exaggeration, or one runs back to a fifteenth-century rural England in which landlords and tenants hardly figured. And the latter is palpable historical nonsense.

Although this is a field of enquiry which has as yet hardly been scratched, two tentative and quite independent conclusions have been posed: that around the turn of the fifteenth to sixteenth century about a fifth of farms were occupied in freehold; that again around the beginning of the nineteenth century about a fifth of farmland was so occupied. As a matter of more certain knowledge, about an eighth of land was owned by farmers at the end of the nineteenth century. The facts pointed to are: one, that before the nineteenth century there had been no long-run tendency for freeholds to disappear; two, that at no time – since the early Middle Ages at least – had the freeholder been a really prominent figure amongst British farmers; three, that the nineteenth century did see a diminution in the amount of owner-occupier farming, but that it was not an event of anything like revolutionary proportions.

The impression that had been put about in the past that some historical epoch had seen a massive thinning out of freeholder farmers seems to be largely myth. Two factors appear to have been responsible for the propagation of this over-excited view. The first is a confounding of the number of those designated freeholders with the amount of freehold land. It evidently was the case until comparatively modern times that very many tenant farmers also held varying amounts of land of their own. A deep anxiety to own at least a scrap of land is a common characteristic of heavily agrarian societies. But with the more strictly business attitudes brought to farming in more industrialised societies, farmers usually wish to conserve their working capital, to employ it in farming itself rather than in a needless acquisition of property. Through the eighteenth and nineteenth centuries the numbers qualifying for the description of freeholder undoubtedly fell off very considerably; but that is no measure of the amount of freehold land passing into landlord ownership.

The second factor which would seem to have led to exaggeration on this issue is the attention given to instances of landlord purchase of freeholds to round out an estate or to complete an intended engrossment – instances which are fairly numerous from at least the sixteenth century onwards. But what in all probability has been overlooked is a roughly counterbalancing sale by landlords of detached and administratively awkward pieces of property or small parcel sales to raise money at times of financial embarrassment or to sustain capital expenditure. There has usually been a tendency amongst historians to think of landlord sales as being sales to other landlords or to those with commercial or industrial fortunes, as obviously was the case in sales of whole estates or substantial portions of them. But as long as the peasant attitude to land which was touched on above persisted, there would be plenty of opportunities for the sale of patches and small units to the farmers of the neighbourhood.

There is one further point which is liable to give rise to confusion on the question of owner-occupiers. That is the classification of copyholders. If these are categorised as owner-occupiers – as with some legitimacy they could be – then undoubtedly one would have a pre-nineteenth-century decline in owner occupation. Through the seventeenth century and even the sixteenth, but most especially the eighteenth, landlords took the opportunity when copyhold farms reverted to them to substitute terminable tenancies; although very probably some copyholds by inheritance where the regular rent was merely nominal were transmuted into freeholds by way of a single quittance payment by the occupant, or even by way of simple default if the admission fine too was so low that the landlord had ceased to bother about it. By the beginning of the nineteenth century the copyhold had become a rare form of tenure, having for the most part given way to the tenancy-at-will or the medium-term leasehold, with the landlord's rights of ownership plain beyond any ambiguity.

It is almost certainly true that the net direction of flow of freehold land altered from time to time according to general circumstances: at times of difficulty for farmers, tending to pass into landlord hands; at times of buoyancy, with relatively high landlord expenditures, tending to pass out of landlord ownership, though at any time the net change was probably fairly slight. The years immediately after 1814 were certainly a time of difficulty; and this, combined with a changing agrarian psychology running through and beyond this particular phase, very probably made of it one in which more freehold land than usual was thrown to landlords and, as a matter of historical chronology, initiated a long-run diminution in the extent of owner occupation.

Although those freeholders who had recently incurred fixed charges were probably the worst hit section of agrarian society, most of their difficulties were common to farmers as a whole. Indeed the form of tenure which seems to have taken the severest shaking was leasehold. The trend towards medium-term leases (five to twenty-five years), which had been a feature of British farming over the previous century and a half, was not only terminated but reversed. The experience of being caught by a high rent while prices tumbled was traumatic – such that ever since the enormous bulk of British farms have been held at will. But it was not only fixed or inelastic rents which squeezed farmers' profit margins. Even when labour is unorganised wages tend to be sticky. Through these years they came down, but lagging behind prices, and the defensive reduction by farmers of labour employed redounded on them in the form of higher poor rates, paid by the occupiers of property. Church tithe was another charge on farmers and in many areas it was paid by way of a modus, a money sum agreed on for a period of years, instead of a fraction (conventionally a tenth, in practice usually less) of the varying yield from year to year. Rectors like landlords often consented to abatements, but overall the real burden of tithe must have risen in the immediate aftermath of the war. All in all, there is no mistaking the fact that the period 1815–22 was one of severe agricultural depression, in which the weak went to the wall and all were edged towards it.

With the partial recovery of prices in 1823 by when, broadly speaking, rents, wages and tithe had swung into line and an industrial boom was helping to draw the rural unemployed off the poor rates, the general agricultural depression can be said to have ended. The Corn Laws which had been allowed to lapse during the war and were re-enacted in 1815 under intense pressure from the agricultural interests, had fixed 80s a quarter as the price below which wheat imports were prohibited, with similar provisions for other grains. With prices having to come down from over 100s a quarter for wheat, the new Corn Laws did not bite very sharply to start with – for the first five years or so it needed only a mildly defective domestic harvest to push prices beyond the prohibition barrier, admitting imports and denying British farmers full compensation for lower than average yields. But by the early 1820s grain prices had come down to such a level that only a catastrophically bad harvest could drive them up to the barrier price; and in fact, after 1820 no foreign corn worth speaking of reached the market until the Corn Laws were modified in 1828 to permit of importation at a wheat price of 52s a quarter, subject to duty of 34s 8d a quarter at that price, falling as prices rose further until it reached a minimum rate of 1s a quarter at a price of 73s. Between 1823 and 1828, then, British agriculture enjoyed more or less normal cost conditions and virtually absolute protection against foreign competition, under circumstances of intensifying demand as population pressure vigorously mounted; and even after 1828 the Corn Laws continued to confer on it a very substantial advantage over foreign rivals.

Yet despite being so favourably circumstanced all was not well with British farming. The return to normalcy exposed a situation which had been steadily constituting itself for many decades and was now very plainly evinced: the existence of a great divide between British farmers. On the one hand there were the stock-raisers of the north and west and those occupants of free-draining soils in parts of the south and east who mixed livestock with a basically arable farming. On the other hand there were those who farmed the low-lying wet clays which covered a good deal of the eastern half of the country, especially towards the interior, maintaining roughly the same sort of overall balance between livestock and arable products as those more fortunately situated on the chalky and sandy soils, though more heavily inclined to cattle than to sheep, especially vulnerable to footrot on damp land. Retrieved prosperity was the perquisite of the stock-raisers, supported by relatively buoyant prices, and of the cultivators of the light soils. For the clay farmers, depression persisted throughout the 1820s and much of the '30s, although hardly with the acute intensity of the 1815–23 period.

The cost gap between those who could cultivate root crops and make optimum use of artificial manures and improved implements and those who could not had become very wide. Common prosperity during the war and common distress after it had masked the difference but now it evidenced itself as a distinction between those who made comfortable profits from farming and those who made little or none, though it was not the sole factor in that distinction: variations in personal efficiency, in landlord outlays, in local weather conditions, in the incidence of animal diseases etc. superimposed their confusing patterns. What it meant was that the marginal farmers – in theory terms those whose costs control prices – were not just a handful of unfortunates scattered throughout the country, but a solid block concentrated on the clays, accounting for a sufficiently large proportion of gross foodstuffs output to mean that prices would always move just enough to keep them in being, but only in odd years, when weather conditions peculiarly favoured the clay farmers over their light soil competitors, enough to yield them normal profits. (Analysis in theoretical margin terms must take account of the 'stickiness' of the situation arising from the historically entrenched position of these producers and their landlords; by contrast with the textbook marginal farmer, brought into activity by rising demand, these would endure subnormal returns for a long time.)

Only when good artificial drainage rendered the clays susceptible in some measure to the progressive light soil agricultural routines could they share effectively in the rewards of a generally favourable situation for farmers. And, considerations of the efficacy of contemporary techniques aside, drainage was an expensive business. Depressed profits and rents did not encourage such undertakings, as they did not encourage outlays on other things, farm buildings, roadways, fences and farming equipment. Even standard expenditure of this kind may have been reduced in the clay country so that although short-run financial benefit was derived from what in effect was capital consumption, the differential disadvantage in point of unit costs may have been widening rather than closing. Certainly it is not until the late 1830s that positive signs of advance in this unhappy sector of British agriculture start to become apparent.

Transport

Not least of the developments affecting the market for agricultural produce were transport improvements, principally by way of the enlargement of the canal network, though the marked improvement of the road system was of some consequence also. The earlier phase of canal construction had only incidentally been of benefit to farmers. By contrast, the canals of this period, whose promotion was concentrated very much in the years 1789–96, and particularly intensively in the 'mania' of 1791–94, were, many of them, built primarily to serve agricultural needs, or at least built with such needs prominently in view. Whereas the first generation canals had hinged on Severn, Trent and Mersey, it was the Thames which constituted the central path governing much of this second generation work. Chief amongst the canals feeding into the Thames (with completion dates) were: Thames and Severn (1789), coming in through central Gloucestershire and south Oxfordshire; the Oxford Canal (1790) running down through open country from Coventry; the Basingstoke Canal (1796), coming up from Hampshire to join the Thames at Weybridge; the Grand Junction (1800), winding northwards from London through the rural Midlands before swinging westwards to reach Birmingham; the Kennet and Avon (1810), a better Thames–Severn link cutting through south Berkshire and central Wiltshire to the Avon at Bath.

Although the linkage of the Thames watershed, and London in particular, with the west Midlands and its canal network was an evident function of some of these projects and all of them in some measure facilitated distribution from the great metropolitan entrepôt, agricultural carriage, both of a local variety and for delivery to London and other major market centres, was plainly a leading consideration. Along with others in primarily rural areas, the Thames-directed canals probably outweighed, in point of capital expenditure involved, the further canal building in industrial and coalmining regions earlier described.[1]

The principal gain accruing to agriculture consisted, of course, in the economising on the cost of moving produce out, but useful too were the lower haulage costs of movements in of artificial fertilisers and animal fodder. However, an overall appreciation of the economic value of the rural canals of this period must incorporate a number of serious qualifications. First, it is perhaps desirable to stress the truism that transport improvement did little to enhance farming yields per acre, already insisted on as the primary challenge confronting agriculture. It was largely only profits, or obversely prices, which drew benefit from lower freight charges. Secondly, even the price benefit was not an unmitigated blessing inasmuch as high cost producers lost something

[1] See pp. 457–8.

of their regional monopolies; and although consumers certainly gained in at least the short run, it would not be an entirely specious argument that the increased exposure of the clay farmers to light soil competition tended to repress rather than sharpen their efforts to improve. Thirdly, and this has already been raised in connection with canals in general, many producers already enjoyed reasonably good transport facilities and thus stood to gain little or nothing from canals – although this obviously is of less relevance when dealing with producers most of whom were necessarily located at some distance from water. Fourthly, even though urban growth and industrial concentration stretched the distances which agricultural produce had to travel, a ubiquitous activity like farming did not generally have to send its products very far to find a market, and livestock, which might move across the country from breeder to fattener and thence to the butcher, continued to travel on the hoof.

Fifthly, shifting the ground of appraisal, business per canal mile was obviously less when catering primarily for a necessarily dispersed activity such as agriculture than when catering for locationally clustered industries. With individual producers unable to transfer close to the canal bank, as manufacturers, generally speaking, could do, some sort of compromise had in effect to be struck between the ludicrous economics of a canal branch to every farmer's backyard and a system which left so many farmers still dependent on land carriage that canal business would be negligible. In fact, this piece of inescapable logic along with the limitations on potential traffic imposed by the third and fourth considerations above meant that it was highly unlikely that a canal which leant heavily on agricultural trade could make money, even if planned with thorough forward market research.

It hardly needs saying that the rural canals of these years were projected on little more than a vague general assessment of likely business. As much as anything else they were prompted by the palpable profitability of the earlier ventures in the west Midlands and south Lancashire and a consequent credulity in canals as potential money-spinners. It is noteworthy that, broadly speaking, these canals, unlike their predecessors, were not promoted and financed by local interests with a well-informed sense of the commercial advantages to be derived, but leant on blind capital, mustered through agencies which hung around the London Stock Exchange, itself facilitating the raising of capital by providing a running market in issued shares and, during the mania phase, effectively serving as a general advertising medium for new canal projects by publicly displaying the appreciating value of shares in those projects already initiated. The 'mania' was essentially a Stock Exchange phenomenon, characterised like others of its kind by share valuations which had little or no reference to the worth of the enterprise involved but were determined by speculative judgments as to market trends. Inevitably the time came when pessimistic judgments outweighed optimism and a painful unwinding process set in. Dependent on investors with little objective guide other than Stock Exchange valuation of canals in general, the wave of fresh promotion subsided with share prices. As against forty-five canals with a combined nominal capital of £6,660,000 launched over 1791–94, the next three years brought forth eight with a capital of £1 million.

Planned for the most part on unrealisable expectations, the rural canals were a grave disappointment to those who invested in them. That in itself was simply personal, not national, loss. These canals were built, and once built were of some real economic benefit to the areas they served. But there is an arguable sense in which national loss resulted. To say that the return to private investors was low or non-existent is implicitly to say that, by comparison with investment ventures which did yield normal profits, the resources of manpower and materials employed in these undertakings produced relatively little of public value; that they represented a waste of limited national productive potential inasmuch as the resources engaged might have been more beneficially employed in other directions.

Technically, what is at issue here is the marginal productivity of capital under the general economic and technological conditions of the times. That in certain fields, up to a certain point, the productivity of capital was high is plain. That it was beyond that point subject to fairly sharply decreasing returns could with some plausibility be contended. If it were accepted that returns did decrease quite sharply and that marginal productivity was low, this could be to say that the resources employed in the construction of the rural canals would not have done any more for society had they been diverted to other investment projects. And indeed it might well be allowed that, on a summary inspection of the economy, nothing stands out conspicuously as capable of employing additional capital to obviously superior effect. In that case, one could say that rural canals were at least preferable to totally unproductive relief projects or simple philanthropy as a way of marshalling savings for redissemination, not only in that they were of some real economic value, but also in that the expectation of a return elicited more than conscience or compassion would have done. Put another way again: postulating that income distribution was such that savings tended to exceed investment capable of normal returns, only a redistribution of income or the employment of savings in low or nil return investment projects would sustain the current level of economic activity; the first alternative would of course yield the greater total social satisfaction but in the lack of it the second was better than neither.

One last general descriptive word on canals is desirable. The vision which had fired James Brindley was substantially realised by the canal building of these years. The 'cross' was completed. The great rivers were linked. With the west Midlands canal complex as a hub, Mersey, Severn, Trent and Thames were interconnected, and in 1814 the Grand Union linked Trent and Thames even more directly. All in all, by then there were few districts of any population density in Great Britain which were not in water contact with one another by fairly direct routes. However, at the risk of tedious repetition, the extent to which this was the work of nature and of earlier river improvers should again be emphasised. And the usefulness of the canal sections of this system of water routes was in some degree impaired by lack of uniformity: canals varied a good deal in width and depth so that barges could not always pass from one to another, necessitating transhipment with the handling costs which that involved. Nevertheless, whatever of reservations as to its economic significance, Britain, which as late as 1770 had lagged conspicuously behind the most forward parts of the continent in respect of manmade transport routes, was by the end of this period, or even two decades earlier, endowed with the most sophisticated internal transport system in the world.

It was not only in its canals that Britain had leaped ahead. These forty-five years saw more done to improve British roads than was to be effected until the motor vehicle age. The essentials of what was involved have been dwelt on in the previous chapter: turnpike trusts and better road engineering. And, also as stressed earlier, the importance of roads for goods freightage was limited, though it may be said that farmers, unable to move their business close to canals when these penetrated rural regions, necessarily depended heavily on roads as feeder routes to exploit such advantages as canals might offer; and, given that agricultural commodities would almost certainly have to travel some way by road, that the loading and unloading costs involved in using canals for part journeys and the possible circuitousness involved might mean that even over distances it was cheaper overall to make the one unbroken direct land haul; so that, as farm produce had to travel further to market, agricultural reliance on roads may have increased even with the proliferation of canals. Even so, the judgment made before that the value of better roads consisted principally in gains not readily susceptible to strict economic evaluation may still stand.

Capital expenditure on turnpikes, spread fairly evenly throughout the period, although in no degree comparable with that on canals, is subject to the same kind of weighting as that already brought to bear on canal investment and can in that sense be assigned a real economic importance – measurable if the relevant data were available. Other than these brief comments the only observation of passing interest to make on roads is on the increasing involvement of central authority in turnpikes, particularly marked from 1815 onwards. The ineptitude to which small self-constituted trusts were prone and the limited nature of their views increasingly prompted Parliament not to renew their authority on the expiry of the Acts (of limited term) under which it was exercised and instead to throw together several old trusts to make one large new one, more likely to incorporate ability and broader views of the public interest. In essentials this was just the old reliance on local capacity writ rather larger. In two particular cases Parliament took the responsibility clean out of the hands of unpaid local gentlemen with a taste for public service and transferred it to salaried officials answerable to itself, creating the embryo of a centrally controlled system of road administration to set alongside the handful of central services already existing – which in fact consisted only of defence, justice and mail delivery. The two cases concerned were the London to Holyhead road, in which twenty-nine trusts were extinguished (1815); and the terminal stretches of the main roads leading into London, involving the extinction of fourteen trusts (1826). An even more ambitious scheme was for a parliamentary route from London to Edinburgh, including the construction of much entirely new road. However that latter feature of the project excited the hostility of local interests, fearing a loss of trade, and the Bill failed to secure a Commons' majority. That was in 1830, happily coincident with the end of this period, for it marked the arrest of what actually turned out to be a false start. Not until quite recent times did central authority again assume direct responsibility for roads. Already by 1830 the more farsighted could see that it was not roads which were to provide national through routes but railways.

Banking

Just as with canals, one of the most prominent features about banks within this period is their proliferation in rural areas. This is not by any means to imply that banking development in industrial regions and commercial centres was anything other than very pronounced. Indeed the first twenty-five years or so of this period witnessed a swelling of bank business and a mushrooming of banking concerns in south Lancashire, the west Midlands, the West Riding of Yorkshire, South Wales and central Scotland which fully merits the epithet revolutionary, while London banking also expanded considerably. Growth in these regions was essentially quantitative and does not require extensive treatment here since its fundamental features remained those already discussed in some detail in the previous chapter. Scottish and London business continued on the fairly sound basis already well established. Elsewhere the trade bill continued to be the key element in most banking operations. The viability of banks continued to be closely correlated with fluctuations in the state of public preferences for cash and in the level of commercial activity. The fact that in some areas, south Lancashire and South Wales most conspicuously, banks were increasingly dealing with the owners of productive concerns, rather than with merchants or mercantile type functionaries, made little difference to the intrinsic nature of their business. The bills such industrialists issued against purchases of materials were of the same character as merchants' bills, and the fixed assets which industrialists commanded were of little interest to banks as forms of security, whether as specific collateral or as a general assurance of capacity to pay: the particular menace banks operated under was pressure on liquidity; whatever money value a blast furnace or a spinning factory might have it was certainly not a readily realisable value.

In Lancashire, where early banking development had been slow, there was the additional hazard that many of the bills in circulation were not genuine trade bills with a specific consignment of commodities to back them, but bills resting only on the personal credit of the men they were drawn on. Of this type particularly common were bills for very small amounts issued in payment of wages under the prevailing scarcity of coin – especially acutely felt in the earlier phase of the wartime inflation, although in its later stages a plentiful issue of Bank of England notes partially overcame the difficulty. More dangerous, though generally less common than these small wages bills, were bills for larger amounts

476

issued to meet debts of all kinds. Of conventionally short term they were really just devices for staving off pressing obligations which could not be met, shading from circumstances where the issuer had a genuine expectation of being in funds when the bill matured to ones of outright fraudulence. Lancashire banks often had to make uncomfortable choices between passing up opportunities of employing funds (along with disobliging valuable customers) and hazarding their liquidity and even their fundamental soundness. Put another way: Lancashire banks could get unintentionally drawn into providing long-term capital finance – which up to a point was a healthy enough trend even if a crude and unplanned one. The same sort of thing doubtless happened elsewhere but Lancashire circumstances fostered it to a peculiar degree: the rapidity of industrial development in a region which was somewhat backward in point of financial institutions more or less forced industrialists to devise credit instruments of their own and, specifically, the lack of note-issuing banks compelled them to contrive their own small paper, with the result that private bank-notes never figured much in Lancashire, the region moving straight from its own personal expedients to Bank of England notes.

Lancashire banks, and others, could, with whatever degree of deliberation, the more safely extend their employment of funds some way beyond genuine self-liquidating trade bills and negotiable gilt-edged securities in that, generally speaking, they were increasingly in receipt of rather more durable deposits as the wealthier provincial shopkeepers, merchants, manufacturers and professional persons came to lodge spare cash with banks, although the proneness of these people to withdraw at flutters of alarm enforced caution on the prudent banker.

Another enlarged source of funds opening up to banks in industrial regions, and to the London banks, was provided by that development of banking in agricultural areas already distinguished as a leading feature of this period. Rural bank business was highly seasonal in character. Funds flowed in through the period immediately following the harvest to be steadily run down again through the rest of the year. Thus for a part of the year rural banks had more money than could profitably be employed locally. The surplus was despatched to London, generally to the metropolitan banker who acted as agent, either to be deposited with him at an agreed rate of interest or with instructions for him to employ it on behalf of the rural bank. Either way the rural bank wanted to be able to retrieve it as farmers' deposits were run down. The short-term bill was of course the ideal form of employment for this kind of money, whether bought by the London bank on its own behalf or on behalf of its rural principal. Through this season of the year, then, banks in industrial regions had usually ample opportunities of having bills rediscounted in London, enabling them to expand their own local discounts or other kinds of short-term loans. This cross-country bill business channelled through London had, by the 1800s, brought into existence in the capital a group of specialist bill-brokers, usually acting for the London agents of the two groups of provincial bankers but sometimes dealing direct with either or both provincial terminals.

At the back of this development lay the drawing of farmers into the ambit of banking, already effected in Scotland but in England very largely the achievement of these particular years, especially of the war years. We might conjecture that a principal initiative in this direction came from established banks in mixed industrial and agricultural regions. (It must be remembered that even for the very end of this period the distinction, made above for the sake of convenience, between industrial and agricultural regions is something of an oversimplification; for the beginning of the period it is to treat of the facts of economic geography in distinctly casual fashion, while for the years which witnessed the first emergence of country banks it is quite groundless.) There would be numerous banks which owed their origin to dealing in bills arising out of the distant commerce in which rural industries were involved and who would be well located to extend their other banking services to farmers, whose dealings were conducted largely or entirely in cash and who had consequently not usually been among the original clients of such banks. In many cases the incentive to comprehend agricultural business might be particularly sharpened by a decline in local industrial activity. Norfolk – its capital, Norwich, in particular – would be a perfect case in point.

Such a decline might well be accompanied by an extension of the market area for local agricultural produce bringing farmers into more frequent contact with dealers, who settled with bills as opposed to the cash with which purely local transactions would usually be effected, and thus fetching farmers to banks in greater numbers to have their bills discounted.

In general, farmer banking seems to have been deposit banking in large degree, certainly to a much greater degree than had been the case with country banking in earlier years. In some cases it may even have had independent roots of its own – growing out of dealings with local general merchant shopkeepers who both bought from and sold to farmers. Farmers might maintain a standing account with such dealers, leaving moneys due on sales of produce in the dealers' hands and drawing on these when making purchases; this is embryonic deposit banking and if accompanied by overdrawing on deposits and accepting the dealers' own notes when withdrawing cash has become fully-fledged banking. It should be said, however, that there is little positive evidence to sustain this piece of historical reconstruction and that it is probable that the early development of farmer banking was very largely by way of an outgrowth from established commercial banking.

The chief agency in the initial growth of farmer banking would, then, be the success of the established banks in inducing farmers to deposit funds with them. In all probability the principal aid which banks enjoyed in achieving this was their own note circulation. As a propaganda medium notes had already demonstrated their usefulness in Scotland. Through this period, when the supply of Bank of England notes (with the possible exception of the immediate postwar years) was increasingly capable of meeting payments requirements, English banks too came more and more to value their note issue for this specific promotional purpose rather than any other. The farmer who had come to accept one kind of bank debt (notes) as safe, would the more readily confide in another (deposits). Or at least if he mistrusted notes he had come by he would have to visit the bank to change them, when the virtues of banking could be expounded to him.

The basis of familiarity and confidence laid by notes was powerfully supplemented by wartime circumstances. High profits brought most farmers more cash than they had ever had before and high interest rates enabled banks to offer attractive deposit terms for sums large enough for the income on them to be a meaningful consideration. High profits brought also heightened anticipations encouraging larger outlays, sometimes beyond ready cash capacity. Opening a deposit account with a bank could be paving the way to a request for a loan – or, alternatively, in Scottish fashion, a loan account could become in time a deposit account. And loans to farmers seemed good banking business at a time when it was difficult not to make money in agriculture. Most of this kind of lending was probably intended to cover increased expenditure on seed, manures, labour, tools etc. which would be recovered within a season or two; but some was perhaps on an avowedly longer-term basis and a certain amount of what was nominally short-term doubtless contrived or was constrained to run on in rather indefinite fashion. Loans not recovered before the postwar price slump

479

were particularly likely to become frozen for a long while thereafter; and although the interest payments, assuming they were kept up, appreciated in real value the strain on bank liquidity might be very severe. It was another of the many lessons teaching bankers that if they were to survive in bad times they had to curb their eagerness to take advantage of good times.

It was within this period that bank policy, the role of bank money in the economy and the function of the Bank of England in particular became the subjects of close public concern and inquiry and of governmental action, with consequences of some weight. That is a theme most appositely woven into the chronological survey of the economy with which this chapter must conclude. The necessity for such an appendage is imposed above all by the war, whose distorting effects on economic trends can only be properly portrayed in their own topical context. Nearly half this period, a crucial phase in historical perspective, lies within the terminal dates of the war, 1793–1815. And, awkwardly, the war was neither of such enormous economic import that the secular tendencies of the economy were largely obliterated by it, as was the case in 1914–18 and 1939–45, nor of merely marginal consequence. In the latter case one could satisfactorily comprehend it with occasional passing references; in the former case one could legitimately void the war period altogether and simply pick up with the enduring effects it left on the economy. Neither being the case it must be treated in its own right.

Foreign trade

Of the sectors into which the economy is divided generally for treatment in this book, foreign trade was the one whose pattern was the most warped by the war and it must largely be dealt with in that particular context. However, it would be sensible to indicate separately the long-run changes in the pattern of British external trade as manifested by a contrast between its general structure in 1785 and that obtaining in 1830. Much of course has already been said which pieced together provides the structural pictures, and its summarisation in statistical form will obviate the need for tedious repetitiveness (Tables II.10–13).

TABLE II.10. *Principal domestic exports, percentage breakdown*

	Woollen goods	Cotton goods	Iron 'raw'	Iron 'manufactured'	Non-ferrous metals and manufactures	Linen goods
1784–86	42	8	7		7	4
1829–31	13	49	3	4	4	6

(The statistical series on which the two rows are based are not strictly comparable. The first is founded on 'official' (fixed) valuations of English and Welsh exports, including exports to Ireland. The second is founded on valuations, at current prices, of United Kingdom exports. The resulting discrepancies, however, cannot be great except in the case of 'Linen goods' where the rise is probably just about fully accounted for by the inclusion of Irish exports for the later years.)

TABLE II.11. *Markets for domestic exports, percentage breakdown*

	Southern Europe	Northern Europe	USA	Asia	British West Indies	Canada	Latin America
1784–86	24	20	21	15	11	5	negligible
1829–31	17	22	17	12	8	5	12

So far as Table II.10 is concerned, nothing need be added by way of amplification to what has previously been said in dealing with the industries concerned, except perhaps to draw attention to the fact that considered from the commodity aspect there was no real gain in point of diversification. Indeed the dependence on textiles became even more pronounced; they account for over two-thirds of all domestic exports at the end of the period.

It is of course desirable to indicate the record of exports in gross. But between the shift in general price level over the period and, more important, the variations in factor cost of the principal items involved, this presents problems. A crude conversion of exports at the beginning of the period on an approximate basis of the prices prevailing at the end would, in rough and ready terms, yield a fourfold increase overall (i.e. the 1829–31 percentages for markets may be multiplied by four to obtain a rough indication of the real growth of each). This is a greater increase than that registered by real national output as a whole, of the order of three-and-a-half-fold, but since much of it was due to the reduction in factor costs the comparison does not indicate that exports were responsible for an increased proportion of national income.[1] In fact over the period as a whole that proportion actually fell off from about one-eighth to about one-tenth. Put alternatively, this is to say in effect that the very considerable extent to which the cotton industry came to lean on export markets was rather more than counter-balanced by a relative shift towards dependence on home markets on the part of other industries, principally the woollen industry.

The markets table (II.11) shows that the additional exports of this period went mostly to the regions already buying British goods in rough proportion to established sales. Such variations as are exhibited merit a few general comments. The differing records of the two major divisions of Europe crudely reflect the somewhat stagnant state of the economies of Spain, Portugal and Italy and the rather livelier condition of those of Germany and the Low Countries. The slippage in the figure for the USA marks that country's first firm steps towards industrialisation, after a phase of extremely heavy buying from Britain, getting under way in the mid-1790s and lasting until the American embargo on British trade (1807), during which the USA was taking over 25 per cent of British exports, surpassing any of the other regions as classified here. Of single countries it was still easily the biggest buyer even at the end of the period, the development of native enterprises in some branches of cotton textiles, metalwares and certain other light industries having done no more than deny a few of its exuberantly expanding opportunities to British suppliers.

The failure of the Asiatic market to expand more rapidly than it did is to be explained principally in the difficulty of competing with native cottons after freight costs had been borne on the much more cheaply produced British varieties. The West Indian record measures the fact that having developed so considerably through the eighteenth century there was not a great deal more room in the islands for continuing economic expansion. The first fifteen years or so of the period saw a

[1] If, for example, the factor cost of a unit of exports were halved and exports increased from 100 units to 1,000 units (i.e. by 10) the return to those deriving their income from exports would only increase by 5; whereas an increase by 10 in real gross national output is an increase by 10 in real gross national income. What this means in plain language is that in the case of exports the benefit from factor cost reduction *per se* goes to the foreign importers; if the elasticity of export demand is one or less the exporting country gains nothing at all (i.e. it gains nothing directly, but resources are released for employment in other fields).

wave of British cottons sweeping aside Indian calicoes, but that brought commercial penetration of this market close to its limits. The great expanse of Canada on the other hand had only slowly been opened up in the past and even the somewhat accelerated rate of settlement of this period did not convert it into a market of great weight despite its almost total dependence of Britain for manufactured goods of all kinds. The really big breakthrough in foreign markets came, as the figures indicate, in South and Central America. This is to be closely associated with wartime events and treatment of it can for the moment be reserved.

TABLE 11.12. *Principal imports, percentage breakdown*

	1784–86	1829–31
Total £ m	14	45
Sugar	17	15
Tea	10	6
Silk (raw and yarn)	6	4
Flax and linen yarn	4	4
Raw cotton	3	18
Iron	3	negligible
Coffee	2	5
Corn	1	4
Hides and skins	n.a.	3
Dyes and dye materials	n.a.	4

(For 1784–86 the percentages are based on figures for English and Welsh imports only, including imports from Ireland. For 1829–31 they are based on United Kingdom figures. The resulting discrepancies would be insignificant. Both, however, are founded on 'official' valuations. This means that while the figures for any one commodity may be directly compared (after adjusting for the overall change in imports) to indicate quantity changes, they ignore any shifts in price ratios. The significant results of this are that actual expenditures on cotton and coffee are somewhat overstated in the 1829–31 figures, the price of both having appreciably fallen relative to other imported commodities.

The 'total' figures are 'official' valuations (with Irish trade excluded from both) and can be regarded as measuring fairly accurately the overall change in the volume of imports even with the shifts in price ratios referred to.

The corn percentages are based on the years 1782–88 and 1829–35 to even out the effects of harvest fluctuations, and in the latter case to indicate the position after the modification of the Corn Laws in 1828; they are net of exports.)

Turning to imports, most of the details in Table II.12 are readily comprehensible in the light of what has been said earlier and their implications need not be spelt out here. One composite change of some significance may however be underlined. On the basis of the commodities listed, some two-thirds of imports at the beginning of the period consisted of consumer goods of a luxury or semi-luxury nature. By the end of the period this proportion had fallen to about two-fifths, raw materials for British industries and an essential consumer item, corn, accounting for the remainder. The importance of this broad distinction is that whereas deprivation of the first category of imports would merely cause certain tastes to be denied, deprivation of the second would initiate a chain reaction of potentially devastating economic consequence. The changing balance between the two categories is a measure of the degree to which the British economy was becoming more intimately geared to an international economy.

Some of these imports were of course re-exported, but here again shifting ratios tended to increase the exposure of the economy to the operation of external factors. Only the incomes of merchants, shippers and those employed in handling goods in transit depended on re-exports. Their total cessation could at any time be borne without grievous harm to the economy at large whereas the loss of necessary imported materials or of markets for domestic exports could precipitate destructive tremors of formidably extensive scope. Although imports for re-exportation, over the period as a whole, increased nearly as much as imports for retention, re-exports came to account for a substantially diminished proportion of total exports, increasing in real value rather less than threefold while domestic exports increased roughly fourfold. (The re-export/domestic export ratio dropped from 30 to 17 per cent at official valuations; but the particular artificiality of official re-export values and the fact that the current price ratio between the two categories changed appreciably over the period void these figures of any real meaning.)

One must not make too much of these shifts in the nature of British external trade. While the relative movements from 'non-crucial' to 'crucial' imports and from re-exports to domestic exports did in themselves heighten the international sensitivity of the economy, this was substantially offset over the period as a whole by the fact, stated earlier, that on balance producers' dependence on foreign markets actually fell off a little, and by the further fact that British buyers on average were to a somewhat greater extent catered for from home supplies. This was in part a result of the direct substitution of British for foreign products, principally iron, but also because the demand for the kind of goods produced in Britain rose rather more rapidly than that for goods produced abroad; in particular the demand for British made textiles (even allowing for their import content) rose more rapidly than the demand for sugar and tea.

Reverting briefly to the re-export trade, it should be said that it experienced a marked change in general character through this period. The tobacco trade which had been such an important element before the American War made something of a recovery in the 1790s when poor market conditions in revolutionary France and the closure of the Amsterdam entrepôt drove American suppliers back on to London; but the trade fairly soon fell away again and was of negligible value from the early nineteenth century onwards. Sugar, after a big spurt under wartime conditions, then ran up against the cultivation of beet sugar on the continent, although about a tenth of sugar imports were still re-exported at the end of the period. The closure of Amsterdam also produced a great upward leap in the coffee trade and, while it slumped rather badly with the peace, approximately a half of coffee imports was being re-exported around 1830. Coffee was by then the last great relic of an earlier era of trade for trade's sake. Increasingly the re-export trade was just an offshoot from Britain's industrial activities. Raw cotton was vying with coffee as a re-export, even though this only absorbed about a twelfth of cotton imports. The stocks of the Liverpool merchants were the obvious resort of European manufacturers caught short in their own markets or too few in number to warrant direct supplies from source. British imports of dyestuffs served European textile industries in the same way, although here the British commercial footing in South America and India from which many of these came also played an important part. Re-exports accounted perhaps for as much as two-fifths of dyestuffs imports, ranking third to coffee and cotton in the general re-export trade.

Perhaps the most striking feature about sources of imports as shown in Table II.13 is the massive share preserved by a handful of small West Indian islands. Nothing perhaps better underlines the continuity between these and earlier decades than this statistical fragment, manifesting the persistence of basic consumption patterns throughout an age generally reputed for its revolutionary character, though it should be allowed that were figures available for 1830 they would almost certainly show the West Indian proportion of imports starting to fall off appreciably. West Indian sugar alone just failed to keep up with the general growth in British imports but its slight deficiencies were made up by coffee, while rum too had a hand in the performance.

TABLE II.13. *Sources of imports, percentage breakdown*

	British West Indies	Northern Europe	Asia	Southern Europe	USA	Canada	Foreign West Indies and South America
1784–86	27	25	21	15	6	negligible	negligible
1820–22	26	15	23	12	13	3	8

(Figures for this purpose are not available after 1822.)

The obvious shifts revealed by the table are the relative drawing away from northern European supply sources and the very marked inclination towards North America; the first would probably, and the second certainly, be even more pronounced by 1830. They are in some part interrelated phenomena, manifesting substantially increased imports of North American timber, tar and pitch at the expense of Baltic supplies, and even of North American grain, though Baltic sources remained heavily predominant for some decades to come. However it is above all cotton imports which account for the great development of the USA as a supplier. By the end of the period three-quarters of British cotton requirements were met by the southern states (the remainder coming from other parts of the Americas and various miscellaneous quarters of the globe); and these probably accounted also for about three-quarters of all imports from the USA.

As with exports, so in this table too Latin America emerges from nowhere with some éclat. The commodities involved consisted principally of dyestuffs, hides and skins, and a certain amount of cotton, but the story of the trade is best related in its military and diplomatic context.

Fluctuations

And so to the bumps and jumps which events contrived for the economy through this period. As already noted, it is the war in particular which compels some sort of a blow by blow account to be offered and it may as aptly be said here as elsewhere that this book does not purport in general to comprehend secular cyclic analysis of the British economy. The case for trade or business cycles of about ten years' duration, imposing a fairly regular wave pattern on the British economy from the late eighteenth century through to the twentieth, seems to have been made beyond dispute, although debate will doubtless persist as to the key agents of cyclic behaviour – stock levels, profit expectations, investment decisions, credit creation, sun-spots or what-not. Since this book in general is essentially concerned with long-run historical trends the trade cycle can legitimately be subsumed rather as variations between day and night time levels of economic activity can be subsumed. In this particular section, however, which is concerned with shorter-run trends, cyclic behaviour cannot be altogether edited out, and, in very compressed form, some account of it is offered in connection with the 'crises' of 1810 and 1825. But while it is hoped that what is said there may be of some help to the uninitiated in understanding this general characteristic of economic life under uncontrolled dynamic conditions, a comprehensive analytic account of the phenomenon is really the province of economic theory, not of economic history.[1] (It may perhaps be usefully mentioned here that this field of investigation has its own vocabulary: 'crisis' and 'depression' do not carry the same burden of eventfulness as they do in ordinary usage; 'crisis' signifies a situation tendency to administer a sharp check to economic activity; 'depression' simply signifies a state in which economic activity is running at a lower level than previously, or even, sometimes, no more than a failure to maintain the same growth rate as previously.)

What of the longer-term cycles, with durations measured in decades, which some observers have discerned at work? There would be fairly wide agreement on the justice of saying that the postulation of such cycles is still pretty speculative; that the raw data is put through a good deal of mathematical processing before it can be made to show up such cycles; and that their subsequent representation as smooth curves is rather more impressive than the tentative economic analyses projected in explanation of them. Indeed their proponents, broadly speaking, do not suggest that they are 'true' other than at that fairly high level of abstraction at which they are capable of application to a wider range of situations than those from which they are actually drawn. They represent attempts to discover generally valid laws of economic change

---

[1] What has earlier been said in connection with banking, particularly on pp. 393–7, is also of some relevance in this context.

which run through the dense and complex welter of specific circumstances which make up any one real life instance. The mathematical
'smoothing' which goes into their construction deprives them of any
title as descriptions of what actually happened in history; and, if it be
allowed that in real life situations the specific elements greatly outweigh the universal elements, then, even with their existence more
conclusively established, their value in interpreting the historical course
taken by any particular economy is sufficiently slight for them to be
passed over in a work whose analytical mesh does not pretend to be
other than fairly coarse.

It was observed at the beginning of this chapter that the economy
enjoyed a particularly favourable conjuncture of circumstances through
the first few years of this period; and, by implication, that the 'Industrial
Revolution' could plausibly be said to have been born during that
phase when all signals seemed to be set at 'go'. The outbreak of war
with revolutionary France in 1793 brought a brief but severe shakeout
as a panic flight into gold constricted trading credit and precipitated the
collapse of quite a number of country banks; but the pressure on
liquidity was eased when the government announced its readiness to
issue £5 million worth of exchequer bills against sound commercial
or bank paper – a tentative step towards a state issued paper currency
to make good the shortfall in precious metal and Bank of England
currency which was all that could command general confidence at
such times of alarm. (The efficacy of this measure – it was not even
necessary to implement it fully – underlines a major contrast between
the two belligerents. Different histories had contrived a situation in
which British government paper was as good as gold even though no
specific assets lay back of it, while the French *assignat*, with the considerable property expropriated from the French church to back it, was
depreciating daily.)

With the currency crisis soon quelled most producers were probably
able to weather the temporary curb on trading activity while running
down raw material stocks and letting stocks of finished goods pile up.
The war closed French ports to British ships but the French trade was
never of great consequence and what there was of it largely continued
anyway, via neutral ports, principally Hamburg; and the French occupation of Holland and the destruction of the entrepôt commerce of
Amsterdam in 1794 brought the massive Dutch coffee trade to London,
along with a sizeable amount of traffic in sugar, tobacco, spices and
other commodities. Interest rates started upwards as the government

moved heavily into the money market, but in general the kind of projects which in the past had shown themselves sensitive to rising interest rates and falling stock prices appear to have shrugged these off in a general atmosphere of confident business expectations. In any event, government war expenditure, whether tax financed or loan financed, was a powerful contribution to demand – experienced most signally by the metallurgical and shipbuilding industries, but of appreciable direct consequence to the textile and leatherworking industries, not to mention the straightforward requirement of men for the fighting services. In major part this represented a transfer of resources, of ambivalent welfare value; but to the significant extent to which it invoked resources which otherwise would have been idle it generated a train of fresh income creation which was unambiguously real gain and which must be reckoned a factor in keeping demand pressure at that pitch which enabled the 'Revolution' to go forward through this initial, and perhaps decisive, phase.

There was however an investment sector which did clearly suffer from government pressure on lendable funds: domestic building. Whether it was the speculative builder – the building craftsman who ventured on his own with minimal capital resources was a common type in the trade – or the prospective houseowner who needed financing, this was an area of the economy which drew heavily on loan funds. To what extent it was actually sensitive to interest rate is questionable; it was perhaps more a matter of lenders' preferences, swinging to this field when other opportunities were not plentiful and swinging away again when they were – certainly into our own times the countertrend character of building activity has been very marked. On this occasion, housebuilding remained at a low level right through to 1803, when other forms of investment activity slackened off. Since the same phase brought two pairs of years (1795-96, 1800-01) in which bread prices accelerated upwards at a velocity which wage rates could not possibly match, buoyant as they were under conditions of keen competition for labour, there can be little doubt that conditions of life for low income groups deteriorated badly up to the temporary cessation of the war in 1802 (Peace of Amiens). The deterioration was probably worst in growing towns, where the need for new housing would have been most acute and where, generally speaking, Speenhamland style poor relief, automatically linked to bread prices, did not prevail.

The harvest of 1794 was bad. The harvest of 1795 was worse. During 1796 some 850,000 quarters of wheat were imported; the highest recorded for any previous year had been 530,000 in 1783. These imports were expensive. They had to be scrambled for in competition with other buyers from north-western Europe (the harvest failure was general); and with so many sailors lost to the Navy at a time when maritime trade generally had expanded considerably British shipping resources were insufficient to fetch this dearly bought grain back from the Baltic, so that neutral shipping space, commanding a premium price, had to be hired.

Both Baltic corn dealers and foreign shippers, made nervous by the war, were apt to require payment in gold, or at least to repatriate their earnings as soon as they had discounted bills taken in payment. The gold outflow occasioned in this way was superadded to that necessitated by the maintenance of military units abroad and the payment of subsidies to Britain's continental allies, in addition, rather ironically, to that resulting from French acquisition of gold in order to replace the now virtually worthless *assignat*, effected largely through neutral Hamburg which in turn drew on London among other gold stock centres.

The great bulk of this gold came of course from the vaults of the Bank of England. Whether the Bank could have borne this strain as it had borne earlier strains was something which was not to be put to the test. In February 1797 the government released the Bank from its obligation to honour its commitments in gold.

In the strictest sense the 'suspension of cash payments' was not an abandonment of the gold standard. Until Bank of England notes were made legal tender in 1812 creditors retained a full right to require payment in gold – unless their debtor was the Bank of England. In practice, the Bank of England had so secured itself in the public confidence that its now unbacked money was just as acceptable as it had been when gold could be got for it at a fixed price. The alarm initially engendered in some quarters was quickly stayed. The banking and mercantile community in London and the provinces, with virtual unanimity, pronounced its readiness to carry on business as normal with a pure paper currency. This stand was facilitated by the fact that the initial suspension was for twelve months only, and its subsequent renewals were on the clear understanding that cash payments would be resumed after the war so that Bank of England notes (and other liabilities) continued in principle to constitute claims to gold capable eventually of being exercised. A number of banks found it necessary to close their doors for a few days until popular opinion had been reassured by the confident attitudes of local establishments, but in general only the merest ripple of disquiet very briefly disturbed money transactions of any kind.

While certain of the specific year by year consequence of suspension must be touched on in their proper order, two running results of it may usefully be indicated straight away. With the Bank of England effectively holding a licence to print money, the government's capacity to borrow to finance war expenditure was in practice unlimited (as long as the Bank's gold holding could support external expenditure). Under this aspect, suspension was really as much a matter of removing any check to the issue of Exchequer bills as it was of freeing the Bank from constraint; and if this were not a chief consideration in the initial decision to suspend cash payments it was certainly a dominant one in the subsequent maintenance of suspension. Secondly, and from a national point of view this was much more important, it meant that inflation did not impair the competitiveness of British goods in foreign markets. Any general rise in sterling costs was, other things being equal, offset by a corresponding depreciation of the pound on the foreign exchanges. The Bank of England had a licence to print money. The government had a licence to borrow. But, of transcendent significance, export industries had a licence to grow.

Of course it might be argued that suspension was the cause of inflation, so that in this last respect it was merely a matter of the condition carrying its own cure. Here one moves into that price phenomena ground which is easily the most treacherous of all the surfaces on which economic history has to play. Wherever one treads it the snares of price theory and the mud of merely partial data lie ready to enmesh and bring down even the most skilful. In common prudence no more is to be attempted here than an indication of the main lines of possible approach.

The available data is abundant enough to make it clear that prices were already rising before suspension. One price series founded on an unweighted range of consumer goods shows an 8·5 per cent increase on the average of the years 1792-96 over the years 1787-91, even with grain excluded – and 15 per cent with grain included. And though any realistic cost of living type index would show a powerful upward movement in the years after 1797, much of it would be due to the necessarily heavy weighting assigned to grain whose price behaviour is quite distinctive. The evidence would not support the attribution of a unique character to post-1797 price trends, so that a purely monetary explanation would not seem tenable. However, that would still leave plenty of scope for a monetary explanation in association with other factors.

Begging the task of attempting to assess the importance to be attached to them, such other inflationary factors as were obviously present may be simply itemised. First, base demand was strong. Rising population and a high level of investment were, right from the outset of the period, pressing on supply factors. Indeed it is virtually axiomatic that the earlier stages of a growth phase, before the benefits of investment are fully felt, will be accompanied by some degree of inflation. And the secular trend of demand was supplemented by heavy government expenditure from 1793 onwards. Second, there is the bearing on prices of the obstructions posed to imports by acts of war. Fortunately for Britain many of her imports came from regions which lay well beyond the range of enemy power and her naval strength enabled the lines of communication with these to be kept open. But between hostile control of certain supply sources and an irreducible amount of roving commerce raiding, with a consequent risk premium on shipping and insurance rates, some rise in import prices was inevitable. The most telling price consequence of this situation was in the case of grain, despite the fact that imports constituted, even in the worst years, only a fraction of total supplies. But with a highly inelastic demand for this commodity, grain imports were, year in, year out, the indispensable marginal element in supply; and it is a first principle of price behaviour that under unregulated conditions it is the cost at the margin which determines prices. Supplies from the Baltic region were especially vulnerable to unfriendly action on both land and sea, rendering them difficult and costly to obtain. With grain the chief single component of living standards it was a potent sector of general inflation.

That last comment is really to run to ground which is ultimately common to all lines of approach to this question. Whether inflation was initiated by increasing the money supply, whether it was demand-engendered or whether it started as a rise in import prices it was bound eventually to assume the blanket character of a cost-push inflation, operating both through consumer goods' prices and hence wage costs and, more directly, through producer goods' costs.

We must return to the immediate aftermath of suspension. In 1797 occurred the first serious check to economic growth since its clear onset in 1785. In all probability a purely secular cyclic arrest was due anyway. The Bank of England's cash difficulties stemmed not only from a loss of gold but also, though less weightily, from its swollen liabilities consequent on increased discounting as trade and government expenditure had expanded. Quite possibly, then, the Bank would have started to curb credit even had gold not been flowing abroad in inordinate amounts. And curb credit it did although it was now under no impelling necessity to do so, since it could print liquidity at will. Of course, formally it could not yet count on suspension being continued after the initial twelve-month period, so that it ought in any event to be establishing such a gold ratio as would enable it then to resume cash payments. Possibly its behaviour through 1797 was primarily prompted by this consideration. However, it does seem clear from the Bank's practice over the next few years, when it could quite safely have ignored gold standard rules, that, admittedly in a fairly latitudinarian manner, it continued nevertheless to observe them, on the principle that as effective controller of the public money supply it should have main regard to the public interest, and that that was best served by regulating money creation with reference to the gold situation.

The Bank's gold stock was fairly quickly reconstituted: 1798 brought a renewal of growth and a fresh surge of investment activity. The pace faltered badly with the very substantial expenditure on foreign corn of 1801 when wheat imports were higher than ever before at 1,420,000 quarters, and each quarter cost about half as much again as it had done at the previous peak of 1796. Imported grain in 1801 may have accounted for close on a fifth of total supplies and its acquisition may have involved the diversion of something like three per cent of national purchasing power from domestic to foreign expenditure, so that on this particular occasion the impact of a bad harvest on the level of domestic productive activity must have been pronounced. The available data suggests that it was in fact of the order of a three per cent drop. The better harvest of 1801 and the cessation of hostilities early in 1802 brought the economy bouncing back again with an investment boom lasting into 1803, with which the first, formative, phase of the Industrial Revolution could be said to have concluded.

For some years after its renewal in 1803 Britain's participation in the war was of a rather nominal variety and it was not until 1807 that it again started to engender particular economic consequences of importance. On 21 November 1806 Napoleon, fresh from the destruction of Prussia at Jena, had issued the Berlin Decrees, commanding the total cessation of trade between the United Kingdom and such of Europe as the Emperor of the French then controlled. But, between the aversion of subject countries to the measure and the consequent disinclination of

Dutch, German and Italian officials to execute it, the corruptibility of French officials when they were installed, and the ease with which the forms of the blockade could be preserved without any real reduction in trade by operating through neutral ports, the Continental System had only a derisible paper existence from its inception right through the first half of 1807. By the end of the year, however, British goods could only reach European markets with great difficulty and in massively reduced quantities; and imports from the continent had become almost unobtainable. The coverage of the blockade had become almost total. By one means and another Russia, Austria, Denmark, Spain and Portugal had been brought within its scope. Malta provided a base for a fair amount of smuggling activity along the Mediterranean coasts; but otherwise only Sweden remained open to provide a colouring of non-British origin to goods intended for Napoleonic Europe; and the superficial forms which had passed benevolent scrutiny in the earlier months of 1807 were now ripped aside with a new found official zeal as the Emperor himself, freed from military preoccupations by his victory over the Russians in June, undertook a much closer personal surveillance of his System. Through the first half of 1808 the rigour of the blockade was fully maintained; and now the effects of French economic warfare were seriously aggravated by similar American measures.

Anglo-American relations had been troubled ever since the beginning of the war by British interference with American shipping to prevent war materials reaching France and, of much more irritative effect, to arrest Royal Navy deserters serving on American vessels. To this already sensitive situation there were now added the Orders in Council (11 November 1807), Britain's reply to the Berlin Decrees. These denied all countries observing the continental blockade any commercial intercourse other than with the United Kingdom – and Britain had the naval strength to make this prescription effective. The underlying strategy was to make economic life so difficult for the countries participating in the Continental System as to force them to abandon it, either openly or surreptitiously. Of necessity, the measure was principally directed against the use of American vessels in the conduct of continental trade – the USA being the only neutral power with sufficient ships to undertake it. It was a measure which had no justification in international law and what it meant in effect was that Britain was prepared to hazard Anglo-American trade in an endeavour to prise open the continental blockade. Despite the anger aroused in the USA the pacifically minded President Jefferson was resolved to stop short of war and contrived a response intended to do the maximum commercial harm to Britain with the minimum of discomfort to America. The Embargo Act (22 December 1807) forbade all American exports to the United Kingdom and a range of American imports thence; those still permitted were the cheaper kind of necessaries, constituting about a half of normal British exports to America. It was not, perhaps, a very skilfully selected strategy since one of its chief consequences was to cut the British cotton industry off from USA raw material supplies at a time when the closure of continental markets for cotton goods had reduced the industry's requirements of raw cotton anyway – and as yet only about a half of Britain's cotton imports came from the USA. Nevertheless, on top of the heavy fall in sales to the continent the partial loss of the American market caused British exports through the first half of 1808 to run at a very low level – approximately 25 per cent below that prevailing a year earlier.

Napoleon's very anxiety to extend the Continental System brought something of a compensating adjustment for British exporters in its train. To bring Portugal to heel he occupied it (November 1807); and the Portuguese sovereign fled to Brazil where, perforce, he had to authorise direct trade with other European countries, which under the old Portuguese colonial arrangements had been forbidden. The Spanish government had been more docile; but the laxity with which the Continental System was enforced in Spain brought it a French army also (March 1808), exciting a popular revolt. Although the 'patriot' government, dependent on British arms and British money, resisted pressure to pronounce the abolition of the old restrictions on colonial trade, its own insecure and uncertain character limited its effective authority and exposed the Governors of the American colonies to the force of local opinion which was generally hostile to the enforced trade with Spain; and a substantial, though not complete, freeing of trade took place in Spanish America through the second half of 1808. Apart from the USA, in limited degree, only Britian was in a position to take advantage of these openings in South and Central America which served to alleviate in some measure the difficulties created by the Blockade and the Embargo.

The popular uprising in Spain had European as well as American consequences. It blew a great hole in the south-western section of the blockade wall, widened with the arrival of a British army in Portugal and its expulsion of the French from that country in August 1808. Quite suddenly the Continental System started to crumble. In the north, through the late summer and autumn of 1808 the island of Heligoland became the centre of an intense contraband trade carried out by small ships all along the facing Danish, German and Dutch coasts. And whether confronted with plain smuggling or with declared cargoes of reputedly non-British origin officials on the Baltic and North Sea littorals reverted to that benevolence, ineptitude or corruption which had made the System a joking matter in its early months. Where this administrative collapse is not to be credited to the moral effects of the Orders in Council, working as it had been hoped they would work, it reflects again the extent to which the operation of the blockade depended on the personal supervision of the Emperor – in October drawn off to Spain and in the following April to Austria, to add to his string of military triumphs.

The Continental System survived on paper; but in 1809 the volume of British overseas trade was larger than it had ever been before and in 1810 it swelled even more. And this despite the fact that diplomatic difficulties with the USA persisted. The Embargo was repealed (15 March 1809) in the face of its unpopularity in the USA itself, but the American government persisted with a policy of commercial pressure on Britain to secure the withdrawal of the Orders in Council and intro-duced in the place of the Embargo the Law of Non-Intercourse, tech-nically an even more stringent measure as far as Anglo-American commerce was concerned for it flatly forbade all trade between the two countries. In practice it meant a resumed flow of American cotton and other supplies to Britain, carried by American vessels clearing USA ports for the Azores, the Canaries, Madeira, Lisbon or Cadiz, some genuinely observing the letter of non-intercourse by transhipping to British vessels at these places, others breaching it with impunity, for there was no effective way of checking on where a vessel actually went once out of port. (This device had not been available under the Em-bargo which had confined all American ships to home waters.) Imports from Britain could not, however, in any quantity be masked and non-intercourse was, then, more grievous for British exporters than embargo. However, non-intercourse was suspended between June and September 1809 as a result of a diplomatic muddle in the course of which the Americans were given to understand, erroneously, that the Orders in Council were to be withdrawn. Between that period of grace, which saw a hectic rushing of cargoes across the Atlantic, a certain amount of concealed entry of British goods through American ports and some smuggling across the Canadian border and in small vessels working out of the West Indies, exports to the USA through 1809 cannot have been far short of normal levels. And 1 May 1810 brought the total repeal of the Law of Non-Intercourse and a full restoration of Anglo-American commerce.[1]

Tight as things had been through the worst phase, roughly summer 1807 to summer 1808, they had been neither severe enough nor protracted enough to cause any grave harm to an economy sustained by a strong internal dynamism. Only the cotton industry, leaning fairly heavily on European and American markets, had suffered with any real degree of seriousness; and even there the dislocation had not been such as to have really apprehensible repercussions on the economy at large.

The blockade in itself could never have sabotaged the British economy, even if its full potential had been realised over a prolonged period. Very crudely speaking, it had about as much capacity for harm as had those purely domestic circumstances which, in peace or war, could turn boom into depression. However, this is to say, amongst other things, that the blockade superadded to an adverse shift in domestic circumstances could seriously exacerbate a depression and impede the recovery of momentum. It was fortunate for Britain that through the years 1807 and 1808 purely internal factors had been conducive to continuing growth – potential growth which the unfavourable external situation had just about frustrated without actually thrusting the economy back in its tracks. But Napoleon had not yet despaired of the Continental System and 1811 brought a conjuncture of circumstances engendering a depression of probably unprecedented gravity, and initiating a decade during which the persistent growth momentum of the previous quarter-century was very largely lost.

It is plain that by the later months of 1810 merchants' stocks were excessive to current demand. It is possible, too, that recent investment in productive capacity had run ahead of actual requirements. It was almost certainly the case that the liquidity of the banking system was unusually low. In brief, all the features of a classic cyclic overreaching of the economy were probably present. Purely secular factors may have been responsible in substantial part for this situation, but there are two

[1] This was just another change of American tactics. Both embargo and non-intercourse had also been directed against France which under the Milan Decrees (17 December 1807) treated American vessels as belligerent should they call at a British port en route to the continent, as the Orders in Council required them to do. The new American policy was to reimpose non-intercourse against either of France or England whenever the other lifted its restrictions on American shipping.

sets of specifically topical factors which quite obviously had a hand in it. First, the recent dissolution of the constraints on external trade had resulted in particularly heavy importation of foreign goods for both domestic and re-export sale – more goods than either home or foreign markets could readily absorb. Secondly, the Bank of England had been steadily slipping away from that observance of gold standard rules which it had broadly continued to practise in the first few years after suspension; and certainly by 1809, at the latest, it had quite consciously abandoned them and had instead come to regard the soundness of the securities against which it granted credit as the prime determinant of the volume of its liabilities. The two things were closely linked. More trade necessitated more trade bills; and the freer the Bank's discount policy the more easily could trade bills be created.

The Bank had in fact switched from a gold-backed currency to a goods-backed currency whose volume fluctuated with the level of trade. The snag in such a practice was that the trade goods in question might sell more slowly or for less than had been anticipated. In one mercantile sector in particular this danger was present in very acute degree: the Latin American trade. The surge of exports to the Portuguese and Spanish colonies through 1808 was founded on speculative optimism rather than on knowledge of the market. Turnover of the sudden inundation of British manufactures was slow and sometimes only effected at giveaway, loss-cutting prices. Even when goods had been disposed of there followed the problem of repatriating the proceeds. There was of course no established commercial network such as would have enabled this to be achieved by means of bills on London or other European centres. It was trade conducted under essentially medieval conditions. Where money could not be brought back as silver or gold it could only get home in the form of goods. South America could offer quite a range of goods; but production and distribution patterns had to be reorientated to meet the novel requirements of British merchants and, further, many of the goods in question were already obtainable more cheaply from other sources. Latin American cotton, sugar, coffee, tobacco and copper were not in normal circumstances fully competitive in European markets, though the cotton and tobacco could find buyers when the USA closed up. Hides, skins, tallow and dyestuffs had a real commercial future but not one which could be secured overnight.

In summary, during this first hectic phase of the Latin American trade both outward and inward consignments were commonly subject to lengthy delays and to disposal at unremunerative prices. As a consequence, bills which had financed initial purchases from home suppliers often could not be met when they fell due. Up to a point, the further extension of credit or the raising of fresh credit could take care of this situation but it seriously impaired the capacity of this sector of the commercial front to withstand pressure. It created an especially vulnerable salient whose collapse could trigger off a general alarm, a consequent freezing of credit and a seizing-up of trading activity. And as a matter of chronological fact it was in this sector that the first signs of weakness appeared.

From July 1810 a number of mercantile concerns which were involved in the Latin American trade were brought to the point of having to default on their bills, though their fundamental balance was perfectly sound. For some while, vigorous action on the part of the Bank of England shored up the situation, the Bank coming to the specific assistance of concerns which it was persuaded would ultimately be capable of meeting their debts, and, more generally, discounting good paper with especial freedom. Under suspension the Bank was released from the dilemma of having to choose between protecting its own gold at a time of pressure and denying others that support which might enable pressure to be stood off. On this occasion that flexibility of response might have been sufficient to stay the potential crisis if it had been only the peculiar difficulties of Latin American merchants which had to be contended with. But, as indicated already, merchants of all kinds were overstocked and were bound eventually to come to the point where, further credit being unobtainable, they would have to accelerate unloading in an endeavour to raise cash, precipitating a downward wave of prices, eventuating in the cash realised on sales being insufficient to cover the bills issued on original purchase. And while it was dealers in imported commodities who were, in general, the worst situated in this respect, export merchants and purely internal traders who had run up stocks with the boom which had got under way from mid-1808 were also, in varying degrees, similarly placed, as were producers in point of either stocks of raw materials or stocks of finished goods. And just as producers might have built up excess stocks so too they might have built up excess productive capacity, resulting then in a temporary cessation of further investment expenditure which could itself have been the initiating factor in a purely cyclic downturn of the economy. Investment expenditure would certainly taper off sharply once a downturn, however initiated, had set in and would thus have operated as an exacerbating factor even if it were not a causal one.

Stock and investment levels can be pointed to as crucial, omnipresent variables under nineteenth-century conditions tending to produce a regularly recurring transformation of boom into depression. Perhaps 1811 was essentially the successor depression to that of 1797, the interval between the two stretched beyond the normal length postulated by trade cycle theory by the disturbing effects of the circumstantially occasioned setbacks of 1801 and 1807–08. But it would be a fool's task to try to disentangle secular from topical among the factors that converted the tremors caused by Latin American difficulties into a pervasively profound disturbance and set at naught the Bank of England's efforts to stop the rot. If anything were needed to turn the probability of setback into certainty, it was provided by the sealing off of northern Europe in late 1810.

Although Napoleon, with the Austrians shattered at Wagram (6 July 1809) and the reconquest of Spain well in hand, had for some while been able to turn his undivided attention to the problem of reducing Britain, he had hesitated to essay a purposeful reimposition of the blockade. Among other considerations he had been held back by the superabundant French harvest of 1808. The consequent low prices threatened to cause serious disaffection among French agrarian and mercantile interests unless export outlets were afforded. Britain was not just the most likely buyer but, with effective naval enforcement of the Orders in Council, the only foreign market which could be reached by sea. The British government was hardly likely to authorise imports of grain from France if the blockade were being rigorously enforced; while with the blockade effectively lifted the British government was prepared to permit not only grain but imports of wine and brandy as well. Through 1809 then and into 1810 – until surplus grain stocks had been cleared – it was reckoned to be in French interests to keep Anglo-European commerce open, even though in so doing Britain was enabled to weather the very bad harvest of 1809 without grave distress. But from the spring of 1810 in the areas under direct French control the blockade was reimposed with enhanced tightness. The coasts opposite Heligoland were flooded with troops and the contraband trade totally extinguished. Dutch and Prussian ports were filled with French soldiers and customs officials. Finally, Swedish facilities were lost to Britain on the commencement of a state of war with England (17 November 1810), forced on a very reluctant Sweden by France.

While in the north the blockade now operated more efficiently than it had ever done before, things were easier in the south than they had been through the worst of 1807–08. Portugal and the southern fringes of Spain, which remained in patriot hands, were open and the land boundaries of these regions could not be policed effectively enough to prevent a fair quantity of British goods passing across them for eventual distribution over quite a wide area. Nor were the Mediterranean coasts rendered impervious to smuggling carried out from Malta. Even with the favourable southern situation, however, exports to Europe through 1811 were some 40 per cent below the 1809 level and imports from Europe were some 65 per cent down.

The re-establishment of the blockade both sharpened the point of actual crisis and deepened and prolonged the subsequent depression. In the first respect its peculiar efficacy was to complete the plight of merchants carrying stocks which had been intended for ultimate disposal in northern Europe. Although many of these commodities did eventually find outlets in the south, the further delay strained credit resources beyond endurance and precipitated a widespread defaulting on bills. In weather like this, the Bank of England abandoned its lifeboat role and looked now to its own safety, declining to touch commercial paper unless its prompt payability was beyond question. The government, somewhat tardily, took over the role in April 1811 making £6 million of Exchequer Bills available, repayable over a year and a half, but so stringent were the conditions attaching to this facility that less than 1·5 million were taken up. (Neither the Bank nor the government were prepared to subsidise stockholders who had guessed wrongly as to future market trends; sufficient credit to see fundamentally sound concerns through temporary difficulties was as much as either would supply at the best of times.)

Banks, country banks most especially, were among the most conspicuous casualties of the crisis, sabotaged by that ironic law which ensures that bankers are under the greatest pressure to meet their liabilities (notes and deposits) at those times when they have the greatest difficulty in realising their own claims (bills and securities). In other words, the whole credit system was plunged into an accumulating crisis of the general type described in the previous chapter. And it should be noted in passing that the vulnerability of the banking system as exposed with particular painfulness on this occasion contributed powerfully to strengthening the view that credit creation should be subject to some form of control other than the private discretion of bankers. The crisis coincided with the publication of the report of the parliamentary Bullion Committee – appointed to consider the advisability of restoring cash payments – which was in effect a thorough denunciation of the Directors of the Bank of England and a strong plea for linking bank credit automatically to gold. Although the Bullion Committee was primarily concerned with the depreciation of the pound on the foreign exchanges, its report lent much weight to the opinion that internal instability resulted from ungoverned credit creation.

Such an opinion was not only widely held by contemporaries but has often been advanced by later historians. An adequate discussion of the issue cannot be essayed here but a couple of observations might usefully be made: first, that some accounts glibly contrive to equate easy credit and reckless speculation; second, that a fairly clear cut distinction must be preserved between initiating a crisis and exacerbating a crisis. Nobody could dispute that the crisis of 1810–11 would not have been so bad had the banking system been more liquid. But it is a far cry from that observation to a picture of a frenzied abandonment of all commercial prudence, inevitably culminating in a wholesale liquidation of stocks and widespread bankruptcies. All credit-financed activities carry some element of risk, as does the least departure on the part of a banker from 100 per cent liquidity, so that it is always open to a retrospective observer to exclaim that credit was 'excessive' whenever an economic setback occurs. Obviously the quantity of credit adequate to sustaining one level of economic activity becomes 'excessive' should that level fall but, equally obviously, it does not of necessity follow that the 'excess' was the cause of the setback; and once recession has set in the question of whether recession is cause and 'excess' effect or vice versa is like asking which of the scissors' blades does the cutting.

The freezing of credit consequent on the severe pressure on liquidity would, in any circumstances, have caused a general depression from late 1810 but one from which recovery would normally have been effected in a matter of months as overexposed positions were liquidated and credit equilibrium re-established. Instead, however, the depression persisted throughout 1811, well into 1812 and though that latter year brought some alleviation it was not until 1814 that the economy recovered anything substantial of its earlier elastic exuberance. The depressive effect on incomes and thus domestic purchasing power of lowered investment and wage outlays, which any setback must bring in its train, was prolonged by the serious checks to overseas sales, deadening the capacity to snap back which the economy could normally preserve for the relatively brief duration of an ordinary secular crisis.

The blockade was maintained at a high level of efficacy throughout 1811 and the first half of 1812. And American non-intercourse was renewed from February 1811 (replaced in March by the Non-Importation Law which modified non-intercourse by allowing Americans to export direct to Britain but preserved the prohibition on imports from Britain), France having proclaimed the repeal of the Milan Decrees in respect of American shipping. June 1812 brought a gain in the form of a change of sides by Russia and Sweden which permitted trade with northern Europe to effect a partial recovery; but the same month also saw the cold war with the USA turn into a shooting affair, anti-British sentiments joining with designs on Canada to ensure the ascendancy of counsels of war over Jeffersonian pacificism in the White House – ironically at almost exactly the same time as commercial discontent in Britain had overborne the British government's bellicosity and brought about the repeal of the Orders in Council – five days after the American declaration of war but some weeks before news of it reached Britain. Had the timing of events been a little different mid-1812 might have seen the beginnings of a renewed economic upthrust. Even the most avid American 'hawk' could hardly have called for war with the Orders in Council withdrawn; and a reopening of the American market might have supplied just the fillip the British economy needed at that time. As it was, open war with America, conducted on a minimal scale, did not so much worsen the situation as frustrate any prospect of a rapid resumption of growth. The cotton industry was handicapped, but not crippled, by the cessation of raw cotton supplies from the USA. Doubtless the industry could have made more of European opportunities through 1813 and 1814 had it been able to obtain the generally cheaper and better quality cotton which the USA could supply instead of having to draw on other sources. But it was far from prevented from taking advantage of the gathering collapse of Napoleon's Europe. And that of course was the leading feature of 1813 and 1814.

In December 1812, as the pathetic remnants of the Grand Army came out of the Russian snow and across the Niemen, the Continental System fell apart, never to be reassembled. The ordinary vicissitudes of war continued to impede Anglo-European trade for another fifteen months, but the worst was unambiguously over. The gradual recovery of economic momentum was transformed into a boom with the surrender and abdication of Napoleon in April 1814, powerfully reinforced by the conclusion of peace with the United States in December, and not seriously interrupted by Napoleon's brief resumption of power in the spring of 1815. But this halcyon period was not to be the launching pad of a fresh long-run upswing. Peace brought its own difficulties. In the first place, the hectic rush to exploit Continental markets built up a great glut of goods seeking outlets, with the natural consequences: price cutting, losses, defaulting on bills, pressure on banking liquidity, tightening of credit. Secondly, with European affairs finally settled at the Congress of Vienna (concluded 8 June 1815) the government lost no time in setting about restoring expenditure to a normal peace level (see Table II.14).

TABLE II.14. *Government expenditure (£ million)*

1814	1815	1816	1817
113	100	71	59

Even more significant is the rapid elimination of deficit financing. In 1814 £35 million of expenditure had to be covered by borrowing. In 1815 this was down to £20 million; and in 1816 to £2 million. In the context of a gross national expenditure of the order of £300 million these figures represent the withdrawal from the economy of a demand element of a very appreciable magnitude; and though the funds in question, taxpayers' and savers', might be expected to find alternative employments, there was bound at least to be a time lag before they did so. From boom, the economy by late 1815 had passed into depression, mild by comparison with 1810–12 but depression none the less, lasting into 1816.

The establishment of a new balance later in 1816 brought about a temporary check to the strong deflationary trend which had set in with the ending of the war and which is perhaps the most obtrusive characteristic of the postwar years. Chronologically, this is the first phase of a long-run price fall reaching on to 1851–52. In some measure the whole may be regarded as a single phenomenon, to be explained as due to the cost benefits resulting from sustained investment in improved productivity, following on an initial period during which investment engendered demand had on balance outweighed the deflationary effects of lower real costs. But the sharpness of the price fall in the immediate aftermath of the war – by approximately a quarter between 1814 and 1816 and by about a further fifth between 1816 and 1821 – gives it a quite distinctive character of its own.

The postwar deflation (1814–21) gives rise to two general questions. First: how far is it warrantable to identify the deflation with depression? Many contemporaries certainly did so to the extent that the six or seven years following the war passed into folk history as ones of grim suffering. Modern research however suggests that following the 1814–15 boom and the 1815–16 recession, the economy bounced back in quite lively fashion to attain a plateau in 1817, on which, however, it more or less stagnated through the next four years or so. Embedded in a long-run history of vigorous growth the postwar years certainly lack lustre but the available data does not support their characterisation as ones of prolonged depression. It seems fair to say that the experience of falling money incomes caused contemporaries to paint their own condition in exaggerated shades of black. A man who has only nine-pence where formerly he had a shilling is very apt to think himself worse off whatever his ninepence can buy. Even more readily persuaded of his ill fortune is the producer who sells goods some while after in-curring the costs of production at a time when the general price level was higher – the instinctive approach of the plain man is to cost at historic value; costing at replacement value is something of an account-ing sophistication. And, whatever of the academic soundness of costing methods, the producer who believes himself to be doing badly is not likely to spend any more on fresh investment than is absolutely necessary; so that the climate of a depression, even without the sub-stance of it to start with, can create the reality through lowered capital outlays, or, at least, can result in growth opportunities going unex-ploited. This in fact is what, crudely speaking, would appear to have been happening in the British economy through the years up to 1821. Investment expenditure was running at just about sufficient a level to keep the economy buoyant, but was not high enough to impart that upthrust which had characterised it through the earlier years of this period.

A rather more specific consideration which may have served to repress investment outlays was the expectation that prices would go on falling until they touched a predictable floor, causing would-be investors to hold back until that floor was reached. And there was such a floor on which many contemporaries believed that prices would rest: that determined by the pre-suspension gold parity price of the pound.

Here we are touching on the second general question raised by the postwar deflation: what caused it? This is just as tricky a question as that posed by the preceding inflation, and much the same range of explanations, put in reverse, are available for the one as for the other. One may invoke demand trends by pointing to the drop in government expenditure and, more protractedly, the comparatively low level of investment expenditure, taking sufficient head of steam out of gross demand to allow the downward tendency of real costs to make itself felt. One may invoke falling import prices as the return of peace freed supply channels. Again it would be grain prices which would dominate this picture and a persuasive coincidence between the deceleration of the general price fall and the levelling out of grain prices once the Corn Laws had become of real efficacy in 1821 lends an attractive plausibility to this line of analysis. Finally there is the monetary approach: the view that it was not at root a matter of the prices of goods falling but one of the value of money rising.

Although a few heterodox voices were raised, the great weight of public and parliamentary opinion was massively in favour of a prompt return of the pound to gold. The 1811 Report of the Bullion Committee enjoyed an enormous prestige and the government had severely tried its supporters at the time by not accepting the Committee's recommendation for an immediate repeal of suspension. Already its request for a temporary extension of the unpopular wartime income tax had suffered a humiliating parliamentary defeat. So, although both the government and the Bank would have wished to shelve indefinitely the question of returning to cash payments, political prudence commanded that something be done, or seem to be done, towards getting rid of the paper pound which critics of the right and left alike identified as the source of every kind of ill. Nor was there even any serious debate as to what the gold price of the pound ought to be: a sound currency was the old currency, convertible into gold at the uniquely valid rate of £3 17s 10½d an ounce.

An immediate return to gold was impossible. Over the last years of the war, only about 5 per cent of the Bank's liabilities were covered by its gold holdings and it could not rapidly build up its gold stock without forcing the market price of the metal well above the old parity; and obviously the Bank could not commit itself to selling gold at £3 17s 10½d an ounce when it could be resold at a premium on the open market. The government induced Parliament to extend suspension until July 1818, lavishing denials of any intention of tricking out the life of the paper pound indefinitely. And the Bank itself certainly appears to have done what it could towards making a return to gold possible. By the beginning of 1817 about a quarter of its liabilities were covered by gold and as a token of intent it undertook to pay cash against its £1 and £2 notes (accounting for a tiny fraction of its total note circulation), and in September it made the more substantial gesture of paying cash against any of its notes issued before 1817. When July 1818 came round the government agreed to a full resumption of cash payments twelve months thence. This was however something of a tongue in cheek attitude. A pair of bad harvests in 1816 and 1817 necessitating heavy imports of grain combined with foreign borrowing in London[1] had led to a large outflow of gold. Between encashment of convertible notes and, probably, a certain amount of voluntary selling on the part of the Bank to check the rising gold price, it had already lost much of the gold which it had accumulated over the previous two or three years. By early 1819 it was almost back to the point at which it had started and in the open market gold stood at £4 3s 0d an ounce.

There could now be no question of resuming cash payments, as promised, in July 1819. To allay the angry suspicions of Parliament, the government agreed to a committee on the question. Well managed, the committee recommended a step by step resumption commencing in February 1820, to be completed by May 1824 at the latest – providing a comfortable breathing space during which the Bank's gold ratio could be suitably fortified or, failing that, during which unforeseen events could occur which would regrettably prevent the committee's recommendations being implemented. As it happened the cynics were put to rout. Far from showing any laggardliness the Bank returned wholly to gold in May 1821. It was enabled to do so, not only because it had built its gold stocks up to and beyond the level reached in 1817, but also because its liabilities had fallen considerably: from hovering close to £50 million in 1816 they were running well under £30 million when cash payments were resumed and had a gold coverage of nearly two-fifths, a very comfortable ratio.

The most particular question that this shrinkage of liabilities occasions is: was it a deliberate achievement on the part of the Bank? And this in essence is just another way of asking if the deflation was at root a

---

[1] Between 1816 and 1818 the governments of France, Russia, Austria, Prussia, Holland, Naples and Denmark all raised loans on London – now taking over the rôle of international money market formerly played by Amsterdam and Hamburg, centres which never fully recovered from the wartime interruptions of their business.

monetary phenomenon. If it were the case that the Bank deliberately curbed credit and thus constricted the money supply, that would provide good ground for arguing that the deflation was the result of monetary policy. The argument could be developed in several different ways: as a straightforward expansion of the quantity theory of money; as a question of the value of money in gold terms; as a matter of checking demand. But these sophistications must be passed over here, the more readily since modern scholarship inclines to the view that the deflation was largely an autonomous phenomenon, fortuitously allowing the Bank's liabilities to contract without any positive action on its own part and thus eventually permitting cash payments to be resumed. This view would have it also, of course, that the general postwar dullness of the economy is not to be explained by reference to a putative protracted credit squeeze on the part of the Bank, but rather that general sluggishness resulted in a diminished requirement of credit.

From late 1821 the economy started to cast off the lethargy of the previous four years. In so far as this might be associated with the resumption of cash payments it could only be by way of the consideration already referred to: expenditures previously deferred now being undertaken in the expectation that the price fall was at an end. But it seems unlikely that this was a major factor in the upturn. Possibly, competitive price-cutting in an endeavour to break through market constrictions, helped by the bumper harvests of 1820 and 1821, initiated a rise in consumer demand which was stimulated further by a wide range of reductions in customs duties under the budget of 1823. The improved situation of farmers by then would also have contributed usefully to enlivening consumer demand. And Latin American markets which had been disturbed by the endeavours of Spain and Portugal to re-establish the *ancien régime* across the Atlantic expanded briskly from 1822 with the effective independence of the former colonies guaranteed by Great Britain and the USA. The spurt in consumer output soon brought in its train a rise in capital expenditure, and by 1824 the economy had swung into a boom of exuberance.

Doubtless the upsurge in production would eventually have engendered its own cyclic check but on this occasion it seems as if before that point was reached an accompanying boom phenomenon blew its top and precipitated a general crisis. The universal atmosphere of high-pitched optimism had set in motion a great tide of speculation, the like of which had not been seen since the South Sea Bubble. Some of it was speculation in commodities, gambling on a continuation of the price rise which the boom had triggered off. But more of it was speculation of a much more hazardous variety – Stock Exchange speculation. Three broad categories of stocks were the subjects of activity: British industrial concerns; Latin American industrial concerns, principally in mining; and Latin American government loans.

Many of the British concerns were founded in sound enough premises. The economy was experiencing a powerful expansion and there were certainly fields of activity in which large capitals were desirable if the full potential of the times was to be realised. Conspicuous were mining (metal ore and coal) enterprises, gasworks (coal extracted gas as a means of public lighting had already proved itself on a small scale), and insurance businesses (fire and maritime insurance were old established activities but the actuarial foundations of sound life insurance were only in the course of being laid). These were areas in which there was much scope and where capital might well enjoy increasing returns. Less prominent but also of some realistic promise were saltmaking, construction, glassmaking, distilling and banking concerns.[1] In brief, these British enterprises were, in general, promoted with some genuine perception of economic realities; and a few of them did go on to lead useful commercial lives.

The Latin American concerns were another kettle of fish altogether. Most of them were founded in utterly chimerical and sometimes fundamentally fraudulent prospects. The enthusiasm for Latin American investment, whether in industrials or government stocks, has to be understood in the context of British reactions to the overthrow of Spanish and Portuguese rule on the American continent. British sentiments – middle-class sentiments at any rate – had been fervently committed to the colonists in their struggles for independence. A keenly felt sense of solidarity with the new states created an immense fund of goodwill towards them and judgments of their economic situations were highly coloured by a lively sympathy with their politics. The bourgeois values whose ascendancy in Britain were apprehended as a main foundation of her commercial achievements were seen to have triumphed over the stultifying principles of absolutism in Latin America and would surely promote there too a vigorous exploitation of those economic

---

[1] Under the 'Bubble Act' of 1720 all these concerns were of very dubious legality. The Act was, however, widely regarded as obsolete. No prosecutions were initiated and the matter was put beyond doubt by the repeal of the Act in 1825. The banking concerns had also the statutory monopoly of the Bank of England to reckon with. They proposed to avoid a breach of this by not issuing notes – which in the opinion of many lawyers would keep them within the letter of the law.

opportunities which under the old decrepit order of things had gone untapped. The credulousness of centuries in the vast potential wealth of the continent still retained much of its allure for the more naïve. It was this climate of feeling that elicited British money for worked out silver mines and governments whose budgets were noteworthy chiefly for the magnitude of their deficits.

In the last analysis it did not really matter much whether or not a sound basis underlay the stocks dealt in. Their prices once impelled upwards by eager anticipations of handsome returns,[1] pure speculation on the course of stock exchange valuations took over as the dominant market force, cumulatively driving prices upwards as long as speculative judgments reckoned on the rise continuing, and bringing them tumbling down once the balance of market opinion tilted the other way. And the good often suffered with the bad in the downslide. The normal practice on first issue was to require only a fraction of the share price in immediate payment, the remainder to be called up later as the enterprise got under way. But, between those who had bought with the sole intention of reselling but had got stranded in a falling market[2] and those who had lost heavily on other share transactions, many calls could not be met and enterprises perished for want of funds. Many of course were doomed to perish anyway. Apart from those which had never rested on anything but empty promises, most were radically flawed by the incompetence of their managements, composed very often of men with little or no working acquaintance with the activity in which they proposed to engage, ingenious enough perhaps in spotting opportunities but ignorant of the practical means of exploiting them. This indeed, not only at this particular time, but for many decades to come, was perhaps the most telling limitation keeping concern size down to family or small partnership scale: the near impossibility of recruiting the echelons of trained managerial staff which larger enterprises would require. The building up of such a corps was bound to be slow since the only effective training ground was employment in management itself; there could be no short cut from owner-managed concerns as the predominant type in any field to those managed by salaried employees on behalf of blind capital. The attempts of 1824–25 to create large-scale businesses from scratch were attempts to gallop

[1] The government loans were of course fixed interest stocks but they were initially issued on very attractive terms, offering yields to redemption of up to 10 per cent, so that they too had highly elastic prices.
[2] Shares with outstanding calls could easily become unsaleable at any price.

when management strength only permitted of walking pace. Doubtless the cleverest of the promoters of these ventures were well aware of their impracticability and simply played on the gullible public eagerness to climb on the economic band-wagon, remunerating themselves with salaries and fees or even by outright embezzlement for as long as appearances could be kept up.

Speculation in volatile shares, assisted particularly by the device of the partially paid share, opened up a new threat to the stability of the banking system. Once share prices started downwards, as they did in June 1825, the pressure for cash mounted. Those who had bought in the expectation of selling at a profit before payment had to be made had now to choose between raising cash to keep their positions open or selling at a loss and having to find cash to make up the difference – and the faster speculative positions were liquidated, the faster share prices fell, raising requirements of cash. Calls on partially paid shares intensified the demand. And soon the pressure extended beyond Stock Exchange circles. Debtors pressed to pay up leant on their debtors, and so the ripples steadily widened until a full-scale credit crisis of the familiar type was abroad, bringing in its train a freezing of trade and general depression – a depression which in point of the rapidity of its onset and of its intensity while it lasted was perhaps the worst yet experienced.

The depression was, however, relatively shortlived. By mid-1826 the economy was pulling out of the trough and by 1827 it had climbed back to the pre-depression level. Much of the credit for this rapid recovery must go to the Bank of England which, instead of opting for safety by reducing its liabilities at a time when its gold reserves were being run down by the general demand for cash, discounted good paper with especial freedom, preserving many banks and mercantile concerns from collapse and contributing powerfully to a freeing of credit and a quick resumption of trading activity.

Although the Bank's behaviour through the crisis was universally applauded, it, along with the banking system as a whole, was widely blamed for having contributed to it, in the terms which had become commonplace since 1810: 'excessive' creation of paper money. And the government was pressed to take measures to bring note issue under strict control. A number of thoroughgoing schemes were aired but the legislation which actually emerged in 1826 was of a rather mouselike character. It embodied three measures. First, banks were forbidden to issue notes of under £5. Parliamentary opinion had somehow seized on the small note as being particularly pernicious and the measure must be regarded as just a sop to that opinion, remarkable only for its quaintness. Secondly, the Bank of England was empowered to open branches in the provinces. This was with a view to promoting the circulation of Bank of England notes at the expense of the notes of private banks. And although the contemporary fixation with notes, rather than with bank credit in general, reveals some rather muddled thinking, the appropriation by the Bank of England of a substantial share of general banking business would certainly have made for greater stability in the banking system as a whole. In the event, however, the Bank only opened a dozen branches and these were prevented by the Bank's notion of professional decorum from competing with the private banks for general business.

Thirdly, the Bank of England's monopoly of joint stock banking in England was breached by permitting other joint stock banks to be established outside of a sixty-five mile radius from London. In the long run this provided an important base for a steady strengthening of the banking structure. It permitted large agglomerations of capital to be recruited in place of the private fortune of an individual or two as the foundations of banking concerns. And the viability of a bank was, in significant measure, a function of its size: the hazards of a run on cash were less when spread over many noteholders and depositors than when they hung on the actions of a relative handful; more particularly, a purely local rush for cash could be coped with when a branch bank under pressure had the resources of other branches to call on. Indeed one might say that it was not so much joint stock banking *per se* which was an element of strength as the branch banking which joint stock made possible. Branches were to the banking system rather what mobile reserves are to an army – the ready means of shoring up sectors under particularly heavy attack and thus preventing a crumbling of the whole front. However the key constituent of banking business was enjoyment of the public confidence. And in the aftermath of 1825 joint stock was not a word well calculated to excite faith. The anonymity of a joint stock concern was another longer-run handicap. People liked to be able to put a face and a character to the person to whom they entrusted their money. For all of their chequered record, the private banks in general had substantial forces of goodwill with which to resist joint stock invasion. It was to take many decades before English banking was dominated by large, heavily capitalised, multibranch concerns.

Vigorous growth, punctuated with sharp crises accompanied by anxious and angry discussions of the credit system were to remain broad characteristics of British economic life for the next half century or so; and on that note we can move on into those years – into a phase which, if general styles can ever be attached to chapters of economic history, might be termed the Revolution consolidated.

Three

1830–1873

From a technological point of view the period 1830–73, indeed one could say almost the whole of the nineteenth century, has a curiously paradoxical character. Effecting an immensity of technical change it yet contributed little to the fundaments of technical knowledge. Its peculiar achievement was not to open doors but to fling back those which had already been partially opened. More specifically, the extension and improvement of mechanical modes of production already devised earlier and the widened employment of steam power are the dominant technological traits of this period. But in one particular field it pushed the work of its predecessors so much further and with such consequences that it may be said to have effected its own distinctive revolution. That was the application of steam power to a mobile tractive unit – the locomotive. The basic technology involved was already a quarter of a century old at the outset of the period, yet its impact on the economy at large had been barely perceptible so far. There is no shadow of exaggeration in saying that over the next four decades or so the railways were the centrally crucial factor in British economic development. They may therefore properly constitute our first theme here.

The railways

The last chapter saw railways just starting to achieve a distinct existence of their own, disentangling themselves from colliery operations to become general public carriers. Two major centres, Liverpool and Manchester, had been linked by rail in 1829 and just as sixty years earlier the connection of these two towns by water had initiated a wave of canal construction so now an age of railway building was launched. It was not of course mere coincidence that the same route was the progenitor in both cases. Transport economics are contained in the formula 'Amount of freight/Distance carried', and no route in Britain offered a better ratio than this. In both cases the lush profitability of the undertaking was an important factor in stimulating entrepreneurial interest in a new transport medium – and in both cases participants in other ventures did not always take full account of the egregiously favourable conditions that the Liverpool to Manchester route enjoyed.

A trickle of railway promotions in the early 1830s swelled to wave-like proportions in the years 1833–37. These undertakings when completed constituted in sum an arterial system, linking up Liverpool, Manchester, Leeds, Birmingham, Derby, Bristol and London, along with a few short offshoots from this system, miscellaneous scraps of track here and there, and lines from London to Portsmouth, to Dover and to Colchester. Ignoring the miscellaneous scraps, this was really a duplication of the basic south Lancashire and west Midlands canal system, fused with a radial system of which London was the hub. Again, the geography of the first railway complex parrots that of the first canal complex for sound economic reasons. The additional London-pivoted rail complex, whose canal counterpart had been much slower in the making, engaged such early attention because railways enjoyed a kind of traffic which canals could never secure: passenger traffic. This was an unanticipated revelation. Pioneering expectations had been founded in the experience of collieries and canals. But the Liverpool and Manchester early demonstrated that people wanted to travel – for business and pleasure – to an extent that no one had dreamed of. And subsequent experience brought further confirmation of the phenomenon, which must be accounted a major factor in galvanising entrepreneurial interest in railways – over longer routes especially, the addition of passenger traffic to goods traffic could make for a profitably high rate of track usage when goods traffic alone might not justify the considerable capital outlay.

The mushrooming of joint stock companies in 1824–25 had already shown that there was a good deal of money about, anxious to associate itself with the opportunities afforded by economic growth. The railways provided a perfect mate for that money. Unlike most other forms of contemporary economic activity, railways could not start life in a small way. The Liverpool and Manchester and a few other early short route companies did finance themselves much in the manner of the early canals, leaning largely on local businessmen who reckoned to benefit directly from better transport facilities. But reliance on this kind of investment capital had soon to be left behind as projected routes became longer and the purposes they proposed to serve more diffuse. The blind but eager capital of the public at large was summoned to finance railway contruction. Virtually inevitably, railway shares soon became the subject of Stock Exchange speculation. 1836–37 was 1824–25 over again – bank and other shares scrambled with railways for public attention. Although the general economic setback of 1837 was not as severe as that of 1825–26 and something of a floor was set to Stock Exchange prices by the fact that, broadly speaking, the companies dealt in had sounder prospects, many fingers got badly burned by railways shares and a bewildered and chastened public drew back from railway investment as hastily as it had first embraced it. Promoters of railway ventures were losing the edge of their enthusiasm anyway as the costs of railway construction mounted: iron prices, always highly sensitive to demand fluctuations, had gone up sharply as track started to be laid; one price series shows bar iron rising from £6 10s a ton in 1835 to £10 10s through 1836 and 1837; and the prices of other railway materials, chiefly timber and bricks, behaved in similar fashion.

Whether it was principally a matter of the deadening of entrepreneurial initiative or of a reluctance on the part of the investing public to part with its money to railway companies, fresh promotions certainly ceased almost entirely over the years 1838–42, though much of the actual execution of projects initiated earlier continued on into these years. Likewise then, it it an open question whether it was the fall in material prices – bar iron down to £5 5s a ton in 1843 and £4 15s in 1844 – or the softening of investors' painful memories which prompted the next bout of railway ventures, getting under way in 1843 and lasting into 1847. This is the phase which has gone down in history as the Railway Mania. The 1833–37 phase had transcended in point of projected expenditure the only precedent – the canal mania of 1791–94. Now it in turn was surpassed in the same magnitude by the promotions of 1843–47.

While in the peak year of the first phase, 1836, the capital authorised to be raised by the requisite Acts of Parliament was £23 million, the corresponding figure for the peak of the mania, 1846, was £133 million. In the context of a gross national income of c. £500 million p.a. this was a figure of staggering size. It was not of course – indeed could not be – all called up at once, but capital of about that amount was in fact devoted to railways over the years 1846 to 1849, when their total called up funds stood at £225 million. (Much of the outlay 1846–49 was of course in respect of ventures initiated earlier and a substantial proportion of the proposals of 1846 itself was never executed.) At the beginning of 1843 some 1,800 miles of railway line had been completed. By the beginning of 1850, when the impetus of mania construction started to run down, there were 6,084 miles open, providing more or less direct rail linkage between all principal centres of population with some quite intricate local clusters of track in the west Midlands, south Lancashire, and the West Riding of Yorkshire as well as in the vicinity of London – primarily due there to the convergence of main line routes – and a rather haphazard branch line service in rural areas. So much in fact had already been put in hand by 1847 that there would almost certainly have been quite a sharp tapering off of fresh promotions even had they not been abruptly checked by the repetition in 1847 of the events of 1837.

Already in the 1830s a few relatively large enterprises had stood out amongst the numerous concerns which constructed and operated[1] the disjointed point to point stretches of track which had constituted the primitive railway system. At this early stage, an enterprise was large in proportion to the distance between the two points which it proposed to link. But as branch lines were built and independent ventures increasingly connected up with one another, the advantages of unified control to make for thoroughgoing operational integration became more and more manifest. And whether effected by share exchange or by outright cash purchase the fusion of two concerns inevitably took the usual form of absorption by a relatively large concern of a smaller one. What in origin were just long line companies, started to move towards ownership of regional complexes. In 1844 there were 104 railway companies in Great Britain but already the top six owned one-third of all track; and the top twelve owned one-half. Further mergers and fresh construction through the mania and its aftermath brought certain companies into the 'fifties within sight of monopolies of all rail traffic over very extensive tracts of territory. At the same time, the mania had left a legacy of much duplication of rail services – from the mid-1840s the government had endeavoured to exercise some kind of planning control through the vetting of railway bills but, short of taking

---

[1] In some early instances railway concerns, modelling themselves on the canal companies, simply constructed the railway and charged tolls on whoever wished to use it. But the evident need to coordinate traffic movements soon led to a fusion of the two functions.

the initiative out of private hands altogether, it could do little more than prevent evident absurdities. (The most notable of these was disparate gauges – though the Act of 1844 enforcing the most commonly used gauge of 4ft 8½in. as a national standard came rather too late; in particular, the spine of the Great Western Railway, the London–Bristol line, had already been completed to a 7ft gauge, committing that company to the broad gauge for the rest of its system and cutting off a large sector of the country from through communication with the rest, until 1892 when the GWR converted to standard gauge.)

The chief feature of the railway history of the 1850s, then, was the endeavour of the larger companies to put things in order – their kind of order – within their respective spheres of operation, by mopping up smaller concerns which offered competitive or complementary services in the interior of their territories and by eliminating alternative routes of larger rivals on their flanks. Although denial of overrunning facilities and sometimes even more bellicose methods (such as on occasion the hemming in of a rival locomotive) were employed in this railway warfare, it mostly took the form of price-cutting. This means was generally ultimately effective when directed by a large company – which could tolerate a loss on part of its operations – against a small one. Although here and there small companies survived either because of their obdurate resistance or, more commonly, because they did not bother their powerful neighbours, by the early 'sixties six English and two Scottish[1] companies utterly dominated the railway scene in point of mileage owned. To these might be added six other English companies and one other Scottish company[2] with relatively little track but operating high intensity services. After a fresh building spate in the first half of the 'sixties, the top eight owned nearly two-thirds of the country's railways – and along with the other seven, nearly seven-eighths.

This division of railway Britain into great principalities could not have taken place without the benevolence of the state. For one thing, parliamentary consent was necessary to mergers or new acquisitions –

[1] *Midland*; *Great Eastern*; *London and South Western*; *Great Western*; *London and North Western*: operating adjoining fanlike sectors pivoting on London. *North Eastern*; *North British*; *Caledonian*: monopoly blocks in the north-east of England, the south-east of Scotland and central Scotland respectively.

[2] *Great Northern*, a long-line company, London to Edinburgh, which appeared a little too late to develop into a large regional complex. *Lancashire and Yorkshire*; *Manchester, Sheffield and Lincolnshire*; *London, Chatham and Dover*; *South Eastern*; *London and Brighton*; *Glasgow and South Western*: operating in the population concentrations indicated by their names.

although in practice Parliament could hardly withhold its assent to the takeover of a loss-racked small company. Even without this specific sanction, railway companies in prudence had to take account of parliamentary and governmental opinion. Although establishment attitudes on economic questions in general were largely shaped by the *laissez-faire* doctrines which by mid-century had fully established themselves as a new orthodoxy, these were heavily qualified in the case of railways by the traditional principle that highways were a public responsiblity; and although it might be considered that that responsibility was most effectively discharged by delegating it to private enterprise, delegation was not construed as dereliction. Whether explicitly spelt out or not, it was universally acknowledged that railways would be left to the play of the profit motive only as long as it was demonstrable in practice that this best served the public interest. The railway companies were hedged about with checks on their freedom of action. These were in some degree concrete checks: maximum tariff schedules and, increasingly, safety provisions – though the former were largely irrelevant, being usually well in excess of optimum commercial rates and voidable in the case of freight under the guise of terminal handling charges, while the efficacy of the latter was for long impaired by the weakness of the state inspection system. Of greater import was the more intangible climate of sentiments in which the railways existed – at its crudest inducing good behaviour on their part for fear of provoking state action against them (and from 1844 a particular sword of Damocles menaced them in the shape of an Act of Parliament giving the government the option of nationalising the railways after 1865); but more subtly and more pervasively by imbuing railway managements themselves with something of a public service mentality. In the immediate context the significance of all this is that had the state and the larger railway companies not been in general accord on the desirability of the merger movement it could never have proceeded as it did. It was conceived of by both as being a sound, sensible rationalisation of the messy, inefficient, wasteful muddle of services which the rampaging exuberance of the 'thirties and 'forties had bequeathed to the nation.

Although the companies concerned had of course financial ends in view in taking over other enterprises, it would be true to say that these did not in general extend to monopoly pricing policies, if only because they would not have been allowed to get away with it. Coordinated through running, more intensive utilisation of assets, economies in overheads: these were the kind of advantages they sought. But often, more than accountancy calculations lay back of railway empire building. Sheer prestige was a coveted end too. The great companies early acquired a strong *esprit de corps*, ostentatiously manifested in the liveries of their rolling stock, the uniforms of their staff and, generally somewhat later, in the architectural pomp of their stations. Just at what point commercial strategy was consumed in the quest for glory one could not say, but undoubtedly some at least of the railway struggles of the 'fifties came to be sustained, if not initiated, by pride rather than prudence – this, most evidently, in the contests between the great companies themselves for traffic in overlapping flanks.

The practical consequences of the diversion of energy and money to railway warfare were two. Very little fresh construction was projected, though the backlog of 'forties' schemes kept constructional activity ticking over quite briskly. Secondly, railway profits tended to be low. By the end of the 'fifties, however, the giants had either won their victories or had decided that feuding was too expensive. Their contests with one another had been particularly costly and singularly fruitless. Thereafter they took to peaceful coexistence; and a system of mutual understanding kept rates evenly balanced over routes in overlap areas. With that, the companies turned to thickening out their systems. The period 1859–66 was characterised by a spate of construction of link and feeder routes, 3,600 miles of track being added to the national network over these eight years, compared with 2,300 over the previous eight.

But though this phase may stand with 1833–40 and 1843–50 in point of rate of construction, it differs radically in point of mode of execution. The risk-bearing capital of the general public had little access to participation in company extensions. The companies financed their building for the most part either out of their own reserves or by raising fixed interest loans. The latter did usually take the form of debenture stock; and although this secure but rather unexciting kind of investment was not without its attractions, much of it was placed privately in large blocks, through the agency of the specialists in this kind of business who were establishing themselves as an important element in the world of finance. In any event it did not cater for the common sort of investor who hoped for 10 per cent plus on his money – and often of course got little or nothing. That such prospects as there had been of earning this kind of return on railway capital were now largely usurped was not evident to a society dazzled by its own recent achievements and persuaded that it was the manifest destiny of capital to fructify in use.

The closing down of former outlets for avid speculative capital coincided with a shrinkage of opportunities for the contracting concerns which the intensive railway building of the 'thirties and 'forties had thrown up. Through the 'fifties, these had often been able to supplement the reduced level of domestic contracts with work on the Continent where railway building was swinging into its stride and where, initially, British engineering and constructional experience were much drawn on. But Continental countries fairly soon bred up specialists of their own. The flow of European contracts started to peter out and fresh company building at home was not enough to keep the contractors as fully occupied as they were accustomed to be. There, then, were investors anxious to get their money into more railways and there, too, were contractors anxious to build more railways.

What followed was very odd. In some cases contractors built lines on their own initiatives with no definite notion as to who was going to operate them on completion, financing the work out of capital raised from the general public, commonly tricked out by stretching credit from suppliers of materials. In other cases the initiative came from towns which had been bypassed by main lines and to which no main-line company considered it worth while to build a branch:[1] Civic pride and the convenience of the townspeople required that the town be put on the railway map; sufficient capital for the venture being unavailable locally the contractor took up a block of shares in the company formed for the undertaking and resold them on the Stock Exchange. The use of the contractor as a front in these and similar ventures ranged inextricably in motive from the convenience of raising capital via a concern versed in such matters through to a fundamentally fraudulent desire to obscure the profitless nature of the whole project; and the contractors' interest might be compounded in varying proportions of a desire to facilitate a project which was to bring him business and the scope afforded him of making a profit on the resale of shares.

Whatever their nature, contractors' shares enjoyed a long-run bulls' market as speculative forces took over on the Stock Exchange. But the general crash of 1866 knocked the bottom out of this kind of business; and this brief and rather bewildering mode of railway promotion was not to be heard of again. The age of new railway ventures was virtually

[1] The economics of branch lines were rather complicated. Receipts on a branch might not cover its costs, yet the branch might justify itself by the extra traffic brought to main lines. Thus a long branch might be an economic proposition even running at a relatively heavy loss while a short branch running at less loss might not because road or water carriage already gave convenient access to the main line.

over. Rounding out work by the established companies kept construction going at about the rate of 300 miles a year up to the end of the 1870s, and right up to the First World War each year brought its quota of a few extra miles of track as demographic and economic shifts called for new services.

Those investors who in the hectic decades had leaped on to the railway band-wagon were in general rather disappointed in the outcome. After the wasteful 'fifties profits picked up in the 'sixties; and in the 'seventies with expenditure on integrating their systems largely behind them most of the railway companies had both enhanced the earning power of their assets and put themselves in a position to adopt a more lavish dividend policy, but even then few paid more than 6 per cent. The trend of dividends thereafter[1] was downwards, partly because much of the later loan-financed investment by the companies (in improved rolling stock, signalling systems, terminal facilities, etc. rather than in extra track) failed to earn enough to cover interest payments, so that, in effect, ordinary shareholders had to subsidise debenture holders. In some degree the discrepancy between expectation and eventuality was just a question of irrationally pitched expectations. But even by cooler standards the return on railway capital was on the low side. At its peak in the 1870s the rate of return averaged out overall at just about 4·5 per cent p.a.

Two general sets of factors contributed to this rather dull experience. First, the lack of controlled planning of the railway system and the resulting inefficiency of capital in many instances; two or more routes where one would have served; routes which could never secure enough traffic to pay their way. Second, the curbs to which railway pricing policies were subject, which prevented their fully exploiting such advantage as they had over other transport media. Despite the inherently monopolistic nature of any rail route, railways lived in a fairly competitive world. Many canals did not succumb without a fierce struggle, slashing charges in an endeavour to stay in business, and here and there succeeding in retaining certain kinds of traffic. As between coastal points, the balance of advantage of trains over ships was often far from decisive. Over short distances road cartage could often offer a more convenient and flexible door to door service. And as between many points railways competed with one another. An uninhibited,

---

[1] A number of the general observations on railways on this and following pages apply, fairly evidently, largely or entirely to the decades after 1873, the themes dealt with not lending themselves very happily to chronological chopping-up.

commercially motivated railway policy could have softened much of the financial effect of this situation: flexible tariffs permitting of relatively low rates where water competition was met, compensated for by high rates where an effective monopoly was enjoyed; and, where necessary, price-fixing agreements amongst railway companies themselves though such practices would be more fruitful when applied to goods freight with its relatively inelastic demand than when applied to passengers, who might well choose to stay at home. These devices were employed by the railway companies in appreciable measure but the concept of railways as a public service constrained the companies in a way from which commercial enterprises generally were free. And the same concept allied with company pride also, on occasions, impelled the railways to maintain unremunerative services and to undertake expenditure of dubious earning potential.

A third factor bearing on railway earnings which may usefully be mentioned, though its greatest relevance is to the decades succeeding this period, is that the marginal productivity of railway capital tended to diminish rapidly from the high rate achieved on initial outlays. In essence this is just a variant way of putting the last mentioned point: investment in improving or extending existing services was commonly of low earning potential. The productivity of capital is of course ultimately a matter of technology. The railways born out of a major technological breakthrough drew little further benefit from technological advance. Through the first two or three decades better locomotives and rolling stock design did make for higher speeds and greater comfort, but improved vehicles cost more to build and whether they led to any operational economies is questionable; while from the closing years of this period railway technology virtually stood still until, well into the twentieth century, other forms of power started to take over from steam. In any event such a large proportion of railway costs arose from initial capital expenditure that once undertaken it would swamp any but very substantial gains arising from reductions in running costs.

This inability of technology to enhance the productivity of railway capital can be viewed from another aspect. Throughout the economy real wages rose steadily through the second half of the nineteenth century; while most sectors were able to enhance the productivity of labour to an extent which offset its increased cost, the railways were unable to do so; and although their quasimonopoly situation enabled them to pass on much of their higher costs to their customers, some part of the burden had to be borne by profits.

Railway shareholders were compensated in some part for the lowness of dividends by their regularity. Passenger business, which increased in every single year up to 1909, ironed out the effects on railway revenue of economic fluctuations. However, most shareholders, whether satisfied or not with their dividends, were powerless to influence railway policy. The great railway companies provide the first general instance of that divorce of management from ownership which was to become an increasingly common feature of economic organisation in the twentieth century.

The sheer size of the chief railway concerns which necessitated raising capital from such numbers as could not possibly participate in the conduct of the enterprises, even had they wished to, had further implications which along with the special characteristics of railway business in itself produced in the great railway companies economic organisms of a completely novel kind. They could learn little from the business units of which the rest of the contemporary economy was composed and had to contrive their own specific mode of functioning. This is a theme which is really both too particular and too extensive to receive much more than a passing acknowledgement here; but in very broad terms something of what was involved should be indicated.

Firstly there was the question of the recruitment and vocational education of the managerial personnel which a large company required in some number. The point has been made earlier that this was a radical source of weakness to the development of large-scale organisations generally, and if it did not undo the railway companies in their early years, it was largely because the intrinsic competitive strength of railways masked managerial inefficiences. There was no obvious quarter to which to turn for managers and the early ones were drawn from a variety of fields. However there was one contemporary organisation which, at least in point of the scale of its operations, bore some resemblance to railway business – the Army. Quite a few of the first generation railway executives were ex-army officers. But on the whole their record did not demonstrate the appositeness of military experience to railway management, though on the purely technical side the recruitment of retired engineer officers for certain posts established itself as something of a railway tradition.

However, if the Army did not continue for long to supply men to general management, it certainly imparted to the railways an enduring code of conduct and attitudes. A reciprocal loyalty between company and employees, whose evident exemplar was the spirit of the regiment, was a central element in railway management in more ways than one. Devoted service brought promotion. And, an experienced staff of its own once constituted, a railway company almost invariably filled its managerial positions from its own ranks, the normal ladder of ascent being grounded in the lower ranges of the middle class from which boys with a certain amount of general education were recruited for clerical employment, the successful mounting eventually to higher administrative rungs, at the top of which lay the post of general manager of the whole company. It was a very insular system, becoming even more so as the loyalty theme drew boys to follow their fathers into company service. A fidelity to established routine was commonly the most commended virtue; and there was doubtless much justice in contemporary criticisms that railway management was often insensitive to the changing requirements of its customers. But, other perhaps than in a greater mobility of management staff as between the companies themselves, there was not much that could have been done to improve the quality of railway management. Until well into the twentieth century the railways remained almost alone in requiring numbers of salaried professional executives, so that there was very little scope for fruitful cross-fertilisation from other fields of commercial endeavour – and, as has been shown in more recent times, the distinctive public service ethos of railway administration does not always blend very happily with the stricter balance sheet mentality which makes for success in commercial activities generally.

Outside experience was available to railway managements: in a formal sense the great railway companies were run from outside. The companies early developed that distinction between direction and management which has been a particular characteristic of large-scale enterprises in Britain ever since. Crudely analysed the phenomenon was, in large measure, the product of class consciousness. In their developed form the companies were important, prestigious, national institutions. The men who attended to their day to day governance had neither the social background nor the compensating personal wealth to fit them for the formal sovereignty of such concerns. So, there had to be a board of directors made up of men with the socially requisite qualifications.

With or without the largely fictional distinction between direction and management the participation of the owner managers of ironworks, coalmines, textile mills, etc. in railway operation was of evident potentially beneficial consequence, and membership of a railway board might conceivably enable the leisured owner of inherited wealth or the successful politician to discover a hitherto buried talent for business. Given the restricted catchment area of railway managers, it was plainly desirable that executive strength be reinforced from other directions. And in one or two cases a capable board, or a capable inner cabinet on a board, did make for noteworthy efficiency. But in general the whole ambience which gave rise to this kind of control structure directly militated against its being of any efficacy. By very definition the board was not a management body. If in the early days there was some sound distinction between general strategy and day to day management issues – the distinction between planning new undertakings and operating ones – once the pattern of railway services had been completed and railway technology provided no new occasion to effect any radical change in operational techniques, the enormous bulk of railway business came under the heading of management. Boards which might have been capable of good work were prohibited by their own terms of reference from usurping the prerogative of the general manager; and if they did overstep their terms of reference they were apt to imperil his cooperation, without which they were pretty helpless. A railway directorship was very much a part-time activity, usually carrying little more than a nominal fee, the post being apprehended as more or less analogous to service on hospital boards or charitable organisations, with the result that very few railway directors had any solid grasp of the details of the business.

It follows from that last fact that, in any event, most boards were not competent to take a useful part in management. On his part, the average general manager can have felt little inducement to treat his board with anything other than surface respect. The social snobbery which was a main ground for the board's existence in the first place must have often been offensive to him and jealousy for his own hard attained position must have tended to make him reluctant to allow of any dilettante invasion of his territory. Generalisation of this kind is of course dangerous. All would depend on the personalities of the particular individuals involved. But it does not seem too much to say that particular qualities of tact and understanding would be required if the talents of managers and directors were fruitfully to supplement and support each other; and that the lack of these attributes must often have led to covert obstructiveness and reticence on the part of managers in their dealings with their boards, with consequent inertia when fresh action was what was needed.

Although as implied already, railway management methods tended to become rather stereotyped, certain novel problems had to be faced before a stereotype could be evolved. Four obvious ones can be distinguished although not much can be said about their solutions here: costing, operational planning, market forecasting and staff discipline.

Here and there we have already briefly noted how the increasing use of expensive fixed assets in certain productive activities gave rise to largely unfamiliar problems in the calculation of unit costs. The problems assumed new dimensions of complexity in railway business for at least four reasons: the very considerable weight of fixed costs in total costs; the wide variety of fixed assets employed (land, track, bridges, signalling equipment, terminal facilities, rolling stock, engineering workshops with their impedimenta, office premises etc. etc.); the difficulties of determining to which service costs were to be attributed (e.g. the apportionment of centrally incurred costs amongst the different operating sectors or of branch line costs among the main lines which they fed); finally, the question of what in any event constituted a unit of railway output. While railway response to these issues may fairly be said to have made a contribution to the development of cost accounting techniques, it must also be said that many of them were evaded or even went unrecognised, and that no British railway management ever had the detailed appreciation of cost effectiveness which would be considered essential to efficient management today. (United States' railway managements were much more forward in this field and from the early twentieth century British railways hesitantly started to learn from them.)

The problem of operational planning was of course linked to the problem of costing in so far as it was a question of securing the optimum 'mix' of the different cost elements involved in providing services. But broadly speaking, the problem was only grappled with in the crudest way at this level. Indeed without sophisticated mathematics and electronic computers it would have been impossible to do much more. It was, for the most part, at a simpler level that the need for operational planning made itself consciously felt: that of coordinating traffic movements with regard to safety, and to providing connections and timings which met the needs of railway customers – a specially arduous task where the cities were closing in on the railway lines, swelling the volume of traffic at the same time as constricting the construction of supplementary track. This was perhaps the exigency which showed British railway management at its best, calling as it did for the professional talents of the 'railwayman' rather than for those of the businessman, and appealing to that strong vocational sense which placed the railway companies as social organisms closer in spirit to the fighting services than to the general run of economic enterprises.

As to market forecasting, here it is largely a matter of the need being evident in historical retrospect rather than of its contemporary recognition and the clear evolution of new managerial techniques in response to it. The essence of the contrast between railways and most other economic activities in this respect is that the latter can usually test the market directly by limited trials of new products or services without hazarding large sums and, furthermore, can often learn much from simply watching the performance of their competitors. While railways were not entirely precluded from these cheap means of securing first-hand information as to what would be saleable, there was obviously no direct way of appraising the future profitability of a new route and the inability to stage an inexpensive trial or learn from other companies, evident in this extreme instance, would apply in varying degrees to other kinds of projects too. In short, railways had a special need of economic intelligence and market research services if they were to exploit fully their opportunities; and while alert management – including the special contribution which directors with outside business interests could make in this field – could, and in particular instances did, make for rewarding new departures, the financial penalties attaching to misjudgments founded on hunch and partial knowledge acted as powerful inhibitions.

The army model for railway management was at its plainest in the sphere of staff discipline. Employee control has in glancing fashion already been touched on as a problem facing large-scale enterprises wherever economic circumstances gave rise to them, right back to the sixteenth century. It was in the last analysis a problem of social conditioning – or in an even more coldly clinical phrase, human engineering. Two particular kinds of response needed to be built into conventional culture before large-scale enterprises could effectively take over sectors of economic activity; the readiness to accept an externally imposed work rhythm; and the disposition to serve an employer's interest when no automatic or immediate penalties or rewards attached to performance. The first was required principally from manual operatives, the second from supervisory and managerial staff and manual operatives engaged on tasks which could not be closely overlooked. Establishment of the first depended very much on the existence of the second among those charged with the direct supervision of operatives.

In the case of commodity production the problem posed could often be evaded by relating the remuneration of foremen, section managers, etc. to output achieved, under what were essentially subcontracting arrangements – much resorted to in the first generation or two of textile factories and established practice in ironworks and coalmines, as well as being a standard feature of large constructional undertakings, including the building of the railways. Railway operation, faced, at least in its early years, with a largely non-conditioned work force, had of its nature very special human problems to grapple with. Much of the work of its manual operatives could not be subjected to constant supervision – and on it often depended the lives of large numbers of people. Virtually none of its work was susceptible to measurement in such terms that remuneration could be directly related to effort or efficiency. It had, then, to evolve its own code of industrial discipline and since the rest of industry had little to teach which was capable of adaptation to its special needs it turned to the Army, whose personnel problems were of a somewhat similar kind.

The relevant point has already been made with regard to a railway company's 'officer' (and the word itself was part of standard railway vocabulary): clerical and administrative staff, with whom might be included the specialists in accountancy, legal and technical departments, although these had a rather autonomous existence with professional codes of their own. To what has been said already on the analogy between railway company and regiment a couple of further observations might be usefully added. The size of most railway companies greatly facilitated, indeed made possible, the use of promotion prospects as a way of welding employees to the company's service. A hierarchy of posts existed of an elaboration which other kinds of contemporary commercial enterprise had no need of, with a consequent inability on their part to offer a continuing scale of rewards for faithful and efficient service. Secondly, the railway companies, along with other developing institutions such as the joint stock banks, the insurance companies, the Civil Service and the Post Office, came to play the same role with regard to the lower middle class as the Army, the Navy and the Church played for the more elevated social orders: that of providing occupations consonant with the canons of social respectability which prevailed at those class levels. Subscription to the values of fidelity and diligence propagated by the company was a badge of class identity.

At the manual operative level, employees were equated visibly with military rank and file by putting them into uniform. The cruder techniques of military discipline, flogging and shooting, were not of course available, but on the deterrent side meticulous regulations, accompanied by scales of fines for breaches, were a central feature of railway discipline; and on the positive side the propagation of a general ethos of loyalty to the service was sustained in some measure by a reciprocal attention to staff welfare. By contemporary standards the railway companies were good employers: while wages were if anything on the low side, employees of some years standing were generally secure against redundancy dismissals; loss of employment through accidents on duty often elicited *ex gratia* payments from the companies; and small pensions were paid to long serving employees.

The management aspect of railways has been dwelt on in a little detail here because railway operation was the first sector of the economy where the problems posed by large scale undertakings became the general experience. In this respect, indeed, the railways were extremely precocious. The scale of operations of the great railway companies by the 1860s, whether measured by capital employed, turnover or labour force, was not to be matched elsewhere in the economy until after the First World War and it has only been in our own times that businesses of such magnitude have become normal in most sectors of the British economy. Chronologically, then, railways were very early precursors of the corporation age; and, given not only the specifically economic but also the wider sociological implications of this, it is of some interest to see to what extent they appear as pioneers of modern techniques of business control. A summary conclusion, founded on what has been said above, would perhaps be that railway management contributed little to later developments in this field, partly because the railway companies did not venture as far as an unambiguous commercial motivation might have impelled them, and in the personnel sphere specifically because they took a course which subsequent social changes rendered increasingly anachronistic. In a jargon phrase, the railway company 'profile' did not fit the requirements of a later age of big business.

The impact of the railways on the economy at large may be considered under two broad heads: the impact of their construction and the impact of their operation. The magnitude of the sums involved in the construction of the railways have already been indicated. The very particular importance to be attached to them is this: it seems to be a fairly general rule of history that in a free enterprise economy where the economic role of government is minimal, money capital will accumulate in the possession of a very small minority of the population, a trend which powerfully reinforces itself whenever modes of supplying goods are such that capital is a major element in their provision, so that the special return which it commands enables capital to accumulate still further; that such an economy is apt to lead to accumulations of money capital in excess of actual investment requirements; and, consequently, that the lack of employment for this excess of saved up purchasing power will result in a deceleration of expenditure – that is, of demand and hence of the rate of economic activity – the effect, of course, being multiplied as the rate of growth of producers' incomes slackens, resulting in decelerating expenditures on their part etc. In other words, a developing capitalist economy is very likely to require a more than proportionate rate of increase in investment expenditure if the pace of development is to be maintained, because it is very likely to be generating a more than proportionate rate of increase in accumulations of money capital (savings).

In this particular case, the indications are that not only was money capital accumulating in this manner but that the level of investment, far from gathering momentum, was by the early 'forties actually starting to run down as the technological revolution in that key growth sector, the cotton industry, neared completion while technology was failing to provide fresh opportunities for investment of a comparable order in other productive sectors – threatening then not only deceleration but actual stagnancy, albeit stagnancy on a plateau of unprecedented elevation. Certainly, the interval between the first two railway construction booms, the years 1840–43, saw the economy at its most sluggish since the 1810s. That in the outcome, then, the British economy lost little of its earlier growth momentum is, on the demand side, to be attributed in very considerable measure to an accelerated rate of investment; and to this, the contribution of capital expenditure on the railways was peculiarly distinctive. Through the fantastic mania years railway expenditure alone must have accounted for roughly a half of all investment. Even in the relatively dull 'fifties it was about a fifth and in the 'sixties it was around a quarter. Although it is probably true that in the absence of railway investment other additional kinds of investment would have taken place to some degree – history does seem to show that a plenitude of capital will itself sometimes prompt investment – there can be no serious quarrel with the judgment that railway outlays were an absolutely crucial variable in the overall investment level, such that without it growth momentum would have been largely lost. And this for the moment without reference to British involvement in foreign railway building, which can be more conveniently discussed in another context.

It is very possibly true that the economic consequences of railway construction in Britain were greater than those of railway operation. This is a theme which as yet must wait on future research before any firm conclusions can be essayed, but there is ground for conjecturing that in respect of actual point to point haulage, rail freightage of goods had no very substantial intrinsic cost advantage over pre-existing transport media; that much of the gains offered by rail transport arose out of two incidental features, themselves the outcome simply of the speed of rail carriage. The first was the ability of railways to offer a passenger service, enabling them to achieve a relatively high degree of fixed assets utilisation – in a sense, railborne goods could be subsidised by passengers whereas waterborne goods could not. The most significant result of this may have been in low density traffic areas, where it permitted a rail line to function economically when a canal could not have done, rather than in high traffic density areas where goods alone might make for optimum utilisation of assets.

The second gain arising from railway speed was the saving in money capital tied up in goods in transit and in stocks; the one for the evident reason that goods spent less time in transit, and the other because businesses could function on lower stock levels when these could be replenished more quickly and more certainly. It is impossible to put even a notional figure to the proportion of total production costs borne by charges on capital invested in goods in transit and in stocks or to the reductions rendered possible by railways. Stray accounts make it clear that such charges could be very high in nineteenth-century business and in the very long run substantial economies were achieved in this respect but as between better transport, more regular market patterns or more efficient stock control as the prime agents of this one could not attempt to choose. But it might be observed that at least by comparison with many countries, such as the USA where a detailed study has suggested that this was an important consequence of railways, Britain with its relatively short lines of internal communication and an already efficient postal service may not have stood to gain very much from simple savings in delivery times.

All in all there is reason enough to adopt a rather reserved attitude as to the overall cost economies arising out of railway facilities in Britain. It will surely never be demonstrated that there were none;

but when the subject has been more thoroughly investigated, it may emerge that they were a good deal less than the central place assigned to railways in most narratives of the nineteenth-century economy (including this one) might suggest. Railways did almost entirely supplant inland water transport and made a big dent in the business enjoyed by coastal shipping, but not much can be inferred from this. A minimal advantage over these other media would have sufficed to achieve it, and in some cases, perhaps, no real advantage at all but simply a command of eager funds with which to fight a price war until a rival water carrier, less favoured by investors' enthusiasm, was driven out of business. The initial fixed costs once incurred, one had to triumph over the other so that those heavy fixed costs could be spread as widely as possible. And this not only from the point of view of the railway companies but also from that of the nation at large: it would have been a gross waste of national resources to apply them to the maintenance of two alternative transport systems. (Though it should be said that the two were in some degree complementary, particularly up to the 1860s while the railways leant heavily on water and road routes as feeders to their own arterial network, canal and cartage business actually increasing in gross as a result. And a few very favourably situated canals, mostly short ones in colliery regions, were strong enough to withstand railway rivalry; others here and there were able at least to keep open on the basis of carriage of certain very bulky commodities such as hay, straw, dung and building stone for which the railways did not contend because the space they took up could be more remuneratively filled with other goods.)

In a final evaluation there remains that which no amount of historical revision can alter and which will always conserve for railways a central place in nineteenth-century history: their passenger business. For the carriage of people, rail represented such an advance over road, in speed, comfort and, above all, cost, as to render comparison between the two almost meaningless. To all intents and purposes it added an entirely new element to living. The gains arising from it cannot be measured, for there is no pre-existing yardstick against which to measure them. Three broad kinds of gain might be identified: the greatly enhanced facility of contact between businessmen, which in a variety of ways must have reduced entrepreneurial errors and eliminated cost-bearing delays; the equally enhanced mobility of labour, both in that a change of residence could be more easily effected and, of greater import, in that a wider geographical spread of jobs became accessible from the one place of residence (although in the long run the encouragement thus given to concentration of enterprises in a few conurbations has, perhaps, created more problems than it originally solved); thirdly, and entirely incalculable, the opportunity afforded of travel for pleasure. The hotels and boarding-houses of Blackpool, Skegness, Clacton, Margate, etc. are far from least among the creations of the railways. This is to touch on themes which could carry us far beyond the scope of this book. Let it simply be said that in any perspective which comprehends all the elements which enter into the business of living, the iron rail and the steam locomotive in combination easily transcend in consequence any other technological innovation of the eighteenth or nineteenth centuries.

Ships

Rail traction was not of course the only form of transport to which steam power was applied. The steamship also stands high among the practical achievements of this period. And with that can be closely linked the iron-hulled ship. The available statistics may conveniently describe the bones of the story (Tables II.15 and 16).

Perhaps the first thing to stress is that considering that the basic technology involved dated from very early in the century both iron and steam were very slow in winning favour among British shippers. Not until 1863 did the tonnage of iron ships built exceed that of wooden ships. Not until 1870 did steam tonnage built exceed sail. And we would have to run on until 1883 before we found more steam tonnage than sail afloat under the British flag, the amount of sail tonnage in use having gone on increasing until 1866. Of the great innovations of the eighteenth and nineteenth centuries, none was slower in making practical headway. Basically, the obstructions responsible for this were human ones – in a summary but not unduly oversimplified phrase, the conservatism of British shipowners and British shipbuilders. It was not of course that these were men whose individual characters were in some myserious way deficient in faculties which entrepreneurs in other fields possessed. Their conservatism was institutionally engendered, partly the doing of the state, partly that of the organisational structure of the two activities themselves.

The state's part was to continue until mid-century to wrap the shipping industry in the comfortable blanket of the Navigation Acts. A good deal of the original elaborate legislative apparatus had already gone by

TABLE II.15. *Shipping tonnage in use in the United Kingdom*

Year	Percentage sail	Percentage steam	Total (mil. tons)
1830	99	1	2·2
1840	97	3	2·8
1850	95	5	3·6
1860	90	10	4·7
1870	80	20	5·7
1873	70	30	5·8

TABLE II.16. *Shipping tonnage built for use in the United Kingdom*

| Period | Sail | | Steam | |
	Wood	Iron	Wood	Iron
1830–34	99		1	
1835–39	93		7	
1840–44	93		7	
1845–49	88		12	
1850–54	75	4	3	17
1855–59	71	7	1	19
1860–64	47	22	1	32
1865–69	35	32	1	33
1870–74	11	14	1	74

the beginning of this period. The dismantling had effectively begun as far back as 1766 with the Free Ports Act, which exempted designated West Indian ports from certain of the restrictions imposed on colonial trade. And although in original intent this had no further view than attracting the vessels of other European powers to these ports so as to facilitate evasion of the barriers imposed by those countries on the entry of British goods into their colonies, it, along with subsequent similar legislation, provided a legal base for a general freeing of the colonial trade as the attempt to control it became more and more pointless, especially so after the loss of America, with the power to regulate the tobacco trade which had been the only colonial commodity of weight really to need legislating into British hands.

By the time of the first substantial reform of deliberately liberal intent in 1825, those elements of the Navigation System which had been concerned with goods entering into colonial trade had, for all practical purposes, vanished. What still stood were the provisions regarding the nationality of vessels conducting trade through British ports. Although the Act of 1825 granted significant relief from these, British shipping retained a substantial measure of protection. Importation of a range of bulk cargoes remained confined to British ships or ships of the country of origin of the goods, and the re-export of extra-European produce remained the exclusive preserve of British vessels – the first of particular value as, apart from the direct protection conferred, it tended powerfully to exclude third party carriers from the general export trade, since, to engage in it, they would often have had to sail in light, rendering the voyage profitless. Most particularly, the surviving elements of the Navigation System protected British shippers in European waters against American competition. Through the first half of the nineteenth century the finest ships in the world were built in the yards of New England.

However, between their legal privileges, the fact that the shipping of other European countries was not, in general, any more efficient, and the further fact that in the remunerative long-distance hauls to Asia and Latin America they encountered little competition, since these regions had few oceangoing vessels of their own, British shippers could contrive a very comfortable existence without bothering to match the effectiveness of the Yankee vessels which monopolised the North Atlantic trade. Indeed, through a period when the volume of maritime trade was expanding vigorously, British shipowners could achieve a handsome growth in business without any particular exertion on their part. As the figures in Table II.15 indicate, British shipping tonnage increased by just about two-thirds between 1830 and 1850. But over the same two decades foreign trade in bulk more than doubled. In relative terms the share of British shipping was declining.

Cosseting by the state would perhaps have been unimportant if there had been lively competition within the very substantial British mercantile fleet itself. That there was not is due in large part to the fact that the industry as a whole enjoyed very much of a seller's market. On the rising tide of trade there was little need to heighten efficiency or lower tariffs to win business. But there was a further factor which militated strongly against novel initiatives: the substantial lack of entrepreneurship within the industry. Shipowning, as it had been for centuries, was still very much a fragmented function. The basic property unit was not the ship but the ship share, usually one-sixty-fourth of the whole.

Merchants, ships' officers and a miscellany of the individuals who drew their livelihood from the business of a port were ship share owners; and few of them depended primarily on shipping profits for their incomes. Thus the pecuniary basis of entrepreneurship was often missing. Few had sufficient financial incentive to interest themselves closely in ways and means of enhancing shipping efficiency. It was an organisational structure admirably suited to marshalling the capital required for iron-built, steam-powered ships; but the very source of its strength in that respect tended powerfully to dissipate the entrepreneurial energy needed to effect a revolution in shipping technology. And such energy was particularly needful in this field.

Plainly, the reorganisation involved was not just a matter of hauling down sails and putting in a steam engine. It necessitated the recruitment of men with the special skills required for handling a steam ship. It necessitated something of a rethinking of the economics of shipping, particularly with regard to utilisation – idle time being especially expensive in the case of steamships with their relatively high capital cost. (This factor alone would call for professional managerial attention of a kind which sail shipping could dispense with.) But above all, it involved a complete recasting of the shipbuilding industry – or rather it necessitated an entirely new shipbuilding industry, so fundamentally different were constructional techniques as between sailing ships and steamships, and of such an enormously greater order were the capital requirements of yards building for steam as against those building for sail. The great leap from one to the other could only be prompted by very strong demand pressure, and the structure of shipowning was not such as to conduce readily to the generation of that pressure. Really, the wonder is not that steam was so slow in taking to the sea but that it did so at all considering the radical institutional changes which had first to be effected. It is noteworthy that other countries were even more behindhand than Britain, and that the few others which did come to build their own steamships in the late nineteenth century were led to do so largely through governmental interest in fighting ships, triggered off by the re-equipment of the British Navy with vessels which completely revolutionised naval warfare.

The chronology of the conversion to iron and steam would support the view that it was the final repeal of the Navigation Acts in 1849 which spurred shipowning and shipbuilding into profound reorganisation in order to meet the now naked challenge of American ships which through the 'fifties won much business from traditional type

British vessels. And as, through the 'sixties, the more enterprising took increasingly to new ships – the most venturesome to steam, the more cautiously progressive to iron-hulled sailing ships (rather faster than wooden-hulled ones and requiring less maintenance attention) – the traditionalists were rapidly becoming uncompetitive. By the end of the decade it was manifest that the combination of wood and sail had no commercial future except for certain very limited purposes.

Through more than half a century of dabbling with iron the builders of wooden ships had had little to fear from the innovators. Suddenly now, in just a decade, they had become virtually obsolete. In 1860 they had been responsible for nearly three-quarters of the tonnage launched in Great Britain. In 1870 they accounted for only about a sixth. And in most cases this meant extinction, not just conversion. Apart from anything else, most builders of wooden ships were located in the wrong places – principally along the Thames estuary and the south-east coast, whereas the future lay with good riverside sites which stood close to iron industries, pre-eminently with Tyneside, Wearside and Clydeside. Here in the last few years of this period were to be found the most considerable productive enterprises in Great Britain. For sheer rapidity of growth these great iron-shipbuilding concerns are amongst the most remarkable phenomena thrown up by the Industrial Revolution and it is to be regretted that we are not well informed as to the initiatives and sources of capital backing them, evidencing as they do an elastic capacity for development which enterprises in other industrial sectors in general do not seem to have shared. But it can and should be said that they could only have emerged out of an industrial context of substantial pre-existing development in the iron and steam engineering trades. The concept of oceangoing steamships was no particular nation's perquisite, but in the contemporary world only Britain could command the practical technological experience and the supplies of iron necessary to translate the concept into economically significant reality.

The swing to steam was not actually as decisive as the construction figures for 1870–74 would suggest. In most years over the next couple of decades iron-hulled sailing ships accounted for more than a quarter of tonnage launched in the United Kingdom, and as late as 1885 sail tonnage launched in that particular year exceeded steam tonnage. Various factors conspired to keep a place on the seas for sail mounted on iron (and later, steel) hulls. On certain regular runs where steady favourable winds could be counted on (e.g. the Australian wool and the Indian tea runs) an iron-hulled clipper had little speed disadvantage as against steamship; and the radius of action of steamships in the earlier years was limited by a combination of high fuel consumption and shortage of intermediary coaling stations. (Or, looked at under a different aspect, payload capacity over a distance was constricted by bunker space.) For long hauls, then, the lower cost sailing ship often retained an advantage – indicated by the fact that until 1894 the average size of iron or steel sailing ships built, at around a thousand tons, was regularly greater than that of steamships. The initial cost was of course a crucial consideration and many shipowners swung to and fro between steam and sail as the price of iron and steel fluctuated: the steamship required much more metal, not only because of its machinery but also because the deck, masts, etc. of a sailing ship continued to be made of wood, so that the cost differential between the two varied greatly with volatile iron and steel prices; through the 'seventies and 'eighties there is a close correlation between orders for sailing ships and export demand for British iron. Not until the triple-expansion engine was perfected in the 1880s, making for appreciably higher speeds and greatly lowered fuel consumption, did technology confer an overwhelming advantage on steam.

Steam's advantage over sail was of course primarily a matter of speed. Over long distances the saving in charges on capital tied up in goods in transit could alone make for significant economies. But the most considerable economies arising out of greater speed derived from the greater number of journeys which a ship could make over any given period, such that even with the higher initial cost the fixed element in total costs was lower per journey. Whether running costs were lower is questionable: a steamship carried a smaller crew than a sailing ship of equivalent size but a sailing ship, of course, did not have to meet fuel costs.

The higher speed of steam was not really due to greater maxima – even with triple-expansion engines few steamships could exceed 15 knots and a fast clipper could make 17 or 18 with favourable winds; but with unfavourable winds a sailing ship might not even be able to clear harbour while a steamship was indifferent to the weather, short of storm conditions. This factor meant also that the steamship was much more flexible; put crudely, it could go where it liked when it liked. And it was in the operation of tramping even more than in liner services that steam was at its most advantageous – at least, when coupled with the international cable facilities which were spreading from mid-century. Steamships, that is to say, were less likely to spend time without cargoes. And, obversely, cargoes were less likely to lie on wharfsides waiting for ships. The combination of steam and cable – particularly the latter in this respect – also allowed stocks to be run at much lower levels, with appreciable economies in consequence, not only by way of the savings on capital but also, in the case of many commodities, through the reduction of loss from deterioration. (If the stock economies resulting from railways were at all important, so to a great degree were those resulting from cable and steamships, which achieved much greater reductions in the delay between order and response. But it may be observed that the amount of real overall gain is disputable. After an initial, once and for all, reduction of stock levels, which does release goods for consumption, there is no further direct addition to the supply of consumable goods. Whether the permanent saving in the amount of capital needed to supply any given quantity constitutes the release of a real factor of production to serve other economic ends depends on whether money capital is to be accounted a real factor of production – a point on which views are apt to differ. The same line of reasoning applies to savings on goods in transit: the total quantity in transit at any point in time is equatable with stocks.)

As indicated earlier, the displacement of sail by steam could only take place in close association with a restructuring of the pattern of ship-owning; specifically, in such a way as to preserve its dispersed character while superadding professional entrepreneurial control. In a sense nothing could have been simpler: the owners of shares in ships only needed to be transmuted into owners of shares in shipping companies. All that was wanting were the initiatives to form and manage such companies. The 'fifties brought a handful of pioneering ventures, particularly in Glasgow and Liverpool, blazing a trail which was followed with growing eagerness through the 'sixties and 'seventies. They were very distinctive figures, these men who assumed the leadership of an industry which had hitherto not known their type at all. Distinctive, not only in their novelty in this particular field, but in the special aptitudes which their kind of business called for and in the relationship in which they stood to the companies whose affairs they directed.

Heavy initial expenditures had to be hazarded on judgments as to the vagaries of international trade for a couple of decades to come – and even the shrewdest judgments of future demand trends were not proof against fluctuations in freight rates occasioned by the supply situation, steam shipping being particularly liable to oversupply because the heavy effective cost of laying up vessels meant that excess capacity, when it occurred, only contracted very slowly. This was further complicated by the equal volatility of ship prices, since shipbuilding capacity was also inelastic in the short run. No other commercial activity called for such finely balanced judgments on basic strategy as this did; a fact reflected in the great variations in fortunes as between different shipping companies.

The other respect in which the shipping companies tended to have a peculiarity of character was that the men who controlled them usually had a substantial financial stake of their own involved, yet were also answerable to a body of co-owning shareholders, whereas, generally speaking, in the rest of the contemporary economy either the directors of enterprises were responsible only to themselves and perhaps their relatives and one or two sleeping partners, or, at the other rare extreme such as the railways, a total severance of management and ownership prevailed. Its hybrid character gave the steamship world an aggressiveness which contrasted sharply with the rather torpid atmosphere in which British commercial life was tending in the later years of this period to become enveloped, bred on the one hand of a reluctance to expand concern size beyond the scope of family control, accompanied sometimes by a thinning of entrepreneurial energy as it passed through the generations, and on the other, of an incentive structure which tended to evaluate fidelity to routine more highly than original initiative. In the shipping business the insufficiently vigorous were liable not only to suffer in their pockets but, where they were not in control of a majority shareholding, to find the company passing into more determined hands. Other, less healthy, consequences followed from this situation. Directors in their anxiety to keep shareholders happy were sometimes tempted to pay higher dividends than was sensible in a business where ample reserves were needed to weather the inescapable periods of profitlessness. And, where majority control was enjoyed, the particular hazards attached to forfeiting it in this rapacious world powerfully reinforced the common reluctance of family concerns to grow by way of recruiting fresh equity capital from outside, with the long-run result that British shipping came to suffer from an excess of inefficiently small or under-capitalised concerns.

(It should be made clear before leaving this topic that what has been said relates to cargo shipping. Passenger shipping in a total economic context is not really weighty enough to warrant here the separate account which would have to be given of it. But, as a one-sentence acknowledgement of it, it can be observed that it took to steam much earlier – nearly all the pre-1850 steamships were passenger vessels – and that it gave rise to much larger companies, such as Cunard and the Peninsular and Oriental, which in their general character more closely resembled the railway companies than they did the cargo concerns dealt with above.)

The iron industry

It is a natural transition from railways and steamships to the iron industry. In certain years the iron requirements of these two users (including foreign demand) may have accounted for over half the output of the British iron industry and in most years they were probably responsible for at least a quarter. Their role then, especially that of the railways, was a key one in sustaining a revolutionary growth rate in the iron industry throughout this period (see Table II.17).

TABLE II.17. *Pig iron output (million tons)*

1830	1840	1850	1860	1870	(1873)
0·7	1·4	2·2	3·8	6·0	(6·6)

This record yields an annual average growth rate of 5·5 per cent over the whole period – the same as that recorded over the previous forty-five years, which is to say that the revolutionary growth phase commencing in or around 1785 persisted to the very end of this period. Indeed its termination may legitimately be dated with a precision to which long-run economic trends rarely lend themselves: September 1873, with the crash on the New York stock exchange and the freezing of American railway orders – after which things were never quite the same again.

As had been the case ever since the big initial technological breakthroughs, this growth was largely engendered by autonomous demand movements. Through the first decade or so of the period, the demand was principally domestic, with railway requirements a prominent element over the years 1836–41; thereafter foreign and home demand were about equally responsible for growth; and with the ending of the domestic railway building boom of the 'sixties, foreign needs, for railway iron in particular, took over as the chief growth agency.

Through those closing years probably rather more than a half of British 'raw' iron went to overseas customers, the proportion having risen fairly steadily from around a fifth at the beginning of the period. Put in a total economic context, iron exports had earned about 0·3 per cent of British national income in 1830. In the early 'seventies they accounted for over 3 per cent.

While at one time or another British iron went to almost every corner of the world to serve almost every one of the multifarious purposes which iron could serve, it was above all certain particular countries in course of equipping themselves with extensive railway systems who called upon British iron suppliers. Towering above any other was the USA, impatiently spanning its immense distances. Even in the 'thirties and 'forties more track was laid there than in Britain. However it was from the early 'fifties that American construction started to assume really prodigious proportions. The Civil War brought a sharp check, but from 1865 activity was fully resumed and swelled to phenomenal magnitude until temporarily arrested by the severe financial crisis of 1873. India, Germany, France, Australia, Russia and Belgium, while not approaching the American scale, were also prominent as buyers of British railway iron, mostly from the early 'fifties and particularly over the years 1867–73 when half the world was seized by a simultaneous frenzy of enthusiasm for railway building.

It was this bunching of railway projects which gave the British iron industry its particular, and somewhat fortuitous, opportunities in foreign markets. While India and Australia would certainly have drawn heavily on British supplies in any circumstances, most of the big buyers of British iron were countries which, by the mid-century at least, were in possession of fully up-to-date iron industries of their own – and in a number of cases, by the time of the onset of the international railway boom in 1867, were technically more advanced than the British industry. They bought British iron not because it was cheaper, and certainly not because it was better than their own iron, but because their own as yet limited capacities could not meet requirements during the more intense demand phases. The British iron industry over the last couple of decades was not reaping the benefits of its own contemporary technological forwardness but that of an earlier generation, which had initiated such a precocious expansion of the industry in Britain that even as late as 1870 it still commanded half the world's iron producing capacity. Railway builders through much of the 'fifties and 'sixties and continuously through the years 1867–73 had no effective option but to buy British. And this straining of world iron capacity brought the further windfall gain of scarcity prices. In the early 'seventies even the most hopelessly inefficient could not help but make money hand over fist out of iron.

British ironmasters, then, throughout nearly all this period could swim happily with the tide of demand. Only during the breathing space, 1841–44, between the two early phases of domestic railway building, was the industry seriously troubled by that excess capacity which its relatively high fixed costs made particularly burdensome. That spell and two or three others of no more than a few months duration apart, the industry could enjoy the comforts of eager courtship by the market. This easy situation meant that the industry was under little pressure to heighten its efficiency – the more especially since internal competition was heavily damped down by price agreements. And technologically the industry of 1873 was in most essentials that of 1830.

One basic advance of considerable importance had been effected in the early years of this period: direct smelting with raw coal, made possible by James Neilson's hot blast (preheating the air blown through the blast furnace to a temperature of 600°F or 315°C) patented in 1828 and first employed for production in 1830. Apart from eliminating the coking stage it also substantially reduced the quantity of coal required, which not only yielded important fuel economies but by leaving more room for ore in the furnace enhanced smelting capacity and thus made for lower fixed costs per unit of output. All in all, it lowered smelting costs by something like a third. But it was not suitable for use with every kind of coal, nor for the production of many kinds of iron. Its most signal consequence was in Clydesdale where it enabled the hitherto unusable backband ores to be employed for smelting. Thereafter little was achieved towards supplying cheaper or better pig. The brand new Cleveland industry, starting up in the early 'fifties, was able to take full advantage of such improvements as there had been in furnace design principally with a view to enhancing capacity, and was conspicuously forward in conserving the waste gases generated by smelting as a cheap ancillary power source. But outside Cleveland, right through to the end of the period, there was little interest in revising smelting techniques and even less in improving puddling methods.

Technical progressiveness is not of course an immutable law of nature. In itself the failure of an industry to achieve continuously significant cost reductions is not necessarily a matter for comment, let alone disparagement. But in this particular case the facts do point to a needless inertia on the part of the British iron industry, at least over the last decade or two of the period. What Cleveland could do, other districts could have done. And, more important, what was being done in France, Germany, Belgium and the United States from the 'fifties onwards could have been done in Britain also. By the later 'sixties acute observers were aware that the British industry while still a giant amongst pygmies was an awkward, clumsy, slow-minded giant, threatened with ultimately going the way of the dinosaur if it did not pay more heed to what the clever little pygmies were doing.

To state precisely what they were doing would carry one much further into technology than lies within the ambit of this book. But the main lines of progress could be crudely classified under three broad heads: reduction of heat wastage (measured against a theoretical optimum the loss of heat at all processing stages in the iron industry was enormous); the application of analytical chemistry to metallurgy with the objects of more efficient use of ingredients, finer control of the product and commercial utilisation of slag residues; reduction of handling costs by way of mechanical aids, improved plant layout and vertically integrated concerns. It would be ridiculous to say that these paths were unexplored in Britain but it is plain that they were not being followed with anything like the scrupulosity and thoroughness of the growing young industries elsewhere.

This sluggishness on the part of the British industry is, of course, in considerable measure to be attributed to the factor already raised: technically backward or not, there was no difficulty in securing orders. And full order books would have a further, more positive tendency, to retard the introduction of new techniques. Plant owners would be reluctant to suspend operations at a time of high profitability in order to allow equipment to be modified or replaced – a consideration applying with especial force to the hectic years, 1867–73 when potential rivals in the international field were coming up particularly rapidly. And at any time of course newly founded concerns had the considerable advantage over established ones of not having embarrassing decisions to take on the economics of scrapping fully viable but technically obsolete equipment to make way for up-to-date substitutes. It could often be the case that it was more profitable to cling to old plant than to lay out money on new, especially under keen demand conditions and consequent lack of market discrimination between producers.

Nevertheless it is clear that the technical backwardness of the British industry is not to be fully explained in terms of lack of incentive, nor even entirely in wider terms of lack of interest in technical improvement. While simple conservatism – a stubborn attachment to the proven and currently profitable – was certainly a major impediment to progress, it would be absurd to represent the industry as totally blind to the possible benefits of innovation. It knew itself after all to be the offspring of technical revolution. A more radical flaw was the general apprehension of technical progress as a matter of chance – a fortuitous, unpredictable, undeterminable element in industrial life – not so much something that was achieved as something that simply happened. Specifically then, the systematic pursuit of technical improvement was an idea which in general was quite foreign to British industry. Investigation and inquiry were not conceived of as a normal regular function of a business concern. Improvement was not part of anybody's job. In the case of the iron industry, chemists and physicists had no place in it. Except in the very last years of the period, when a few more forward-looking concerns had come to embrace research within their organisation, hardly anybody in a British ironworks had any clear idea of what went on inside a furnace. Tried rules of thumb governed production processes. As long as they worked nobody was very concerned to know why they worked – which meant amongst other things that when a new idea did present itself, nobody was really competent to evaluate it.

The iron industry, British industry in general and, in fact, British society at large, was not organised for the purpose of effecting a continuous revision of technology, nor even for the purpose of exploiting current technology to the full. Britain had led the world in recasting its economy in an industrial mould; but it lagged in restructuring itself so as to sustain and accelerate the developments which a particular conjuncture of circumstances had initiated. The point at which this is most plainly true is education. From the elementary to the most advanced level virtually nothing had been done towards reshaping educational curricula and methods with a view to fostering the knowledge, skills and aptitudes which could be of service to industry. At the one extreme, thrift, sobriety, honesty, diligence and a proper respect for one's betters, along with the elements of literacy, numeracy and Christian doctrine were the objects of education; at the other extreme, Latin, Greek and pure mathematics; and at intermediate levels varying combinations of the two sets. It was in brief an educational structure which pretended that the world of industry did not exist. Even had industry wanted more chemists, physicists, etc., or manual workers with a technical grounding, it would have been hard put to find them in Britain, though it would have done rather better in Scotland than in England.

But there is more than a simple deficiency of certain vocational accomplishments involved in this question. There is a whole set of establishment attitudes which regarded industrial life with something approaching disdain and contempt, with effects ranging well beyond the exclusion of technical and scientific subjects from educational curricula. While in any society purely pecuniary ambitions are a primary motivation of human behaviour, social esteem is also a coveted end and the means whereby it can be secured control and contain the pecuniary impulse. In this context, while begging the detailed sociological analysis which the issue really merits but which lies beyond the competence of this book, what is being urged in crude terms is that the British upper class, whose canons of respectability set the standards for society at large, ruled, essentially in self-defence perhaps, that industrial activity had a low honorific value; that, among other reasons, British industry was tending towards inertia because Britain did not really prize industrial achievement very highly. It is perhaps suggestive that the Great Exhibition of 1851, that ostentatious display of British industrial accomplishments, was the idea of the German prince consort; the lofy derision with which it was received by *The Times* was doubtless an accurate enough reflection of the sentiments of that newspaper's readership.

One might even go on to argue the view that the family firm represents an aping of the family estate and, thus, an endeavour to claim for it the same kind of social respectability as went with the possession of broad acres. Whatever the merits of such a thesis it must at least be observed in the present context that this was another structural feature tending to inhibit continuous progress, for the evident reason that blood is no guarantee of efficiency. And the iron industry left less room for new entrants than most; partly because the suitability of any particular product could only be established by lengthy use, so that there was a natural disposition on the part of buyers to cling to familiar suppliers; partly because of the relatively large initial capital required to commence business in this field.

We have drifted from the iron industry into much wider – and deeper – waters. But it has been advised drifting. Iron was the first major British industry to be overtaken by more energetic rivals – technically overtaken within this period, although the consequences in sales terms had not yet made themselves apprehensible. Iron was the industry where the running down of the entrepreneurial drive of the early revolutionary years first makes itself evident. And the general features of British life which have been the subject of comment above stand out particularly in an international comparison of iron industries. In the years to come it was the German and American industries which supplanted the British in many of the world's markets; and it is to Germany that one would point as an exemplar in technical and scientific education, and to the USA for a prime instance of a society uncluttered by inhibitory social hangovers.

After so much on the technical languor of the British iron industry, it becomes necessary to say that what was to prove the most radical breakthrough since Cort was of British origin: a cheap steelmaking process – in fact two cheap steelmaking processes. Only the most cursory references have been made here to steel hitherto. It was used where a fine cutting edge was required, for watch springs and a few other trivial special purposes where its peculiar combination of hardness and capacity to withstand strain or impact was essential. It was of course an ideal multipurpose metal but ruled out wherever ordinary iron would serve by its higher cost. Steel was expensive because with existing methods the process of adding the carefully gauged amount of carbon to pure bar iron (itself, expensive, imported charcoal smelted iron) so as to achieve a homogeneous metal of the correct carbon content (around 1 per cent) could only be effected on a very small scale, with consequently very high fuel and plant costs per unit of output; and, furthermore, it yielded ingots which were impracticably small for most purposes.

The ideal solution to the problem of making cheap steel was a process for refining pig iron which could be arrested at whatever point at which the requisite quantity of carbon remained in the melt. This was what Henry Bessemer proposed to achieve with his 'converter', patented in 1856, in which air was forced through molten pig at high pressure, burning out the carbon and other impurities. Bessemer's expectations were not fully realised. He was unable to control the burning sufficiently precisely to make steel direct, while it also transpired that the technique left an undesirable form of oxygen in the metal and, furthermore, failed to eliminate phosphorous. The last defect could be overcome by smelting with non-phosphoric ore. Robert Mushet provided Bessemer with the answer to the oxygen problem by incorporating manganese into the process, with the extra benefit of further toughening the metal – and, in his own judgment and that of recent students of the question, received very inadequate recognition for his contribution. As to steelmaking, there was nothing for it but to reduce the pig to pure bar and then to add the requisite carbon. It was not quite what Bessemer had originally hoped for, but it was, nonetheless, cheap steel – that is steel with a low enough price premium over puddled iron to offer possible long run economies on account of its longer working life. And a few years later William Siemens offered an alternative technique which did permit of fine enough control to directly transform pig iron into steel.

Siemens's basic contribution was not a steelmaking technique as such but a furnace, more accurately, an 'open hearth', heated by circulating currents of hot gas, making for both a much higher degree of heat utilisation and more flexible heat regulation than could be obtained in conventional reverberatory or direct heating furnces. It was of potential benefit in any high temperature melting process and was in fact first employed in glassmaking. Its first application to steel was in melting down scrap steel, and then in 1865, by a French iron concern, Martin's, to the reduction of a mixture of molten pig and scrap to new steel. Although in the same year Siemens himself started making steel without using scrap, the Martin method was found preferable for most purposes and, when the swing to steel had been fully effected, was the technique employed in most open hearths. This is, however, to run ahead of ourselves. Even in the very last year of this period only about a tenth of British pig iron ended up as steel – this, fifteen years after Bessemer himself had pioneered the way by setting up his own steelmaking business in Sheffield.

In the light of the fact that steel was ultimately to sweep iron aside, this was just inching forward when, retrospectively, one might have expected transformation on a par with that which had succeeded Cort's development of puddling and rolling. But it must be borne in mind that steel, whether made in the converter or in the open hearth, was still more expensive than puddled iron. Given that most articles of ferrous composition had a normal working life of ten, twenty or more years, it was bound to take that kind of period of time to demonstrate that despite its higher initial cost, steel did work out cheaper. In a number of possible applications, of course, the potential benefits did not consist solely, or even at all, in the greater durability of steel but in its greater strength enabling such a reduced weight of metal to be used as made immediately for lower costs, even permitting of mechanical operations which hitherto had not been practicable at all; possibilities of that general nature being also opened up by steel's cutting powers. But whatever the application only protracted experience could abundantly demonstrate its feasibility, commercial or technical.

Whatever the rate of adoption of steel in later years, there could be little sound reason for expecting it to have been much higher than it was within the bounds of this period, the more particularly since Bessemer charged high licence fees while his patent lasted. When it expired in 1870 the iron industry was caught up in the great international railway boom during which it had neither the incentive nor the spare resources to attend to such as might be interested in buying steel in any quantity – all this supplemented by the special consideration that the non-phosphoric ores required for either converter or open-hearth only occurred, in Britain, in Cumberland, which sustained no more than the tiniest iron industry. Fairly evidently smelters would be at least reluctant to sever themselves from the local ores on which their businesses were founded. However, the question of whether or not to make a different product is essentially one decided by the market rather than by autonomous action on the part of producers themselves – it was users who would really settle the iron versus steel issue.

It remains to indicate something of the geographical shifting about within the British iron industry (see Table II.18).

The outstanding trait is perhaps the development of the industry in Scotland where output increased some twentyfold between 1830 and 1852. Thereafter further growth was much slower and Scottish output settled down at around a million tons per annum in the early 'sixties. The tremendous initial upthrust was of course due to the introduction of the hot blast and the consequent exploitation of the blackband ores in the Clydesdale region, which for some two decades or so made Clydesdale pig the cheapest in Britain and would have been a source of serious embarrassment to other producers had it not been for the very buoyant demand trends of those years. The ease with which Scottish pig – and cast – could find markets elsewhere in the country doubtless explains the slow development of bar iron manufacture in the region. What there was was produced largely to meet local requirements, and although textile machinery from the beginning was quite an important source of local demand, it was not really until the great increase in steamship construction on the Clyde that Scottish iron-smelting became integrated with a regional industrial complex. The great extension of the market for iron shipbuilding and associated engineering trades, getting under way from around mid-century, coincided happily with what otherwise might have been the beginning of a period of difficulties for the Scottish smelters. The blackband ores were becoming thin, costs were levelling up with those of other producers, and Cleveland had emerged as most favoured smelting district. Scottish furnaces could not have continued for long to lean on outside demand.

TABLE 11.18. *Geographic distribution of national pig iron output 1830–73 (percentages)*

	1830	1852	1873
Total (mil. tons)	*0·7*	*2·7*	*6·6*
South Wales	41	25	12
South Staffs. }	31	28	10
North Staffs. }		3	4
Shropshire	11	4	2
East Midlands	7	6	7
Scotland	5	29	15
Lancs. and N. Wales	4	1	9
North-east	1	5	13
Cleveland	—	negligible	18
Cumberland	negligible	negligible	7

('East Midlands' denotes those adjoining parts of Derbyshire, Nottinghamshire and the West Riding of Yorkshire of which Sheffield is the centre. For the later years 'Scotland' signifies very largely the Clydesdale region. For the earlier years 'Lancs. and North Wales' refers chiefly to the area around Wrexham; in 1873, chiefly to the Furness district. 'North-east' denotes Tyneside and Durham.)

The emergence of Cleveland is the other most conspicuous feature of the period – even more striking perhaps than the earlier rise of Clydesdale since the Cleveland industry was born out of nothing, the presence of iron ore in the district only being determined in 1850 but giving rapid rise to an industry clustered around Middlesbrough which by 1872 had become the leading producer of pig in the country – and, as noted earlier, the most efficient. Cleveland's growth would have been even more dramatic had it possessed coal of its own. As it was a substantial fraction of its ore went across the Tees into south Durham, which accounts for most of the output labelled 'North-east', 1873, in Table II.18. However, on balance it was usually more advantageous to bring the coal to the ore, rather than vice versa, and it was Cleveland it-self which smelted the greater part of its ore, generally in integrated con-cerns – another point of efficiency – which within this period devoted themselves principally to rails, their coastal situation being especially suitable in catering for the foreign market; it was Cleveland above all which grew fat on the international railway boom of 1867–73: of the two million-odd tons added to annual national sales of iron over those years Cleveland's share alone was about 700,000 tons.

The development of Cleveland and south Durham brought about the steady rundown of the iron industry around Tyneside and Wearside which, on the basis of the local market, had expanded considerably through the first couple of decades of this period, particularly in the puddling branch, the region's pig output being heavily reinforced by Scottish supplies.

As presented in Table II.18, two other regions exhibit noteworthy development over the later years of this period: Lancashire and Cum-berland. However in this context these two largely constitute the one district, the part of Lancashire principally concerned being Furness, geologically part of the orefield which runs down the Cumberland coast. From the early years of the period south Wales had been in-creasingly supplementing local ore resources from this field; but hitherto the unsuitability of Cumberland's coal for coking had told against the maintenance of anything but a trivial amount of smelting in the area itself. In the early 'sixties, with the first active stirrings of interest in Bessemer steel, its unique non-phosphoric ores prompted the foundation of new enterprises there, initiating a movement whose most rapid progress occurred in the decade immediately following the end of this period.

Complementing the rapid growth of smelting in certain districts through the second half of this period was the relative decline of other districts. Most manifest is the falling away of the Black Country which had maintained vigorous development into the 1850s, but then abruptly not only started to lose its relative placing but entered on an absolute decline, briefly reversed at the height of the international railway boom but immediately and sickeningly resumed thereafter. Although the region was coming to labour under certain disadvantages, to be touched on, the difficulties of this well-rooted industry seem fairly plainly to be attributable in substantial measure to its own human failings. The stubborn conservatism of the South Staffordshire ironmasters became notorious. If not very much was being done elsewhere in the country to heighten cost efficiency and adjust the nature of products more closely to user requirements, virtually nothing was being done in the Black Country, which seems to have leant almost entirely on its historical reputation and the fallout from demand explosions for any orders over and above the core element which it could fairly reliably count on from the metalware trades of the Birmingham region. In partial mitigation of this sorry record it may be said that the district's ore deposits were running down (but were as yet far from exhausted), and that its inland location put it at something of a disadvantage in catering for the export demand which was of gathering consequence through the period. It should also be pointed out that though the fortunes of the puddling branch would seem to have followed a roughly parallel course to those of the smelting branch, Black Country puddlers were still responsible for as much as a quarter of total British output of bar iron at the end of the period, having come to draw heavily on outside supplies of pig.

It was in south Wales that, particularly from the later 'fifties, dwindling local ore supplies presented the most acute problem. By the end of the period they sufficed for only about a third of the iron made in the region, whereas Staffordshire, although finding it convenient to draw some ore from a distance could still get by on its own. Cumberland ore and, in increasingly significant quantities from the late 'sixties, Spanish ore made up the growing deficit, enabling south Wales to bump along at that output level of rather under a million tons per annum which it had attained by the later 'fifties. Its ability to sustain itself under adverse supply conditions may be attributed in some part to a relatively high degree of technical efficiency – it was accounted the most progressive of the older iron districts – but more importantly to its geographical location. This was of consequence in several respects: it eased the cost burden of fetching ores from Cumberland and Spain; it facilitated export sales, especially to the USA; but it had too a more specific significance: the south Wales iron industry was becoming increasingly drawn into the tinplate business which, with the prominent development of canned foods from the mid-'sixties, was running on a swelling tide of demand and more than anything else from then on was what preserved south Wales iron output from steady decline. Traditionally drawing on convenient Cornish tin supplies, south Wales was well placed to supplement these with imports, figuring from mid-century and accounting for nearly a half of requirements by the end of the period; and, of course, also well placed to drive an export trade in tinplate. In fact the region was easily the world's most important supplier and provided a creditable instance of deft adjustment to changing conditions.

Two words should be added for the sake of completeness on the other districts listed in the table. Shropshire was held fast by limited coal and ore resources and by the end of the period was on the threshold of a steady decline into oblivion. The east Midlands sustained itself on the market base of local engineering industries and on the abundance of local coal but the relatively high cost of having to draw ore from outside and its inland situation limited its external sales scope.

Engineering

Reference has been made to engineering industries as a demand element in the iron trade. And although, as already insisted, railway requirements must be distinguished as the special agency of a 'revolutionary' growth rate in iron throughout this period, the industry would still exhibit a very healthy growth rate even with railway and ship metal subtracted from its output. Much of what would remain would consist of the orders of the machine makers. While in 1830 a substantial proportion of British iron output would still have ended up in the form of domestic utensils and ornaments, simple tools, nails and the like, by 1873 that traditional kind of market was of slight importance to the industry as a whole, though still of appreciable weight in the Black Country, and a chief importance of iron to the economy at large was as the base material of mechanical production.

Some general indication of the advance of machinery through this period is afforded by the calculation that steam power generated by stationary engines in 1830 cannot have exceeded in gross 100,000 horsepower whereas in 1873 it was over a million horsepower. In the textile industries the use of steam for all basic operations was now virtually universal; the need for steam engines in coalmining had increased very considerably; intensifying urbanisation had swung flourmilling heavily over to steam; the metalworking and engineering trades had devised techniques which permitted them to use steam for certain kinds of operations; garment and shoe makers had started to employ it in a modest way; pottery, glass and paper manufacturers had virtually abandoned water for their powered operations; printers had taken to steam; agriculture was making increasing use of it in various ways; and there were other less noteworthy users. The iron industry was of course a very big user, accounting for a quarter of total steampower generated for production tasks.

All this plainly signifies tremendous growth on the part of the steam-engineering industry, no more than a rather exotic fringe element in the industrial economy of 1830 and, what there was of it, largely concentrated in the Birmingham region. Fairly steadily, but most intensively from mid-century onwards, the industry developed not only in its heartland but in all the districts where steam power was intensively used: the textile districts, clustered round Manchester, Leeds and Glasgow (in the last given further successive boosts by the rise of the Clydesdale iron industry and then by that of steamship construction on the Clyde); the Tyneside-Wearside region, with a similar development of iron and steamship business building up a market on a base laid by the steam engine needs of the region's collieries; south Wales, where coal, iron and tinplating orders sustained steam engineering; and the Sheffield, Derby, Nottingham triangle, where collieries and ironworks again supplied a base market.

In the case of collieries and ironworks, the essential novelty was not their requirements of steam power, which antedate this period, but the full emergence of specialist concerns to cater for these requirements, which earlier had commonly been attended to by steam-using enterprises themselves, purchasing such materials and hiring such technical expertise as they could not supply from their own resources. The appropriation of these functions by specialist concerns reflects both the extension of the market to the point where it could support them and the increasing technical complexity of steam engineering, notably from the mid-'forties when the development of compound engines made for much higher pressures and correspondingly greater efficiency, but called also for special skills in their design and construction. The rise of marine engineering led to further specialisation, steamship engines representing an entirely new order of magnitude, some of them running to over 500 h.p. when few land engines exceeded 100 h.p. But although engines for the larger vessels were the work of specific marine engineers, who were sometimes shipbuilders as well, many smaller vessels must have been engined with the products of general steam-engineering concerns on and around Clydeside, Tyneside and Wearside.

The special case of combined marine-engineering and shipbuilding firms aside, none of these concerns was very big. It should be stressed, as it has been already in the previous chapter, that they were not so much manufacturing as assembling enterprises; that what are here distinguished as steam-engineering concerns were really only the synthesising element in a complex of trades, the whole tending towards an increasing subdivision of functions, interlocking not only with steam engineering specifically but with engineering generally in the widest sense – an intimidating tangle which has so far defied detailed research.

Retrospectively, it is fairly clear that this organisational structure was not such as to make for optimum efficiency. Broadly speaking, optimum efficiency is achieved with continuous production runs of standardised products, geared with planning and technical control of preceding processing stages. Judged by this criterion, the suppliers of steam engines could hardly have been worse situated, exercising as they did only minimal control over both their own product and the supply of their materials. As producers they were little more than contractors, custom working to specific orders. Not only did this mean that it was difficult to standardise on a suitably limited number of models but also that activity levels were very apt to fluctuate considerably. But, while in the later years of this period, discerning observers had come to perceive the desirability of a rationalisation of this industrial complex, it was not a move which could readily come about as a result of spontaneous decisions from within.

In the first place, customers wanted engines which met their particular power requirements and fitted in with their particular plant layouts. The steam engine suppliers could only standardise to the extent that the steam engine users were able and prepared to standardise. Had the steam engine business been in the hands of a few large concerns they might have had the bargaining strength to force acceptance of stock models on the users. But the field was occupied by a relatively large number of small concerns precisely because of the nature of the market – erratic and therefore presenting particular hazards of excess capacity if one attempted to grow too quickly; and beyond a certain growth point it would become needful to extend vertically as well in order to guard against underutilisation of resouces on account of possible supply bottlenecks, multiplying then the amount of capital which would have to be hazarded. Size might eventually bring its rewards in the shape of a market conditioned to standardisation and a consequent ability to even out demand fluctuations by producing for stock. But in the interim the pioneers were very likely to be killed off by intolerable losses. In a phrase, what was good for the economy as a whole was not necessarily good for individual business concerns. In the steam-engineering field, as in others, there was safety in diffusion, both horizontal and vertical.

What has just been said was not of course the only factor bearing on the organisation of steam engineering. Factors common to British industry as a whole, reluctance to expand beyond family scope, the problem of recruiting managerial personnel, operated here too. And there was a further special factor, distinctive of much of the whole variegated range of engineering trades. Concerns were usually the foundation not of the common type of entrepreneur but of working engineering craftsmen – in many of the early cases in particular, genuine innovators seeking to develop and exploit their own notions. Vertical disintegration was inevitable under these circumstances: these men had usually only the scantiest capital resources and thus had to depend on outside suppliers for materials. And as long as the market for engineering products was expanding rapidly and the general size of concerns was small there was abundant scope for the capable craftsman to venture on his own – itself limiting the capacity of existing concerns to grow, by siphoning off the personnel who would be needed for responsible positions in any kind of multicellular concern. As much as is known of it, the early history of British engineering reads like a page of Genesis: Watt begat Bramah, Bramah begat Maudslay, Maudslay begat Whitworth, and so on. It will be appreciated also that this kind of initiative, often prompted more by the creative urge than by the profit motive, commonly did not run in its ambitions to commercial empire-building; and that it tended to engender a professional *esprit* which valued craftsmanship more highly than cost efficiency.

We have slid now from steam engineering in particular to general engineering and although all of the general observations just made apply equally over much of the engineering range, at least one and that the most important sector has a distinctive history of its own: textile engineering. Already by the beginning of the period, in its cotton branch at least, this was a fully fledged industry, clearly standing out as an entity from the mishmash of metalworking trades which constituted the rest of the contemporary engineering industry. Nevertheless, in common with other engineering industries, it has not yet been the subject of thorough historical investigation and in offering any account of it one has to lean uncomfortably heavily on general impressions.

As to its growth, one may confidently say that it was very vigorous throughout this period, not merely matching that of the cotton industry itself, but running ahead of it, as over the first decade or two the swing to power looms was finalised and, increasingly throughout, as exports of cotton machinery rose. By the end of this period it was an industry characterised by relatively large individual concerns, with labour forces of five hundred plus, maintaining continuous production runs of standardised items – concerns that is with a strong enough position not merely in the British but in the world market to be able to disdain the whims and fancies of buyers, strong enough to dictate the technological structure of the cotton industry according to the criteria of cost efficient engineering. Indeed things seem to have come to the point where a new cotton manufacturing enterprise neither needed, nor effectively was able, to make independent decisions other than to choose which engineering concern it should order its plant from and which of the specialist industrial building concerns should erect for it premises of stereotyped design. Along with the ready availability in Lancashire of suitable labour this indicates that entrepreneurship in the cotton industry had become a virtually automatised function, once the initial decision to engage in business had been taken and the requisite capital raised – a situation most manifestly indicated in the decade immediately following this period during which 373 new cotton manufacturing companies were founded in Britain, explicable only on grounds of the great simplicity of entering the field. Lacking in colour and the element of the heroic which characterised the 'revolutionary' phase, this kind of situation is a mark of the evolution towards an organisational structure in which the margin of human error is minimised and the exploitation of human skills maximised by functional specialisation at that level of concern size which offers major efficiencies of scale. Cotton textile engineering does, then, seem to stand out as an industry which achieved notable development in balanced integration with the sector of the economy which it served.

It must, however, be said that the apparently smooth evolution of cotton engineering must have tended both to depend on and to make for relative technological stability, in cotton manufacturing and machine manufacturing alike. The basic design of all the cotton machinery in use throughout this period was already soundly established at the outset. Machine manufacturers were never brought to that acutely uncomfortable point of having to choose between scrapping valuable plant on the one hand and running the risk of technical obsolescence on the other, with the inevitable difficulties and setbacks which either decision would occasion. And, implicitly, it was not really in their own interests to promote investigation which would tend in that direction. This is by no means to suggest technical stagnancy. Fairly continuously, basic equipment was being modified; the cotton industry drew steady cost benefits from the technical liveliness of the machine makers. It is in respect of its own production methods that cotton engineering might be said to have shown a certain sluggishness. Like all British engineering trades it prided itself, and justifiably, on the high level of operative skills which it maintained. And it is perhaps true that as a result it interested itself less than it might have done in the development of machine tools. Certainly it is true that for all its high standing and general vigour it was not among the more forward sectors of British engineering in the employment of power and mechanical aids. But only much more detailed inquiry than has so far been undertaken could establish to what extent, if at all, it could have drawn additional benefit from contemporary technology in this field.

Information on machine-making for other textiles is very sparse. Development would have been a crude function of the extent of mechanisation and the breadth of the market; which is to say that it presumably lagged behind that in cotton engineering. Even by the end of the period other kinds of textile engineering had not bred up concerns which approached the biggest Lancashire enterprises in point of scale. Nevertheless stray indications point to lively and progressive activity in both woollen and linen engineering in the Leeds, Bradford, Halifax, Keighley area.

Of other branches of engineering, one to develop with particular prominence over the last couple of decades of this period was agricultural engineering. Already early in the nineteenth century there had emerged concerns producing ploughs, harrows, seed-drills, rollers, etc. of standardised designs for extensive marketing along with stock replacement parts, edging out local craftsmen working on an *ad hoc* basis. In the 1830s some of these concerns added steam-powered threshing machines to their range. But it was from the early 'fifties that the market for these and for steam ploughs, and steam reaping and mowing machines expanded particularly vigorously, throwing up some concerns which rivalled the cotton engineers for size. Lincoln housed several of these but there was no marked tendency towards concentration and agricultural engineering was spread fairly widely throughout the eastern cornlands which constituted its major market.

The development of agricultural engineering bears the clear marks of technological alertness and organisational efficiency; and one would be disposed to rank its achievement along with that of cotton engineering if it were not for the fact that while British cotton engineers led the world, British agricultural engineers were only second, and a rather poor second, to the Americans. British agricultural machinery was largely American in inspiration. And when, mostly just beyond this period, capacious export markets started to open up, it was American suppliers who won the lion's share.

The bald comparison is, however, a good deal less than fair to British agricultural engineering. Cotton engineering had as a domestic market base the largest cotton industry in the world. And although odd instances can be found to the contrary, it is virtually an economic axiom that an industry's potential is given by the scale of its home market. With agricultural engineering all the advantages in this basic respect lay with America. Not only was there more farming in the United States – an immense amount more by the end of this period – but American circumstances conduced more to the adoption of agricultural machinery. Hired labour was expensive because of the ease with which men could obtain farms of their own; and the same factor, an abundance of land, encouraged extensive rather than intensive farming so that greater acreage per unit of crops created a sharper need for mechanised working methods. Given that America had by mid-century built up a substantial industrial capacity, it would have been remarkable had that capacity not been applied in this field and had America not taken the lead in this particular branch of engineering. If British concerns, both in respect of the machines made and of the techniques employed in their manufacture, were largely imitators of the Americans they were at least competent imitators; and if they paled beside their American counterparts their like was not to be found anywhere on the Continent, proximity to which enabled them to maintain a strong competitive footing in the shadow of American suppliers. (America in fact only started to export to the Continent in significant amounts from about 1870; before that British concerns enjoyed most of the market, which was, however, very small up to then, Continental agriculture in general lagging well behind British in the adoption of machinery.)

No specific reference has been made so far to what was probably the largest group amongst the engineering trades: the manufacture of railway equipment. This is an activity which poses certain problems of treatment. In the first place a variety of items come under the heading 'railway equipment' and there is bound to be a large degree of arbitrariness in any classification of them. Any attempt at a comprehensive coverage would be out of place here and the matter may be simplified by touching only on the major items: track, rolling stock and loco- motives – and of these track manufacture, by direct rolling, was the business of the iron industry, and has already been attended to in that context.

Rolling-stock production, like many other engineering trades, was a diffused function meandering away for many of its components into the crisscross complex of metal- and woodworking crafts at large. Even so, the concerns engaged in assemblage ranked among the larger contemporary industrial enterprises, with labour forces of up to and beyond a thousand; and it would seem they achieved something approx- imating to machine-belt production through the employment of mechanical handling and lifting devices. Relatively speaking, it appears to have gone much further than most other industries towards hori- zontal concentration, a sprinkling of firms in the Birmingham region and a few other places sharing the market, home and overseas, between them. This phenomenon is explicable by the obvious inclination of the railway companies to order in large homogeneous batches and by the freedom of the market from the sharper fluctuations to which those for other kinds of capital goods were liable and which tended to inhibit growth in concern capacity.

Locomotive construction also gave rise to large undertakings. The greatest of these, however, were not distinct concerns but the workshops of the principal railway companies – which would seem to have been the most considerable of all contemporary industrial enterprises in point of numbers employed, although much of the labour was engaged on repair and maintenance rather than on construction. The acreage required for these great engineering establishments necessitated their location away from existing industrial concentrations: Crewe (LNWR) was created out of the open countryside; the sleepy little market town of Swindon sunk its identity in the new community founded on its outskirts by the GWR; Derby was boosted into the ranks of industrial towns by the workshops of the Midland Railway settled on its fringes; the Great Northern had a similar impact on Doncaster, as, less strik- ingly, did the other great companies in those places where they located their engineering works.

Despite their insulation from competitive pressures these under- takings seem to have been keenly sensitive to considerations of technical efficiency. Indeed, it may be that their independence of the market and of profit and loss accounts gave them a licence to experiment with a latitude which contemporary commercial concerns would not have allowed themselves; while the scale of their operations, automatically proportioned to those of the massive companies of which they were part, afforded special scope for organisational efficiencies and effective dictatorship towards suppliers of components and materials, obviating the difficulties which smaller engineering concerns were apt to encounter in embarking on novel departures. Much of the pioneering works in the application of standardised production methods and machine tools to heavy engineering seems to have been undertaken in the railway company workshops; and their reputation as schools in engineering practice was second to none. But of course the very fact that the workshops were not engaged in production for the open market renders them unsusceptible to any sort of comparative economic evaluation and really confines them to a place in the history of technology.

There were a few independent concerns building locomotives. In the early railway years, before the great companies dominated the field, there was scope for supplying the numerous enterprises which were too small to warrant constructional works of their own; and the survival of some of these continued to provide a small market for the independent builders, who also won foreign orders. However the industrialised, or industrialising, countries fairly soon came to meet their own requirements – locomotives being awkward things to ship – and it was only with the intensified railway building in the underdeveloped parts of the world in the late nineteenth and early twentieth centuries that at all substantial export opportunities proffered themselves; and even then the independent concerns remained dwarfed by their company counterparts.

We have now gone about as far as one can go in an inspection of the engineering industries without becoming intolerably entangled in a jungle of tool and component makers of a thousand and one varieties, linked together by endlessly ramified interconnections, completely obliterating such shadowy distinction as can at any time be preserved between the engineering trades specifically and the metalworking trades at large – and even spilling over into the working of other, non-metallic, materials. Of other kinds of engineering activities, the manufacture of mining equipment should be acknowledged as evidently of some importance. But in the current state of historical knowledge it is impossible to say how far it was the business of specialist concerns or how far mining enterprises themselves attended to it in conjunction with suppliers of parts and materials. The same ignorance must be pleaded with regard to the manufacture of machines, or the more complex kinds of equipment, for other purposes. One clearcut exception to this general obfuscation may be indicated: the manufacture of sewing machines, first dabbled with in Britain in the 1850s but dominated from 1870 by the Singer concern set up in that year at Clydebank, near Glasgow, by the parent American company; this was perhaps the most sophisticated engineering concern in Britain at the end of this period, making extensive use of power and machine tools to turn out thousands of machines of uniform design a week.

Reference has now been made more than once to machine tools and something, in general terms, should be said of their significance and the extent of their use. A machine tool may be defined as a device, hand-operated or powered, capable on simple actuation of fashioning a material to a given shape and size. The types of such devices in use in this period fall mostly into the general categories of cutting, stamping and drilling tools; and the advantages to which their use could give rise may be broadly summarised as acceleration of the rate of output of operatives and standardisation of product.

Apart from the obvious consideration of the ease or difficulty of devising such tools for any particular purpose, their utilisation would of course be determined by the cost advantage they offered over hand-working methods; and it is very needful to stress that cost considerations might well tell against the adoption of machine tools. Any machine tool would almost certainly suffer from two disadvantages as against hand methods: the device itself would be more expensive than the hand tools which it could replace; and it would be more inflexible than hand tools, i.e. incapable of as wide a variety of tasks. Thus a concern producing different varieties of articles at different times might find it cheaper to use one set of omnipurpose hand tools rather than several sets of specialised machine tools, even though the machine tools, if continuously employed, would do their particular jobs more cheaply. And the potential economies arising from the use of machine tools might not consist in reducing the cost of a particular task but in the overall economies made available by uniform components, through permitting of continuous production runs, the elimination of delays in matching different components to obtain a fit, and, in the case of equipment in use, the ability to supply replacement parts directly from stock instead of having to wait for a new part to be made. In fact, within this particular period, it seems probable that the gains arising from standardisation were more commonly the potential attraction of machine tools, rather than the direct working economies. And for many purposes it was possible to achieve the requisite degree of precision using gauges to check highly skilled handwork.

Clearly, therefore, the introduction of machine tools was not just a function of inventiveness and adaptability but, in at least equal measure, of the nature of the particular task, of wage rates, and of the character of a particular manufacturer's market. Consequently comparison between different industries in terms of their use of machine tools is apt to be meaningless without a detailed consideration of their different circumstances. In particular caution is necessary in making any general comparison between British and American industry in this respect. It is true that, with increasing plainness from the 1840s onwards, American industry was more forward than British industry in taking to machine tools. But this discrepancy is subject to a number of explanations of which the backwardness of the British may well be the least. In some instances, lower wages and more skilled hand craftsmen could mean that a British concern would derive no advantage from machine tools where an American concern, whose circumstances were otherwise similar, would. More generally, the difference in market conditions can explain a good deal. In the later years of this period, the sheer size of the American market permitted of a degree of concentration on a limited range of products and a consequent capacity to use specialised machine tools to a degree which, as a simple matter of population mathematics, was not possible in Britain. However, it is probably true that in this respect size was of less consequence than the more stubborn insistence of British customers on having their particular needs or fancies precisely catered for; and, as treated of already, British concern size was certainly a good deal less than the optimum which could have been sustained – i.e. the markets of potential machine tool users were excessively variegated. And here one is moving into that ground where it becomes increasingly difficult to distinguish between straightforward entrepreneurial failings and incapacities occasioned by general economic structure which it was beyond the competence of any individual entrepreneur to remedy.

In very broad terms it would seem that the makers of engines, machines and steam ships were more forward in the adoption of machine tools than the general run of metal- and woodworking trades, whether it were a matter of devising tools themselves or of borrowing American ones. Many of them, however, made their own tools; and even at the very end of this period it is doubtful if anything which could in the full sense be described as a machine tool industry existed in Britain, few if any concerns having gone further than selling some of the tools which they made for themselves. In other words, even in the most advanced areas, the market for machine tools had not been extended to the point where it could support specialist suppliers, with the efficiencies which would accompany functional subdivision. In the USA on the other hand a fully-fledged machine tool industry was now well established and though, as stressed already, that does not necessarily point to a culpable backwardness in British engineering, it did mean that, as an international market for machine tools developed in subsequent decades, it was not a British industry which was poised to exploit it.

Of all major sectors of the British economy, unquestionably the most backward, in the sense of having experienced the least technical and organisational development, was that comprised of the general metalworking trades, with which can be associated the woodworking trades. To any generalisation covering such a wide variety of activities there are almost bound to be particular exceptions; and straightaway the more distinctive exceptions to this generalisation should be noted. The most comprehensive exception relates to the group of manufactures for which wire was the basic material. Wiremaking itself had been undertaken with powered machinery since as far back as the late sixteenth century but it is, fairly precisely, in the course of this particular period that pins, needles, wood-screws, wire net articles and wire ropes became the subject of powered production methods, often of American design, and factory organisation, although even by the end of the period very few of these factories seem to have run beyond a couple of hundred employees and some of them still found it more economical to employ water rather than steam power. The extensive nailmaking industry had a somewhat similar history. Powered machinery for certain kinds of nails first established itself in the 1840s, by which time the important American market was being lost to the native machinemade product, and gradually extended its range; but domestic nailmaking survived into the twentieth century. The manufacture of hand guns was transformed in much more abrupt fashion by the establishment in 1858 of a government factory at Enfield, modelled directly on its American counterpart at Springfield and equipped with American machinery, prompting a similar venture by the Birmingham Small Arms Trade, originally just an association of the 'masters' who exercised a 'clothier type' function amongst the varied skilled component makers who had hitherto constituted the hand gun industry. In 1861 the association transformed itself into the Birmingham Small Arms Company but its factory at Small Heath had to push along on the leftovers from government requirements and sporadic foreign orders; it was not until the 1890s when it took to making bicycles that BSA became a household word. Britain was not to throw up a commercial gunmaking concern like that founded by Samuel Colt – but then the gun had not quite the place in the British way of life which it had across the Atlantic. Powered lathes suitable for the working of a certain range of wood artifacts were another American importation, getting under way from the 1850s but hardly giving rise to concerns of any substantial scale until towards the end of the century.

There was of course a range of heavy iron articles produced by means of steam-powered rolling mills, slitting machines, hammers and stamps, but these really belong with the iron industry, as do cast iron articles, integrated as they often were with the business of ironmaking. And apart from the cases where the use of capital intensive equipment gave rise to factory organisation there were a few metalworking activities which were factory housed for other, special, reasons, such as steel-pen-making, dating from the 1830s, where the number of different but quickly executed processes needed to convert a strip of steel into a nib made it particularly desirable to congregate them under one roof; or the development from around mid-century of foreign markets for branded edge tools where the uniformity of product appearance and quality necessary to the preservation of the market placed a special premium on close supervision of operatives.

Moving away from these and a handful of other instances of factory organisation which could be cited, we start to wander into a world which still at the end of this period contains essentially medieval elements. Quite commonly, simple manually operated lathes and presses were adopted through these years but without engendering any modification of organisational structure. The domestic worker was still far from being a rarity – sometimes highly skilled with a long formal apprenticeship behind him – perhaps working by himself, perhaps the master of a small labour force. Some domestic workers enjoyed a real economic independence; and those employed in a small workshop might reasonably anticipate setting up on their own one day. Others were the effective employees of a mercantile intermediary who supplied the materials and disposed of the finished product or were no more than the outworkers of a factory enterprise. It was even possible for the independent artisan or the small master to make use of power for ancillary operations like grinding and polishing: power hire concerns existed on whose premises steam powered operations could be carried out for a fee, or in which a small workshop could be rented. Here in this polyglot field, then, even as we enter the last quarter of the nineteenth century we find the 'Industrial Revolution' as yet only very partially realised.

The coal industry

Associated with most of the developments dealt with so far in this chapter lay that one activity in respect of which Britain had been particularly generously endowed by nature: coalmining. We have seen that in the preceding period the business of raising coal had not been the subject of any noteworthy advance; that it had only been dragged into growing at a rate commensurate with that registered by the economy as a whole by the special requirements of the iron industry. In brief, Britain had an abundance of coal resources, but technology was unable to confer on them that special scope for intensified exploitation which other more dynamic industries had come to enjoy. In essentials that situation remained unchanged throughout this period also. If coalmining now joined the ranks of 'revolutionary' industries in point of growth rate achieved, it was primarily because of autonomous demand developments. It was pulled along in the wake of the iron industry, of gasworks and of the railways and other steam power users. The figures shown in Table II.19 show an overall annual growth rate of 4·25 per cent,

TABLE II.19. *United Kingdom coal output* (*mil. tons*)

1830	1850	1870	(1873)
22·5	49·5	110·5	(128·5)

maintained fairly evenly throughout the period – to be contrasted with the 2·25 per cent of the preceding forty-five years. And it was extended industrial use which was chiefly responsible for this performance. Domestic consumption, which had still accounted for about a third of total output in 1830, had fallen to about a sixth by 1873. However that still signifies a notable increase in *per capita* domestic use – not far short in fact of a twofold increase. In plain language homes were better heated and more food was cooked.

Rising real wages – from about mid-century – were in part responsible for this, but there is another agency which must be reckoned a significant secondary factor in stimulating coal use generally – although its overall consequence would certainly have been greater in the case of domestic than in the case of industrial users. This agency is, of course, the railways. It must be stressed that the impact of railways on coal prices was very variable – considerable in some market areas, none at all in others. It was a function both of the distance between source and point of final sale and of the freighting service which was displaced by a rail route. The first explains why, in general, industrial users did not stand to gain as much as domestic users: if they were heavy coal burners they would in all probability be already located close to coal. But, given that for users remote from source transport costs were the dominant element in coal prices, freight economies whose consequences might be imperceptible in the case of other commodities could have appreciably significant results in the case of coal. And the gains arising from rail linkage would be particularly marked if it was a shipping service which was displaced, since the greater speed and reliability of rail would permit stock levels to be cut. This was of special advantage in the case of coal where irregular demand necessitated higher stock levels, and thus capital charges, than served for most other commodities.

It hardly needs saying that it was the London market which met these conditions in pre-eminent degree. Coal first reached London by rail in 1845 though it was not until the early 'fifties that rail movements started to become of any consequence and not until 1867 that the quantity exceeded shipborne coal. But by 1873 about two-thirds of London's coal came in by rail. Available price data suggests that in real terms London prices for north-eastern coal fell by about a fifth as a result of rail transport – and for lower grade coals the fall was probably greater since Midlands coal, generally less suitable for domestic burning, could now reach London in partial competition with supplies from the northeast. London was, however, quite exceptional. No other major market centre could have benefited from rail freightage as the capital did. And in relative terms London was not as important a market as it had earlier been. In 1830 9 per cent of gross national output was consigned to London. In 1873 that proportion stood at 6 per cent.

Although, as just indicated in the reference to Midlands coal reaching London, the railways did in some cases extend the market range of collieries and make for a new competitiveness between districts, they did not result overall in any profound rearrangement of the market patterns already shaped by natural and canal transport facilities. Working of the north-eastern field was from the 1830s extended into the interior of south Durham which, before the railways, had been denied access to outside markets. But the depth at which much of this coal lay – over 1,000 feet – had been the basic reason for its neglect in the past and it was the increasing cost of mining elsewhere in the field which prompted interest in it, even before the coming of the railways; it would almost certainly have been opened up anyway and, in the absence of railways, linked to the sea by canal. And there were other particular localities, now provided with rail contacts, which had not earlier been endowed with canals because the volume of local traffic had not then warranted it. But in general, the balance as between the various coalfields remained largely unaltered throughout this period. Only in Scotland, mainly in the first couple of decades of the period, was development egregiously rapid; and there of course it was prompted by the dramatic growth of the iron industry.

There were, however, certain shufflings about for which the railways along with other factors were responsible. The north-eastern field leant relatively less on outside home markets and relatively more on industrial demand from the region itself; and by the end of the period to a very appreciable extent on export markets. In the west Midlands there was something of a reverse shift; the running down of the Black Country's iron industry in the later decades of the period being largely compensated for by enlarged sales to outside markets. South Wales also found compensation for slackened growth on the part of its iron industry in outside sales, particularly overseas. In the east Midlands wider rail-penetrated markets made for rather more vigorous growth than that sustained by any other coalfields bar Scotland. The order of this is indicated by the official statistics collected from 1854, for rather awkwardly defined regions: for a region comprising Yorkshire, Nottinghamshire, Derbyshire, Leicestershire and Warwickshire (the last two smaller producers not being part of the east Midlands field) the proportion of total national output rose from 17 per cent in 1854 to 21 per cent in 1873. The north-east still surpassed any other coalfield at the end of the period with 23 per cent of the total – a fractional slippage from its 24 per cent of 1854.

The development of overseas markets has just been mentioned as of importance to the north-east and to south Wales. As a proportion of gross national output, exports in 1830 had stood at 2 per cent, having just started through the previous five years to climb beyond the negligible level at which they had run at any earlier time – i.e. excluding sales to Ireland. Growth was steadily maintained throughout this period. By 1850 6·5 per cent of output was going abroad and by 1873 nearly 10 per cent, exports in gross having risen from half a million tons at the beginning of the period to twelve million by the end. Nearly all of this came from the coastally situated fields of the north-east and south Wales, for whom export markets had become of considerable consequence, accounting in fact at the close of the period for about a quarter of these regions' output, the north-east being principally occupied in supplying countries bordering the North Sea and the Baltic, and south Wales in supplying France and the Mediterranean countries. Thus was Britain drawing the benefit of industrialisation and population pressure on fuel supplies on the Continent, in a field which she was uniquely well placed to exploit. Although, naturally, Continental industries tended to congregate on their own coalfields, these do not exist in profusion and none of them is coastally situated. Particularly while Continental railway services were still in only a skeletal state in many areas, coal users, industrial, domestic or transport, who for one reason or another could not cling close to coalfields often found the north-east of England or south Wales to be their cheapest source of supply.

Coal, then, had a peculiar place amongst British exports, of which it accounted for about 5 per cent by the end of this period. With all other commodities of any weight, exports were a function of relative economic forwardness. With coal, exports were a function of geology and geography. It was the only item of primary produce which Britain exported in significant quantities.

The textile industries

On that note we may move on to the industry which at the end of the period as at the beginning was Britain's most considerable exporter – and that without any natural advantage whatsoever: the cotton industry.

The figures in Tables II.20 and 21 indicate a continuation through the first decade and a half of this period of the trend of the 'twenties: maintenance of a 'revolutionary' growth rate, sustained about equally by home and foreign demand. Viewed under technological and organisational aspects as well, what in the previous chapter was designated as

TABLE II.20. *Average annual growth rate of output of cotton goods* *(percentages)*

1830–35	1835–40	1840–45	1845–50	1850–55	1855–60	1860–65	1865–70	1870–73
5·75	5·75	6·75	1·25	6·00	4·25	− 6·75	8·25	4·75
							1·50	

TABLE II.21. *Average annual growth rate of export of cotton cloth* *(percentages)*

1830–35	1835–40	1840–45	1845–50	1850–55	1855–60	1860–65	1865–70	1870–73
6·75	5·25	7·00	5·75	6·00	7·00	− 4·25	8·50	3·75
							2·25	

the second phase of the cotton industry's revolution, getting under way in 1821, may be run through fairly precisely to 1846. Its characteristics warrant only a summary repetition here: power weaving, steam power, medium- to large-scale concerns, housed in specially designed premises and often integrating spinning and weaving. From 240,000 in 1830 the numbers of hand loom weavers fell to 57,000 in 1846, virtually all employed on very fine work, mostly in Scotland, although there was also something of a concentration of them in Bolton; they probably then accounted for some 2 or 3 per cent of output, the remainder being the work of power looms. Of power used in the industry, by 1846 about seven-eighths was steam-generated. The labour force of the average Lancashire manufacturing concern then numbered close to 500 and the odd giant touched 2,000, although in Scotland, responsible for about a tenth of output, concerns on average were only about half the Lancashire size. Scotland had always devoted itself largely to muslins and other high quality fabrics, in which fields relatively limited market scope, higher capital requirements and greater problems in adapting powered machinery to the work tended to check concern growth.

The onset of generally adverse economic circumstances beginning with the failure of the European potato crop in 1846, followed by a run of bad grain harvests, and embracing the commercial crisis of 1847 and the subsequent depression which lasted into 1848, marks in a clearcut way the close of an era in the history of the cotton industry. The abrupt intrusion of these topical factors of course exaggerates the suddenness of the change, but it is evident that they more or less coincided with the secular arrival of the industry at the end of a road which it had been following since 1821. Just as the very low 1·25 per cent growth for the quinquennium 1845–50 is in considerable measure a reflection of circumstances peculiar to those years, so the apparent return to a fully 'revolutionary' growth rate in the following quinquennium is in large part due to the especially depressed base of measurement; and the recalculation of these rates as an average of 3·5 per cent over the whole decade, 1845–55, affords a better indication of the secular situation.

In gross achievement terms the new situation can be crudely categorised as one in which growth proceeded at a merely 'normal' rate by contrast with the 'revolutionary' rate of earlier years. (The effects of the American Civil War obscure the long-run record of the industry through the latter part of this period. Nevertheless, although its expression as an annual average is a highly artificial procedure, a comparison between the levels of output and exports of 1873, by when a return to normality had taken place, and that of 1860, on the eve of the Civil War, may stand as a measure of performance, capable of being directly compared with earlier growth rates.) An overall comparison of the phase 1845–73 with that of 1821–45 yields average annual growth rates of 2·75 and 6·75 per cent respectively.

A glance at the figures in Tables II. 20 and 21 suffices to indicate the weight of foreign demand in sustaining such continuing growth as there was after 1845. Indeed a closer calculation on the assumption that around a half of output was being exported in the mid-'forties would lead to the conclusion that home demand actually fell over the 1845–73 phase. (Output rose in the ratio 100–210, exports in the ratio 50–166; conclusion: home purchases fell in the ratio 50–44.) Considering that over the same period the population of Britain increased by 38 per cent this is rather surprising. In some part it is to be explained away by the nature of the data used in calculating output – figures for raw cotton consumption: some reduction in wastage of the raw material was achieved during the period in question; that, however, could hardly be estimated as higher than the eighth which would yield approximately constant home purchases (and raise the overall growth rate to 3 per cent) – but would still leave a fall of close on a third in *per capita* consumption of cotton goods. And as far as quantity is concerned we must credit this as being an accurate enough indication of the truth of the matter. It does not take any account of possible changes in the quality of cloth bought in the home market and there is every reason to suppose that with rising real wages over the period in question there was a general shift away from the cheaper towards the more expensive ranges of materials. Other data does in fact suggest an increase of the order of 50 per cent in actual domestic money expenditure on cotton goods – and much the same in real terms since cotton manufacturing costs seem to have been lowered to an extent which about offset the general rise in prices which set in from 1851–52. Even this however is equivalent only to a 1·5 per cent annual rate of growth of the home market – and represents an absolutely minimal increase in *per capita* consumption.

Plainly by the mid-'forties near saturation point had been reached in the home market. The British populace was already buying about as much cotton cloth as it wanted. Income increments were henceforth devoted largely to other things. Further cost reductions ran up against a rigidifying demand. And much the same phenomenon can be observed in established overseas markets on the continent of Europe and in the USA, the pattern complicated by the build up of native cotton producing capacity, particularly in the cheaper kinds of cloth, and, of reverse effect in the case of the USA, massive population growth.

That which can be isolated then as the specific agency of a continued sturdy though decelerated growth on the part of the British cotton industry is a greatly extended market scope in areas which hitherto had been of only slight relative importance; Asia and Australasia. It was from the middle 'fifties that these regions started to open up to British cotton goods with particular rapidity. In the case of Australasia, of course, this is to be explained largely in simple terms of a much intensified rate of settlement and an almost total lack of local manufacturing industries of any kind. In the case of Asia, with its very considerable population and its own anciently established textile trades, it was a matter of the increasing competitiveness of Lancashire goods, carrying them across a market threshold, partly by means of lowered production costs, partly on account of the more abrupt reductions in freight costs to these distant markets as iron-built ships took to the oceans and, probably more important, as railways, albeit thinly scattered, pushed into the interior of the Indian subcontinent, which from a commercial British point of view constituted the principal part of Asia.

But, as the percentage figures indicate, this momentum was not sustained. Migration to Australasia did not build up after the American fashion. Asia was too poor to possess any very elastic capacity for absorbing European manufactures. And all the while the richer countries of the Western world were closing such gaps as still remained between the competence of their own cotton industries and that of Great Britain, in most cases with British-made machinery. By the end of this period cotton had become an industrial laggard. It had of course constructed for itself a position of immense strength and prestige, and in absolute terms it was to be many decades before that position even started to be sapped. But the task of sustaining a dynamic economy to which it had once contributed so much was henceforth to be borne by others and cotton was to share in only meagre fashion in the benefits of economic growth, national and international.

From technological and organisational aspects 'revolution' really came to an end in the mid-'forties. This is by no means to say that the achievement of cost efficiencies ceased. As indicated already, it was market circumstances not its own sluggishness which curbed the industry's progress. And as further indicated when dealing with cotton engineering, it had by the later years of this period attained that kind of developmental level at which a high degree of efficiency could be maintained without benefit of heroic initiatives. It would seem in fact as if the industry right though the second half of the nineteenth century was fairly steadily effecting real cost reductions of the order of 0·5 per cent p.a. – hardly comparable with the achievements of the revolutionary years but quite respectable nonetheless. But they were achieved without further modification of any radical kind in the structure of the industry.

There was one fairly basic technical advance whose adoption runs all the way through and a little bit beyond this period: the self-acting mule, in which the movable carriage as well as the spindles were power-operated. Patented by Richard Roberts in 1830 it was soon adopted for the very coarsest yarns but was only slowly improved for spinning finer yarns and was not in universal use until the 1880s. Increased use of the self-acting mule apart, however, the industry of 1873 was in nearly all essentials the same as that of 1845. Concern size had already by the mid-'forties reached its optimum point and showed no further general tendency to increase although with a stable balanced relationship secured between the weaving and spinning branches of the industry, many integrated concerns shed one or other activity and concentrated their entire resources in a single department.

This situation in which decisive economies of scale were achieved up to a certain point but in which, beyond that fairly modest point, little or no further advantage arose, was an important factor in keeping the industry in an economically healthy condition and in preserving it from the strictures often directed at many other sectors of the contemporary economy. On the one hand it left no scope for the kind of small, ill-ordered concerns which proliferated in many of the metalworking and engineering trades. On the other it prevented the sort of stultification which could result from the quasimonopolies of established concerns when the high initial cost of entering a field acted to exclude fresh recruits. There were of course at any time plenty of old-established family concerns in cotton but the price of their survival was a constant alertness to the doings of newcomers to the industry. Money, certainly, was an essential passport for admission. Basic plant and premises would run out at a sum of the general order of £50,000. But building contractors and machinery suppliers, eager for business, might grant generous credits and the quantity of actual cash required would commonly not exceed the capacity of a small partnership of comfortably off individuals close enough to the industry, as most Lancashire people were, to have a fairly shrewd idea of what they were doing.

There were other factors which simplified entry to the industry. For one, as just implied: its intense localisation, making for easy contact between entrepreneurs, financiers and personnel of all grades, operative, supervisory, managerial, and, thus, the ready coordination of the human elements of a new concern. For another: the relatively uncomplicated nature of the industry itself, turning out a fairly uniform product for a reasonably stable market, using standardised production methods, and thus less plagued by hazards and uncertainties than most other industrial activities. Such was its situation, in fact, that from the early 'seventies new concerns in the spinning town of Oldham could be floated on the hard won small savings of cotton operatives, shopkeepers and the like; although it should be said that the townspeople of Oldham must have had something of a peculiarity of character as no other spinning town ever threw up a counterpart to the 'Oldhams Limited'. (As the designation implies, these were companies formed under the Limited Liability Act of 1855 which exempted shareholders in any company constituted in accordance with the provisions of the Act from liability for the debts of the company beyond the extent of their share subscriptions, paid or uncalled. However, whether in this or in any other case limited liability played any part in stimulating investment interest seems very doubtful. There is no distinctive difference between the general patterns of public investment before and after the Act such as would confirm the opinion of the proponents of the measure – and of many later commentators – that needed capital had previously been inhibited by unlimited liability. All the evidence in fact from the whole of the nineteenth century points in precisely the reverse direction – to the unwillingness of entrepreneurs to employ the capital for which the moneyed public was so eager to find outlets, with or without limited liability.)

Something finally should be said of the impact of the American Civil War (1861–65) on the industry. It was, of course, pronounced. Regularly since the mid-'thirties just about four-fifths of the industry's raw cotton requirements had been met by the USA. By the close of 1861 only the utterly diminutive quantities which the Confederacy could slip through the Union naval blockade were reaching Britain. And when Lee surrendered the army of Virginia at Appomatox on 9 April 1865 the Cotton Belt offered nothing worth speaking of except its testimony to the savage thoroughness of Sherman's march to the sea. Nor did the 'Reconstruction' years promote the rapid recovery of cotton cultivation in the exhausted South. It was not until 1871 that American supplies regained their prewar level. Well before then, however, the British industry had ceased to be gravely discomfited by the lack of American cotton. By the end of 1865 it was probably getting as much cotton as it could use, given that it was a higher cost material with which it was then being supplied and that the consequently higher price of the finished article had a dulling effect on demand. This was mostly Egyptian and Indian cotton whose greatly extended cultivation had been prompted by the disappearance of the cheaper American article from the market.

That response had not been an overnight one. Throughout 1862, 1863 and 1864 an intense cotton famine had prevailed the world over; and what little there was to be had commanded prices of up to five times the prewar norms. Not only then was a tremendous cut-back in output enforced by the sheer lack of raw material but, since such escalated costs could not be passed on to the customer without killing the market stone dead, such production as was maintained for the sake of keeping plant and labour employed and commercial contacts alive was commonly profitless. It is an impressive measure of the innate strength of the Lancashire industry that after three harrowing years it could bounce back with such resilience immediately raw material supplies enabled it to resume profitable production at something approaching a normal level. And the Lancashire record may be vividly contrasted with that of the Scottish industry, crippled beyond recovery by the cotton famine. The great bulk of Scottish mills ceased production entirely during the war, and of those that subsequently reopened many had been so loss-racked that they were driven to final liquidation within a few years, thus providing Lancashire with extra market room which was eagerly snapped up by new concerns through the 'seventies and the early 'eighties.

The Civil War situation may well have engendered another particular effect, perhaps touching the whole of the industry though probably affecting Scotland especially closely. Many customers driven to alternative, usually more expensive, materials, during the cotton famine may not have fully reverted to cottons when these became available again. Scottish muslins very likely lost unretrieved ground to French silks, whose much greater freedom of entry to the British market under the Anglo-French trade treaty of 1860 coincided so closely with the enforced drop in muslin sales.

The woollen industry quite certainly drew immense, if only temporary, benefit from the difficulties of cotton as the figures in Tables II.22–24 make clear.

TABLE II.22. *Powered machinery employed in the woollen industry* (000s)

TABLE II.23. *Persons employed in the woollen industry* (000s)

Year	Spindles	Looms	
1856	3,112	53	167
1861	3,472	65	173
1867	6,976	119	262
1871	4,958	115	239

Plainly there run through these figures secular trends both as to gross output and as to mechanisation; and we must endeavour to obtain some notion of what the long run record of the woollen industry was through the whole of this period. The data available for that purpose is not very satisfactory but the estimates of domestic raw wool consumption shown in Table II.24 would give an accurate enough account of the general order of output growth.

TABLE II.24. *Domestic raw wool consumption: annual averages (million lb)*

1830–34	1835–39	1840–44	1845–49	1850–54	1855–59	1860–64	1865–69	1870–74
171	178	188	210	241	263	312	374	436

Average annual increases (%)

	0·75	1·00	2·25	2·75	1·50	3·50	3·75	3·00

Source: E. M. Sigsworth and J. M. Blackman, 'The woollen and worsted industries', in *The Development of British Industry and Foreign Competition, 1873–1914*, ed. D. H. Aldcroft.

Over the early years of the period these show much the same sort of record as that sustained through the 'twenties: a growth rate roughly commensurate with the rate of population increase. A measurable quickening of the pace can be dated from just before mid-century, but even gathering momentum as it did it never started to assume anything like 'revolutionary' proportions, although it is worth pointing out that over the later years of the period the woollen industry was growing more rapidly than the cotton industry.

The industry's market situation was such that although by the opening of the period it leant heavily on home demand, exports only accounting for around a fifth of its output, there was little that it could do to promote domestic consumption of woollen cloth. Where substitution was possible wool could make no substantial headway against cotton: pound for pound raw wool was two to three times the price of raw cotton. And when some sort of an appreciable margin started to open up between mass purchasing power and basic needs, it was not for the most part devoted to more varied or elegant clothing. The exceptional years of the American Civil War apart then, such growth prospects as the industry had lay mostly in the relatively small export field. It suffered, that is to say, from a low growth potential gearing.

A spurt in important trans-Atlantic sales engendered by the American boom of the early 'thirties was a useful but shortlived stimulant; and though exports of yarn had started to build up from zero in the late 'twenties and grew with prodigious momentum up to mid-century – and with persistent vigour into the 1860s – their value was at any time small in a total output context; and their basic effect was to equip foreign cloth manufacturers with the means of resisting competition from British weavers. It was not until just around mid-century and most intensively from the early 'sixties that British woollen cloth started to make substantial advances in foreign markets, such that by the end of the period some two-fifths of its output was going abroad, representing roughly a fivefold increase compared with the approximate doubling of home sales, an achievement to be attributed in indeterminate measures to its technical superiority over other producers on the one hand and autonomous expansion of sales scope in its principal North American and Continental markets on the other.

There is, however, a close correlation between the export record of the industry and its adoption of powered machinery. Behind the upsurge in yarn exports lies the finalisation of powered spinning, completed for worsted yarn by *c.* 1840 and for woollens by *c.* 1850, while a serious bottleneck in worsted spinning was after numerous attempts wholly relieved with the rapid introduction of several different efficient combing machines from the late 'forties. The inability of the weaving side of the industry to make full use of this enhanced spinning capacity explains the development of an export trade in yarn, levelling off as the extension of powered weaving enabled the industry profitably to employ the yarn itself in the exploitation of foreign markets for cloth. By about mid-century virtually all worsteds were power-woven and the same was in general true of woollens by about the end of this period. Thus if the onset of 'revolution' in the woollen industry be dated from the first employment of the flying-shuttle on a significant commercial scale, it had taken just about a century to resolve itself.

And even then, while the worsted industry, closely resembled cotton in its organisational structure, the woollens industry, producing a greater range of fabrics, for the most part of a finer quality, still contained numerous small concerns specialising in certain types of material of limited market scope, an appreciable number of them, in the West Country and in other scattered places, continuing to employ water power – not to mention the survival of independent handworking spinners and weavers, mostly in Scotland. The output of these last was statistically insignificant and in all probability no longer represented production for remote local markets as it still had done a couple of decades earlier, but a catering for sophisticated metropolitan markets, on the very strength of its being 'handwoven'. More generally, the existence of a clientele which was quality and design conscious rather than cost conscious afforded scope for the West Country to retain a substantial market footing by the side of the more favourably located

West Riding industry as coal became a main base of production methods. The West Riding's cost advantage in this respect was in any event limited, partly because fuel costs were a relatively small proportion of total costs in the case of expensive fabrics and partly because by the time powered weaving was extended to high grade woollens a comprehensive railway network had narrowed the differential in coal prices. The result was that although by mid-century the West Riding had all but totally expropriated the manufacture of worsteds it housed only about a half of the woollens industry – a proportion which it was not subsequently to increase.

It should be finally be added that any potential check to the industry's growth capacity by way of raw material problems was fully obviated by the great extension of sheep-farming in Australasia and, over the closing years of the period, in South Africa. By mid-century a third of the industry's wool requirements were met from abroad and by the end of the period nearly twice as much wool was imported as was raised at home, though by then enhanced farming efficiency had enabled the annual domestic wool clip to be increased by about a third, meeting about three-fifths of the industry's enlarged requirements so that a substantial proportion of the imported wool could be spared to sustain what had become an important re-export trade.

To the extent that the British (i.e. excluding the Irish) linen industry could ever be said to have experienced a 'revolutionary' phase it should probably be dated as *c.* 1815–*c.* 1860, through which powered spinning extended itself to cover virtually the whole range of yarns; and within which powered weaving, slowly from *c.* 1830, quite rapidly from *c.* 1850, enlarged its territory to cover all but the finest fabrics (always, in any event, an Irish speciality). The purely British industry never assumed a fully rounded character. The West Riding and west Lancashire, the chief English spinning centres, at any time through these years wove up only a fairly small fraction of their yarn, a large part of it always going across to Ireland. From the 1850s the Irish, rather tardily, were themselves taking to mechanised spinning and the English industry was entering on a slow decline, which by the early twentieth century had brought it near to extinction. In and around Dundee, a more authentically integrated industry did establish itself; and the town itself was, by the 1860s, as thoroughgoing an instance of a one industry town as any in the kingdom, some 85 per cent of its working population of about 45,000 being employed in linen manufacture, and over a half of these in the town's ten largest concerns. Even Dundee, however, was from *c.* 1870 surrendering the linen business to Ireland and was taking increasingly to jute – for sacking materials, carpet backings and the like. All in all, the British linen industry's output had probably hit a plateau by *c.* 1860 and was only temporarily prevented from moving into decline by the cotton famine – from which, however, it was the Irish industry that drew the most substantial benefit. At the height of its international technical precocity, in the mid-'fifties, the British industry may have exported as much as a half its total output, much of it to the USA. But at any time it looked a rather poor cousin by the side of King Cotton.

The silk industry was another to start on a downward path within this period, when the Anglo-French trade treaty of 1860 abruptly exposed it to the full blast of French competition. Up to then it had enjoyed more or less continuously growing prosperity as wealth accumulated in the pockets of the middle and upper classes who formed its clientele. Although the quality of its finished fabrics never won the esteem which French goods commanded, its throwing machinery, resting on a strong general textile engineering base, was, at least in the early years of this period, reputed the best in Europe; and the British industry was as forward as any in applying steam power to weaving – gradually doing so from the 1830s, although at any time extension was slow and into the twentieth century a good deal of silk cloth was woven on hand-looms. In addition to its use for pure silk fabrics increasing quantities of silk yarn were being used with worsted in Bradford and other West Riding towns – a practice given encouragement in 1857 when Charles Lister devised a method of spinning yarn from very low grade – and thus very cheap – silk waste. And this constituted a particular sector[1] of the British silk industry which, at least for a while, could remain largely indifferent to the incursion of French fabrics. (Subsequently the French – and others – moved strongly into this field.)

Before leaving the textiles industries it should be observed that within this period garment-making started to move towards mechanisation and factory organisation. The inspiration was almost entirely American,

---

[1] It was a very particular sector. The yarn was *spun*, not *thrown*, i.e. made in essentially the same way as yarn from cotton and wool fibres.

triggered off by Singer's sewing machine, invented in 1850 and, though neither the first nor the only practicable machine, greatly superior in most respects to any of its rivals; if others were its equal in design Singer's advanced production methods gave him the advantage in price. Cutting machines soon followed. But even by the end of this period only a minute amount of power was employed in garment manufacture, such factory housed machines as there were being almost entirely hand- or foot-operated, while a number of tasks were still invariably done with needle and scissors, both on and off the premises. These factories in gross employed on the premises no more than 10,000 persons, some 1,500 of them in Leeds where the first readymade clothing factory in Britain had been founded in 1856.

The sewing machine, however, was being more widely adopted than these figures might suggest. While readymade clothing was slow in winning market favour there remained the traditional bespoke trade, ranging from the independent tailor or dressmaker catering for a low income clientele in the immediate locality to large Savile Row concerns with perhaps several dozen employed in a central workshop and even more maybe as outworkers. The sewing machine could find a place here too, even amongst those independent tailors and dressmakers or quasi-independent outworkers who could not raise the purchase price of what was a fairly expensive device but were enabled to acquire one via the Singer hire purchase scheme. Progressive marketing techniques were not the least element in the Singer success story. The same facility could also contribute to household use of the sewing machine but the very scanty evidence available suggests that the sewing machine was not adopted for homemade clothing until a little later in the century when cheaper, though less efficient, machines were developed.

The knitted goods industry, still essentially a hosiery industry, was very slowly applying power to its frames throughout this period, and drawing in from the surrounding countryside into Leicester and Nottingham. But power's margin of advantage was slight, so slight that the hosiery masters generally found it more advantageous to cling to domestic production than to move their businesses into factories where they would be subject to the restricted working hours and other conditions imposed by the Factory Act of 1850 and other legislation. An Act of 1874, extending statutory control to domestic workers, seems to have been instrumental in greatly accelerating the conversion to power knitting – although hand frame working survived into the twentieth century.

Boot and shoe making had a history closely similar to that of garment manufacture: partial mechanisation from the 1850s on an American model, but with very little use of power. With boot and shoe design less prone to fluctuations in fashion, standardisation was more easily attained, and, although within this period little difference was yet discernible in Britain between the organisation of the clothing and the shoe industries, the USA had already gone a long way towards turning the latter into a full factory industry and towards mass production of cheap readymade footwear. Over succeeding decades imported American machinery steadily 'revolutionised' the British industry.

The precocity of the USA in the mechanisation of garment and, more particularly, footwear manufacture will have been remarked. The same phenomenon has earlier been noted in connection with some engineering and associated industries. And it is worth pointing out that special explanations in terms of market conditions which were there urged cannot be readily invoked in these cases. There remains of course the simple difference in gross market size but that is of no relevance here since optimum concern size was plainly attainable well within the limits of the British market. There also remain, maybe more tellingly, the differences in wage levels. But if the decisiveness of that consideration be doubted, then any disposition to argue that the assumption by the USA, from around mid-century, of the leadership in creative technology is not to be wholly explained in strictly economic terms would, perhaps, find its most solid grounding in the record of the garment and footwear industries. Of course, as implied already, readymade clothing had a mass of market prejudice to overcome in Britain; but in a comparative evaluation this might be found to reduce itself to the more effective promotional and selling methods of the American producers.

Chemicals

It is a fairly natural, if not immediately obvious, transition from the textile industries to the chemical industries. These, like the engineering industries, are a polyglot group lumped together under an omnibus description more from convention and convenience than any rigour of definition. In the literal sense the designation would cover all manufacturing processes in which a transmutation of substances is effected by chemical action and would thus extend to the smelting of metals, the making of glass, pottery, paper, soap, paint and a variety of other activities which are not customarily included under the label chemical industries. And, again like the engineering industries, there is an inevitable degree of arbitrariness as to when to allow them a place of their own in a narrative of this kind. Even apart from those conventionally excluded from the scope of the designation, a number of activities involving chemical processes can be run back to very early times. Finally, any treatment here of this variegated collection must confine itself to a selection of those chemical industries which for one particular reason or another warrant a special reference. These can be reduced to four commodities: soda, bleach, synthetic dyestuffs and synthetic fertilisers. Of these, three were intimately associated with the textile industries with whose growth their own was closely connected both as effect and as cause.

The manufacture of soda (sodium carbonate) was at any time the most considerable of the quartet. It is the basic ingredient of soap and scouring agents of any kind; and, while the increasing use of domestic soaps was certainly an important demand element in the growth of the industry, it was its employment in the preparation of textile materials which lent soda a special importance. In a variant form it was also essential in the making of glass and in certain other minor activities. For centuries, millennia even, it had been extracted from various kinds of vegetable matter to serve these purposes. The innovation with which we must deal consisted, then, not in its use but in the manner of its production; an innovation which stands as the first major contribution of theoretical chemistry to industrial practice. It derived from the identification by the French chemist, Duhamel, in 1736 of soda and hydrochloric acid as basic constituents of common salt, and the determination by another French chemist, Le Blanc, in 1789, of a practicable method of separating the soda from the salt by the addition of sulphuric acid. However as things then stood, the price of both sulphuric acid and salt precluded any significant commercial exploitation of this basic work in Britain. Current techniques involved the use of large quantities of expensive nitre for the production of sulphuric acid. But, in building on the basic research of their fellow-countryman, Lavoisier, two further Frenchmen, Clément and Désormes, in 1806 demonstrated that nitre functioned only as a catalyst in integrating oxygen with sulphur to produce the acid and that as long as an abundance of air was admitted during the process only very little nitre need be used. Between this discovery and the development of more efficient equipment for production on a large scale, the price of sulphuric acid which had stood around £30 a ton at the time of Le Blanc's breakthrough had fallen to about £3 a ton by 1825, when the price of salt was drastically lowered by the abolition of the heavy excise duty which this readily taxable commodity had hitherto borne. Soda, which had cost £36 a ton in 1820, sold for £18 a ton in 1830, and with further improvements in plant design was down to £5 a ton by mid-century.

As the figures make plain, the combination of French science and British engineering had effected revolutions in the production of both sulphuric acid (which served other purposes as well) and soda which can stand full comparison with those achieved in metallurgy and textiles. And although it was in France, naturally enough, that the commercial production of Le Blanc soda first established itself, the British industry, resting on a base of superior development in coal, metallurgy, engineering skills and transport facilities, once launched, fairly quickly overhauled its French counterpart, and by mid-century even numbered northern France among the export markets which took more than a quarter of its output, the USA, with no soda industry of its own, being a particularly big buyer to meet the needs of its growing industries.

Well before soda manufacture in Britian had been able to take effective advantage of cheap sulphuric acid, the closely associated manufacture of chlorine bleach had done so. Chlorine had been a completely unknown substance until 1774 when it was detected in gaseous form by the Swede, Scheele. In 1785 the French chemist Berthollet recognised its potentiality as a bleaching agent but it was not until 1799 when Charles Tennant and Charles Macintosh developed a process for converting the gas into a powder that production on any substantial scale was commenced – in Tennant's own St Rollox works, near Glasgow. The chlorine itself could be extracted from more than one base material but when sulphuric acid prices had started their downward slither this established itself as the material of choice and bleach prices took an even more dramatic course than those of soda: 1800: £140 a ton; 1820: £60 a ton; 1850: £14 a ton.

Catering as they did for the same textile markets and making common use of sulphuric acid, the manufacture of both bleach and soda came often, though not invariably, to be undertaken jointly, along in a number of cases with the production of sulphuric acid for outside sale as well as for internal use. The result was that the leading concerns in the field ranked amongst the larger of contemporary enterprises. St Rollox, the greatest of them all, covered by the 1840s a hundred acres of ground, and though the industry was not a labour intensive one, employed over

1,000 persons. But despite the presence there of St Rollox, Glasgow was not the principal centre of the industry. As might be expected, Lancashire encompassed a major concentration, situated to the west of the cotton country and in the heart of the Lancashire coalfield, clustered around St Helens, Warrington and Widnes. Rather more surprisingly, Tyneside rivalled and even surpassed the Lancashire concentration, its coal and its convenient situation for delivery to continental markets contriving to outweigh its distance from home textile centres and from the Cheshire rock salt deposits. (The local sea-salt industry had been steadily succumbing to the much more cheaply transported Cheshire salt ever since the early canals had started to fine down the freight cost burden under which the Cheshire producers had earlier laboured.)

Over the very last years of this period, the fusion of soda manufacture and bleach manufacture was given additional impetus by two roughly contemporary circumstances. Although their consequences were only to work themselves out fully in the couple of decades following this period, they may conveniently be referred to here. The first was the introduction from the late 'sixties of effective methods of employing the hydrochloric acid which could be very cheaply derived from the residue left by soda manufacture to replace sulphuric acid in the production of bleach. This made soda manufacturers into almost automatic joint suppliers, able to distribute their cost burden amongst the two products at discretion – or, put another way, to subvent the cost of producing one substance from the proceeds of the sale of the other.

The second circumstance was the development by the Belgian, Solvay, of an effective method of extracting soda from salt by the use of ammonia and carbon dioxide in such a way that the ammonia was retrievable and thus capable of being used repeatedly, affording considerable cost economies, although bleach was not obtainable. Solvay rapidly built up the large-scale production of soda by this method – he became one of the Herculean figures of European industry – and by the end of this period British producers were starting to feel the edge of Solvay competition in both home and foreign markets. In the following years, as other Continental manufacturers took increasingly to the Solvay method, British producers fought back, not by scrapping existing Le Blanc plant and converting to Solvay but by adding the by-product bleach to their output and cutting their soda prices.[1] For some

[1] One or two British concerns did become Solvay producers, notably Brunner-Mond, founded as such in 1874. This rapidly became the largest individual concern in British chemicals, and eventually constituted the core element of ICI.

while this proved a very effective response and in an expanding world market British soda sales continued to grow in the face of Solvay competition. But by the later 1880s the quantities of bleach being spewed out by British soda manufacturers had run way ahead of demand, and fierce internecine competition had set in as concerns endeavoured to sustain their sales of bleach in order to support competitive soda prices. Of course, the more bleach prices were cut, the less capable was bleach manufacture of subventing soda manufacture. The answer was to limit bleach output and by restricting supply to maintain such bleach prices as would enable soda prices to be kept competitive, provided of course that the price of the bleach did not have to be raised to such a level that bleach produced by other methods could undercut it – the margin of advantage over other methods was, however, such that there was ample room for manoeuvre in this respect. In 1890 the United Alkali Company, incorporating the great bulk of soda/bleach producers, was formed to effect this strategy. That it did not in the outcome succeed in maintaining the production of Le Blanc soda was probably due less to any radical defect in the strategy than to the closing up of outlets for bleach, as the major Continental countries and the USA developed bleach manufacturing of their own behind tariff walls.

As to the third significant chemical industry which was bound up with textiles, the manufacture of synthetic dyestuffs, there is a good deal of arbitrariness in singling out 'synthetic' from 'natural' dyestuffs. While some of the latter were derived more or less directly from various vegetable substances, others necessitated quite elaborate processes, such as to give them a fair claim to the style of 'chemical industries'. The essential distinction consists in the fact that while 'natural' dyes are *extracted* from a naturally occurring substance, 'synthetic' dyes are chemically *constructed* (*synthesised*) from the distillations of several substances which are not in themselves dye sources. There is also a more fundamental, technical, distinction. To the extent that the manufacture of natural dyes involved chemical processes it dealt with inorganic structures, while the manufacture of synthetic dyes involves the composition of organic structures. In a strictly economic analysis none of this really matters – especially when within, and indeed some way beyond, this period, the output of natural dyestuffs greatly exceeded that of synthetic dyestuffs. The justification for affording the synthetic dyestuffs industry special treatment, when previously the natural dyestuffs industry has earned no more than passing mention in connection with the textiles industries, consists in the degree to which synthetics leant on fundamental chemical research, the operational scale on which their commercial production had to be undertaken and their interconnection with other industrial activities.

We have seen already the debt owed to pure science by the makers of soda, bleach and sulphuric acid. But the processes involved in these instances were not of great complexity and it is not beyond credulity that they could have been stumbled on by chance and developed by trial and error in the same way as the smelting of metals and a variety of other transmutative processes had been developed through history (though it should be allowed that the rapid improvement of manufacturing plant could never have taken place without a clear understanding of what it was that the plant was required to do). With synthetic dyestuffs it is flatly inconceivable that they could ever have appeared or their range have been extended without an enormous amount of basic and meticulous chemical research – although as we shall see the initial specific breakthrough was a matter of accident.

In the simplest of summaries the work involved the identification of the behavioural characteristics of molecular substances when isolated from the intricate organic compounds in which they occurred in nature and their reassemblage in stable form so as to yield materials of given attributes, either in imitation of known materials or as entirely new materials vested with particular desired characteristics. The basic theory was propounded by the German chemists Wöhler and Liebig in 1828 and subsequently refined in detail by various others, mostly German and French. By the 1850s synthetic substances were being produced in a number of laboratories but none of these early experiments had yielded materials of practical applicability until in 1857 an eighteen-year-old English chemistry student, William Perkins, dabbling with aniline, a substance earlier isolated in Germany, found that he had unwittingly produced a purplish dyestuff. Sheer luck brought Perkins to this discovery, but he was in fact an extremely able chemist and a competent man of business. Under the name 'mauve' he started production of his find on his own account and, by the time he retired from business at the age of thirty-five with a comfortable fortune made, had added a number of other synthetic dyestuffs to his output range and was the most considerable manufacturer of synthetic dyes in the world. Their range was however still very limited. Although the broad lines of future research had been indicated by Perkins's work, the development of further synthetics was as yet a hit and miss affair – with the misses enormously outnumbering the hits; even the occasional hit was commonly not translatable into a commercial proposition without a great deal of further work both on alternative chemical procedures and on plant design. After Perkins, virtually all the research and most of its practical application was undertaken in Germany. Britain, after its precocious start in this new industrial field, was left way behind.

While this contrast of German thrustfulness and British inertia only made itself commercially felt from the mid-'seventies onwards, the essentials of the situation already existed some years earlier and are of relevance not only to the manufacture of synthetics but, in some measure, to industrial performance generally. These essentials were two: the much more advanced state of scientific education in Germany along with the much greater number of scientists turned out; and the much greater readiness of German industry to employ these scientists, both for day to day control and management posts and for research, and in the latter case to provide adequate facilities and to finance systematic long-term investigations of unpredictable outcome. The greater attention given to scientific education was due in substantial part to the keener belief in the practical usefulness of science but it did pre-date the industrial exploitation of scientific knowledge on any significant scale and must be accounted as part of that general cultural phenomenon which in the eighteenth and early nineteenth centuries had manifested itself most sharply in the contrast between France and Britain in point of enthusiasm for scientific inquiry – and Germany before she found her own feet looked to France as the exemplar of the arts of civilised life.

The matter must not be overstated. Ever since the seventeenth century science had been acknowledged as a laudable pursuit in Britain; it could always count on at least token patronage from the establishment – and in Scotland on more substantial support. Nevertheless it enjoyed a much greater prestige in France, and later in Germany, than in Britain. Any explanation of this phenomenon can only be speculative and would, anyway, lie beyond the competence of this book. The mere fact itself goes some way towards explaining the greater number of scientists amongst the personnel, including owners and directors, of German industrial concerns. A university education for the sons of the middle class was standard in Germany while it was still rare in England, except as a preparation for the the Law or the Church; and with science enjoying the academic standing which in England was confined to the classics and mathematics, the simple pursuit of a conventionally reputable education was as apt to result in a scientist as in anything else. Many of the 'scientists' to be found in German concerns were not engaged in scientific work at all and, indeed, were perhaps no more competent to do so than many gentleman graduates of Oxbridge were to construe Ovid at sight. But if a mere counting of heads would exaggerate the real weight of science in German industrial life, it remains true that it was much greater than in Britain.

In addition to the sociocultural explanations of this there is also that given by the structure of German industry once it had started to go any way along its own 'revolutionary' path (say, from *c.* 1860). Concern size was larger than in Britain; and research economics are strictly a function of size: since the same body of research will serve for any quantity of output, the unit costs of research fall continuously with increased output, and, obversely, can become deterrently high at low output levels. This consideration applies emphatically to the manufacture of synthetics, which necessitated high research outlays which sometimes had to be carried for years before any return was earned on them, with the further implication that concerns in this field needed a spread of products so that established items could pay for the development of new lines. Moreover, the question of research aside, the nature of the plant used and the multiple distillations obtained from raw materials, effectively enforcing multiproduct operation,[1] also conferred decisive advantages on the large-scale concern. Once entrenched, then, the position of the great German synthetics concerns was almost impregnable against any normal commercial challenge. No sane entrepreneur would hazard the capital required against the accumulation of vital scientific and technical knowledge commanded by the Germans. (During and immediately after the First World War, with the help of government finance and a flat prohibition on imports a fairly substantial British synthetics industry was created out of the scraps which, since Perkins, had supplied a few of the simpler products.)

One must not proceed too hurriedly from the particular to the general. The state of science and industrial appreciation of its potential was utterly decisive in ensuring German ascendancy in synthetics. But synthetics are a very special, not a representative, case. And although science, chemistry rather than physics, had a contribution to make in other fields – in iron and steel for instance, as indicated earlier – and although British backwardness, both in the attention given to scientific

[1] The practical scope of synthetic chemistry was rapidly widened from the mid-seventies. By the early years of the twentieth century it comprehended virtually the whole colour spectrum in dyestuffs, certain perfumes and flavours, a number of drugs (chiefly antipyretics, hypnotics and analgesics, including aspirin), and a couple of explosives.

education and in the use made of what there was, was an ultimate source of weakness in these fields, there were vast tracts of industry to which contemporary science had little or nothing to offer; textile manufacture, engineering, shipbuilding, coalmining and myriad lesser trades. Given that the resources of any one economy are finite, it may reasonably be argued that the optimum balance of advantage lay in leaving activities founded in advanced scientific knowledge to those best equipped for them and devoting one's own resources to other, abundant, opportunities. This would be to imply that Britain gained rather than lost in allowing the synthetics business to pass to Germany; although it is of course no kind of justification for the neglect of science in potentially beneficiary sectors to which a large body of other resources was already committed. Then it could amount to spoiling the ship for a hap'orth of tar.

Finally, as a general observation on research investment from the standpoint of the individual concern, it should be said that even when science might have something to offer it does not necessarily follow that it is good business economics to endeavour to exploit it; there is never any guarantee that research outlays will pay for themselves; and it is not an uncommon experience when research does come up with something of major benefit that its application lies in somebody else's field. The financing of research has posed a perennial problem ever since the first recognition of its desirability. With its potentially endless ramifications, interconnections and overspills, there can be little prediction of the extent and nature of its results. He who pays the piper cannot really call the tune. So, who should pay the piper? The state? Academic institutions? Philanthropy? Business concerns? When, as tended very much to be the case in nineteenth-century Britain, each can find good reasons for believing it to be properly a charge on the others, the result is inertia even in the midst of a general consensus on the desirability, in principle, of action.

What, in summary analysis, has led to particular attention being given to the development of synthetic chemicals, notwithstanding their restricted footing in Britain and their fairly limited serviceability,[1] is their role as indicators of economic sophistication. Only a relatively highly developed society could command the knowledge, skills, materials and

[1] It is really only with synthetic fibres, plastics and a greatly widened range of pharmaceutical products that synthetics industries can be said to have come to occupy a place of substantial importance in modern economies generally – and for the most part this is a post-World War II phenomenon.

capital needed for their production. They could only have succeeded, never preceded, substantial progress in the industrial arts generally. And to what has already been said to this effect, one final note should be added. The principal source of the base substances used in synthetics was coal tar, a residual product of coking coal. To have burned massive quantities of coal just for the sake of these byproducts would have been ludicrous economics. In other words, the pre-existence of numerous coke ovens in the iron industry and of gas works was an essential economic base of the synthetics industry. By the same token the growth of synthetics made a useful contribution to lowering iron and gas costs by providing a market for what formerly had been largely unremunerative waste, requirements of tar for other purposes falling well short of supplies. Such were the quantities of tar extracts which the German synthetics industries came to require that their own considerable supplies were inadequate and they had to draw quite heavily on British sources, which benefited, then, even in the absence of any substantial synthetics industry in Britain itself.

The last of this quartet of chemical industries, synthetic fertilisers, claims a place here less on account of the industry itself than because the general theme of advance in chemical knowledge which has been taken up can appositely be extended to comprehend soil chemistry, since it was over the first couple of decades or so of this period that the foundations of this science, which had for a long time attracted speculative attention, were soundly laid. This achievement was essentially the work of the German, Liebig, and two Englishmen, Lawes and Gilbert. Liebig's contribution was to sort out the work of numerous predecessors, of very varied value, and, with the addition of important work of his own, to synthesise a comprehensive theory of the elements of plant growth.[1] And it was Lawes and Gilbert, working from 1835 on Lawes's estate at Rothamsted, converted into an experimental farm station, who confirmed, with certain modifications, the accuracy of Liebig's conclusions. By the mid-'fifties, in place of the conjectures and surmises, some of them very wide of the mark, which had still prevailed a quarter of a century earlier, it was decisively settled that the principal constituents of vegetable growth were soluble phosphates, potash (potassium carbonate) and nitrogen. In the case of the last, some uncertainty still prevailed as to the requirements of different kinds of plants and the extent to which plants could derive it from the air, not completely cleared up until 1881

---

[1] The first edition of his *Chemistry in its Application to Agriculture and Physiology* was published in 1840.

when it was fully demonstrated that leguminous plants manufactured their own nitrogen and imparted some to the soil (a good two centuries after their fertilising quality had first been appreciated in practice), and that other classes of plant needed nitrogenous matter in the ground.

The primary importance of all this belongs of course in the context of agriculture. Its industrial consequences were relatively slight, for all of these basic constituents either occurred in usable form in nature or could be very simply obtained from readily available substances: nitrogen, from the Chilean nitrate deposits; potash from various sources but, after 1860, chiefly from the unique natural accumulations at Stassfurt (Germany); and phosphates from Peruvian guano (sea-bird droppings) or by grinding either bones or the basic slag remaining in steel furnaces (useful of course to the iron industry in the same way as a synthetics market for tar was). A particularly rich form of phosphates was obtainable by processing bones with sulphuric acid and gave rise to 'superphosphates' manufacture, which constituted the synthetic fertiliser industry.[1] Superphosphates were, however, expensive and many farmers continued to use the cheaper form so that the growth of an agricultural chemicals industry was slow; by the time it had attained any size the extent of its agricultural markets had become slight in a gross economic context.

An industry which has already received passing mention and which, in a strict sense, was also a 'chemical' industry is gas supply. It was noted in the previous chapter that the boom which culminated in 1825 was accompanied by a spate of gas undertakings – as a group, probably the soundest of the varied ventures of that frenetic phase. Already by the opening of this period nearly every town of over 10,000 inhabitants (of which there were then about a hundred) was on gas – though as yet domestic use was probably fairly limited and the lighting of streets and of industrial premises would have accounted for the bulk of consumption. It would seem to have been fairly precisely through the 1830s and 1840s that household use of gas light[2] became widespread, stimulated

---

[1] Not really 'synthetic' in the sense in which the term has earlier been used. 'Artificial' would be a better term but is usurped to describe any fertiliser other than animal dung.

[2] Gas for heat did not become available until 1885 and into the first couple of decades of the twentieth century remained of restricted use. Gas for powering light engines was dabbled with in the 1860s, became quite widely adopted in the 1880s, chiefly in various metal-working trades, was briefly toyed with for heavy work, and then rapidly gave way to electricity in the early years of the twentieth century.

by a price fall of roughly a half, due partly to more efficient gas engineering and partly to the snowball effect of increased consumption, which permitted fixed costs to be spread more widely. By mid-century very little of urban Britain was without local gasworks – and most of the villages and rural homesteads which lacked a supply were never to be put on the gas map. As yet uncontemplated uses for heat and power aside, further growth prospects for gas, like many other commodities, lay in the enhancement of the purchasing power of that very substantial fraction of the population (getting on perhaps for a half) whose income left little or nothing to spare after basic necessities had been met and for whom gas light was an unwarrantable luxury.

Although fixed costs on production plant, pipes and terminal fittings, constituted a substantial proportion of total costs and gas production was an unambiguously capitalist industry, it did not give rise to much in the way of heavily capitalised concerns. The odd company in the great cities may have incorporated capital of over £50,000 but there were numerous concerns with capitals of under £10,000. The service area of any one gasworks was confined to the built-up block in its environs. In London, Liverpool, Glasgow, Manchester, Edinburgh, Bristol and Leeds there was scope for, though little advantage in,[1] large-scale operations, but in the rush to exploit gas these cities generally got carved up into the territories of several concerns. Here there was some overlapping, with wasteful duplication of mains and fierce, though generally shortlived, company feuds. Even some smaller towns had a plurality of services. With capital costs working out at something like £1 per head of population, even a single works serving a town of 50,000 was not of gross dimensions. And practically all the gas companies were single works undertakings. There were no gas tycoons. With no scope for operational integration of different works, there was no call for the talents of the empire builder; indeed a works once established there was little need of entrepreneurial or managerial skills of any kind. Production was a simple routine affair and marketing a more or less automatic function, within very constricted geographical confines. Once household consumption became dominant, demand was almost somnolently regular; and cost structure was uncomplicated: set fixed costs, labour and coal costs. (With their open market volatility the latter might have been a troublesome feature but, although no positive in-

[1] Above a certain low level the principal economics of scale arose from greater utilisation of mains, i.e. costs fell with intensified consumption in a given area but mere geographical expansion yielded little or no cost gain.

formation is to hand, it seems likely that with predictable requirements, gasworks obtained their coal at fixed contract prices.) Gas was thus an ideal home for local capital seeking a comfortable return with a minimum of personal attention required.

The real entrepreneurs were perhaps the men who built the gasworks, closely resembling, though not of course in the scale of their activity, the roughly contemporaneous railway contractors and engineers. Like the railway builders they roamed widely, even abroad; their fortunes fluctuated sharply as investment enthusiasm for gas rose and fell with the upswings and downslides of the economy as a whole (the gas boom phases were 1820-25, 1831-36 and 1843-47); and when credit was easy but orders insufficient, they built their own gasworks, issuing shares, borrowing and letting suppliers go unpaid until they found buyers for them.

The simplicity of gasworks management along with the necessarily monopolistic situation of suppliers (tempered by the price sensitivity of consumers) not only attracted private capital but also suggested gas to be a suitable subject for municipal enterprise. From the earliest days a few local authorities had built their own gasworks, but it was not until the very last years of this period and through the following decades that any significant quantity of the national gas supply started to pass into the hands of public bodies. As late as 1913 nearly two thirds was still privately supplied.

The earlier inactivity of local authorities is to be explained less by reference to *laissez-faire* orthodoxy than by the simple absence of consolidated municipal authorities in many of the larger industrial towns, which were in general the first to take to gas, until the Municipal Reform Act of 1835; and, more generally, by the commonly moribund condition of such corporations as there were, until revivified by the same Act which, in any event, still left many smaller towns without an authority of their own. In brief, then, gas had already come to most towns before a competent local authority existed; and it took some decades of muscle flexing before the post-1835 corporations felt themselves capable of taking over from private enterprise – necessarily a slow business anyway, as long as the state observed a neutrality of attitude on the matter.

Housing

Another field in which, in the light of later history, one might expect to find local authorities acting is housing. In actual fact, a small amount of philanthropic work aside, this remained exclusively private enterprise territory throughout this period. Housing is of course one of the prime constituents of living standards and if little has been said about its provision in earlier sections of this book it is essentially because the house-building industry is one that has hardly any history, its techniques and organisation having changed very little over the centuries. At any time the most that could conceivably be offered by way of an account of its record would be a measure of its gross output, but before 1785 there are no statistics on which to base calculations. And even with abundant statistical indications of the quantity of housing constructed, one would still be very far from any accurate appreciation of dwelling standards. A house is just the nub element in a complex of environmental facilities: air, light, space, sanitary services, playgrounds, and so on. In other words – and it hardly needs saying – a calculation of bricks and mortar per head of the population is not an adequate measure of home conditions.

No attempt can be made here to assess in detail the changes in this intricate complex. Plainly, they were in substantial measure a function of urbanisation; and the impact of rapid urbanisation in Britain on home conditions is a matter of some notoriety, as is the gradual awakening of the Victorian conscience to the enormous gap between the residential environment of the general body of the working class and that of the more comfortably off – a movement whose most prominent landmarks are the Public Health Acts of 1848 and 1875, the Local Government Act of 1871, and an Act of 1879 enabling local authorities to finance public housing schemes – measures which are noteworthy less on account of any immediate results engendered than as admissions of responsibility on the part of the political establishment. What can be said here, then, on the house-building industry specifically must be set against a broader background of probably deteriorating environmental facilities up to mid-century or so and of a very gradual amelioration thereafter.

Perhaps the first thing to stress about the building industry is its magnitude. In this particular period buildings of all kinds would have accounted annually for some 4 or 5 per cent of gross national output – among industrial products, headed at the beginning only by cotton

goods and woollen goods, and, towards mid-century, by coal as well.[1]
This comprehends industrial and commercial premises; residential
buildings accounted for about two-fifths of the industry's output,
about 2 per cent of gross national output. And the proportion of
national income expended on housing was much higher – probably
over 10 per cent. Sites, in shortest supply where people were densest,
had to be paid for; the same concentration factor meant that existing
houses generally commanded a scarcity premium price (a 'rent' in the
technical sense); and, most weightily, the majority of occupants were
unable to raise the purchase price of a house and therefore had to draw
on somebody else's capital to accommodate themselves. Interest
charges, whether openly on a mortgage loan or, much more commonly, effectively concealed in a rent, were in fact, as they still are, the
major element in housing costs. What it all comes to is that housing
leaned on an industry which was unable to achieve any intrinsic cost
economies, on an inelastic supply of land and on the provision of capital
whose price showed only the most moderate of tendencies to fall.[2]
While sooner or later through the late eighteenth and the nineteenth
century, clothing standards, dietary standards, heating standards,
standards of enjoyment in fact of almost all consumption goods,
drew some substantial benefit from enhancements of supply capacities,
housing standards derived only minimal advantage from the revolutionary transformation of the economy.

On the other hand, it does not appear that there was any long run
regression in housing standards in the strict sense of accommodation
space *per capita*. The very imperfect statistical data available from 1785[3]
makes it plain that from 1793 to the end of the first decade of the nineteenth century the rate of house-building failed to keep pace with
population growth, but suggests that from then on the net addition to
the country's housing stock may have slightly exceeded the increase in
population, and that by the 1840s the housing situation may have been
back to what it had been in the early 1790s. From 1851 onwards a

[1] If classified as a single group metal artifacts would also exceed buildings – as, briefly,
would 'raw' iron and steel alone over the very last years of the period, at least in current
value terms.

[2] Consols yielded $3\frac{1}{2}$ per cent around 1830 and $3\frac{1}{4}$ per cent around 1873. Other interest
rates presumably moved in similar fashion.

[3] An annual record of brick output. Apart from its obvious imperfections as a measure
of house output – varying proportions as between houses and other brick built structures,
shifts as between brick and other building materials – there is no 'norm' base to which to
relate it, i.e. that rate of brick output needed to maintain housing standards at a given level
of population cannot be positively determined.

direct, though not fully trustworthy, indication of changes in housing levels is afforded by the count of houses made from then on at the decennial census. These show an inching up in houses *per capita*: 1851, 0·1914; 1861, 0·1956; 1871, 0·1990 – or in the rather more meaningful terms of the fall in numbers to each house: 5·22; 5·11; 5·03.[1] Since the proportion of children in the population rose fractionally, this, to its diminutive extent, represents, not a decrease in family size, but a decrease in the number of families sharing accommodation. (Expressed as average annual growth rates to afford comparability with growth rates elsewhere cited, the increase in the housing stock for the successive decades represented rates of: 1851–61, 1·25 per cent; 1861–71, 1·50 per cent.)

There was at work through the two decades 1851–71, what was probably the only factor of any weight to make a contribution towards easier housing throughout the nineteenth century; cheaper delivery prices in many places of bricks, slates and other building materials as the railway network spread to points which had drawn little or no benefit from the earlier canal system. That this largely explains the marginal improvement in the housing situation over those decades is suggested particularly by the fact that after a further minute improvement as recorded by the 1881 census, that of 1891 shows no further *per capita* gain; and although those of 1901 and 1911 show resumed improvements, these can be fully accounted for, and more, by a decrease in family size.

Housing was to remain, as it does to this day though in attenuated degree, the blackest patch in an economy which continued to heap up wealth in historically unprecedented fashion. Indeed, it is virtually axiomatic that, in a growing free enterprise economy, the conditions of its supply ensure that housing will lag badly behind other sectors. No other sector is so capital intensive; yet the huge bulk of those wanting houses neither command capital of their own nor can effectively compete as borrowers with those seeking capital for productive investment. (The same lag has occurred, it may be added, in socialist societies which, more deliberately, have preferred to devote capital to other purposes rather than to housing.)

[1] The comparable figure for 1951 was 3·53.

Agriculture

If housing is one major component of mass welfare which is very apt not to participate in general economic growth, foodstuffs are another which can be threatened by a lack of resilience in supply factors. In the previous two chapters we have seen British agriculture contriving, with a substantial measure of success, to feed an unremittingly expanding population under the constrictions of a limited supply of land. This period, of course, brought no demographic respite. From 16·1 million in 1830 the British population had grown to 26·8 million by 1873 and was then nearly four times as great as it had been when the long-run population increase set in in the 1740s. Data of any precision is lacking but the crude inferences which can be drawn from such statistical material as there is suggest that grain output having rather more than doubled since the 1740s ceased to rise any further in the 1840s and started on a gentle decline from around mid-century. Table II.25 indicates the likely general trend of the wheat supply situation through the period as a whole.

Let it be made clear straightaway that the gradual diminution of corn output from the ceiling of the 1840s does not denote a contraction of British agriculture as a whole. It can be estimated that gross agricultural output rose by something like 50 per cent through this period, suggesting that output of farm produce other than corn rather more than doubled, i.e. ran appreciably ahead of population growth, so that *per capita* consumption of dairy produce, potatoes, meat, etc. probably increased on balance by more than a third. Plainly, the resources applied in these directions could have been devoted to maintaining a continuing expansion of the basic foodstuff, wheat. Equally plainly, domestic wheat output could not indefinitely have been kept fully in step with population growth without a positive reduction in *per capita* standards of consumption of meat, etc. In other words, by some point in time in the third quarter of the nineteenth century the multifarious requirements of foodstuffs occasioned by rising population had finally outrun the productive capacity of British land. And, under these conditions of competing demand pressures on an increasingly inadequate supply capacity, the average British farmer evidently found that profit maximisation lay in persistently edging more towards livestock. But it was a matter of edging. The very modest rate of decline in corn output makes it abundantly clear that corn-growing continued to be a remunerative activity.

TABLE II.25. *Wheat supplies, 1830–71 (annual averages)*

	1830–36	1837–43	1844–50	1851–57	1859–64	1865–71
Net domestic output (mil. cwt)	57	60	61	57	55	50
Net imports (mil. cwt)	5	10	14	20	31	35
Total supplies (mil. cwt)	62	70	75	77	86	85
Imports as % of total	8	14	19	26	36	41
Per capita consumption (cwt)	3·6	3·7	3·7	3·5	3·6	3·4
Price (per quarter)	53s 9d	61s 3d	51s 7d	57s 10d	48s 2d	53s

(The domestic output figures given in this table are notional. Their point of departure is the round figure of 50 million cwt for 1865–71, arrived at on the base of the acreages under wheat officially recorded from 1867 and an assumed yield, net of seed-corn, of around 14 cwt an acre. This departure figure has been worked backwards using the trend data contained in S. Fairlie, 'The Corn Laws and British wheat production', *Economic History Review*, vol. 22 (1970). The import figures are derived directly from the official statistics but also contain an element of approximation. The table here refers to Great Britain and wheat brought in from Ireland is therefore classed as imported, as it is in the official figures up to 1842. After 1842, however, the official figures relate to the United Kingdom. It has been assumed that British imports from Ireland 1843–57 ran at the same average level as 1837–42 and thereafter ceased – an assumption crudely founded on the Irish output statistics, which exist from 1847 onwards. The use of UK figures after 1842 also involves the inclusion of imports by Ireland but these can never have been more than a tiny fraction of the total and the resulting error is probably rather more than counter balanced by another defect: the simple summing of imports of grain and imports of flour which would understate imports relative to domestic output, calculated in grain terms.)

It is important to stress the fact that corn continued to pay; important because it underlines the point that the great growth in corn imports throughout this period occasioned no serious harm to British agriculture. Crudely speaking, imports supplied that portion of the market which the British farmer was not interested in supplying. The real danger, in fact, was not that British farmers would be undone by foreign competition but that foreign supplies would be insufficient to meet requirements. It is against that background that the repeal of the Corn Laws in 1846 must be understood.

The repeal of the Corn Laws was of course an event of more than strictly economic significance. Historians have become rightly suspicious of those simple clichés which comprehend great phenomena in definitions of the block interests of socio-economic groups. But it does seem impossible to improve on the representation of the repeal of the Corn Laws, considered as a political phenomenon, as a triumph of the middle class over the upper class – a triumph in which British conservatism acquiesced, with that shrewd sense of self-preservation and that instinctive apprehension of politics as the art of the possible which, with almost incredible regularity, have always served it at times of potential disaster. On this occasion indeed, enlightened conservatism, headed by Sir Robert Peel, actually anticipated the crisis and itself effected the overthrow of its own interests; and although the unenlightened and slower minded rump then threw its precocious leader overboard, it was no more than a few years in catching up with his quicker perceptions of the facts of life.

Charged as it was with so much passion the protracted debate, indoors and out of doors, on the Corn Laws cannot be easily penetrated to touch the springs of quieter, less emotionally committed, judgments which perhaps ultimately settled the question. But it is difficult to believe that, despite the agonised predictions of disaster from landlord spokesmen (predictions which the Anti-Corn Law League was not especially anxious to rebut, the downfall of landlordism being precisely the outcome hoped for by many League supporters), and that behind the polemical rhetoric, cooler minds were unaware that there was not surplus grain enough in the whole world to flood the British market; that it was competing demands from other grain necessitous regions which, much more than the Corn Laws, were checking and would continue to check the flow of foreign grain to Britain; that repeal would do no more than place Britain on an equal footing with the many other seekers after the limited supplies of the few grain surplus regions; that Britain could certainly not afford to forgo her own grain output, and that gross European demand would keep international corn prices quite buoyant enough to ensure an adequate return to the British grower; in brief, that the ostensible ground of political battle, the struggle for paramountcy between the industrialist interest and the landlord interest, was not really in issue at all. In storming and carrying the citadel of the Corn Laws the industrialist interest had, in a real sense, won a tremendous victory, but one of that kind, not unknown in military history, where after both assailants and defenders have committed massive resources to a particular position, it is subsequently realised that the position was not of major strategic importance at all – a fact which had perhaps been appreciated by sharper minds all along.

How far Peel and other contemporaries perceived the delicate balance obtaining between British grain output, British grain requirements and the state of the international grain market is in the last analysis of less importance here than the fact itself. And that fact, already subsisting a good decade before repeal and radically distinguishing the circumstances of 1846 from those of 1815, was the product of sustained population growth throughout Europe, including Britain, unaccompanied by any corresponding opening up of new grain sources. The wheat supply table (II.25), indicates clearly the British consequences of this situation both in the steady upward move of imports before repeal and in the failure of imports to accelerate immediately after repeal. The latter part of 1846 – the Corn Laws were repealed in June – and 1847 did actually see a massive leap in combined grain imports by the UK. At official valuations they amounted in 1847 to £16 million as against a previous all time high of £6 million (1839). However the bulk of this was destined for the relief of Ireland where the failure of the potato crop had, quite literally, left the greater part of the populace totally without food. Maize, previously imported in only trivial amounts, constituted a large fraction of the grain imports of 1847, it being the only grain cheap enough for sale or free distribution to the Irish peasantry.

The *per capita* consumption figures point to the inelasticity of foreign supply sources in the decade or so following repeal; to their inability to spare for Britain any more than, or even as much as, the bare minimum necessary to keep total supplies in step with population – a phenomenon confirmed by the upward tendency of prices.

From the late 'fifties, however, there are signs of something new starting to stir. In Table II.25 it shows up in the marked, though not momentous, acceleration of imports – in point both of absolute growth and of percentage of total supplies – in the rise in *per capita* consumption and in the pronounced drop in prices. From somewhere, cheaper and more abundant wheat was starting to flow. Table II.26 indicates the sources.

Russia was of course a traditional, if rather spasmodic, source of supply. The gathering momentum of her wheat exports from *c.* 1860 is to be explained less by the opening up of new lands than by internal transport improvements, facilitating the movement outwards of grain from

TABLE II.26. *Sources of wheat imports (annual averages)*

Period	From Russia		From USA and Canada	
	Mil. cwt	% of total imports	Mil. cwt	% of total imports
1850–54	3·2	19	1·8	11
1855–59	2·6	16	2·7	17
1860–64	5·1	18	12·1	42
1865–69	10·1	34	5·9	20
1870–74	11·8	30	18·5	47

remoter parts of the interior, very possibly at the expense of the local peasantry who could not match international market prices; and although Russian supplies continued in very erratic fashion to be of periodic importance to Britain, Russia, with its own steadily growing population, was hardly an authentic grain surplus country. Even in North America the race against world population was not won in suddenly decisive fashion. The cutback in exports to Britain over the years 1865–68 presumably reflects the spurt in American population which followed the Civil War, just before the massive surge across the Mississippi and into the Great Plains had got fully under way. This, in the decade or so immediately following this period, utterly transformed the world grain supply situation and, by the mid-'nineties, had reduced the British wheat grower to a position of virtual redundancy. But in the immediate context it is needful to stress that even the leap in North American exporting capacity of the closing years of this period left the British consumer still primarily dependent on home output – and left prices still chiefly determined by the quality of the domestic harvest: it was a cluster of bad harvests that was responsible for the sharp jump in the average price level through this last phase. (It is improbable, however, that the drop in *per capita* consumption was caused by higher prices. This would seem to be not a topical but a secular phenomenon: the onset of a move away from bread as the basic element in the diet of the masses as rising wages permitted of a more varied and attractive diet.)

Allowing that the higher prices scored up in certain years over the final phase of this period were due to poor harvests we can distinguish the late 'fifties as inaugurating a new era of lowered grain prices. On the face of it this might be expected to have bitten deeply into farmers' profit margins and to have ushered in a new period of difficulty and distress for British agriculture. That it did not is, in summary terms, to be explained by two things: significant reductions in real farming costs had been achieved – were, indeed, a part cause of the price fall; and the average British farmer was leaning increasingly less on wheat revenue for his income. To put this situation in perspective we must go back to the beginning of the period under review.

In the last chapter we left British farmers in two broad groups, the prosperous and the poor, crudely coterminous with the light soil and the primarily livestock farmers in the one case and with the clay farmers in the other. From the late 1830s the clay farmers started to pull out of the trough in which they had languished for over two decades. The higher corn prices sustained over the years 1837–42 constituted the initiating factor in their recovery. In itself this was just prosperity regained at the expense of the community at large, and the price relapse of the mid-'forties would have lowered the clay farmers back into the depression from which they had briefly emerged. Many probably did revert to their former profitlessness for varying periods and the extent to which the clay farmers as a body succeeded in effecting an enduring improvement in their condition is a matter of some uncertainty and controversy. However, if remaining less advantageously situated than their light soil counterparts, it does seem to be true that the heavy soil farmers did not experience a general and persistent return to their pre-1837 miseries. From the 1840s two sources of succour were becoming available to the men on the clays. The one was imported oil-cake – cheap livestock fodder which permitted increased numbers of cattle to be maintained on grasslands and profitable advantage to be taken of the expansive market for milk and beef. The other was efficient drainage. Machinemade and machinelaid pipes replaced handworked tile or stone-paved channels, offering both lower costs and better performance.

Fairly clearly, the retreat from corn, already noted, was largely the doing of those clayland farmers who expanded oilcake fed herds at the expense of their arable. Equally clearly, the scope for this kind of repatterning of farming practice on the clays was far from being infinitely elastic. Notable as it was, the growth in demand for livestock produce could not induce any massive abandonment of corn growing as long as there was no profound slump in corn prices. The clays remained mixed farming regions with no more than an increasing bias towards cattle. And it was as mixed farming lands that most progressive contemporaries regarded them when urging the benefits of drainage. While the clays remained water-soaked their occupants were held fast in the grip of antiquated farming practices. With decent drainage, it was argued, not only would cereal yields be directly raised but the range of root crop routines, productivity-enhancing implements and artificial manures which were the basis of light soil prosperity would become fully available to the clay farmers also. There is no doubt in retrospect that the anticipated advantages of the new drainage technology in the clay country were not in the outcome fully realised. In the first place a good deal had still to be learned about drainage techniques – specifically as to the depths at which the pipes should be laid – and many contemporary installations were less than fully successful. In the second place good drainage alone will not convert clay into the effective equivalent of free draining sandy or chalky soil and the notion that once drained the whole gamut of light soil practices could be immediately applied to the heavy soils was misconceived. Nevertheless, if contemporary expectations were overpitched, drainage of the clays could certainly do nothing but good and the third quarter of the century took to the task with enthusiasm.

A drainage system being a permanent enhancement of the values of the land was naturally a charge on landlords rather than farmers. Working out at around £5 an acre it involved an outlay of a sum equivalent, in rough and ready terms, to four years gross rental income. Many landlords did not possess that sort of ready capital, and few of those who did would have been willing to freeze it all in a drainage system which would probably take twenty years or more to return it via increased rents. Thus while landlords' personal resources doubtless provided a significant fraction of the capital raised, outside sources had to make a heavy contribution if the task of adequately draining the five million acres[1] or more which stood to benefit substantially was to be put in hand with any rapidity. How far existing financial institutions might have responded to this need – and how far in practice they did respond – one cannot say. The 'West End' banks had in the past financed a good deal of landlord expenditure via mortgage loans. But the general trend of bank policy throughout this period was away from this rather illiquid kind of lending. On the other hand, the insurance companies found mortgage loans a suitable form of employment for

---

[1] Perhaps as much as twenty million acres could have been drained to some advantage but this would include a large amount where drainage would have been commercial lunacy.

some part of their swelling funds. In the outcome, however, the two principal outside sources of drainage finance were the government and the specialist drainage concerns.

Peel had attempted to soften the blow of repeal by creating a drainage loan fund of £2 million in 1846,[1] and this was supplemented by another £2 million in 1850. These were revolving funds and by the end of this period had supplied about £7·5 million to financing drainage. The drainage concerns, dominated by the Land Improvement Company, had by then perhaps found £4 million.[2] As the cumulative total then laid out on new style drainage was probably between £20 million and £25 million this suggests that about half was raised by landowners themselves from personal resources and privately arranged loans. One way or another this mobilisation of capital over the last three decades or so of this period, most intensively over the last two, probably resulted in more being devoted to land drainage alone than had been applied to all forms of long-term agricultural investment over any comparable period in the past. Throw in landlord expenditures on farm buildings, roadways and other permanent fixtures and this phase is unique in point of the capital committed to agriculture, and thus in point of the capital burden assumed by landlords.

So far as landlords themselves are concerned, there is little doubt that, appraised by normal commercial standards, their investment decisions proved a major strategic blunder. Even while the good times lasted they failed to earn a return on their outlays commensurate with those derived on outlays in many other sectors of the economy; and when, just beyond this period, rents started to slither downwards, many of those who still had outstanding loans were paying out more in interest than they were drawing in rent increments. But to proceed from these facts to any general characterisation, favourable or unfavourable, of the landlord class, or to any general statement as to the potential efficacy of their capital had it been employed in other ways, are

---

[1] It has been argued (D. C. Moore, 'The Corn Laws and high farming', *Economic History Review*, **18**, 1965) that this fund was no mere sop to landlords but an element, along with repeal, of a deliberate agricultural reform policy. This contention has not so far won general acceptance and would need to be more abundantly demonstrated before it could do so.

[2] Where the drainage companies got their money from is a matter which has not yet been investigated. It seems unlikely that much of it came out of their own share capital. Bank credit and, perhaps more weightily, insurance funds may well have constituted a large part so that, indirectly at least, these may have been important sources of drainage finance. If insurance funds did figure it is very possible that the drainage companies only acted as brokers in the placing of mortgage loans.

manoeuvres to be undertaken with great caution. In the first place much of this was projected as *very* long-term investment – much longer than any usual industrial investment undertaking. It is only with the advantage of hindsight that one knows positively that it was not to be granted the anticipated term to justify itself. And, as stressed already, right through to the end of this period the market situation required – and remunerated – agricultural growth.

Secondly, the failure of landlords to make as much hay as they might have done while the sun shone must, amongst other things, be understood against a background of conventional landlord–tenant relationships which was strongly biased against sharp rent responses to altered cost and price situations, preferring gradualist adjustments and slow swings from phases when landlords were the chief beneficiaries to phases when farmers were the chief beneficiaries: *c.* 1850–73 was the farmers' phase succeeding 1815–*c.* 1850 which had been a landlords' phase.

Thirdly, and more imponderably, landlord investment cannot be treated as if it were purely commercially motivated. This is in some degree true of almost any period in British history but maybe particularly of the third quarter of the nineteenth century when the ascendancy, social, political and economic, of the landed establishment was coming under serious challenge but while there still seemed a strong chance of successfully resisting that challenge. Landlord investment must surely in some measure be understood as a counter-response, partly to the accusation of parasitism, partly to the danger of being overtaken in point of wealth by industrial capitalism. The percentage certainly mattered but it mattered equally that it be earned from land and that it be seen to be of communal benefit. For landlords to have endeavoured to switch their capital into industry, or to employ it in any 'anonymous' fashion, would have been to surrender – even on honourable and profitable terms, a surrender which would have been to acknowledge their defeat as a class.

Turning to the thesis that agricultural investment represented a misapplication of national resources, three points may be made. First, that the relatively low return accruing to landlords is not necessarily a measure of the social return. In fact it is quite evident, as indicated above, that a substantial part of the return went to farmers. So many factors enter into the equation that it would be impossible to isolate that element of farmers' incomes which was in fact a return on the landlords' capital; which is to say that it is impossible to know whether the capital could have been more fruitfully applied in other sectors.

Secondly, and this only needs to be said because of possible ambiguities in some formulations of this question, there can be no sense in arguing from the experience of later years (when there is no doubt that the return, whether secured by landlords or by farmers, was way below any acceptable norm) with reference to returns *then* being earned on other kinds of new investment. Real resources cannot be stored; refusal to employ them at one time does not make any more available at a later time.[1] Expressions such as the 'overcapitalisation' of British agriculture with reference to the years after the mid-'seventies are peculiarly dangerous in their implication that had it then been possible to liquidate the capital tied up in British agriculture it would have become available for other purposes (such as building a time machine?).[2] Any comparison must be with alternative applications at the time of the investment. Such a comparison should extend over the whole lifetime of the alternative – i.e. beyond the mid-seventies if necessary. But between ordinary depreciation and technological obsolescence this would not tell against much of the agricultural investment if the return on it before the mid-'seventies was comparable with the contemporary return on the alternative.

Since it has already been said that the social return on agricultural investment cannot be measured, there is really not much point in taking the matter any further. But a third point may briefly be made. Were it demonstrable that higher returns could have been secured on alternatives, it still does not automatically follow that such alternatives would have been accessible to the providers of agricultural funds. With contemporary concerns in most industrial fields commonly reluctant to take in outside equity capital or charge themselves with the servicing of much loan capital, it is questionable how much extra capital would in fact have found its way into really useful fields, and highly probable that much of this hypothetically diverted capital would have joined the massive stream flowing into the numerous public flotations, home and foreign, of the period, whose earning potential was frequently much more suspect than that of British agriculture.

This issue of the rationality of landlord investment has carried us fairly far afield and has left untouched the question of most immediate

---

[1] This is not of course true of very rare materials – nor in the very long run of any material. But it is true of labour and thus for all practical purposes of resources generally over any time run which may be sensibly reckoned with.

[2] It might be intended to mean that *money* capital would be released to supplement a supply kept short by institutional defects. But it is hardly credible that anybody would argue that such a shortage prevailed in Britain over the years in question.

import in the particular context of farming costs and output: the benefit accruing to the land as a direct result of that substantial element of capital expenditure which was devoted to drainage. In the current state of knowledge, however, little can be added to the vague observations already made to the effect that in general not as much advantage as had been anticipated was derived from drainage. So far as the clay farmers are concerned it seems likely that, to the indeterminate extent to which they improved their lot, the shift towards oilcake-fed cattle was more efficacious than the installation of drains. But such margins of uncertainty leave plenty of room for positing some significant gain from drainage both directly and indirectly via the 'high farming' which it rendered possible.

Much of this high farming consisted of practices already well established in many light soil areas but, particularly after 1853 when grain prices picked up sharply, convincing farmers and landlords that repeal of the Corn Laws had not sounded their death knell, it added to existing progressivism a much more discriminating use of artificial fertilisers, derived essentially from the basic research of Liebig and Lawes and Gilbert, and, of more modest extent, an increased use of steam power. The threshing machine was general on large farms by mid-century and over the next couple of decades hand-threshing became virtually extinct but the lead set by the USA in other agricultural applications of power was followed rather haltingly. There was still a good deal of hand-reaping and mowing even at the end of this period and farms on which the steam tractor had become a universal prime mover were model show pieces rather than representative commercial units. Quite commonly, of course, farm size was not large enough to justify the use of powered machinery. There were something like 300,000 farmers (excluding smallholders) in Britain, less than 20,000 of whom farmed more than 300 acres – these accounting, however, for close on a third of total farm acreage. Five farmers out of six worked on 150 acres or less. And these proportions remained more or less constant throughout this period. (The likelihood is that any marked tendency for farm size to increase had ceased from around 1815–20 with the virtual finalisation of enclosures.) How much further a growth in unit size could have profitably gone is difficult to say. Doubtless the bulk of the 100,000 or so who farmed less than 50 acres would be demonstrated on a clinically economic appraisal to have been operating appreciably below optimum efficiency, but these accounted for less than 10 per cent of total farm acreage. And while it is probably true that farms in the 50–300 acre range, representing about 60 per cent of farm land, were in general too small to make full use of powered machinery, it is not as if power were a crucial element in agricultural economics. The modest cost advantages to be derived from it could easily have been offset, if unit size were increased, by the attenuation of immediate control in an activity in which so much depends on the watchfulness of the individual farmer. (Much loose comment on nineteenth-century agriculture is plagued by false analogies between farm and factory. Even with mid-twentieth-century techniques few farms can be successfully managed on machine-belt principles. American farming was much more highly mechanised but it is very doubtful if it was any more efficient.) In any event even to raise the question of any substantial increase in farm size is really to go beyond the permissible limits of hypothetical history. The wholesale evictions necessary to effect it would have been socially and politically intolerable, while it is difficult to see where the working capital for the larger farms would have come from: landlords would scarcely have added this to their already considerable fixed capital burden and ordinary private capital would not have been lured in quantity into a field so notoriously prone to misfortune. In practice, farm size had to be scaled to the personal capital resources of individual working farmers.

Through this period a particular factor limiting the capacity of individual farmers to make their capital extend to the financing of larger farms was the growing capital intensiveness of British agriculture as it became more and more biased towards livestock, not only on the clays where it commonly meant a contraction of corn output but also on the light soils where the self-promoting sequence roots–livestock–manure–corn could permit of a swelling output of both. It is indeed arguable that on the clays at least farmers would have benefited from a *reduction* in farm size, allowing them to concentrate their capital resources on stocking farms given over to the dairy and meat production which increasingly offered higher returns. But even on the clays, arable and pasture farming were integrated activities. Whatever the routine, manure assists corn growing. And in varying degrees, roots of one kind or another could be cultivated on drained clays. There could be no hurry to disturb a balance which was currently profitable for the uncertain advantages of more intensive livestock farming, particularly when the rudimentary cost accounting methods of most farmers made the accurate attribution of cost elements and determination of profit margins on each of several products quite impossible.

Ill-informed as to the precise sources of profits most mixed farmers could do no more than tentatively feel their way towards an optimum balance. And as long as the market balance was not in course of rapid alteration the lag in adjusting the pattern of farm output cannot have occasioned much in the way of profitable opportunities missed. It was only in the couple of decades following this period, as the bottom fell out of the market for home produced grain, that the need for a radical repatterning of agricultural effort became imperative. In any event, while farmers' profits within this period might have benefited from an acceleration of the swing to livestock, that large section of the populace which ate bread because it could afford little else required every ounce of wheat got out of British soil.

It remains to indicate something of the changing market conditions which made for such intensification of livestock farming as occurred. Detail is lacking as to the rate of development of its different branches but it seems highly probable that the most expansive was dairy farming. The crucial factor here was again the railways. Although the railway companies were rather slow in providing the special facilities which milk carriage properly required and a fully adequate system of milk distribution was not established until the 1880s, from much earlier the milk market had been transformed by rail transport and milk must have become a commonplace in the homes of the urban masses where formerly it had been a rarity. Butter being less perishable and, more important, too expensive to command a really extensive mass market, would not have benefited from rail transport in the same degree but would certainly have drawn significant advantage from it.

Rail speed also revolutionised the movement of meat-yielding animals. Weight was no longer lost in long treks across country and feeding costs en route were slashed. But measured against the total costs of meat-raising these gains were not of a major order and certainly there is no question of a radical revision of meat-eating habits in this period. The principal growth factor here was simply population, requiring a minimum two-thirds increase in weight of meat raised from a more or less fixed amount of land. *Per capita* consumption probably edged up but hardly by very much until the very last years of the period, when higher wage levels would have started to add significantly to the range of habitual meat-eaters. Before that, such upward tendency of mass purchasing power as there was was still being largely directed, so far as food was concerned, to increasing consumption of potatoes and milk – and, even more, of the imported commodities, tea and sugar.

611

Finally, the accelerated development of the woollen industry from about mid-century gave new opportunities to sheep graziers, not only in Australasia but in Britain also. The wool supply situation, in fact, was rather similar to that of wheat. Even as imports grew whatever the British farmer could provide was wanted until, with wool as with wheat, the later 'seventies and the 'eighties brought a massive extension of the capacity of regions against whose natural advantages British agriculture could not hope to compete.

Money and banking

The last chapter concluded with the observation that periodic crises and accompanying debates on the monetary system remained endemic features of British economic life throughout the period 1830–73. More precisely identified, these crises struck in 1837, 1839, 1847, 1857, 1866 and 1873. A full diagnosis of each would lie beyond the purport of this book, as would any adequate discussion of the respective roles of specific topical factors and secular cyclic ones in their occurrence. If in what follows some reference is made to the circumstances contributing to these crises it is only for the sake of rendering their general nature as comprehensible as seems needful for the purpose in hand, which is their implications for the monetary institutions which had to bear much of their brunt and which, rightly or wrongly, were commonly held responsible for their onset.

In broad terms, all these crises partook of the same essential nature as those referred to in the last two chapters: a sudden rise in the demand for 'cash' against paper or book assets – of either domestic or foreign origin – severe pressure on banking liquidity, a consequent contraction of credit and a downturn in general economic activity – the extent of the latter being very variable and open to attribution to 'real' factors, stock levels, investment swings, harvest yields, etc., raising analytic issues which we are here pledged not to discuss.

The crises of 1837 and 1847 have already been referred to in dealing with railways, where it was suggested that they were analogous to that of 1825 in being characterised by speculative transactions on the Stock Exchange, inevitably culminating in a collapse of share prices. To that it should be added that in each case the transition from a bulls' market to a bears' market may not, as it actually happened, have been an autonomous Exchange phenomenon but one precipitated by a contraction of the credit necessary to sustain speculative dealings, the contraction originated by the Bank of England in an endeavour to protect its gold reserves, which on each occasion were being subject to an external drain: in 1837 caused by American purchases of gold to enable the United States to return to a gold-based currency; in 1847 caused by the heavy importation of grain to supply famine-stricken Ireland.

The crisis of 1837 may have had an American origin; that of 1839 quite certainly had. The specific triggering factor was perhaps, as in 1847, a gold outflow occasioned by unusually heavy grain imports; but the points of vulnerability to the consequent curbing of the Bank's discounts were not, on this occasion, occupied by British speculators but by American ones – in chief, one particular American speculator, the Bank of the United States[1] which had been attempting since 1836 to hold a gigantic corner in Liverpool-consigned cotton by discounting its own bills and other American securities in London. By September 1839 it could no longer stretch its credit far enough. The cotton corner caved in and a chain reaction was set in motion which ran from London to Philadelphia, from there throughout America and then back across the Atlantic to Britain, where the fixed interest bonds of American states and associated banking, railway and canal concerns were held in great number by banks and mercantile houses engaged in Anglo-American trade – bonds whose payability depended directly or in-directly on the credit of the Bank of the United States and whose consequent devaluation brought British banking liquidity under sudden and serious pressure, with all the wider repercussions which that implies.

The quick succession of crises in 1837 and 1839 lent a new urgency and virulence to demands for a stricter system of credit control. Already in 1833 the modest legislation of 1826 had been marginally supplemented: by opening up the London region to joint stock banks provided they did not issue their own notes; by making Bank of England notes legal tender (to economise on internal use of gold); and by exempting the Bank of England from the legal interest limit of 5 per cent in respect of its discount operations. This last has a special interest, of which more in a moment. The first two represent further attempts to give effective expression to the principle that the crucial factor in the avoidance of periodic crises was the preservation of some

[1] Since 1836 no longer a government-privileged institution but just the largest bank in the USA. The termination of its charter had been one element in that policy of President Andrew Jackson, of which the restoration of gold was another element, which sought to release the American farming community from the reputed grip of the banking interests of the eastern seaboard cities.

sort of balance between the volume of notes in circulation and the nation's, largely the Bank of England's, stock of gold. This principle was by now common to almost all participants in the great money debate which had been more or less continuously conducted since the early days of the century – the alternative principle, briefly urged and operated by the Bank of England in the years around 1810, that the stock of goods, not the stock of gold, was the proper determinant of the money supply having been thoroughly discredited.

What was matter for lively controversy was the determination of the correct balance between notes and gold and the mechanism by which that balance should be preserved. Views on the resolution of these questions ranged from the simplicity of fixed one hundred per cent gold backing for notes to the imprecisions of flexible gold ratios according to the day to day judgments of bankers. The disputants were divided not only on points of monetary theory but on the practical question of how far the Bank of England could be relied on to judge accurately of the proper balance and to take discretionary action to ensure that balance. And this was both a matter of the adequacy of available banking techniques and of the readiness of the Bank of England to prefer the role of central bank to that of commercial bank. The partial exemption in 1833 of the Bank from the operation of the usury laws[1] was an attempt to confer on it an additional instrument for controlling credit creation and protecting its gold holdings: a flexibly increased discount rate could be used to choke off borrowing in a less arbitrary fashion than brute refusals to discount; and, through the general increase in interest rates which it would engender, foreign funds could be attracted to London to check an external outflow of gold. In contemporary practice the ability of bank rate alone to achieve either of these ends was very limited. Borrowers, especially in periods of speculative enthusiasm, had a high degree of insensitivity to interest rates: 'hot' money movements played only a small part in international gold flows, the lack of a fully multilateral system of international payments and special requirements of gold (such as that of the USA in 1836–37) being the chief flow agencies, while such interest seeking movements of funds as there were, were primarily governed by long-term interest rates which had only a very attenuated sympathy with fluctuations in bank rate.

Whatever the possible efficacy of flexible bank rate it could have none if the Bank were not prepared to employ it for these ends; or rather,

[1] The usury laws were effectively abolished in their entirety in 1854.

since the Bank would certainly in its own interests do what it could to check on actual gold outflow: if the Bank were not prepared to raise the rate for the purpose of stemming its own discounts, as distinct from raising it to take commercial advantage of the demand for credit. The 1833 provision, in a manner of speaking, put the Bank on public trial: would it conduct itself as a central bank and move ahead of the market or would it conduct itself as a commercial bank and move with the market?

The sharp antitheses of the question blur, however, when applied to real life. Sudden penal increases in bank rate would be as apt to cause a crisis as to forestall one. In practice, the distinction between an active curb on the money market and a passive response to the market was one buried in the minds of the Bank's directors. And in its public utterances the Bank showed an ambiguity of attitude. It acknowledged that public responsibilities devolved from its key role and its note-issuing privileges, but it also insisted that it had a duty to its shareholders. All in all, its numerous critics found in the events of 1837 and 1839 enough to hold the Bank guilty of having contributed to them by failing to restrict credit, either from culpable neglect or from the inadequacy of the means at its disposal. The pressure mounted for a statutorily ordained rule of control. And the Bank itself was not averse to the notion of release from the embarrassments of discretionary power and the yapping of its critics. From this body of feeling there emerged the Bank Act of 1844.

The 1844 Act took its departure from the generally held identification of notes with credit. It was not denied that other forms of money were used but notes were the most widely employed form and their volume, it was believed, governed the total volume of all forms of money. Its object, then, was to appoint a stable balance between notes and gold by centralising note issue in the Bank of England, the repository of most of the nation's gold, and by compelling the Bank to regulate its note issue according to its gold state. It avoided the extreme of requiring one hundred per cent gold backing, aiming only at such a gold ratio as would meet any likely requirements of gold against notes, and acknowledged the special position of Scotland, which had never except in the most nominal way operated on a gold backed currency, by exempting that country from its provisions. In summary form, it laid down: (1) No newly founded bank thenceafter could issue notes. (2) No existing bank which did not currently issue notes could thenceafter do so. (3) Any bank currently issuing notes was to forfeit its right to do so on merger with any other bank. (4) Banks continuing to issue could not do so beyond an amount equivalent to their average issue over the twelve weeks preceding 27 April 1844. (5) The Bank of England, separated into distinct Issue and Banking departments, could only issue notes to the amount of gold held by the issue department *plus* £14 million *plus* two thirds of the permitted issue forfeited under (3). (The curious-looking (3) represents an attempt to achieve the ultimate extinction of private issue in a way that was compatible with the age's notion of property rights.)

Three years after the passing of the Act, the crisis of 1847 necessitated the temporary suspension of the limits on Bank of England note issue, as did the crises of 1857 and 1866. The Act, that is to say, was acknowledged to be incapable of application in precisely those conditions which it had been framed to prevent. It was in fact a monumental irrelevancy. Credit was in practice no more governed by bank notes than bank notes in practice had been governed by gold. For the panic-engendering threat of an exhaustion of gold it had simply substituted the panic engendering threat of an exhaustion of notes. And whenever that threat was about to materialise it had to be alleviated by removing the limits on note issue,[1] reopening the Bank of England's gold store to whatever demands the volume of money in circulation might make on it.

Ironically, the Act's inability to achieve that control of the money supply which it purported to secure ensured that it was merely an irrelevancy and not a new source of danger to the economy. Sustained raising of the level of economic activity through the decades following the Act required a roughly corresponding increase in the supply of money. Alternatively put, a failure of the money supply to increase would have frustrated economic growth.[2] In the outcome, however, the Act had erred not only in underestimating short-run elasticity between notes and money supply, but in missing the secular trend for cheques, and even bonds and securities which bypassed the banking system altogether, to replace notes in the settlement of transactions – i.e. a diminishing norm notes/money ratio. Had the Act not so blundered it would not have survived. That it did survive – until 1914 – was in the

[1] In 1847 and 1866 the mere assurance that the potential note supply was unlimited was enough to stay alarm. Only in 1857 was it found necessary to issue beyond the 1844 limits.
[2] In theory an increased velocity of circulation could permit of growth with a fixed money supply. But it is not easy to hypothesise a mechanism which would automatically adjust velocity in such circumstances.

short run due to contemporary inability to devise any generally acceptable replacement along with the readiness to sweep it under the carpet whenever it became dangerous, and in the longer run to the diminished proneness of the banking system at large to fail under pressure. (The foregoing remarks have been addressed to the central feature of the 1844 Act, the attempt to control the money supply. The extinction of private note issue, undertaken in the course of this purpose, may be allowed to have been a desirable object in itself in so far as noteholders at times of alarm might seek to encash private notes where they would rest easy with Bank of England notes.)

Although Peel, Prime Minister, Chancellor of the Exchequer and architect-in-chief of the 1844 Act, seems to have conceived of the Act as an ultimate safeguard against overissue rather than as a fully automatic system of credit control, the Bank of England inclined towards apprehending it in the latter sense and to the consequent view that credit control was now mechanically attended to by its Issue department, leaving the Banking department free to pursue an ordinary commercial discount policy. That is not to say that it considered itself to have unbridled licence to discount continuously as freely as its resources would allow, if only because the Bank itself might be a sufferer in any crash resulting from an overextension of speculative positions to whose build up it could, as a chief source of credit, contribute powerfully – and nobody believed that the Act was foolproof against a total abandonment of all but the most shortsighted commercial view on the part of the Bank. But it is to say that the Bank which had, over the previous decade or so, been edging towards a passive lender of secondary resort role, waiting for borrowers to come to it rather than going down into the marketplace itself, now entered much more freely into everyday discount business. And, more weightily, it is to say that the Bank considered itself absolved from any requirement to evolve new, more effective, techniques of central bank operation, and absolved also from any strict obligation to come to the rescue of the banking system as a whole at times of pressure, as it had done conspicuously in 1825. Neither had it before the Act ever pledged itself to such a line as a matter of principle, nor after the Act did it in practice leave the banking system entirely without support at moments of crisis; but an explicit acknowledgement of a permanent duty to discount good paper at bank rate might have steadied nerves in crises and in practice relieved it of much of the pressure which uncertainty and apprehension generated at such junctures.

All in all, the 1844 Act, if it did not occasion actual regression, certainly arrested for a good two decades the evolution of central banking in England. Until the late 'sixties the Bank continued to take the view that it was just a very large commercial institution, in its peculiar gold-holding role governed by statutory regulations, and for the rest grudgingly conceding that it could not be totally indifferent to the wider repercussions of its actions. The crisis of 1866, however, does seem to have had a traumatic effect. Certainly over the closing years of this period and through the immediately following ones, in both avowed principle and in operational practice, the Bank of England rapidly transformed itself. By 1880 it had withdrawn entirely from ordinary commercial discounting, was in clear intent employing bank rate in penal fashion, when necessary engaging in open market operations[1] to make it bite, and was professedly prepared to act as lender of last resort on all good paper.

The disappearance of crises from the British economic scene from just around the end of this period marks the close of an era in the history of the monetary and banking system; an era which could be said to have begun towards the middle of the seventeenth century and whose essential characteristic is a slow – and often painful – institutional and psychological adjustment to the phenomenon of 'created' or 'fictitious' money – a sort of economic Frankenstein, which men had made but had taken over two centuries to learn to control. The year 1873 is perhaps a peculiarly suitable date with which to terminate this era, being as it was one of potential rather than actual crisis – a crisis stayed by a developed capacity to handle the phenomenon. But it was not only, or even primarily, the evolution of the Bank of England towards an authentic central bank rate which made for the taming of the monster. Nor indeed was it solely a matter of autonomous adjustments to money. Exogenous factors, diminishing the force of the sort of circumstances which could create a potential crisis situation, played a part too: a more fully multilateral international payments system, curbing the violence of gold movements; factors fining down the extremes of speculative activity which in its various forms could contribute so powerfully to crisis: better international communications and the development of 'futures' dealings restrained commodity speculation; a more generally informed awareness of the real extent of profit

---

[1] In the years in question: itself borrowing from the money market in order to draw enough liquid funds out of the commercial banks as to compel them to refuse discount facilities, thus forcing the bill dealers to come to the Bank of England.

possibilities braked down on share and investment speculation. But perhaps the most important developments in making for greater stability of the system were the closely associated strengthening of the structure of commercial banking and increasing confidence of the general public in that structure.

The virtues of joint stock banking, and more specifically branch banking, were dwelt on in the last chapter. Progress towards concentration of banking capital and towards geographical diversification through this period was, admittedly, uneven and not especially rapid. The boom of 1833–37 did bring a great increase in joint stock foundations, both by way of entirely new concerns and by way of the fusion of existing concerns accompanied by the recruitment of outside capital – generally to finance expansion but sometimes just a liquidation for cash of some part of the original owners' share in the business. By the time of the 1844 Act something like a half of the country's banking business was in the hands of joint stock concerns – and more joint stock capital was vested in banking than in any other activity bar the railways. But while they constituted larger capital concentrations on average than did the private[1] banks, these joint stock concerns, about 120 in number, were by later standards still very small and their operations were still highly localised, a number of them having no branches at all. Quite often joint stock was little more than a propaganda medium, it being expected that shareholders in a bank would keep their account with that bank. And the 1844 Act, framed to take advantage of the current vogue for joint stock, quite evidently placed a check on the extension of joint stock business. Peel and his advisers had badly miscalculated in supposing that the enthusiasm for merger would, under the issue forfeiture provision of the Act, lead to the rapid extinction of private notes. At the end of this period, over half the 207 banks issuing in 1844 were still doing so and the proportion of total private issue rights surviving was rather higher since it was generally the smaller issuers who had disappeared. The right of issue was in fact jealously guarded, not lightly surrendered against the advantage of merger. Even where it was not a direct source of profit – and with lower liquidity ratios becoming safe it was more likely to be – it still had an advertising value and, moreover, a simple prestigiousness. Just how much weight is to be attached to this specific inhibition one could not say but it is clear that through the

---

[1] An unfortunate ambiguity attaches to 'private' used with regard to banks, sometimes, as here, denoting non-joint stock, sometimes especially in connection with note issue, denoting all banks other than the Bank of England.

three or four decades following the Act private banking lost no more ground and even perhaps, in an expanding market, gained some; while only a handful of joint stock concerns grew (by absorption of lesser banks) with any marked freedom, and none achieved a truly national network. By the end of this period the London and County had about 150 branches, the National Provincial nearly as many, but these were the only two in the hundred-plus class, while some half a dozen others counted fifty-plus each. And although some mergers between joint stock banks had taken place, fresh ones had been founded so that the total number of distinct joint stock concerns in 1873 was almost exactly the same as it had been in 1844.[1] Nevertheless, in combination, the strong initial intrusion of joint stock between the Acts of 1826 and 1844, and the more continuous dropping out of the smallest and most frail private banks, along with a certain amount of private merging which stopped short of going joint stock, roughly halved the number of separate banking concerns during this period; a period which must have seen the volume of bank liabilities at least triple and possibly increase by a good deal more. Concentration had certainly not occurred in the degree to which it was to be experienced over the next forty or fifty years, and banking was still very regional in character. But organisation had within this period recorded substantial, if gradual, gains in point of the solidity and resilience of its component members.

It was not only in respect of the greater risk spread via more customers per bank and of the greater mobility of funds via branch banking that structure had been fortified. The asset composition of the average bank was much better geared to its liabilities in 1873 than it had been in 1830. Banks in close and informed touch with mercantile life in great trading centres had always been able to employ their funds with due regard to security and liquidity, and such enhanced viability as they came to enjoy through this period would be largely due to considerations already raised. It was the common type of country banker, private or joint stock, with no obvious local outlets for his funds whose situation showed the most marked improvement. Already in the previous chapter we noted the emergence in London in the early years of the nineteenth century of a class of bill brokers whose particular vocation it was to find employment in trade bills for the surplus funds of the country banker. Through this period that facility was greatly extended, and

[1] All the figures of bank numbers in this paragraph relate to England and Wales only. Scotland's established joint stock and branch banking system experienced substantial growth but no essential change through this period.

added to by the evolution of many of these bill brokers into bill dealers, operating on their own account with bank funds borrowed at call or short notice. The advantage of either broker or dealer to the banker was that it gave him the effective services of men thoroughly familiar with the bill market. But the dealer offered two further advantages: he bore the risk – the broker did not normally guarantee the bills he supplied – and the funds loaned could be more quickly retrieved than on a bill whose maturity had to be awaited. In practice, of course, the distinction was not quite as clearcut: the broker could not supply many bad bills without losing his business and if the dealer misjudged his bill acquisitions so badly as to bankrupt himself, the bank just had to line up with his other creditors. As to liquidity: if money was easy a bill could always be rediscounted, and if money was really tight the dealer might not in fact be able to pay on demand. The differences were ones of degree rather than kind. And the degree was such as to make an important new class of highly liquid assets available to banks, such that they could lower their cash ratios, enlarge the income-earning proportion of their assets and thus reduce the temptation to dabble with unwise forms of lending to make up for a high proportion of 'dead' money carried.

The specific liquidity advantage offered by the dealer was of interest to all kinds of banks, not just country ones with problems of access to suitable forms of lending. Especially from about mid-century onwards a good deal of both metropolitan and provincial bank money was in the hands of the discount houses – as, with a growth in stature, the bill dealers came to be styled. And it should be pointed out that, while the immediate position of the banks benefited from the development, financial structure as a whole was only strengthend to the extent that bill dealing was increasingly committed to a keenly specialised professional expertise; and that the liquidity of the system as a whole was impaired to the extent that banks lowered their cash ratios. Effectively it meant that an individual bank wanting cash in a hurry drew it from other banks via the discount houses. At a time of general pressure for cash this obviously could not work; and with less cash currently in the system the burden on the ultimate source of cash, the Bank of England, was increased. And the actual pressure on the Bank came specifically from the discount houses, when they found their normal cash sources, the private banks, closed up. So long as the Bank was an active competitor with the discount houses in the bill market, it resented being expected to bail them out at times of difficulty. In practice it did do so;

but until the Bank withdrew from ordinary commercial discounting and constituted itself as an authentic lender of last resort, the threat always lurked of the whole house of cards being brought down by the collapse of the bill dealers.

Towards the longer end of bank asset range the period brought both problems and solutions, of a kind, to those problems. The problems ran back to about 1820. For over forty years before that date, war and the aftermath of war had almost continuously kept interest rates on government securities up to four, five, six and even more per cent. But from 1820, odd years of minor budgetary deficit and those of the not very expensive Crimean War (1854–56) apart, the state ceased to borrow and, indeed, even started on the task of clearing off its mountain of debt: from £840 million in 1820 the National Debt had fallen to £732 million by 1873 – although it was still easily the largest debtor institution in the country and its outstanding fixed interest securities still the most important class of long-term and readily negotiable asset available. With money actually coming on to the market from the government, the return on government stock edged downwards; from mid-century onwards it usually hovered between 3 and 3¼ per cent – not calculated to yield very handsome bank profit margins.

At the same time a variety of other fixed interest stocks were becoming available, offering not only better rates but a range of maturity dates which permitted the careful banker to graduate his portfolio so as to ensure a fairly regular fall in of cash. These were the bonds and securities of home and foreign railway companies and other public utilities – the foreign ones often carrying an official guarantee of interest – and those of overseas governments, central, provincial and local. Over the whole range there was of course very wide variation in real security, from such as Latin American stocks (which were pure gamble) to Indian and colonial government stocks which could be deemed to be underwritten by the power of the British government (which was, however, punctilious in refusing any formal guarantee). Although bankers made some costly mistakes in their selections from the range, most conspicuously in their heavy purchases of USA securities in the mid-'thirties, and the temptations of 7 and 8 per cent returns were not always as rigorously resisted as sound banking dictated, with a modest degree of discernment – especially from the mid-'fifties onwards – 4 and 5 per cent could be earned with only minimal risk.

All in all, over the last couple of decades of this period, loans to the bill market, trade bills, British government and other fixed interest securities, an institutional mechanism which gave ready access to those and in all normal circumstances permitted of their ready realisation,[1] lent British banking an asset spread ensuring that balance between safety, liquidity and profitability which is the essence of successful banking. With the greater part of its funds thus properly deployed, British banking could the more safely allow some part to be devoted to financing long-term productive investment. How far it went in this direction, and how much further it could usefully and sensibly have gone, are questions which lie beyond the scope of available data. On the one hand, in formal principle bankers set their faces much more firmly than before against this illiquid kind of lending and one may imagine in particular that the branch manager in a joint stock concern was not permitted the latitude of personal judgment that the owner of a private banking business might sometimes allow himself in financing a local business venture. On the other hand, it is certainly the case that overdraft accommodation, nominally liable to short notice recall, could on occasions run on indefinitely and, in effect, provide long-term finance. Such laxity would hardly be extended to the adventurer struggling to launch an enterprise, nor would it normally be of sufficient extent to be of much assistance to the established enterprise set on a planned course of substantial build-up of capacity. But that considerable sector of the British economy which was in the hands of single owners, families, small partnerships, with well-rooted businesses and only modest growth ambitions may well have found this sort of thing useful in helping to finance those marginal additions to unit capacity which in sum constituted a major component of national economic expansion. And this informal provision of investment capital aside, there was also that subscription to railway and other public utility debentures already referred to. Neither as a proportion of total bank funds nor as a proportion of total fixed investment can these forms of bank finance have been large but they might claim a place worth entering on a list of contemporary fixed capital sources which would, however, be dominated by retained profits, private financial contacts and funds openly invited from the general public.

Strengthened organisation and sounder asset structure brought cumulative gains: fewer bank failures enhanced public confidence; enhanced public confidence reduced runs on banks at times of crises and diminished the number of failures. After the crisis of 1825 bank

[1] The internal telegraph system, generalised by about 1865, was a useful element in this respect.

mortality declined at each succeeding one and those of 1857 and 1866 did no more than expose one or two cases of internal rot which sooner or later was bound to have been fatal anyway. In fact, the banks in more senses than one were distinctly further removed from these two crises than from earlier ones. Both 1857 and 1866 were the culminating points of massive booms in world trade in which Britain was a major participant, not only in respect of the actual goods involved but also as a source, or a prop, of the credit which sustained the booms. Much of this credit did not emanate, directly at least, from the banking system. The conventional trade bill element in it was supported largely by the discounting activity of the London bill dealers, while a fair amount of it took more unconventional forms: bonds and shares of railway contracting concerns, railway companies and other corporate organisations, as well as simple credit arrangements with suppliers which did not take negotiable documentary form. In 1857, indeed, much of it was not even of British origin but had been remitted to London for realisation or had been accepted by British suppliers against overseas orders. The USA figured prominently amongst its generators and it was a severe price set back on the New York stock exchange which triggered off the crisis.

The crisis of 1866 was more of a domestic event, speculative railway building at home and dealing in Indian cotton for delivery to Liverpool being major contributory factors, while the specific triggering agent in this case was the spectacular crash of the great discount house, Overend and Gurney, not essentially due to its discount business but to its having dabbled widely and unwisely in other fields.

On both occasions the banking system at large had come under severe pressure, but the pressure had been successfully withstood and it was the 1844 Bank Act and the Bank of England amongst banking institutions whose defects were the most clearly exposed. But 1866 was the last event of its kind. Only seven years later all the ingredients of the 1857 crisis were again present: a marked increase in world trade, buoyed up by a variety of credit instruments and closely associated with a feverish burst of railway building; the USA again very much to the fore and taking a headlong fall with the Wall Street crash in September of 1873, whose shock-waves had by early November pushed London bank rate up to 9 per cent. Yet there was no genuine crisis in Britain, no fiercely intense pressure for cash, no suspension of the 1844 Act, no great wave of bankruptcies in commercial circles and no downturn in the general level of economic activity. The credit system had come of age.

The economic role of the state

In dealing with the credit system reference has been made to the role of the state, while at other odd points also the issue of state economic policy has been raised. It is a theme which must be treated in its own right.

Eighty years ago Arnold Toynbee in a famous course of lectures which gave historical shape to the idea of an 'Industrial Revolution' said: 'The *essence* of the Industrial Revolution is the substitution of competition for the medieval regulations which had previously controlled the production and distribution of wealth' (my italics). And for many subsequent decades the notion that this putative revolution in habits of mind was an integral and crucial element in the transformation of the economy remained historical gospel. Examination questions required Adam Smith and *The Wealth of Nations* (1776) to be ranked with Richard Arkwright and the water frame, with James Watt and the steam engine, and with the other great names and events which in a simpler age of historiography than our own could constitute the 'Industrial Revolution'. Nowadays all has changed and of Toynbee's assertion nothing substantial survives. We know now that the edifice of medieval regulation had been falling into desuetude since the seventeenth century; that long before Adam Smith gave it a fully explicit and evolved doctrinal utterance, an attitude which amounted to *laissez-faire* in practice had prevailed in state counsels, though not absolutely; and that at no time after Adam Smith did the principle that the economy should be left to the ungoverned play of the profit motive ever secure a total ascendancy. Above all, we are a great deal more sceptical of the force of grand abstractions in determining political behaviour, a great deal more suspicious of the authenticity of reputed ideological convictions when cited in support of this or that programme of action – or inaction, and a great deal less readily persuaded of the pervasive bearing of such programmes on the course actually taken by the economy.

It is not so much that the surface history of state activity in the economic field cannot still be made to square with the Toynbee thesis. The story of a steady lifting of officially interposed checks to free competition still stands up to historical scrutiny, if the original sharpness of definition is allowed to blur both in respect of chronology and in respect of material extent. What cannot be accepted is that the motives and calculations lying behind this sequence reduce themselves to a single economic dogma, and, equally, that a phase of historically unprecedented growth on the part of the British economy is to be uniquely, or even substantially, explained by reference to a collection of legislative reforms.

Having said so much it would perhaps be as well to suggest straight away the broad terms of an alternative general representation of the state's part in the economy through the late eighteenth century and the first three-quarters or so of the nineteenth – after which the pressures of a fairly thoroughly democratic electorate start to exert their special effects. So far as internal regulation is concerned, the only question of real weight is not how far the state went in scrapping existing controls, but how far it was prepared to go in placing new limits on economic freedom. Already by the second half of the eighteenth century, the law of the market ruled unchallenged throughout nearly all sectors of the internal economy. Succeeding years just saw the final sweeping away of one or two special survivals and a certain amount of clearing out of long dead lumber from the statute book. On the more important question of new conditions which might suggest the need of state intervention to limit the free play of market forces, establishment response might be summarised as having been founded in a pragmatism with which a measure of social conscience was intermingled, a pragmatism which had prime reference to the interests of the moneyed classes who composed the political nation.

To account for the limited extent of state intervention in the economy there is no need to invoke the imperious sway of an abstract doctrine but simply the fundamental fact that wealth was being accumulated as never before. Why should the beneficiaries of this process wish to interfere with its operation? Where at odd points the economic mechanism seemed defective in serving their ends, they were perfectly ready to employ the power of the state. Control of the monetary system was entrusted to the law. The public transport system was kept under continuous public surveillance. And while in the end it was decided that it was not necessary to commit the railway network to state ownership, the telegraph network was removed from private ownership and incorporated with the state postal service in 1870. The telegraph companies were fully, indeed over fully, paid for their property. And, more generally, regard for property rights was a cardinal feature of establishment attitudes. But this is hardly matter for comment in the case of a property-owning establishment. If anything is matter for comment it is the growing extent to which it was acknowledged that property had its duties as well as its rights, and the increasing degree to which property was compelled by law to perform its duties: legislation on conditions of employment in factories and mines; legislation requiring ratepayers to pay for public health and education. That by later standards this sort of thing was of restricted efficacy is, in this particular context, of much less significance than the fact that the nineteenth century brought a swelling amount of it whereas the eighteenth century had felt no need for it at all. None of this is to say that the principles of the classical economists were not often on the lips of public men. Doubtless the occasional conscience was stilled by the 'iron law of wages' and the satisfaction of a fortune enhanced by the reflection that one had been but moved by the 'hidden hand of God'. But the particular vocabulary of politics and social justification cannot in itself be treated as an important fact of history.

It is when one turns to the external regulation of the economy that the classical economics lays a claim to having been authentically efficacious in refashioning the techniques of commercial policy. The objective of external commercial policy was, in the nineteenth century as in the twentieth, the maximisation of national wealth. The need to insist on this truism is that in the mouths of its most vocal spokesmen such as Richard Cobden and John Bright, the policy of free trade could take on a quasireligious aspect, contriving to suggest that in abolishing tariffs and other protective devices one was serving a divinely appointed purpose; that protection was not just an error of commercial judgment but a mighty offence in the eyes of the Lord; that it was Britain's providential mission in the world to bear free trade along with Bibles and breeches to the unevangelised. Nothing perhaps has contributed so powerfully to the British reputation for sanctimonious hypocrisy than the world's experience in the nineteenth century of the pulpit style in which it was urged to cooperate in making Britain richer. From the particular viewpoint of a historian what is troublesome is that the gospel was preached with such earnestness that even today it still leaves its marks on general accounts of nineteenth-century British history, the rise of free trade being commonly described in tones which would be more apposite to the rise of Christianity and a sequence of calculated commercial measures described as the gradual unfolding of revealed truth. After generations of a representation of nineteenth-century commercial policy as a question of moral rectitude, it seems extraordinarily difficult even for professional historians to get back to a simple appraisal of it as a question of commercial advantage and, while not necessarily ignoring the curious rhetoric often attaching to it – which is at least a point of sociological interest – to treat of it as essentially a reflection of the changing status of Britain in the international economy.

The rule of commercial judgment which the nineteenth century added to the formation of external economic policy and which could with some legitimacy be said to have been the special contribution of the classical economists was that in the long run a country could only expand its exports in the proportion to which it expanded its imports.[1] Now politicians, notoriously, are not takers of the long view. The clear recognition of this long-run truth by no means revolutionised the conduct of British commercial policy. There was no important step taken which can be unambiguously attributed to this specific argument; those which could be justified in such terms were also capable of justification in other terms as well. It was for the most part short-run considerations which led to wide-ranging tariff reduction and abolition. But it must be allowed that this movement proceeded further and faster on account of the belief that to facilitate the entry of imports was to promote opportunities for exports. That is, however, to say that the grand principle of the free trade purists simply supplied added momentum to a course which would have been pursued anyway. Leaving aside for the moment one or two measures which might be argued as exceptions, it is to insist that the lines of nineteenth-century commercial policy were set by criteria which already prevailed in the eighteenth century and that the differences in actual outcome reflect not any radical revision of principles but a radical change in objective circumstances. If there were a revolution in official thinking on tariff policy it had taken place around the end of the seventeenth century and the early eighteenth with the endeavour to weigh in commercial considerations with fiscal considerations in the shaping of the customs structure.

To come closer to particulars: to the very considerable extent to which nineteenth-century tariff reform had the objects of diminishing the burden of duties on raw materials borne by British manufacturers and of increasing the cost efficiency of the revenue system, it was acting in a fully established tradition. What was new was the extent to which the nineteenth century could further the aim of simplification of the system by scrapping duties of formerly protective effect on goods which were now largely or wholly excluded by the superiority of the

[1] The ultimate *laissez-faire* argument was that consumer satisfaction was maximised by such international specialisation as comparative regional costs would freely determine. But in this pure form it subsumed full international mobility of labour – neither an assumption which fitted the actual facts nor a goal which any state was likely to set itself. If this argument had any bearing on the formation of policy, it was only by way of directing attention to consumers' interests, while preclassical economic thinking had been largely preoccupied with producers' interests.

British product – duties, that is, which had become void of any substantial value, commercial or fiscal, and served only to clutter up the rate books and complicate the work of customs officers. Another nineteenth-century circumstance which permitted either of general reductions or of the abolition of particular low yield, administratively inconvenient, tariffs was the fact that after 1815 imports in gross grew much more rapidly than government expenditure. In brief, an immense proportion of the nineteenth-century tariff reform, and one might say all of that contained in the two great batches of 1825 and 1842, is fully explicable by reference to official aims which were already old at the beginning of the century and to economic circumstances which allowed these aims to be carried into far-reaching effect.

Two types of tariff reduction in which the new free trade doctrine might be considered to have played a more decisive part are left out of account in that last statement. The one relates to a kind of circumstance which had not in any serious way confronted an earlier age: one where a British commodity in enjoyment of a protective duty was unable fully to supply an important domestic need. Here it was a matter of weighing the respective interests of home producers and home consumers. The outstanding instance in point is, of course, that of corn. The considerations attaching to the repeal of the Corn Laws have already been noted and all that need be summarily repeated here by way of reminder is that, while at the level of public controversy the issue was cast very much in terms of Free Trade *versus* Protection, this was to oversimplify and distort the essential facts of the matter. However, it would be as much a misrepresentation of the case to pose repeal as just a pragmatic preferring of the welfare of bread eaters to the profits of farmers and the rents of landowners as it would be to pose it as just a triumph of one economic theory over another. If the issue was decided in favour of consumers, it was in at least some significant part because the wider ranging argument of the Free Trade purists conduced to that resolution. And the same observation may hold for the repeal in 1853 of the duties on imported tin, lead and copper which involved essentially similar considerations, with the British producers of these metals, which were already having to be imported to supplement home supplies, in the place of farmers and landlords and the users of the metals in the place of the bread-consuming public – and with the free traders, so to speak, the arbiters in preferring the interests of one to those of the other. But what it is sought to stress here is that in this kind of case there was a direct collision of economic interests which had to be decided one way or the other, whether or not a principle of purportedly universal applicability offered itself as sovereign arbiter.

The type of tariff reduction which is most clearly attributable to free trade doctrine is that which exposed a protected industry to serious foreign competition in a case where there was no real need of the imported product; where the home producer was sacrificed to provide putative export opportunities for other home producers; where the intention was to shift labour and capital away from an activity which in an international comparison was inefficiently conducted towards ones in which these resources would find optimum employment, whatever the hardship caused by the immediate dislocation; in other words, a move which could only be economically justified in authentic *laissez-faire* terms.

The fact of the matter is, however, that anyway into the nineteenth century, Britain had only one industry of any extent which could offer itself for sacrifice in this way: the silk industry. It was sacrificed. But even here the manner of the sacrifice leaves room for arguing that the measure fell short of being a perfect embodiment of Free Trade doctrine, though some may feel that the argument belongs more to a handbook of casuistry than to an economic history. Protection for the silk industry was given up under the Anglo-French Trade Treaty of 1860. Since this was a reciprocal arrangement, France lowering duties on a range of manufactures, it can be contended that the silk industry was bargained against concessions of calculated equivalence; that it was swapped instead of being unilaterally deprived of that protection to which by the pure lights of free trade it had no claim anyway; that to qualify as a genuine free trade measure it should have been sacrificed for the speculative advantages which that doctrine posited, not for precisely prescribed ones. But in whatever terms the dismantling of protection for British silk goods is to be explained, the important point in this context is that it was the only industry of weight in respect of which commercial policy could have clearly evinced a belief in the correctness of the classical analysis.

This one case apart, it was not of any fundamental consequence whether British statesmen were devotees of *laissez-faire* economics or not. British manufactures could go unprotected because they no longer had any need of protection. Tariff policy could concentrate on restructuring the system of duties so as to yield such revenue as was needed with the minimum of administrative effort and expense, and with as little taxing of economic enterprise as was consonant with that end. To repeat oneself: the nineteenth-century economy enabled a tariff policy inherited from the eighteenth century to be pushed to a conclusion.

The economy in its external aspects

The essential contention of the preceding paragraphs has been that so far as external economic relations were concerned the crucial change occurred not in the principles governing commercial policy but in an intensifying integration of the British economy with the world economy which permitted of, and to a degree compelled, a radical simplification of the tariff system. Put in a single broad context, this intensification may be summarised by saying that at the outset of the period about one-sixth of total national income was earned abroad; by mid-century that proportion had edged up to about a fifth; and by the end of the period it had shot up to about two-fifths. These figures of course comprehend both 'visible' and 'invisible' transactions. Turning first to visible trade the process may be stated more particularly as shown in Table II.27.

TABLE II.27. *British foreign trade as percentage of gross national income*

	1831	1841	1851	1861	1871
Retained imports	14	16	18	27	30
Domestic exports	10	11	14	19	25

(These figures are derived from the relevant base data contained in B. R. Mitchell and P. Deane, *Abstract of British Historical Statistics*, with the UK trade values contained there notionally adjusted to allow for the Irish element.)

The levels attained by the end of the period need no verbal commentary to invest the figures with rhetorical impact. What may usefully be stressed is the abruptness of the upturns, especially in regard to exports. Expressed in this manner exports had been gently declining from around the beginning of the century up to the early 'thirties, when the movement more or less levelled off, and then suddenly leaped upwards in 1849.

Graph II.3a affords a more detailed chronological indication of the behaviour of exports, illustrating the contrast between the quarter-century 1849–73 and the preceding years, as well as demonstrating how

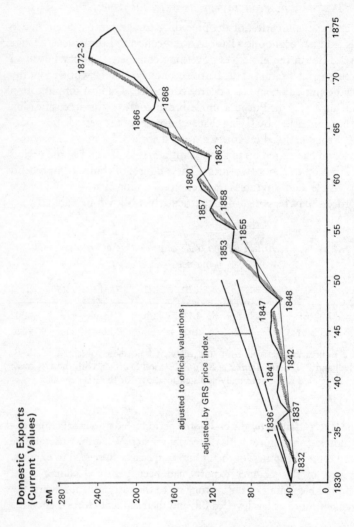

Domestic Exports (Current Values)

£M

adjusted to official valuations

adjusted by GRS price index

GRAPH II.3A. *Export values 1830–75*

Percentages of Total Domestic Exports

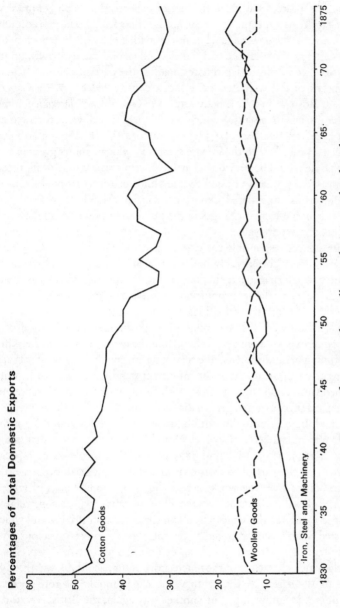

Cotton Goods

Woollen Goods

Iron, Steel and Machinery

1830   '35   '40   '45   '50   '55   '60   '65   '70   1875

GRAPH II.3B. *Exports of cotton goods, woollen goods, iron, steel and machinery, 1830–75*

the upsurge of that quarter-century took the form of a broken series of bursts. As a direct statistical measure of exports, the graph is not very satisfactory. As a measure of *real values* it suffers from taking no account of changes in the general level of prices, with a consequent tendency to overstate growth after the early 'fifties and to understate growth up to that time. It would be legitimate to adjust the current values 1830–50 by means of the weighted price index constructed by A. D. Gayer, W. W. Rostow and A. J. Schwartz (*The Growth and Fluctuation of the British Economy 1790–1850*) which would yield a 'real' value for 1850 of £94·5 million, on a base of £38·3 million for 1830. But the applicability of such a procedure to the intense spasms in which exports grew in the later phase would be very questionable since price changes during those spasms were primarily caused by the same keen international demand conditions as engendered export growth. A price index would not reflect genuine secular changes in the purchasing power of money and to discount export values by it would in effect be to discount the very circumstances responsible for export growth. As a measure of *volume* the graph very considerably underrates achievement up to about mid-century when marked reductions in the factor costs of textiles, constituting a very large proportion of total exports, were still being effected.[1] (At 'official' valuations exports in 1830 were £61·2 million; in 1850 they were £175·4 million.) Thus the usefulness in itself of a record of exports at current values, as in the graph, is more as marking the timing of significant change than as measuring the magnitude of such change which, from the most important standpoint – that of income earned from exporting – is most satisfactorily indicated by its representation as a proportion of gross national income, as in Table II.27 above.

Graph II.3b helps to distinguish the agency chiefly responsible for the intermittent character of export growth. The export booms culminating in 1847, 1853, 1857 and 1873 coincided with phases of especial growth on the part of exports of iron and machinery. In other words, these booms were the work of periodic international bursts of investment in fixed equipment – above all, in railways, whose construction abroad exhibited the same convulsive character as in Britain, and which reacted with peculiar potency on the world's most capacious iron industry. As effectively noted earlier,[2] the 'boom – crisis – depression' cycle which characterised the nineteenth-century economy was through the third quarter of the century more commonly of foreign than of domestic authorship; put another way again, the British economy

---

[1] On the implications of this see p. 482n.   [2] See p. 624.

of this phase was very much an 'export led' economy – in the sense that the most volatile of the major variables involved was export demand. Yet this feature should not be overstressed. The boom which broke in 1866 consisted in substantial part of a domestic railway construction spate; and the admittedly strong export element in the boom was principally supplied by a leap in woollen exports (rounded off with an increase in cotton exports as they recovered from the American Civil War), reflecting not so much intense international demand conditions, such as engendered spurts in exports of producers' goods, as the final attainment by the British woollen industry of the kind of competitive advantage which the cotton industry had secured decades earlier; that is to say, it was a 'secular' rather than a 'cyclic' phenomenon. More generally, while it is proper to emphasise the special role of international investment booms in prompting particular bursts of export acceleration, this should not obscure the strong base trend, persisting through boom and relapse, not only of exports of consumer goods, which might be expected to show a constancy of tendency, but also of producers' goods which could find ample markets even in the absence of special boom conditions. Indeed, iron benefited from the railway booms as much by way of the steep price rises engendered as by way of an increase in physical sales.

The details of the principal long run shifts in the pattern of British foreign trade have already been indicated in dealing with the particular economic activities concerned and it will suffice here to summarise them in broad statistical form with a minimum of further commentary (Table II.28).

TABLE II.28. *Principal domestic exports* (*percentages*)

	1829–31	1850–52	1872–74
Cotton goods	49	39	31
Woollen goods	13	13	13
Linen goods	6	7	4
Hardwares	4	4	2
Iron and steel	3	9	14
Machinery	0·5	2	4
Coal	0·5	2	5
Chemicals	—	1	4
Re-exports as percentage of total exports	15	14	19

TABLE II.29. *Markets for UK exports (percentages)*

	Northern Europe			Southern Europe	
	Domestic exports	Re-exports		Domestic exports	Re-exports
1829–31	21	—	1829–31	18	—
1854–56	13	*33*	1854–56	25	*49*
1872–74	18	*28*	1872–74	28	*53*

	USA			Latin America	
	Domestic exports	Re-exports		Domestic exports	Re-exports
1829–31	19	—	1829–31	13	—
1854–56	20	*4*	1854–56	9	*2*
1872–74	14	*7*	1872–74	9	*3*

	Asia			Africa	
	Domestic exports	Re-exports		Domestic exports	Re-exports
1829–31	12	—	1829–31	2	—
1854–56	13	*3*	1854–56	3	*2*
1872–74	15	*3*	1872–74	3	*1*

	Canada			Australasia	
	Domestic exports	Re-exports		Domestic exports	Re-exports
1829–31	5	—	1829–31	0·5	—
1854–56	4	*1*	1854–56	9	*7*
1872–74	4	*2*	1872–74	7	*3*

	West Indies	
	Domestic exports	Re-exports
1829–31	10	—
1854–56	3	*1*
1872–74	2	*1*

(The separate figures for 'Northern Europe' and 'Southern Europe', 1829–31 are not directly comparable with those for later years. In 1829–31 the designations refer to ports of entry, 'northern' denoting all ports north and east of the Franco-Belgian frontier, 'southern' all others including those of the Ottoman Empire. In 1854–56 and 1872–74 they refer to ultimate destinations, 'northern' denoting Scandinavia, Russia, Germany and the Austrian Empire, 'southern' the remainder, including the Ottoman Empire. The principal effect of the change in classification is to transfer the Low Countries from 'northern' to 'southern'. Re-export figures are not available before 1854.)

Of the domestic commodities exported, nothing need be said which has not been said already in one connection or another. Table II.29 (markets) however merits a few brief observations. The reversal over the later part of the period of the long established trend for Europe to decline in relative importance is particularly noteworthy. Coal had a prominent hand in this and so had the tardy breakthrough in woollen textiles. Rail penetration of market areas was of assistance, particularly in Russia where the railways also greatly facilitated the movement out of grain, enhancing the country's external purchasing power. But more impressive than the opening up of backward Russia is the great increase in exports to the most forward parts of the Continent: Germany, the Low Countries and France (Table II.30). Here the increase was a

TABLE II.30. *UK exports to Russia, Germany, Holland, Belgium and France (current values, £ m., annual averages)*

Period	Russia	Germany	Holland	Belgium	France	Total domestic exports
1850–52	1·3	7·7	3·7	1·1	2·4	74·6
1872–74	8·1	27·9	15·8	6·5	17·0	250·4
Increase by factor of	*6·2*	*3·6*	*4·3*	*5·9*	*7·1*	*3·4*

function precisely of the rapidity of industrialisation in countries which were now passing through their own 'revolutions', and could do so the more easily for being able to draw on Britain for iron, machinery, coal, chemicals, etc., bypassing bottlenecks in their own supply capacities.[1] The USA of course was going through the same phase; but here, self-sufficiency in much of the industrial field was attained earlier than on the continent – American engineering precocity has already been remarked on – and it was largely America's exceptional requirements of iron for her gigantic railway programme which prevented an even greater drop in her relative standing among British export markets.

There remain the 'underdeveloped' parts of the world, whose outstanding importance for Britain was as purchasers of cotton textiles through those decades when the Continent and the United States were building up cotton industries of their own to such an extent that already by the 1850s only particular, specialised – though commonly expensive

[1] In the case of France, the Anglo-French trade treaty of 1860 played a particular part in opening up her markets to British goods.

– products of the British industry could gain market access in the greater part of these territories. The failure, for varying reasons, of the Latin American and West Indian markets to expand at a rate commensurate with the general growth of world trade was compensated for by the intensification of Australasian settlement and the breakthrough achieved in Asiatic, particularly Indian, markets. And these gains were consolidated by the steadfast refusal of the British government to permit India to impose the protective tariffs needed to allow her ancient cotton industry to readjust to the new modes of production.

The re-export trade had already, as seen in the previous chapter, shed much of its old eighteenth-century character as Britain's own heavy requirements of certain imported raw materials had effectively appointed her as the warehouse to which many parts of Europe resorted for supplies. This new character became more pronounced with the growth, markedly from the 1860s, of the flow of wool from Australia, too remote for Continental or American manufacturers to establish direct commercial contacts, and promoting London as the world's principal wool market. By the end of this period, wool had become the leading item of re-exportation.

TABLE II.31. *Principal re-exports as percentage of total re-exports, 1872–74*

Wool	Cotton	Coffee	Tea	Hides and skins	Dyestuffs
17	13	9	5	5	4

The growing weight of foreign trade in the British economy has been stressed at the beginning of this section. It can hardly be over stressed: 25 per cent of national income earned from exporting; 30 per cent of national income expended on imports – these are proportions of awesome dimensions. And the peculiarly crucial role of imports is even more acutely underlined in Table II.32.

TABLE II.32. *Share of selected imports (percentage of total)*

Period	Cotton	Corn	Sugar	Wool	Tea	Metal goods	Silk goods
1854–56	15	13	7	5	2	2	2
1872–74	14	14	6	6	3	3	3

(Figures on a comparable base are not available before 1854.)

Nearly a third of the massive swelling import bill was incurred in supplying Britain's two leading industries and in providing a basic food-stuff (after allowing for about one-sixth of the cotton and about two-fifths of the wool being re-exported by the end of the period). The proportion over the closing years would have been even higher had not relatively cheap Russian and American corn recently become available in quantity; the increase in the value of corn imports was therefore less than proportionate to the increase in their volume: while the table indicates that corn imports, by value, increased only fractionally more rapidly than those of cotton, by volume, corn rose more than threefold as against cotton's rise of about two-thirds.

The continuing high rankings of sugar and tea among imports, at a time when the total was growing so considerably, is of course indicative of high rates of increase in the consumption of these commodities. In fact advances in mass purchasing power through this period appear to have been devoted to a large extent to these two items, making a significant contribution towards swelling the import bill.

TABLE II.33. *Per capita consumption of sugar and tea*
(annual averages in lb)

	Sugar	Increase by factor of	Tea	Increase by factor of
1829–31	18·7		1·25	
1850–52	27·1	*1·5*	1·94	*1·6*
1872–74	50·6	*1·8*	4·11	*2·1*

The remaining two items in Table II.32 may stand as representative of a still fairly small but significantly growing category of imports: manufactures, finished and semifinished. Imports of silk goods are a special case since their increase resulted from the deliberate sacrifice of the British industry under the Anglo-French trade treaty – with even more drastic consequences than are suggested by the leap from £3·7 million of imports from France in 1860 to £15·8 million in 1870, since much of the 1860 figure would have consisted of yarn for working up in Britain. Yet consequence as it was of a conscious act of state policy rather than an autonomous economic phenomenon, the surrender of the silks market to foreign manufacturers was really only a sharply defined particular instance of an ineluctable general trend. Britain could not indefinitely command every branch of manufacturing industry, the more so as industry became more variegated and more ramified; others were bound sooner or later to overtake her in particular branches. More important, Britain could derive positive advantage from letting such branches pass into other hands, releasing her own resources for employment in fields for which she was particularly fitted.

The silk manufacture had always been a hothouse plant in Britain and would have withered whenever the protective walls came down. Metal goods provide a clearer illustration of the general trend referred to, though here too special factors account for much of the rise. The bulk of these metal imports consisted of crude tin, copper and lead, reflecting not so much intensifying international specialisation as dwindling home supplies of the relevant ores. Domestic tin ore output reached its peak in 1871, copper in 1856 and lead in 1870. But well before these dates output had started to lag behind requirements and, increasingly, had to be supplemented from foreign sources, usually in metallic form, the bulky ore being expensive to move.

TABLE II.34. *Retained imports of crude metal*
(annual averages in '000 tons)

Period	Tin	Copper	Lead
1845–47	0·3	0·0	1·9
1872–74	6·4	21·0	63·2
Domestic output 1872–74	9·8	5·3	57·8

Of more searching significance is the iron and steel constituent of these metal imports, although as yet this accounted for little more than a quarter of the total.

TABLE II.35. *Retained imports of iron and steel*
(annual averages in '000 tons)

1829–31	12·4
1850–52	30·4
1872–74	174·3

While the rise over the earlier part of the period marks nothing more than increasing requirements of the special purpose irons which had always to be imported, that of the later part, particularly evident from the mid-1860s, denotes a recourse to Continental suppliers for varieties of iron produced in Britain in circumstances where the Continental products won preference on grounds of cost, suitability or delivery dates. Belgium in particular had developed an iron capacity well in excess of her own relatively modest needs and won orders not only in Britain but also in foreign markets which Britain was accustomed to supply. However, portentous as it might be, this was as yet an event of marginal proportions: the iron imports of the closing years of the period had about 6 per cent of the value of exports and were equivalent to about 3 per cent of total British output.

In gross, then, the import bill was under pressure from several directions – and this, starting from a point in time when a chronic deficit on the balance of trade had already set in: the last time Britain had shown a trade surplus had been in 1822. This need occasion no surprise when it is recalled that export growth from the mid-1780s had consisted very largely in the great increase in cotton exports, an increase whose *value* was far from commensurate with its *volume*, with the result, noted earlier, that exports in gross had come to earn a diminished proportion of national income; and the greatly swollen volume of cotton exports had necessitated a corresponding increase in imports of the raw material. The subsequent course of the trade balance is illustrated in Table II.36.

TABLE II.36. *Trade deficit 1830–75*

Period	Annual average £m	As percentage of exports	As percentage of national income (approx)
1830–39	17	32	4
1840–49	23	35	5
1850–59	27	23	5
1860–69	55	27	7
1870–75	54	19	6

The economic effort needed to correct the imbalance is indicated by the percentage figures. If that effort had had to be applied in the field of physical goods, either by way of a sacrifice of imports or by way of a diversion of goods from home to foreign buyers – on the strained assumption of the requisite foreign markets being found – the impact on material living standards would have been pronounced. The availability of other means of earning foreign exchange was of key consequence.

TABLE 11.37. *Invisible external earnings 1831–75*
(*£m annual averages*)

Period	Shipping	Financial services	Investment income	Overall surplus on current account
1831–40	8	4	13	4
1841–50	13	4	17	6
1851–60	23	7	29	20
1861–70	40	12	51	37
1871–75	51	16	83	79

(The figures are derived from A. H. Imlah, *Economic Elements in the Pax Britannica*, 1958.)

It should be pointed out first of all that the conventional measurements of balance of payments items, followed here, contain an element of misrepresentation: exports are valued 'f(ree) o(n) b(oard)', i.e. exclusive of freighting costs, imports are valued 'c(harges) i(nsurance) f(reight)', i.e. inclusive of freighting costs. In the case of imports, while this provides a proper measure of the economic effort required to procure them, it overstates the foreign exchange costs to the extent that the goods were carried in British ships, that is, it overstates the trade deficit. This is compensated for by crediting payments made by British customers to British shippers among external earnings from shipping, though such payments are not true external earnings. (True external shipping earnings would consist of earnings on the carriage of exports and of earnings on third party freights. If one assumed that British ships participated in equal proportions in import and export carriage, and also that third-party freights equalled the excess of import freights over export freights – i.e. Imports = Exports + Third party – then the overstatement of external shipping earnings, and of the trade deficit, would amount to one-half of recorded shipping earnings. But, while such assumptions would be reasonable enough with regard to the *value* of goods carried, they could not be made with regard to *bulk* of goods carried, apt to be very variable and the chief determinant of shipping costs. Thus, without a detailed investigation, no figure could be quoted for the magnitude of this distortion but it can certainly be said that it would be substantial.)

The role of British shipping, then, as an earner of foreign exchange is considerably overstated in the figures above. Furthermore, the striking rate of increase in shipping earnings should not be regarded as a measure of the competitive efficiency of British shipping services. The increase by a factor of rather more than six is to be set against the increase in overseas trade by a factor of rather more than five. The somewhat faster rate of growth of shipping earnings can probably be fully accounted for, and more, in the longer average distance of hauls as trade with the East expanded and in the increasing weight of bulky commodities, corn, coal, iron, machinery, heavy chemicals, etc., among the goods entering into British overseas trade. In fact, until the very last years of the period, the share of British shipping in carriage into and out of British ports showed no general tendency to rise; nor is there any reason to suppose that the British share of third-party freights increased either. And while the closing years did see British shipping starting to secure a clear international advantage through the application of steam to maritime transport, this was of limited benefit as far as earnings of foreign exchange were concerned, since the advantage consisted precisely in the fact that one paid less for steam haulage – and world demand for shipping is not primarily determined by shipping costs but, autonomously, by the quantity of goods seeking carriage. Put technically, the demand for shipping is a derived demand with a low price elasticity, so that, other things being equal, a reduction in shipping prices means a fall in shipping revenue. However, these qualifications having been entered, the fact that Britain undertook significantly more than a half her own inward and outward freighting, along with a certain amount of third-party carriage, meant that even while doing no more than holding her relative position as a shipping nation, she earned increasingly more from shipping services as the volume of international trade expanded.

The particularly significant effect of what has just been said is that shipping earnings were a function of overseas trade. The same is true in substantial degree of 'financial services', since a good deal of this mixed category consisted of the bill acceptance[1] and brokerage business

[1] To 'accept' a bill is to undertake to meet it – in the case of the kind of business referred to here, the undertaking being given against default on the part of the original 'acceptor'.

involved in that role of international mercantile centre which London had been playing since the decline of Amsterdam and Hamburg during the Revolutionary and Napoleonic Wars. This role was extended in scope as Britain became a major supplier of goods to the world at large, with the consequence that sterling as a much used currency became a widely employed international medium of exchange – a development greatly helped by the internal political stability and avoidance of serious warfare which distinguished Britain among the nations of the world in the century after 1815. The 'bill on London', particularly from about mid-century, came to hold a unique place amongst the world's monetary instruments. Also from around mid-century dated the particular development of an international marine insurance business – again functionally related to the expansion of world trade.

A third type of international financial service which was becoming increasingly remunerative from the 1850s was the arrangement of loan facilities in Britain for foreign borrowers. This was business of the somewhat misleadingly named 'merchant bankers' who commonly came to it via acceptance business in foreign bills, and whose names have become part of the folk-history of international finance: Rothschild, Baring, Hambro, Goschen and others.

The fees earned in the provision of these various services were useful in rectifying the external payments account, but as the figures make plain they were at any time a relatively minor element among invisible receipts. Given that they, along with shipping earnings, were in significant degree linked to trade levels, these items could not be looked to to convert a large standing deficit, itself a function of trade levels,[1] into the increasingly substantial overall surplus which was being earned from the mid-'fifties. In other words, this surplus must be ascribed primarily to 'investment income', not just because of the comparative magnitudes of the items involved, but because this item was largely independent of trade levels (which is not to say at all that trade levels were independent of overseas investment). Put another way again, shipping and financial services operated as a kind of built-in corrective

Acceptance houses might also do a certain amount of discounting and general lending but their chief business was guaranteeing bills – a business founded on a close familiarity with trade and traders and on their international reputation which conferred a high standing on bills accepted by them.

[1] Because in practice an increase in exports was very apt to engender an increase in imports, both by way of a greater requirement of raw materials and by way of the income generated by export sales being expended on imported goods – to the extent, probably, that any rise in exports would eventually engender a more than corresponding rise in imports.

to the trade deficit because they were automatically linked to it; but by the same token they could not run away ahead of it; only investment income, an autonomous variable, could do that.

The issue of investment income and the overall external surplus is something of a chicken and egg matter: a substantial surplus could only be won out of such income; investment abroad could only take place to the extent of the surplus, since capital can only be exported out of what remains when current liabilities have been met. However the distinction of chicken and egg need not bother us here. The period opens with perhaps £200 million worth of assets located abroad, returning an income of around £10 million p.a. And both the origins and composition of this capital stock are obscure. Some of it, perhaps much of it, obviously consisted of West Indian estates and other such property within the 'Empire'. A good deal besides was probably made up not of physical assets but of liquid capital and 'goodwill', the stock in trade of British merchants based abroad – in Riga, Hamburg, Oporto, Bombay, etc. These were types of foreign income source whose development had not necessarily required much in the way of capital export in the past. They were as much the fruits of enterprise as of investment, developed through the exploitation – in whatever sense the reader cares to take that word – of indigenous resources. However, already by 1830 Britain's foreign investment portfolio included a selection of that type of asset which in the years to come was to predominate: securities and shares, whose holders for the most part were merely passive recipients of interest payments and dividends. The soundest element in this range consisted of the loan stock of various European governments, most of it dating from the years immediately after 1815 when war-racked Europe had resorted to London to finance the reinstallation of the *ancien régime* – led by France, whose ironic need was for funds to pay the reparations levied by the victorious allies. In terms of paper valuation these loan stocks would have been overshadowed by the mass of scrip thrown up in the investment boom of 1821–25, most of it, as seen in the previous chapter, centred on Latin America. But by 1830 much of this could have been bought by the barrow-load for halfpence.

The subsequent course of foreign investment is indicated in Table II.38.

The changes in level and their timing are perhaps the most important features of this picture, but firstly the nature and geographical direction of the capital flow can be briefly detailed. The drop from the 1821–25

TABLE 11.38. *Foreign investment 1816–75 (£m annual averages)*

1816–20	7	1836–40	3	1856–60	26
1821–25	10	1841–45	6	1861–65	22
1826–30	3	1846–50	5	1866–70	41
1831–35	6	1851–55	8	1871–75	75

(These figures are simply the balance on current account net of bullion movements, and therefore measure capital exports *less* capital imports. Information on capital imports is very sparse. They were certainly small and probably consisted very largely of sterling balances held by foreign banks etc. for international payments purposes. The trend of the above figures may be taken as reflecting closely the trend of capital exports, whose absolute amount would be a little greater than shown.)

level indicates, among other things, the souring effects of the Latin American experience on the attitudes of the general investing public. Not for another quarter of a century were flotations designed to lure the blind capital of uninstructed affluence again launched in any number. The American bonds which were responsible for an upward spurt towards the mid-thirties were taken up very largely by mercantile and banking concerns[1] – to their cost, as has been seen already. Similarly, the French railway securities which lay back of the miniboom of the mid-'forties were for the most part placed privately, often through British promoters and contractors who were commonly closely connected with these enterprises. The underlying groundswell from which these wavelets occasionally broke out would have been composed of private investment of a traditional kind, a certain amount of capital outflow in association with fresh settlement in Australia and Canada, and a little privately negotiated borrowing by European governments.

It was the mid-1850s which brought the general investing public back on the scene, as the world's need of capital outran the resources of private and professional contacts. It was, of course, railway construction programmes which, above all, necessitated this increasingly massive recourse to British funds – in some cases because indigenous savings were insufficient in amount, in others because the habit of confiding one's hoardings to anonymous organisations had not yet been learned. In Britain the habit was being well learned, along, at least in the case of foreign investment, with its cautionary lessons. Only the lesser part of

[1] On these bonds, see p. 613.

the investment of these years went into ordinary, risk participating, shares; the bulk went into railway stocks carrying a government guaranteed dividend or, in greater quantity, into fixed interest securities, issued by governments – national, provincial, municipal – themselves undertaking the building of railway systems and/or ancillary facilities, telegraph networks, roads, docks, etc., along with the provision of other public utilities such as urban tramways, gasworks, water supply and sewage systems, street paving and lighting – in extra-European regions, often in close association with the railways which had brought urban communities into being.

British capital did flow into other fields as well, but not in great quantity. As in Britain itself, industry in the world at large did not often look to the general public for investment capital and much of what there was in the way of British investment in general economic enterprise overseas took place in association with British initiatives, with the capital commonly found by the entrepreneurs themselves. Ventures in Spanish iron-ore mining, Malaysian tin-mining, Australian sheep-farming and, rather more surprisingly, Texas cattle-ranching provide instances of this sort of thing, along with a handful of cases of British industrial concerns founding overseas branches. But in general British entrepreneurs found plenty with which to occupy themselves at home.

Some foreign railway undertakings were in whole or part British promotions, with railway contractors looking for work often to the fore. This was true of a number of the early European railways and, continuously, of a good deal of the Latin American railway system – much of it, however, dating from the decades beyond this period. And in a particular sense it was wholly true of the Indian railway network which was British in every respect bar geographical location: initiated in effect by the British government, with military as much as commercial considerations in mind, financed almost entirely from Britain, and designed, constructed and operated by British engineers, contractors and managers. But the bulk of the British capital that went abroad over the last couple of decades of this period was called for and managed by the host countries themselves. With the particular exceptions mentioned Britain's role was that of *rentier*, not of *dirigeant*.

Persistently throughout this phase the principal recipients of British capital were the USA (the Civil War years aside) western Europe, India and Australia; while over the last decade or so Russia, the Ottoman Empire, Egypt and, very markedly, Argentina, were coming to figure prominently. The broad consequences are illustrated in the approximations shown in Table II.39.

TABLE II.39. *Stock of British overseas assets, 1830–73 (£m)*

1830	1850	1873
200	300	1,050

of which Europe and Near East	USA	India	South America	Australia
320	270	170	135	85

As observed already, the timing of these capital flows is of particular interest (see Graph II.4).

Two relationships merit attention: that between capital exports and domestic investment; and that between capital exports and exports of goods. It will be recalled that the phases of greatest investment at home were the railway bouts: 1833–37, 1843–47, and, of lesser intensity, 1860–66. To the first two phases there correspond spates of capital exports commencing around the same time but slackening off earlier, in 1835 and 1844–45, while that of 1860–66 is accompanied by a strong but halting rise in capital exports, 1862–65, which failed to top the peak reached in 1859. This seems to indicate fairly plainly that circumstances which encouraged investment at home had a stimulating effect on investment abroad as well; but also, that the potential flow of capital abroad was in part diverted into domestic channels. It suggests, perhaps, that fluctuations in the readiness of savers to part with their funds, or in the availability of spare funds, were a crucial factor in determining the volume of capital undertakings – by contrast with the variant suggestion that the volume of capital undertakings was determined by entrepreneurial decisions. But it could also be argued that in so far as domestic and foreign investment booms were railway centred, their more or less simultaneous onsets reflect relatively low prices of railway materials, prompting entrepreneurial ventures both in Britain and overseas – with foreign enthusiasms getting choked off as competition for British materials, to which all had to resort, made them increasingly difficult and expensive to get. Whatever explanation is to be offered for the phenomenon,

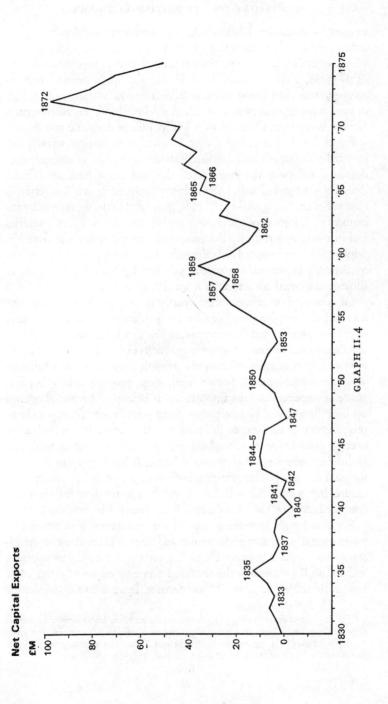

Net Capital Exports
£M

GRAPH II.4

its most important implication is that funds which would flow into domestic ventures when these were available could also be drawn abroad. More significant than the partially repressed foreign investment booms of 1833–35, 1842–44/5 and 1862–65 and the freely soaring ones of 1853–59 and 1866 (most marked from 1870–72[1]) – phases in which domestic investment was at a relatively low level. In other words, foreign investment filled the gaps left by lulls in domestic investment.

Put in the most meaningful way, investment in foreign railways had essentially the same economic implications for Britain as investment in domestic railways: the engendered demand came back to Britain, directly as export demand for railway equipment, and indirectly as export demand for goods of all kinds, generated in the short term by the immediate injection of purchasing power into the recipient countries and in the longer term by the economic expansion in those countries which railways promoted or facilitated; and the long-term effect worked in Britain's favour on the supply side too by lowering the costs of moving imported commodities from remote interiors.

Of course, these effects varied greatly in magnitude; and there was no absolute necessity to any of them: engendered demand did not have to expend itself in Britain – there were few tied loans, although British suppliers sometimes had to grant long credits or accept bonds and shares in payment; the extent of economic growth consequent upon railways was very variable; as in Britain itself, some projects were a hopeless waste of resources and the importance to Britain of territories opened up by railways was plainly not uniform – not every foreign railway probed great grain belts or sheep ranges. But, while it is true that the average pound invested abroad did not secure the same return to Britain as did the average pound invested at home, Britain's place in the international economy – her situation both as exporter and importer – did ensure her substantial benefits, probably greater benefits than any country before or since has derived from external investment.

For a strikingly clear indication of the correlation between British international economic performance and foreign investment, comparison should be made between Graph II.4, recording capital flow overseas, and Graph II.3 recording the course of domestic exports (p. 632). In a real world subject to so much 'interference' by crosscutting factors the

[1] For the sake of ease of reference to the graph, the terminal dates given in the text are those of the calendar years in which values were at a minimum/maximum; the actual turning point may have occurred in an adjacent year. Redated to mark turning points the phases cited would read: 1833–35, 1842–45, 1862–66, 1854–59, 1867–73.

'fit' between these two graphs is a real statistician's delight. The export graph registers eight troughs and eight peaks. In both cases to all but one there corresponds a capital flow trough or peak occurring in the same or in one of the two preceding years – reflecting the timelag in the feedback of export demand. (The exceptions are the export trough of 1832 with the capital flow trough coming a year *later*, and the export peak of 1853, with the capital flow peak coming three years earlier – too early, perhaps, to signify a correlation.)

'. . . it is true that the average pound invested abroad did not secure the same return to Britain as did the average pound invested at home' (above). In that case would Britain not have done better to have kept all her capital for domestic employment? Economists will appreciate straight away that the question is improperly formulated: it is not the comparative *average* returns we should question but the *marginal* returns. In plainer language, the fact that the capital *actually* employed at home yielded more benefit to Britain than that sent abroad signifies nothing; what is at issue is whether that sent abroad would have been more beneficial if employed in *unexploited* fields at home. Any resolution of a hypothetical issue of this kind depends on what other hypotheses one is prepared to pose. If, in the case of this particular question, one makes the solitary assumption of capital remaining at home the answer is that in all probability it would have been of less benefit. If, on the other hand, one is prepared to assume certain changes in domestic economic institutions as well, one could say confidently that at least some of the capital which went abroad could have been more beneficially employed at home.

Coming closer to cases: given the actual structure of domestic investment, more idle capital at home would hardly have done much more than further encourage those all too numerous public flotations of the period which, when they were not prompted by outrightly fraudulent designs on the eager savings of a gullible public, were commonly characterised by hopeless incompetence and mismanagement. (The general type has already been noted in connection with the boom of 1824–25 and, while this sort of thing was edged aside by the generally sounder railway and banking promotions of the 'thirties and 'forties, the 'fifties and 'sixties saw a resurgence – given particular encouragement by the Limited Liability Act of 1855, relieving shareholders of liability for company debts.) Capital flowed into these dubious quarters because it could not gain access to more solid undertakings, once the railways had ceased to draw heavily on the general investing public.

And there were undertakings which on a clinical appraisal could have put additional capital to effective use.

The iron industry, most manifestly, could with advantage have vested capital in extra capacity, up to date equipment and structural reorganisation. Yet even in this very plain instance, while one might start off with ascribing the failure to recruit readily available capital to simple lack of enterprise – founded in complacency, reluctance to admit outsiders, etc. – one fairly soon starts to run into much more ambivalent ground: the balance between the short-run losses involved in modernisation and reorganisation and the long-term gains; the problems of recruiting managerial personnel; market resistance to product standardisation, etc.

In another general instance which comes readily to mind in this context – the engineering industries where the gap between reality and hypothetical optimum might also have been narrowed with the assistance of outside capital – ambivalences of this kind crowd in on first contemplation. And so on. Throw one set of 'Ifs and Buts' into the historical record and in no time they are multiplying like house flies in summer. It is perhaps better, and certainly easier, to cling to the straight facts. Industry did not ask for more capital. Transport probably got more than was needful. Agriculture has already had to face the charge that it used too much. Capital went abroad because it was not wanted at home.

As one final word – and that without venturing again into the realms of hypothesis – the point may usefully be made that this whole issue only raises itself because of the relatively high level of domestic savings. With a greater average propensity to consume, the purchasing power represented by the capital in question would have gone direct into consumption goods. It hardly needs saying that the society we are dealing with was not one whose consumption wants had been satiated. Crudely put, this society saved to the extent that it did because those with the wants had not the money and those with the money had not the wants. This involves a theme which so far has only been taken up incidentally or by implication but which merits direct explicit utterance in concluding an account of an epoch which could with justification be said to have brought a 'modern' economy into being. Capital is so much a central element in such an economy that we find the word 'capitalist' the most apt label with which to describe it. This capital is constituted out of savings – abstention from consumption cedes resources for application to the accumulation of productive equipment.

The more is saved, the more capital is constituted and the more productive power can be accumulated – and it is of course the productive power of 'modern' economies which is their fundamentally significant characteristic. Starting then from a 'pre-modern' position only a society maintaining a high rate of savings can effect the transformation with any sort of rapidity (meaning by 'rapidity', over decades rather than centuries). And in that pre-modern position there are only two possible situations in which such a rate of savings will be maintained: either a coercive authority will enforce it, or wealth will be unequally divided to such an extent that a great deal of it is concentrated in the hands of those who have so much that after all their normal consumption wants have been satisfied, a large surplus still remains to them. But, and this requires equal emphasis, in a private enterprise economy there is no continuing certainty at all that investment opportunities will exist to the extent needed to absorb the volume of savings; and, if not, that economy will suffer from a deficiency of demand, i.e. will operate at a level below its real capacity. Thus the inegalitarian income structure essential to getting a 'revolution' under way is at the same time a continual threat to its maintenance. This chapter opened with railways. It can properly end with them because it was above all investment opportunities provided by railways, at home and abroad, which stayed that threat through the years we have been considering.

Four

1873–1914

The economy in 1873

Several hundred pages back, a bird's eye survey of the British economy in 1740 was offered (pp. 317–24). A century and a quarter or so on in historical time let us repeat the exercise along similar lines.

Britain now occupied the centre of the world economic stage. She was the model by reference to which other countries set their own economic aspirations. She commanded a larger share of international trade than any other country, with the corollary that for many countries she was their most important trading partner. She was the world's primary source of international capital. Her currency was a principal medium of international exchange. Her *per capita* wealth exceeded that of any country except the USA. But here on this last count a reservation interrupts the superlatives – a reservation which pertains less to Britain's inferiority to the USA than to the manner in which wealth was distributed in Britain. Between 1785 and 1873 average *per capita* wealth had approximately tripled in real terms. Even the most pervervid protagonist of the 'optimistic' school in the 'standard of living debate' would never have contended that *per capita* wage incomes did anything more than double over the same period and the consensus of recent cooler judgments is that they in fact increased by a good deal less, rising minimally if at all up to the mid-1840s and showing a powerful upward tendency only from the early 'sixties. And all this starting from a highly inegalitarian base. If the period in question was not one in which the rich got richer and the poor got poorer, on all the available though inadequate evidence it was one in which, up to the 'sixties at least, the upper classes accumulated wealth as never before while the lower classes experienced only a marginal alleviation of their condition.

There were of course variations within wage incomes. A highly skilled engineering craftsman might around 1873 be taking home £80 a year, a casual labourer perhaps no more than £25. But this was the difference between simple comfort and serious deprivation – and perhaps two-fifths of the population were materially deprived to the point of inability to sustain normal health and vigour. The differential range of wage incomes becomes exiguous when set against the four, five and even six figure incomes which receivers of rent, interest and profits commonly commanded. (And it must be remembered that the tax system, far from tending to even out such discrepancies, positively aggravated them. Income tax at fourpence in the pound, with effective exemption for wage earners, did little to redress the regressive bias of a revenue system which leant heavily on duties on a narrow range of mass consumption goods.)

This prolonged failure of wage incomes to match the rise in other incomes – such that when wages did start decisively upwards the gap to be closed was enormous – gives rise to two general questions. What kind of incomes had taken the lion's share of the increments to national wealth through these decades of sustained economic growth? Why was it that wage incomes only started to participate substantially in that growth from the early 'sixties?

The first question is not as easy to answer as might appear at first sight. Reasonable attempts can be made to estimate factor shares in national income over the period in question; but through an age of structural change these do not go very far towards answering our question. The share of wage earners actually rose. But what this reflects is the disappearance in many trades of the small master and, probably more weightily, the steady *proportionate* fall in the number of farmers among income recipients – of persons, that is, whose income would be accounted profits – and a corresponding increase in the numbers living off wages. By the same token the share of profits in gross would have fallen. But this says nothing of the course of the *per capita* income of profit earners. No useful information is available about the trend of such incomes, though it is very possible that intensifying competitiveness, promoted particularly by transport improvements, trimmed profit margins. (One probable exception of some weight would be the iron industry, experiencing almost uninterruptedly keen demand under inelastic supply conditions.) However, it would be quite impossible to assign mathematical values to the elements involved; and if it were the case that profit rates on the whole contracted, one would have to balance that against the larger average scale of the enterprises of profit earners. In any event the distinction of 'profit' as a special type of return is a very artificial procedure. In practice it is quite indistinguishable from the return to capital. And the same observation holds true in some degree for rent. Gross rental income from agricultural land probably increased more than fourfold in real terms between 1785 and 1873 while the number of rent recipients may be assumed to have remained much the same, so that this could in rough and ready fashion be contrasted directly with the threefold increase in total *per capita* income. But a significant amount of this represented the return on capital invested in bettering farm land. Urban rentals likewise were compounded of a return on mere ownership and a return on capital vested in property development – both capable of being very high in areas of population concentration.

Capital it is that stands out most conspicuously as the factor appropriating a continuously larger slice of the national cake. It has been estimated[1] that between 1785 and 1873 the annual rate of capital formation increased from 5–6 per cent of national income to 12 per cent. Allowing for a slight secular decline in interest rates this indicates that the return to capital about doubled its share of national income. And, while the bases for such a calculation are very uncertain, this return by 1873 cannot have accounted for any less than a quarter of total incomes and may have been as much as a third or more. Indeed, on the face of it this kind of record is what one would expect. The shift to capital intensive forms of economic activity is a fundamental trait – in a sense *the* fundamental trait – of British economic development over the period in question.[2] Given this, only a very substantial fall in interest rates could have

[1] By P. Deane and W. A. Cole, *British Economic Growth, 1688–1959* (1964), pp. 263–6.

[2] It might usefully be pointed out that this is just a matter of historical fact, not one of theoretical necessity. A new technology may demand no more capital than the old. Nor is there any advantage in a shift to capital intensiveness *in itself*: money capital is not a *real* factor of production – it is merely an institutional factor which, in certain societies, is needed to command labour; a shift from a labour intensive mode of supplying a particular good to a capital intensive mode which leaves costs unchanged does not effect any overall gain by way of economising on labour – it merely transfers labour from the production of that good to the production of the capital good(s) in question. (Of course it may be the case at any one time that in *real* cost terms the capital intensive mode is superior but is not utilised because of a high interest rate/wages ratio and that a subsequent fall in that ratio will lead to its adoption.) Returning to the point at issue: it did *happen* to be the case that the new technologies becoming available in Britain were more demanding of capital than the old.

checked the absorption by capital of an increasing share of national income – and, as seen in the previous chapter, the tendency for savings to run ahead of domestic investment, which would have served to bring interest rates down and in fact did so in fractional degree, was substantially offset by the increase in foreign lending.

Capitalists, in the literal sense of the word, need not constitute a distinct group of income recipients. The saved portions of incomes of all kinds could make up the capital fund; and incomes of all kinds could then be supplemented by the return which capital rendered. In historical fact, wage earners could make no contribution worth speaking of to capital formation. A high level of saving could only be sustained by the wealthy, and it was their retention of a high proportion of the income secured from capital outlays which enabled the capital fund to be continuously enlarged at the rate it was; thus as long as economic development necessitated a continuing intensification of capital investment the income of the wealthy was bound to grow with exceptional momentum.

Here indeed we have the semblance of an answer to our second question: why had wage earners participated in such slight degree in the benefits of economic growth? If it were true, as it was, that, along the path followed by the economy, capital necessarily secured a relatively large return, then as a matter of logic labour could win only a relatively small return. Yet this is no answer – no more than is the variant formulation that the build-up of productive capacity necessitated abstention from consumption and that this was achieved by keeping wages down. Neither answer does any more than analyse *what* happened; neither indicates *why* it happened. Specifically, the actual mechanism by which wages were determined is not identified. And the truth of the matter is that this mechanism cannot be positively identified. We have no adequate, generally agreed, theory of wages for this purpose. To institute a search for one here is beyond the scope of this book. All that can effectively be done – and that purely negative – is to dispose of any naïve notion that a simple supply and demand theory, such as one might use to account for short-run wage movements, would serve. It would not, partly because it does not seem to fit the, admittedly scanty, historical data: there does not seem to be any close correlation between long-run wage movements and long-run employment levels, indeed such records as there are do not suggest any secular change at all in employment levels; and partly because the usual way of invoking this type of analysis is to posit redundancy as a result of labour-saving devices. Such a procedure is open to two fundamental objections: (1) that all the factual indications are that in anything but the very short run the increase in output more than compensated for the fall in requirements of labour per unit of output; (2) that, as a matter of theory, the demand curve for labour under these conditions has not made a simple shift but has changed shape, so that no *a priori* prediction can be made as to the direction of movement of the point of inter-section; in plain language, an employer may not need as much labour as formerly but he is prepared to pay more for what he does need because he can get more out of it. (The 'redundancy' approach is sometimes buttressed with rising population. But rising population is simul-taneously an increase in the labour supply and an increase in the level of demand, and is, then, self-cancelling in this respect. It has not been unknown for rising population to be invoked as a demand factor to account for the adoption of labour-saving devices and then as a supply factor to account for depressed wages!)

Great wealth by all known standards. An unprecedentedly inegali-tarian distribution of that wealth. These are twin characteristics of the British economy of 1873. The primary historical process producing them was the application of capital to new modes of supply. Capital had been so applied in all sectors of the economy – in agriculture, in transport, in industry, and, effectively, in export markets and import sources. Its efficacy and overall economic significance in these various fields has been considered at appropriate points in the preceding chap-ters. What it is sought to stress now in making a conscious contrast with the Britain of 1740 is the extent to which the process had transformed the balance of the economy. In 1740 agriculture had been the central economic activity, not only on account of its sheer weight relative to the whole but also because of the way in which the level of agricultural efficiency controlled economic performance generally. In 1873, while agriculture was still an important activity and the most crucial of all productive activities, Britain was, in the full sense of the term, an industrial nation. Industry's output was now three times that of agricul-ture and was currently growing at a rate of about 2 per cent p.a., whereas agriculture was on the point of contracting.

Industry had not only swelled enormously in gross importance. It had changed profoundly in character. And prominent amongst the human consequences of that change was the massing of people in urban agglomerations. Rural industry was not quite dead but as a demographic factor it had become negligible. Of a total population of 27 million in

1873 about 9 million lived in just nineteen solidly built-up urban blocks comprising more than a hundred thousand persons each:[1] London, Manchester, Merseyside,* Glasgow,* Birmingham,* Tyneside,† Leeds,† Sheffield,† Edinburgh,† Bristol, Bradford, Nottingham, Stoke, Wearside, Hull, Dundee, Plymouth, Portsmouth, Leicester. (Precise population figures for these cannot be given because of uncertainty as to what fell within the 'solidly built-up' area, but London, so defined, would have comprised something over 3 million; Manchester around 750,000; those marked *, over 500,000; †, over 250,000 and the remainder under 250,000.) At the opposite end of the density scale, fourteen English rural counties had either completely or very nearly ceased to grow at all even though the national rate of population growth was still very high at around one per cent p.a. In the mountain wilds of the Celtic fringe the same was true of six Welsh counties (out of twelve) and of eighteen Scottish counties (out of thirty-three). While urban Britain struggled to squeeze ever-increasing numbers into its few square miles, rural Britain was on the point of depopulation.

An even more specific product of the changed character of industry was the industrialist: the outright owner of premises, plant, tools, materials – of the whole physical apparatus of production – possessed of undivided sovereignty over the entire productive process and in undisputed enjoyment of the surplus of revenue over costs. This concentration of functions was not universal throughout the economy. At the one extreme older, more diffused forms of organisation still survived here and there and at the other, dispersed ownership had led, in the case of the railway companies and some other instances, to the complete severance of management from ownership. But the industrialist as defined was the archetype, almost the folk hero, in a society grounded in that application of capital to industrial technology of which he had been the chief contriver.

One simple way of describing the extent of economic change effected by 1873 might be to say that we are now confronted with an economy that is recognisably 'modern'. It is a world that we of today could find our way round in. Or at least, the 1970s would find less to wonder at in the 1870s than the 1870s would have found in the 1770s. In the preceding chapters we have, so as to speak, made our way through a great divide and emerged on the frontiers of familiar terrain. It has been a slow, and perhaps tedious, journey. Unavoidably so, for

[1] The towns listed are not the administrative entities but the built-up areas centred on them.

one of its chief objects has been to chart with some precision the paths along which the economy found its way across that divide – strange paths which no other economy had ever traversed and which have warranted a certain degree of meticulousness in retracing them. But having come out in territory where the landmarks are more readily identifiable, we can legitimately proceed at a brisker pace. The fairly close sector by sector plotting which has been undertaken up to this point can for the most part be discarded in favour of an approach devoted to general trends rather than particular incidents.

Such a switch is in any event more or less forced on us by the subject matter. Hitherto, the national economy could, without intolerable distortion, be identified with a fairly small number of particular economic activities. From here on the increasing variegation of the economy renders such a procedure less and less permissible, while an attempt to encompass this variegation in adequate detail would run to unendurable length. The more modest objects of the remaining chapters, then, will be principally to delineate the general course of gross economic performance and to trace the evolution of those specific traits which characterise the economy of more recent times by broad contrast with that of the 1870s. However, for the period at present in question there is one key sector of the economy which continues to insist on special attention: the iron and steel industry. It so insists, in some part, because its particular history experienced an especially sharp change in character in the years following 1873 and, in other part, because much of the general economic change of this period can be related to, or pointed by, its individual record.

Iron and steel: a case study

The significant history of the British iron and steel industry over this period is substantially contained in three events: (1) the abrupt cessation of 'revolutionary' growth; (2) the rapid loss of international predominance; (3) the decisive conversion from iron to steel. The relevant statistics are given in Graphs II.5 and 6[1] and Tables II.40 and 41.

In 1873 the world for a time stopped building railways and the British iron industry had to wait seven years before it once again contrived to sell as much as it had been doing on the eve of the September

---

[1] In contrast to an ordinary arithmetic graph, where equal intervals represent equal increments, equal intervals in these graphs represent equal rates of change; and the slope of the graph line is a measure of growth rate.

Movement of U.K. Pig Iron Output 1830 – 1910-4
(Values for Indicated Years up to 1860;
Five Yearly Averages thereafter)
(Semi-Logarithmic Scale)

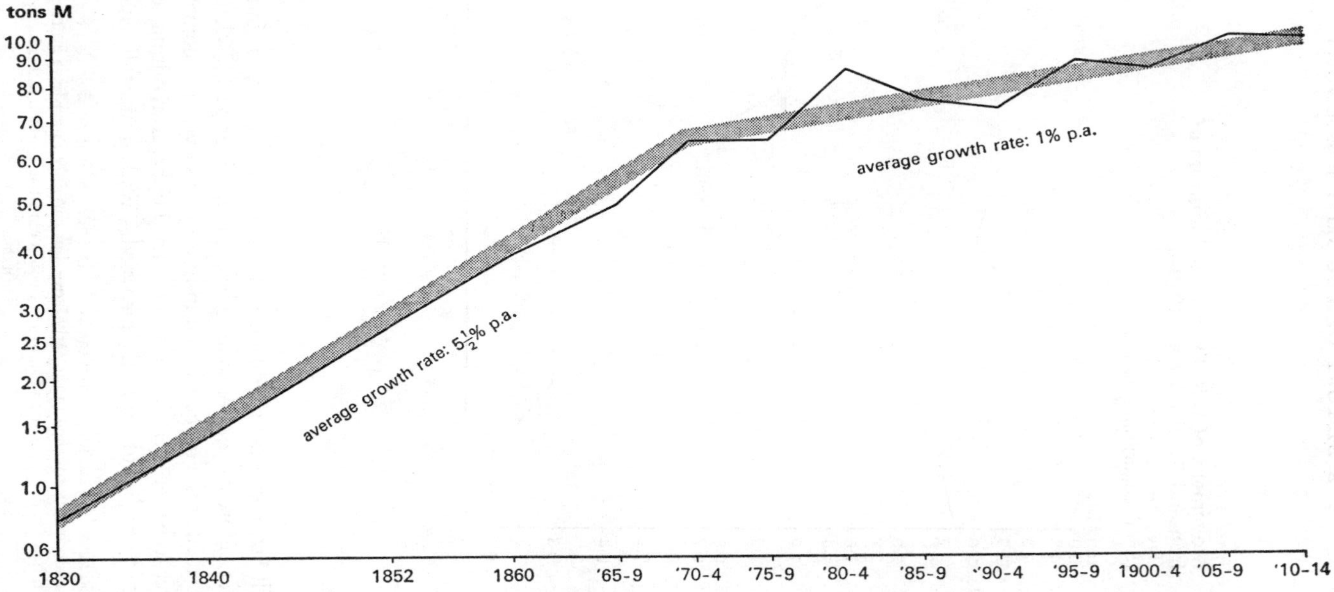

tons M

GRAPH II.5.

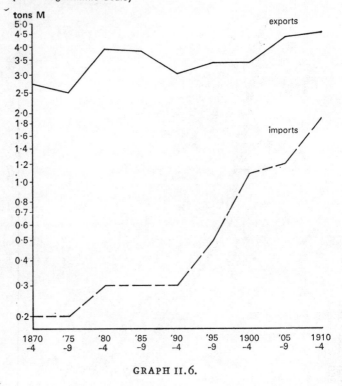

Movement of U.K. Exports and Imports of
Iron and Steel 1870–4 – 1910–4
(Five Yearly Averages)
(Semi-Logarithmic Scale)

GRAPH II.6.

Wall Street crash. As far back as the data can carry us, the industry had
never before run on for so long below a previous peak. What might be
described as the longest boom in history was over. Its momentum was
never to be recovered. Nor was the level of bar iron output achieved in
1872–73 to be subsequently surpassed.[1] With powerfully augmenting

[1] So far as one can judge from the available evidence. It is possible that the earlier level
was again briefly touched in the early '80s – but certainly much less remuneratively: bar
which had fetched £12 10s a ton in 1873 could command only £6 15s in 1880.

TABLE II.40. *UK iron and steel output as percentage of world total*

	1875–79	1880–84	1885–89	1890–94	1895–99	1900–04	1905–09	1910–14
Pig iron	46	41	35	29	28	20	18	14
Steel	35	33	30	24	20	15	12	11

TABLE II.41. *UK steel output expressed as percentage of pig iron output*

1871–74	1875–79	1880–84	1885–89	1890–94	1895–99	1900–04	1905–09	1910–14
8	14	22	36	42	49	58	62	74

(With the available data the figures in Table II.41 are the best indication that can be had of the swing from bar iron to steel. But the expression

$$\frac{\text{Steel}}{\text{Pig iron}}$$

is not in itself an accurate measure of the balance between steel and other kinds of iron, since it takes no account of pig wastage in transformation, nor of exports and imports of pig, nor most importantly, of the use of scrap in steel making.)

rapidity the world from the mid-'seventies was taking to steel. Already by 1873 the combined American and German steelmaking capacities exceeded that of Great Britain, even though their combined pig iron capacities were still only a half of the British. The huge British industry was caught on the wrong foot, still poised to produce bar when the future lay with steel. And as Table II.40 indicates, it never really succeeded in getting on to the right footing. The landmark dates in its loss of international strength are: 1886, surpassed by USA in steel output; 1890, surpassed by USA in pig output; 1893, surpassed by Germany in steel output; 1901, surpassed by Germany in steel exports; 1906, surpassed by Germany in pig output; 1910, surpassed by Germany in total iron exports. By 1913 United States steel output was four times and German two and a half times that of Great Britain. And these ratios were not just functions of population differences. The USA produced one and two-thirds times as much steel per head of its population; Germany one and a third times; and little Belgium nearly twice as much.

Before probing a little more closely into the competitive situation of the British industry, the market trends associated with this record should be broadly indicated. The 'eighties brought the last of the great world railway booms; and what was still the world's largest iron industry could not help but benefit from it. But it is notable that on this occasion demand from the USA was very largely for pig iron. America's rolling-mills could already turn out double the British rail output and looked to Britain only for the crude material to work on. Germany too, into the 1900s, continued to draw fluctuating quantities of pig from Great Britain. Thus was Britain reduced effectively to the role of primary producer, supplying the relatively cheap base materials for secondary, and more remunerative, processing. Only one British processed item continued to find substantial markets in the 'developed' world: tinplate, exports of which rose more than fourfold between 1870 and 1891, when they were abruptly tariffed out of the American market. Other processed items by the early 'eighties had to look mainly to 'underdeveloped' regions for markets – and naturally such regions had not the purchasing power to buy in great quantity.

At home the petering out of fresh railway building through the 'seventies was only just about balanced by the growth of shipbuilding and such increase as there was in economic activity generally. For about a decade and a half from the early 'eighties through to the mid-'nineties, the domestic market ceased to expand; 1896, however, brought the onset of a long run shipbuilding boom which lasted with brief interruptions until 1913. These were the halcyon years of British shipbuilding. Not only did a vigorous expansion of international commerce bring a notable increase in both home and foreign mercantile orders, but the intensification of Anglo-German naval rivalry gave rise to the construction of warships on a prodigious scale. Other engineering industries too, including the newcomers, the cycle and motor vehicle manufacturers, found new or substantially extended markets.

All in all between 1896 and 1914, home consumption of iron and steel increased by something like two-thirds, approaching once again after a long lull the momentum which had been sustained for decades into the 1870s. Yet the output of the British iron and steel industry over this same buoyant phase increased by only about one-third. And this through a time when on top of the growth of the home market, 'underdeveloped' territories – India, Australasia, Japan, China, South Africa, Latin America, Canada – were greatly accelerating their imports of iron and steel. This might be termed Phase Two in the international decline of the British industry. If Phase One be the period during which Britain failed to hold a substantial share in the massively growing American and German markets, Phase Two is the period during which Britain was being edged aside in third-party markets which she had hitherto dominated and where the advantages of geographical situation and established connections, reinforced in some cases by political ties, lay with her.[1] More humiliatingly, Phase Two is the period during which substantial tracts of Britain's own home market were lost to German, Belgian and American exporters.

What went wrong? Let it be said straight away that there can be no prospect of arriving at a comprehensive answer within the ambit of these pages. In appraising the international situation we have to deal with five different general categories of metal (four steels and puddled iron) each susceptible to numerous further subdistinctions both in point of chemical composition and mechanical fashioning, all finding different sorts of markets; and with producers operating under greatly varying cost and supply conditions and standing in widely discrepant relationships to their markets. There can be no possibility of isolating one or two simple variables as responsible for the differing records of national industries. The most that can be done here is to indicate the broad lines of the requisite comparative appraisal.

As significant a line as any along which to make an initial approach to this intimidating issue is that of Britain's relationship to her foreign markets for iron. It is a crude truth that despite the extent to which the British industry, by the early 'seventies, had come to lean on export sales it was not orientated towards foreign markets. It had grown up with developing British uses for iron. It produced what the home market wanted and sold to foreigners whatever they might require from its normal, domestically orientated, range. But, this said, it is a point of intricate delicacy to determine just when, if ever, it, or certain sections of it, could with commercial advantage have turned with more deliberation to catering for foreign users. Up to the 1870s the issue is really an empty one. What Britain required and what the world required were much the same thing. Specifically, the industry which had evolved to meet British railway requirements was perfectly adequately geared to meet foreign railway requirements. Furthermore, as seen in the last

---

[1] Canada, which could much more easily be supplied by the USA, is an evident exception. On comparative geographical situations, it should be remembered that while much of the British industry was coastally located, the German and American industries lay well inland.

chapter, foreign demand tended very much to be spillover demand, erratic and unpredictable. To have sought to settle down in its wake would have been to hazard a very rough passage. And not only did the home market offer greater stability; it was, right through to the end of the 'seventies, the largest single market in the world, still at the close of the decade accounting for about one quarter of world consumption. Thus up to the 'seventies, every evident consideration had conspired to wed British producers to British users. By the end of the 'eighties things were very different. British consumption was probably not much more than one-eighth of the world total and Britain's pattern of iron use had become appreciably different from that of the world at large as paths of economic development diverged. Plainly, integration with the home market could no longer provide a strategy for dynamic advance.

The British industry, then, could only have continued to participate substantially in a growing world market by purposefully redirecting itself towards meeting world requirements. But this is by no means to say that that option was in practice available to it. The 'world market' of which we are speaking consisted in very large part through the decisive 'seventies and 'eighties of the USA and Germany, the two countries which were themselves developing iron and steel industries with exceptional momentum. The maintenance of 'revolutionary' growth did not depend in any weighty degree on the retention of a strong competitive position in third party markets. Indeed it was only from the mid-'nineties that Britain's position in such markets as a whole was seriously troubled. The specific necessity was to keep up with the American and German industries *in their own markets*.

Could the British industry have successfully reorientated itself to the planned cultivation of these markets? Could it, that is, have turned its great productive capacity in this direction so as to be able to secure an established pitch in the market place which, while it could no more have frustrated American and German development in iron and steel than it could have arrested Niagara Falls, would have assured the British industry a substantial share in these second wave 'Industrial Revolutions'? More meaningfully put, does the failure so to adjust, and with it the loss of growth momentum, point to impassable constrictions or to human inadequacies?

The adjustment had to be profound. And it had to be rapid. Before 1870, at the earliest, there would have been little commercial wisdom in a foreign-based strategy; after 1890, at the latest, the way in was closed, barred by the developed power of the American and German industries entrenched behind tariff fortifications. Indeed the reference to tariffs might well be thought to resolve our questions. These countries had become determined on excluding imports and, sooner or later, they would push their tariffs high enough to ensure that they did so. Germany embarked on an increasingly protectionist policy from 1879; and the United States had taken decisively to protection with the secession and defeat of the free-trade minded South, although it did not assume an absolutely exclusivist character until the 'Mckinley Tariff' of 1890. But the more of the market exporters secured in these countries while they could, the more averse would domestic consumer interests be to their exclusion. At least, the effort to live in competition with the German and American industries in their own markets, even if it had eventually to be given up, would have helped to brace the British industry to face such competition in other markets when it came. We cannot explore here the complexity of ifs and buts involved in the outcome of a hypothetical campaign in German and American markets. What can and should be remarked on is that nothing of the kind seems to have been even contemplated. This industry, which had been so handsomely treated by the market in the past, either saw no reason to anticipate harsher times ahead, or, if it did, considered their occurrence as being beyond the bounds of its competence.

Such a remark should not be converted into a *post hoc* reproach or criticism. It is no part of our business here to play God, dispensing praise and censure out of an all-knowing wisdom. What is our business is to observe that the economic environment in which the British iron and steel industry lived changed with very great rapidity through the 'seventies and 'eighties, and that entrepreneurial behaviour patterns did not change with it. More specifically – although inevitably with much oversimplification: in the past, entrepreneurship had been largely a matter of organising a works which autonomous market forces could be relied on to keep employed; now, if growth were to be sustained, entrepreneurship had to comprehend economic intelligence, forward planning, deliberated market strategy, etc. – and, it might be added, the readiness to set up behind tariff walls if these proved too high to climb.

The hypothesis that a newly calculated programme for German and American markets might have served to sustain 'revolutionary' growth assumes not only a rapid and radical reforming of entrepreneurial thinking but also an intrinsic competitive efficiency. This is in fact a very large assumption. We have already seen in the last chapter that the British industry had become technically behindhand in comparison with the German, French, Belgian and American industries. A decision to meet these industries on their own ground would have entailed the readiness and the ability to match them technically. No such decision was made; and the technical gap instead of being closed became positively wider. By the beginning of the twentieth century the British industry had abandoned any pretence to technical forwardness; and its notion of rebutting criticism was to protest its willingness to examine techniques which had already been proven abroad, and which it commonly succeeded in satisfying itself would not for one reason or another serve in Britain. Germany and, in lesser degree, France were the acknowledged leaders in metallurgy; in plant engineering, the USA.

It was not that the inventive flair was conspicuously lacking in Britain. A number of the ideas exploited abroad had been anticipated or paralleled in Britain. What was lacking was research and development *organisation*.[1] Particularly illuminating and significant is the history of the last of the fundamental technical breakthroughs: the Gilchrist-Thomas process which made it possible to produce steel from phosphoric pig, in either the Bessemer converter or the Siemens open hearth, and thus released cheap steelmaking from the constraints of scarce non-phosphoric ores. British discovery though it was and dating from 1879, still in 1896 only 15 per cent of British steel was made from phosphoric ores, as against *c.* 90 per cent in Germany and *c.* 60 per cent in the USA; and although the pace of change then quickened, in 1914 the proportion was as yet only 43 per cent.

In itself this record does not necessarily constitute any kind of a comment on the British industry. The basic[2] process was intrinsically more expensive than the acid process. As long as good quality non-phosphoric ores were readily and cheaply available, it might be said that there was little reason to take to making basic steel. The reason for German adoption of it was that Germany's most extensive and most suitably situated ore field, that of Lorraine, was phosphoric – without Gilchrist-Thomas German steel development would have been a much more arduous affair. Britain, on the other hand, not only possessed non-phosphoric ores in Cumberland but could also, from South Wales and the north-east coast, draw easily on Spanish ore supplies. Yet the extent to which Britain clung to acid steel was perhaps ill-advised. All around, basic yielded the more satisfactory metal, especially as against acid

[1] See p. 546
[2] In the standard terminology 'basic' denotes the use of the Gilchrist-Thomas method with phosphoric ores, 'acid' the unmodified techniques used with non-phosphoric ores.

Bessemer, which except when very carefully made was of unreliable durability under strain and did not lend itself well to welding and riveting – and it was not until the late 'eighties that the converter started to give way to the open hearth in Britain; up to then the bulk of British steel output consisted of what in point of quality was the poorest of the four general types of steel (acid Bessemer, basic Bessemer, acid open hearth, basic open hearth).

None of this of course amounts to saying that Britain should have abandoned a steel which she was well placed to manufacture cheaply and which was perfectly satisfactory for many purposes, prominently for rails. But competitive power could have been strengthened by a more diversified output.[1] And, in the particular context of technical competence, part of the reason why Britain took so slowly to a method which she had pioneered was that its successful establishment on a regular commercial basis required the resolution of certain problems of plant design and ore blending which the German industry was more effectively organised to grapple with than was the British.

The need to raise the level of technical efficiency did not go entirely unrecognised. The Iron and Steel Institute had already been founded in 1869 for the exclusive purpose of promoting investigation of technical questions. Through its meetings and publications it served as a useful clearing house for technical information, but it was no more than a talking shop and the talk could only be of what was being done outside its walls. In the works themselves the employment of chemists became standard, but their role was rarely anything other than the subservient and poorly paid one of making routine analyses of materials, often with inadequate equipment; and the employment of professional engineers to deal with questions of plant design was quite unknown.

In the country at large there was, it is true, a rapid awakening to the way in which social and economic change had outdistanced the fragmentary and anachronistic educational system. The Education Act of 1870 laid the base of universal primary education. But although there now existed a consensus that education for the masses was a good thing, few concerned themselves closely with defining its aims and content and with ensuring that it was purposefully and usefully related to the real needs and aspirations of those whom it was supposed to serve. But at least, the days of illiterate employees – sometimes in posts of responsibility – rapidly became a thing of the past. At more advanced

---

[1] The case for basic steel gained particular strength from the 1890s as Cumberland and Spanish ores became poorer and more expensive to fetch.

educational levels, while technical and scientific instruction and inquiry definitely remained poor cousins in the family of higher learning, the period did see a good deal done towards the provision of the appropriate facilities.

It was very much a piecemeal achievement, the work of various local and private initiatives, and the result was a rather ramshackle, patchwork structure, but it would be broadly true to say that the continuing backwardness of British industry in fields where technical and scientific expertise were called for was due much more to the failure of industry to invoke the available facilities than to the shortcomings of the educational system. And if there was justification in the protestation, heard often in iron and steel quarters, that technical and scientific education was too academic, insufficiently practical, then much of the blame for that lay with industry itself. In particular, the iron and steel industry was big enough, wealthy enough, and important enough, to have associated itself much more closely than it did (which in fact was hardly at all) with the nurturing and shaping of technical and scientific education in Britain – and in the Iron and Steel Institute it possessed a ready-made instrument for that purpose.

The disposition of the industry to exploit the potential contribution of chemists and engineers is a fundamental point of reference in any consideration of comparative technical efficiency. However, even the best will in the world could not engender optimum efficiency irrespective of circumstances. Works' size and structure was commonly a limiting factor. Perhaps the most obvious respect in which this was true was in regard to research. The unit costs of research are fairly strictly a direct inverse function of volume of output.[1] British works were not only smaller than the giant ones becoming characteristic of the American industry, which might be said to have enjoyed the benefits of a corresponding market scale, but also smaller than German and even French plants. (Here again the Iron and Steel Institute could have been useful in providing central, jointly financed research facilities where the smallness of firms precluded their undertaking their own research.)

Even if the British industry was content, as generally it was, to leave exploration to others, techniques devised abroad were not necessarily capable of adoption in scaled down British works – as indeed the British industry was only too ready to assure its critics. The lessons of metallurgical research could usually be applied, given the readiness to do so, on any scale; but the kind of advance in plant design and machinery which

[1] See p. 590.

the Americans led was tailored to large outputs and long continuous production runs, for example, to blast furnaces producing over 200,000 tons p.a. around 1900, when the most capacious British furnace did not exceed 50,000.

In some instances, imitation of the best American practice was ruled out not only by considerations of scale but also by the disintegrated structure of the British industry. One must not generalise too freely about the virtues of integration, i.e. fusion of all or some of the different stages in steel manufacture. The separation of processes was an ancient feature of the British industry; and increasingly, the fragmented geography of materials and markets dictated functional disintegration. As between certain stages there were no strictly technical advantages in fusion – leaving open for the moment the question of whether there were other kinds of advantages. In the particular context of American technology the form of integration which offered distinct advantages was that between pig iron production and the conversion of pig into steel. In Britain, in marked contrast with the situation in the USA and in Germany, only a minority of blast furnaces were attached to steel works, precluding, for this if no other reason, the adoption of those American techniques which were designed to effect economies in the transition between the two.

At the later processing stages, the fashioning of billets, slabs, plates, sheets, etc., a further factor hindered adoption of the powerful high speed American machinery. The continuous production runs, without which it was not commercially practicable, could rarely be sustained in Britain where the market insisted on having its steel in a variety of dimensions. In the USA, massive producers like Carnegies successfully conditioned the market by practising a discriminatory pricing policy as between 'standard' and 'non-standard' dimensions. In Germany, the United Societies of German Architects and Engineers agreed on standard sections in 1883. Britain did not follow suit until 1903 but even then the limited scale of operations of many British works prevented anything like full advantage being taken of the new situation to install American-style machinery.

Any contrasting of British and American technology must of course be undertaken with delicacy. The difference in the size of home markets must be continuously appreciated and, of particular weight here, so must the higher level of American wages. American methods were capital intensive because labour was dear; and their capital intensive methods were most efficient on a large scale – which is to say that such methods might not yield any cost advantage in Britain where labour was cheaper; or, at least, that the incentive to raise the scale of operations so as to most effectively accommodate American-type technology was not as sharp in Britain.[1] However, the same consideration does not apply in contrasting Britain and Germany, where wages were lower and which yet, on top of its own contributions to iron and steel technology, drew much more on American practice than did Britain. And if this is to be explained in terms of the larger scale and greater integration of German enterprises, then in what terms are these in turn to be explained?

We should at this stage make explicit a distinction which has not yet been drawn out: that between scale and extent of integration of a single works and scale and integration of a single concern which might embrace several separate works. In the latter respect Britain had nothing to compare with the colossal United States Steel Corporation which on its creation by merger in 1901 produced nearly twice as much steel as the entire British industry put together and spanned the whole range of processes from ore- and coal-mining upwards. Nor were there British counterparts to the Krupp and Thyssen enterprises in Germany. There were indeed by the early twentieth century a number of British concerns involved in steel which were large by any contemporary standards obtaining elsewhere in British industry. However, nearly all of them were the result of fairly recent mergers and few were primarily steel-making concerns – both observations applying to a group composed of firms principally involved in shipbuilding and armaments: Vickers, Armstrong Whitworth, John Brown, Cammell Laird, William Beardmore (half owned by Vickers), Palmers; and to Stewarts and Lloyds who were primarily tube makers. Guest, Keen and Nettlefolds was also the result of recent mergers creating a very variegated enterprise scattered through South Wales and the Black Country. Steel-making was, however, its central activity and it can be associated here with three other concerns which were primarily steelmakers although integrated both forwards and backwards as well: Blockow Vaughan, Dorman Long and Cargo Fleet, all Teesside enterprises. Again, two of these figure only by virtue of recent combinations. Blockow Vaughan stands alone as a relatively heavily capitalised concern whose essential

[1] The matter could be put the other way round: American industry could afford high wages because of its superior technology. As a matter of historical chronology it seems proper to treat high wages as primary to begin with, explaining them as due to an abundance of land. But the further one moves from frontier days and the more industrialised the American economy becomes, the more reasonable is the reverse representation.

business was steelmaking and which had a history as such reaching back beyond 1899 – in fact, back to 1874.[1] And as steelmakers none of these four around 1905 would have had an output as high as half a million tons a year, a total then exceeded by probably about ten German firms and, even in the shadow of United States Steel, producing around twelve million tons a year, by some six or seven other American concerns. This was the kind of class that a single *works*, integrating pig iron and steel, needed to be in to take full advantage of plant on the American model. And of the four British *concerns* named, only Blockow Vaughan concentrated its pig iron and steel business in the one works.

Technical efficiency is not of course the only kind of efficiency that scale may offer. On the other hand, big is not necessarily good. Just how far the large merged enterprises which have been mentioned sought and attained economies in administrative overheads, marketing expenses etc. is difficult to say. Whether the assured supplies and outlets which vertical integration afforded brought real economies and not merely an easier life for management is again something that cannot be confidently pronounced on. But one does have the impression that commercial advantages which did not embrace positive considerations of efficiency were commonly a dominant factor in the formation of these companies. Reduction of competition and control of materials appear to have been chief ends in view. Certainly, the obtrusive position in this group of the shipbuilding/armaments companies – Vickers and Armstrong Whitworth easily outdistanced any of the others mentioned in point of scale – should not go unremarked. These were components of a military-industrial complex in which cost efficiency was a very subordinate consideration. When the Admiralty wanted a Dreadnought it did not go shopping for cut-price offers, and it certainly did not go looking abroad.

Such instances as there were of large British firms involved in one way or another with steel did not for the most part make for notable efficiencies in the business of steelmaking. If steelmaking were to achieve comparability with American and German standards what was needed were more firms on the model of Blockow Vaughan,[2] to which Germany had perhaps a dozen counterparts. So we come back to the question: why this discrepancy between British and German structure?

[1] It should be said that the Guest element in Guest, Keen and Nettlefold had in itself constituted a long established and substantial steelmaking business.

[2] Blockow Vaughan is held out as an exemplar in respect of its scale and structure. Although it had in the past been perhaps the most forward of British steel makers, from the 1890s, for reasons which are obscure, it lost much of its dynamism.

In some part the answer is that the British industry was the captive of history while the German industry started with a clean slate. The German industry was able to achieve a high degree of geographical concentration – not of course the same thing as concern concentration but obviously conducive towards it – because German steel-using trades grew up in the wake of steelmaking and naturally chose locations close to steel – in the Ruhr and, to a lesser extent, in the Saar-Lorraine area. In Britain the situation was more complicated. Here the 'Revolution' had been very much a textiles led one, resulting in the location of a good deal of engineering industry in south Lancashire and the West Riding, regions with little or no ore or ready access to it. The west Midlands, of course, had conjoined metal using trades and a base iron industry, but iron-smelting was now running down there and, in any event, its metal trades long clung to puddled iron. Shipbuilding – a steel user of growing importance – had of necessity chosen different sites again, near the iron industries of central Scotland and the north-east coast. The steel industry of the north-west coast had grown up on its unique non-phosphoric ores in industrially virgin territory. South Wales had had a somewhat similar history – abundant ironmaking materials but little local industry. The same pattern obtained for the slowly emerging industry of the Scunthorpe region, founded on the extensive and easily worked Lincolnshire ores, but under the disadvantage, shared with the north-west, of having to draw its coal from outside. Thus cross-cutting considerations of markets and materials had contrived to disperse the British industry quite widely and militated against the emergence of large concentrated enterprises.

A second factor which had operated on the scale and structure of British steelmaking firms was the relative slowness with which steel found market favour in Britain. The big pig and puddled iron makers as a result tended to hold back, and most of the early entrants in the field neither commanded large capitals nor owned blast furnaces. And although some of these pioneers went under and others developed, many survived without growing much larger or integrating backwards into pig iron. This was particularly the case with open hearth steelmaking in which, for technical reasons, it was possible to get launched on a smaller scale than in Bessemer steel and where, also, the advantages of working in conjunction with blast furnaces were not as pronounced. Britain, in fact, took to the open hearth more rapidly than any other country – primarily because from the mid-1880s it was realised that acid open-hearth steel was much more suitable for ship plates than acid

Bessemer, a fact which could with profit have been appreciated much earlier.

Yet these considerations are relatively minor. Indeed they would be of little relevance except in the context of what was the fundamental factor curbing growth in concern size: the lack of expensive growth in the market for British iron and steel. German firms grew rapidly because their markets grew rapidly. Given the same rate of market growth the British industry could have engendered concerns of a scale and efficiency which, if it did not eliminate incorrigibly small competitors, would at least have confined them to local or special markets, and which, within the areas over which the industry was dispersed, would have permitted of the dominance of a small number of optimum-sized enterprises, along perhaps with a certain amount of geographical reconcentration.

This was the kind of recomposition which the British industry had come to need. And if it were not to be generated by market expansion there were only two other ways in which, hypothetically, it could have been brought about: by a forward aggressive policy on the part of those few concerns who were already within reach of optimum scale economies, directed to capturing the markets of smaller producers; or by a programme of voluntary, cooperative 'rationalisation', achieved by extensive mergers, the subsequent closure of smaller or poorly located works and the transfer of their output to the best potential sites. Either strategy would have been very costly in the short run. The first would have involved bitter and protracted price warfare – to which this industry with its high fixed costs was rootedly averse. The second would have meant writing off a great deal of expensive and still viable plant, and would have necessitated an appeal to outside funds for a project whose short-term prospects would hardly have allured the average private investor.

The second strategy was ultimately to be adopted, but only in the black days of the late 1920s and early 1930s with the industry on the brink of disaster and with substantial financial assistance from the Bank of England and a consortium of the commercial banks. In the years we are concerned with at the moment, and this should be stressed, the industry was not as a whole in any difficulty; it was merely failing to develop as it had done in times past and as its chief international rivals were now doing. Conditions were not buoyant but they were comfortable enough for most. No sense of urgent alarm existed such as might move the industry to radical and expensive departures from its familiar routine.

In distinguishing lack of market expansiveness as a fundamental causal element in the situation, we have come full circle. It was precisely the failure to achieve market growth that initiated our inquiry. There is a strong temptation to allow this to have been cause rather than effect, sufficiently accountable for by the natural advantage of the German and American industries in their own markets, the more especially when fortified by tariff protection. But even if this were conceded as a primary explanation of performance over the phase 1873–96 when continuing growth depended very much on retaining a strong footing in these markets, it still leaves the loss in the later years of substantial tracts of home and third party markets to be explained. Can this be done in terms other than those of the relative inefficiency of the British industry?

One possibility is that raw material costs had become higher in Britain. In detail, this is a fairly intricate question involving considerations of different kinds of coal and ore and their locations relative to steelmaking centres. Let it be simply resolved here by saying that on balance the British industry, assuming the readiness and the ability to make the most of things, was about as well placed as any other major steel industry. Coal was still abundant, although not always in quite the right place; and where domestic ores were not serviceable, foreign ores could be brought in cheaply enough.

A second possibility is that labour costs were higher in Britain. Britain in fact occupied an intermediate position in this respect. British wages were not nearly as high as American but were a little higher than German, which in turn were higher than Belgian. Low labour costs must certainly be accounted a significant element in Belgian competitive strength but the German advantage in this respect does not seem to have been large enough to warrant any great weight being attached to it. The more nostalgically minded among British employers – those who hankered after the days before 'employer' had supplanted 'master' – did quite commonly diagnose trade unionism as the source of competitive weakness; but wider agreement was to be found for another thesis: that Britain was the victim of 'dumping'.

Over the last decade or so of this period 'dumping' of foreign steel and its implications were the most hotly debated of all topics bearing on the British industry. And the debate is still alive among economic historians. Two separate though interrelated issues of contention can be distinguished: the extent and nature of dumping; and whether protective measures should have been taken against it. At one extreme what

676

was argued was that the German steel industry was purposefully bent on the destruction of the British industry by dint of building up a capacity to flood the British market with steel at prices below prime cost (i.e. the sum of labour, material and other variable costs), the losses so sustained being recouped from high prices charged in the protected home market; and that Britain must resort to tariffs to preserve her steel industry from extinction.

Receding from this extreme is a range of views: (1) that dumping (defined as sale below prime cost) did regularly take place, not with a view to destroying the British industry but, less malevolently, as a result of the general expansiveness of German industry which, in the case of steel, could run the hazard of excess development because this safety valve existed: (2) that dumping in the strict sense did not regularly take place, but that the Germans practised a multiprice commercial policy, as commonly does any industry which sells in more than one market, including, confessedly, the British iron and steel industry itself – a policy which at times of depressed home market conditions might mean spasmodic selling abroad below prime cost. (This observation would apply with particular force to the Americans, who figure less in the debate because they did not at this time regularly cultivate European markets, only seeking to sell in quantity there when home conditions were slack.) (3) Finally, that the whole issue was a red herring: that foreign competitive strength was primarily due to lower real costs; and that if the British industry could not match these costs it was positively desirable that it give way to superior production centres and permit the resources which it employed to be redeployed into activities for which Britain was better suited. Crudely represented, this last was at the time the majority view in establishment circles at large. It was what prevailing economic orthodoxy taught and as long as predictions of impending disaster for the British industry were believed, as they were by most thinking persons, to be unwarrantable scaremongering, its academic logical conclusion could be contemplated with equanimity – British iron and steel output through the 1900s was, after all, rising more vigorously than it had been doing for a couple of decades.

As a topical public question, the issue was, in any event, not an isolated one and was rarely argued on its own merits. In contemporary political debate it figured only as an element in the challenge thrown out to the now venerable policy of free trade by Joseph Chamberlain with his imperial preference programme. For Chamberlain, protection was only incidental to imperialism: commercial preference could only be extended to the Empire by tariff discrimination against non-Empire countries. And, as a political issue, tariffs on steel were caught up with the much more explosive matter of tariffs on food – and went down with the 'dear bread' charge with which the Liberal party steamrolled its way through the polls in the general election of 1906. Looking back, it is plain that tariffs for steel should at least have been allowed a discussion of their own, detached alike from 'Empire' and 'dear bread'. Whether or not German practice amounted to dumping, German steelmakers certainly regularly sold abroad at prices below those they charged at home. And their home prices could only be maintained by stifling competition – externally by tariffs, internally by cartels. One does not need to construe German competitive strength as due wholly or even substantially to German tariff policy to appreciate that there was a better case for granting some measure of tariff protection to British steel than was allowed to emerge at the time. But one cannot lightly proceed beyond the strict terms of this observation. In particular, the situation in the 1900s cannot be equated with that of the 1930s when tariff protection was finally conceded. In the 1900s the industry was not in the throes of depression; as noted earlier, it was in fact expanding. And if tariff protection would have enabled it to expand faster, the price, in the short run at least, would have been paid by those British steel users, export industries among them, who drew the benefit of cheap imports – imports not only from Germany, with its arguably 'unfair' export prices, but also from free-trading Belgium.

Industrial performance: the general record

Foreign tariffs, Britain's persistence with free trade, intensifying international competition, loss of growth momentum, the problems of adjustment to changed circumstances, issues of technical and entrepreneurial efficiency – all those considerations which have figured in our discussion of the British iron and steel industry, have their varying places in any appreciation of the record of British industry as a whole over the years 1873–1914.

A summary representation of that record in some kind of overall context can be statistically afforded. At the beginning of the period British industry accounted for about 30 per cent of the world's output of manufactured goods; by the end of the period that proportion was down to 14 per cent. Again, at the beginning Britain supplied about

Percentage Growth Rate of U.K. Industrial Output

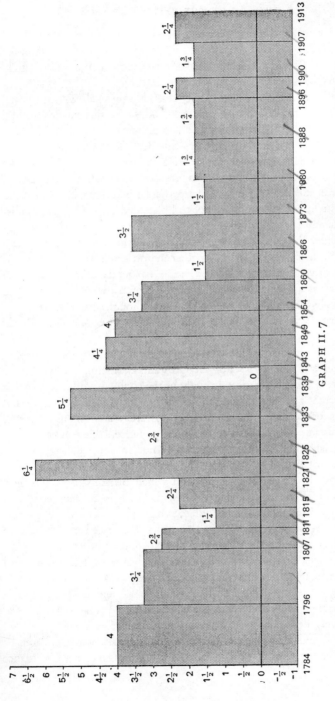

GRAPH II.7

(The periods represented here vary from four to eight years in length. They constitute an attempted compromise between periods so short that the fluctuations would divert attention from the trends which the graph is designed to draw out and periods so long that significant movements within them would be suppressed. However, performance within the periods chosen was not always very uniform nor do the dates selected necessarily mark turning points. The base data is taken from W. G. Hoffman, *British Industry, 1700–1850.*)

40 per cent of the manufactured goods entering into international trade; by the end that proportion was down to 25 per cent. Set in the context of Britain's own historical experience the matter may usefully be stated at rather greater length. (Graph II.7).

The broad traits revealed closely resemble those already noted and examined in the case of iron and steel. And the parallel extends further: as with that particular industry, it was principally the USA and Germany who were stealing Britain's thunder. However, it should also be observed that neither the relative international decline nor the deceleration in growth rate are as pronounced in this general instance as in iron and steel. A study of that particular industry is instructive and suggestive; but its lessons are not to be applied sweepingly and indiscriminately to British industry at large. No other industry of weight was under the same novel necessity to contend with its chief foreign rivals in their own markets. No other industry, that is to say, found its competitive position so suddenly and so stringently altered. For British industry as a whole the world changed more slowly. But it changed nonetheless certainly in the long run, although in some cases the long run was not to work itself out until after the First World War.

The long run in question was characterised not only by the emergence of other great industry states, the USA and Germany, but by a steady process of industrialisation throughout the civilised world, proceeding at different rates and taking different forms from region to region but always proceeding, always moving towards more industry, never towards less. Once the way had been pioneered this was inevitable. Industrialisation in other countries is not in some strange way a measure of British inadequacy. The remarkable thing is British precocity and the length of time through which Britain's precocious lead was held. What should raise eyebrows is not Britain's falling share in production of and trade in manufactured goods but that, three-quarters of the way through the nineteenth century, her share had been as huge as it was. Nor did the increasing participation of others in industrial activities necessarily work to Britain's disadvantage. The resources of any one country are limited, particularly when that country is a small, already densely populated island. As imagination and technology added to the range and variety of goods which mankind could supply, it was positively desirable, even from a purely insular viewpoint, that the material and human capacities of a continuously widening area be recruited to this or that particular task. It was argued earlier for instance that it may well have been to Britain's advantage to let synthetic chemicals pass to Germany.[1]

Britain was and remained a country fitted by history and by geography to be a major industrial power. What the years now under review brought was the need to find a role which was at one and the same time related to her own industrial past and adapted to a new world of widespread industrialisation. It was not important that Britain retain 40 per cent, or any given percentage, of international trade in manufactures. Indeed, in so far as such an expression is an inverse function of the volume of international trade, a decrease would point to more favourable conditions for Britain. What was important was that British industry continued to expand export sales to such levels as would ensure that export earning in gross kept step with the import expenditure which general growth would generate. And what was even more important still was that industry, now the central sector of the economy, seized those opportunities which provided the opportunity of sustaining general growth in a changing world.

Hypothetically, of course, pressure on export performance could have been relieved by a restructuring of the economy in such a way as to concentrate output effort more on the home market, provided it took such a form as to reduce the marginal propensity to import, either by the direct substitution of home for foreign produce, or by capturing demand increments for the kinds of goods which were produced at home. Such capturing did indeed take place to some extent – largely, however, because particularly rapid growth occurred in sectors which, of their nature, could not be the subjects of international trade: education, defence, medical services, gas and electricity supply, travel and entertainment, etc. As a result, exports expressed as a proportion of national income reached their peak in the 1870s and imports in the 1880s, when the accelerated swing to foreign foodstuffs was substantially completed. But even if the requirement to export for balance of payments reasons became somewhat less urgent, it remained urgent enough by any standards: about 30 per cent of national income was being expended on imports over the closing years of this period.

It follows from all this that, of the statistics cited in initiating this theme, the most significant are those describing the record of industrial growth rate. What kind of judgment should they evoke? Should we emphasise the sharp drop which they reveal? Or should we stress the continuation of growth on a base which, judged by any historical

[1] See p. 591.

standards, was of considerable elevation? Do we treat the figures as evidence of weakness or of strength? We could take the line that earlier growth momentum had resulted from exceptional and unrepeatable opportunities, and that if the rate now compared unfavourably with that being achieved in a number of other countries, as it did, it merely reflected the tardiness of those countries in getting their 'Revolutions' launched. We could, on the other hand, argue that British industry had become set in the methods and attitudes of an outdated generation and, most specifically, was failing to hold and extend export markets in the face of competition from younger, more enterprising industries – a line of argument already pursued in the case of iron and steel. But even before we come to testing that line of argument as applied to industry in general, we should confront a more fundamental question. The deceleration we are faced with – is that to be understood as a demand phenomenon or as a supply phenomenon?

A strong case can in fact be made for treating deceleration as originating on the demand side. The case is a simple one and has, in effect, already been made.[1] The high and rising rate of investment expenditure of the past ceased to be sustained; and although the enhancement of mass purchasing power which had already set in was maintained into the 1890s, the resultant shift to consumption expenditure was insufficient to make up for the loss of demand impetus. In the not excessively oversimplified phrase of one historian, the course of events after 1873 might be styled 'What happened when the railways were built'.[2] Expressed as a percentage of national income, investment has been estimated to have moved as shown in Table II.42.

The split between home and foreign investment makes it difficult to estimate the impact of these variations on demand. While investment at home contributed directly and wholly to demand, investment abroad only did so to the extent to which it was translated, directly or indirectly, into export orders for British goods. (Parenthetically, it can be noted here that by 1914 the stock of British capital abroad had risen to about £4,000 million, of which some £1,500 million had come in the great surge of 1905–14. Very little of this was now held in Europe, investors' attention having become heavily concentrated on six regions, as follows, with approximate indications of their share of the total: USA,

[1] See pp. 652–3.
[2] W. W. Rostow, 'Investment and the Great Depression', *Economic History Review*, **8**, no. 2, 1938. It should be said that Professor Rostow's concern here was to explain the long-run price fall after 1873 and that he did not in fact accept that output rate of growth showed any significant decline.

TABLE II.42. *Investment at home and abroad, 1864–1913*
(as percentage of national income)

Period	Investment at home	Investment abroad (net)	Total investment
1864–73	7·3	4·4	11·7
1874–83	8·0	3·1	11·1
1884–93	5·8	5·2	11·0
1894–1903	8·2	2·2	10·4
1904–13	6·4	6·3	12·7

(Source: P. Deane and W. A. Cole, *British Economic Growth*, pp. 332–3.)

20 per cent; Latin America, 20 per cent; Canada, 15 per cent – most of it dating from the 1905–14 phase; Australasia, 10 per cent; India, 10 per cent; South Africa, 10 per cent – prompted particularly by the gold and diamond discoveries of the 1890s.) Broadly speaking the feedback benefit of investment abroad would have fairly steadily tended to decline through this period as the recipient countries turned to indigenous suppliers or to exporters other than Britain, to satisfy the demands which British capital had initiated. Funds flowing to North America in particular were increasingly likely to expend themselves in the USA. Latin American countries remained rather more attached to British suppliers but, again, in diminishing degree as German, Belgian, French, Italian and US exporters won increasing favour there – sometimes even for railway equipment for enterprises in which British management was added to British finance. Of the major recipients of British capital, Australasia, India and South Africa were the most loyal to the hand that fed them. But even in the Empire import patterns were becoming more diversified.

All these trends become particularly pronounced over the last decade or two of this period, which is to say that the waves of capital surging abroad with gathering momentum from 1905 – continuously from 1907 exceeding the amounts invested at home – were of clearly attenuated capacity to engender demand for British goods. Bearing this consideration in mind, one might tentatively speak of the level of demand creating investment resting on a plateau into the early 1880s; then dipping sharply; effecting a partial recovery in the late 1890s; and, very possibly, falling off again as foreign took over from home investment from around 1907.[1] Taking the whole period 1785–1914 briefly under

[1] Table II.42 does not of course locate turning points with any precision. For these reference must be made to the original source.

broad review from this angle, we might sketch a picture of investment bouncing upwards at the outset of the period to exploit new technological opportunities; checked by the difficulties of the 1810s; resumed very vigorously at the beginning of the 1820s; from the mid-1830s receiving spasmodic powerful boosts from railway construction and, after mid-century, from foreign capital projects, which through this phase had a powerful feedback effect; then hitting the plateau already referred to. The overall effect would be to establish a rough correlation between investment, considered as a demand agency, and industrial growth; and thus to lend weight to the contention that post-1873 industrial deceleration can, at least in part, be understood as a demand phenomenon.

Another factor which may properly be included on the demand side is the effect of foreign tariffs, designed deliberately to depress or even extinguish export demand for British goods. Varying greatly, as they did, from country to country in respect of range, rates and duration, a charting of their precise effects would require a book in itself but it is obvious that, over the twenty years or so from the late 1870s onwards, the build up of tariff protection for native industries in western Europe and the USA appreciably curbed demand over the whole span of major British exports, bar coal, although in the longer run the competitive efficiency of the industries whose development was thus promoted rendered tariffs increasingly needless as a way of excluding British goods.

To the extent that we incline towards a demand explanation of industrial performance we are leaning towards an acceptance of a substantial degree of inevitability in the deceleration. There is an evident truth in saying that industry could produce no more than was wanted. At the same time it might be true that industry itself could have acted on demand. It might be the case that industry could itself have usefully maintained a higher level of investment, with the twin effects of injecting an extra element of demand into the economy and of further stimulating demand through cost reductions; and the latter would be efficacious not only in home but also in foreign markets. We cannot help but come back to the issue of a possible failure on the part of British industry – a failure to seize opportunities for growth, a failure to achieve efficiencies which would have enabled it to deal more successfully with foreign competition, a failure to employ fruitfully larger and potentially remunerative amounts of investment capital.

The notion that there was untried scope of this kind can only be tested by looking more particularly at the various branches of industry.

Before essaying that there are a couple of considerations of general relevance which can be aired. There is firstly the fundamental question of the effort which British society was prepared to devote to economic performance. Man does not live by goods alone. Leisure and relaxation have to be sacrificed for output. And the extent of sacrifice which is felt to be worth while is apt to vary a good deal from time to time and from place to place. There is plenty of evidence to suggest that the British populace was coming to value leisure more highly than it had done in the past and to be less ready to sacrifice it than were the peoples of other countries such as Germany. The working day was becoming shorter. The weekend was creeping into Saturday. The annual holiday was becoming a generalised institution. Even within working hours the rhythm of effort was being relaxed. The people of Britain were choosing to sweat a little less. The rewards of enhanced productivity can be taken either in more goods or in less labour. Who will insist that they should always be taken in goods?

A second consideration bearing on industrial performance generally is the course of prices (see Graph II.8).

This record itself needs explaining. But, as on earlier occasions when we have been threatened with the complications of price theory, the matter will again be sidestepped here. As always there is a broad choice between 'real' and 'monetary' explanations. A 'real' approach might distinguish a persistent downward trend operating on the supply side, through fairly continuous cost reduction, checked between 1853 and 1873 by countervailing demand engendered by railway and associated investment projects in many parts of the world, breaking through again as investment demand fell off after 1873, to be reversed once more by the international trade boom getting under way from 1896. A 'monetary' approach would see precious metal supplies failing to keep pace with the growing volume of transactions until the Californian and Australian gold discoveries of the late 'forties and early 'fifties; but, with these petering out, prices forced down again until revived by South African gold in the 'nineties. Apart from interpretation, dispute can arise over the facts themselves. A manageable representation of prices requires the construction of an aggregated index number series whose composition and weighting can always be argued with, at least with regard to its measurement of slight movements and its identification of turning points. Where there is not pronounced and sustained movement in a particular direction there can be endless quibbling as to what is to be accounted short-run 'disturbance' and what is to be accounted long-run 'trend'. In this case only the steady downward drift *c.* 1873–*c.* 1896 is free of such difficulties. However, since that is the phase which chiefly concerns us here and since we are evading interpretative polemics, we can treat it as an unambiguous base of reference and return to our original point of departure, the bearing of prices on industrial performance.

Wholesale Prices in Britain, 1821 – 1913
(1900 = 100)

GRAPH II.8. *Price movements, 1821–1913*

Deflation is not good for business. Profit margins are squeezed when price levels fall through the interval between incurring production costs and selling the goods, and when interest, rent and wage charges cannot be promptly adjusted to price changes. On top of this real reduction in profits, which commonly may not be very great, there is the experience of falling money profits, not necessarily adjusted mentally to the higher purchasing power of money.[1] In brief, falling prices are apt to have a souring effect on business expectations and to inject a note of doubt into assessments of fresh investment projects. The marked upturn in investment outlays in the decade following 1896, when price trends were reversed, would lend support to this approach – though one could of course argue that the cause and effect relationship was the other way round, i.e. from investment, through engendered demand, to prices, while the subsequent sagging again of industrial investment over the closing years of this period would necessitate an independent explanation. It should also be borne in mind that the price fall was a worldwide phenomenon and therefore does not provide a ground of distinction between the situations of British industry and of faster growing rivals.

Less work and lower prices doubtless had some bearing on performance in all branches of industry, but all branches did not perform alike. We must briefly indicate something of the varying experiences of the different branches of British industry.[2]

In any league table of industrial performance, pride of place should probably go to the business of building steamships. On any assessment – growth rate, international competitiveness, technical and organisational efficiency – this industry stands up to critical scrutiny very well, though a note of reservation can creep in over the closing years of the period. Shipbuilding represented, one might say, Britain's last bid for industrial pre-eminence. It was the last major industrial sector in which Britain took the lead and held it. Still in 1914 some three-fifths of the world's tonnage was built in British yards – twenty years earlier it had been about four-fifths. Crudely speaking, British shipbuilding on the eve of the First World War stood in something the same situation as the British iron industry had occupied on the eve of 1873 – an international colossus in point of sheer capacity but one which, having pioneered the techniques and large scale organisation on which the business was founded, had, perhaps, started to fall behind others, most particularly the rapidly growing German industry, in sustaining progress in methods. The parallel with the earlier international precocity of British iron holds good also in respect of the market base of achievement. In both cases, the fact that Britain took to using the article in question much earlier than others initiated advanced development, gradually extended

---

[1] Further references to these considerations can be found in Part I, pp. 110–11, where the like but opposite effects of inflation are raised, and Part II, p. 505.
[2] Many of the particular points made in compressed fashion in what follows on individual industries have already been made more amply in the previous chapter.

to comprehend export markets as the British example was imitated elsewhere. In the case of shipbuilding, it will be appreciated that no other country conducted anything like the volume of maritime trade which Britain did. Pre-eminence in this field was something to be expected rather than applauded.

The much lesser amount of seagoing trade conducted by other countries also meant that export opportunities were bound to be somewhat limited. Notwithstanding its command of such a preponderance of world capacity, only about a quarter of the industry's output in the early twentieth century was built for foreigners and this accounted for rather less than 2 per cent of total exports, although allowance should be made for the considerable quantity of secondhand tonnage sold abroad which might effectively double these proportions, and, furthermore, for the foreign traffic won by British-owned ships, impossible to distinguish from British traffic but whose extent is broadly indicated by the fact that British ships handled more trade in and out of American, French, Belgian, Dutch and Italian ports than did ships of those nationalities themselves and conducted a quarter of the seagoing trade of Britain's nearest maritime rival, Germany – and it was, of course, more remunerative to build ships with which British owners could conduct other countries' trade than to export the ships themselves.

If shipbuilding can be distinguished as an industry which made a special contribution towards supporting a dynamic rate of economic advance under changing conditions, the same cannot be said of the cotton industry which with average annual growth rates, in quantity terms, of 1·25 per cent for overall output and of 1·5 per cent for exports, was putting in a performance below the national industrial average, and could be said to have dragged down the performance of industry as a whole – in quite appreciable measure, given the weight of this particular industry in the whole. Yet this narrowly mathematical way of putting the matter can be dangerously misleading. Diagnoses of the relatively sluggish rate of British industrial growth which distinguish the slow increase of large, historically developed sectors as a prime agent of retardation certainly focus attention on a central feature of the situation. But, unthinkingly construed, they lend themselves to the inference that momentum was to be recovered by withdrawal from such sectors and the transfer of resources to young, freshly developing sectors. The implied argument that Britain somehow erred in not abandoning activities which made a substantial contribution to material welfare and to incomes for the sake of concentrating on much more marginal activities is to make a fetish of growth rates at the expense of absolute levels of achievement, which from any meaningful human viewpoint are what really matter. In no circumstances could cotton any longer achieve the 3 or 4 per cent growth rates which would impart a powerful momentum to the economy at large. But this is much more a comment on the extent of its past achievement than one on its current feebleness. Britain still in 1914 had the most capacious and the most efficient cotton industry in the world. It had met the growth of rival industries in Europe and the USA and the erection of tariffs to shelter them with a shift to the finer fabrics which by dint of Lancashire skills continued to penetrate recalcitrant markets, although the constricted market scope at this end of the price range forced it into a much increased dependence on Asiatic, chiefly Indian, markets where under conditions of open competition it could not be seriously challenged, as was also the case of course in its own home market, taking about a fifth of total output. All in all, British cotton goods sold wherever they could reasonably be expected to sell. But a commodity of diminishing marginal utility which had already penetrated nearly all of the world's markets could not look for fresh conquests of any great extent.

British woollen fabrics had never enjoyed the same commanding international position as British cottons had won; yet the British woollen industry was, at the beginning and end of the period alike, the world's leading producer. Export sales were hard hit by the growth of a tariff protected industry in the USA, which had been a market of very considerable weight, and the industry never again attained its export level of the early 1870s. But ground was held in Continental markets, fresh opportunities were found in the Empire, the Far East and Latin America, and the British industry, over the period as a whole, seems if anything to have increased its share of international trade in woollen goods. Ironically, the market in which it suffered most, apart from the USA, appears to have been Britain itself, where a change in fashions initiated in the 1880s led to a swing to French worsteds which the British industry made only a very half-hearted attempt to meet. But this affected only a particular sector of what was a very varied market and one which, by contrast with cotton's market, was starting to reflect the effects of increasing mass purchasing power, of which the British industry by and large took ample advantage. Nevertheless the woollen industry's ability to capture something of incremental expenditure with its varied range of fabrics could never make for growth rates of a 3 or 4 per cent order. In broad terms, it must be classed with the cotton industry as an already developed sector, continuing to maintain a generally high level of competitive efficiency but subject to distinct market limits on its expansion potential.

The three sectors detailed so far were those in which British industry continued to lead the world and in which checks on advance could fairly be said to have been set by external conditions rather than by internal shortcomings. However these sectors accounted, according to the 1907 Census of Production for only about 11 per cent of total net industrial output. (Cotton, 6 per cent; Shipbuilding, 3 per cent; wool, 2·5 per cent). If we shift attention to a group comprehending engineering (6·5 per cent), iron and steel (4 per cent) and chemicals (3·5 per cent) we move into that theatre in which criticisms of British industrial performance have found their most vigorous play. Here it is that suggestions of technological inertia, entrepreneurial ineptitude, base defects in technical and scientific training, radical weaknesses in organisational structure, lack of responsiveness to new opportunities, have been raised the most freely. Here it is that the market scope offered by a world in course of equipping itself with the means of industrialisation might be expected to have supplied particularly abundant opportunities to that country which had first achieved industrial maturity; an area, that is, in which the advantages of having taken the lead might be thought to have been enduringly decisive; and where, as a consequence, the historical experience of actually being overtaken and of being confined to a modest growth rate in the midst of dynamic world demand seems at first sight to offer ground for the sort of charges just detailed.

However, that case studies soon involve one in intricacies which defeat comfortably dogmatic simplifications has already been demonstrated in our consideration of iron and steel, while something of the even more complex situation of the engineering and chemical industries, with their numerous subdivisions, has been indicated in the previous chapter. These latter industries, indeed, with ramifications lending themselves to very fine specialisations, were precisely of that nature which permitted a high degree of international differentiation, with advantage to all concerned. Here, especially, a recitation of American and German strengths must not be offered as a definition of British weaknesses. And, in any event, British performance in these fields does not expose itself to crude reproach with the same blatancy as in iron and steel. Measured in money values (i.e. unadjusted for price changes) iron and steel exports increased one- and two-thirds times over this period as a whole. Exports of machinery (including vehicles) increased fivefold and exports of chemicals threefold. Alternatively expressed, while iron and steel exports edged up from 9 per cent to 10 per cent of the total, machinery rose from 2 per cent to 8 per cent and chemicals from 2 per cent to 4 per cent. Plainly, these two, engineering particularly, were not sluggards. What is at issue is whether under exuberantly expansive market conditions growth in these sectors might not have been even more rapid.

One important branch of British engineering, but only one, did maintain an unquestionable international pre-eminence: textile engineering. Only in the heavily protected USA market was any serious setback experienced and even there the native worsted industry, admittedly small, continued right up to 1914 to draw the huge bulk of its machinery from Britain. In export markets, American textile engineers could not live with the British, and while competition was experienced from German, Austrian and Swiss firms, this did little more than take some of the cream off Britain's worldwide sales. A massive home market base was a major source of strength, but the alert export orientation of the industry is exemplified by the readiness with which it took to the manufacture of cotton ring spinning machinery – an American innovation which, within this period, found little favour with British cotton spinners.

Yet it was organisational efficiency and operative skills rather than technological forwardness which remained the bases of British competitive power in textile engineering. In other engineering fields which Britain had pioneered, such as steam engines and railway locomotives and rolling stock, much of the expanding market scope was taken up by German and American suppliers. There remained, however, plenty of room for the British product, and there was no question here of any absolute setback. If on the Continent and in North America more advantageously located German and USA concerns commanded the bulk of the market, British firms were little disturbed in most of the Empire and were able to retain a reasonable market share in other areas such as South America and the Far East, while the British market itself remained almost exclusively the preserve of home manufacturers. With the advantage of the lead earlier obtained in these branches, a less fragmented organisational structure might well have made for a more impressive performance, but the record does not suggest gross backwardness: it speaks more of others catching up than of Britain falling behind.

The picture which is starting to emerge, then, is one of continuing, though not necessarily unchallenged, strength in fields where the original initiatives had been British and where accumulated skill, experience and market reputation were major assets – with the lurking implications that things were rather different in more novel developments. One particular sector which embodies this theme is agricultural engineering. Threshing machinery, early developed in Britain, was exported continuously in considerable quantity. So were steam tractors. Yet over this extending range as a whole the British industry was not only outclassed by the American – which was more or less inevitable – but came to be closely rivalled, in such markets as the Americans left, by the German industry, a late starter in the field.

Machine tools tell a similar story. British industry was strong towards the heavy end of the scale, encompassing the tools used in steam-engine, locomotive and ship construction. But, notwithstanding a phase of rapid adoption of American methods to cater for mass production of bicycles in the 1890s, in the medium and light machine tool ranges Britain could not stand comparison with the USA and Germany, either in point of technical initiatives or of output – the latter being the more important, since the capacity to imitate can be just as valuable as the capacity to invent. Again, American forwardness may be related to American circumstances, but the superiority of Germany, coming up from behind, is difficult to account for in terms other than greater ingenuity and greater enterprise on the part of both producers and users of machine tools. Indeed, where circumstances are broadly comparable, machine tools may perhaps serve as a handy test of relative levels of attainment in engineering generally. Their use signifies an elastic output capacity, free of the difficulties of recruiting and training a specially skilled labour force. It points to costs low enough to be able to command the breadth of market essential to their economic utilisation; and to a market structured and conditioned to the acceptance of uniform articles susceptible to continuous flow production. As Germany came to lead Britain in machine tools it is not surprising to learn that she led also in other developing branches of engineering. And these years, of course, brought not only growth and extension in pre-existing sectors but the creation of brand new fields of engineering activity.

One such field, bicycles, has just been referred to. Here actually was a novelty in which Britain forged ahead in rather impressive fashion. By the early 1890s, the bicycle in all its modern essentials had been fully evolved; and in a flurry of enterprise and capital raising a substantial industry came into being in the Birmingham-Coventry area, characterised by extensive use of machine tools, standardised production methods and prices low enough to command a broad, though not quite mass, market both at home and overseas, easily outselling the German industry, its nearest rival, in third-party markets. Yet the very vigour and efficacy of the British thrust in cycle manufacture only highlights the relative weakness of the effort in other, more considerable, fields of new endeavour.

On the face of it motor-car manufacture had a record comparable to that of cycles. Starting from absolute zero in 1896 Britain by 1913 had a motor industry turning out 34,000 vehicles a year, which at a gross market value of around £15 million put the industry among the leaders of the engineering trades. But it was in imitation of German and French initiatives that the British industry was launched and, although on the purely technical level Britain soon bred individuals and firms who were fully the peers of their Continental counterparts, in gross output terms it continued to lag. In this high potential field, in which a strong engineering and metallurgical base could count for so much, Britain right through to 1914 remained in the rather humiliating position of being a net importer, although, by then, imports consisted principally of chassis and components from France and Germany while exports were very largely made up of finished vehicles (selling mostly in Empire markets).

However, the most significant and most invidious comparison is not that between the Continent and Britain but that between Europe as a whole and the USA, rolling out 485,000 cars a year by 1914. This was no consequence of inventive precocity. America borrowed the motor car from Europe. But, in borrowing it, America transformed it. What France, Germany and Britain offered as a rich man's toy, America converted into a mass consumption good. Of course, the depth of the market which the American industry contrived to plumb was in significant part a function of American incomes; but that was by no means the whole of the story. Entrepreneurial imagination, 'creative' selling and the harnessing of engineering talent to the design of production systems no less than to the design of motor cars – these were the features that intrinsically distinguished the American from the European motor business. The nature of the American achievement is the measure of Europe's failure. Here was the making of a second 'Industrial Revolution'. But it was only on one side of the Atlantic that the prospect became a reality before 1914. As someone has said, America is the oldest country in the world because she was the first to enter the twentieth century.

The impact, actual or potential, of the motor car cannot be measured in any ordinary cost-benefit way. It was not so much an improvement as an entirely new product, to be grouped along with the wireless and the aeroplane as elements in a wholly novel range of experience which technology and science were now making possible – although up to 1914 only the motor vehicle among this trio had acquired any serious economic significance. Indeed, the period now under review saw questing mankind ripping aside the veil beneath which the physical universe hides its prowess and potentiality in a manner which gives these years a very special place in the history of science and technology. That boundless command of nature which the High Renaissance had exuberantly envisaged but which, through subsequent centuries, had proved so slow in realisation was now being achieved. However, much of what was now becoming understood had to wait before ingenuity and a deepening of knowledge could render it capable of wide-ranging practical application and the social and economic consequences of this massive intellectual achievement were as yet limited. Up to the outbreak of the First World War its most important practical manifestations were in the development of new forms of power.

Steam power, a main base of the first Industrial Revolution, suffers from inflexibility, non-transmissibility and the bulkiness of the fuel used, as well as, in the case of regions remote from coal, the cost of the fuel. Flexibility and transmissibility could be supplied by electricity which, generated from a central station, made the use of power in small and/or irregular amounts commercially practicable. In certain circumstances, electricity could also make power available where the bulkiness or the cost of coal had precluded or limited the use of steam power; for example, electric traction for neighbourhood transport services; hydro-electricity in mountainous regions distant from coalfields. A more widely serviceable answer to the problems posed by bulk and cost of coal was supplied by oil-fired engines. Oil occupies only half the space of the energy equivalent in coal and, in practice, requires even less storage space on account of its fluid capacity to fill volumes of any shape or size, with the direct implication that where storage space was valuable – most evidently in oceangoing ships – oil could offer significant working economies over coal, and the indirect implication that being as a consequence cheaper to move it would have a lower delivered price than coal in many parts of the world.

Here, then, were two new forms of power answering a complex of needs and capable of extensive application. In our present context the question is: how did British industry respond to the consequent demand, home and foreign, for the novel types of equipment required? The answer is: not as resiliently as a number of other countries. The British electrical engineering industry was not only overshadowed, with almost tedious predictability, by the American and German industries, but in competitive efficiency it also compared poorly with Swiss, Belgian, Swedish and even Hungarian enterprises. This undoubtedly was a 'second wave' opportunity which Britain failed to seize. It was not that Britain was slow in taking to electricity. From the time of its very first commercial application to telegraphy in the 1840s, Britain had been quick, if not to lead, at least to follow, taking briskly to electric lighting from the early 1880s, electric traction a little later, and, the last but ultimately most important application, to electrical powering of machinery, mostly in the 1900s. Right up to 1914 Britain was one of the world's biggest users of electricity, exceeding Germany in absolute, and even more in *per capita*, terms. Furthermore, Britain had early developed a strong telegraphic equipment (largely cables) industry, which continued to hold a leading place amongst world suppliers in this particular branch of electrical goods. Yet when the various kinds of demand coalesced to engender a powerful boom in electrical apparatus from the mid-1890s, British users had to draw heavily on German and American suppliers; and although the degree of dependence on imports fell off in the early 1900s this was largely because the two great American combines, General Electric and Westinghouse, had found the British market sufficiently rewarding to set up large subsidiaries to supply it direct. Indeed, with an offshoot of the German Siemens concern as another, earlier established, main component of the industry in Britain, the extent to which an authentically British electrical engineering industry existed at all was slight. This British located industry, as one should perhaps style it, did build up something of an export trade in electrical machinery, accounting at the close of the period for about 6 per cent of engineering exports – and about 0·5 per cent of all exports – a puny total in the face of world demand and one which leant heavily on Empire markets, with their partiality for British supplies, and on South American markets where British-promoted enterprises were prone to order British.

The story is much the same with oil-fired engines. From the early 1890s, very successful light engines were made by British engineering concerns, many of which sold abroad in coal-less areas for use in tractors and a variety of low power operations. But when the big, complex, technically exacting diesel engine came on the scene British manufacturers left the field to Germans, Swiss, Belgians and Swedes, not to mention Danes and Hungarians. Here is a plain case of inward-lookingness. As a land engine, there was little use for the diesel in cheap coal Britain; while as a marine engine, in which capacity its potential advantages were considerable, its high initial cost frightened British mercantile shipowners, although others, the big German shipping lines and the British Admiralty among them, were less timid. Without a substantial home market base, British engineering concerns were not prepared to take the plunge into those foreign markets where the diesel commanded a keen interest.

Finally, and very briefly, two less important engineering sectors in which the theme of British inertia in the face of new technologies is manifest may usefully be noted: watches and office machinery – the first an ancient product but which from as early as the 1860s was becoming the subject of new mass production methods in the USA and Switzerland; the second, comprehending typewriters, cash registers and adding machines, an entirely novel range, with a history of blue-prints and patents reaching back into the first half of the nineteenth century but only transformed into a commercial proposition by American methods from the 1880s. In the one, American techniques were being copied in Britain from the late 1880s with a measure of success sufficient to check the flow of imports. In the other, reliance on deliveries from the USA was diminished only when American manu-facturers set up branch plants in Britain.

Turning to chemicals, where the increasing sophistication of processes and the widening range of products presented new challenges at the same time as worldwide economic growth presented new market opportunities, we must forswear any attempt at detailed examination of British performance. The broad traits are plain enough and the fairly careful distinctions which need to be observed between different branches of engineering can be safely abandoned in the case of chemicals.

In the great majority of its numerous branches this was an industry group demanding such accumulations of technical and material resources that only the most extensively developed economies could support it. Chemicals were the almost exclusive prerogative of four countries: the USA, Germany, Britain and France. With a world market expanding exuberantly in quantity and range, none of these four could hardly help but grow. But of the four Britain's growth was easily the slowest. Entering this period ahead of the other three put together in what was still a fairly limited field, Britain preserved a strong international position until about the mid-1880s. Thereafter the others grew much more rapidly, and by the end of the period Britain had fallen way behind the USA and Germany, and was only just keeping its nose ahead of France. In many of the newly developed branches, synthetics conspicuously, Britain came to lean on imported supplies; and imports grew much faster than exports, so that by the early twentieth century *net* exports had become quite small. Lack of well-trained chemists, disinterest in exploiting such expertise as there was, a reluctance to finance research – these fairly evidently were the basic reasons for British weakness in this field, in which indeed, it could fairly be said, no serious attempt to stay the pace with Germany was made, once technical leadership in chemicals had clearly been assumed by that country.

This brief review of British performance in selected industrial sectors has been directed towards elucidating the question: were there about through the period 1873–1914 growth opportunities which British industry missed? And this ought not to be confounded with any 'top of the pops' kind of assessment. An international comparison, where it is available, can serve as an indicator of performance against a yardstick of general possibilities. But, as urged already, it was not necessarily to Britain's overall economic advantage to appropriate every possibility. Furthermore, growth opportunities were not necessarily most ample where international competition was keenest. Our concern here is with growth – and with relative international achievement only in so far as that provides a criterion of growth. Where that criterion is not available, assessment of performance is much more difficult. To indicate just one such sector, though that a very important one: coalmining, which by 1890 had clearly established itself as Britain's premier industry and in 1907 was measured as accounting for 15 per cent of net industrial output. Maintaining a fairly constant growth rate, in gross physical output terms, of 2 per cent p.a. it was in foreign markets that coal sales grew with especial momentum: coal tonnage exports increased at an average rate of 4·25 per cent p.a. between 1873 and 1913, by when they accounted for around a quarter of the industry's output and about a tenth of all exports. But this performance is not susceptible to any meaningful international comparison. It was a simple function of geography and of autonomously determined demand; or, put in obverse form, British coal sales were not governed in any very significant degree by the relative cost efficiency of the British industry. (Indeed, measured in output per man/hour terms, coalmining was easily the most retrograde of major British industries, although it would be impossible here even to attempt to assign the responsibility for this as among the inescapably increasing inaccessibility of the coal measures; the minuscule scale of many of the hundreds of different colliery enterprises; and failings on the part of both management and labour, along with the reciprocal antagonisms between the two.) Here, one might almost say, was growth for the asking. And perhaps the most important feature is that the British market itself did not ask for a great deal of growth: subtract export sales and the rate of output increase drops to 1·5 per cent p.a. – a figure which, while it doubtless reflects in some degree more efficient ways of burning coal, is principally just another comment on the overall rate of British industrial growth.

By throwing in coal we have raised our coverage of British industries to about 40 per cent of the total as constituted in 1907. (The major groups omitted are: food, drink and tobacco (processing), 12 per cent; building, 7 per cent; apparel, 6 per cent – none of which lend themselves with any ease to evaluation in terms of exploitation of growth possibilities.) It cannot be pretended for one moment that what has been said here permits of any simple diagnosis of Britain's industrial situation, or of any straightforward appreciation of the level of industrial performance. That there were certain weaknesses is plain; but the degree to which these impaired overall performance is difficult to determine with any kind of exactitude. The record undoubtedly offers evidences of entrepreneurial sluggishness, technological inertia, inefficient organisation, but equally compels great reserve in generalising these phenomena as central explanations of industrial performance. About all that one might properly permit oneself by way of simple generalisation would be that whichever of the various lines of approach and analysis are followed they all tend to converge at the one point: the maturity of the British industrial economy, whether it be the maturity of the old dog who cannot be taught new tricks or the maturity of the hardened traveller who has nowhere left to go.

The forms of business life

If one can legitimately speak of the maturity of the system, the system in question might clumsily be defined as that of individualist capitalism, and that to which it was to give way as that of corporate capitalism. The later years of this period may be identified as those in which the transition was initiated, although the movement was by no means rapid and as early as 1914 large tracts of the economy were still totally unaffected by it.

In a full perspective the rise of corporate capitalism has perhaps been a phenomenon of as profound an importance as that of the individualist capitalism which it has supplanted. Unlike its predecessor, it has not been intimately and necessarily associated with major technological transformation, and the extent of the strictly economic advance of which it has been an agent is not comparable in degree with that achieved by the Industrial Revolution. But under other aspects, it has changed things in ways that we are still seeking to identify and come to terms with. An essay in analysis of this multifaceted change would have to roam well beyond the scope of this book but two core characteristics may be briefly mentioned. The one is its introduction into business life of *la carrière ouverte aux talents*: the substitution of management by right of ability for management by right of inheritance – with both the provision of career opportunities over a broad social spectrum and its requirement of a society conditioned to breeding the appropriate type of salaried personnel.

The second characteristic relates to the question of power. The large oligopolistic concern which has come increasingly to dominate the economic scene possesses power – over prices, supply, incomes and employment – of an order which the smaller individualist concern of the former régime, merely one among many in conditions of open competition, could never command. At the same time, this power is depersonalised and diffused. The concern exists independently of any individual or group of individuals; and its power is spread, smeared one might say, throughout its elaborate structure. To speak of the divorce of ownership from control is a common way of describing this phenomenon of depersonalisation and diffusion. Yet this is really an attempt to fit the phenomenon to a set of concepts from which it has escaped. The old notion of ownership has become void of any real sense when applied to a mass of shareholders who own nothing but the periodic right to such payment, if any, as the directors may at their effective discretion appoint. Nor is it as if a board of directors, possessed of no formal security of tenure, can in the full sense be said to be in control of a large complex concern, whose performance is effectively determined by the decisions and actions of a management hierarchy and organised labour. Ownership has no substantial existence and control has no definable location.

The above outline has run well ahead of the period immediately in hand. It is only in very recent times that the type of socio-economic organism described has proliferated into most sectors of the British economy – although it could be said to have already become a standard type in the American economy by 1914. And, even within our period, many of such truly large-scale concerns as did emerge retained characteristics inherited from an older order of things. However, if any point in time can be distinguished as inaugurating the epoch of corporate capitalism in Britain it must be the later 1890s, if by 'corporate capitalism' one means to refer to enterprises whose elaboration of structure put them beyond the comprehensive sovereign power of the old style of capitalist entrepreneur and which, having once broken through the limits set by the constricted financial and managerial resources of the older form of organisation, had come into possession of an indefinite growth potential – not necessarily of course exploited. (It will be appreciated, that 'corporate' is not used here in a legalistic sense, or indeed with any rigour of definition.)

There was no evenness about the onset of the phenomenon. At one end of the economic front it had set in much earlier than the 1890s. The great railway companies have already been cited as prominently precocious instances. No other industrial enterprises were, within this period, remotely to approach them in point of scale of operations. At another extreme there were sectors which had not even effected the transition from domestic industry until the last years of the nineteenth century or the early years of the twentieth: various metal- and wood-working crafts only came into factories with the adoption of electrical power; and boot and shoe manufacturing only with the generalisation of American machinery; while much garmentmaking remained the province of domestic workers up to and beyond 1914. The history of structural change is a variegated one; but the 1890s do claim a special place in it: of the forty-five British industrial concerns with a nominal capital of more than £2 million in 1905,[1] twenty-seven had been

---

[1] The data relating to 1905 is derived from P. L. Payne, 'The emergence of the large-scale company in Great Britain, 1870–1914', *Economic History Review*, **20**, (1967): 1905 has no

constituted under their current style between 1894 and 1903, twenty-two of them in the particularly intense phase of company promotion 1896–1901, and of the eighteen already in existence by 1894 some had only moved into this class since then by dint of subsequent takeovers or extensions.

Fairly plainly, the later 1890s in particular did set loose forces tending to subvert an economic order founded on the family and small partner-ship concern, although, equally plainly, the old order retained an abundant capacity for survival. These forces might be distinguished as four: exploitation of the intrinsic cost economies of large-scale or vertically integrated operations; extension of the field of activity of superior management talent; reduction or limitation of competition; and, of a rather different nature, a desire on the part of owners of private businesses to liquidate their property in whole or part for cash – especially potent when there was the prospect of getting more than the business was worth. Of these, the last two were unquestionably the most decisive in the great majority of instances of growth by way of merger. And it was by way of merger, rather than by way of internally engendered expansion, that the bulk of the largest of contemporary concerns emerged. Growth on a dynamic base of scale efficiency and man-agement strength was very much the exception rather than the rule.

Individual cases have of course individual explanations and generalisa-tion can be dangerous, but there is a striking uniformity of character to a block of thirteen companies, ranking among the largest in the coun-try, eleven of which date from what might be termed the 'merger mania' of 1896–1901. The thirteen, arranged in industry groups with dates of formation, are: Salt Union (1888), United Alkali (1890), Fine Cotton Spinners (1898), Bleachers' Association (1900), Calico Printers (1899) Bradford Dyers (1898), British Cotton and Wool Dyers (1900), Yorkshire Wool Combers (1899), English Sewing Cotton (1897), Linen Thread (1898), Wall Paper Manufacturers (1899), Associated Portland Cement (1900), Imperial Tobacco (1901). All of these represented amalgamations of several, in most cases numerous, indivi-dual concerns, very few of whom had themselves attained any substan-tial size. And in all of them the individual concerns of which they were constituted retained a great deal of autonomy, central sovereignty being

significance other than being the date for which this author supplies the data. By 'industrial' is meant manufacturing and mining; principal categories excluded are transport, com-merce and finance.

absolute on only one issue, price. They were, in effect, only more formal and permanent expressions of the pricing agreements which the industries concerned had habitually sought to contrive – with the additional feature that the general investing public was afforded the opportunity of participating in the prospective benefits of controlled prices. Proportions of the shares in the newly formed companies were offered for open subscription, the remainder being taken up by the constituent concerns themselves, who thus exchanged their businesses part for cash and part for shares, not uncommonly at valuations which greatly flattered them.

Very few of these ventures achieved anything like the degree of commercial success extended in prospect by their promoters. They were founded in nothing more substantial than their reputed capacity to control prices and thus profit margins. In practice, however, the fields in which they operated were relatively easy to enter and price maintenance fairly soon foundered on fresh competition, or in some cases on competition from established concerns which had not been gathered into the combines – whose founders seem commonly to have underestimated the extent of market control needed to make dictated prices stick.[1] But even if profits rarely reached anticipated levels, sheer size conferred durability. Corporate capitalism had its foot firmly in the door and was not to take it out again.

Two other very substantial groups may be associated with these price fixing combines, in that, within them also, concern growth was largely due to an anxiety to curb competition and, again, proceeded by way of merger. These groups are the banks and the breweries. At first sight, these may not seem to have much in common with each other nor with the combines just referred to. Banking and brewing were, and remained, keenly competitive businesses. What was sought by the large concerns in these fields was not the ability to dictate prices but protection against competition by means of securing assured points of contact with their clienteles. What the tied house was to the brewery, the neighbourhood office was to the bank. Of course, both kinds of business had an established history of concern growth, in the case of banking reaching back to the Act of 1826 and in the case of brewing back even to the early eighteenth century. But, while earlier growth had been primarily due to endeavours to secure the various kinds of

---

[1] The Imperial Tobacco Company should be excepted from these remarks. It not only retained but enlarged its original share of the market; and, after some initial teething difficulties, proved a conspicuously profitable undertaking.

efficiencies that went with scale in these fields, its marked acceleration through the years now in question reflects above all a scramble for captive custom. In the case of banking, this meant the acquisition by the large joint stock concerns of small private banks with their local good-will; in the case of brewing, the acquisition by the breweries of licensed premises which, since the introduction of restrictive licensing in 1869, enjoyed an effective legal privilege in the sale of beer. In both cases as the scramble reached a crescendo in the 1890s and early 1900s the prices offered reached levels which few owners of private banks or 'free houses' found themselves able to resist.

Alongside these acquisitions went mergers between the concerns engaged in the scramble, commonly directed towards rationalising and integrating the rather ramshackle individual networks which had been built up. The result was a much increased degree of concentration in both businesses; but in brewing its extent was limited by the inability of any one brewery to make deliveries over an area of more than a few miles radius, with the consequence that although some very large concerns emerged in metropolitan areas, there remained over a thousand brewing firms scattered throughout the country. Nevertheless the big metropolitan brewers ranked among the greatest of contemporary enterprises in the early years of the twentieth century; fifteen of them in 1905 had a capitalisation of over £2 million each. In banking concentration went a good deal further. By 1914 the huge bulk of the country's banking business was in the hands of twenty English and eight Scottish concerns.

Simplifying a little, the types of large-scale concern so far noted could be said to have embodied the principle of affiliation rather than that of integration. The price-fixing combines did not envisage close operational fusion of the enterprises they embraced; and bank branches and brewery-owned pubs are, of necessity, semi-autonomous elements in their parent concerns. If we are hunting for instances of an evolved corporate capitalism with its peculiar opportunities and problems and vested with those characteristics which distinguish it most clearly from individualist capitalism, we find it only very partially established in these areas, in which the degree of decentralisation ensured that within new forms much survived in substance from the older order of things, including very often the retention of a strong family character.

Outside these essentially defensive affiliations, instances of large, operationally integrated enterprises, sustained by and offering full scope for strong central management remain few and far between all the way up to 1914. Rail transport remained the only field where such enterprises were the characteristic type. The liner shipping companies provide another parcel of instances but tramp shipping, accounting for the bulk of maritime transport, remained the province of the hybrid type of concern remarked on in the previous chapter. Heavily capitalised concerns had always dominated the insurance business (other than that undertaken collectively by Lloyd's underwriters), but this was business of a uniquely simple and routine character and did not necessitate the sort of elaborated decision making structure which is here being insisted on as a hall-mark of corporate capitalism. Shopkeeping, rather paradoxically, remained the breeding ground of tiny businesses in their thousands while throwing up a handful of firms whose turnover was to be measured in millions of pounds: the chain-stores, Boots, ABC, Lyons, Liptons, Home and Colonial; the department stores, Whiteleys, Harrods, Selfridges; the furniture stores, Maples, Waring and Gillow – all of them to be explained less in terms of scale economies than of shrewd perceptions of a new sensitivity on the part of the shopping public to lay out, presentation of goods, shop décor, brand image, etc.

Within the range of what is normally understood by 'industry', where the intrinsic advantages of scale are commonly greatest, what is most striking perhaps is the continuing rarity of enterprises which were plainly bent on a dynamic drive to achieve the rewards of size and, as a consequence, evolving into fully fledged 'corporations'. J. & P. Coats (sewing cotton) and Lever Bros (soap) are conspicuous. So are Brunner Mond, a distinguished exception to the generally indifferent British record in chemicals, and Courtaulds, progressive pioneers of the first artificial fabric, rayon. Even these were still in the transitional stage from family concern to depersonalised corporation, the founders or descendants of the founders still being in effective control of all four.

Two oil companies, Shell and Anglo-Persian, came to considerable size on the basis of a rapidly growing market over the closing years of this period. In one sense, these two companies had radically different structures: while Shell remained the private property of a tightknit Anglo-Dutch consortium, Anglo-Persian was, in a manner of speaking, a public company in the fullest sense of the term, the British government being a major shareholder, for the sake of assuring oil supplies for the navy. At the same time, they were alike in having widely flung undertakings to administer, necessitating elaborate management hierarchies such as to place them along with the railway companies as prototypes of the modern corporation.

A group of eleven large companies involved in steel has already been considered and the conclusion reached that, big as they were, they did not attain that size to which a vigorous pursuit of optimum efficiency might have led; and that the motives behind their formation were commonly defensive ones.[1] Nevertheless, and despite the frequent persistence of a strong family element, these may be accounted corporate concerns in the rather elusive sense in which the term is being used here. Indeed iron, steel, shipbuilding and armaments were the sectors of the industrial economy in which, by 1914, the old type of pure family concern or small partnership had become rarest. There were few firms in these fields in which ownership had not been diluted in some degree by the admission of outside capital, and not very many either in which day to day management was not in the hands of salaried professionals, although utlimate control usually rested with a board of directors on which the original ownership was well represented.

This type of 'mixed' concern was by 1914 to be found in some number throughout the economy. Side by side with the big public flotations, and indeed more persistently, had gone privately arranged sales of blocks of shares in smaller concerns. Diffusion through two, three and more generations had often in itself caused ownership to become quite widely spread; and those heirs who had no active part in a business were particularly likely to sell off their holdings in whole or part, perhaps to diversify their income sources, perhaps to raise expendable cash. Inactive participants would also tend to be averse to ploughing back distributable profits; and growth capital which had formerly been internally engendered might now have to be raised from outside. At the same time the passage of generations could lead to increasing reliance on hired managers for the conduct of a business. In this sort of way, then, the family character of concerns could become gradually attenuated, without any clearcut transition to a new form intervening. And, while in one way or another old-established closed concerns were slowly being opened up, the scope for newcomers to enter business in a small way was becoming narrower.

By the early twentieth century, technology had created a situation in which relatively large initial capitals were needful to break into many profit making activities. Building, garment manufacture, retailing and road haulage were perhaps the only substantial sectors which still offered enterprise armed only with a few hundred pounds the prospect of a modest fortune – along of course with the much greater likelihood

[1] See pp. 672–3.

of bankruptcy. In new fields of endeavour, cycles, motor cars, electrical apparatus etc., pioneers needed substantial financial backing if they were to get into the market. But 'substantial' here does not mean millions or even hundreds of thousands of pounds; and none of the companies created in these fields had by 1914 remotely approached the big brewing or steel concerns in point of size. If the old-fashioned family or small partnership concern was gradually ceding the field, it was not, for the most part, to the great corporation but to companies whose scale of operations commonly did not surpass that of many well-established family businesses and which often were organised around a dominant founding personality, intimately identified with the concern in the manner of the individualistic entrepreneur of the past. But if for the moment developments did not throw up many enterprises of a radically novel character and constitution, the widening diffusion of ownership was creating concerns whose proprietors were essentially *rentiers*, equably disposed towards reorganisations which might be resisted in privately owned businesses, apt to be as much a way of life as a source of income. What was going on might be described as a kind of softening up process, fashioning firms of a greater malleability and receptivity and making them readier future subjects for conversion into, or absorption by, the fully fledged business corporation.

This chapter has so far addressed itself to two themes which must figure prominently in any account of economic change and development in Britain over the last hundred years or so: the response of British industry to new opportunities on the one hand and growing competition on the other; and the emergence of new forms of business life, carrying implications that range well beyond the issue of economic efficiency. If we add two other particular themes it would be fair to say that we have gathered together the essentials of what has transformed the economy of the 1870s into that of the 1970s. The additional themes are: the increasing weight of the state in the national economy; and the changing patterns of incomes and consumer spending. Although neither of these provide matter of profound import in the context of the years up to 1914, there is enough of substance to them to warrant their introduction at this stage.

The economic role of the state

State activity in the economic sphere may conveniently be considered to take three forms: (1) expenditure on goods and services; (2) control and regulation; (3) redistribution of income. This distinction does not necessarily relate to particular kinds of measures or even to particular intentions; but, broadly speaking, the last two will only figure prominently as a consequence of deliberate economic or social policy while the first will always figure in some degree whether or not any such policy is being pursued. However, the crude volume of state expenditure is obviously a function of the number of fields in which government, central or local, chooses to act. In other words, as long as we are

TABLE II.43. *Expenditure (net of national debt charges) by central and local government as a percentage of national income*

	%
1873	7
1883	10
1893	11
1906	13
1913	14

(1906 is given because of defects in the available figures for local expenditure and the special effects of the Boer War on central expenditure in the immediately preceding years. The base data used is derived from Mitchell and Deane, *Abstract of British Historical Statistics*, pp. 367–425 and is not quite what it ought to be for this purpose. The figures used for central government expenditure and national income relate to the United Kingdom while those used for local government expenditure relate to Great Britain only. Furthermore, there are no figures for local Scottish expenditure before 1893. Here, Scottish expenditure has been assumed to bear the same ratio to English and Welsh in 1873 and 1883 as it did in 1893. The consequent errors in the percentages given would not be large and would have no significant effect on the trend shown.

National debt charges have been excluded since the primary object here is not to measure expenditure *per se*, but to provide a yardstick of government activity through the dates given; and the great bulk of the national debt arose out of pre-1815 military activity. Local government debt charges are, however, included since they largely related to continuing activities, conspicuously trading services, and constituted an integral part of the cost of those activities.)

dealing with what may handily be termed a minimalist state, government will occupy no special place in an economic narrative unless warfare, the business of even the most minimalist of states, involves it in heavy expenditures. Minimalism, sanctified as *laissez-faire*, had characterised British government for over half a century through the post-1815 era. But as we move through and beyond the last quarter of the nineteenth century, state activity, under one or other of the forms we have distinguished, comes to loom more conspicuously in the economic sphere.

As a spender, the gross record of the state through this period is given in Table II.43.

In rough and ready fashion, broad components of this growing body of expenditure can be distinguished (see Table II.44).

TABLE II.44. *Objects of central and local government expenditure other than national debt charges (percentages)*

	1873	1883	1893	1906	1913
Military	34	27	27	25	25
Social services (i.e. education and health)	8	11	16	22	23
Other goods and services	48	55	48	47	42
(of which postal, water, gas, electricity, transport and harbour services)	—	—	—	(22)	(26)
Poor relief, old age pensions and national insurance benefits	10	8	7	6	10

(The source data is the same as above. Its use for this purpose gives rise to various difficulties which have not been resolved here and the table should be regarded as very crude, serviceable only as indicating general trends.)

Reported in these statistics we have the onset of a 'revolution'. Like many other of history's 'revolutions' this has been a gradual one, born out of no sudden convulsion in human affairs and achieved by men who quite commonly would have trenchantly disowned any revolutionary intent. No one political creed or party has borne special responsibility for it. No one governmental programme has been a chief architect of it. It has been a revolution of bits and pieces, apprehensible as a unified sequence only in hindsight – that viewpoint which can always make a wood out of miscellaneous trees. It is however an authentic revolution which, willy-nilly, has transformed a minimalist state into an interventionist state, and has contrived an economy in which government, whether it wishes it or not, has become the principal *dramatis personae*.

Within the period immediately in question, it was in the field of education that new measures had their most considerable effect on the level of governmental expenditure. A series of statutes following on the founding measure of 1870 established a comprehensive system of free and compulsory primary education, while the Act of 1902 brought public finance to secondary education as well – in both cases the bulk of the charge falling on local, rate supported, authorities. An educated population had come to be regarded as a categoric social necessity. There was not, however, the same concern to ensure a healthy population. Public hygiene had for some time been the object of growing activity and the Public Health Act of 1875 prescribed sanitary standards which effected the eradication of a good deal of the filth and squalor in which infection had luxuriated through much of the nineteenth century. But, while the state was taking care of prevention, cure remained largely a private responsibility. Treatment, of a kind, had always been available to the destitute under the Poor Law, and some local authorities were coming to provide hospital services over a broader social range; but the great bulk of British hospitals continued to be maintained out of patients' fees and charitable donations. General practitioner services were made available to those in employment under the National Health Insurance Act of 1911, mostly financed out of statutory contributions from employees and their employers.

No less impressive than the financial consequences of new governmental initiatives in the social welfare field is the weight by the close of this period of expenditure on what are usually styled 'trading services' – the 'postal etc.' group in Table II.49 conprehending services which were self-financing. Less eye-catching, because not for the most part the outcome of major pieces of legislation, this was 'creeping socialism' at its most insidious – an untrumpeted edging aside of private by public enterprise over a steadily widening field. Mail delivery, to which were added telegraph, telephone, savings bank and money remittance services, had been an ancient function of that special agency of central government, the Post Office; but the others in the group, water, gas, etc. were the business of local authorities; and it is worth stressing that it was not, for the most part, Whitehall which was the responsible agent in the extension of state activity of this period but the town hall. Centrally enacted legislation created the statutory framework and, in certain fields, specifically imposed duties on local authorities. But councils all over the country were increasingly extending the ambit of their little empires beyond the bounds of their strict statutory responsibilities. The gathering vigour and purposefulness of local government is not least among the major traits of the history of Britain through the late nineteenth and early twentieth centuries.

Particular initiatives in particular fields for particular reasons – if these add up, as they do, to a substantial amount in gross expenditure terms, they do not at the same time add up to an integrated socio-economic programme or philosophy. The state was becoming an increasingly important participant, but had as yet little inclination to direct or manage the economy, to fashion it to given proportions or to manipulate it towards given ends. Control and regulation as a form of state activity need, then, occupy no space in this chapter.

Nor can income redistribution claim much attention although it would be true that the bias of state financial operations was reversed through this period. A budget which on balance had exacerbated income differentials in 1873 was by 1914, to a very modest degree, operating to narrow them.[1] Movements on both the expenditure side and the revenue side had conjoined to produce this effect. On the expenditure side outlays on education were chiefly of benefit to the less well off. There was an element of state subsidy to the National Insurance Acts of 1911 which financed medical care and sickness benefit for all wage earners and unemployment benefit for those, about two million in number, in certain trades peculiarly liable to employment fluctuations, while the statutory contribution from employers can for practical purposes be accounted a tax on them, specific to financing these services. And from 1909, old age pensions of 5s a week became payable out of central government funds – although in some measure these, along with sickness and unemployment payments, simply served to shift some of the burden of distress from local poor rates, which remained the principal instrument of income transference; an instrument which, if coming to be employed with a little more flexibility and compassion, continued to be directed solely to the relief of authentic destitution and to leave a mark of social disgrace on those whom it touched.

On the revenue side, a growing proportion of state income was

---

[1] This is not true if account is taken of debt interest, paid for the most part to the well-off. Whether or not account should be taken of this factor would seem to depend on whether or not the holders of government debts would have found alternative uses for their money in the absence of state borrowing.

coming from levies which, where they were not actually progressive, were at least not positively regressive as duties on mass consumption commodities, tea, sugar, tobacco, beer, etc. tended to be. Income tax, payable only on incomes of over £100 p.a., rose from 4d in the £ in 1873 to 1s 2d in the £ in 1914. Surtax became payable on incomes of over £5,000 p.a. in 1911. A new system of death duties had been introduced in the budget of 1894. All in all, while direct, income related, taxes had accounted for 22 per cent of central tax revenue in 1873, they accounted for 46 per cent in 1914.

Little that had been done so far had purposefully sought to use the power of the state to redress the inegalitarianism which the free play of social and economic forces had brought about. Only the Liberal government which came to power in 1906 – at a general election which in returning forty members of the recently founded Labour party had manifested a newly articulate discontent with the old order – had deliberately set about a very modest transfer of wealth from one set of pockets to another. But, even without deliberation, the tide had started to turn. As state expenditure, for one reason or another, had swelled, it had been acknowledged, explicitly or implicitly, that the financial burden should fall where it could be borne without discomfort. A notion of social justice had insinuated itself into a revenue system which hitherto had had regard only to tax yields and ease of administration.

Incomes and expenditure

The drift of state activity was towards an alleviation of the condition of the masses. But it was a slow drift and its overall achievements by the end of this period were not of much more than marginal consequence. If conditions of life for most people improved through these years, the improvement owed relatively little to the benevolence of the state. That there was improvement is abundantly clear. The pronounced upward trend of real wage rates which had got under way in the 1860s was more or less continuously maintained until the end of the century – by when, the evidence suggests, they were some 80 per cent higher than they had been around 1860. The more impressionist picture derived from information about the style of working-class life supplies some of the meaningful detail to the bare statistical data: more abundant and attractive diet, better clothing, more comfortably furnished houses (without, however, a corresponding improvement in houses themselves), a wider range of leisure and entertainment activities. The music hall, the working man's club, professional sport, the popular press, the annual seaside holiday are all distinctive products of the late Victorian and Edwardian age. Thrift had its share too, testified by the swelling funds of friendly societies, of building societies (these, however, though working-class in origin, tended to assume more of a middle-class character), of trade union benefit schemes, of those insurance companies which specialised in the small policy – conspicuously the Prudential – of the Post Office and Co-operative societies' savings banks, not to speak of thousands of local burial clubs, wakes clubs, Christmas clubs, etc., innocent of anything like audited accounts.

To call this prosperity would be an excessive straining of language. It was no more than comfort. And even that was by no means a universal experience. If coalminers, pre-eminently, and skilled and semiskilled workers in most branches of industry scored substantial gains, agricultural labourers, who had shared in the general advance of wages through the 'sixties and early 'seventies, achieved only a fractional further betterment of their condition as farming struggled to adjust to the rising tide of imported foodstuffs. Women workers, especially in the two groups, domestic service and garment manufacture, which accounted for about three-fifths of all female employment, experienced little improvement of their lot. And the mass of unskilled, irregularly employed, general labourers, whatever ill-recorded advance was achieved at this level, remained trapped in a vicious circle of poverty: inadequate nutrition, enfeebled constitutions, diminishing earning power once middle years had been reached; with the cycle often accelerated by excessive recourse to life's only solace, beer. Perhaps, indeed, the most pronounced effect of income movements through the last quarter of the nineteenth century was to widen working-class differentials. While the coalminer, the steel furnace man, the engineering craftsman, could maintain a life of dignified comfort, detailed surveys of the late nineteenth and early twentieth centuries revealed that about thirty per cent of the population lived in a state of deprivation.

But if the persistence of real poverty on an extensive scale must receive every emphasis, the considerable increase in real wages which was the experience of the majority of workers through to the end of the nineteenth century still stands as one of the period's most prominent phenomena. How is this increase, which can fairly precisely be dated to c. 1860–c. 1900, to be explained? It was observed earlier that we lack any general theory of long-run wage levels, but in the case in question now, we can attempt to do without one by settling for a sequence of short-run movements as a chief agency. Within the phase 1860–1900 the increase in *money* wages came very largely in a series of bursts: 1863–66, 1870–73, 1882–84, 1888–90, 1896–1900. These bursts coincide closely with spates of intensified economic activity and low levels of unemployment. And labour was now showing a new-found ability to exploit its periodic scarcity. Moreover, money wages which had been jacked up during these spates fell back little, if at all, in the intervals,[1] even though these were commonly marked by very high levels of unemployment. It is difficult to resist the inference that we are here confronted with a new actor on the economic stage: durably organised trade unionism, capable of extracting advantage for its members from good times, and, perhaps even more important, of defending them from bad.

Certainly, the years in question are the years of consolidation and muscle-building on the part of the British trade union movement. The bubble unions of earlier decades which had been contemptuously burst by employers were, from the 1850s, being replaced by less visionary minded organisations, prepared to work with the system rather than against it, ready to bide their time and their funds, building up a solidly attached membership as much through their benefit schemes as through their fighting prowess, acquiring an aura of Victorian respectability and gradually swinging the employing classes from vehement hostility through grudging acceptance even to a positive preference for organised labour as making for more manageable industrial relations.

There was, then, more to this development than the swagman's 'Stand and deliver!', with the strike as the weapon of intimidation – although it should never be forgotten that this crudity always lurks at the very centre of trade-union/employer relationships, however sophisticated their forms. On the one side, there was a new set of pecuniary ambitions. Labour, historically, had habitually acquiesced in the customary valuation placed on it. Occasionally, the spirit had revolted and thrown itself into millennary movements whose prophets run from John Ball in the fourteenth century to Feargus O'Connor in the nineteenth, and which were usually as shortlived as they were futile. Always, of course, there had been individuals of egregious ambitions, but these had sought advancement by breaking out of the ranks of labour. Now the notion was rooting itself that labour as such

---

[1] This was not wholly true of certain industries, conspicuously coal and iron where wages, in the short run, were often price-linked and where sharp price fluctuations brought correspondingly sharp wage fluctuations.

could rightfully and reasonably look for a steady augmentation of its income; that the working man could aspire to something of the material comforts and pleasures that his 'masters' enjoyed. And to make the point fully, stress in this last sentence must go on 'steady' and 'something': millennarianism, or its latest variant, socialism (in its rigorous sense), had little part in this attitude. The existing capitalist order was frankly accepted, but as a régime which, with prudent tactics, could be made to yield more to those who served it with the work of their hands. On the employers' side, there was a realistic recognition of the change in labour's posture and of the fact that it was a development which they could live with, or at least that war to the knife, however satisfying to the sentiments of the more bloody-minded among them, would do more harm to their purses than would timely concessions. A measured appreciation by each side of the strength of the other and some acknowledgement of an area of common interest were creating a new pattern in industrial relations.

This sober, sturdy unionism was by no means established throughout the working population. It was peculiar to the skilled and semiskilled, and to certain industries, conspicuously textiles, iron and steel, engineering and shipbuilding – to which may be added coalmining, in which union organisation was equally strong but where industrial relations were continuously marked by naked reciprocal hostility. Only buoyant market conditions, permitting both wages and profits to expand simultaneously, kept in check the savage bitterness which was to unleash itself so destructively in the coalfields in the 1920s.

A skilled membership made a union doubly strong: blackleg labour could not readily be found to counter a strike; and relatively high earnings enabled the union to accumulate fairly substantial funds. By the reverse token, successful union organisation of the unskilled was difficult, the task commonly aggravated by the casual nature of unskilled employment; and although from the 1880s onwards, and especially after 1900, the so-called 'New Unionism' was recruiting adherents in growing numbers, its fighting strength was suspect which, along with the revolutionary syndicalist socialism which many of its leading personalities professed, served to excite an aggressive, union-breaking counter response from employers. A handful of famous victories were won but whatever ultimate sociopolitical importance might be attached to the movement, the total extent of its gains in immediate terms of pounds, shillings and pence on wages was not of great moment.

Acknowledging that union organisation was at its most efficient among skilled workers, the broadly contrasting income experience of the skilled and unskilled does lend weight to the view that trade unionism was a main agent of increased wages over the four decades *c.* 1860–*c.* 1900. This leaves unexplained the much less favourable course of wages after 1900. In real terms, wages on average were no higher, even somewhat lower, in 1914 than they had been in 1900. Two things appear to have been responsible for this. One, that although the secular economic growth trend was much the same as it had been through the previous quarter of a century or so, there was a long run of years without one of those particularly intense accelerations of activity such as had come at more frequent intervals in the past and which, as seen, had enabled money wages to be pushed sharply upwards. Taking the analysis a little further, the diversion of investment capital abroad from around 1905 would seem to have taken the steam out of the domestic boom which was then getting under way and which as a result only went off at half-cock, frustrating a fresh major break-through of money wages. This flow of capital abroad engendered something of a compensating effect in the form of 'feedback' export demand. But as noted earlier, the 'feedback' potency of overseas investment had become attenuated. It was not until 1910 that something of an export-led boom got moving and even then money wages could only manage a fairly modest rise.

The second factor curbing real wages was the reversal from 1896 of the downward course of prices which had characterised the years from 1873. After 1900 such increase as there was in money wages was cancelled out by rising prices. Indeed the dominant determinant of real wage incomes throughout the period 1873–1914, bar the phase 1896–1900, was not the course of money wages but the course of prices. One should, however, understand this statement as a description of a formal mathematical phenomenon, not as a definition of efficient causality. In other words, it would, fairly plainly, be wrong to suggest that real wages, up to 1900, rose to the extent that they did *because* prices fell; that real wages were the passive subject of prices. The manner in which money wages rose through much of the 1860s, in the bursts referred to between 1873 and 1896, and through the phase 1896–1900, makes it clear that wages, under the right conditions, had a powerful capacity for self-impelled action and compels the conclusion that they *actively* maintained such money levels as permitted them to rise in real terms during the 'Great Deflation'.

At the same time it must be acknowledged that the particular behaviour of food prices did act as a kind of *deus ex machina*, an agency which operated on real wage levels without operating on profit margins – other than those of farmers. If the prices of all commodities had behaved in identical fashion, an increase in real wages while prices fell must have been entirely at the expense of profits, assuming for the sake of argument unchanged productivity. But if food prices fell faster than other prices, an increase in real wages could occur even while money wages were lowered to preserve profit margins.

Food prices did fall a good deal more sharply than prices generally between 1873 and 1896. Grain in particular came tumbling down. Wheat which in 1872–74 had averaged 57s 2d a quarter, averaged 26s 6d in 1895–97. Potato prices fell nearly as steeply. Milk and home-killed meat remained much firmer but cheap bacon and ham was arriving in growing quantities from North America and Denmark, while from the mid-1880s effective refrigeration techniques were giving access to the grasslands of North America, Argentina and Australasia with their abundant potential as low cost beef and mutton producers. Cheap foreign sources of butter and cheese were also being tapped and, at the same time, tea and sugar prices were slithering downwards as extended cultivation multiplied supplies. In fact, the last two or three decades of the nineteenth century brought an extension of the world's food raising acreage which makes the phase unique in international economic history. And no country drew greater benefit from it than free-trading Britain, prepared to let its own food producers go to the wall in the interests of its food consumers. By the turn of the century, however, the frontiers were beginning to close in and world population was again coming to press on an agricultural capacity now losing the elastic resilience which it had briefly and exceptionally enjoyed. Food prices hereafter moved in broad sympathy with the general price level; and the windfall advantage which wage earners had drawn as the margins of agriculture had been thrust back was not to be repeated.

To the extent that higher real wages were a function of lower food prices, this was gain for wage earners at no cost to employers. Was the cost then borne by farmers? Are we witnessing here an effective transfer of income from the agricultural community to the industrial prole-tariat? Were higher living standards for the urban masses bought at the price of rural distress? Put in the plainest terms: did cheap imported foodstuffs undo British agriculture?

There is no simple answer to these questions. If the wheat market had largely to be ceded to foreign suppliers and what remained to the British producer brought only a miserly return, the buoyant market for fresh meat and milk was preserved. Moreover, livestock needed feeding. Although imported animal fodder met much of the need, the scope for enlarging domestic output of oats provided some compensation for diminished wheat acreage; and brewers continued to insist on home-grown barley.

The commercial opportunities that survived offered no prospect of sustaining the expansive profitability which many farmers had enjoyed through the preceding decades, but deft adjustment to changing conditions could enable a comfortable livelihood to be retained. And the sort of adjustment required was one which British agriculture was already making in shifting away from wheat towards livestock. It was not, then, a radical change of direction that was called for but a prompt and powerful acceleration of a pre-existing movement.

In these circumstances, fortunes varied greatly with individual acuity and flexibility. Broadly speaking, the clay farmers, who had already gone furthest in the requisite direction, were the most forward in getting their arable down to grass and cushioning themselves against disastrously low grain prices, while the light soil farmers were the slowest in breaking with the classical, grain pivoted, arable rotations which had served them so handsomely in the past, but which now left them exposed to the full blast of foreign competition. The almost uninterrupted fall of grain prices from the mid-'seventies to the mid-'nineties was too fast for the reflexes of many of the latter, and only the subsequently firmer prices enabled them to re-establish their bearings in a drastically changed world and find a reasonable measure of prosperity in routines whose balance as between wheat and barley, on the one hand, and animal fodder, on the other, reflected the balance of market prices. At the same time, low bread prices – along with low potato prices, low tea prices, low sugar prices, low cheese prices, low beer prices – and the rising real wages which were a part consequence of them were a positive assistance to the suppliers of fresh meat and milk, whose produce was a particular object of incremental purchasing power. Imported meat supplies, of course, siphoned off some of the demand which otherwise would have fixed on home-killed beef, mutton and pork. But this was largely hypothetical rather than actual loss: cheap cured and refrigerated meat was bought by those who had formerly subsisted almost entirely on a diet of bread, potatoes and cheese. Indeed, it might be that there was a degree to which the availability of an intermediary foodstuff facilitated the transition to fresh meat as a growing number of wage earners became able to afford it.

Averaging out – but remembering that the average amalgamates widely discrepant cases – farmers' incomes in real terms would seem to have just about maintained themselves, even through the period of most rapidly mounting foreign competition. To a degree, this was achieved at the expense of the incomes of two other agrarian classes: landlords and labourers. In the traditional cornlands of the south-east, rents sometimes crumbled to merely nominal values, behaving as classical theory teaches rents will behave on marginal land, which, until adapted to changed circumstances, was what British wheat-bearing land had become. But rents on pastureland kept up, and a fair number of landlords owned urban or urban fringe property, whose rising value could more than compensate for declining agricultural rents. Taken *en bloc*, landlord fortunes were substantially conserved. It was agrarian wage incomes which submitted to a major reduction. Even this was the consequence not of a cut in wage rates – which indeed edged upwards in real terms, though not to the extent of wages generally – but of a cut in the number of wage earners. Between the censuses of 1871 and 1911 the number of agricultural labourers fell from 988,824 to 665,258, reflecting above all the shift from labour intensive arable farming to labour sparing pasture farming. And the broad indications are that the very sluggishness of farmers in effecting this transition ensured that the run down of the agricultural labour force occurred sufficiently gradually to permit of a fairly smooth absorption of the redundant elements in the agrarian population by other sectors of what was a growing, if not exuberant, economy.

All in all, then, while individual cases of distress among farmers, landlords and labourers were numerous, British agriculture contrived to change roles without having to endure a phase of cataclysmic upheaval. Its new role was certainly a secondary one, both in the sense that incomes derived from agriculture now accounted for a greatly reduced proportion of total incomes – over the whole period, from about 15 per cent to about 5 per cent – and in the sense that British farmers had ceased to be the principal source of supply of the nation's foodstuffs.

Possibly, even probably, some of the ground ceded to foreigners could have been held had home producers shown more alert and resolute adaptation to changing circumstances. Nothing that British farmers could do would have enabled them to compete with the produce of the vast open spaces of the Americas and Australasia but, on the face of it, Danish bacon and butter might well have met with more strenuous opposition from British suppliers. This, however, is to operate in the margins. Only a return to protection could have preserved a place of central economic importance for British agriculture. As a matter of deliberate policy Britain, alone among the major countries of the world, allowed farming to be reduced to a subsidiary role in her national economy. And the gain thereby secured was that the mass of the British population enjoyed a higher standard of living than was to be found in any other populous country, bar the USA. If Germany by 1914 produced one and a third times as much steel per head of her population as did Britain, *per capita* meat consumption in Britain exceeded that of Germany in just about the same proportion.

While, as stressed already, this by no means implies that real poverty was not still widely prevalent in Britain, it does imply that Britain had approached closer than any other country, the USA again excepted, to that level where daylight starts to show between society's primary wants and mass purchasing power, to that point where wage earners are floated off to join the other classes of society as buyers over the whole range of consumer goods and services. To put it another way, such development leads to a stage where the differences between the various classes of society in point of material comforts are ones of quality and quantity rather than of fundamental style of life, with an erosive effect on class differentiations as at least one set of status symbols loses its distinctiveness; while, under an economic aspect, it creates opportunities of widening the range of application of mass production methods. However, within the period at present in question it is a matter of an approach towards this level, rather than of its attainment. What might with rhetorical licence be styled 'the consumer revolution' could not be said to have yet begun in the Britain of 1914.

In its higher reaches at least, working-class life style had certainly gained much in point of ease and comfort, but it was still clearly distinguishable from middle-class life style, though it would be true to say that the most clearcut distinction consisted not in the type of goods purchased but in whether or not domestic servants were employed. (The 1911 census counted $2\frac{1}{2}$ million domestic servants – 14 per cent of the total employed population and outnumbering any other general category of employees.) Certainly too, the half century or so up to 1914 had seen a growing attention paid to the consumer. Advertising, packaging, shop design were directed to securing his, or more commonly her, custom in a manner that would warrant speaking of a retailing revolution. Yet while in some degree this witnesses to such an extension of consumer purchasing power as to elicit novel attempts to court it, much of it can be explained in other terms: the massing of shoppers in urban agglomerations, reinforced by the more rapid access to shopping centres afforded by rail and electric tram services; the growth of a national press, supplying a medium for propagating brand images; the diversion of entrepreneurial talent to selling as the deceleration of economic growth and the advantages of established concerns blocked fresh opportunities in manufacturing. And it should be noted that this novel attention was often directed to the middle-class rather than the working-class customer: the department stores, such as Whiteleys, Harrods, Selfridges – perhaps the most distinctive developments in retailing – were after the doctor's wife, not the bricklayer's.

In brief, the rise in real wages did not go far enough to convert any substantial segment of the working class into an essentially new kind of market. But it came close to doing so. Had the momentum of the increase in wage purchasing power over the decades c. 1860–c. 1900 been maintained through the closing years of this period, Britain might have been entering the threshold of 'the consumer revolution' by 1914. It is at least a mathematical truth that a projection of the smoothed real wages curve for 1860–1900 through to 1914 gives a value some 25 per cent above that actually attained – a value in fact which was not to be reached until the early 1930s.[1] A little fancifully perhaps, we might on this basis identify the decade or so preceding the First World War as a phase in which the British economy missed the opportunity of changing into a higher gear, one with a drive supplied by the domestic purchasing power of a high wage economy, à l'Américaine.

Of course, one cannot treat wages as an autonomous variable in the complex equation of a national economy. There is bound to be a great deal of circularity in any attempt to link wages and level of economic performance. And to the extent that there was an exogenous determinant of real wage levels, in the shape of international food prices, their levelling off from around the turn of the century eliminated a factor which had earlier been favourable to real wage movements. However, we are left with one variable that was both indigenous and,

---

[1] This statement refers to wage rates, as distinct from actual wage incomes (i.e. no allowance is made for variations in unemployment). If the high unemployment of the 1930s is taken into account, it is probably true that wage incomes did not reach the value in question until the Second World War.

to a degree, autonomous: investment. Quite plainly, had the £1,500 million or so of capital which flowed abroad between 1905 and 1914, or any substantial part of it, been retained for domestic investment, it must have conduced to the generation of higher wage incomes; although the magnitudes would obviously have depended very much on what sort of undertakings were financed by this hypothetically diverted capital. And while it is only the absolute level of wages that is strictly in issue here, it may also be observed that a particular effect of this spate of foreign investment was to widen again the income differentials which since c. 1860 had been tending to close (ironically, at just that time when a Liberal government of mildly radical temper was putting through a programme designed to achieve a measure of income redistribution in the reverse sense). With the reduced feedback earlier commented on, a high proportion of the return to Britain on this foreign investment consisted of the direct return to the investors in the form of interest and dividends, a return, that is, exclusive to the moneyed classes. Once again, the rich were getting richer while lower income groups were doing little more than marking time.

Five

1914—1939[1]

The last chapter indicated four themes which, it was suggested, constitute between them the essentials of what has transformed the economy of the late nineteenth century into the economy of the 1970s: (1) the response of British industry to new challenges and new opportunities; (2) the growth of the business corporation; (3) the increasing degree of state involvement in the economy; and (4) the changing structure of income and expenditure patterns. Along with some account of gross economic performance through time these will provide the substance of our two concluding chapters. Needless to say, these are not isolated topics. Rather are they closely interconnected. (Only the issue of state involvement could be said to have a significant autonomy of character, pertaining as it does in substantial part to independent developments in the realm of ideas and ideals.) And it is especially true of the period now in question that the extent of development in the particular directions indicated was controlled above all by the level of gross economic performance.

Gross economic performance

The outstanding characteristic of the performance of the British economy in the years between the two world wars can be expressed in one word: waste. And that in turn can be very simply exemplified (see Graph II.9).

---

[1] A more accurate description of the chapter would really be, 1919–39 since it does not purport to treat of the war years except in so far as the postwar situation requires reference to them.

722

Unemployment, 1919 – 1939

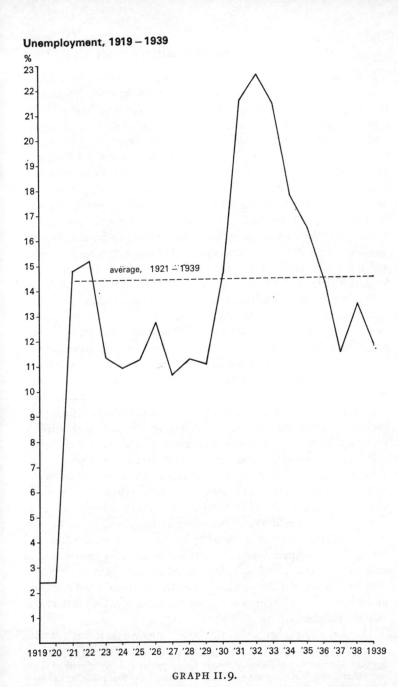

GRAPH II.9.

(Up to 1923 the base figures are those of trades unions recording unemployment amongst their membership; thereafter they relate to workers covered by National Insurance. Neither are comprehensive and the true global rate of unemployment at any time was probably somewhat higher than indicated here. Source: Mitchell and Deane, *Abstract of British Historical Statistics*, pp. 65, 67.)

If one takes a rate of 2 per cent as signifying 'full' employment, i.e. as marking the irreducible minimum of 'frictional' unemployment in a free society,[1] then the margin between the 2 per cent level and the actual rate of unemployment can be taken as a good measure of 'waste' – of productive resources available but unused. Discounting 1919 as a year in which many were still held in the armed forces and 1920 as a year of rather artificial postwar boom, this measure indicates a 'waste' rate of just about 12·5 per cent of the country's economic potential on an average of the interwar years as a whole. And if allowance is made for a degree of under-recording in the data used and for the 'short-time' working to which a number of industries resorted in place of laying off workers, a figure of 15 per cent is probably a more accurate measure – and this before taking any account of the cumulative booster effects which a high level of employment and demand would have engendered.

In a total human analysis, the most profound import of all this mathematics relates to the unemployed themselves, to the pinch-penny existence to which it reduced them, to the repeated heart in mouth scrambles at the news of a job going somewhere or, perhaps worse, the passive resignation to joblessness in a world of 'No vacancies' which just did not want to know. Here however, in a work devoted to the fairly strict economic, it is the other, colder face of the coin which is to be shown: the unemployed as so many ciphers of productive capacity. As such, the figures disclose a radical failure on the part of the British economy. They speak of a vast opportunity missed. They spell out an awful indictment of a system of economic organisation which confronted simultaneously, in the very person of each unemployed worker, with real human wants and the means of satisfying them was yet unable to match the one to the other. For here, it is not essentially a matter of the arguable, marginal weaknesses which in the decades before the war may have been responsible for some loss of growth momentum and international competitiveness. Here it is a matter of a central flaw in economic structure. And indeed, it should be made plain at the outset that the flaw was not one peculiar to the British economy but one lying at the heart of that international economic order of which Britain was but one member.

Translated into other terms, this 'waste' meant that it was not until

---

[1] Post-1945 experience has in fact shown that it is possible to get close to 1 per cent but it would be proper to make some allowance for the greater mobility of workers in our own times as a result of better transport facilities (private rather than public) as well as for labour 'hoarding', i.e. the retention by employers of workers not currently required against an anticipated need for them in the near future.

1924 that industrial production surpassed the level reached eleven years earlier in 1913 – having just about reattained it in the boom year of 1920, only to fall back sickeningly again. And the fact that this level had been briefly touched in 1920 makes it clear that the slowness in topping it was not due to any impairment of productive capacity inflicted by the war. The war in fact caused little enduring harm, and none of any persistence. Britain had not been a battlefield and, apart from negligible damage caused by the odd Zeppelin raid, had not suffered at all from the physical destruction of productive equipment. Shipping losses had been high, but by 1922 there was no shortage of ships relative to the quantity of goods seeking carriage. Factories which had shifted to war production obviously lost a certain amount of time in reconverting, but this process, along with the release of manpower from the armed services, had been completed by 1920. Nor, extending the range a little, had the liquidation of certain overseas assets to meet the exigencies of war-time external finance gone anywhere near the point of so reducing investment earnings as to threaten Britain's capacity to pay for imports of raw materials etc. In brief, there is no question whatsoever of attributing, in any direct kind of way, economic performance after 1920 to any lingering consequences of the war. Indeed, the only pronounced circumstance of economic relevance which belongs to the aftermath of war worked very much in Britain's favour. As the world reverted to something resembling normality, there arose a surge of demand for goods of all kinds to make up for wartime losses or deprivations. And this at a time when much of the industrialised world was incapable of responding. The north-eastern industrial quarter of France along with Belgium had suffered fearful devastation; elsewhere political turmoil, sometimes accompanied by rampaging inflation, often impeded economic activity. Britain was much better placed than most to take advantage of this situation and of the high prices which it generated. These were halcyon months for nearly all sectors of the community. But their like was not to be experienced again for three decades.

It is not that the British economy in the longer run failed to grow. Between 1913 and 1939 industrial production increased to an extent equivalent to an annual average growth rate of about 1·5 per cent. (As a way of stating growth rate itself this would be very artificial since the period is cut across by the war, 1914–18, and the great slump, 1929–33. The object here is simply to contrast 1939 with 1913 in a way which permits comparison with earlier advances, expressed in previous chapters in growth rate terms.) This is not much below the *c.* 1·75 per cent recorded for 1873–1913 and if one allows for the marked difference in rates of population increase (1873–1913: 1 per cent p.a.; 1913–39: 0·5 per cent p.a.) the *per capita* increment in the later period is actually higher. Through the principal growth spates themselves, quite impressive rates were maintained: 1923–29, 3·5 per cent p.a.; 1934–37, 7·75 per cent p.a. But all this only serves to underline the magnitude of the output forgone. It makes it plain that the ingredients of a major economic advance were there all the time. If this kind of performance could be sustained by an economy operating so far below full capacity, what might it not have done had it been organised to employ all its resources?

Unemployment was not of course an unprecedented phenomenon. But neither in magnitude nor duration had there been anything in earlier history which could stand comparison with the unemployment of 1921–39.[1] The prevailing system of economic organisation had worked well enough in the past. What overtook it now so as to cause it to function so defectively?

There is an extent, but only a modest one, to which the record of these years is simply a continuation of prewar trends. Competitive weaknesses constricted market opportunities, and with them output and employment levels. The steel industry, in particular, continued to lose ground to foreign rivals once European steel producers had got back on their feet (say from 1923), the widening of the technical gap between British and other steelmakers sometimes being furthered by reconstruction from scratch after wartime devastation. Exports, in tonnage terms, never returned to prewar levels, while imports between 1924 and 1931 regularly topped their previous record of 1913. The result was that, notwithstanding the broader domestic market base created by the growth of the motor vehicle industry and other new or developing steel users, total British output of steel and puddled iron (the latter rapidly dwindling to insignificance) having risen above the 1913 level during the war and in the boom of 1920 did not again surpass it until 1927, only to be plunged into the great slump two years later.

From 1932 onwards, however, the situation assumed a very different aspect. Reduced to its lowest level of output since 1895–96 and struggling against a mass of cut price imports (the consequence of a huge excess in world capacity), the industry was at last granted the protection

---

[1] Trade union records of some comprehensiveness reach back to 1867. Before 1921 these disclose only two years in which unemployment exceeded 10 per cent: 1879 (11·4 per cent), 1886 (10·2 per cent); and the worst eighteen-year stretch revealed is 1877–95 (6·1 per cent).

for which it, or at least sections of it, had clamoured for so long. As the domestic economy as a whole lifted itself out of depression, steel output soared upwards. At the peak of this steep ascent, in 1937, tonnage produced was 35 per cent above the previous high, scored in 1929, and 46 per cent above the 1913 mark. Of course, achieved as it was in a protected market, this powerful recovery is no measure of the industry's efficiency. And the continuing depressed level of exports is a positive indication that competitive strength remained low. Nevertheless, it would be true to say that the industry was, at last, purposefully directing itself to repairing the technical and organisational defects which for half a century or more had marred it. What the confidence bred of an assured place in the home market did not provide towards moving it to reconstitute itself was in some part supplied by the government, which in return for protection laid an obligation on the industry, in admittedly broad terms, to serve the national interest. An official watch-dog was appointed in the shape of the Import Duties Advisory Committee, which acted on producers through the newly formed British Iron and Steel Federation, the latter being the creation of the industry but, in form at least, of a suprasectional character, expressed in its having an independent chairman, and vested with extensive sovereignty over the industry as a whole.

Heightened efficiency must always in itself be reckoned as economic gain; and to the extent that the steel industry in these post-1932 conditions did improve its efficiency, some real advantage was secured to the economy. But in the case of an underemployed economy, one man's gain can be another man's loss when improvement means labour redundancies. In stepping up its output the steel industry through these years raised its requirements of labour, but not proportionately. To achieve the 35 per cent increase in output between 1929 and 1937 it needed to increase its labour force by only about 14 per cent and through 1937 unemployment in the industry was still running around 11 per cent. Only in the context of a much greater total economic dynamism could advance by any single sector generate its full benefit potential.

Steel was not the only industry to experience particular market difficulties through the years of waste. Coal suffered more grievously. Output never regained the 1913 level, and presumably never will. Diminished competitiveness had a hand in this. Notwithstanding something of a technical revolution in the industry – machine-cut coal increased from 8 per cent of the total in 1913 to 61 per cent in 1939 –

output per man-shift rose much less rapidly than in Germany and Poland, Britain's chief rivals in foreign markets. For this the industry's fragmented structure and its hideously bad labour relations must bear a good deal of responsibility. Britain's share in the international coal trade fell from 55 per cent in 1913 to 40 per cent in 1937. However, a retention of relative standing would not have radically altered the total picture. Between the two dates total output fell from 287 million tons to 240 million tons and exports from 73 million tons to 40 million tons. Preservation of the 1913 share in international trade would have raised the 1937 figures to 255 million tons and 55 million tons respectively. Much more important in limiting sales scope were the greatly accelerated conversion from coal to oil at sea and the considerable economies effected in coal consumption right across its usage range, constituting one of the most noteworthy, if not among the most flamboyant, of technological advances of these interwar years. To supply just one instance: in Britain itself the 3·1 lb of coal required to produce a unit of gas in 1913 had fallen to 1·3 lb by 1938. We return to a point already effectively made: that the British coal industry should run down because of improved techniques in the generation of heat and power was all gain, provided that the resources released were absorbed elsewhere.

The contraction of the coal industry was slow and halting. The contraction of the cotton industry was rapid and more or less continuous. On the basis of raw cotton consumption and taking the 1913 figure as 100, output by 1925 was down to 74 and by 1939 to 60. The explanation of this is fully contained in another piece of statistics. Exports of cotton cloth (1913 = 100) ran: 1925, 66; 1939, 27.

This was a disaster which Britain was utterly powerless to check. Since as early as the 1820s the cotton industry had been losing foreign markets as other countries mastered the fairly simple and cheap techniques of cotton goods production, gradually extending their competence from the coarse to the more taxing fine linens; and the British industry had been continually forced to increasing dependence on the more economically primitive parts of the world. Now it ran out of world. The Far East which had been left to it up to the First World War was rapidly travelling the same road as other former markets had earlier gone, the war itself by interrupting British supplies having given it a vigorous shove. India, largely producing for herself, and Japan, more of an exporter, joined the ranks of major cotton producers, with the decisive advantages over Britain of proximity to local markets and raw cotton sources and of cheap labour. The game was up, finally and irrevocably. Only Lancashire's skills in the finer specialities permitted it to be brought to a close with a degree of gradualism – protracting it even into the years after the Second World War.

In broad statistical terms the record of cotton is roughly paralleled by that of shipbuilding. Taking the 1,660,000 tons launched on an average of the years 1910–14 as a base (100), output for 1925–30 was 81 and for 1936–38 it was 44. Its unemployment record was fearful: between 1924 and 1939 it averaged 36 per cent, as against a national average of 15 per cent, never going below 20 per cent and in the years 1932–33 hitting the almost incredible figure of 62 per cent. Nothing can serve to hide the story of human wretchedness contained in these unemployment figures. But the statistical suggestion of an industry on the brink of, if not already into, a state of final collapse is misleading. The enormous discrepancy between the shipbuilding unemployment figures and the national average is in some part to be explained by the exceptional expansion of the work force in the postwar boom, at its peak bringing 3·8 million tons under construction in British yards as against a previous all time high of 2·6 million tons, and by the inevitably slow withdrawal from the industry in the years of subsequent redundancy of men living in areas where few, if any, other kinds of employment were available. The same boom also goes some way towards explaining the depressed output levels of later years. It left the world glutted with ships – at a time when international maritime traffic was anything but ebullient. Through 1921–29 the volume of international trade only just crept above its prewar level, world economic growth tending much more towards national self-sufficiency than had earlier been the case and, furthermore, being increasingly directed towards sophisticated products of low bulk/value ratio requiring relatively little shipping space. At the same time, faster and better designed ships meant that any given quantity of gross tonnage could now carry a greater quantity of goods than the same amount of pre-1914 tonnage. All in all, the world after the collapse of the 1920 boom may well have required less ships than it had done before the war, and found itself endowed with more.

The onset of a universal slump in 1929 completely cut the ground from under the feet of shipbuilders the world over. By 1933 British launchings had fallen to a derisory 133,000 tons (= 8 on the 1910–14 base). And while the general economic upturn setting in from 1933 brought some solace to the shipyards, the resort of virtually every country in the world to protection as a solution to economic ills had a doubly damaging effect on the prospects of the British shipbuilding industry. Protection in general operated to keep down the volume of international trade: right up to 1939 it was well below pre-1929 levels. Protection of shipbuilding in particular, by means of subsidies etc., operated to divert foreign orders from British yards.

Shipbuilding, then, through nearly the whole of this period was confronted with quite abnormal market conditions. But sooner or later these conditions would pass. Sooner or later world shipping needs would grow again. Unlike cotton, shipbuilding had not entered on an irreversible decline. It could never expect to recover the international pre-eminence which it had enjoyed in the decades before 1914; the overwhelming advantage which it had then commanded in point of sheer capacity could not, in the nature of things, have lasted, and steadily through the interwar years it had been eroded as others, conspicuously Germany and Japan, expanded their capacities. Doubts could be raised also about the competitive efficiency of British yards – particularly perhaps with regard to oil-burning ships in whose development Britain had lagged behind. But the fact remains that when war came again to Europe in 1939 Britain still easily outdistanced any other country as a builder of ships and was ready, when peace should return, to pit herself against the world.

This brief survey of four major industries which experienced especial difficulties through these years and which exhibited particularly high rates of unemployment should serve to make it plain that there can be no question of ascribing gross economic performance to some common endemic weakening of British competitive ability, of representing the interwar years as the culminating stage of an enfeebling disease whose symptoms were already visible in earlier decades. Certainly, there were remediable inefficiencies, of the kind discerned in earlier chapters, whose rectification would have alleviated conditions. Equally certainly, they do not constitute a central explanation of the interwar record. An extension of the survey to other 'distressed' industries – wool, linen, pottery – would disclose as wide a variety of factors (including for example the sudden ascent of the hem-line) in play as observed in the case of the four considered. Perhaps the only all-embracing remark applicable to these industries is that they all had to contend with a changing environment. And as a contribution to analysis of the situation that does not take one far. The economic environment had been changing for centuries. Indeed the whole of economic history is but the record of change and of adaptation to it.

One has not identified anything very distinctive in saying that times were changing.

Nor does the notion that the key to the interwar situation lies in a palsy of British enterprise in the face of change stand up to even casual scrutiny. Let us remember that in *per capita* terms industrial output was growing more rapidly through this period as a whole than it had been doing in the four decades before the war. If there is any warrant for speaking of human shortcomings vitiating the performance of the pre-war economy, then the interwar years must be distinguished as a phase in which these shortcomings were being remedied. In most of the fields in which there is some *prima facie* evidence for raising this kind of accusation against the prewar economy the interwar years saw a new upsurge of enterprise. In chemicals, development had been boosted by the war and the consequent severance from German supplies, and a succession of mergers culminated in 1926 in the creation of the giant Imperial Chemical Industries, capable of sustaining the research effort so necessary to this sector. In electrical engineering development through the 'twenties and early 'thirties was largely on the heavy side (generators, etc.) as the basic electrification of the country was pushed through, the quantity of electricity generated increasing about seven-fold between 1918 and 1938; in the later years it was more on the appliances side, electric bulbs, irons, heaters, cookers, vacuum cleaners, refrigerators, radios, and so on as growing domestic advantage was taken of the electricity network. Electrical equipment for industry was also an expanding sector throughout the period. In motor vehicles Britain was the first European country to remodel her industry on the American pattern and by the early 'thirties, she had become Europe's leading producer – still of course lagging far behind the USA but closing the gap somewhat through the 'thirties.

Not that over the range comprehended by these categories Britain came to assume any position of international eminence: there is no question here of retrieving industrial leadership. If the post-1918 world could be said to have had an industrial leader then it was the United States. But the time had passed, if it ever existed, when international supremacy was the standard to which economic performance was to be referred. Rather is it a matter of whether or not Britain conformed to the general pattern of economic change and development set by a group of 'advanced' countries. British hesitancies, in the areas considered, through the prewar decades provided ground for suspecting the formation of an increasingly anachronistic economic pattern. British endeavours in these areas through the interwar years served to dispel any such apprehensions. And the fact that Germany or France, Sweden or Switzerland, Italy or Japan were doing as well or better in this or that direction is of little relevance in any general critique of the level of British economic achievement. One could point to particular patches in the British industrial economy of the 'twenties and 'thirties which emerge badly from an invidious international comparison. Performance in machine tools remained very poor by American and German standards until the last couple of years of the period, when the pressure of rearmament needs served to narrow the gap. In rayon manufacture, where the British firm Courtaulds had been the leading prewar pioneer and in which British textile skills might have been expected to provide a powerful advantage, British output in the interwar years was successively surpassed by that of the USA, Italy, Germany and Japan – although the industry was one of the fastest growing in Britain and Courtaulds remained among the world's major firms in the field, with subsidiary or affiliated concerns in a number of other countries. One can also make the point that in those areas, such as chemicals, where Britain made up ground it was with the assistance of protective tariffs, conferred either by the McKenna duties of 1915, originally a wartime measure designed to economise on shipping space and foreign exchange but allowed to remain after the war, or by the Safeguarding of Industries duties of 1921 and subsequent years, designed to sustain industries deemed particularly vital to national security; while from 1932 virtually the whole of British industry was hastily brought under the umbrella of a 20 per cent or $33\frac{1}{3}$ per cent duty. But all this is simply to say that the industrial economy of Great Britain, like that of any other industrialised country, was not impervious to the buffetings and vicissitudes of international trade and competition. One cannot stress too strongly the exceptional character of that brief phase in the world's history when one country alone had crossed the threshold of industrialisation and could for the while command a universal market with haughty ease. That Britain now had to jostle for a living was simply a reassertion of normality.

One summary way of putting the fundamental point being urged here is to say that the failure of the interwar economy – and measured against potential it was a massive failure – cannot be primarily ascribed to sociological causes. A conspicuous lack of enterprise (using the word to comprehend all the forms of human effort which enter directly into economic activity) cannot be distinguished as a chief cause of economic shortcomings. Obversely, the sources of economic malfunctioning were themselves economic in character. In its primary task, that of translating human wants into effective demand, the economic mechanism had lost its efficiency.

It cannot be pretended that that last observation amounts to an analysis of the situation. It is no more than a particular way of describing it, with no greater advantage than directing attention to the line which an analysis ought to pursue. And let it be said that the business of history is not to prescribe retrospective cures for economic ills – a relatively easy task with the advantage of hindsight – but rather to indicate why these ills came to pass; and that in the case in question historians are still very far from an agreed explanation with any pretensions to completeness.

The broad chronology of the years of waste is plain enough. Three distinct phases can be distinguished: 1921–29, 1929–33, 1933–39. Performance through the last two of these phases can, to a significant degree, be correlated with manifest trends in the international economy and to that extent then are fairly readily explicable, if one begs the question of why the international economy behaved as it did. It is its performance through the first phase which poses the most taxing analytical problems.

A broad area can easily be identified as a breeding ground of much of the trouble. The particular difficulties of the established staple industries, steel, coal, textiles and shipbuilding, between them accounting in the early 'twenties for just about a third of total net industrial output, plainly lie close to the heart of the matter. (And given that many different factors were responsible for these difficulties there is an element of pure ill chance in the conjuncture of events which the economy of the 'twenties had to face.) There is an obvious truth in saying that, had these industries been able to sustain their prewar dynamic, unemployment and the waste it implies would have been much less. But in itself this does not take us very far. In the first place, while it is true that many of the conditions bearing on these industries were in one sense or another exogenous ones, there still remains a degree to which performance in this area was a function of the general level of economic activity, enclosing the analyst in a vicious circle. In the second place, and here is the crux issue: why did not other sectors absorb the resources unwanted by the 'distressed' industries?

An answer which immediately suggests itself is: inertia. *Labour*, certainly, can be a very immobile factor of production, both geographically and occupationally. But a quick piece of statistics serves to dispel any picture of a large body of static, unwanted labour, capable of absorption had it been more mobile. In those two of the faster growing industry groups which registered the lowest unemployment figures, electrical goods and motor vehicles, the rates 1924–39 were 8 per cent and 10 per cent respectively, and for 1924–29, 6 per cent and 8 per cent. No doubt Oxford, Luton and Slough had a much happier time of it than Jarrow, Oldham and the Rhondda Valley, but greater mobility of labour would have done no more than share out the misery more evenly.

The argument that *capital* clung to sectors yielding a low return in terms of output and employment generated when it could have been put to work in high return sectors can, up to a point, be better sustained. The capital reserves of firms in the distressed sector naturally tended to go back into the industry. Banks and other standing creditors not uncommonly found more money to put into reconstruction schemes which offered a prospect of restoring their original investment to profitability. The general investing public could sometimes still be induced to subscribe at least to debenture loans, on the strength of historic reputation and the book value of assets. And such capital injections were commonly far from fruitless. In many cases they did revivify an ailing business and in many others they checked what otherwise would have been a much more disastrous decline. It should be remembered that, of the four most conspicuously distressed industries, steel bounced back before 1939, shipbuilding was eventually to recover, coal remained of key economic importance and even cotton retained some fully viable branches. Nevertheless it must be true that average return on investment in these industries was appreciably below that on investment in, say, engineering, chemicals and motor vehicles. And, in terms of output and employment generated in Britain, there is an obvious form of investment on which the return was lower still: overseas investment. Without returning to the dizzy levels attained immediately before the war, this through much of the 'twenties was running at quite a high rate (on average 2·3 per cent of national income).

But the point in this context is not whether the money capital going in these low return directions *could* have been more beneficially employed but whether, as things stood, it *would* have been more beneficially employed; that is, were there high growth potential activities in which entrepreneurs found themselves unable to secure capital because it was going elsewhere? The Macmillan Committee, appointed in 1929, did report widespread difficulty among small businesses in raising capital, compelling the conclusion that there was a degree to which fresh enterprise was thwarted for lack of capital. But since the most conspicuous growth potential areas were ones in which firms like Imperial Chemical Industries, Associated Electrical Industries and Morris Motors operated the difficulties of small businesses does not take us very far towards explaining why growth in these areas was insufficiently rapid to draw off unwanted resources from other areas. (The argument here has dwelt on *money* capital. It is needless to pursue it with regard to *real* capital when dealing with an economy which was underemployed across its whole range).

If we allow that the labour was there, that the capital was there and, as argued earlier, that the enterprise was there, we have effectively ruled out the supply side as containing the explanation of inadequate growth. We are driven on to the demand side. Here export demand offers itself *prima facie* as the most crucial variable. And indeed, in a certain sense, we have here the answer, whole and entire, to our question. Taking exports 1909–13 as a base (100) their volume through the post-war years may be calculated as shown in Table II.45.

TABLE II.45. *Exports, 1920–38*

1920–24	1925–29	1930–34	1935–38
75	84	60	66

Since in the base period export demand amounted to just about one-fifth of total demand, these figures manifest a withdrawal of very significant magnitude from the total. That, one might say, wraps it up. The British economy plunged below capacity because export demand fell off. But we have only answered our central question by evading it. The fall off in export demand is for the most part just the obverse side of the coin to the weakness of the established staple industries. We have simply come back to the same place through a different door. To ask why newer growth sectors did not absorb unwanted resources is, largely speaking, to ask why domestically orientated industries did not take over as pace setters from export orientated industries. Looked at this way, diminished exports are a symptom of the condition, not the cause. In an extensively industrialised world, the newer industries could not look for export markets on the relative scale which the older staples had once enjoyed. If one takes that as given, then it is not export demand that one should put the finger on but domestic demand. It is the failure in the past to build up a sufficiently powerful head of domestic demand which, in this view, explains the inability of the newer industries to draw in idle resources and expand as productive potential permitted. It also explains, in some part, the weakness of the older industries, which obviously would have derived some benefit from a higher level of domestic demand. Moreover, it would follow from this that the situation had a strong tendency to self-perpetuation. If deficient demand be an explanation of unemployment, unemployment, meaning unremunerated individuals, makes for depressed demand.

Monocausal explanations, of course, can never do justice to the complexity of the real world. Export demand was not entirely autonomous. Old and new industries alike could certainly have done something more to stimulate it. A foreign exchange rate which more accurately reflected relative prices and costs would also have helped exports. As it was, postwar exchange rates were badly out of line. While the British monetary authorities exerted themselves to get the pound, after its wartime depreciation, back to its old gold parity, finally taking the plunge into formal restoration in April 1925, others took delighted advantage of the total collapse of the old stable order to strike rates which undervalued their currencies, with consequent advantage to their exporters. Continuously between 1920 and 1931, when Britain was again driven off the gold standard, the pound was overvalued relative to the currencies of all the major trading nations outside the sterling area. The postwar international monetary chaos had itself impeded that growth of world trade in which Britain could reasonably expect to share – and it was in the hope that stability of the pound, still a major international currency, would serve to stimulate world commerce that sterling was put back on gold at a rate which was known to overvalue it.

One must point out too that launching new industries can involve difficulties. Goods which are 'lumpy', i.e. come only in large and relatively expensive units, may require a considerable reshuffling of expenditure patterns before full market breakthrough can be achieved. (Hire purchase type schemes can of course overcome this difficulty, and indeed go further by inducing people to buy what they cannot afford. The latter, however deplorable on a personal level, can be of positive general benefit in an underemployed economy when the demand thus induced leads to new investment, which in turn generates extra income, conceivably to the point where the improvident buyer finds himself able to afford the article after all. (The tardiness in promoting hire purchase in Britain – it only started to become generalised in the 'thirties – might thus be accounted a failing.) More generally, novel goods which are not substitutes for current articles of consumption have to wait on the development of consumer taste – by contrast with the situation of goods which are substitutes, e.g. cotton cloth in the early Industrial Revolution, and which are, then, entering an already prepared market. Thrustful advertising will help to accelerate market adaptation. But, in any meaningful welfare calculus, advertising is of uncertain value. A want satisfied must always be accounted a welfare gain. That the same is true of a want excited is a good deal less clear. Anyway, the fact may be noted that in advertising, as in hire purchase, Britain lagged behind the USA.

Considerations such as these having been entered, we can return to the view that the principal agency of inadequate growth was deficient domestic demand; or, put more fully, that the shift into domestically orientated industries, which was a necessary condition of sustaining such a growth rate as would fully employ available resources, was retarded by lack of demand. And if any kind of sense is to be made of this contention it must be taken as an observation on the state of income distribution. To say that domestic demand was inadequate relative to productive potential can only mean that insufficient income had passed into the hands of those with a high propensity to spend – and for practical purposes that signifies the lower income groups. In this analysis, the crucial years were those, 1900–14, during which the upward course which wages had been following through the previous four decades or so was arrested. It was, the argument would run, the consequent loss of purchasing power momentum which prevented the postwar economy, or even the late prewar economy, from being carried into the initial stages of that age of mass consumption and high employment which, in the actual event, was not to get properly under way until after the Second World War.

The preceding paragraphs have addressed themselves most specifically to the years 1921–29, but most of what they contain applies to the whole run up to 1939 and the particular pattern of events through the phases 1929–33 and 1933–39 can be regarded as having been superimposed on this general pattern.

Economic history, dealing as it does in sequences rather than incidents, throws up few memorable dates. One of those few is 1929.
Folk history has it that the Great Depression[1] started with the Wall
Street crash of the closing days of October 1929, and folk history has a
right to have it so. An event of the extent and magnitude of the Great
Depression insists on a theatrical onset. It is only dull pedantry which
points to earlier, clinically statistical evidence of incipient depression;
and in any event, whether the month be June or October, the year
was certainly 1929. It was a worldwide phenomenon. Britain simply
imported it; and, in fact, never suffered from it to the same intense
degree as did most other parts of the world. Indeed, as will be seen,
Britain even drew a measure of advantage from it.

Although inquiry will doubtless continue, economic historians seem
to be fairly satisfied that the Great Depression can be largely attributed
to two circumstances. One, the downward slither of the prices of
primary produce as worldwide advance in agricultural techniques
made for a rapid increase in output at a time when the rate of population growth in the industrialised world had slackened off. With a
generally inelastic demand for primary produce farm incomes fell off
and with them the demand for industrial produce. Two, the cessation of
American foreign lending which had played an important part in
sustaining international trade through most of the 'twenties. For this,
events on Wall Street were largely responsible. From 1928 American
fundholders were turning to the lure of their own stockmarket, either
participating themselves in the biggest bull market ever or, more
prudently, providing the funds, at 10 per cent or more, for those
brokers' loans which were such a potent force in keeping the market
headed skywards. And after 1929 of course such investible funds as
were still afloat were very chary of venturing out of harbour.

For Britain, then, the Depression started as a sharp downturn in
exports; and from there steadily communicated itself to nearly every
other sector of the economy, reaching its greatest depths in 1932. Its
impact was huge. But its implications are fully contained in the unemployment graph (p. 723) and its immediate causation is quite plain.
It is not so much the Depression itself on which we need linger here but
the subsequent recovery, which in Britain was a good deal stronger
than in others among the older industrial nations, though not as strong

---

[1] In the past British economic history has had a 'Great Depression 1873-69'. The absurd-
ity of this designation has by now been abundantly exposed and the unenviable title can be
assigned exclusively to that place in world history which has a unique claim to it.

as in certain countries still in course of industrialisation, such as Japan and Sweden, for whom the Depression was little more than a momentary interruption of rapid growth – not to mention the Soviet Union, completely insulated against these capitalist disorders.

The strength of recovery in Britain was, in significant part, a function of the relative moderation of the British depression. (To speak of the relative moderation of the Great Depression in Britain is of course to underscore its intensity elsewhere, e.g. industrial production [1929 = 100] in Britain fell to 89 in 1932, in the USA and Germany alike it fell to 53.) This moderation is broadly assignable to two factors. Britain had not been through a preceding investment boom and therefore had not on hand the great glut of productive capacity which commonly existed elsewhere and which operated to keep new investment expenditure heavily depressed through subsequent years – in the USA net investment (gross investment *minus* capital depreciation) was consistently *negative* from 1931 through to 1935. This of course is to say little more than that those who have not risen very far do not fall very far. A more authentically beneficial factor, from Britain's viewpoint, was the tumbling price level of primary produce. One index of food and raw material prices shows them falling from 100 in 1929 to 69 in 1933. And for Britain, to a unique degree, this was largely a matter of falling import prices. For Britain, that is to say, falling prices did not bespeak falling incomes. Notwithstanding the downward pressure on money wages, the real wages of those in employment steadily rose through the depression years. Indeed, they rose more rapidly over the years 1929–33 than they had done through the preceding four years 1925–29. The fact that so many were not in employment did take all the gilt off this piece of ginger-bread, but even so the impact on gross wage incomes of this, the deepest depression ever, was surprisingly mild: calculated *per capita* as 100 in 1929 they fell to 95 in the trough of 1932. Salary earners, a component of growing weight in the population, very possibly improved their lot, deriving similar advantage from falling prices and being more likely to retain their jobs – although teachers, a substantial segment of this group, had to submit to a 10 per cent cut in salary in 1931 in conformity with prevailing economic orthodoxy.

In our context here the most specific implication of the course of wage and salary incomes is the very modest degree to which the level of domestic consumer demand was diminished.[1] Or, put another way, the

[1] A secondary implication of falling import prices was that with her relatively elastic export position and her relatively inelastic import position Britain might otherwise have

pressure of depression was borne largely by savings, found for the most part out of those types of income which were pretty roughly savaged, profits and interest.

To summarise the preceding paragraphs: of the four main heads under which total expenditure may be distinguished (investment, consumption, export, and government expenditure), Britain in respect of two of them fared a good deal better than many other countries. The British economy, one could say, did not fall through the floor in the manner of the American economy. A platform was retained from which recovery could be fairly rapidly effected.

Depression started in Britain in the export industries. Recovery was not to be founded in the same quarter. Though Britain did participate in the movement of world trade up out of the abyss of 1932–33, neither world trade in general nor British trade in particular were to regain their 1929 levels before the outbreak of the Second World War. Recovery, in the sense of getting back to and beyond 1929 levels of economic activity, had to be grounded in the home market. What was in any event desirable, as we have already seen, was converted into a categoric imperative by the manner in which all the industrialised countries, Britain amongst them, sought to claw their way out of depression by securing their home markets to their own producers through tariffs and other restrictive devices.

Britain shed the incubus of an overvalued currency in 1931 when a flight out of sterling forced her off the gold standard and the pound was left to find its own level.[1] With more deliberation, efforts were made to promote exports by a series of bilateral agreements with countries to whom Britain was an important customer, and by the general agreement on Imperial Preference between Britain and the Dominions which emerged out of the Ottawa Conference of 1932. These agreements did have the effect of boosting exports to the countries concerned, but the debate persists to this day as to whether what was gained on the swings was not lost on the roundabouts as competition was diverted to other markets, and as other countries, notably Germany, followed the British lead into bilateralism. But whatever gain may have come from these manoeuvres, or from any others that might have been essayed, there

run up a growing trade deficit. As it was the volume of imports fell by only 13 per cent between 1929 and 1933 while the volume of exports fell by 37 per cent, yet the trade deficit actually *decreased*.

[1] From 1932 onwards the pound was subject to the operations in the foreign exchange market of the Exchange Equalisation Account which kept it close to the depreciated value then reached.

was not the least prospect of floating Britain into economic resurgence on a tide of rising exports.

Given that clear and vigorously sustained recovery did set in from 1933, what got it going? The government had not been idle in the face of economic disorder of such unprecedented magnitude. It was, after all, a Labour government which was in office at the onset of depression; and this was succeeded in 1931 by a 'National Government'. In form this was a union of all parties, presenting a common front to the nation's ills, though in effect, since the bulk of the Labour party repudiated the coalition and the much reduced Liberal party split over it, a Conservative government which retained as titular head the Labour prime minister, Ramsay MacDonald, who had inspired the idea. However, under either political colouring the government's view of its own competence was a limited one: broadly summarised, the creation of background conditions favourable to economic recovery. Coming closer to particulars, this amounted to three things: a balanced budget, tariff protection, and cheap money.

A balanced budget meant higher taxation and reduced expenditure. As every student of elementary economics nowadays knows the correct prescription for treatment of depression is *increased* government expenditure. Yet in this context the balancing of the budget must probably be reckoned as a positive contribution towards promoting recovery. Businessmen were taught by the economic doctors of the day that the country's future hung on government restraint. Business confidence demanded a balanced budget; and without it, investment in the private sector would have sagged, almost certainly to an extent which would have outweighed any 'pump-priming' public sector deficit such as Keynes and his fellow heretics were urging. (Britain pursued the 'wrong' policy and recovered. The USA adopted the 'right' policy and floundered on in depression through the rest of the 'thirties.) Moreover, foreign fundholders were as unenlightened as British businessmen. A budgetary deficit would have meant a continuing critical balance of payments position and, among other consequences, the impossibility of operating a cheap money policy.

The effects of the shift from free trade to protection, which was decisively contrived with the tariff legislation of 1932, are difficult to assess. Against the gains secured in the home market by protected producers is to be set the long-run loss in foreign markets as a result of the chain reaction: diminished imports by Britain – diminished sterling earnings abroad – diminished purchases from Britain; while in the immediate outcome there is the loss to consumers of cheap imported goods to be reckoned with. Whole volumes incorporating these and other more sophisticated considerations have been devoted to weighing the pros and cons of protection. The refined calculus needful for a precise resolution of the question can be dispensed with here. The area over which home-produced and imported goods competed with one another was relatively narrow; and the area within which the fairly moderate tariffs of 20 or $33\frac{1}{3}$ per cent were of crucial consequence was a good deal narrower still. In a total context the difference, one way or another, was marginal. And of single industries only one of weight, the steel industry, had its market situation palpably transformed by protection.

If the consequences of a balanced budget and of new tariffs are open to argument, there is no question but that low interest rates were favourable to recovery. However, while it is plain that the ability to borrow cheaply will promote rather than retard investment, all the evidence suggests that, between any normal limits of movement, interest rate levels are only a very minor consideration in entrepreneurial investment decisions; and few would be disposed to argue that the rapid de-escalation of interest rates after the sterling crisis of 1931 had been resolved[1] had any powerful bearing on productive investment. That still leaves one kind of loan-financed undertaking to be taken into account: house purchase. And in fact, economic historians – a species much given to interpretative polemics – are surprisingly unanimous in according residential building a central role in the recovery from the Great Depression.

Cheap money bore on house-building in several ways. Most obviously, low interest rates reduced the cost of a mortgage. (Interest charges will usually account for at least a third of mortgage repayments.) However, building societies did not bring their rates down to the full extent of the drop in interest rates generally, most societies' rates came down slowly from a high of 6 per cent to $4\frac{1}{2}$ per cent (i.e. by 25 per cent) while the yield on Consols, for example, fell from 4·6 per cent to 2·9 per cent (i.e. by 37 per cent). The relative attractiveness of building societies as depositories for funds was therefore enhanced, and more money was available for mortgage lending.

[1] The authorities had sought to pursue a cheap money policy since early 1930, bank rate being kept below 4 per cent between March 1930 and July 1931. The flight out of sterling forced it to 6 per cent in September 1931 but from February 1932 it came down step by step and rested continuously on a 2 per cent floor between June 1932 and August 1939.

Likewise low interest rates enhanced the relative attractiveness of rent-yielding property as a form of investment and thus encouraged building for letting. At the same time as operating on the demand side in these ways, easy money operated on the supply side, through increased bank lending to builders,[1] who usually depend heavily on bank credit to see them through the interval between construction start and completed sale.

It was not easy money alone which initiated the housing boom that got under way in 1933. Steadily since 1914 the stock of houses had fallen further and further below the nation's needs. During the war the diversion of men and materials to other tasks had cut deeply into new building; and subsequently the failure of interest rates to revert to pre-war levels (the return on Consols, 1920–29, averaged 4½ per cent as against 3 per cent, 1905–14) dulled the attractiveness of building for letting, while the persistence with rent control on existing houses, introduced as a wartime measure to check the free market consequences of the housing shortage, meant that tenants had little incentive to buy houses for themselves. And although local authorities had increased their output of houses way above prewar levels (virtually zero), this was quite insufficient to make up for the huge shortfall in private building.[2] Sooner or later a housing boom had to come. Easy money, along with a number of autonomous factors, including the beginnings of rent decontrol, something of an improvement in building efficiency with consequent cost advantages, and a relaxation of building society policy on deposits and repayment periods, ensured that it came in 1933.

To explain the housing boom in terms of the previous shortfall in house-building is really to particularise a general point already made: output in Britain was not held back by an accumulation of durable goods inherited from an earlier upswing. And to explain the housing boom in terms of easy money is to postulate purchasing power capable of taking advantage of the situation – which again is to refer back to the fact that throughout the depression consumer incomes had succeeded in maintaining a relatively high floor level. Put together, this is to say that the general conditions which got the housing boom going would

[1] Properly speaking this was a distinct phenomenon, the consequence not of low interest rates, to which builders were no more sensitive than other entrepreneurs, but of the availability of bank funds, partly as a result of credit creation by the Bank of England (in support of low bank rate), partly as a result of diminished bank borrowing by other entrepreneurs during the depression.

[2] To a large extent of course local authorities and private builders were catering for separate markets.

facilitate recovery in other sectors also, once any one sector had generated sufficient expenditure to impart a clear upturn to the economy. And in fact, following quickly on the heels of housing came other consumer durables, conspicuously motor cars and electrical appliances, supplying further momentum through the heavy investment expenditures which production of these goods required. By the end of 1933 the economy was clearly on the move again.

Recovery was pronounced and recovery was vigorous. Moreover, recovery was effected on the basis of the home market. Strategically, so to speak, the economy emerged from the depression properly deployed, or at least on the way to proper deployment. The years 1933–37 saw it grow at a rate which had not been rivalled in even the headiest years of the Industrial Revolution. But although the base was the right one it was still not broad enough. In 1937 the advance stopped in its tracks and, despite the special stimulus of rearmament expenditure, had made little further movement forward when war came again to Britain in September 1939. Carried forward by domestic consumption expenditure the economy had once again run up against its inadequacy; and had been brought to a halt with over 10 per cent of the labour force – over 10 per cent of its productive potential – still unemployed. The way to sustained growth had been glimpsed but not grasped.

The business corporation

The quarter-century preceding the First World War had seen the old individualistic order starting to give way here and there to forms of corporate capitalism. Yet by 1914 the fully elaborated corporation was a very rare form of business life in Britain. By 1939 it had become a perfectly normal, if not quite representative, type across a great range of economic activities. And while such tendencies as there had been towards corporate capitalism before 1914 had often been impelled by motives which did not embrace economic efficiency, the development of the interwar years was principally sustained by a drive towards the productive advantages of scale. This is not to say that the price or market fixing goals which had been conspicuous objects of the prewar combination movement ceased to be common aims of business strategy. Quite the reverse in fact. Shrinking markets and falling prices, through the interwar years, became the familiar experience of many sectors of the economy and drove increasing numbers to seek protection in defensive alliances of one kind or another.

The unhappy history of most of the earlier combines counselled against resort to outright fusions of concerns but the 'twenties and 'thirties in Britain were the high years of restrictionist producers' associations – variously, concerting prices, dividing out markets, allocating output quotas, conducting centralised selling or tendering arrangements, even sometimes pooling profits for distribution according to agreed formulae. In the most thoroughgoing instances such associations effectively differed from the older combines only in that membership of them was terminable. Nor was it the case that restrictionism was peculiar to distressed industries. Indeed, while associations of this character were in general most frequent where conditions were harshest, they were often at their weakest in such circumstances, when desperation drove many to break the rules to win orders which would temporarily keep noses above water; and some of the most effective associations were to be found in healthy, growing industries. In cotton, for instance, where the air was continuously thick with restrictionist schemes as sales tumbled downwards, it was only when statutory agencies were created in 1936 and 1939 that 'weak selling' was brought under effective control; while on the other hand, one of the most rigorously observed of price and output agreements was that of the Electric Lamp Manufacturers Association (1919) operating in a continuously expanding market.

In fact, there is perhaps no more distinctive trait of the interwar years than the galloping loss of faith on all sides – business, academic, political – in the efficacy of free competition as a means of promoting economic wellbeing. The country itself, one might almost say, became an association for the protection of profits. To the few surviving disciples of *laissez-faire* it was the age of national apostasy – which, among other things, serves to demonstrate the feebleness of the merely doctrinal in shaping economic attitudes.

If then, the combine of essentially monopolistic intent figured little among the corporate formations of this period, it was because businessment found the association a more satisfactory device for securing its reputed advantages. However, if this is to say that the fundamentally defensive motives which had commonly prompted the creation of large corporate concerns in earlier years, were, under other forms, no less active during these years, it should not obscure the fact that, alongside them, more aggressive, empire-building forces were now coming into play much more freely than ever before. Variously, an appreciation of the intrinsic advantage of scale, or integration, an awareness of the selling power of standardised brand images sustained by massive advertising, a concern to exploit strong management by extending its range of application, were making with growing forcefulness for the creation of business units of that sort of size and character which identifies them as fully fledged corporations.

Before saying something of the general movement adumbrated in the last sentence, we should perhaps take brief note of three particular fields in which somewhat peculiar circumstances had already, by way of successive mergers, engendered concerns of substantial size: railway operation, banking, and brewing.

The need for integrated services had become obvious at a very early stage of railway history and by the 1860s had resulted in the vesting of the huge bulk of track mileage in a handful of great companies – the first, and very precocious, instances of the fully elaborated corporation. Succeeding decades, however, brought only a very gradual further increase in the size of these companies until in 1921, under statutory compulsion, integration took a great leap forward with the concentration of railway operation in four massive concerns (Great Southern, London North Eastern, London Midland and Scottish, Great Western).

Banking, which by 1914 had achieved a somewhat similar degree of concentration as railway operation, also moved suddenly on to a new level of integration as a burst of major mergers over the years 1917–20 resulted in the emergence of the 'Big Five' (Barclays, Midland, Westminster, National Provincial, Lloyds). In brewing, however, which over the couple of decades preceding the war had been through a phase of concern expansionism roughly analogous to that experienced by banking, the movement now lost a lot of its momentum. The scramble for pubs had already gone about as far as it could go with commercial advantage. Indeed, in their anxiety to block one another, many breweries had acquired pubs which proved to be more of a liability than an asset. Furthermore, beer sales were fairly steadily falling – due partly to greatly increased excise duties and partly to a change in popular drinking habits. However, if this operated to check concern growth by way of internal expansion, it also served to accelerate the tendency towards concentration as small local breweries found sales dropping below viable minima and were forced either into extinction or into selling out to the big metropolitan breweries, who might acquire them for the sake of their pubs if these lay within the wider delivery range created by motor transport. It is above all the disappearance of the country breweries which is reflected in the fall in the number of separate brewing plants from 2,889 in 1920 to 885 in 1940. Among the larger breweries there was not much further consolidation by way of amalgamation until the late 1950s and the 1960s.

One consequence of this checking of the rate of enlargement of brewing firms was that these now slipped well down the table of large-scale manufacturing concerns, having as a group been headed earlier only by a body of steel, shipbuilding and armaments concerns. The fact that brewing, an activity which above a certain level does not derive any significant technological economies from scale, had earlier figured so highly is above all a comment on the very limited extent to which the corporation had penetrated into British economic life up to 1914. By 1939, the big breweries had been overtaken, in this kind of ranking, by literally dozens of other concerns. And conspicuous among these were firms operating in those sectors which were expanding the most rapidly through this period and which, as it happened, commonly stood to draw considerable advantage from large scale operations.

The supreme instance in point here is the motor vehicle industry, in which the rise of the corporation was essential to its transformation along the lines pioneered by the USA. In 1922 there were eighty-eight firms producing annually some 90,000 vehicles of all sorts of shapes and sizes, with no one firm in command of anything more than a very small segment of the market. By 1937, when annual output was running at around 500,000 vehicles a year, the number of firms was down to twenty-two, and six of these held three-quarters of the market, the other firms largely confining themselves to special vehicles of limited sales scope. The 'Big Six' consisted of Morris, Austin, Ford (an affiliate of the American concern), Vauxhall (an almost defunct concern in 1928 when it had been taken over and revitalised by the American firm, General Motors), Rootes (originally motor dealers, now manufacturing vehicles under the Humber, Hillman, Commer and Sunbeam-Talbot brands, having taken over the original producers in the early 'thirties when they had been on the point of collapse), and Standard. It was in these six corporations that was heavily concentrated the capital and the technical and management skills which by the mid-'thirties had come to sustain the most sophisticated motor industry in Europe.

Dominance on the part of a few is often the preliminary to reciprocal arrangements designed to preserve the balance of power. With so much to lose, the children of mammon commonly deem it more prudent to treat than to fight among themselves. And, indeed, the initial rise to dominance is more frequently the outcome of well judged dynastic marriages than of successful warfare. It is, then, of some interest to note that the motor vehicle business was, and remained, fiercely competitive. Those who reached the top had fought their way up; and had to continue to fight to stay there – though after new markets had been carved out with the slashing price reductions which mass production methods had made possible, culminating with the £100 car in 1934, model competition was generally preferred to price competition. Mergers had played only a minimal part in the rise of the 'Big Six'. Of the numerous firms which had disappeared, far more had ended up in the hands of the official receiver than in the comfortable embrace of a former rival. Hard won markets could prove equally hard to hold. Singer, for instance, had grabbed 15 per cent of the car market by 1929 and then ranked third to Morris and Austin. Thereafter its decline was almost continuous. Even Morris and Austin found the going hard in the 'thirties. Between 1932 and 1938 their combined share of the car market fell from 60 per cent to 44 per cent, the chief gainers being the 'Americans', Ford and Vauxhall, whose share rose from 11 per cent to 28 per cent.

Contrasting strongly with the motor corporations in point of the atmosphere in which it lived, but in its own way no less a product of the wind of change blowing through British industry, was Imperial Chemical Industries, the most ambitious of the great corporate formations of these years. It was the creation of a single-stroke merger of 1926 between four concerns, themselves among the larger of contemporary enterprises: Brunner Mond, United Alkali, Nobel Industries, and British Dyestuffs. Through subsequent years it absorbed a number of other firms. Operating as it did over a very variegated product range, one could not define its market power by any single, simple calculation. But, especially when account is taken of the deterringly massive accumulations of capital, technical knowledge and patent rights needful to enter most of the fields in which it was active, its sheer size must be reckoned to have conferred on ICI a near impregnability against all but the most ruthless or most reckless rivalry.

Yet it would be plainly wrong to give ICI the same character as those prewar combines whose overriding purpose had been the elimination of competition. The ability to bargain on equal terms with the great European (chiefly German) and American chemicals concerns, over such things as prices, patents and markets was a major element in the strategic thinking which inspired the original merger and informed subsequent policy. At the same time, however, there was at work a determination to endow the industry with that research backing in depth which was essential to competitive strength in the field, and, more generally, to fuse the numerous and disparate elements of which this sprawling enterprise was composed into an efficiently melded and reciprocally supporting whole. Indeed, in the early days concern to fashion a thoroughly integrated business resulted in excessive executive centralisation and it became necessary to restore some degree of administrative autonomy to individual components. But if the lessons needful to effective management of an enterprise of this scale and character took some while to learn, the role of ICI in rooting a strong chemicals industry in a country which hitherto had put up a very indifferent performance in the field must be reckoned to have been of crucial importance.

The history of development in the electrical goods industries has a broad similarity to that of chemicals. Here too, pronounced progress is to be associated with structural recomposition and the creation of new corporate enterprises. A product range which runs from radio valves to massive generating plant, comprehending a host of highly differentiated products in between, cannot be the subject of any simplified representation and we must content ourselves here with merely taking note of the extensive tracts of territory which, through a mixture of mergers and internal growth, had by 1939 come into the possession of three companies: Associated Electrical Industries, General Electric and English Electric.

Aircraft construction was an industry where the nature of the product would compel large-scale organisation once any substantial market existed. That condition was only rather tardily fulfilled. The war had given a powerful temporary boost to aircraft manufacture, but through the 'twenties military establishments were being kept at a low level and civil aviation was only in the proving stage. Through the 'thirties, however, the scope of air travel was rapidly extended and over the closing years a crash programme for building up the RAF was being pushed through. By 1939 aircraft manufacture, which ten years earlier had barely moved out of the garden shed stage, had become big business. Hawker Siddeley (an amalgamation of several pioneering concerns) and De Havilland had become companies of first division stature. Aircraft were now a weighty element in the multifaceted Vickers group; and Rolls Royce were well set on that course which was to make aero-engines their most important, if not their most distinguished, product.

Steel may be grouped with motor vehicles, chemicals, electrical goods and aircraft to form a quintet of major manufacturing industries in which technological considerations argued powerfully for large-scale operations. We have seen that already by 1914 the classical type of modestly sized owner-managed concern was fading out of the steel scene; we have also seen that the evolution towards concerns of a radically changed scale and character had not proceeded at all as rapidly as pure considerations of economic efficiency would have dictated, in fact that steel stood out as an industry very much in need of fundamental reorganisation. Up to 1914 the situation was obscured by the generally comfortable conditions which the industry enjoyed, notwithstanding its steady loss of international competitive strength. It was the hard times of the 1920s, rounded off by the Great Depression, which made plain the urgent need of a new strategy. For many within the industry of course, an essential preliminary was a home market secured to them by tariffs; for some, undoubtedly, tariff protection, insulating them against the consequences of their own weaknesses, was a fully sufficient end in itself. Before 1932 there was very little spontaneous movement towards radical reorganisation. A succession of mergers through 1917 and 1918 had thrown up United Steel; but this was wholly inspired by the purely commercial advantages of guaranteed sources and outlets for the component concerns, who stood in a vertical relationship to one another and who under the merger arrangements preserved their operational autonomy. A series of acquisitions of more truly integrationist intent was that effected by Dorman Long, culminating in 1929 in their absorption of their famous neighbour Blockow Vaughan. In broad terms this should be accounted an instance of amalgamation for the sake of exploiting strong management, Blockow Vaughan having for some time been in rather inept hands while Dorman Long was one of the most capably run steel firms in the country.

This last was a shot-gun marriage. Blockow Vaughan were only brought to the altar by their bankers, Barclays, who threatened to foreclose on an overdraft of £1 million if the wedding did not go through. It was not an isolated instance of banking pressure. By the late 'twenties most steel concerns were heavily in debt to their bankers. Few had any prospect of being able to redeem their obligations in the near future and some were even unable to meet the interest payments due. This situation brought a new actor on to the stage: the Bankers' Industrial Development Company, formed in 1930, a consortium of bankers headed and inspired by the Bank of England, in the person of its

Governor, Montagu Norman. Under Norman's leadership British banking seemed for a while to be moving towards that close engagement with the control of industry which had earlier come to characterise industrial structure in Germany and, in lesser degree, the USA. If in the end the movement did not go as far as at one time it looked to be doing, there was none the less a phase during which Montagu Norman became a central figure in the reorganisation of the British steel industry, even of British industry at large, since the BIDC's operations were not confined to steel though it was most active in that field.

Taking advantage of the financial frailty of firms, Norman aimed to dictate a thoroughgoing 'rationalisation' of the steel industry by means of its reconcentration in a few geographically consolidated units under the directorship of able men of his own choosing.[1] Many firms, of course, were not so completely at the mercy of their bankers as to be delivered into Norman's hands; and after 1932 the Import Duties Advisory Committee and the British Iron and Steel Federation took over much of the strategic planning role for which Norman had cast the BIDC. Moroever, general economic recovery, by restoring profits, enabled many firms to retrieve their financial independence. But the Bank of England, either directly or through the BIDC, was the architect of three major pieces of reconstruction: the fusion in 1928 of Vickers and the loss-ridden Armstrong Whitworth; the subsequent hiving off of the steelmaking interests of these two firms and of Cammell Laird, and their reconstitution as the English Steel Corporation (1929); and the merger of five troubled Lancashire concerns into the Lancashire Steel Corporation (1930). The same agency had a hand in the big Scottish amalgamation which emerged as Colvilles (1930), and in the planning of Guest, Keen and Baldwins which combined the South Welsh steelmaking interests of Guest, Keen and Nettlefold and of Baldwins – the two firms remaining separate in respect of their other activities.

None of the various amalgamations detailed had any very sensational results in the immediate outcome. Here and there, unsuitable plants were closed down and output concentrated in better endowed works. More generally, financial and management structure were strengthened. But little was done for the moment towards exploiting the potentially considerable technological advantages which scale proffered – not that market conditions during the depression were anything but profoundly

---

[1] It is perhaps worth remarking that Norman, who had earlier taken a high *laissez-faire* line, seems to have been moved to action in order to forestall intervention by the Labour government of the day.

unfavourable to expensive new investment. All the same, the way was being cleared for the kind of new departures which only the very big could finance and sustain. And in more unobtrusive fashion, two other important concerns were through the 'twenties and 'thirties steadily picking up smaller enterprises in their particular fields and coming into possession of such substantial shares of the market as could support plant on an American scale. These two were Stewart and Lloyds (tubes) and Richard Thomas (tinplate). And these two it was who were responsible for the most eye-catching new ventures in steel of the interwar years. In 1934 Stewart and Lloyds opened their new £3 million works at Corby, in the middle of open country, where ore from the adjacent Northamptonshire field went in one end and finished tubes came out the other, to the amount of nearly half a million tons a year by 1939. In 1938 the first continuous steel strip mill in Britain, erected by its American designers, went into operation at Ebbw Vale where the brand new, fully integrated works of Richard Thomas had cost £12 million, making them the most expensive single project ever undertaken in British manufacturing industry up to that time.

While Corby and Ebbw Vale were the only ventures of the period which started from scratch, there were also a number of major extensions of comparable sophistication and cost which were undertaken in the transformed circumstances of the mid- and late 'thirties: by Guest, Keen and Baldwins at Cardiff; by the Lancashire Steel Corporation at Irlam; by Colvilles at Clydebridge – without naming other projects whose cost would be counted in mere hundreds of thousands of pounds. Tardily, but with rapidly gathering decisiveness, steelmaking was becoming concentrated in units proportioned to the massive capital requirements of up-to-date technology.

Away from those areas where the nature of productive techniques made for significant efficiencies of scale and where, as a consequence, size was commonly essential to competitive strength, the corporation becomes more haphazard in its incidence, more the product of accidents of history or of exceptional personalities. Yet if chance factors commonly initiated the phenomenon, from that point on it generally had a powerful tendency to self-reinforcement. The corporation, that is to say, was more likely to go on growing than the 'individualist' concern; or, at least, the 'individualist' concern would commonly have to make the jump to corporation stature if it were to stay in a field which the corporation had invaded. It is of course needful to introduce the qualifications contained in 'tendency', 'likely', 'commonly', etc. in making generalisations of this kind. No simple, stereotyped model can be constructed to describe the process, and no useful discussion of it could be essayed outside the pages of a volume specially dedicated to the topic. But very broadly speaking there are three general types of factors involved: first, those which confer a competitive strength on the large concern as against the small concern (apart, that is, from strict cost economies), among which the ability to build up brand loyalty through extensive publicity may be particularly powerful in certain fields; second, those which enable the large concern to survive in bad times when smaller rivals may go under, leaving the field clear when growth possibilities return – of particular weight through this period. Finally, and of a rather different order, there is the much more uninhibited growth motivation of the corporation as against the individualistic concern, apt to contain itself within the limits of the financial and managerial capacity of its owners. Indeed, making a hardy foray into collective psychology, there would seem some warrant for suggesting that growth, rather than profits, is the supreme object of corporation behaviour – or, at least, that the corporation appraises itself by reference to gross profits rather than rate of return on capital invested.

In the boldest of summaries, this would seem an area to which the 'threshold' concept is peculiarly applicable: a sector may run on for decades without crossing the threshold into corporate capitalism; but once it has done so, the further extension of the corporation is likely to be rapid, either by way of the growth of the pioneering corporations (itself sustainable by internal expansion or by external acquisitions) or by way of the transmutation of a gathering number of individualist concerns into corporate concerns. Some such thesis seems essential to any explanation of the speed of spread of the corporation through these years when contrasted with its very slow earlier headway.

Such in fact was the extent of the corporate invasion that it really becomes easier to indicate the sectors which remained largely immune to it than those which were subject to it. However a few more names can be dropped as a token measure of the phenomenon.

Two outstanding instances of the power of extensive advertising are supplied by the Imperial Tobacco Company and Lever Bros, the latter associating itself with two Dutch margarine concerns to constitute Unilever in 1929. Two great cocoa and chocolate concerns, Cadbury and Rowntree, provide other conspicuous exemplars of the art of cultivating brand loyalty. The selling power of a name was no trifling element either in the great growth of Dunlop, the tyre manufacturers.

Capable management was of course crucial to substantial growth in any field, but outstanding instances of strong management at work are supplied by Pilkingtons (glass), Courtaulds (rayon), Tube Investments (light metal tubes etc.) and the Metal Box Company (cans etc.). The first of these, rather remarkably, was able to recruit talent enough from within the Pilkington clan and funds enough from retained profits and private loans to remain entirely in family hands until 1970.[1]

The Imperial Tobacco Company aside, the most expansive of the combines of 'merger mania' origin was Associated Portland Cement (Blue Circle) – due partly to more competent management than it had been blessed with at its formation and partly to a policy of buying up its competitors whenever they became too successful. Other concerns of prewar date to attain considerable stature include the two oil companies, Shell and Anglo-Iranian (formerly Anglo-Persian). And so one might run on through concerns like the British Aluminium Company, the British Match Corporation, the British Sugar Corporation, Tate and Lyle, BSA, London Brick – to mention some whose title or reputation serves to identify them – and extend into retailing where the corporation continued to encroach on the small man, with names such as Marks and Spencers and John Lewis to add to those thrown out in the previous chapter. But the point has perhaps been made. It really is easier to enumerate the blank spaces.

It is not that within the areas mentioned the small individualist concern wholly disappeared from the scene – either in these or later years. At any time, there have been very few fields in which there have not been particular corners which can successfully be occupied by the small producer catering for some confined or specialist market. Indeed, from its lofty height the great corporation will often miss or disdain opportunities of restricted scope; or, as a matter of deliberate policy, it will leave initial exploitation to those closer to the ground and buy them out if the venture proves rewarding. The dominance of the corporation is not to be equated with the extirpation of the individual entrepreneur.

---

[1] Diffused ownership and management by professional, salaried executives have earlier been offered as distinguishing characteristics of the 'corporation'. However in the last analysis it is its size and elaboration which define it – a size and elaboration such as to put it beyond the normal competence of an individual or a family. No classificatory scheme can fully reckon with exceptional individuals or families. Apart from the Pilkington family other 'rogues' would be William Lever (Lord Leverhulme) who remained in absolute control of Lever Bros until his death in 1925 and William Morris (Lord Nuffield) who for a long time similarly controlled Morris Motors. For the few cross-cutting cases of this kind one should perhaps devise a special category of 'family corporation' to denote concerns which while still 'family' were 'corporate' in the scale and nature of their operations.

Nor, taking another tack, should one make the mistake of supposing that the logical ultimate in the rise of the corporation is monopoly: oligopoly, certainly; monopoly, rarely. Except in special circumstances, a monopoly or near monopoly situation positively invites fresh entry, offering a strategic situation of superb simplicity and the virtual certainty of being able to shake enough apples off the one groaning tree to make the effort worth while. The history of Associated Portland Cement and of Wall Paper Manufacturers (another 'merger mania' combine earlier enumerated), two among the few British concerns to get close to a pure monopoly position, exemplify the point. The great chunk of the motor car market secured by Morris in the late 'twenties lured the Americans, Ford and General Motors on to the scene, and the even larger share of the soap market won by Lever Bros likewise brought Proctor and Gamble across the Atlantic. Imperfect competition – the characteristic order of the corporation age – is not to be thought of as a transitional stage in some ineluctable degeneration of perfect competition into monopoly.

Returning to the point of departure. The extent of 'corporate' territory by 1939 is most handily indicated by noting those sectors in which the concern of 'individualist' type still predominated. Shop-keeping must be accounted such a sector, notwithstanding the continuing incursion of big chain and department stores, particularly in apparel and groceries. Including the co-ops[1] these conducted just about a third of all retail sales by 1939. But the other two-thirds were in the hands of what are to be reckoned the most individualist of all business units.

Those impossibly polyglot groups, mechanical engineering and metal manufactures provide somewhat similar contrasts: in a number of particular quarters, concerns of fully corporate character predominated; in others, enterprises whose capital would not run beyond four or five figures continued to prevail.

These areas aside, the principal sectors in which the corporation was for the most part conspicuous by its absence might be itemised as: agriculture, textile manufacture, garment manufacture, boots and shoes, building, coalmining, woodworking, printing (other than newspapers), road haulage (goods), shipping (tramp cargo). (And of these,

---

[1] The Co-operative Wholesale Society might itself be reckoned one of the most considerable of 'corporations' from the time of its foundation in 1864. But it, along with the co-operative movement as a whole, is of such a distinctive character that a mere passing reference could not apprehend it while an adequate treatment would take one much further into the sociopolitical than lies within the competence of this book.

agriculture, garment manufacture, building, woodworking, printing and road haulage might be further distinguished as sectors in which the *very small* concern – with, say, less than 20 employees and £10,000 capital – was still common.)

Perhaps the two most interesting cases in this list are textile manufacture and coalmining – seedbeds of individualist capitalism. In these minimal capital requirements obtained which were quite high by historical standards. The small *man* had long ago been driven from these fields. Yet the small *concern*, small, that is, by the standards of the corporation age, continued to prevail at a time when it was ceding place over much of the rest of the economy.

Some part of the explanation of this undoubtedly lies in the historical record. Tradition-conscious families clung to enterprises which had become as much a way of life as a source of income. A more specifically economic explanation can be found in the fact that, beyond a certain level, textile and coalmining technology offered few or no further economies of scale. And market conditions through these years offered little possibility of significant concern growth by way of internal expansion, while poor profit prospects were unlikely to lure funds and enterprise to the promotion of mergers. At the same time, the notion of salvation through 'rationalisation' was a very active one in textiles and coal throughout this period. Reorganisation by way of the creation of a small number of financially and managerially strong concerns, involving the closure of the most inefficient works or mines, the adjustment of output to real demand levels and the elimination of cut-throat competition – this was the kind of 'rationalisation' programme which in variant forms was continuously being urged on these industries. And in cotton such a project did get launched when the Lancashire Cotton Corporation, backed financially by the Bankers' Industrial Development Company, was formed in 1929 with the aim of acquiring two hundred of Lancashire's spinning factories and then 'rationalising' them – when, it was reckoned, the Corporation would command capital assets worth £29 million. Although this aim was not realised in full, the Corporation must be grouped amongst the industrial giants of the 'thirties.

There were also concerns of corporate scale and character in various branches of textiles: the 'merger mania' combines, engaged in the ancillary processes, bleaching, printing, dyeing and wool combing; J. and P. Coats and the English Sewing Cotton Co. who, working in close association, master-minded the thread market; Courtaulds, and a newcomer, British Celanese, in rayon. But the central processes involved in the manufacture of the two chief fabrics, cotton and wool, remained very much the territory of the family concern, the closed partnership or the small company.[1] By the side of the Lancashire Cotton Corporation there persisted many one-works cotton-spinning enterprises, while woollen spinning and the weaving of both of the two principal materials remained almost exclusive to such units.

Incomes and expenditure

The term corporate capitalism is one way of describing the form of economic organisation which through these years was supplanting the individualist capitalism of the past. Another would be: bureaucratic capitalism. Indeed in the most literal sense, it is not the corporation which has replaced the type of owner-manager who fashioned the nineteenth-century economy but the bureaucrat. The corporation is an abstraction. The flesh and blood reality is the elaborated bureaucracy which plans, decides and takes action. Sociologically, one might say, the salaried bureaucrat is the twentieth-century's most distinctive product; and it has been urged more than once in earlier parts of this book that the tardiness of appearance of the large-scale organisation is to be explained, not by sole or even primary reference to the economic environment, but also by the absence from society of this type of individual, without whom no complex organisation could have more than an ephemeral paper existence. The sequence of underground shifts and strains which culminated in society throwing up the type cannot be plotted here, but there is no mistaking the fact that the interwar period saw it coming with a rush. Salary incomes, which in 1914 probably accounted for about 5 per cent of total incomes, accounted for around 15 per cent in 1939.[2]

There was a good deal more to this than simple substitution of salaried managerial personnel for profit-earning owners. In Parkinsonian fashion complex organisations tend to breed administrators – the whole requires more administration than the sum of its parts. And

---

[1] Cotton spinning in particular had been fairly prolific of concerns characterised by diffused share ownership and management by salaried professionals but of limited scale and of a very parochial character – neither 'individualist' nor 'corporate', in the loosely defined senses in which these terms have been used here.

[2] It depends of course on what one means by 'salaries'. In rough and ready intent it is here confined to the incomes of administrative and professionally qualified employees, with a lower limit of say £250 p.a.

in addition to bureaucrats there were technocrats. The growth industries, motor vehicles, electrical goods, chemicals, rayon, aircraft, were founded in sophisticated technology and science and engendered a consequent need for highly trained specialists. Older industries, conspicuously steel, were also employing scientists and engineers in greater numbers than they had done in the past. The public sector too was an expanding employer of salaried personnel, particularly in local government where a greatly extended range of responsibilities was being undertaken. All of this in turn generated a need for enlarged secondary and higher education facilities. Teachers constituted a substantial element of the swelling corps of salaried employees.

It was this proliferation of salary earners which made for the most considerable change in income composition through the years between the wars. Largely as a consequence of it incomes from employment rose from 47 per cent of total incomes in 1914 to 62 per cent in 1939. How much significance is to be attached to the change it is difficult to say. A good deal of it was more in the nature of income transmutation than of income redistribution. What had formerly been the profit income of the entrepreneur became the salary income of the manager. On the other hand, a fair proportion of this body of salary earners did represent a group of relatively scarce skills or aptitudes which society for one reason or another required in increased quantity. To that extent, there was a genuine shift away from the remuneration of mere ownership of the physical means of production towards the remuneration of labour, albeit a special kind of labour. And although the ability of certain skills to command a special return could conceivably be as pernicious in its effects as that of property, skills are not inheritable in the manner of property, and skills do not have property's capacity for self-accumulation. A shift towards the remuneration of skills is generally a shift towards egalitarianism and a wider diffusion of purchasing power.

Our most specific concern here is not with egalitarianism as a social phenomenon but with income distribution as a determinant of expenditure, on the assumption that a more egalitarian distribution makes for a higher level of expenditure. And that element of increased salary incomes which was secured at the effective expense of the income returns to property concentrations would seem to have accounted for a good deal of such rise as there was in consumer expenditure through these years, most notably through that phase 1933–37 which lifted Britain out of depression. The new houses and, more especially, the motor cars and electrical appliances which figured so prominently in the recovery, were pre-eminently the purchases of middle-class salary earners.

Contrariwise, the failure of the majority of employment incomes, wages, to achieve anything like a commensurate increase has already been suggested as a central explanation of the general flabbiness of economic performance. Only through the brief postwar boom were wage incomes able to achieve any really substantial advance – only to lose all the ground won when the subsequent recession and deflation brought money wages spinning downwards and unemployment cut deeply into the numbers of earners. From the trough of 1922, money wage rates kept at a more or less stable level through to the depression and the continuing downward movement of prices, led by food prices, enabled real wage incomes to move modestly upwards despite a steady unemployment rate of 10 per cent plus; and, as seen already, the accelerated slide of prices during the depression went a long way towards counteracting the effects on wage incomes of cuts in rates and massive unemployment. But it was only from 1935 that economic conditions permitted of general and sustained trade union pressure to force money wages up again.[1] Unemployment remained high by any historical standards and this both restricted the increment to wage incomes in gross and took something off the edge of trade union militancy. The increase secured was appreciably less than would have been obtained under conditions of full employment; and much of it

[1] The following figures are illustrative:

	Number of industrial disputes	Working days lost
	(Annual averages)	
1930–34	412	5,000,000
1935–38	844	2,100,000

The inverse relationship may be explained this way: high profits encourage both wage demands and ready concessions, i.e. frequent but shortlived disputes; low profits and high unemployment discourage wage demands (or resistance to wage cuts) and heighten employer obduracy, i.e. infrequent but protracted disputes.

It may conveniently be pointed out here that profits are probably the principal determinant of wage rates under conditions of organised labour, an employer's readiness to cede to wage demands being primarily governed by how much profit a strike will cost him. The rate of unemployment would normally be a factor of much less weight. On the employers' side it would hardly enter into the matter at all since, unless unemployment were huge, an employer could not hope to replace a striking labour force with 'blacklegs'. On the trade union side, however, the prevailing rate of unemployment would be of more consequence: a general climate in which a steady wage was prized would tend to inhibit any action which hazarded it; more potent, perhaps, would be the question of finding alternative temporary employment for the duration of a strike. But in the last analysis the weight of these considerations would be a function of the likelihood of a strike achieving quick success, i.e. of the likelihood of an employer giving way.

was swallowed up as prices swung upwards again. On the outbreak of the Second World War real wage incomes *per capita* were only about 20 per cent higher than they had been twenty-five years earlier – and only marginally above the level briefly touched in 1920. However, there would be some warrant for picking on 1935, rather than on the more obvious 1939, as marking the onset of that sustained hoist of wage incomes which has transformed expenditure patterns in Britain, even though its impact before 1939 was of very slight consequence in a total economic context.

One gets a somewhat different picture if no account is taken of unemployment. Wage *rates* by 1939 were rather more than 30 per cent higher in real terms than they had been in 1914. And certain kinds of workers, in the motor vehicle and electrical industries for instance, enjoyed both more regular employment and more rapidly increasing wage rates than did the general run of labour. Few working-class households boasted a car in 1939, but some very favourably circumstanced ones did, along with a fridge and a washing machine. The sharp social contrasts of Victorian and Edwardian Britain were beginning to blur as the most fortunate members of the working class became able to afford middle-class indulgences – although a more effective blurring agent was the growing amorphousness of the middle class itself, with the multiplication of salaried employments of ambiguous status. Indeed 1939 has a tantalising effect on the economic historian. Taken in gross the income and expenditure pattern was still much the same as that of 1914. But unemployment was coming down; wage incomes were going up, without benefit of adventitious price falls; here and there evidences of new consumption standards were peeking through. Was the system finding its own way towards the 'consumer revolution'? Or did it really take six years of war and a radical rethinking of public policy to put it on the threshold?

Returning to actuality. The gross increase of 20 per cent or so in real wage incomes could not support any broadly based restructuring of consumer habits. A good deal of the increase went on a rearrangement of diet: less bread, more eggs, butter and vegetables, the substitution of butchers' meat for bacon. Cigarettes took a certain amount: tobacco consumption *per capita* rose from 2·2 lb in 1914 to 4 lb in 1938. Radio sets and electric irons, at a few pounds each, were very generally acquired in the 'thirties; and many households managed to afford more expensive vacuum cleaners as well as spending more freely on general furniture. The cinema provided a widely popular new form of entertainment – although the ninepennies on a Friday or Saturday night worked out cheaper than an evening at the pub and the cinema must be reckoned an important factor in the great drop in beer consumption from the heady prewar levels, releasing a significant slice of working-class income for other purposes.

In the upper ranges of working-class incomes, the fall in interest rates from 1933 and the easier payment terms of building societies enabled a substantial number to become owners of their own homes – although the strictly financial benefits of this only materialised fifteen or twenty years later when mortgages had been paid off. And from the lowest ranges, slum dwellers were being moved into council houses, mostly in the 1930s under the provisions of legislation of 1930 and 1935 – not always with enthusiasm since council rents, subsidised as they were, were generally higher than the evacuees had been accustomed to paying. But the principle that it was the business of the state to ensure adequate housing for everyone at moderate rents did not succeed in entrenching itself. Confronted with the acute postwar housing shortage, the government in the first hectic flush of victory had, indeed, imposed such a statutory duty on local authorities in 1919 and had provided that the Treasury would pick up the bill for the deficit. However, it soon recoiled from the mounting cost of providing homes for heroes and in 1921 repealed the measure. Treasury subsidies for local authorities' house-building were restored by the Labour government in 1924 but on a much more limited scale; and amid the prevailing insistence on governmental economies, these were scrapped in 1933, leaving central funds available only for assisting slum clearance schemes. Nevertheless, under one Act or another local authorities did build 1·4 million new houses between the wars, while a further 0·5 million privately built houses were also subsidy aided, constituting between them 42 per cent of all houses built over the period. Through the 'twenties and early 'thirties these certainly prevented a bad housing situation from becoming a great deal worse, and through the 'thirties they represented substantial headway towards the eradication of those pools of overcrowding and squalor which had for so long characterised the poorest quarters of the towns and cities of Britain.

The role of the state

Subsidised housing has brought us within the confines of the final theme with which this chapter has to deal: the economic role of government. The overall record of state spending may be indicated by continuing in Tables II.46 and 47 the series initiated in the previous chapter (pp. 707, 708).

TABLE II.46. *Expenditure (net of national debt charges)*
by central and local government as a percentage of national income

1913	14
1925	20
1937	25

A more or less unremitting expansion of state activity of one kind or another is immediately revealed. Before essaying any consideration of the component elements, two implications of the simple magnitude may be stressed. The one is the extent to which state expenditure was enlarging its power to determine movements of the economy as a whole. It is true that within this period the opportunities thus afforded of a deliberate use of state expenditure as an instrument of economic policy were not taken; specifically, instead of seeking to increase state expenditure in order to supply a deficiency of private expenditure policy sought rather to curtail it in such circumstances. Nevertheless, once a particular type of expenditure has been set in motion it is in practice extremely difficult subsequently to reverse the movement; the great economy drive of 1931, despite retrenchment in particular quarters, was unable to reduce central government expenditure in sum – although it did effect a modest reduction in total government expenditures. Willynilly, state spending did tend to operate in 'countervailing' or 'contracyclic' fashion and to supply a more or less continuously upward bias to economic trends.

The second general implication of the simple magnitude of state expenditure involves the same sort of considerations as have been already raised in introducing the large business corporation on to the scene. The state as employer, as supplier, as customer is vested with an effective power independent of that which it enjoys *qua* state, and which, when deployed over an extensive area, may well be more pervasive than that which it exercises in the name of its formal sovereignty. And of course, the wider this area the more elaborated the bureaucratic apparatus required, meaning at one and the same time a need for the appropriate type of personnel and a diffusion of effective control of the machine. In much the same way as ownership becomes an empty concept in connection with the big business corporation, so the notion of democracy or of responsible government may become attenuated in connection with the organs of state. Indeed, one might say that the further state activity extends and the more large-scale organisations come to predominate in the private sector – the two historically have been roughly parallel processes – the more the department of state and the business concern become assimilated as socio-economic organisms.

One final comment on the gross record before turning to the particulars: while the figures indicate a continuous upward trend, they also suggest a sharp jump between the immediate pre- and post-war years; a more detailed year by year plot would demonstrate such a jump very clearly. This is no statistical accident. In some part it is to be accounted for by a specific consequence of the war: disablement and bereavement pensions, which of course steadily dwindled from their immediate postwar peak. In greater part, however, it reflects less specific but more enduring legacies of war, operating on both the expenditure side and the revenue side. On the expenditure side the war served to spotlight certain deficiencies in the existing order, particularly in housing, more generally in that standard of diet, medical care, etc. which had resulted in two-fifths of military conscripts being found unfit for active service – deficiencies which once clearly exposed could not subsequently be ignored. In some degree too, wartime exigencies had drawn the state into financial involvements which could not always be readily cast aside or which, at least, helped to break down traditional reservations on the role of the state. This kind of breaking down of customary limits, however, operated most powerfully on the revenue side, providing the finance for a sharp extension of government activity. Rates and types of taxes which would have been electoral suicide before 1914 had become normal experience by 1918. A Chancellor of the Exchequer could court popularity by reducing income tax to 4s in the pound, when prewar it had never gone above 1s 3d. Beer drinkers who had contributed £13 million to the revenue in 1913 could be induced to pay £80 million in the 1920s without exciting anything more than maudlin reminiscences about the days when a pint could be had for a penny.

Coming closer to particulars, the broad components of expenditure can be distinguished as shown in Table II.47.

TABLE II.47. *Objects of central and local government expenditure other than national debt charges (percentages)*

	1925	1937
Military	14	19
Social services – direct provision	11	16
Social services – cash benefits	25	20
Housing	5	5
(of which subsidy)	(1)	(1·5)
Trading services	21	20
Other goods and services	25	20

(The base data is derived principally from A. T. Peacock and J. Wiseman, *The Growth of Public Expenditure in the United Kingdom* (1967), *passim*. In adapting it for this purpose certain adjustments, containing an element of approximation, have had to be made and the figures given are subject to a margin of error – almost certainly no greater than 2 in any of the values stated.

The change of source and the rearrangement of categories precludes any close comparability with Table II.44, p. 708. 'Military' in both tables should be more or less directly comparable. The sum of the two 'Social services' in Table II.47 and the sum of 'Social services' and 'Poor relief . . .' in Table II.44 are not really comparable although the excess of 'Social services – cash benefits' over 'Poor relief . . .' may be taken as some indication of the change in the volume of money payments. 'Trading services' (Table II.47) includes one or two minor services not given in the subgroup, 'postal . . .' (Table II.44). The small amount of prewar housing expenditure is included in 'Other goods and services' in Table II.44.)

Taking the items in order, and delving a little below the statistical surface: the course of military spending reflects above all changes in the international political and diplomatic climate; from the relatively low level at which it was maintained through the 'twenties and early 'thirties, when disarmament conferences, peace pacts and the League of Nations were hopefully looked to as harbingers of a new international order, it started upwards again from the mid-'thirties as it became apparent that old devils were very far from having been exorcised. It is, then, an item whose fluctuations relate principally to events beyond our orbit here – of primary significance, only in so far as the fall in its share of total government spending by comparison with the pre-1914 era is a kind of obverse measure of a general shift in the role of the state: a shift away from 'minimalism' towards 'interventionism'.

Amongst the 'interventionist' activities which are our primary concern here, the chief interwar contribution to the two major social services which were directly provided, health and education, was to fill out the framework already in existence by 1914 rather than to extend its range. In the immediate postwar years there was a rapid increase in expenditure under the National Health Insurance scheme, which had not come into fully effective operation before the war and whose burden had in substantial part been borne by the military medical services during the war. Subsequently, enlarged health expenditure was largely the work of local authorities, who greatly accelerated their push into the hospital sector, formerly sustained principally by charitable agencies. By 1939 over two-thirds of all hospital beds were under local authority management and the way was clear for a simple transition to a fully nationalised hospital service. In education, the fully evolved primary school system found the demand placed on it declining as the birth rate fell – the number of children attending state elementary schools dropped from 6·05 million in 1914 to 5·04 million in 1938. There was, however, plenty of room for improving school buildings and equipment and for raising the teacher/pupil ratio. Between items such as these and a considerable extension of the school meals and medical services, expenditure on primary education continued to move upwards – apart from the years 1932–35 when the cut in teachers' salaries made for economies in this, the major component of education expenditure. It was, however, to the extension of secondary and higher education that activity was particularly directed. Public expenditure at these levels rose from 16 per cent of total state educational spending in 1914 to 25 per cent in 1938 – although that still left a lot to private financing: quite apart from the purely private schools, including those confusingly called 'public schools', about a quarter of state and grant aided secondary school costs and about a half of university costs were met from fees and endowments etc.

Perhaps the most striking contrast with prewar times is afforded by the considerable proportion of total state outgoings which now took the form of straight cash payments to beneficiaries. Some part of the jump above prewar levels is to be accounted for by war pensions: 7 per cent of total spending in 1925 and 3 per cent in 1937, the difference being almost entirely responsible for the fall of the share of 'cash benefits' in the whole between these two dates. The bulk of this item, however, reflects the operation of compulsory, state managed, insurance schemes, to provide security against sickness, unemployment, death and old age. The measures of 1911 had taken health insurance as far as it was to go – although it was only from 1920 that the scheme got fully into its stride – but the scope of unemployment insurance was greatly extended beyond its limited 1911 coverage in 1920, and a retirement and bereavement pensions scheme was launched in 1925.

The health insurance scheme proved an auditor's delight, receipts continuously exceeding expenditure – such that in 1932 its accumulated balances could be used to bail out the distressed retirements pensions scheme. Even this latter did not run into really serious difficulties – original actuarial miscalculation combining with reduced receipts during the depression to produce a deficit of a fairly modest order. With the unemployment insurance scheme it was a very different story; its behaviour constituted the rankest of offences against all sound insurance principles. Continuously in the red – the deficit covered by Treasury loans – from within a few months of inception in its extended form, it lost all but the sorriest semblance of an authentic insurance scheme with the onset of the depression. From then on, it was really no more than a convenient institutional channel for the disbursement of government relief for the unemployed.[1]

One effect of the extended coverage of centralised schemes run, at least in principle, on an insurance basis was to take much of the strain off the locally administered and financed Poor Law – a strain which almost certainly would have proved intolerable under the continuously high unemployment of the interwar years. It is not that this made for any reduction in the sums expended by local authorities on poor relief. Indeed, throughout the years from 1921 onwards these ran at about three times their prewar levels. What it did mean was that local poor relief could now be concentrated much more closely on these particular areas of distress which lay beyond the competence of the national social security schemes; and that rate conscious councils could adopt a somewhat more generous and humane approach towards these areas without fear of precipitating an unmanageable cost escalation. The 'workhouse' associations of the Poor Law had bitten too deeply into popular consciousness for it ever to be able effectively to reconstitute itself on a new model, but something of an attempt was being made – one which was given explicit expression in 1929 when the style 'poor

---

[1] From 1931, when contribution rates were raised, the receipts of the Unemployment Fund did cover 'in benefit' disbursements. Payments to the unemployed who had run out of benefit were met out of Treasury subventions. In 1937 these 'unemployment allowances' were transferred to a separate Unemployment Assistance Fund.

relief' was amended to 'public assistance' and responsibility for its administration was transferred from the old boards of guardians to the ordinary local authorities, county councils, etc.

State activity in the housing field has already been attended to and the only feature which warrants a further comment here is the somewhat anomalous nature of the activity as between 'social services' and 'trading services', when much the greater part of costs was recovered out of rents charged to tenants.

Coming finally to trading services proper, operating on self-balancing accounts: the slight decline in their proportionate rating when set in the context of a growing total reveals a steady expansion of this kind of activity; an expansion in fact over its whole range, of which the most important elements were as before, postal (the only one operated by the central government), water, gas, transport and electricity services – with the last showing the highest rate of growth. Broadly speaking, however, this expansion did not represent a further extension of the public sector at the expense of the private but a more or less even rate of growth of the two in the fields concerned, with the result that a very varied pattern of services continued to prevail over the country as a whole: here one drew gas from a municipal authority but travelled on the trams of a commercial concern, elsewhere the reverse obtained, and so on. No close study of this area has yet been undertaken and it is difficult to say why the tendency for local authorities to take over from private agencies, which had been very pronounced in the three decades or so before the war, now tapered off. Possibly it reflects the fact that earlier takeovers had often been of low profit concerns and that without compulsory acquisition powers local authorities could not get their hands on the more profitable enterprises still remaining in private control. Possibly it is due to the greater preoccupation of local authorities with housing, hospitals, roads, etc., drawing attention away from trading services. Possibly it is to be ascribed to the waning of the Liberal party which at the local level had earlier been particularly forward in effecting 'municipalisation'. Labour councils may have preferred to wait for nationalisation and Conservative councils may have had a preference for private enterprise.

If in general the swing from private to public enterprise did not proceed much further through the interwar years, the period did throw up a new kind of institution, the semi-state body or public corporation, charged with general statutory obligations to provide a nationwide service and ultimately answerable to the government but vested with complete autonomy within these limits. The first two public corporations came in 1926 in the shape of the BBC and the Central Electricity Board, the first familiar enough to need no introduction, the second responsible for the construction and operation of a national electricity grid,[1] designed to ensure optimum utilisation of generating capacity. Both of these of course constituted very special kinds of cases. In the one, a public tax financed monopoly was the only practical alternative to advertising financed radio; in the other, centralised coordination was essential to efficiency; the simplest way of achieving it was the creation of a single monopolistic organisation – with evident dangers if it were constituted as a private profit-making concern. The general issue of public *versus* private enterprise had little place in these particular ventures. Nor could it figure much in the creation of the British Overseas Airways Corporation in 1939. With its limited market base and high costs a regular long distance air service was not a paying proposition. The private concerns maintaining such services had only been kept going by subsidies from the government, concerned with the maintenance of national prestige and with military considerations. Their amalgamation into a unified public concern represented little more than the logical conclusion of the situation.

One other organisation merits reference here: the London Passenger Transport Board, created in 1933 to operate all tram, trolley, bus, underground and tube services in the Greater London area, hitherto provided by a variety of municipal and private enterprises. It differed from the three public corporations mentioned in that its competence was restricted to a particular area, being more in the nature of a special kind of local authority with precedents in the Metropolitan Water Board (1905) and the Port of London Authority (1910); and it differed also in being partly privately owned, the commercial concerns taken over by it becoming shareholders.

Of little immediate weight either in a gross economic context[2] or in the context of the 'political' debate on nationalisation, the most particular significance to be attached to these bodies is as models for the organisation of those fairly extensive sectors of the economy which were to pass into public control in the years after the Second World War.

We have now started to verge on the question of policy itself: its

---

[1] A long-distance transmission system; the CEB neither generated electricity nor sold it to final users.

[2] Expenditure by these bodies is *not* included in Tables II.46 and 47, the requisite information not being readily available.

principles, purposes and intentions. If one bears in mind that of the twenty-one years between the two wars eighteen were years of what was in name or effect a Conservative government – that is, of a party whose supreme strength has always been its studious avoidance of the doctrinaire – and that the remaining three were of Labour governments which were never in command of a parliamentary majority, it will be easy enough to credit that policy was not characterised by any great rigour of principle, consistency of purpose or clarity of intention. However, two broad generalisations are permissible: in all political quarters there was a fairly deliberate drift towards policies of redistributive intent and effect; and in a much less deliberate way government was increasingly drawn into active involvement in the conduct and management of the nation's economic life.

The agencies of redistribution on the expenditure side have already been noted: the education service; subsidised housing; general practitioner medical services under the National Health Insurance (for workers only, the lack of provision for dependents being perhaps the most conspicuous shortcoming in the range of social services); local authority hospital services; cash payments under the three insurance schemes (including therein unemployment relief met by Treasury subventions); old age pensions (most of them in the course of being replaced by contributory pensions); poor relief (from 1929, 'public assistance'). The collection certainly witnesses to a concern for social welfare which could hardly have been envisaged even as late as, say, 1900. Compassion, a sense of social justice, an awareness that poverty was not so much a mark of individual failure as of a failure on the part of society as a whole – these were sentiments which had in the past been very slow in gaining a footing in establishment circles but which by 1939 had come close to passing for commonplaces. However, sentiments, and their accompanying rhetoric, do not constitute a concerted programme of action. More specifically in this context: while particular measures to meet particular contingencies had been framed on the broad principle that the well off should contribute to the assistance of the badly off, no government ever contemplated a calculated manipulation of the fiscal system as a whole in order to achieve some given measure of income redistribution; and the gross effect actually achieved in practice was determined as much by the unplanned conjuncture of fiscal elements as by deliberate redistributive intent.

Intent manifested itself most plainly in the insurance schemes, in which state and employer contributions well outweighed employee contributions – although the ultimate amount of state support for the unemployment insurance scheme was really determined by the brute force of events, compelling a choice between state subvention on a completely unenvisaged scale and the total collapse of the scheme. Taxes proper followed a more haphazard course. The war had necessitated a great increase in tax revenue which, largely for reasons of administrative simplicity and certainty of yield, was obtained in major part from direct taxes: income tax, surtax and death duties, which fell mainly or entirely on the comparatively wealthy. At the same time, however, there was a big increase in duties on alcohol and tobacco, commodities for which demand was relatively inelastic. And these emergency dispositions of the tax system were substantially conserved to sustain the rising peacetime expenditure of the subsequent years. The overall effect was to produce a rather curious pattern as far as the incidence of taxation at different levels was concerned.

From income levels of about £500 p.a. upwards the system was quite sharply progressive: the married man with three children in 1934 was paying away in taxes about 13 per cent of an income of £500 p.a., but about 50 per cent of an income of £20,000 p.a. However, up to incomes of £500 p.a. the system tended to be regressive, the result above all of the alcohol and tobacco duties, assisted in lesser measure by tea and sugar duties. The married man with three children in 1934 paid in taxes about 17 per cent of an income in the £100 to £200 p.a. range (comprehending the huge majority of wage incomes) if he were an 'average' smoker and drinker; and even the total abstainer in this range paid taxes at a slightly higher rate than his counterpart in the £250 p.a. to £500 p.a. range.[1] It was into this latter range that there fell the great bulk of the period's most distinctive income recipients, the salary earners; and it was this new middle class which, largely accidentally, was the particular favourite of the tax system. However, even across its regressive range the system took more in absolute terms as income rose – and a great deal more as income passed beyond the £500 p.a. mark. Given that expenditure on the social services was almost entirely for the benefit of the working class, the net result was that the state had become the agent of an appreciable, though hardly substantial, effective redistribution of income. Rough and ready calculations suggest that for most of this period the one tenth or so of the population with incomes of above £250 p.a. (which may be taken as marking the upper limit of

[1] The percentages quoted are taken from U. K. Hicks, *The Finance of British Government 1920–1936*, (1938), pp. 270–7.

wage incomes) and in receipt of close on a half of total incomes, financed in effect the whole of state outlays other than on social services and through the social services contributed about 4 per cent of their income to the support of those on less than £250 p.a.

If a fairly consistent social policy can be ascribed to interwar governments, economic policy was little more than the plaything of events. Circumstances enforced actions, but no clear guidelines existed to lend any continuity of purpose to the actions taken. The received body of economic theory addressed itself to a hypothetical equilibrium situation in which perfect competition, perfect mobility of the factors of production, perfect entrepreneurial knowledge and wisdom were assumed, and which analysis demonstrated to result in the optimum deployment of resources. It was a model which had corresponded sufficiently closely to the facts of economic life in pre-1914 Britain to induce general acceptance of its appositeness as a basis of policy – or, rather, as a justification for no policy. Confronted with disequilibrium, evident imperfections and a resource utilisation which plainly fell well short of the optimum, the classical economics could offer nothing to the statesman; and the new economics of which John Maynard Keynes was the chief architect was still struggling for a hearing when war again came along to impose its peculiar imperatives on economic policy. Deprived of help from the experts, it is no wonder that the mere politicians could at best contrive little more than *ad hoc* responses to particular exigencies, and often found themselves unable to contrive any response at all. Conservative governments may have been readier to invoke *laissez-faire* principles in defence of inaction, but Labour governments, rhetorically committed to the use of state power, were similarly devoid in practice of broadly efficacious policies. The closest approach to a political programme for coherent action was that contained in the Liberal election manifesto of 1929, *Can Lloyd George do it?* – which, however, did nothing to stay the precipitate decline of the Liberal party.

There is, then, little possibility of imposing an ordered pattern on the series of expedients which one government or another resorted to in this or that field; and what follows, in concluding the general theme of the economic role of government, can be little more than a simple recitation, much of it merely a summary digest of matters scattered about in what has gone before.

The war had brought about a great extension of state control and regulation, and though the years 1919–21 saw an almost frenetic scrapping of almost all of this wartime apparatus, certain relics did survive. Before handing the railways back to private control in 1921, the government sought to ensure a more rational and efficient organisation by enforcing the reconstitution of the old companies into four new ones. The railways had always operated under the close eye of the state; and when railway revenue slid downwards under the pressure of competition from road transport, the government sought to redress the balance with motor vehicle and petrol duties and the limitation of public carrier licences; while in 1935 the state-owned Railway Finance Corporation was set up to provide loan facilities for a business whose diminished profits now precluded it from raising capital in more conventional ways.

Coalmining was another activity which the state had taken over during the war and where, even more than in the case of the railways, there was need of reorganisation. With its numerous high cost pits which could only pay their way under abnormal demand conditions, and its reciprocally vicious labour relations, it was an industry which threatened to destroy itself unless taken firmly in hand. It was, indeed, a very hot potato – too hot for the government of the day which in 1921, notwithstanding the recommendation of the Sankey Commission (1919) that it remain permanently in state hands, abruptly handed it back in the same condition as it had found it. But the difficulties of an industry of such weight and consequence could not be lightly shrugged aside. Subsidies in support of wages were found in an endeavour to buy peace in the coalfields, until in 1926 the government wearied of the matter and decided to allow the industry to sort itself out in the crucible of industrial warfare. As a means of resolving the wages issue for the while the crushing defeat sustained by the miners in the great coal strike – briefly and ineffectually supplemented by a fiasco of a general strike – was decisive; but even when able to dictate their own wage terms, many of the smaller colliery enterprises remained in a very parlous condition. Willynilly, the government was drawn back into involvement with coal.

The Coal Mines Act of 1930 envisaged an enduring long-term solution to the industry's difficulties through the amalgamation of enterprises and the formation of a small number of strong multicolliery units in place of the hundreds of concerns which currently littered the industry. The Coal Mines Reorganisation Commission, vested with compulsory powers, was created to effect this strategy, but its powers were so hedged about with qualifications that not a single compulsory merger was achieved, though the Commission did successfully promote a few voluntary amalgamations. Originally intended as temporary measures to see the industry through the reorganisation phase, other sections of the Act provided for the fixing of minimum prices and the allocation of output quotas to individual collieries, with the object of maintaining adequately remunerative price levels – the system to be operated by the industry itself under the general supervision of the Board of Trade. This in practice became the most effective feature of the statute. It could not, however, be thought of as anything other than a palliative; and in 1938 the government took a step towards more direct control when it nationalised all unworked deposits, giving the state the effective determination of the future shape of the industry.

Agriculture may be distinguished as the third of a trio of major economic activities with which the state had become involved during the war and from which it subsequently never fully disengaged itself. During the war policy had been directed above all to raising the output of cereal crops. Considerable success was achieved, and in the immediate aftermath of the war the government was encouraged to entertain the notion of effecting an enduring reversal of the decades' old decline in British grain output by persisting with the guaranteed price scheme operated since 1917. But the bursting of the postwar boom and the consequent steep deflation brought a hasty change of mind as the cost to the state of making up the difference between market price and guaranteed price mounted to utterly unenvisaged proportions. In 1921 the scheme was abruptly scrapped and farmers were left to find their own salvation. Nevertheless the conviction implanted by the U-boat campaign, that British agriculture should be kept at at least some minimum level of viability, did not fade away entirely. In the hope of shoring up farming with a new prop, legislation of 1925 sought to promote the cultivation of beet sugar by a system of subsidies, with the eventual consequence that about a quarter of British sugar consumption was met from homegrown supplies. And against the background of a worldwide glut of foodstuffs and of the Great Depression which was in substantial part a consequence of this phenomenon, and later of the growing menace of another war in which Britain might again be thrown back on her own resources, the state through the 1930s built up an increasingly complex apparatus for the support of British agriculture.

Acts of 1931 and 1933 provided for the creation of marketing boards for various commodities – voluntarily constituted by producers themselves but, once established, vested with statutory authority to conduct all sales of the commodity concerned, with the aim of ensuring stable prices and predictable incomes for producers. Import quotas and tariffs ensured that such arrangements were not undone by controlled foreign supplies. A guaranteed price scheme for wheat was reintroduced in 1932, financed by a duty on imported wheat. State financial support for milk and meat producers was afforded from 1934. Other measures subsequently supplemented and reinforced these provisions. By 1939 the state had thoroughly infiltrated the business of farming and had, in effect, become a full partner with the farmer himself in deciding what was to be raised and in what quantity. And as a more or less direct consequence of state support, agricultural output (expressed as a fraction of gross national product) which had probably hit its lowest point around 1930, at about 3·5 per cent, thereafter started, very slowly, to climb upwards again.

No other sector of the economy elicited state intervention on the scale of agriculture. Elsewhere, government activity was very much a matter of bits and pieces. Here and there, research assistance was afforded under the auspices of the Department of Scientific and Industrial Research, created during the war. Some firms were enabled to raise government guaranteed loans under the Trade Facilities Acts of 1921–27 – concerned chiefly with promoting exports. An export credit guarantee scheme was run by the Board of Trade from 1921 and was very widely used. But neither in terms of state expenditure nor in terms of general economic benefits secured were these measures of any great consequence.

As has been indicated either in the immediately preceding paragraphs or in earlier parts of this chapter, the depression played a very particular part in drawing the state into closer engagement with the economy. Purely electoral considerations, if nothing else, required that whether or not anything effective was done something must seem to be done. The principal measures taken – balancing the budget, conferring tariff protection, lowering interest rates – have already been noted and summarily appraised. Ironically, schemes for the direct relief of unemployment were sacrificed to the canons of financial orthodoxy. The Unemployment Grants Committee, which since 1921 had disbursed funds for public works, fell to the economy axe of 1931. But the dribble of projects which it had financed had made no contribution worth speaking of towards creating employment, indeed none at all in the long run since the Committee had had no powers to initiate schemes of its own and was confined to making grants to permit of the acceleration of undertakings already planned by local authorities. Throughout the period, in fact, official thinking remained profoundly sceptical as to the value of direct employment schemes; and although, under the Special Areas Act of 1934, four regions where unemployment was particularly high – south-west Scotland, west Cumberland, Tyneside and South Wales – were the subject of a specific unemployment policy, this was more fertile of investigations and reports than of efficacious actions.

Perhaps the most interesting product of the measures precipitated by the depression was the Import Duties Advisory Committee, created in 1932 to determine whether and to what extent particular industries should receive tariff protection and empowered to recommend stipulations to be attached to the grant of such protection. It was, thus, an agency through which the state could act on the structure and behaviour of industry while stopping short of the appearances of direct intervention; and, if in practice it was only on the steel industry that the IDAC acted to much effect, it may serve as an exemplar of the sort of relationship which the governments of these years in general sought to cultivate with private enterprise: one founded in the formal principle of entrepreneurial independence but leaving room for cajoling, coaxing, nudging and every now and then a little discreet arm-twisting on the part of the state. Often, of course, officialdom could see nothing for it but to leave private enterprise to sort things out itself as best it could; and there was little disposition, even when Labour was in office, to replace private by public enterprise or to question the key role of profits in sustaining economic performance. If anything in the nature of a general principle can be discerned at work, it was that of helping business to help itself. The stabilisation of profits was a central feature of policy measures for coalmining and agriculture, of the rationalisation of the steel industry as programmed by the Bank of England and later the British Iron and Steel Federation in conjunction with the Import Duties Advisory Committee, and of legislative schemes for the two other chief 'depressed' industries, cotton and shipbuilding.

Cotton in 1936 was endowed with the Spindles Board, charged with buying up and extinguishing surplus spinning machinery, the cost to be met out of a levy on surviving spinners. This endeavour to eliminate cut-throat competition was followed up in 1939 by legislation creating an apparatus for fixing compulsory minimum prices – whose introduction, however, was overtaken and rendered pointless by the outbreak of war.

The shipbuilding industry had provided itself with its own equivalent of the Spindles Board when it created, in 1930, the National Ship-builders Security Ltd to buy up and dismantle the least efficient yards. Unanimously supported by the shipbuilders themselves, this venture did not require statutory powers, but it had the warm approval of the government of the day and its initial capital was provided by the Bankers Industrial Development Company, a creation of the Bank of England. And the effects of the reduction in shipbuilding capacity which it brought about were supplemented by the British Shipping Act of 1935 which sought to promote orders by granting subsidies to trampship owners who scrapped old tonnage and built new.

Hesitant, fumbling, tentative, ill-ordered, piecemeal, makeshift – these adjectives inevitably suggest themselves in any attempt to ascribe a general character to economic policy through the years 1919–39. And in the last analysis, its interest consists not in its practical consequences, which set in total perspective were fairly slight, but in the record it yields of the intellectual response of political and governmental institutions to a succession of circumstances for which little in previous history had prepared them and for which no preformulated strategy was available. But that is a study which must be regarded as beyond our purview here. If a valedictory comment is called for, the most appropriate might be that an economic policy characterised by uncertainty in large part reflected the uncertainty of direction of base economic trends themselves through the years in question.

Chapter Six

1939–1970[1]

The last two chapters have steadily run down on detail in favour of the delineation of certain broad trends which have been proffered as defining the essential character of economic change and development in Britain over the last hundred years or so. This final chapter in particular purports to do no more than offer the most generalised of macro-economic surveys over a terrain which must be reckoned the province of the economist rather than that of the historian.

In historical perspective this period is characterised by two outstanding traits: its growth record and the economic role played by the state – phenomena which are so closely interlinked that no meaningful account could attempt to treat them separately.

The economy in gross: prosperity, problems and policies

With the conclusion of the Second World War the British economy moved into a phase of sustained growth such as it had not experienced since the termination of the great international railway boom in 1873. The potential which had been so prodigiously wasted through the interwar years was, at long last, brought into effective and remunerative activity. As against the crippling levels of the 'twenties and 'thirties, the average annual unemployment rate, up to 1970, consistently ran below 2·5 per cent, and most of the time below 2 per cent. More or less as a direct consequence of this, industrial production in 1969 stood at a level commensurate with a rate of increase since 1939 of *c.* 2·75 per cent p.a. – to be contrasted with the *c.* 1·5 per cent p.a. of 1939 over 1913,

[1] As in the previous chapter the war years as such are not discussed here.

and achieved with a labour force which has grown rather less rapidly than in the earlier period.[1] Discounting the war years and the immediate postwar period, industrial production 1950–69 grew at a rate of *c.* 3 per cent p.a.; and, more significantly perhaps, sustained this rate in fairly constant fashion throughout.[2]

Intimately associated with this reinvigoration of the economy has been a radical rethinking of the economic function of government. Already through the interwar years government had been increasingly disposed to tinker with the economy, patching up this or that rent, plugging this or that hole. Now it added to that readiness to undertake specific repair jobs an acknowledgement of an overall responsibility for the general level of economic activity. This acknowledgement had its founding declaration in the wartime coalition government's White Paper, *Employment Policy* (1944), which opened with the words: 'The Government accept as one of their primary aims and responsibilities the maintenance of a high and stable level of employment after the war'; and went on to sketch out a Keynesian economic strategy founded on the management of gross demand by means of variable budgetary deficits/surpluses.[3]

As the White Paper itself had recognised in advance, no deliberated policy was in fact needful to ensure full employment in the immediate aftermath of the war. Far from there being a problem of sustaining such a level of demand as to employ the available manpower, there was a pressing problem of stretching manpower resources to meet the multi-

[1] Since 1966, while population has continued to rise, the labour force has actually *declined.*

[2] Since 1945, industrial production has fallen short of its previous peak in only two years: 1952 and 1958. Additionally, the phases 1955–58, 1960–62 and 1965–67 were ones in which growth was well below the 3 per cent average. (Figures for industrial production have been preferred to figures for gross domestic product throughout this book; partly because estimates of industrial production reach back much further in time, permitting of continuous comparability; partly because the services element in GDP is measurable only in expenditure, not physical output, terms, with the result that what may be genuine gains show up as losses, e.g. elimination of an intermediary dealer, cessation of an unwanted transport service, reorganisation so that one civil servant can do the work formerly done by two; or, put the other way round, rising GDP *might* reflect nothing more than rising inefficiency.)

[3] As originally envisaged this did not involve a total abandonment of 'orthodox' budgeting. The image of the Chancellor as 'housekeeper' died hard and the White Paper conceived of him as continuing to balance government revenue and expenditure over a run of years. It was not until about 1950 that it was fully accepted in the Treasury that the budgetary deficit/surplus had no significance other than as the adjusting item in bringing the desired level of gross national demand into line with the predicted level of gross national supply.

farious demands being made on them. These included demand for consumer goods denied in the overriding cause of armaments production during the war; demand for capital goods to make up the deficiencies caused by wartime destruction and the running of productive equipment beyond normal replacement point, or to permit of reconversion from military to civil production – both consumer and producer demand originating not only at home but abroad as well, at a time when balance of payments requirements made it imperative to respond to such foreign demand as fully as possible; a peculiarly urgent demand for houses; and the continuing, if much reduced, demand for men to sustain the military establishments necessitated by the Cold War. And on top of quantitative shortages there were the qualitative ones resulting from six years during which the huge majority of young men had been trained for nothing but warfare.

When, in the absence of a full employment policy, might the post-1945 economy have relapsed into depression in the manner of the post-1918 economy? It was a question which had occupied the compilers of the White Paper who, though studiously cautious in making any explicit prediction, seem to have thought a downturn could be expected within three years of the end of the war. It was a question which was very much on the mind of the first postwar Chancellor, Hugh Dalton, who framed his policy with an eye as much to the anticipated deflation as to the current inflation. It was in fact a question which figured prominently in all sorts of quarters through the first couple of years after the war. But thereafter the question slid below the horizon. The turning point never came. The pressure of demand generated by postwar exigencies imperceptibly became the pressure of demand generated by a vigorously growing economy. The year 1950–51 can probably be identified as the stage by which the special consequences of war had faded away. (By the end of 1951 nearly all the elaborate apparatus of controls, which the war had necessitated and with which the postwar Labour government had continued to contain the problems of shortages, had gone and a Conservative government had been returned to power on an election slogan of 'Set the People Free'.) But neither at this stage nor at any subsequent point did any Chancellor have to implement measures in specific execution of a full employment policy.

This is by no means to say that governmental commitment to full employment was, in the actual outcome, an irrelevancy. No government which was guided by the old principles of financial rectitude would have persisted with the outlays on housing, health and education,

779

along with the military expenditures – massive by any historical peace-time standards – which have been continuously maintained since the war against a background of recurring foreign exchange crises. The substitution of the principle of 'macro-economic' budgeting for that of 'housekeeping' budgeting permitted successive governments to go on financing policies which the older canons would have ruled to be prohibitively expensive. Government did not need to pursue a specific 'full employment' policy because government was committed to social and military programmes generating expenditure fully sufficient to ensuring 'full employment'. And the costing of these programmes by reference to real national resources rather than by reference to a hypothetical 'taxable capacity' allowed them to be run to the limits of national productive capability. In a word, full employment policy became subsumed in general policy.

Ironically, the most insistent problem with which in the outcome postwar governments had to contend was not that of supplying deficiencies of demand but that of containing excess demand. If an unemployment graph defines the magnitude of the failure of the inter-war economy, a prices graph may stand as a measure of the pains and penalties of full employment and continuous growth in postwar conditions.

Inflation since 1945 has been a source of concern on several grounds, not all of them amenable to rigorous analysis. In the first place, there has been a feeling, strongly entertained in certain quarters, that a stable currency (i.e. stable money values) is a prime virtue in itself. This kind of money fetishism, as old as money itself, is nonetheless potent for being fundamentally irrational. In a modified, and quasirationalised, form this sentiment manifests itself as a commonsense aversion to having to pay more for something than one did formerly. The fact that one's income has risen by a compensating, or more than compensating, amount is not necessarily seen to be a relevant consideration. To be able to have one's cake and eat it is a universal human aspiration. The house-wife in particular seems apt to be much more impressed by higher prices than by a fatter wage packet – and housewives constitute a half of the electorate.

Inflation, then, as a public issue has been infused with a large measure of emotiveness carrying it well beyond the ground of its strictly economic implications. And a further consideration which has also served to heighten the emotive content of the debate is the socially discriminatory effect of inflation: as between those whose incomes can readily adjust to rising prices and those on fixed or inelastic money incomes. But, while this consideration has often figured prominently in political polemics, as a matter of objective fact, the numbers on such fixed or inelastic incomes have not been great and inflation *per se* could

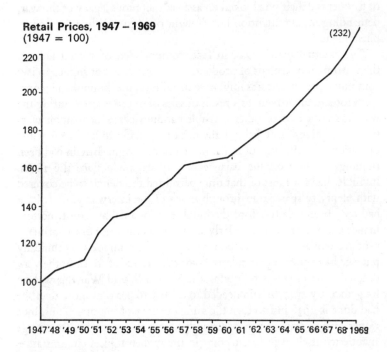

Retail Prices, 1947 – 1969
(1947 = 100)

GRAPH II.10.

not be said to have operated as an important agent of income transference or to have created a social problem of serious extent.

We come, then, to that feature of inflation which has been of the most profound significance in a strictly economic analysis: its bearing on the external balance of payments. And the balance of payments situation has, in fact, been the great shadow cast across the very real achievements of the postwar British economy.

For the first couple of years after the end of the war, inflation and the balance of payments problem were, and were treated by policy makers as, two quite distinct phenomena. A measure of inflation had been fully anticipated; and strong measures to check it were deliberately eschewed for fear of precipitating a depression on the 1921 model. The potentially injurious social effects of steep rises in the prices of basic commodities in short supply were firmly held in check by the maintenance of wartime rationing and price control measures. Meanwhile, the huge balance of payments deficit was looked on as an autonomous legacy of the war, demanding urgent attention but thought of as essentially a temporary phenomenon.

This external deficit was, in fact, compounded of several factors: the wartime impairment of productive, and hence exporting, capacity; continuing heavy overseas military expenditure; the diminished income from foreign investment as a result of sales of overseas assets during the war; the reduction of other invisible earnings consequent upon wartime disruptions. But behind these fairly specific difficulties lay the operation of a tendency of much more remote origin. Britain had been running a deficit on the balance of physical trade since the 1820s. Invisibles had for most of that time permitted this deficit to be covered with plenty to spare. But through much of the interwar years Britain had only been able to afford the indulgence of a flabby export performance because of the particularly steep falls in the price of the primary produce which constituted the major part of her imports. Technically put, she had enjoyed particularly favourable terms of trade. In the very different circumstances following the Second World War this was no longer so. By 1947 Britain needed to export 16 per cent more than she had done in 1938 just to earn the same quantity of imports. Thus, by a rather savage coincidence, a seriously disadvantageous secular change manifested itself at just that point in time when topical circumstances were making exceptional difficulties. And a strategy which had originally been designed to close a temporary gap left by the war had to adapt to effecting an enduring rectification of Britain's external economic relations.

In the immediate postwar situation, reliance was placed on the apparatus of physical controls which had been built up during hostilities and which had served to keep the wartime deficit within some sort of limits. The deficit which had then remained had been covered by credits from the USA under the lend-lease agreement. Although in August 1945 lend-lease was abruptly terminated, in December a new American loan agreement was negotiated which, it was then believed, would tide Britain over until normality was restored.

Controls did their job very efficiently. By 1947 while the *volume* of imports was being held at 78 per cent of its 1938 level, the *volume* of exports had risen to 109 per cent of the 1938 amount, achieved by dint of according preferential treatment to exporting industries in the allocation of supplies and by arrangements with such industries, conspicuously the motor vehicle industry, to withhold deliveries to the home market in favour of foreign sales. Yet for that year the deficit on the physical balance of trade was £425 million. (And, with overseas military expenditure still running at a very high level, the deficit on invisibles was £120 million.)[1] It was plain that the balance of payments problem was not merely a transitory product of the war; and that a much more thoroughgoing shift into exports was needed than could be achieved by any *dirigiste* policy – or, at least, by any one that stopped short of comprehensive nationalisation. Physical controls could operate directly and to any desired effect on the import side, but only indirectly and with limited efficacy on the export side. Furthermore, controls in general were becoming increasingly unpopular at home and import controls in particular ran counter to the aspirations of the General Agreement on Trade and Tariffs (GATT) to which Britain along with most of the other major trading nations had set her hand and which was directed towards a freeing of international trade from the numerous obstructions which had been interposed during the 1930s. With the special autumn budget of 1947 may be dated a long sequence of measures

[1] The total deficit of £545 million was fully accounted for, and more, by the deficit with the 'Dollar Area' (the USA, Canada, and some other American countries), which amounted to £571 million. Into the 1950s it was this 'Dollar Gap' which was the particular object of concern.

British was not alone in running a large deficit with the USA, the only major economy to emerge unscathed from the war, and up to 15 July 1947 had protected her precious dollar holdings by refusing to convert sterling earned by other countries (including the very substantial sterling balances accumulated by certain countries during the war) into dollars. A condition of the American loan agreement had been that convertibility should be restored by 15 July 1947. On the restoration of convertibility there was a great rush of sterling holders to exchange into dollars and on 10 August convertibility had again to be suspended. Thereafter sterling remained inconvertible until 1958, the threat of a dollar drain remaining a serious one even when the overall balance of payments had moved into surplus. (Although formal convertibility was not restored until 1958, in practice the Bank of England was freely providing dollars against non-resident sterling from 1955.)

which, in essence, have sought to bring the balance of payments under control by a calculated repression of 'excess' or 'inflationary' demand.

Although the rationale behind this policy has been essentially the same throughout, the precise terms of its presentation and of the tactical thinking informing it have varied somewhat through the years. Up to about 1950, while imports were still being attended to largely by means of direct controls (easily the most effective means of doing the job), 'excess' demand tended to be defined as that which drew too much output into the home market and away from export markets. Through the 'fifties, more emphasis was thrown on demand repression as a way of holding down imports. (Additionally, the Conservative governments of these years inclined strongly to the view that inflation was an evil in itself, i.e. irrespective of its balance of payments repercussions.) More recently, the policy has commonly been represented as a question of keeping prices down in order to maintain the competitiveness of British goods both in foreign and home markets. But these differences are no more than ones of formulation: crudely speaking, between posing the matter in terms of demand itself and posing it in terms of the price levels which demand engenders. Represented in any terms, the endeavour has been to bring about such an adjustment of gross expenditure propensities as to effect a decisive realignment of the British economy in its relationships with the rest of the world.

Limitation of demand has been a persistent policy note since 1947. Yet it would be wrong to create the suggestion of a single strategy pursued unwaveringly throughout. In the first place, and most important, demand repression was never allowed to go so far as to hazard full, or near-full, employment or to risk any protracted interruption of economic growth. Successive governments have sought to hold a balance, often a precarious one, between what have been, in the short run at least, the fundamentally antithetical aims of a sound balance of payments position and a high level of domestic economic activity. And it must be accounted some sort of a success that, up to 1970, it was never needful wholly to abandon one in the cause of the other. Secondly, there have been breathing spells during which Britain has been in surplus, although at no stage has there been a sufficiently large surplus for a sufficiently long period of time to quieten all balance of payments anxieties. Thirdly, the techniques of anti-inflationary policy have varied through time. And fourthly, the topical circumstances giving rise to successive balance of payments crises have not always been the same, although it is arguable that the fundamental cause has been an identical one throughout.

It is no part of the purport of this chapter to offer a blow by blow account, but some attempt to put these observations into historical perspective can be made.

Although in the autumn of 1947 the Labour government embarked on a policy of restraining demand by means of budgetary measures, i.e. drawing purchasing power out of the system via taxation, it continued to lean heavily on direct controls and on a formally non-coercive apparatus of guidelines, requests and exhortations, aimed, variously, at industry – to keep up the export drive; at the banks – to restrict non-essential lending; at the trade unions – to exercise wage restraint; at the populace at large – to be hard-working, cooperative and patient in the face of deprivations. The mixture was not unsuccessful. While, in quantity terms, imports continued to be held well below prewar levels, exports went from peak to peak. Devaluation, in 1949, of the pound against the dollar, from $4·03 to $2·80, greatly strengthened British exports in the all important American market. By 1950 Britain was able to show an overall surplus of £221 million on current account. The immediate postwar crisis could be said to have been resolved. However, this is to say little more than that it was now possible to contemplate a régime in which people could have what they wanted, a régime in which the consumer was once more sovereign.

The outbreak in mid-1950 of the Korean War, with its accompanying menace of a third world war, precipitated an international wave of stockpiling of basic commodities and an escalation of their prices such that Britain once again went heavily into the red (to the amount of £425 million for the year 1951). After the long haul into the clear this was a wretched setback. But it was only a temporary one; and it did not seriously inhibit the Conservative government, returned in late 1951, in going about its programme of 'setting the people free'.

The years 1952–59 may conveniently be identified as a first phase in the attempt to reconcile economic freedom and growing prosperity with a sound external situation. Two things lent the period a particular unity: its balance of payments record and its selection of economic policies.

At first glance, the balance of payments record bears quite a favourable aspect. In only one of the eight years was there a deficit on current account; and in that one (1955) the deficit was a mere £92 million. On the other hand, the average surplus over these years was no more than

£170 million. It was not enough simply to cross the magic line between deficit and surplus. A 'substantial' surplus was needful, and £170 million was not 'substantial'. Such a surplus was inadequate against two tests. It was insufficient to match the funds, government and private, for that level of investment abroad which a country of Britain's international standing and aspirations needed to maintain in both her own interests and those of capital deficient countries. And it was insufficient to build up Britain's holdings of gold and 'hard' currencies to something even approaching parity with the huge volume of foreign holdings of sterling[1] (or alternatively to pay off these claims on sterling). In fact, after long-term capital flows abroad had been covered, there was nothing at all left for this purpose. The consequences of this frailty were, to cite the most conspicuous instance, made very plain in 1957 when, following a devaluation of the franc, a widespread apprehension that Britain would also have to devalue led to a flight out of sterling which within a couple of months had carried off a quarter of the reserves before the rot was successfully stopped.

It was, then, a continuously uncomfortable, though never openly disastrous, situation to which policy was addressed over these years. And it was a policy from which much had been expected. The Conservatives had assumed office amid warm professions of faith in the efficacy of 'monetary' policy. Direct controls, already being cleared away by the Labour government, were to be scrapped, and private enterprise set loose to do its work in the free market conditions which were its natural habitat. Even the moral exhortations which Labour had freely indulged in were thought inappropriate to the environment which the new government wished to foster. Budgetary measures were to continue to play a part in governing the level of economic activity; but the kind of strategy envisaged did not leave a great deal of room for them. On the revenue side the endeavour was to be to get tax rates down and thus heighten incentives; and on the expenditure side there was no serious intention of economising on the social and military policies inherited

[1] Much of this dated from the war, when countries supplying Britain had been unable to repatriate their earnings. Over the years in question these sterling liabilities were around five times the amount of Britain's gold and hard currency holdings. The situation was not fully as alarming as this ratio would suggest since most of these sterling claims were held by 'sterling area' countries (the British Commonwealth, bar Canada, and a few other countries), whose reserves they were and who would not seek to encash them except to meet their own non-sterling deficits. Nevertheless, between the fact that Britain's reserves had to cover any such deficits and the fact that the sterling claims held by other countries were commonly enough in themselves to clean Britain out, the situation was a persistently parlous one – as it still is.

from the preceding government. Scope for tactical manipulation of the budget would therefore be limited. The problem of reconciling effective control of the overall level of demand with the maximum of economic freedom seemed most happily answerable by recourse to monetary techniques, which the Labour government had almost totally ignored but which now suggested themselves as a precise, delicate, continuously flexible system of economic management.

A proper analysis of the 'monetary' strategy of the years 1952–59 would lie beyond the competence of these pages. But it seems fair to say that it was in the outcome a complete failure. The truth of the matter appears to be that there was no general agreement in responsible quarters as to what a 'monetary' policy was – and hence, evidently, as to just how it might be used. In its most thoroughgoing sense, a monetary policy is one that aims to control the supply of money, on the principle that the level of economic activity is determined by the volume of money in circulation. If the principle be sound – and this is a hotly debated issue – a government should be able to operate a simple brake and throttle system of control by means of continuous regulation of the money flow, of which it itself is in effect the source. While every now and then there were hints and suggestions that this is what was meant by the so-called monetary policy of the 'fifties, no attempt was ever made by the authorities to hold to a given level of money creation. At the Bank of England – which under Labour had been effectively relegated to a merely administrative role in economic affairs but which under the Conservatives retrieved much of its prewar participation in policy making – and in 'City' quarters generally, monetary policy seems to have been most commonly understood as interest rate policy. Thinking in these circles appears to have been shaped largely by the manner in which up to 1931 the Bank had contrived to regulate external money movements by means of flexible interest rates; and apart from a rather hazy belief that investment and stock-carrying decisions were sensitive to changes in interest rates the internal effects of such changes do not seem to have been very closely attended to. Thus though variable bank rate[1] was the most prominent feature of the new monetary policy, its relevance to current circumstances was not very clear. Its historical role had been that of smoothing out the violence of short-term external money flows but, apart from its evident incapacity to effect any enduring adjustment of a chronically unsatisfactory balance of

---

[1] Between 1932 and 1951 bank rate had remained almost continuously unchanged at 2 per cent.

payments, its ability to stem a genuine panic flight out of sterling such as that of 1957 was very dubious.

Conventionally the term 'monetary policy' was extended to cover two other kinds of measures – both of them of a fairly crude and blunt variety and certainly invested with nothing of the supple magic which on its initial adumbration the new strategy was reputedly possessed of. The one was a series of requests or requirements to the commercial banks to limit their advances: this was a simple continuation of the practice of the Labour government. The other was statutory limitation of hire purchase agreements in respect of initial deposits and length of repayment periods. Both were in breach of the declared principle of economic management on a free market basis; and their designation as elements of monetary policy may, perhaps, be understood as a concern to maintain the letter of this principle even while offending against its spirit.

Monetary policy in effect, then, was not the single, integrated technique of pervasive effect which early rhetoric had suggested. Most particularly, it did not in the outcome provide an effective substitute for budgetary policy, which under the last Labour Chancellor, Hugh Gaitskell, had achieved a new prominence and which, as things turned out, was in practice the centrepiece of Conservative economic strategy. By the end of the 'fifties this had been frankly acknowledged and while the measures which had gloried under the title continued to be employed as ancillary instruments by successive Chancellors little more was heard for nearly a decade of the omnicompetence of 'monetary policy'.

The turn of the 'fifties and 'sixties brought more than one change. Not only was budgetary policy formally reinstated as the prime instrument of immediate economic control but increasing attention was being given to long-term strategy. The first postwar Labour government had been heavily preoccupied with the exigent problems of the moment, and so far as it gave any attention to the overall posture and structure of the economy was inclined to suppose that nationalisation was somehow taking care of that. The Conservatives in their turn found that a precariously poised balance of payments position and persistent inflation gave them plenty to think about, and were inclined to suppose, in their fashion, that private enterprise was spontaneously taking care of long-term growth. In any event, the notion that a high and sustained rate of growth was a fully practicable proposition was slow to establish itself in any quarter. What was originally a simple 'full employment' policy was some time in translating itself into an explicit 'growth' policy.

When R. A. Butler (then Chancellor of the Exchequer) asked in 1954, 'Why should we not aim to double the standard of living in the next twenty-five years?', this was as much a musing interrogative as a declaration of intent; and over the next few years the government's determination to have a 'strong pound' overrode such growth-mindedness as was taking root. Demand repression between 1955 and 1958 did eventually, and briefly, curb inflation, but the penalty paid was an industrial production index which stood at 106 in 1958 as against 105 in 1955. Growth, while increasingly acknowledged as a proper end of economic policy, was something to be deferred until Britain had turned the corner into 'solvency'. At the same time, however, the view was gathering strength in wider circles that sustained and vigorous growth was not merely desirable in itself but also contained the answer to the balance of payments problem.

Through much of the 'fifties the balance of payments problem had commonly been thought of as consisting in an excessive propensity to import.[1] In the last analysis of course, the question of whether the weakness lay on the import side or on the export side is analogous to the question of which blade of the scissors does the cutting, but there was both a secular reason and a topical reason for picking on imports as the troublemaker. In a secular view: Britain had over the previous hundred years and more built up a consumption pattern which was strongly import orientated. Britain, to a distinctive degree amongst the major countries of the world, had become client to others over a great range of primary commodities; and the one natural material with which Britain was well endowed, coal, was as a fuel increasingly giving place to oil. To check further accentuation of this already strong import bias could seem particularly needful. In a more topical view: through the earlier 'fifties there was not much scope for raising exports further above the high level to which they had been driven by 1950. The basic post-war retooling boom was over but, outside North America, it had not yet been succeeded by high levels of mass consumption. The markets for greatly expanded exports were simply not there.

By the later 'fifties, however, it was becoming increasingly plain that considerable economic progress was being made in Western Europe and certain other parts of the world; progress which was going well

---

[1] That is, when it was not being thought of in the more nebulous terms of maintaining 'confidence in the pound'. The gnomes of Zürich, to use the journalese of the times, were understood to be impressed by high interest rates, increases in purchase tax, rising unemployment and other signs of economic masochism on Britain's part even when the balance of current payments was not under any immediate threat.

beyond anything that could be regarded as mere 'postwar recovery'. Between 1955 and 1960 industrial production in Western Europe rose by 40 per cent, as against 13 per cent in the United Kingdom.

This record was felt to have two implications for Britain. One: it suggested the possibility of achieving a much higher growth rate than was currently being registered or even contemplated. Two: Britain's sluggish export performance could no longer be ascribed to market limitations but was, rather, a reflection of deteriorating competitiveness.

From just about 1960 a new economic strategy was being formulated. Its fundamental premise was that if a trouble-free run up could be secured and if producers could be assured of a sustained growth momentum, coordinated, long-term investment planning could then make for a novel degree of economic efficiency – with not only the promise of something like a 4 per cent p.a. growth rate but also that of an international competitiveness which would provide an enduring solution to the balance of payments problem.

In its most thoroughgoing form, this style of thinking envisaged a close engagement of the government in the requisite planning: by determination of a practicable growth rate; by commitment to such budgetary and other macro-economic policies as would be needful to the sustenance of such a rate; and by itself attending to that coordination of individual investment plans which was the lynchpin of the strategy. In this form, it naturally commended itself most to the Labour party, which had always professed great faith in the virtues of planning, though while in office between 1945 and 1951 its 'plans' had never been of much more than a hand to mouth variety. The Conservative government of the day was a good deal more dubious about the short-run consequences for the pound of an unambiguous expansionist policy and was suspicious of the *dirigiste* undertones of the strategy – whose watchword, however, was 'coordination', not 'coercion'. But, at least in general terms, the notion of deliberated growth was being received with growing enthusiasm in official quarters; and in any event the state, through the public corporations, the local authorities and certain central government departments, was itself responsible for more than 40 per cent of total investment, and thus, willynilly was already substantially involved in investment planning. In its broad principles, the strategy of salvation through planned growth was a bipartisan one, although in the outcome it was never to be fully implemented by either party.

An essential precondition was the avoidance of acute foreign exchange crises such as would force the authorities back on repressive measures. As to this, there was a good deal of optimism in the early 'sixties, when the feeling was current that out of the errors of the 'fifties had been learned the correct techniques for effective short-term management of demand. Taxation measures along with hire purchase controls, it was reckoned, were highly efficient if employed with sufficient promptitude: promptitude in diagnosing 'overheating'; promptitude in applying corrective action. And, since the mid-'fifties, a great deal had been done to improve the speed and accuracy of official economic intelligence agencies, while in 1961 the cumbersome, ritualistic, parliamentary procedures necessary to taxation adjustments were shortcircuited by empowering the Chancellor to vary commodity taxes and employers' National Insurance contributions by simple statutory order. (These were the so-called 'regulators', the second of which in fact was never used.)

With, as was hoped, short-run fluctuations under control, deliberate long-term planning could be effected on the basis of a predictable future. Since, in fact, short-run fluctuations were not brought under control the long-term strategy never really got off the ground. There is little point in doing much more here than itemising the agencies created with a view to achieving efficiency. The first was the National Economic Development Council ('Neddy') set up in 1962. Its membership consisted of individuals drawn from the employers' side of industry and from the trade unions; supported by a permanent staff of statisticians and economists. Its role was never precisely defined. The first task it was set was to determine what sort of growth the economy as a whole might be capable of over the next few years and what the implications of such a growth rate would be for individual sectors; but what active part it was then to play in realising any given target was never made clear. In the outcome it slipped away into the wings after the publication of 1963 of its first report on future growth prospects. More continuously active have been the Economic Development Committees ('little Neddies') set up from 1964 on the model of NEDC but specific to particular industry groups and positively charged not only with the collection and dissemination of economic intelligence in their fields but also with the recommendation, either to the government or to the industry concerned, of any general measures calculated to heighten efficiency. In origin these EDCs were conceived of as principal instruments in the realisation of the 'National Plan', elaborated by a new creation of the Labour government returned in 1964, the Department of Economic

Affairs. This, in general intention, was to be the ministry responsible for detailed long-term economic planning, leaving the Treasury, the traditional economics department, with the responsibility for overall short-run control: and the DEA's 'National Plan', produced in 1965, replaced the earlier NEDC report as the gospel for growth. In fact, neither DEA nor 'National Plan' survived the vicissitudes of the next few years.

In the pursuit of strength through efficiency the Labour government brought into being two further institutions: a set of Regional Councils and Regional Boards, created between 1964 and 1966; and the Industrial Reorganisation Commission, established in 1966. The regional bodies were founded as a sort of geographically based counterpart to the industry based EDCs, although, in form, their competence extended well beyond the narrowly economic to embrace social considerations as well, while, in fact, they never became much more than ancillaries in the decades-old programme of creating jobs in areas of particularly high unemployment.[1]

The IRC is perhaps the most interesting creation of these years of Labour government, founded as it was by a political party traditionally profoundly suspicious of concentrations of capitalist power for the very purpose of promoting combinations in the private sector. £150 million were put at its disposal to facilitate any reorganisation scheme which carried the clear promise of greater efficiency or, under subsequent legislation of 1968, any project at all of benefit to the national economy.

There was, then, no lack of agencies concerned in one way and another with planning and efficiency. But the original dream of a smooth escalation of external strength could hardly have been more violently shattered. Over the years 1960–68 the average annual deficit on current account was £110 million, most of it the result of huge shortfalls in 1960, 1964, 1967 and 1968, each of them aggravated by precipitate repatriations of funds on the part of foreign holders of sterling. In gross, the total currency flow out of Britain between the end of 1959 and the end of 1968, as officially recorded, was £3,500 million, nearly four times the amount of the reserves at the outset. Only massive borrowing from the International Monetary Fund and foreign bankers enabled this to be covered.

Against this kind of background there could be no possibility of pursuing the consistently expansionist policy which the pristine growth

[1] One uses the past tense since at the moment of writing (1971) it does not appear that the new Conservative government envisages much of a role for these bodies.

strategy had prescribed.[1] It was not that a high growth rate was repudiated as an explicit policy aim; but that all too often it was found necessary to postpone it. However, the struggle to create conditions which would permit of uninterrupted growth of a 4 per cent p.a. order was by no means abandoned. While conventional budgetary and monetary measures were being invoked to cope with immediate external difficulties, a quite different tack was also being tried in the hope of bringing a more enduring discipline to bear on inflationary tendencies: an 'incomes policy'.

Among economists the argument had long been common that Britain's persistent inflation was not so much a 'demand pull' as a 'cost push'[2] phenomenon, with the implications that demand repression techniques alone could not get to the heart of the problem. Among politicians, often persuaded of the force of the argument in abstract, there had always been great diffidence and uncertainty as to the practicability of translating it into an active policy. The first postwar Labour government had had, in the mixture of coercion and cajolery with which it conducted economic affairs, an 'understanding' with the trade unions. But this had broken down under the strain of the price rise engendered by the Korean War; and the Conservative government on taking office had made no attempt to renew it: 'free market' principles were as valid for wages as for anything else. And although as disillusionment with 'monetary policy' set in there was a growing hankering after some attempt at directly checking wage increases, the government was certainly not prepared for a head-on collision with the trade unions, who in turn were equally emphatically not prepared to cede anything of the bargaining strength which after decades of struggle had only just started to give the working man an at all substantial share in material prosperity. By the early 'sixties, however, with sterling coming under increasingly severe pressure, with export uncompetitiveness being distinguished as Britain's chief weakness, and with wages rising more rapidly than ever before, the feeling in favour of some attempt to apply a brake gathered strength in official circles. In 1961 the Chancellor, Selwyn Lloyd, proclaimed a 'pay pause' for six months; and this was succeeded by the definition of 'guiding lights', percentage rates which wage increases should not exceed. No power of enforcement was taken;

[1] No possibility, that is, by the canons which prevailed in official quarters. There were – and are – those who argued that growth *per se* was the only proper object of economic policy and that the pound, or the reserves, should be left to whatever end unqualified growth brought them.

[2] Rising wages – higher costs – higher prices – further rising wages – etc.

nor was the prior agreement of the unions sought. It was an exercise in moral intimidation. And by and large, the unions declined to be intimidated.

The Conservative government had never hoped for anything more than a temporary respite, during which world inflation might catch up with the British article and equate competitive costs. It had never supposed that it could engage that cooperation of the trade unions which would be essential to the successful operation of a permanent incomes policy in a free society. The Labour government returned in 1964 hoped otherwise. The National Board for Prices and Incomes which it set up in 1965 was founded on four essential principles which, it was felt, gave a permanent incomes policy a real chance of working. The first principle was that an 'incomes policy' should not be just a 'wages policy'. While the impossibility of submitting most other kinds of incomes to close and detailed supervision was recognised, the NBPI was given full powers of inquiry into profits, salaries etc., and was to assess wage increases in the light of the course of incomes generally. In brief, it was to ensure that wages got their fair share of the cake. Secondly, while the NBPI was to have reference to a 'norm' prescribed by the government, it was not to be rigidly bound by this and could approve wage increases in excess of the 'norm' on either equitable or economic grounds. Thirdly, the NBPI was as responsible for prices as for wages; responsible, that is, for preventing wage increases automatically converting themselves into price increases, eroding both real wage gains and competitiveness in world markets. A clear onus was to be placed on management to absorb moderated wage increases in higher productivity. Fourthly, though this was more implicit than explicit, it was recognised that the pursuit of absolute price stability was a fool's mission; that, while increases in money incomes should be correlated with increases in productivity, some degree of 'wage creep' was inevitable; and that all that could be looked for was to keep British inflation roughly in line with world inflation.

All in all, this added up to an incomes policy of a realistic flexibility. It acknowledged the inescapable limitations to which any incomes policy which stops short of totalitarianism is subject – including the limitations of statutory authority: the NBPI had no power to enforce its recommendations; and the government had no power but to refer prices and wages issues to the NBPI. The very hope of its effectiveness lay in the fact that it was a programme to which industry and the trade unions had voluntarily subscribed; and the authority to be enjoyed by the NBPI was the moral authority which this consensus conferred on it.[1]

It may be, of course, that the inescapable limitations which the programme acknowledged are crippling ones; that a permanent incomes policy is inoperable in conjunction with economic freedom and a high level of employment. The NBPI never had a chance to find out. It was, if it was anything, an organ for the governance of the secular trend of wages and prices. But within months of its foundation, with a huge haemorrhage in the balance of payments, the government was recruiting it as an instrument in a policy of brute deflation. In 1966 it was formally incorporated into the apparatus of statutory control, directed to the enforcement of a complete wages and prices standstill, with which the government had equipped itself. Although this apparatus, never intended as anything other than an emergency measure, was dismantled through 1967 and 1968, the whole philosophy informing the original incomes policy was destroyed beyond retrieval. And from mid-1969 wages bounded upwards with hitherto unparalleled velocity.

By then, the devaluation of the pound, to which the government had finally resorted in November 1967, was taking effect on the balance of payments. Through 1969 and 1970 Britain earned a surplus on current account which was fully satisfactory by any standards. And with the Chancellor's foot coming off the brake, though not on to the accelerator, industrial production which had almost stood still between 1965 and 1967 started firmly upwards again. Indeed, amid all the furore about the balance of payments and despite phases of severely repressive governmental policy, industrial production between 1960 and 1969 as a whole grew at the respectable rate of $3\frac{1}{2}$ per cent p.a. Such a rate might well have been cause for self-congratulation were it not that others were continuing to do better. The Common Market countries (Western Germany, France, Belgium, Holland, Luxembourg, Italy) achieved a 5 per cent rate (1960–68); and all of them, bar Italy, probably enjoyed a higher general standard of living by the end of the 'sixties than did Britain.

(At the moment of writing Britain seems to be entering a new policy cycle. The recently returned Conservative government has announced its intention to 'disengage': business is to be left to cultivate its own garden; the trade unions are to be left to their own sense of national responsibility as far as wage claims are concerned; the IRC and the

[1] Its suprasectional character was emphasised in the appointment, by the Labour government, of a former Conservative minister, Aubrey Jones, as its chairman.

NBPI have been abolished; but the government will of course continue to employ such macro-economic measures as are needful – and there have been noises suggestive of measures to control the money supply.)

If this chapter is heavily given over to government policy in the face of inflationary pressures and balance of payments problems, that does at least make for an accurate reflection of contemporary preoccupations. And in the context of this book the justification for the bias must be that this is a theme which only emerges within this period, the remainder of the chapter being concerned with themes whose basis has already been laid.

Other aspects of state activity

There have of course been other economic issues with which government has concerned itself, in a period which has been characterised by the ubiquity of government. Three further fields of regulatory activity may be briefly adverted to here. The one is a continuation of the 'depressed area' policy inherited from the 'thirties. Since the war a varying system of tax allowances and grants (the latter disbursed particularly lavishly, even indiscriminately, by the Labour government between 1966 and 1970) have been employed positively, in conjunction with the negative powers of the Board of Trade (latterly the Department of Trade and Industry) to withhold Industrial Development Certificates, in order to steer new ventures away from the west Midlands and the south-east to south Wales, the north-west, the north-east and central Scotland. But while 'depressed' has certainly become a complete misnomer for these areas, unemployment there has continued to be higher, and earnings lower, than the national average.

If regional policy has been something less than thorough, and of uncertain efficacy, the same has certainly not been true of agricultural policy. Already by 1939 the government was wholly committed to sustaining British agriculture. Subsequent measures elaborated and finalised the prewar strategy, through a system of direct grants and price support payments by means of which the government effectively determined the quantity and range of agricultural produce and the remuneration of farmers. Thus backed, agriculture has been one of the most dynamic sectors of the postwar economy. Total agricultural output in 1969 was just about 90 per cent higher than it had been in 1938 – achieved on a slightly reduced acreage and with a labour force cut by nearly 60 per cent. If there were an 'agricultural revolution' in Britain it occurred *c*. 1950–*c*. 1965, when most of this gain was registered.

The third field of regulatory activity to be touched on here is the control of monopolies and restrictive agreements among producers. While these had given rise to disquiet between the wars, the overwhelming feeling in favour of 'rationalisation' and against self-destructive cut throat competition had stayed any attempt at statutory control. But with the market well able to look after efficient producers in the postwar years, the balance of feeling swung strongly in the opposite direction; and there have been three major pieces of legislation: the Monopolies and Restrictive Practices Act 1948; the Restrictive Practices Act 1956; and the Resale Prices Act 1964. Of these the last has been the most effective, at least in the sense that it did achieve its immediate and simple aim of putting an end to the practice whereby a supplier compelled a retailer, under threat of cessation of supplies, to charge a given price.[1] And in the case of certain goods, the Act was followed by appreciable retail price reductions.

The other two Acts were of a much more complicated nature. They created the legal presumption that monopolies (a monopoly was statutorily defined as control of one-third of the market) and agreements among separate producers covering the conditions of supply of goods were contrary to the public interest; but provided for quasi-judicial procedures in which in any individual case the contrary might be proven. Neither Act was very clear, as no Act could be, how 'the public interest' was to be established; and the decisions of both the Monopolies Commission, which has not had much to do, and the Restrictive Practices Court, which has had a great deal to do, have been the subject of lively criticism by economists, the general burden being that these bodies take a very simpliste, and not always fully consistent, view of the facts of economic life.

The state has, of course, been much more than simply a regulatory agency. The figures given in Table II.48 may serve as an indication of the extension of total state activity.

---

[1] In general, the object of the practice, which had been spreading since the late nineteenth century, was to protect the supplier against pressure to lower his, wholesale, prices. Most retailers approved the system, which secured them against price-cutting competition.

TABLE II.48. *Public expenditure (net of national debt charges and current expenditure of trading services) as percentage of gross national product*

1937	1949	1959	1969
22	38	38	50

(As the style indicates the basis of this table is not the same as that of Tables II.43 and 46 in the two preceding chapters. It should also be borne in mind that the inclusion of transfer payments – National Insurance benefits etc. – in all three tables precludes their use as measures of resource utilisation on the part of the state.)

Behind these figures lie four main developments. The first, of a rather miscellaneous variety, might be termed 'economic support', and would embrace expenditure on roads and other ancillary facilities, a variety of grants to particular sectors or even, sometimes, to particular firms, and fundamental research and development – particularly in the aerospace, electronics and nuclear power fields. (Through the 'sixties over a half of total R and D expenditure in the country was financed by the state.) Expenditure under this general head rose steeply under the Labour government of 1964–70, in the furtherance of its 'efficiency' programme.

The second general head is: military. While this has soared way above its prewar levels in absolute terms, it was held at a fairly constant 6 or 7 per cent of GNP throughout the 'fifties and 'sixties.

The third, and much more substantial development, has been in the field of social welfare. Summarily defined, the achievement here has been to weld together and round out the bits and pieces which had been accumulating since 1909. Nothing that has been done could be said to have been radically new. What was essentially new, however, was the comprehensiveness of the approach and the priority accorded to its implementation. In a burst of activity, 1944–48, a 'Welfare State' was fashioned out of the assorted elements inherited from previous decades. An Education Act (1944) created a fully comprehensive system of free secondary education.[1] In 1946, a single universal National Insurance

[1] No state system of university (or other higher) education has ever been instituted, but direct central government grants to universities have risen very considerably – from 32 per cent of total university income in 1938 to 70 per cent, of a greatly increased total, in 1968. At the same time local authorities followed an increasingly liberal policy in awarding grants to individual students, such that by the early 'sixties a grant had become virtually automatic on securing a place.

scheme replaced the different partial schemes already in existence, and was backed up by a family allowances scheme and, from 1948, by National Assistance (restyled Social Security in 1966) payments which comprehended those not covered by National Insurance – replacing the former, local and variable, Public Assistance and the special Unemployment Assistance. In 1948, what was perhaps the crowning piece of this welfare apparatus was put in place: the National Health Service, providing free medical care of all types for all the people, and constituting what has probably been in the world at large the most widely admired of all postwar British achievements.

Although expenditure, in real terms, on this range of social services has shown a continuously upward tendency, there have been two particularly explosive bursts: in the immediate aftermath of the institution of the services and during the second spell of Labour government. Between 1964 and 1970 expenditure on education rose by 44 per cent in real terms, on National Insurance and other cash benefits by 35 per cent, and on the National Health Service by 42 per cent. Whether one describes this as governmental extravagance depends entirely, of course, on what sort of share of a finite GNP one considers should be applied in these directions. It is a fact that, notwithstanding the heavy early expenditure, school and hospital buildings and equipment etc. were very inadequate by the highest professional standards; that the share of GNP devoted to these purposes had subsequently been allowed to slip; and that National Insurance and other benefits had not kept pace with the general rise in real incomes.

A fourth element in the public welfare structure has been housing – although it should be borne in mind that the greater part of the cost of public housing is, eventually, recovered from rent-paying tenants. (Up to the late 'fifties the overall proportion being thus recovered was about 60 per cent, subsequently going up to about 70 per cent.) Continuously since 1948 the number of houses built by local authorities, with considerable central government assistance, has run way above pre-war levels. However, here as in other welfare sectors the rhythm has varied. In the immediate postwar years, the Labour government projected a housing programme whose aim was not only to make good wartime deprivations but to effect a substantial general rise in housing standards. With the prevailing shortage of men and materials this programme was not easy of execution; and the increase in local authority building was only made possible by a near total prohibition of private building. The successor Conservative government, which had promised the country 300,000 houses a year (under Labour, in its later years of office, the rate had been about 200,000), initially persisted with the priority accorded to local authority building which rose to an all time high of 240,000 houses in the years 1953/54. But thereafter the government increasingly favoured private building, so that, while the overall target of 300,000 was more or less continuously realised, local authority completions fell to a level of about 120,000 through the late 'fifties and early 'sixties.

On Labour's return to office in 1964, while the general housing situation was immensely better than ever before, there were still pockets where authentically bad housing conditions survived; and, more pervasively, the general level of expectations had swung upwards with the growth of mass prosperity through the previous two decades or so. The new government set itself the very ambitious target of 500,000 houses a year, the needed effort to come about equally from the public and the private sectors. Although, in the outcome, the balance of payments situation forced a heavy cutback in projected public housing expenditure[1] and achievement fell well short of target, both private and local authority building increased quite substantially. The out-turn was an average 400,000 houses a year, 1965–69; and public expenditure on housing rose by 30 per cent, in real terms, between 1964 and 1970.

One important general aspect of social policy remains: the extent to which it has aimed at income redistribution.

So far as the tax system is concerned, there has been no general attempt to give it any more steeply progressive a character than it had attained as a result of high wartime income tax rates, partially lowered again through the first decade of peace, by when income tax stood at 8s 6d in the pound (1938/9: 5s 6d) and surtax in the range 2s to 10s (1938/9: 1s 3d to 9s 6d, over the same income spread). Indeed, the continuous rise of money incomes, accompanied by only modest elevations of exemption limits, has operated to diminish the effective progressiveness of income tax, while the raising in 1961 of the surtax floor from £2,000 to approximately £5,000 (for earned incomes) removed much of the progressiveness across a substantial band of incomes. Roughly speaking: by comparison with the prewar situation,

---

[1] Housing is really the only major item of state expenditure which lends itself to the sort of flexible control necessary to short-term demand management (i.e. 'budgetary policy' has for the most part to operate on the revenue side).

the overall effect has been significantly to reduce disposable personal income at very high income levels, but to leave distribution below such levels much as it had been.[1]

On the expenditure and services side the chief effect of public policy, on a pre- and postwar comparison, has been to create much more favourable circumstances for the lower income family – through family allowances, family size related social security benefits, the National Health Service and the education system[2] – and, in lesser degree, for the old and disabled. However, over a very wide range between lower and higher incomes the social services, taken as a whole, do not have any very pronounced redistributive character. The 'middle class' makes as much use of the National Health Service as the 'working class', a great deal more use of state or state aided education beyond school leaving age, and participates fully in National Insurance, even if – less prone to unemployment – it probably makes fewer claims to benefits. Only local authority housing remains a peculiarly 'working-class' service. And for one thing, this, rather notoriously, often fails to direct assistance to where it is most needed; while, for another, subsidised housing has a partial counterpart in the tax allowance on mortgage interest charges (or since 1967, the government payment in lieu of the tax allowance) available to private house purchasers.

Across a very broad area, then, neither revenue nor expenditure policy has been of any distinct redistributive intent. While the extremes of an older inegalitarianism have certainly been eliminated, no political party has sought to continuously narrow the substantial inequalities which have remained. Explicitly in the case of the Conservative party, implicitly in the case of the Labour party, an appreciable measure of inequality has been considered essential to economic efficiency.

Even at the lowest levels, where it has been declared policy to effect a substantial rectification, the proclaimed goal of the elimination of poverty cannot be said to have been fully realised. Amongst the old, a failure of communications has often prevented assistance reaching the needy, although a big propaganda campaign in 1966 and 1967 does seem to have had considerable success. More of a hard core problem has been posed by the combination of a large family with the persistence of

---

[1] The regressive 'kink' of the interwar years (see p. 770) has, however, disappeared as a result of purchase tax on a wide range of commodities in the place of excise duties on a narrow range of articles of mass consumption.

[2] This last has been of much less benefit to lower income groups than, theoretically, it could be, such groups not availing themselves of secondary and higher education facilities in anything like proportion to their numbers.

certain low wage employment sectors, resulting in a family income below that obtainable in state benefits were the earner out of work. In late 1970 a system of family supplements, payable on top of income from employment, was introduced in an endeavour to meet this problem.

A few paragraphs back it was said that the postwar growth of state activity has taken four principal forms. The fourth of these is only very partially reflected in Table II.48. This is the great extension of trading services undertaken by public agencies. The 'nationalisation' programme of which this was the result was entirely the work of the 1945–51 Labour government, subsequently undone in some part by its Conservative successor. It embraced electricity and gas services, much of which were already in the hands of public authorities; the coal industry and railway services, with which the prewar state had already become involved and over which some extension of public control was inevitable; the Bank of England – little more than a formal change; road freightage (along with certain other miscellaneous transport services) and the steel industry – in the face of intense opposition from the Conservative party which later returned them to private enterprise;[1] the hiving off of BEA from BOAC; and, of course, the preservation of the BBC and the London Passenger Transport Board (transferred to the Greater London Council in 1970), as well as leaving other passenger transport services in the hands of such municipal authorities as operated them.

On the pattern originally created for the electricity grid and for broadcasting, the newly nationalised industries were entrusted to public corporations, whose precise responsibilities, however, and whose part in any overall governmental economic programme remained for a long time rather unclear. Nationalisation was originally effected on the general principle of the 'socialisation' of industry, i.e. the substitution of public service for private profit as the motivating dynamic. But under the first Labour government the practical implications of this principle

---

[1] Certain elements of British Road Services (later, the National Freight Corporation) were retained by the Conservative government. After its return to office in 1964 Labour tacitly acquiesced in the Conservative pattern of road services but renationalised steel, in which, it appears, the new Conservative government is now prepared to acquiesce. Even denationalised the steel industry remained under close government supervision, exercised through the Iron and Steel Board.

were never very closely defined; and, in its earlier years, the succeeding Conservative government tended to look on the public corporations, or such as it could not sell off, as rather tiresome encumbrances.

It was not really until the early 'sixties that any very articulate philosophy was evolved for the public corporations. What then emerged embodied three elements. First, the clear identification of the public corporations, as types of economic organisms, with private corporations: efficiency, even competitive efficiency (as monopolies the public corporations cannot have a great deal of competitive scope) was to be as fully the object of public as of private enterprise, and profitability to be the yardstick of efficiency. (Profitability as a yardstick is not of course the same thing as profitability as an object in itself; and this identification of public with private corporations owed a good deal to a heightened awareness that profits *per se* had ceased to play their classical role in big business psychology.) Secondly, that social benefits and social costs, not susceptible to ordinary profit orientated accounted procedures, should govern the decisions of the public corporations, but that responsibility for taking account of these should rest clearly with the government, leaving public corporation managements unambiguously dedicated to profit measured efficiency. Thirdly, that, commanding as they did key sectors of the economy, the public corporations would play a particularly important part in 'planned growth'; that their close relationship to the government would ensure an intimate and responsible engagement with centrally coordinated planning; that through them the pace could be effectively set for the economy as a whole. (This last kind of thinking was largely peculiar to the Labour party and constituted the rationale to Labour's renationalisation of steel. But since 'planned growth' never got going this sort of strategy never really came into play.)

However conceived of, the public corporations have been there, constituting a massive state presence in amongst the body of private enterprise. As implied already, the weight of this presence cannot readily be measured in expenditure terms.[1] But Tables II.49 and 50 provide two alternative measures of the place of the state, in its various forms, in the economy of 1969.

---

[1] In the composite figures which it publishes, the Central Statistical Office excludes the current (self-balancing) expenditures of the public corporations, counting only their capital outlays as part of public sector spending. This procedure, perforce, has been followed in Table II.48.

TABLE II.49. *Employees in public service as percentage of total employees*

Public corporations (including Post Office)	National government services (including armed forces)	Local government service	Education	Health	Total in public service
$8\frac{1}{2}$	$4\frac{1}{2}$	4	$4\frac{1}{2}$	$3\frac{1}{2}$	25

(The Education and Health figures contain an element of rather arbitrary approximation in separating out those engaged in the public sector from those engaged in the private sector.)

TABLE II.50. *Fixed capital formation (including house building) by public bodies as percentage of national total*

Local authorities	Public corporations	Central government	Total by public bodies
22	19	6	47

The business corporation

It is not a very big step from the public corporations to private corporations. Indeed – and the point has been half made a few sentences back – one of the features of contemporary economic history has been the extent to which what might be called the morphology of the two has been increasingly assimilated. While the public corporation has come to take its private counterpart as a working model, the private corporation, activated by values much closer to those of the bureaucrat than those of the primitive entrepreneur, has become increasingly sensitive to considerations of social responsibility and has often had to take its major decisions in close consultation with the government or, at least, with careful reference to government policy. (In the extreme case of the aircraft industry the private corporation has been even more closely bound to the government than the public corporation.) Nor is it as if the public corporation has succeeded in creating, or even tried to create, a distinctive pattern of management-labour relations. Such hopes as certain early socialists entertained of fashioning a new kind of link between the worker and his work have proved utterly nugatory. The public corporation is as depersonalised as the private. In brief, the fact

804

that one kind of corporation turns over some part of its profits to a group of private individuals or institutions and that the other does not has no serious significance, nor has the fact that in the one the chief executives are appointed by the government, and in the other by their fellows – with the fairly important reservation that an inefficient private board may be swept away by a takeover, while the government may be slow in proceeding against an inefficient public board.

Any attempt to follow in detail the extension of corporate activity was abandoned in the last chapter. All that will be said here is that the movement ceased almost entirely during the war and did not proceed very much further over the next dozen years or so, apart from the entry on to the scene of the crop of public corporations. For this, the apparatus of wartime and postwar controls – limitation of materials supplies, licences to produce, curbs on capital flotations – was, obviously, largely responsible, operating in one way or another to check both internal expansion and growth by way of merger. Evidently too, expansion mindedness was a little slow in taking root again, even after these checks had been removed; and it may be that the Restrictive Practices Act of 1956, by outlawing agreements amongst separate producers, provided the initiating impulse to the resumed merger movement which started to gather strength in the late 'fifties. Whatever triggered it off, it rapidly assumed, and retained, mania proportions. By the mid-'sixties there was hardly a company chairman in the country who was not looking over his shoulder to detect signs of an (unwanted) takeover bid or a (wanted) merger proposal[1] – if, that is, he were not himself engineering such a move. In 1966 the government joined in, with the creation of the Industrial Reorganisation Commission. At the same time, the generally accelerated rate of economic growth after 1958 provided more scope for internal concern expansion; and the Restrictive Practices Act may well have done something towards ensuring that growth opportunities were seized the most abundantly by the most efficient, making for rapid expansion on the part of some and hastening others into extinction or absorption.

With this wave coming on top of the steady build-up of the interwar years the result, in the most generalised of terms, was that by the end of the 'sixties the concern of authentically corporate character (as distinct from that of essentially individualist character) had become not

---

[1] In the conventional terminology it is a 'merger' when the two boards are in agreement, a 'takeover' when one goes over the head of the other and acquires sufficient shares to give it control.

merely a common, nor even just a predominant, but virtually the exclusive type throughout a great part of manufacturing industry, and was widely prevalent in other sectors of the economy.

Making an attempt at a statistical measurement of the dominion of the corporation:[1] if, somewhat arbitrarily, one took the employment of at least £10 million investment capital and of at least 1,000 persons or of £5 million and 2,000 persons as defining the corporation, then in 1969 there were around five hundred private concerns in Britain which met the test, of which some three-quarters were engaged in manufacturing industry. Those so engaged were responsible for some three-fifths of all private sector employment in manufacturing industry. Even more striking, perhaps, is the part played by 'super-corporations'. Of the five hundred odd 'corporations', about ninety were defined by minima of £100 million capital and 10,000 employees or £50 million and 20,000 employees – of these about seventy-five to be classed as engaged in manufacturing industry. These ninety alone accounted for about three-fifths of the total investment capital of the five hundred; and those in manufacturing industry for around two-fifths of all private sector employment in that area.

Combining private with public corporations (of which only the British Steel Corporation was principally engaged in manufacturing): there were eight public and twenty-five private concerns employing over 50,000 persons each, the public ones totalling 1,800,000 and the private ones, 2,300,000. Between them, these thirty-three enterprises were responsible for just about 18 per cent of all employment in the country.[2]

As implied already, outside manufacturing industry and the public sector – and excluding also banking and insurance – the corporation continues to be kept at arm's length, although agriculture is the only at all extensive activity from which it remains more or less completely excluded. In retailing, the small man has been largely pushed off the High Street – particularly after 1964 when the Resale Prices Act exposed him to the price cutting competition of the supermarket – but retains a place around numerous corners and even, in some branches, in the town centre. He continues, by the side of some very large enterprises, to

[1] The figures which follow do not take any account of financial institutions and property companies.

[2] The top eight employers were: Post Office (417,000); National Coal Board (410,000); British Rail (275,000); British Steel Corporation (254,000); General Electric (228,000); Electricity Council (208,000); Imperial Chemical Industries (197,000); British Leyland (196,000).

preserve an active role in the huge building industry and in the various branches of the much expanded catering trade. The garage and petrol station business is another which has expanded very considerably and in which the small entrepreneur has figured prominently; but on the repairs side the big main dealer and garage chains have won an increasing advantage and on the petrol side the garage proprietor is little more than the agent of a giant oil company. In road haulage, if the small man has largely disappeared, his successor is still more apt to be the smallish company rather than the large corporation; as is also the case in general printing. Tramp shipping too retains something of its old individualist character. And an assortment of other service activities continue to afford scope for individual enterprise. Even within manufacturing industry, while the corporation is everywhere present, there remain tracts within which the individualist concern can contrive to coexist, conspicuously in many areas of the intensely, and even increasingly, variegated metalworking and light engineering trades, in garment manufacture, in woodworking and in certain parts of the much contracted textile industries.

Finally, and in rather haphazard fashion, two ancillary features of corporate life in Britain at the commencement of the 'seventies may be briefly mentioned. The one is the incursion of American enterprise and capital. Although there was nothing new about this – it has a continuous history running back to the closing years of the nineteenth century – it came to assume particularly large proportions from the late 'fifties. By 1970 American-owned concerns were responsible for about an eighth of the output of British manufacturing industry; and the phenomenon was particularly luridly illustrated in the state of the British motor industry, where, of the four concerns which virtually constituted it, three were American owned (Ford, Vauxhall, Chrysler – the last by acquisition of the former Rootes). The giant British Leyland was, however, a good deal bigger than any of the Americans; and the situation in the motor industry was not paralleled anywhere else, although the American presence was also conspicuous in chemicals and mechanical engineering.[1]

The second feature is the substantial shareholding in most British corporations which had come into the hands of the 'institutions': insurance companies, investment and unit trusts, pension funds. These, it seems, by 1970 held around a half of the total issued capital of all

[1] Petrol refining and/or distribution, tyre manufacture and foodstuff processing were also activities with a strong international flavour, containing, in addition to purely British enterprises, Anglo-Dutch, American, French, Italian, Swiss and Belgian concerns.

companies quoted on the Stock Exchange. This phenomenon, gathering particular force from the mid-'fifties, was a product of two things: growing personal wealth over a broad middling income range, from which savings have been largely channelled into the 'institutions'; and inflation, which has diminished the attractiveness of fixed interest securities and mortgage loans, and correspondingly enhanced that of profit-participating ordinary shares – in the case of insurance companies and pension funds operating to modify their asset structure; in the case of investment and unit trusts, more a matter of a great expansion of their kind of business as the private investor sought the knowledge and expertise of the professional investment manager.

The phenomenon may be exemplified by the record of British insurance companies, who in 1937 held 10 per cent of their assets in ordinary shares but 25 per cent in 1968. Including debentures and preference shares, the proportion had risen from 34 per cent to 44 per cent – of a total which, in money terms, had increased more than ninefold. However, whether anything more than a curiosity value is to be attached to the phenomenon is arguable. Obviously it places a great deal of power in the hands of a relative handful of institutions. But, in the first place, these institutions have, up to now, made it a fairly firm rule not to interfere in the management of the companies in which they have such a substantial interest. And, in the second place, it is not clear that it would make a great deal of difference if they did. The 'institutions' are themselves 'corporations'; and just how power is shared between the board of ABC Producing Co. in respect of its own affairs and the board of XYZ Insurance Co. would not seem to matter very much. Probably the most important consequence of the situation arises in the case of a takeover bid, when professional investment managers can, presumably, make a more competent assessment of the bid than the ordinary private shareholder.

Incomes and expenditure

We come finally to what in the ultimate analysis is the most significant question of all: what have economic developments since 1939 signified in terms of the material standard of living of the people of Britain?

Setting the answer first of all in broad historical perspective: the thirty-odd years of this period saw the living standards of the mass of the populace rise as they had never done over any comparable stretch in the past, or, indeed, over any hundred-year stretch in the past – or, for that matter, throughout virtually the whole of previous history. The attainment of high mass consumption standards is very peculiarly the achievement of these years. The figures in Table II.51 afford some more precise indication of the phenomenon.

TABLE II.51. *Average per capita income of wage earners, 1850–1969 Index numbers (1939 = 100)*

	1850	1900	1939	1950	1959	1969
Real	45	82	100	174	210	266
money			100	260	463	833

What should immediately be stressed is that this has in only modest degree been a direct result of income redistribution, as is made fairly clear in Table II.52.

After a sharp encroachment on other incomes during and immediately after the war, when wage rises were accompanied by price and other controls which prevented profit makers etc. from keeping pace, the share of wages in gross has in fact fallen. While the actual fall is due in large part to a diminishing proportion of wage earners in the working population, the most important implication here is that the great rise in real wage incomes is primarily the product of overall economic growth, in which all personal income recipients have participated very abundantly; and such shifts as there have been since *c.* 1950 in the shares of personal incomes of all kinds are due much more to relative shifts in numbers than to relative shifts in *per capita* returns. (These shifts in numbers need only a parenthetic comment here, being readily explicable in the light of what has been said earlier, either in this or the previous chapter. The increase in salary earners reflects the continuing particular growth of employment in government, education, 'corporations', and in activities calling for professional qualifications – although it should be said that the Central Statistical Office's concept of 'salary', followed in Table II.52 and embracing roughly all white-collar workers is a good deal more generous than that employed earlier on p. 757n. The increase in National Insurance and other benefits is largely a reflection of the increasing proportion of old people in the population. The extension of corporate enterprise explains the fall under 'Incomes from self-employment and non-corporate enterprise'. It can also be mentioned

TABLE II.52. *Income shares (before tax deductions)*

	As percentage of national income		As percentage of total personal income	
	1939	1950	1959	1969
Wages	39	45	43	42	37
Salaries	22	23	21	24	27
Employers' contributions to National Insurance, pension, etc. funds	2	5	4	5	6
Total income from employment	63	73	68	71	70
National Insurance and other state benefits	(As transfer payments excluded from 'National Income')		7	8	10
Incomes from self-employment and non-corporate enterprise			13	10	8
Rent, dividends and interest			12	11	12
	37	27	100	100	100
Undistributed pre-tax surplus of companies (on same base)			21	17	16
	100	100			

(Public sector excluded)

here that the apparent secular decline (relative) in 'Undistributed pre-tax surplus of companies' is deceptive, the 1950 figure being exceptionally high on account of restraint on dividend distribution at the time.)

To establish the mathematical fact that the increase in wage incomes – and we may broaden this to comprehend all incomes from employment – has been due much more to a larger cake than to a larger share of it is not necessarily to demonstrate that redistributive forces have been of minor consequence. We must reckon with the possibility that redistribution, even of a fairly modest order, has been an important factor in enlarging the size of the cake in the first place. And, posing the issue in its wider terms, we cannot quit this period and its historically unparalleled mass prosperity without raising the general question of what conjuncture of factors engendered such an increase in gross wealth. But, if we ought to raise the question, we cannot hope to supply the answer. The corpus of analytic literature on economic growth is already considerable, but it is still far from providing any commonly agreed on and fully articulated general theory. Economic growth remains something which lends itself much more readily to description than to explanation. And, in any event, that multivariable, dynamic complex which is an economy in course of growth, more especially, one in course of transition from a low to a high growth rate, could only be properly explained by the use of models of formidable mathematical sophistication.

What can be done here, in the simplest of terms, is to indicate some of the variables which look as if they ought to have an important role in any equations which purported to tell us why the post-1939 (or post-1945) economy has behaved as it has done.

It was urged in the last chapter that the explanation of the weakness of the interwar economy is to be sought on the demand side. If this be accepted then the primary causes of post-1939 resurgence should lie in the same quarter.

The war itself, of course, screwed up economic activity, and with it employment and income levels, to a very elevated pitch. But economic effort was devoted very heavily to warfare and there was no automatic guarantee that it would be wholly transferred to civil pursuits on the return of peace. On the other hand, it is probably easier to make the transition from a high-demand-level war economy to a high-demand-level peace economy than from a low-demand-level peace economy to a high-demand-level peace economy. The war in itself, then, should probably be accounted one of our variables.

The war too had more specific consequences. While demand for civilian goods was in some degree restrained by the curtailment of purchasing power through high taxation and inflation, in substantial measure it was also held in check by simple shortages, whose inflationary consequences were moderated by rationing and price control. There was thus a reservoir of pent up purchasing power which, on release, supplied a useful, though exhaustible, boost to demand. Of more enduring consequences were two redistributive factors: high direct taxation rates and the gain of employment incomes at the expense of other incomes.

Here we come back to our jumping off point. And two things ought to be stressed in qualification of the remarks earlier made on the limited degree to which redistribution has figured in the growth of employment incomes. The one is that Table II.52 relates to *pre-tax* incomes. Taking a long reach of history into perspective (for our concern is not only with the contrast between the interwar and postwar phases): the two wars, as we have seen, successively imparted sharply progressive twists to the tax system. Since the wars, the proportion of disposable income left with lower and middling income groups relative to that left with very high income groups has been a great deal more than in the pre-1914 era, even though no government has pursued a consistently redistributive policy.

The second qualification to earlier remarks is that, although there has not been any persistently large transfer of pre-tax income, there was quite a sharp readjustment effected between 1939 and *c.* 1950, not subsequently undone, and that, ever since then, there has been a certain amount of continuous redistributive 'creep', if one reckons in Social Security benefits.

Of most significance in this context is the extent to which redistribution has, in effect, taken the form of transfer from the highest to the lowest – accentuated by the fact that since 1939 it has generally been those towards the bottom of the wage scale who, in relative terms, have done best out of rising wages. Such a direct top to bottom movement should make for a more pronounced shift from saving to expenditure than would a general concertinaing of incomes. And it is, of course, just that kind of shift which is significant here.

The role of government spending was stressed at the outset of this chapter where it was asserted that the commitment in principle to 'full employment' has, in the outcome, mattered a good deal less than the commitment in practice to heavy social and military expenditures; that the full employment principle has really been of consequence in a negative way: by preventing the sort of government retrenchment which might otherwise have taken place on one plea or another.

Finally, on the demand side, there is export demand. This indeed has been the most dynamic of all postwar demand factors. In volume terms, UK exports in 1969 were running at a level three and one-third times above that of 1938, having since their return to prewar levels in 1946 grown, though not in fully even fashion, at an average rate of nearly 5½ per cent p.a. Considered as a demand phenomenon, this has, of course, been due to circumstances outside of Britain; circumstances whose essence has been international economic growth of an order well surpassing that of Britain itself, occurring against a background of substantially, though far from wholly, liberalised national trading policies.

If, at the various points at which overall economic performance since 1873 has been appraised in this book, most attention has been given to demand factors, it is because the view has been taken that the most crucial variables have lain on that side; that the technology, whether of native or of foreign origin, needful to sustain growth of a 2 to 3 per cent *plus* order has generally been available; that defects in structure, socio-logical or economic, have never been of really central consequence, and that such defects as were present were being rapidly remedied between the wars. At least, the contention has been, supply capacity was never very severely tested. More or less continuously since 1939 supply capacity *has* been severely tested. And if it has not responded as fully as many would wish the fact remains that it has sustained a rise in mass living standards without precedent in British history.

In a full historical perspective, what is most remarkable about the period is that it has combined the high rate of capital formation needful to continuous and vigorous growth with this increase in mass welfare.[1] Mathematically appraised, in *per capita* terms the crude growth rate has been no greater than the average sustained over the long 'revolutionary' boom *c.* 1785-1873. But, in sharp contrast with that earlier high growth run, whose returns were largely confined to a small minority of property owners, the post-1945 phase has distributed its benefits about equally among all sectors of society. It has contrived to create the requisite capital stock without conferring a peculiarly favourable return on a small capitalist class. And, in the broadest of terms, this contrast would seem explicable by two circumstances. First, the contemporary pro-viders of capital have not sought the same rate of return as their 'revolutionary' predecessors. This is most evidently true of the state which, in its various forms, provides such a large proportion of con-temporary fixed capital. But it would also seem to be true in some degree of the private corporation, which, it can plausibly be contended,

---

[1] This, of course, is far from having been a peculiarly British achievement. Western Germany, France, Belgium, Holland, Luxembourg, Italy, Switzerland, Denmark, Sweden, Norway, Iceland, Ireland, the USA, Canada, Australia, New Zealand, Israel, Czecho-slovakia, Hungary and Eastern Germany have all, to varying degrees, done much the same thing.

is more growth-minded and less profit-minded than the industrialist of the revolutionary age. Secondly, and perhaps a good deal more important, strong trade unions in our own times have been more capable of exacting a growth return to labour – and have been more bent on doing so – than was the working class of the earlier era; and with the ironing out of cyclic behaviour and spasms of high unemployment they have been in a much better position to bring sustained pressure to bear on employers. What may be called sociological factors, as much as strictly economic factors, appear, then, to have been the agencies of mass participation in growing wealth.

There is a further circumstance, bearing, not on income allocation as between factors of production, but on allocation as between persons, which has been gathering force since the early 'fifties and which may be expected to become of increasing potency in the future: a great increase in personal savings. From the time of the Great Depression, the burden of saving, that is of accumulating money capital, had been very largely assumed by corporate enterprises and public authorities. But since 1950 the proportion of gross national savings coming from the personal sector has moved as follows:

TABLE II.53. *Personal savings as percentage of total savings,*
1950

	1950	1955	1960	1965	1969
	5	23	26	28	28
Excluding Central Government from total	8	27	27	35	40

(The lower row is really the more indicative for these purposes, the Central Government item consisting largely of the net national purchasing power withdrawn via taxation, fluctuating considerably with annual budgetary policy, and not really savings in the ordinary sense.)

In other words, the public at large has once again started to supply considerable quantities of investment capital, and to draw a return on it. What is of consequence in this context is who makes up this investing public. It cannot consist in any significantly large part of the very wealthy, because progressive taxation does not leave enough income at very high levels to contribute more than a small fraction of this volume of savings. Furthermore, the indications are that, through the broad middling band of incomes, contemporary propensities to save do not vary very much with income. The suggestion, then, is of a participation in the return on capital which bears some sort of proportion to income, of a move towards a 'property owning democracy'.

It is not that the new savers directly invest in great quantity. Much of the saving goes into endowment and life insurance and pension funds, whence it finds its way into productive investment – the stock and share holdings of the 'institutions', earlier commented on is the other side of the coin in question; and a good deal, too, goes into financing house purchase – whether as building society deposits or as payments by house purchasers themselves, when the return is the rent or mortgage interest charge saved. Nor is it as if the movement has as yet significantly modified the pattern of wealth distribution (as distinct from income distribution) inherited from preceding decades, or even centuries, which retains a pronounced inegalitarian character:[1] and the movement would have to persist for some decades into the future before it would effect any substantial modification of the pattern. Nor, finally, can it be that the new saving extends all the way down the income scale. It probably goes a good way down, into wage earning brackets, though this can only be speculative; but there certainly is a level at which it peters out rapidly. And if the phenomenon persists, and has been correctly interpreted here, it threatens to open up a new wealth gap; one whose principal manifestation is likely to occur in about thirty years time as a glaring contrast amongst the elderly: between those with a fully owned house and comfortable retirement funds and those with neither.

If an increased rate of personal saving has been a signal consequence of swollen incomes, it has, nonetheless, accounted for only a small fraction

---

[1] Calculations founded on estates liable to death duties show no significant change in distribution since the early 1950s, though, from the beginning of the century up to then, death duties had been having a slow but steadily erosive effect towards the very top of the scale. The figures for 1968 suggested that 3–4 per cent of individuals (excluding property-less wives and children) possessed wealth of over £10,000 and that these accounted for 55 per cent of all personal wealth. However, any redistribution which had been taking place since the early 'fifties would hardly even start to show up in death duty figures until into the 'seventies.

of personal income. Even at 1969 levels, savings took no more than 8 per cent of total personal incomes (after deduction of tax and National Insurance contributions). Some more detailed indication of the disposition of the remainder can round off our appreciation of mass living standards in the new age of growth.

This is a theme which lends itself to fairly clear chronological subdivisions: 1939–45, 1945–50, 1952–70. The first needs little commentary. Incomes rose but there were shortages of nearly all consumption goods. Nevertheless, the leap in employment and in wage rates did make for an edging up of average consumption standards. Most notably, dietary standards improved, at least by the calorie test if not by the palate test. The malnutrition of serious degree and extent which had persisted in Britain right up to 1939, particularly among children of large families, was abruptly extirpated by the apparatus of rationing, price controls and welfare services. If the war deprived four-fifths of many of their accustomed pleasures, it brought, in a utilitarian calculus, more than counterbalancing gains to the other fifth.

The phase 1946–50 brought more widespread gains, but still at a fairly basic level. Growing purchasing power was chiefly applied, as the goods gradually returned to the shops, to raising the variety and attractiveness of the diet yet further above prewar levels, to better and more elegant clothing, to furniture and the simpler kind of household appliances – in brief, more or less a continuation of interwar trends. By the beginning of the 'fifties, however, mass purchasing power was ready to start spilling over. The 'consumer revolution' was about to begin.

And this is a phenomenon which can be accorded a precise onset without a grotesque straining of the facts, in a field which rarely permits of chronological meticulousness. Controls and shortages had earlier prevented a more gradual seepage of mass purchasing power into wider areas; and the outbreak of the Korean War in June 1950 administered a sharp temporary check to extension as steeply rising prices momentarily ran ahead of incomes and the government was forced into severe demand repression in defence of the pound. But 1952 saw momentum recovered, in a Britain which had now shaken off its wartime legacies. The way was open for the consumer to come into his own.

Although expenditure on nearly every item increased in some degree, the emphasis has been on consumer durables: motor vehicles, television sets, refrigerators, washing machines, other electrical appliances, household furnishings and fittings. And among these the motor car has been king. In 1951 there was a private motor car to every 6·1 households in Britain. In 1969 there was one to every 1·5 households. Consumer durables as a whole, along with motor vehicle running costs, which had accounted for 7 per cent of total consumer expenditure in 1951, accounted for 12 per cent in 1968–69 – which while expressing the rate of past growth also suggests plenty of scope for further extension.

Other elements of the good life have, in more variable fashion, attracted heavy expenditures. Alcohol and tobacco, after an earlier lull, came back strongly over a phase 1954–61, accounting between them for around 13 per cent of consumers' expenditure; in the case of alcohol, it was less the brewers than the distillers and wine importers who drew the benefits of the new affluence. Clothing had a minor boom during 1959–65, as the teenagers took over where mum and dad had left off. Many, though by no means all, house tenants could absorb the steep rise in rents which followed on the substantial measure of de-control introduced by the 1957 Rent Act, and still look round for something nicer and pricier. And more capacious and comfortable living conditions generally are reflected in the great rise in domestic electricity and gas consumption which got under way from 1959. Last to be mentioned here but by no means least is a polyglot group whose record almost exactly parallels that of consumer durables: 'services', which took 8 per cent of consumer expenditure in 1951 and 13 per cent in 1969. Restaurants, pubs and hotels are the single biggest element in this group but its full membership beggars description. Its composite role may, however, be summarised: 'Why do it yourself when you can pay someone to do it for you?'

And there, writing on 10 January 1971, we may leave the British economy and its history. The book must end somewhere; and as aptly, or as inaptly, on this as on any other note. It cannot write *finis*. This book must stop but the economy, and the incessant process of change intrinsic to any modern economy, goes on.

Reading List and Index

Reading List

This is a reading list – not a bibliography, let alone a list of sources. And a reading list is strictly utilitarian, aimed at meeting a clearly definable need. This one is primarily directed to the A level student and his teacher; and is to be understood in the light of that aim, and, in particular, with reference to the following principles:

> Nothing is included which could not reasonably be regarded as within the competence of a capable 17–18-year-old student, or which is beyond the usual requirements of an A level Economic History syllabus.

> Indications of the level of ease/difficulty have as their basic criterion the 'average' A level student.

> With certain deliberate exceptions, the comment following each entry is not intended as a thumbnail critique but merely as an indication of the nature of the work. These comments are to be read in conjunction with the title of the work.

> Only a very few of the most important of these articles obtainable solely in the original journal of publication are included.

> A full entry is given just once, either in the section to which it has most relevance or on the first occurrence of the item. Elsewhere, an item included more than once is mentioned by its author and short title followed by a reference to the full entry.

1 CARUS-WILSON, E. M., ed. *Essays in Economic History*, 3 vols, E. Arnold, 1954–62.

Reprints, with the non-professional reader in view, a selection of important articles from *Economic History Review* and other journals. The most useful of these are separately mentioned below with a cross reference to this entry. (In most cases these itemised articles are not accompanied by a comment, the title commonly being sufficient to describe them and their mere inclusion a warrant that they are useful and not excessively taxing.)

Part One

1086–1475
(a) General

2 LIPSON, E. *The Economic History of England*, 3 vols, A. and C. Black, 1931.
Covers period *c.* 1000–*c.* 1700. Dated, both in content, at certain points, and, more tellingly, in general approach. As yet unreplaced, however, in breadth of coverage.

3 CLAPHAM, SIR JOHN *A Concise Economic History of Britain from the Earliest Times to 1750*, Cambridge University Press, 1949.
In the absence of up-to-date general works covering the period 1086–*c.* 1600 the choice must lie between (2) and the relevant parts of this, less dated than (2) but much more sketchy; although the early chapters of (4) are, perhaps, to be preferred to either.

4 POLLARD, S. and CROSSLEY, D. W. *The Wealth of Britain, 1085–1966*, Batsford, 1968.
A study of long run-change in gross national wealth and in its distribution. The earlier chapters are, of necessity, cast in very broad terms and can handily be used as a general survey history of the period 1085–1689. Thereafter the book becomes increasingly more closely engaged with its special theme and is an invaluable synthesis of a considerable body of data bearing on that theme.

5 LOYN, H. R. *Anglo-Saxon England and the Norman Conquest*, Longmans, 1962.
Very useful for those concerned with pre-Domesday period. Concluding chapters cover Norman settlement.

6 MAITLAND, F. *Domesday Book and Beyond* (1897), Collins (Fontana), 1960.
A literary classic most of whose major findings have stood the test of time. Rather too dense for the beginner seeking only a broad survey.

7 MILLER, E. 'The English economy in the thirteenth century', *Past and Present*, vol. 28, 1964.
A brilliantly succinct survey which must take the place of a modern general treatment of the period.

8 POSTAN, M. M. 'The fifteenth century', *Economic History Review*, 1st series, vol. 9, 1938.
See footnote on p. 60.
9 BRIDBURY, A. R. *Economic Growth, England in the Later Middle Ages*, Allen & Unwin, 1962.
Written essentially as a counter to (8). Very serviceable as a brief general treatment of period *c.* 1348–*c.* 1500.

(b) The Agrarian Sector

10 POSTAN, M. M. 'Medieval agrarian society in its prime: England', *The Cambridge Economic History of Europe*, 2nd edn, Cambridge University Press, 1966, vol. 1.
Covers period *c.* 1000–*c.*1500. See footnote, p. 59. Should be regarded as absolutely compulsory reading.
11 LENNARD, R. *Rural England, 1086–1135*, Oxford University Press, 1959.
Draws on a substantial body of particular examples to sustain its cautious but lucid conclusions. Rather more concerned with lords and their estates than with peasants and their villages.
12 HILTON, R. H. *The Decline of Serfdom in Medieval England*, Macmillan, 1969.
Pamphlet. See footnote p. 60.
13 BISHOP, T. 'Assarting and the growth of the open fields', article reprinted in (1) vol. 1. Covers 11th–13th centuries.
14 KOSMINSKY, E. 'Services and money rents in the thirteenth century', article reprinted in (1), vol. 1.
15 TITOW, J. Z. *English Rural Society 1200–1350*, Allen & Unwin, 1969.
Booklet. Brief, thorough and readable on the central issues.
16 LUCAS, H. 'The Great European Famine of 1315, 1316 and 1317', article reprinted in (1), vol. 2.
17 HILTON, R. H. 'Peasant movements in England before 1381', article reprinted in (1), vol. 2.

(c) Industry and trade

— SCHUBERT, H. *History of the British Iron and Steel Industry* (37).
18 CARUS-WILSON, E. M. 'An industrial revolution of the thirteenth century', article reprinted in (1), vol. 1. The impact of the fulling-mill on the English woollen cloth industry.

19 CARUS-WILSON, E. M. *Medieval Merchant Venturers*, Methuen, 1967.
A collection of articles covering the cloth industry as well as trade.

20 POWER, E. *The Wool Trade in English Medieval History* (Ford Lectures), Oxford University Press, 1941.
The published version of a short set of lectures devoted, in fairly broad terms, to the place of wool in the English economy of the 13th, 14th and 15th centuries.

21 POWER, E. and POSTAN, M. M. *Studies in English Trade in the Fifteenth Century* (1933), Routledge, 1966.
A collection of individual contributions which make for a very substantial, if not quite comprehensive, coverage of the topic.

22 POSTAN, M. M. 'The rise of a money economy', article reprinted in (1), vol. 1. A major piece of debunking.

1475–1740
(a) General

— LIPSON, E. *The Economic History of England* (2).
— CLAPHAM, SIR JOHN *A Concise Economic History of Britain* (3).
— POLLARD, S. and CROSSLEY, D. W. *The Wealth of Britain* (4).

23 RAMSEY, P. *Tudor Economic Problems*, Gollancz, 1965.
Brief. The best available substitute for a modern general socio-economic history of a period (*c.* 1480–*c.* 1610) in which there is much that remains uncertain and contentious.

24 FISHER, F. J. 'Commercial trends in 16th-century England', *Economic History Review*, 2nd series, vol. 10, 1957.
A good deal more extensive in its coverage than title would suggest and a valuable adjunct to (23).

25 WILSON, C. *England's Apprenticeship, 1603–1763*, Longmans, 1965.
Broad but quite detailed socio-economic coverage, with attention to political aspects. Very readable.

26 JOHN, A. 'Aspects of English economic growth in the first half of the 18th century', article reprinted in (1), vol. 2. The case stated for imputing a firm upward base trend to the period.

— MATHIAS, P. *The First Industrial Nation* (43).
— ASHTON, T. *An Economic History of England: The Eighteenth Century* (45).
— ASHTON, T. *Economic Fluctuations in England, 1700–1800* (46).
— MITCHELL, B. R. and DEANE, P. *Abstract of British Historical Statistics* (41).
— DEANE, P. and COLE, W. A. *British Economic Growth* (42).

(b) The Agrarian Sector

27 THIRSK, J., ed. *The Agrarian History of England and Wales*, vol. 4, Cambridge University Press, 1967.
Covers period *c.* 1500–*c.* 1650. Its monumental dimensions should not deter since it is composed of a number of self-contained contributions, of variable usefulness for the non-specialist student. A well balanced coverage of the central themes can be obtained from chapters 3, 4, 7 and 9.

28 KERRIDGE, E. *Agrarian Problems in the Sixteenth Century and After*, Allen & Unwin, 1969.
Deals with tenurial issues, enclosures and their social implications. Brief but fairly tough going. The author's frenetic concern to discredit a book written sixty years ago (TAWNEY, R. H., *The Agrarian Problem in the Sixteenth Century*, 1912; Harper & Row, 1967) rather upsets the balance of what is an important work of scholarship.

29 JOHN, A. H. 'The course of agricultural change, 1660–1760', essay in (50).

(c) Foreign trade

30 RAMSAY, G. D. *English Overseas Trade during the Centuries of Emergence*, Macmillan, 1957.
Covers period *c.* 1450–*c.* 1750. Narrative rather than analysis. (May usefully be cross-checked with PARRY, J. H., 'Transport and trade routes', *The Cambridge Economic History of Europe*, 2nd edn, vol. 4.)

31 MINCHINTON, W. E., ed. *The Growth of English Overseas Trade in the 17th and 18th Centuries*, Methuen, 1969.
Reprints a number of articles which, along with an original introduction, make for a very thorough short coverage of the topic.

32 DAVIS, R. *A Commercial Revolution? English overseas trade in the seventeenth and eighteenth centuries*, Historical Association, 1967.
Pamphlet. Largely devoted to period *c.* 1650–*c.* 1750. Perhaps to be preferred to the same author's articles reprinted in (31).

(d) Other particular topics (order broadly corresponds with that followed in this book itself)

33 FISHER, F. 'The development of London as a centre of conspicuous consumption in the sixteenth and seventeenth centuries', article reprinted in (1), vol. 2. A key piece of socio-economic history.

34 OUTHWAITE, R. B. *Inflation in Tudor and Early Stuart England*, Macmillan, 1969.
See footnote p. 108.

35 NEF, J. U. *Cultural Foundations of Industrial Civilisation*, Harper & Row, 1958.
A brief work whose boldness of purpose rather exceeds its actual achievement. The strict examinee may safely ignore it. But those interested by the title should at least find it thought provoking.

36 NEF, J. U. 'The progress of technology and the growth of large scale industry in Great Britain, 1540–1640', article reprinted in (1), vol. 1.
The fullest statement in any one place of the thesis of an 'Industrial Revolution' 1540–1640.

37 SCHUBERT, H. *History of the British Iron and Steel Industry*, Routledge, 1957.
Runs from prehistoric times to c. 1750. A simple account, largely devoted to technological developments.

38 NEF, J. U. *Industry and Government in France and England, 1540–1640*, Russell and Russell, New York, 1968.
Short. France and England are kept separate in the text; and the English part remains the most useful treatment of this major topic.

39 TAWNEY, R. H. *Thomas Wilson's Discourse on Usury (1572)*, Longmans, Green, 1925.
Tawney's long introduction to this reprint of a sixteenth-century work provides not only the authoritative account of the legislation of interest taking but a valuable review of sixteenth-century economic attitudes in general.

40 LASLETT, P. *The World We Have Lost*, Methuen, 1965.
A set of essays on some loosely related socio-economic themes pertaining to the sixteenth and seventeenth centuries. Interesting rather than informative.

— JOSLIN, D. 'London private bankers' (68).

Part Two

1740–1873
(a) General

41 MITCHELL, B. R. and DEANE, P. *Abstract of British Historical Statistics*, Cambridge University Press, 1962.
An invaluable work of basic reference. (Very little data before

c. 1690 or after 1939. Can be brought up to date with the official *Annual Abstract of Statistics*.)

42 DEANE, P. and COLE, W. A. *British Economic Growth, 1688–1959*, Cambridge University Press, 1964.
Essentially concerned with measuring, rather than explaining, the quantifiable aspects. Chiefly useful as a work of reference for the more advanced student. Mainly devoted to period *c.* 1750–1914.

43 MATHIAS, P. *The First Industrial Nation. An Economic History of Britain 1700–1914*, Methuen, 1969.
Similar in projected level to this book itself, but rather more abundant and somewhat differently ordered coverage of period concerned.

44 HOBSBAWM, E. J. *Industry and Empire – an economic history of Britain since 1750*, Weidenfeld & Nicolson, 1968.
Sui generis. In form, a survey account of the period *c.* 1750–*c.* 1965. In fact, a long essay by a very gifted, some would say dangerously gifted, historian. Should be regarded as compulsory reading as long as the reader does not allow himself to be uncritically carried along by the author's rhetoric.

— WILSON, C. *England's Apprenticeship* (25).

45 ASHTON, T. S. *An Economic History of England: the eighteenth century*, Methuen, 1955.
Invaluable for the background. Less useful as an account of change and development.

46 ASHTON, T. S. *Economic Fluctuations in England, 1700–1800*, Oxford University Press, 1959.
Short. Chapters 1–5 afford an indication of the general circumstances bearing on the level of economic activity. Chapter 5 is especially useful as a brief guide to the monetary and banking system. Chapter 6 can serve as a very handy narrative summary of the course of the eighteenth-century economy in a macro-economic aspect.

47 ROSTOW, W. *British Economy of the Nineteenth Century*, Oxford University Press, 1948.
Short. The pioneering, and so far the only comprehensive, attempt at fitting the history into an articulated economic 'model'. Should at least be looked at, once a fair grasp of the basic history has been acquired. The more venturesome may conjoin it with the same author's *Stages of Economic Growth*, Cambridge University Press, 1960, which essays a universal thesis, drawing much on the British historical experience. Neither require of the reader any significantly

higher level of economic sophistication than does this book itself.

48 CHECKLAND, S. G. *The Rise of Industrial Society in England, 1815–1885*, Longmans, 1964.
Broad but quite detailed socio-economic coverage. Very readable.

49 CLAPHAM, SIR JOHN *An Economic History of Modern Britain*, 3 vols, Cambridge University Press, 1932.
Covers period 1820–1914. Massive in scope. Dated in approach. Still very valuable as a work of factual reference.

50 PRESSNELL, L. S., ed. *Studies in the Industrial Revolution*, Athlone Press, 1960.
A collection of twelve original essays by different authors, ranging rather more widely than title would suggest. All of them can be read with profit but those separately itemised here as (29), (69), (70) are especially valuable for the more advanced student.

(b) The Industrial Revolution (general)

51 FLINN, M. W. *The Origins of the Industrial Revolution*, Longmans (Problems and Perspectives), 1966.
A thorough and critical consideration of the historical foundations of 'Revolution'. Requires close reading, but not excessively taxing. Very strongly recommended as an adjunct to this book itself, which nowhere makes of this central issue an explicit theme for separate treatment in its own right.

52 MANTOUX, P. *The Industrial Revolution in the Eighteenth Century*, Cape, 1928.
A classic now overtaken in certain respects by more recent scholarship. But used with caution, still very illuminating.

53 DEANE, P. *The First Industrial Revolution*, Cambridge University Press, 1965.
Covers central economic developments of period *c.* 1750–*c.* 1850. Not quite a general economic history since focused on 'revolutionary' aspects, for coverage of which should be regarded as compulsory reading.

54 DEANE, P. *The Industrial Revolution in England, 1700–1914*, Collins, 1969 (vol. 4, section 2 of *The Fontana Economic History of Europe* – published in separate parts).
A somewhat misleading title. In fact, a broad analytic examination

of the central factors making for economic growth, mostly over the period *c.* 1740–*c.* 1860.

55 LANDES, D. S. *The Unbound Prometheus: Technological Change and Industrial Development in Western Europe since 1750*, Cambridge University Press, 1969.

A magnificently ambitious effort at a comprehensive comparative study of the origins, nature and consequences of technological change. Britain, as the pioneer, naturally gets a good deal of attention. Although one of the most literate pieces of modern economic history writing, much of it demands very close reading; and it is not suitable food for novices. (An earlier, and shorter, version appeared as 'Technical Change and Development in Western Europe, 1750–1914' in *The Cambridge Economic History of Europe*, vol. 6, 1965.)

56 POLLARD, S. *The Genesis of Modern Management*, E. Arnold, 1965.

Covers period *c.* 1760–*c.* 1830. Throws a great deal of light on a key, and previously neglected, aspect of the Industrial Revolution. Hardly a book to start off with; but indispensable to a proper understanding of the sociological implications of industrial capitalism. Fully readable.

57 TAYLOR, P. A. M., ed. *The Industrial Revolution in Britain: Triumph or Disaster?*, Heath (Problems in European Civilisation), 1958.

A collection of articles and book excerpts, starting with Karl Marx, dealing with the concept, chronology and general consequences of the Industrial Revolution. Very illuminating as a record of the historiography of the Revolution.

58 DOTY, C. S., ed. *The Industrial Revolution*, Holt, Reinhard and Winston, 1969.

Same sort of thing as (57), including, in fact, some of the same material, along with selections from more recent work which round off the 'standard of living debate', left unconcluded in (57).

(c) The agrarian sector

59 CHAMBERS, J. D. and MINGAY, G. E. *The Agricultural Revolution, 1750–1880*, Batsford, 1966.

A fairly abundantly detailed but quite straightforward account. Over the relevant period (62) is to be preferred.

— JOHN, A. H. 'The course of agricultural change, 1660–1760' (29).

60 PARKER, R. A. C. *Enclosures in the Eighteenth Century*, Historical Association (Aids for Teachers), 1960.

Pamphlet. A handy brief survey.

61 MINGAY, G. E. *Enclosure and the Small Farmer in the Age of the Industrial Revolution*, Macmillan, 1968.

Pamphlet. Fully described by title.

62 JONES, E. L. *The Development of English Agriculture, 1815–1873*, Macmillan, 1968.

Pamphlet. A thoroughly expert treatment.

(*d*) *Other particular topics* (*order broadly corresponds with that followed in this book itself*).

63 FLINN, M. W. *British Population Growth, 1700–1850*, Macmillan, 1970.

Pamphlet. A careful – and skilful – charting of the technical and interpretative problems of this knottiest of issues.

64 COLEMAN, D. C. *The Domestic System in Industry*, Historical Association (Aids for Teachers), 1960.

Pamphlet. A very useful brief account. Particularly recommended to those using Part 2 only of this book itself.

65 ASHTON, T. S. *Iron and Steel in the Industrial Revolution*, Manchester University Press, 1951; 3rd edn 1963.

Covers period *c.* 1700–*c.* 1800. Essentially a narrative account of the central technological developments and of the personalities and firms involved, including a chapter on the early development of the Watt engine.

66 BIRCH, A. *The Economic History of the British Iron and Steel Industry, 1784–1879*, Cass, 1967.

Broad general coverage. Padded out with longish section on selected concerns, which ordinary reader can happily skip.

67 EDWARDS, M. M. *The Growth of the British Cotton Trade, 1780–1815*, Manchester University Press, 1967.

Perhaps a little on the specialised side for inclusion here. But of modest length, not especially taxing, and concerned with a key industry through a crucial phase.

68 JOSLIN, D. 'London private bankers, 1720–1785', article reprinted in (1), vol. 2. (Since this item is the only one specifically devoted to banking in this list it should be said that it figures only because of its appearance in (1). The body of specialist literature on money and banking is abundant but all of it falls, for one reason or another, beyond the limits of this list.)

69 PRESSNELL, L. 'The rate of interest in the eighteenth century', essay in (50), dealing with a prominent and contentious topic.

— MINCHINTON, W. E., ed. *The Growth of English Overseas Trade* (31).

70 POTTER, J. 'Atlantic Economy, 1815–60: the U.S.A. and the Industrial Revolution in Britain', essay in (50), illustrating the importance of the USA in British industrial development.

71 BAXTER, R. 'Railway extension and its results', article reprinted in (1), vol. 3.

72 HABAKKUK, H. *American and British Technology in the 19th Century*, Cambridge University Press, 1962.
Full of insight on comparative technological progressiveness. But very demanding.

73 WARD-PERKINS, C. 'The commercial crisis of 1847', article reprinted in (1), vol. 3. A convenient case study of one of the periodic crises referred to at points in this book itself but nowhere examined in detail.

— POLLARD, S. and CROSSLEY, D. W. *The Wealth of Britain* (4).

1873–1970
(a) General

— MITCHELL, B. R. and DEANE, P. *Abstract of British Historical Statistics* (41).

— HOBSBAWM, E. J. *Industry and Empire* (44).

74 ASHWORTH, W. *An Economic History of England, 1870–1939*, Methuen, 1960.
Comprehensive without being exhausting. A little too tough for the novice.

75 SAYERS, R. S. *A History of Economic Change in England, 1880–1939*, Oxford University Press, 1967.
A useful short general survey.

— MATHIAS, P. *The First Industrial Nation* (43).

— ROSTOW, W. *British Economy of the Nineteenth Century* (47).

— CLAPHAM, SIR JOHN *An Economic History of Modern Britain* (49).

76 ALDCROFT, D. H. and RICHARDSON, H. W. *The British Economy, 1870–1939*, Macmillan, 1969.
A deceptive title. The great bulk of the book is made up of eight previously published articles of the authors', devoted to particular, though certainly important, macro-economic themes. These articles are of a strongly econometric bent and fall for the most part beyond

the upper limits of the criteria of this list (as well as often exemplifying the econometric delusion that to quantify is to explain). The book, however, does contain an extremely useful 'Bibliographical Survey' which gives the guts of a considerable body of recent and important literature on the general theme of British economic performance 1870–1939.

— DEANE, P. and COLE, W. A. *British Economic Growth* (42).

77 SAUL, S. B. *The Myth of the Great Depression in England (1873–1896)*, Macmillan, 1969.
Pamphlet. Very rapidly buries (presumably for good and all) the style 'Great Depression', and devotes itself primarily, and extremely competently, to an analytical consideration of the course of prices, wages, output and international competitiveness. Considering its brevity it may properly be regarded as compulsory reading.

78 POLLARD, S. *The Development of the British Economy, 1914–1967*, 2nd edn, E. Arnold, 1969.
Packs a considerable body of lucidly presented information into a not excessively big book. Indispensable as a work of reference. Perhaps a little too wearing for continuous reading.

79 YOUNGSON, A. J. *Britain's Economic Growth, 1920–1966*, Allen & Unwin, 1967.
Essentially a critical survey, in moderate detail, of economic policy against a broadly sketched background. A little too taxing for the novice. The more initiated will distinguish between statements of fact and expression of the author's judgments.

— FLINN, M. W. *British Population Growth* (63).

80 PREST, A. R., ed. *The U.K. Economy: a manual of applied economics*, revd edn, Weidenfeld & Nicolson, 1970.
The contemporary economy set in the context of the history of the last decade or two. Intended primarily for economists, and demanding some degree of economic literacy, it promises to be an extremely convenient way of keeping one's economic history up to the minute if the practice, so far followed, of new editions at two yearly intervals is kept up.

(b) *Industry*

— LANDES, D. *The Unbound Prometheus* (55).

81 ALDCROFT, D. H., ed. *The Development of British Industry and Foreign Competition, 1875–1914*, Allen & Unwin, 1968.

A very useful set of short studies, by different authors, of a number of British industries in a comparative international context. For supplementary, rather than central, reading.

— HABAKKUK, H. *American and British Technology in the 19th Century* (71).

82 ALLEN, G. C. *British Industries and Their Organisation*, 4th edn, Longmans, 1959.
Succinct accounts of the problems and progress of selected major British industries, chiefly over the period 1920–58. (Earlier editions, running back to 1933, have different chronological coverage.)

83 DUNNING, J. H. and THOMAS, C. J. *British Industry: Change and Development in the Twentieth Century*, new edn, Hutchinson University Library, 1966.
Short and lucid on the leading changes in the overall pattern, mostly over the period *c.* 1930–*c.* 1960.

84 CARR, J. C. and TAPLIN, W. *A History of the British Steel Industry*, Blackwell, 1962.
Covers period *c.* 1860–1939 in copious fashion.

85 BURN, D. *The Economic History of Steelmaking, 1867–1939*, Cambridge University Press, 1940.
Shorter but much more densely analytic than (84).

(c) Economic policy

— YOUNGSON, A. J. *Britain's Economic Growth, 1920–1966* (79).

86 DOW, J. C. R. *The Management of the British Economy, 1945–60*, Cambridge University Press, 1965.
Perhaps too technical and too detailed for inclusion here. Parts III and IV are quite certainly for the professional economist only. But Parts I and II provide a very useful review of policy measures for those with a modest degree of economic literacy.

87 BRITTAN, S. *The Treasury Under the Tories, 1954–64*, Penguin, 1964.
A short 'popular' – but not vulgarised – account of economic policy. (An expanded version, *Steering the Economy*, 1971, brings the story up to 1969; but the additional matter is a good deal more detailed and rather impairs the appeal of the original which consists very much in its deft brevity.)

(d) Other

— POLLARD, S. and CROSSLEY, D. W. *The Wealth of Britain* (4).

Index

xxvii

6

Building industry, 31–2, 83, 375, 459–
460, 489, 698, 705, 742–3, 755–6,
799–800, 807. See also Housing
Bullion Committee (1811), 502, 506
Bullionism, 86–7, 304, 306
Byzantine Empire, See Levant, The

Calais, as Staple, 90–1
Caledonian Railway, 518n
Calico, see Cotton cloth
Calico Acts, 254–5, 356
Cammell Laird, 672, 751
Canada, trade with, 481, 482, 486, 603,
636, 716; British investment, 683
Canals, 366, 372, 382–5, 457–8, 470–4
522, 533
Cannon, see Armaments
Capital, sources and employment, 27,
30, 32–3, 40, 43, 45–6, 55–6, 68, 74–5,
90, 97–8, 114–17, 120, 123, 125, 133–
135, 136–8, 142–4, 147–9, 151–2,
159–60, 162, 181, 194, 196, 203, 204,
206–7, 208, 213, 214–17, 223–4, 238,
246, 248–9, 250, 252–3, 256–7, 263–4,
267–9, 271, 272, 273–4, 275–8, 290–2,
323–4, 339–40, 348–9, 352, 369–70,
372–3, 379–81, 384–5, 389–92, 420–3,
426, 429–30, 464–6, 472–3, 476–9,
489, 509, 512, 515–17, 520–1, 522,
531, 536–7, 540–1, 575–6, 594–5, 597,
598, 605–8, 620–3, 624, 648, 651–2,
683, 705–6, 734–5, 804, 806, 807–8,
814–15. See also Investment
Carding machine, 345, 352, 355–6, 359,
434
Cargo Fleet, 672–3
Carron iron works, 366, 367, 369–70, 446
Carta Mercatoria (1303), 58
Cartwright, Edmund, 356, 427
Central Electricity Board, 768
Chancellor, Richard, 203–4
Charles I, and patents of monopoly,
161, 165
Charters, see Town charters
Chemicals, 583–93, 690, 696–7, 731,
748–9
exports, 585, 635, 691, 697; imports,
697

Cheshire, salt industry, 31, 243, 262,
313, 382, 383, 586
Chester, maritime trade, 57, 122, 212,
312
Children, employment of, 330, 421,
428
Chlorine, see Bleach
Church, and 'just price', 22–3; and
usury, 46–7, 168; and towns, 20; and
'high farming', 43; finances and
wool, 46, 55. See also Religious
attitudes
Civil War (American), economic
effects, 543, 572, 576–7
Civil War (English), economic effects,
228–9
Class structure and its implications,
175–6, 525, 526, 547, 601–2, 607, 719,
760
Cleveland, iron industry, 544, 551–2
Clothier, see 'Domestic System'
Coal, use of, 147–8, 247, 248, 364–7
Coal industry and trade, 31, 83, 127–37,
241–3, 265, 314, 371–2, 377, 382,
416, 449, 453–8, 567–70, 697–8,
727–8, 755–6, 772–3, 802
exports, 129, 242, 313, 407–8, 569–70,
635, 637, 697–8, 728
Coastal trade, 265, 314
Coats, J. and P., 704, 756
'Cockayne's project', 119–20, 121, 159
Coffee, consumption, 410
imports, 295, 410, 483, 486; re-
exports, 295, 409, 485, 488, 638
Coke smelting (iron), 243, 364–6, 441
Cologne, merchants of, 52–3
Colvilles, 751, 752
Combing machine, 434, 579
Commissioners of Sewers, 263
Common Law and Equity, and cus-
tomary tenures, 72, 189, 193, 237;
and 'free trade', 163; and guilds, 154
Commons, see Agriculture, commons
Commutation of labour services, 38–
40, 44, 63–7 passim, 72
Concern size, 29–31, 32–3, 82–3, 134,
144, 145, 147–9, 249, 250, 253, 256–7,
323–4, 349, 369–70, 372–3, 374, 375–

Iron, industry—*contd.*
  442–7, 449, 453–5, 542–53, 641,
    652, 660–77, 690, 705, 726–7, 750–
    752, 802
  use, 4, 377
  exports, 444–6, 481, 542–4, 635, 662–
    667 *passim*, 690–1, 726, 727; im-
    ports, 56, 83, 244–5, 246, 363, 366,
    442, 483, 640–1, 662, 676–8, 726
  See also Metal Manufactures
Iron and Steel Institute, 669, 670
Italy, trade with, 50, 86, 96, 200–1, 209,
  307–8, 342, 482; woollen industry,
  50

Jacquard loom, 438–9
James I, and 'Cockayne's project', 119–
  120; and patents of monopoly, 163–5
John Brown, 672
Joint-stock companies, 165–6, 248–9,
  250, 280–1, 287–9, 290–2, 384, 472–3,
  509–11, 512, 515–16, 540–1, 619–20
Journeymen, see Labour(ers), indus-
  trial
'Just price', 22–3
Justices of (labourers) the peace, 65–6,
  170, 172–3, 193, 265, 266

Kay, John (flying shuttle), 344
Kay, John (water frame), 354
Kendrew, John, 437
Kennet and Avon Canal, 471
Kent, agriculture and rural society, 10n,
  37; copperas industry, 147; salt
  industry, 31. See also Weald
Kett's Rebellion (1549), 186
King, see State, The; individual
  monarchs
Knights, maintenance of, 2, 3
Knitting frame, 123–4, 257

Labour services, see Commutation;
  Villeinage
Labourers, agricultural, numbers, 10,
  37, 70, 188, 718; position of, 63–7
  passim, 187, 236, 337–8
  industrial, numbers, 79; condition of,
  25–6, 30, 31, 32, 75–8 *passim*, 116–

117, 153–4, 249, 252–3, 256–7, 320,
  323–4, 347–9, 421, 529–30. See
  also Hand-loom weavers
  See also Statute of Artificers; Wages
Lacemaking, 257
Lancashire, population, 320; linen
  industry, 122, 254, 362, 580; woollen
  industry, 28–9, 123; coal industry,
  129, 243, 372; engineering industries,
  451–2, 555, 557–9; chemicals industry, 586; canals, 372, 382, 383; railways, 515; banking, 476–7. See also
  Pennines; Cotton industry
Lancashire and Yorkshire Railway,
  518n
Lancashire Cotton Corporation, 756
Lancashire Steel Corporation, 751, 752
Lead, industry, 31, 83, 145, 248–9, 280,
  373, 447
  exports, 53, 84–6, 373; imports, 640
Leaseholders, see Agriculture, land
  tenures
Leeds, population, 659; woollen indus-
  try, 344; garment manufacture, 582;
  engineering industries, 555, 559; and
  river improvement, 262
Leghorn, as entrepôt, 210
Leicester, population, 659; woollen
  industry, 27; hosiery industry, 123,
  582
Leicestershire, see Midlands; Midlands,
  East
Lepanto, Battle of (1571), 208
Levant, trade with, 52, 56, 86, 96, 208–
  209, 307–8, 310
Levant Company, 208–9, 213, 309
Lever Bros., 704, 753, 754n, 755
Lex Mercatoria, 48, 154
Limited Liability Act, 575–6, 651
Lincoln, population, 4; woollen indus-
  try, 27; agricultural engineering, 559
Lincolnshire, sheep farming, 50, 80,
  185; salt industry, 31; linen industry,
  362
Linen, industry, 122, 254, 361–2, 437–8,
  439, 580–1
  cloth, exports, 361–2, 406, 407, 438,
  481, 581, 635; imports, 52, 122,

Rivers—*contd.*
261–4, 382–3. See also individual
rivers
Road haulage business, 522, 533, 755–6,
802, 807
Roads, 265–6, 385–6, 474–5
Roberts, Richard, 574
Roebuck, John, 367
Rolls Royce, 749
Rootes (motors), 747, 807
Royal African Company, 278–9, 309
Royal Bank of Scotland, 398–9
Rum, imports, 486; re-exports, 409
Rural communities, character and
composition, 3–4, 6–12; industry and
trade in, 20–1, 113–18, 243, 320
Russia, trade with, 204–5, 246, 304–5,
343, 366, 543, 602–3, 637; British
investment, 647
Russia Company, see Muscovy Com-
pany

St Rollox works, 422, 585–6
Salary earners, 739, 757–9, 809–10
Salt, industry, 31, 83, 147–8, 160, 243,
262, 313, 372, 382, 383, 586
supply of, 4, 5
exports, 31, 86, 313; imports, 4, 53,
83, 86
Saltpetre, imports, 209–10
Sandwich, maritime trade, 97
Sankey Brook Navigation, 382
Sankey Commission (1919), 772
Savings, investment and demand, 104–
107, 223–6, 275–81, 291–2, 386–7,
417, 473–4, 489, 504, 505, 530–2,
652–3, 682–4, 721, 737, 739–40, 758–
759, 778–80, 811–13
Scandinavia, trade with, 95. See also
Denmark, Norway, Sweden
Scotland, coal industry, 128, 135, 458,
569; iron industry, 446–7, 544, 550–
551; engineering industries, 452, 550,
555; shipbuilding, 538; linen industry, 254, 362; cotton industry, 432,
571, 576–7; canals, 458; banking, 398–
401, 476. See also Dundee; Glasgow
Scriveners, 275

Secular movements, see Economy,
long run movements
Serfdom, see Villeinage
Selective breeding, see Agriculture,
meat production
Self-acting mule, 574
Seven Years War (1756–63), economic
effects, 355, 396
Severn, traffic on, 129, 143–4, 242, 244,
263, 264
Sewing machine, 563, 582
Shipbuilding industry, 32–3, 83, 459,
534–5, 537–8, 555, 672, 673, 687–8,
690, 705, 729–30, 775–6
Shipping industry, 57, 83, 86, 206–7,
210, 265, 292–3, 313, 534–42, 688,
755, 807
external earnings, 642–3
Shoe manufacture, 583, 700, 755
Shropshire, sheep farming, 80; coal
industry, 129, 457; iron industry,
144, 244, 369, 370, 551, 554; lead
industry, 31
Siemens, William, 549
Silk, industry, 252–4, 362–3, 438–9,
581, 630, 639
goods, exports, 406; imports, 56,
209, 214, 252–4, 362, 411, 483,
638–9; re-exports, 409
Silver industry, 31
Singer Sewing Machine Company,
563, 582
Slave trade, 244, 295–6, 310, 410
Slavery, in medieval England, 9
Smallpox, 62, 101, 230, 325, 327
Smeaton, John, 366
Soap industry, 148, 251, 377, 416
Social class, see class structure
Social policy, see State, The
Soda manufacture, 584–7
Soho works, 368. 370, 375–6
Somerset, see West Country; South
West
South Africa, British investment, 683
South Eastern Railway, 518n
South Sea Bubble, 283–90
South West, population, 319–20;
sheep farming, 34; woollen industry,

Sulphuric acid, 584–5

Summer diarrhoea of infants, 231, 325

Sunderland, population, 659; coal trade, 314, 458

'Suspension of Cash Payments' (1797–1821), 490–1, 493, 498, 499, 502, 506–7

Sussex, salt industry, 31. See also Weald

Sweating sickness, 101

Sweden, trade with, 244–5, 246, 304, 313, 366; iron industry, 244–5. See also Scandinavia

Swindon, 561

Sword Blade (Company) Bank, 282–283

Synthetic fertilisers, 592–3

Synthetics, 587–92

Syphilis, 101

Tariffs, see Customs duties

Taxation, nature and incidence, 277, 381, 655, 710–11, 763, 770–1, 800–1

Tea, consumption, 378–9, 410, 639

Tea, imports, 295, 410, 483, 638–9; re-exports, 295, 409, 638

Tennant, Charles, 585

Textile engineering, 451–2, 557–9, 560, 691

Thames, traffic on, 128, 136–7, 263, 264, 471

Thames and Severn Canal, 471

'Three (Two) Field System', see Agriculture, crop rotation and fallowing practices

Throwing machine, 124, 253–4, 362

Tin, industry, 30–1, 83, 145, 218, 247–8, 249, 250, 372–3, 447

exports, 30, 53, 83, 84–6, 208, 209, 218, 247, 372; imports, 553, 640

Tinplate industry, 247, 370, 372, 447, 553–4

exports, 553–4, 664

Tobacco, consumption, 760, 817

Tobacco, imports, 215, 216, 294–6, 313, 410; re-exports, 294–5, 301, 304, 313, 409, 412–3, 485, 488

Town charters, grant of, 19–20

Towns, government of, 18–20, 21–3, 41, 264; economic life and character, 16–18, 20, 75–8, 321–2; and woollen industry, 79–80, 118, 121, 171; and cotton industry, 432; and river improvement, 263; gas supply, 593–594; living conditions, 328, 489, 596. See also Guilds; Markets; Population, Urban; Local government

Trade, External, 4, 28, 30, 31, 50, 51–9, 78–9, 80, 83–4, 84–98, 112–13, 115, 118, 119–21, 122, 129, 140, 174, 200–19, 231, 238–9, 242, 244–5, 246, 247, 252–4, 255, 257, 258, 259, 292–314, 319, 342–4, 355, 361, 362, 363, 366, 372, 373, 406–13, 420, 422, 423–5, 433, 436, 442, 444–6, 480–6, 488, 489–90, 493–504 passim, 508, 542–4, 553–4, 558, 560, 562, 569–70, 571, 572–3, 578–9, 580, 581, 585, 600–3, 631–41, 662–7 passim, 678–80, 681, 683, 684, 688–693 passim, 695, 696, 697–8, 716, 726, 727, 728, 729–30, 735–6, 740, 741, 774, 782–3, 812–13

N.B. Commodities and countries are included above, but are also referenced separately.

Trade, Internal 45–9, 71–2, 137

See also Coastal trade; Corn trade; Rivers; Roads; Wool trade

Trades unionism, 713–15, 759, 793–4, 814

Trading Companies, and 'Free Trade', 162, 163–4, 309–10, 313–14

Trent, traffic on, 129, 263, 264

Tube Investments, 754

Tull, Jethro, 236

Turkey, see Levant; Ottoman Empire

Turnpike trusts, see Roads

Tyneside, see Newcastle; North East

Typhus, 101, 230–1

Unemployment, relief of, 710, 766, 774–5

United Alkali Company, 587, 701, 748

United States of America, trade with, 422, 425, 431, 433, 481, 482, 486, 495,

496–7, 543, 573, 579, 581, 585, 603,
636, 637, 664, 689, 691, 695, 696,
716; British investment, 613, 624,
647–8, 682–3; cotton cultivation,
422; iron industry, 663–4, 668, 670–3;
engineering activities, 560, 564–6,
583, 691–3, 695, 696; shipping
and shipbuilding industries, 536;
wages and living standards, 560,
671–2
United Steel, 750
Usury, Law and doctrine, 45–7, 168–9,
340, 385, 613, 614

Vauxhall (General Motors), 747, 748,
755, 807
Vermuyden, Cornelius, 181
Vickers, 672, 673, 749, 751
Village, see Rural communities
Villeinage, 7–9, 35–9, 63–8
Virginia, settlement, 215–16

Wages, movements of, 220–1, 231,
655, 657–8, 711–15, 718, 720–1,
739, 759–60, 809–10, 812
regulation of, 25, 65–6, 154, 170,
172–3
Wales, South, coal industry, 129, 135,
242, 457, 569–70; iron industry, 141,
142, 144, 244, 246, 446, 447, 551,
553–4; copper industry, 250; engineering industries, 555; canals, 457.
See also Tinplate industry
Walkers' iron works, 369
Wallpaper Manufacturers, 701, 755
War of American Independence (1775–
1783), economic effects, 343, 395–6,
412–13
War of 1812, economic effects, 503
Warfare, economic effects, see Hundred Years War; Civil War (English); Seven Years War; War of
American Independence; Revolutionary and Napoleonic Wars; War
of 1812; Civil War (American);
World War I; World War II
Warwickshire, see Midlands, West
Watch manufacture, 449, 696

Water frame, 350–5, 359, 420–1
Water power, use, 28, 30, 82–3, 138,
143, 144, 149, 253, 366, 369, 425,
432, 434, 565, 579
Watt, James, 367–8
Weald, The, extent of, 4; agriculture,
235; iron industry, 30, 141, 142, 246,
446
Weapons, see Armaments
Wearside, see North East; Sunderland
Weaver Navigation, 262, 312–13, 382
Weavers' Act (1555), 171, 173
Wedgwood, Josiah, 375–6
West Country, population, 57, 103,
320; sheep farming, 34, 80; woollen
industry, 28–9, 79–80, 118, 120, 121,
258, 343–8 passim, 437, 579–80
'West Indians', and formation of com-
mercial policy, 299, 302
West Indies, trade with, 244, 255, 294–
295, 301–2, 308, 312, 355, 362, 407,
409, 410, 425, 431, 481, 482, 485–6,
636; economic relationship with
England, 301–2, 407, 645; sugar
production and trade, 294, 302. See
also Barbados
West Riding, see Yorkshire
Westmorland, woollen industry, 28–9.
See also Pennines
Whitehaven, maritime trade, 313
Wilkinson, John, 368, 369
William I, and Domesday Book, 2, 7
William Beardmore, 672
Williams, Thomas, 373–4
Wiltshire, see West Country
Winchester, population, 4; woollen
industry, 27
Wine, consumption, 53, 54, 211
imports, 52, 53, 56, 57, 84, 86, 209,
211, 306, 307; re-exports, 295
Wire manufacture, 144
Woodlands, extent of, 4, 127; rights in,
11
Woodmongers, London Fellowship of,
136–7
Wool, trade, organisation of, 41, 49–
51, 89–91, 114, 118
exports, 50–7, passim, 83–4, 174, 202;